Intimate Relationships

Where are we? Where are we going?

second edition

L O V E

Tai J. Mendenhall, Ph.D.
Elizabeth J. Plowman, Ph.D.
Lisa J. Trump, M.S.

Kendall Hunt
publishing company

Cover image © Shutterstock, Inc.

Kendall Hunt
publishing company

www.kendallhunt.com
Send all inquiries to:
4050 Westmark Drive
Dubuque, IA 52004-1840

Printed in the United States of America

Dedications

From Tai Mendenhall:

I dedicate this book to my wife, my family, and my students. To my wife, Ling, for growing with me every day in a love and intimacy that I cherish more than any words could convey. To my family, for inspiring me to follow my heart, chase my dreams, and enjoy the journey. To my students, for challenging me with their curiosity, heartening me with their passion, keeping me humble, and teaching me more than I have ever taught them.

From Libby Plowman:

I dedicate this book to my love, Christian, and my family. To Chris, for his generosity, playful spirit, and handsome smile . . . he floats my boat. I never imagined I would have a partner who I would admire so much. I thank him for sharing this big adventure! To my Mom, Dad, and Andrea, for their love and encouragement every step of the way – through every endeavor. I thank them for teaching me what love and family is all about.

From Lisa Trump:

I dedicate this book to my husband, my family, my friends, my students, and my mentor. To my husband, Miles, for lovingly encouraging me daily to be a better version of myself. To my family, who instilled in me the values of perseverance and humility. To my friends and peers, who make me laugh on tough days and show me support. To my students, for their energy, vulnerability, and willingness to grow. And to my mentor, Tai Mendenhall, for believing in my potential and encouraging me along the way.

From Tai, Libby, and Lisa:

We dedicate this book to the memory of Dr. Wayne Caron, who created the original course, FSoS 1101: *Intimate Relationships* at the University of Minnesota. We thank him for his energy and inspiration, wisdom and kindness, love and support – for all of our students – in their own personal journeys of learning, risking, and growth.

Contents

Foreword   xi

Acknowledgement   xiii

Introduction   xv

Tai J. Mendenhall, Ph.D., LMFT; Lisa J. Trump, M.S.; Jaime E. Ballard, M.S.; Elizabeth J. Plowman, Ph.D.
  Learning about Intimacy (without the infomercial)   xv
  Approaches to Teaching Intimacy   xvi
  Approaches to Understanding Intimacy   xix
  Motivations for Learning (and Acting upon Learning) about Intimacy   xx
  And So, our Journey begins . . .   xxii

1 Intimacy: What Is It? How Do We Develop It?   1

Lisa J. Trump, M.S.; Tai J. Mendenhall, Ph.D., LMFT
  Evolutionary Theory of Attraction   2
  Filter Theory of Attraction   3
  Wheel of Love   5
  Triangular Theory   7
  Love Styles   9
  Putting it all Together   10

2 Attachment: How Where We Have Been Influences What We Do in Relationships   13

Kirsten Lind Seal, Ph.D., LMFT; Jennifer Doty, Ph.D.
  Overview of Attachment Theory   14
  Attachment in Romantic Relationships   18
  So What? What Now?   23

3 Personality and Intimate Relationships   27

Noah E. Gagner, M.A., M.Ed., Lisa J. Trump, M.S.
  What is Personality?   28
  Assessments of Personality   30
  Personality and Dating   32
  Personality and Social Media   35
  Application   38

4 **Gender Socialization and Relationship Formation: What Is It and What Has It Got To Do with Me?   43**

Jane E. Newell, Ph.D., Anna I. Bohlinger, Ph.D., LAMFT
Gender Socialization and Relationship Formation   43
The Feminine Mystique: Consumerism and the Post-War Era   47
Gender and Culture   53
Gender and Religion   53

5 **Social and Cultural Contexts of Meeting and Dating   63**

Jennifer L. Doty, Ph.D.; Tai J. Mendenhall, Ph.D., LMFT; Jonathan J. Kleba
A Short History Lesson: Social Contexts and Relationships   65
Relationships in Today's Market Economy   66
Technology in Relationships   69
What We Don't Know   72

6 **Dances of Intimacy: Patterns of Communication, Boundaries, and Specific Barriers   77**

Kirsten Lind Seal, Ph.D., LMFT; Elizabeth J. Plowman, Ph.D.; Jaime E. Ballard, M.S.
Communication   78
Dances of Intimacy   83
So Really—How Do We Change?   88
Conclusion: When Intimacy Dances Work   89

7 **Boundaries: Where I End and You Begin   93**

Elizabeth J. Plowman, Ph.D.; Damir Utrzan, M.S.
What are Boundaries?   94
The Ripple Effect of Relationship Ponds: Family Systems Theory   99

8 **Authenticity in Intimate Relationships   111**

Anna I. Bohlinger, Ph.D., LAMFT; Elizabeth J. Plowman, Ph.D.; Tai J. Mendenhall, Ph.D., LMFT
What Do We Know?   112
Authenticity and Social Change   114
The Johari Window   115
Why Didn't You Call: The Subjective Version   118

9 Intimacy Killers   121

Jennifer L. Doty, Ph.D., Carrie L. Hanson, Ph.D., LMFT; Matthew A. Witham, M.A., LMFT; Alejandra Ochoa; Tai J. Mendenhall, Ph.D., LMFT

The Four Horsemen   123
Couples and Money   125
Jealousy   127
Infidelity   128
Violence and Relationships   130
Alcohol and Relationships   133
What We Don't Know   134
Application   135

10 Intimacy Healers   141

Christina J. Robert, Ph.D., LMFT; Anna I. Bohlinger, Ph.D., LMFT; Holli M. Kelly-Trombley, Ph.D., LMFT; Lisa J. Trump, M.S.

The Sound Relational House   142
Love Languages   145
Communicating Your Love Language   149

11 Uncharted Territory: Long Distance Relationships in College-Age Commuters   153

Polina N. Levchenko, Ph.D.; Cigdem Yumbul, M.S.; Tai J. Mendenhall, Ph.D., LMFT

Long-Distance Relationships Among Young Adults   155
Common Myths About Long Distance Relationships   156
Review of What We Know about LDRs   157
Specific Cases of LDRs   162
Application: Succeeding in an LDR   163
What We Don't Know   164

12 The Influence of Culture on Relationships   167

Tisa A. Thomas, M.A.; Dung M. Mao, M.A.; Meghan N. Mao, RN

Race, Culture, and Ethnicity   167
Minority Groups in the United States   169
Intermarriage: History to Present Day   173
Ethnicity and Intermarriage   174
Challenges for Minority Families Integrating into the United States   177
Cultural Competence   179
Future Research on Culture in Relationships   180

13 Religion and Spirituality in Intimate Relationships   185

Julie A. Zaloudek, Ph.D.; Gregg T. Schacher, Ph.D., LMFT; Elizabeth J. Plowman, Ph.D.

Religion and Spirituality   186
What We Don't Know   193

14 The Role of Ritual in Relationships   197

Elizabeth J. Plowman, Ph.D.; Gregg T. Schacher, Ph.D., LMFT

The Role of Ritual in Relationships   198
What We Know about Family and Couple Rituals   199
What We Don't Know   205

15 Sexual Intimacy   209

Lisa J. Trump, MS; Polina Levchenko, Ph.D.; Tai J. Mendenhall, Ph.D., LMFT; Brian J. Willoughby, Ph.D.

Sexuality: Physiology or Psychology?   210
Sexuality with Friends and Strangers   216
Sexuality within Intimate Relationships   218
Areas for Further Development   223

16 Queering the Family   229

Kyle Zrenchik, Ph.D., ACS, LMFT; Anna I. Bohlinger, Ph.D., LMFT; Jeni L. Whalig, M.S.; G. Carnes

Queer Theory   230
Alphabet Soup: What Do All of Those Letters Mean?   231
Coming Out   232
What About the Family?   233
Same-Sex Couples   235
Intimate Relationships for Our Transgendered Loved Ones   239
Asexuality   243
What We Don't Know   244

17 Compassion and Forgiveness in Intimate Relationships   249

Mary T. Kelleher, MA, LMFT; Kirsten Lind Seal, Ph.D., LMFT; Jaime E. Ballard, MS; Tai J. Mendenhall, Ph.D., LMFT

Compassion   251
Forgiveness   260
Compassion and Forgiveness Together   264

18 Relationships Across the Lifespan 267

J. Max Zubatsky, PhD, LMFT; Stephanie Trudeau, M.S.

Long-Lived Relationships 268
Sustaining Long-lived Relationships 269
Theories About Long-Lived Relationships 273
Relationship Decisions 279
Stressors in Long-Lived Relationships 282
What Would You Do? 284

19 Are Intimate Relationships Good for Your Health? 289

Diego Garcia-Huidobro, M.D., M.S.; Jerica M. Berge, PhD, MPH, LMFT, CFLE

The Intersection of Intimate Relationships and Health 290
Intimate Relationships and Health Behaviors 290
Intimate Relationships and Chronic Disease 291
Intimate Relationships and Mental Health 291
Theoretical Explanations Regarding the Connection between Intimate Relationships and Health 292
Family Communication and Health 295
Strengthening Intimate Relationships to Improve Health 298

20 Where have we been? Where are we going? Charting the Course in Our Intimate Journeys 305

Elizabeth J. Plowman, Ph.D.; Tai J. Mendenhall, Ph.D., LMFT; Lisa J. Trump, M.S.

What is Intimacy? 305
Where Have We Been? 306
Where Are We Going? 307

Author Bios 311

Foreword

The first edition of *Intimate Relationships: Where have we been? Where are we going?* was the result of a collaborative project led by Dr. Tai Mendenhall at the University of Minnesota (UMN). As the instructor for an innovative course about relationships, Tai engaged several of his doctoral students (who were training—or had trained—to be college-level instructors) and undergraduate students (who were taking—or had taken—the class) to write a new textbook. Everyone involved contributed their perspectives, expertise, and stories—and the ensuing cohorts of students who used the book loved it! They told us that they could hear their own voices, and see their own lives, reflected in the narratives of others who came before them who struggled with similar struggles, embraced similar joys, and embarked on similar paths. We now welcome you to this text's second-edition, wherein we continue together on this amazing journey!

According to Erik Erikson, the development of intimate relationships is a principal psychosocial task during young adulthood. This explains why so many of us—from all walks of life, academic majors, and university programs—are drawn to this topic. We want our relationships to thrive, especially during a time when everything inside of us seems to beg for answers to our deepest longings.

Research involving young adults taking the UMN *Intimate Relationships* course is now serving to—alongside informing this revised text—advance new work in this exciting field. For example, in an analysis that I conducted regarding students' autobiographical papers (which they wrote to demonstrate their understanding and integration of course concepts with personal lived-experience), we found that "syntonic isolation" (to feel good and function well when alone) is essential to the health and well-being of our intimate unions. One student wrote:

> If I were to remember only one thing from this class . . . it is that my partner and I are both unique individuals, and that by viewing the relationship as two (instead of one), we shall be greater for it. To lose our individuality in the relationship would be a great loss. If I am in a relationship and I am not proud of who I have become, I won't be proud of who "we" become. I must love myself before I can love the rest of the world.

This wisdom, as you will see in this book, is one of the keys to extraordinary couplehood. We must first, as Tai would say, take care of the person who we are with 24-hours per day. From there, we can grow together.

As you participate in this exciting course, I invite you to engage in it fully and personally. Look at where you have been. Gain understanding about, and learn from, your own history. And then look at where you are going. Charge forward with newfound wisdom, purpose, and resolve.

Jane E. Newell, Ph.D.
Department of Family Studies & Social Work
Miami University
Oxford, Ohio

Acknowledgement

Thank you to Sarah Aulik, Adam C. Baker, Angelica Belko, Grace Blomgren, Korrina Griffith, Makayla Larson, Nicholas Lebrun, Gannon Raguse, Titi Russell, Jennifer Showers, and Yeeleng Vue for all of your help in offering feedback and revisions to this text. We could not have done it without you!

Introduction
What is Intimacy?
A Journey Now Beginning, Always Evolving . . .

Tai J. Mendenhall, Ph.D., LMFT
Jaime E. Ballard, M.S.

Lisa J. Trump, M.S.
Elizabeth J. Plowman, Ph.D.

Department of Family Social Science
University of Minnesota

Have you ever found yourself watching television in the middle of the night because you couldn't sleep, only to stumble upon an infomercial by the latest relationship guru who has somehow figured out all of the secrets to a perfect relationship? As you watch couple after couple give their testimonials about how watching these simple DVDs—that you can get now for only three easy installments of $19.95—has saved their marriage, improved their sex lives, and otherwise transformed them into something that anyone seeking intimacy would want to be, you think, *Maybe I should buy this . . . After all, none of my relationships have worked out so well, have they?* As happy as you may have been when they started (*they always start out great, don't they?*), they've always failed in the end. Maybe the relationship that you are in right now is "okay," but it's certainly not the dynamic, romantic, amazing union that these couples on TV seem to have. *Maybe, just maybe . . .*

The reality here is that we—as humans—have been trying to figure out intimacy or "love" (however defined) for eons. Some of our oldest known texts deal with the subject, and over the years we have tried to articulate guiding principles regarding how to attract and choose an ideal mate, understand major "do's" and "don't's" to keeping said mate, and somehow achieve an outcome that we presume to be universally desired (e.g., living "happily-ever-after"). And yet, book after book, guru after guru, infomercial after infomercial, DVD after DVD, and relationship after relationship, our quest continues.

LEARNING ABOUT INTIMACY (WITHOUT THE INFOMERCIAL)

This book is based on a course at the University of Minnesota (UMN) called FSoS 1101: *Intimate Relationships*. It was originally designed by Dr. Wayne Caron, who was a lecturer in the UMN's Department of Family Social Science. When Wayne tragically passed away in late 2007, Dr. Tai Mendenhall (who had been one of his teaching assistants a few years earlier) was asked to take over the course in honor of Wayne's memory. Since this time, the structure and format of *Intimate Relationships* has carried forward in the way that Dr. Caron envisioned: in a collaborative and humble manner, wherein learning is seen and cherished as a reciprocal process between teachers and learners. Professors teach students, students teach professors, and students teach each other. Teaching "assistants" are "team-teachers," and they work actively in the co-construction of new knowledge, lesson plans, and teaching/learning strategies and methods. They don't just give a guest lecture now and then, or serve as paper-graders sans engagement with the content.

And so, this book is not a text that was written by Dr. Caron, or later by Dr. Mendenhall. It's not put together by a single person who is recognized or labeled as an "expert" by nature of the letters that appear at the end of his or her name. It is, instead, the culmination of multiple voices—including

Corresponding Author: Tai J. Mendenhall, Ph.D., LMFT; University of Minnesota; Department of Family Social Science; 1985 Buford Ave.; 290 McNeal Hall; Saint Paul, MN 55108. E-mail: mend009@umn.edu.

formal instructors, several cohorts of previous team-teachers, and even previous students—and thereby represents a whole that is unequivocally more than the sum of its parts. There is no single relationship guru here; we—as the authors—are still learning every day about intimacy. Further, we each view intimacy through our own unique perspectives, informed by our personal experiences as well as our innate characteristics. As a result, we would be doing quite a disservice, at the very least, by communicating one sole perspective on what constitutes intimacy. What this text represents is where we are today in our collective wisdom. What we know in the years to come may or may not be the same. Some of it probably will be. Other things will likely be newer, slightly altered, better articulated, and potentially even completely different. Indeed, the more we learn, the more questions we have.

APPROACHES TO TEACHING INTIMACY

A formal literature review, casual walk through the "self-help," "psychology," or "relationships" section(s) of *Barnes & Noble Booksellers*, or search on Google, Bing, or any other electronic search engine, will yield you an enormous selection of texts and resources to guide you through the complex waters of "intimacy." If you had time to read them all (and you never would!), you would find that sometimes these texts overlap and agree with each other. Other times they could not be more different. There are four main approaches to teaching intimacy, and we will use all of them at different points in this text. We briefly discuss each below.

The "Guide to Living" Approach

Many of us seek answers to questions such as: *"What do I need to do to find the perfect mate?"*, *"How can I get a date?"*, *"What am I doing wrong?"*, *"How can I attract the 'right' man or woman?"* These types of questions lend themselves to "how-to" manuals in which authors are quite happy to answer your questions. If this approach is helpful to you, examples of these texts—as optional/additional reading—are listed in Figure 1. There are books about the "game(s)" of dating,

complete with methods of self-presentation and ways to talk (or not talk), text (or not text), and flirt (or play hard-to-get). There are guides that describe everything from one's first encounter with a potential mate to down-the-road questions about commitment and "happily-ever-after." There are books that focus primarily on early stages of dating (e.g., picking somebody up at a bar, getting him/her to say "yes" to a second date); these tend to be heterosexually-oriented, often pitting the sexes against each other in a manner whereby one has to know the "rules" that the other plays by in order to get what s/he wants.

FIGURE 1 Examples of "how-to" manuals for relationships

- *The Rules: Time-Tested Secrets for Capturing the Heart of Mr. Right* by Ellen Fein
- *Not Your Mother's Rules: The New Secrets for Dating* by Ellen Fein
- *The Unspoken Rules of Online Dating for Men* by Eve Margrett
- *Act Like a Lady, Think Like a Man* by Steve Harvey
- *The Truth about Men Will Set You Free: The New Science of Love and Dating* by Pat Allen & Don Schmincke
- *The Real Rules: How to Find the Right Man for the Real You* by Barbara De Angelis
- *Online Dating Photo Rules for Men* by Grace O'Malley

Other texts begin in the phase(s) after initial dating has begun, focusing instead on how to keep something good from fizzling away or dying. These tend to be less "men versus women" in tone, and instead begin to emphasize attention to the person we are all with 24 hours per day (i.e., *our own personal self*) as key to a successful union (see Figure 2). For example, in Carter-Scott's *If Love is a Game, These are the Rules*, the very first rule—before anything else—is that YOU get YOURSELF together. While not academic in its tone, this wisdom is without doubt empirically supported. It echoes sentiments put forth by Dr. Leo Buscaglia and other highly respected teachers and researchers for the past 50 years. They tell us what we sometimes—frankly—do not wish to hear: Have you ever noticed that every time you break up with somebody, you sit there with your friends, your family, your diary, or maybe even your bartender, and talk about all of the ways that the next partner you will be with will be different? *He'll be more family-oriented, better with money, less obsessed with his looks, and value education like I do. She will be more physically affectionate, less messy around the house, more spontaneous and less-concerned with having everything planned out, and like waterskiing like I do.* But think about it . . . Have you ever noticed that the common theme across all of your relationships, every single one of them (that has failed), is YOU? Yes, compatibility is important. But you must consider what you bring to the table. You are the common denominator in all of your relationships. What do you, or have you, contribute(d)?

As we realize—and admit, come to terms with, and act upon—this, we can begin a process of growth that is essential to relational success. But true growth requires reflection and awareness. It is to this wisdom that much of this book will speak.

FIGURE 2   Examples of self-improvement texts for relationships

- *How to Be a Better Wife to Your Husband or Your Partner & Strengthen Your Bond While Deepening Your Love* by David Petar
- *How to Be a Better Lover* by Greg Andrews
- *Be a Better Partner Handbook* by Debbie Lamb & Paul Lamb
- *Understand Yourself, Understand Your Partner* by Jennifer Schneider & Ron Corn
- *The Husband Book: A Guy's Guide to Marriage* by Harry Harrison Jr.

The "Head, Heart, and Gut" Approach

Human beings are immensely complex creatures, comprised of overlapping and mutually-influential systems that are biological, psychological, behavioral, social, and even spiritual in nature. Anybody who has ever gotten butterflies in their stomach when nervous, not been able to sleep because s/he couldn't "turn his/her brain off," acted (or not acted) in particular ways because of what friends, family, or religious/cultural groups would think, and so forth, knows this. Chapter 1 of this text will highlight contemporary understandings of how these different "pieces" of our lives fit together in relation to intimacy, and it is important to know that we are only just beginning to make sense of it. Examples of texts that consider the interacting nature of these different systems and their influence on intimacy are found in Figure 3.

FIGURE 3   Examples of biopsychosocial/spiritual texts about relationships

- *Passionate Marriage: Love, Sex, and Intimacy in Emotionally Committed Relationships* by David Schnarch
- *Sex God: Exploring the Endless Connections between Sexuality and Spirituality* by Rob Bell
- *Sex and the Soul: Juggling Sexuality, Spirituality, Romance, and Religion on America's College Campuses* by Donna Freitas
- *Intimacies: Love and Sex Across Cultures* by William Jankowiak

Six Blind Sages and the Elephant Approach

There's an old story that works well as a metaphor for understanding intimacy, and it is helpful to keep in mind while reading this text. The story tells of a world long ago when different peoples and groups were beginning to contact and learn about one another more than ever before. In one remote village, rumors about a strange animal—called an "elephant"—from a distant land began to spread, and the townspeople asked their sages (the profoundly wise men of the community) to travel to this land and return with stories and a better understanding of what this animal was.

Interestingly (or perhaps so that the message of this story can work), the town's sages—all six of them—were blind. They traveled to the far-away land and each touched the elephant. When they returned they all reported very different things. One sage said that the elephant was like a large tree. Another described it as a large leaf; another still, like a huge wall; and a big snake; and a sharp spear; and a rope. Of course, if you think about this, they were all right and they were all wrong. The sage who said that the elephant was like a tree was probably touching its leg; the wall, its flank; the large snake, its trunk, and so on.

And so it is with intimacy. As we embark upon this journey together, we will talk about many things together, from dating and courtship to creating a lifelong legacy during one's senior years. We will talk about communication, boundaries, relationship "dances," ways that we hurt each other, and ways that we can heal. We will talk about sex, conflict and violence, and different "languages" that we use to speak our heart's wants and feelings. All of these represent a part of intimacy, just like the sages spoke about different parts of the elephant. None of them present a "whole" picture, but taken together, something coherent begins to form.

The "Lost in the Woods" Approach

Finally, as we learn about intimacy—and more specifically, why we do the things we do, how we can do things differently, and what we are seeking and working toward along the way—it is important to understand that: (a) knowledge means nothing unless acted upon, and (b) acting is best advanced when informed by knowledge. In other words, it is important to act—but *think before you do it.*

In particular facets of military training, soldiers are often taught to "hug a tree" for a moment before charging into action when they are dropped into enemy territory. What this means is that is important to take a moment, or even just a fraction of a moment, to assess one's surroundings and get a sense of the lay of the land before doing anything. If a soldier can notice the denseness of the wilderness to the right and the shallow valley to the left, s/he can reorient and consider how best to move forward. Indeed, thinking first in this situation could mean the difference between life and death. Now, relate this concept to the uncharted territories of relationships. If you take a moment to think—for example, during an argument—you can get a sense of the circumstances that are affecting you and your partner, and orient yourself to what actions are needed in that moment. You can then act with compassionate and respectful communication, listen with an open mind and stance, or otherwise do something to help allay what is wrong or repair what is broken. To not think is to put a relationship that you might cherish with all of your heart at risk—a relationship, though, that can be destroyed in a moment of anger. And how many of us can think about our past relationships and not remember many of the good times (or even just the neutral times), but will forever recall that moment when somebody screamed or said something unkind or hurtful? As you learn the information in this book, we encourage you to *use* the knowledge you gain in your own relationships. Think first, then act.

APPROACHES TO UNDERSTANDING INTIMACY

Across the different books, resources, and teachings that are out there, it is also important to understand what "type" of knowledge that you are learning represents. This is not important so you can engage in an academic exercise of categorization per se. It is so because you can critically consume what you are learning, and position it with other things—like parts of the elephant—that are being presented to you. We briefly discuss, below, three "types" of knowledge: Traditional, Modernist, and Postmodern approaches.

Traditional Approaches to Intimacy

Traditional approaches to intimacy are derived from knowledge that is held by those espousing it as timeless, eternal, or even divine (or at least informed by the divine). This is knowledge that is found in conventional and sacred religious texts, like the Christian *Bible*, the Jewish or Islamic *Torah*, the Taoist/Daoist *Tao Te Ching*, the Theravada Buddhist *Pali Manuscript* or innumerable other written spiritual guides.

The manners in which these texts are interpreted, taught, and used to inform our decisions and behaviors in intimacy depend heavily on the groups or subgroups employing them. For example, some Christians maintain that premarital sex, gay and lesbian relationships, and divorce are all sinful, whereas other Christians (following the same religious text) maintain that these things are permissible in the eyes of their God. Arguments between different groups using the same guiding texts are both commonplace and rarely resolved because they challenge important and foundational beliefs. Subgroups simply presume that the other is following its deity's teaching incorrectly. However, those who follow traditional approaches—no matter the specifics of their viewpoints—are united in their reliance on long-standing knowledge and texts to provide guidance in intimacy.

Modernist Approaches to Intimacy

Modernists believe that knowledge is driven by empirical (i.e., observable, measureable) data. Empirical data come from "cutting-edge" research that builds upon previous investigations in the never-ending quest to fill the gaps in knowledge and scientific literature. What we know to be "true" through this lens is what we know to be verified with studies that have explored complex phenomena to make sense of what was heretofore unknown. Examples of modernist knowledge include contemporary understandings of homosexuality as a normative variation of human experience (based on genetics and brain structure research), categorizations of the principal ways in which people experience Western-notions of love (called "love styles"), and the manners in which our current relationship functioning are influenced by early experiences and attachment with caregivers.

It is important to note, too, that research conducted in this manner is not always about hard numbers, experiments, and statistics (called "quantitative" research). "Qualitative" research represents a broad field of inquiry that is driven more by interviews and observations than surveys, tests, or bio-indicators. Contemporary understanding of people's experiences—for example, what it is like to break away from one's cultural group that chooses a mate for you to instead choose a mate for yourself—is often best captured through these types of research methods. Whether quantitative or qualitative, modernist approaches to intimacy pose questions and then seek answers through gathering and making sense of data that are related to the content of study.

Postmodern Approaches to Intimacy

Postmodernism moves beyond notions of "truth" that are espoused by traditionalist (i.e., "because God said so") and modernist (i.e., "because the data say so"), and instead maintain that there are multiple "truths" (i.e., plural) related to any variety of social phenomena. What this means is that one person's version of what is true or real is true or real for him/her, but his/her version of truth does not necessarily apply to you. In fact, your experience of reality may be very different—but this does not make it any more or less "real."

We know, intuitively, that there is merit to this admittedly more complex and messy way of seeing the world. For example, siblings who grew up in the same family oftentimes report very different experiences with their parents, their childhood neighborhood, or how holidays usually went. Two partners in a couple often experience the relationship they are in together differently. One hundred people could go outside and look at a tree, and they would see it in unique ways depending on where they were standing, the manner in which the sun was in (or not in) their eyes, or even in accord to the ways that their senses gave information to the brain (e.g., some people have great eyesight and others are colorblind, some people might have had a front-row view while others' view was obstructed, some may have been close enough to smell the tree's flowers, whereas others may not have noticed the tree had flowers at all). In these examples, is one sibling, one partner, or one tree-observer more "right" in his/her view? Of course not.

This book, and the class upon which it is based, is explicitly postmodern. The collection of information within this text has been informed by numerous individual "truths"—from teachers and students alike—and is likely to be interpreted slightly differently from reader to reader as a result of our individual experiences and ways of understanding. We want to honor that many people regard very highly the teachings from a religion or faith they hold dear. We also want to honor that sometimes people are hurt by such teachings and faiths, and thereby desire to find different ways to experience or behave in their world(s). We want to honor the efforts of science and the knowledge its investigators uncover and offer to us. And we want to encourage you, the reader, to take all of this in through your own unique eyes, experiences, viewpoints, belief systems, and any—and every—thing else that makes you uniquely you. Make it your own. Create your own meaning. Create your own truth.

MOTIVATIONS FOR LEARNING (AND ACTING UPON LEARNING) ABOUT INTIMACY

As we proceed in this book, it is also important to think about your own motivation(s) for learning about intimacy. There are several—unique and overlapping—to consider.

Personal Interest and Growth

Most of us, arguably, want to learn about intimacy so that we can "do" intimacy better. Almost all of us have had our hearts broken before, felt the intolerable pain of a lost love or wondered if we would always be alone, wanting so much for something that we can never seem to reach or hold on to. Many of us have also done the heartbreaking, sometimes because we could not bear the idea of being broken-up with first, other times because we could no longer tolerate something that simply wasn't working any more. Some of us have been abused in relationships—emotionally, physically, or sexually. Others have perpetrated the abuse. But arguably all of us—by nature of picking up this text and reading it—want to grow in intimacy and love. Wherever we have been, we all want to go some place different. Some place better.

Developing Skills

Once we have this desire to grow in intimacy, we must learn new skills. By learning about intimacy, we gain new ways of acting and reacting to others with whom we hope to build something extraordinary. We learn how to communicate authentically, break through socially-prescribed scripts guided by stereotypical notions of gender or beauty, solve problems collaboratively, challenge and change personally, and heal from past hurts (so they don't keep following us into the future). We can take all of this insight and do our relationships henceforth "on purpose." Gone are the days of "ready, fire, aim!"

Advancing the Helping Professions

Many students and learners who take coursework in intimacy are not solely focused on their own growth and development. Rather, they want to help others to have healthy relationships, either as future clinicians (e.g., individual-, couple-, or family- therapists) and/or researchers. And as they (we) do this, we begin to see and embrace the notion that we all—as human beings—are biopsychosocial/spiritual creatures. As our understandings about intimacy are broadened to include knowledge and sensitivities across a variety of disciplines (e.g., Neurology, Psychology, Couple and Family Therapy, Social Work, Sociology, Religious Studies, Anthropology), so do our competencies in collaborating with colleagues outside of our own field(s) and in better connecting-the-dots to facilitating clients'/patients' journeys in healing and growth.

Addressing Social Concerns

Across all of human history, social structures—formal governments, extended kinship networks, cultural/ethnic groups, religious/faith doctrines—have informed, encouraged, and hindered the ways in which we join together as couples, families, and communities (large and small). In the United States, for example, it was not long ago that White people were legally forbidden to marry any person who was not White. Only recently, the United States permitted legal unions between homosexual partners, who love each other and desire many of these same things that their heterosexual counterparts took for granted. In other countries, however—even today—interracial unions are not permitted, and homosexual people are imprisoned or killed for not conforming to heterosexual norms. Divorce, commonplace here in America, is outright forbidden in other parts of the world. And so on. Whether it be about who you can be with, how you can be with him/her, how many "hims" or "hers" there are, or many other "ways" of being in relationships, our social structures have always told us what we can and cannot do.

Studying intimacy equips us, as professionals and as citizens, to challenge what we believe is not in our best interests, and to uphold what we believe will strengthen us. In many Western countries, for example, anti-homosexual laws are beginning to wane (in the same manners that anti-interracial marriage laws did) as research shows time-and-again that homosexuality is not pathological or morally deviant. We also know that marriages between young children and adults are developmentally dangerous to the children; therefore, our governing structures have adjusted to not allow this. As we—in an increasingly "small" world—continue to advance our understandings of intimacy, so too will our governing structures (hopefully!) respond and adapt.

© miker, 2014. Used under license from Shutterstock, Inc.

AND SO, OUR JOURNEY BEGINS . . .

In the pages and chapters that follow, the authors will introduce a variety of relationship topics that we behold as essential to your—our—journey in understanding and growing in intimacy. This knowledge and erudition are paired with personal reflections, exercises, inventories, and experiential sequences that are integrated and introduced in the on-line components of this textbook. All of these things, taken together, are oriented in a manner that will push you to take personal and interpersonal responsibility for your own change and growth. Sometimes what we talk about will be engaging and enjoyable for you. Other times it might be painful and difficult. But take it all in, think about it, and apply what is most relevant and meaningful for you. We wish you only the best as you embark upon this extraordinary journey.

Intimacy: What Is It? How Do We Develop It?

Lisa J. Trump, M.S.
Tai J. Mendenhall, Ph.D., LMFT
Department of Family Social Science
University of Minnesota

LEARNING OBJECTIVES

- Articulate how intimacy functions across a biopsychosocial/spiritual continuum
- Understand key evolutionary facets of intimacy processes
- Understand how filter theories serve to narrow down choices in potential intimate partners
- Understand how relationships evolve over time according to leading theorists in the field
- Understand and articulate the six principal "love styles"

INTRODUCTION

As discussed in the introduction, intimacy is a concept that people have been trying to define for ages. Previous theorists have attempted to operationalize intimacy and have failed to get a complete grasp on it due to its evolving and individual nature. As a result of this arduous process with a potentially unattainable goal, we, instead, have looked to several established theories that inform how we understand the concept of intimacy. The theories presented in this chapter are some of the ways we've attempted to make sense of the concept of intimacy, knowing and being explicit about the fact that it's a constantly evolving and moving target.

Intimacy Along a Biopsychosocial/Spiritual Continuum

When you stop to think about intimacy, what comes to mind? Do you think about what it *feels like* to be intimate with another person? Do you pay more attention to how you *interact* with those around you differently after entering into an intimate relationship? Do you focus on the *thoughts*—both joyous and anxiety provoking—that come to your mind? We would imagine that for the majority of people, the running scripts in our heads consider all of these things and more. To capture the essence of our complicated selves, the biopsychosocial model was originally proposed by George Engel (1977). This holistic approach examines how different parts of our being—the biological, psychological, social, and spiritual—connect to and influence one another. Under this model it is assumed that one aspect of our health, such as our psychological health, cannot truly be teased out from the others. To fully understand one's psychological health, it needs to be looked at in the context of the other aspects of health.

Previous research as well as our personal experiences has repeatedly demonstrated the link between intimacy and our physiology. A common experience of this is in getting ready for a first

Corresponding Author: Lisa J. Trump, M.S., University of Minnesota; Department of Family Social Science; 1985 Buford Ave.; 290 McNeal Hall; Saint Paul, MN 55108. E-mail: buch0245@umn.edu.

date—your stomach might feel like it's filled with butterflies or that it's doing summersaults, your palms might be sweating, and if you're really nervous, your body might even be shaking slightly. Studies, too, have exemplified associations between physiological health and relationships. For example, an interesting study by Kiecolt-Glaser and colleagues (2005) investigated the relationship between positive and negative marital interactions and partners' physical health. Each participant received a suction blister on his or her arm and the couples were randomly placed into one of two groups: those directed to engage in a positive, supportive interaction and those directed to discuss a marital disagreement. The blisters healed slower for the couples engaging in negative interactions than for those interacting in a positive manner. As you can see from this example, the link between our relational experiences and our physiology is significant.

In addition to our physical health, our experiences of intimacy contain the ability to influence our psychological, social, and spiritual health, too. Think back to the example of getting ready for your date. You probably had thoughts running through your head like, *Will s/he like me? What will we talk about? Will our personalities match?* Intimacy, or lack thereof, can directly influence our anxiety and depressive levels, our self-esteem and perceptions of self-worth, and our motivation and ambition/drive, to name a few. Further, relationships and intimacy often bleed into our social experiences and health. If after a few months of dating, you're feeling fulfilled in your relationship and feeling good about yourself, your ways of interacting with others in your social context might look different than if you're feeling unfulfilled, anxious or discontent with your relationship. For example, your experience of comfort and support from your partner may transfer to an increased level of courage when interacting with others.

Lastly, our spiritual health, however one defines it, is intertwined with intimacy in an intricate manner. This component of the biopsychosocial/spiritual model is the most debated by scholars due to its individual, personal nature and the fact that not everybody identifies as being a "spiritual person." Those who do identify spirituality as an important aspect to their being often experience a direct link between their relationships and experiences in spirituality. For example, those who feel loved by their partners might attribute that experience to being blessed by a higher power. Or perhaps those in the midst of a challenging, hurtful relationship might become frustrated with a higher power for not providing wisdom for how to handle the situation(s).

This theory posits that we are complex beings; we cannot isolate out one sole component to fully explain our experiences in relationship with others. Rather, our experience as a whole is defined by the interaction between the biological, psychological, social, and spiritual components. Only focusing on or attending to one aspect of our self with regard to intimacy is a simplistic approach that arguably will fail to capture the true reality of our experiences.

EVOLUTIONARY THEORY OF ATTRACTION

The Evolutionary Theory of Attraction was developed by David Buss as an extension of Darwin's (1859) Theory of Natural Selection. The basis of Darwin's theory was that individuals within a community compete against one another for valuable resources, and those who are best equipped to compete have a higher likelihood of survival. In addition to resources that fulfill one's basic needs, such as food and shelter, key reproductive resources held by those of the opposite sex are also being competed for. Because individuals vary in their capacity of the reproductive resources deemed most valuable, those with the "best" resources are most sought after by those of the opposite sex. Darwin later extended his theory to encompass what he termed as *sexual selection* (1871), which describes the evolution of valuable characteristics that increase the likelihood of successful mating. Just as animals evolved and grew heavy horns or learned mating dances and calls to increase their chances of mating and survival, we too, as humans, have evolved to become more desirable.

Much of the work by Darwin focused on the process of selecting a member of the opposite sex, and how it differed by gender. In his early observations, Darwin discovered that females were significantly more discriminative in their mating than were males (Buss, 1988; Grammer, Fink, Møller, & Thornhill, 2003) and, as a result, males competed against one another through displays of their valued characteristics and resources. Darwin termed the process of competing against one another for the attention of the opposite sex as *intersexual competition*. Although much of the time members of the same sex were directly competing against one another in the pursuit of reproductive success, there were other forms of competition that were less directly confrontational. In some instances, the competition was much more subtle, even to the point of one never coming face-to-face with his or her competition. As individuals competed for reproductive resources, they developed skills in locating potential mates, demonstrating mate-attracting behaviors, acquiring and displaying resources that are highly desired, and altering aspects of their appearance (Buss, 1988). Although both sexes adopted certain reproductive strategies to make themselves more desirable, the specific alterations were largely guided by one's gender.

Research by Buss (1987) focused specifically on gender differences in mate selection. According to the Evolutionary Theory of Attraction, the primary purpose of love is to propagate one's genes to ensure survival across generations. (It is crucial to note that homosexuality was not considered in this particular theory due to its emphasis on reproduction.) Under this Evolutionary Theory, males' primary task is to spread their genes to ensure that children would be conceived, whereas the female's task is to seek out a mate who would provide resources long-term to ensure that children would survive. This naturally positions the sexes against one another (males as aggressors and females as defenders). As a result, males more so than females show greater interest in physical attraction and a healthy, youthful appearance. In contrast, females show preference for males who demonstrate their ability and willingness to invest and provide social, psychological, and material resources. In other words, males look for signs of reproductive fitness (e.g., youthfulness) whereas females look for signs of exclusivity (e.g., ability to provide).

Although this theory stems from early research in the mid-1800s, there is support for the notion that the same genetic and social drives are still active in how we socialize today. Both males and females use certain tactics to compete against other same-sex members for attention from the opposite sex. Women often focus on altering their appearance by wearing makeup and selecting clothes that adhere to the current styles. For example, a woman going to a party with other women will want to make sure that she wears her most flattering outfit and has her hair done to stand out from the group and attract attention. Women are also more likely to use the tactic of acting nice, soft, and more passive as compared to men. Men, on the other hand, often use the tactics of boasting and displaying expensive possessions, such as a brand new Lexus, to demonstrate their financial success (even if it's not an authentic display of such). They are also more likely to demonstrate their athletic abilities and strength. In the study by Buss (1988), effective tactics shared by both sexes included: humor, manners, sympathy, and good grooming. Interestingly, this study also revealed that the demonstration of overtly sexual and provocative tactics by females are mainly effective for short-term sex partners, but are not as effective for attracting a long-term mate.

FILTER THEORY OF ATTRACTION

The Filter Theory of Attraction proposed by Duck and Craig (1977) depicts the process of narrowing down the dating pool of all potential partners by different considerations at different levels of attraction and compatibility. The narrowing down process considers attraction across the external (e.g., physical attributes), impersonal (e.g., attitudes toward events or objects), and interpersonal (e.g., attitudes about other individuals) domains (Duck & Craig, 1977; Miller & Todd, 1998). As each individual considers what s/he deems as attractive, the weight of each of these three components shifts according to his or her individual preferences. What you find physically attractive is likely to be different than the next person you pass on the sidewalk. Further, what you find attractive today is likely to be different than what you found attractive 10 years ago. Yet, we all go through a similar process of filtering down to arrive at the one or few potential partners for us.

The Filter Theory is appropriately named due to its resemblance of a filter—it has a widened mouth at the top and then narrows down to a small opening at the bottom. We begin the process at the top of the filter and slowly make our way down by going through the different stages of the filtering process.

Filter Theory of Attraction

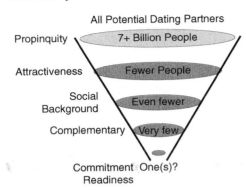

Prior to beginning the process of narrowing, each individual begins with a pool of all potential dating partners—all seven billion (and counting) people on the Earth today. The first step of narrowing is termed *propinquity*—considering those who are in close proximity to you. An individual who is residing in Switzerland is not likely to be a potential partner for one living in Alaska—the regular commute would be terrible. Therefore, environmental factors, and more specifically proximity, allow for communication—both verbal and nonverbal—to take place and for us to continue filtering out those we see as a potential match. However, due to the increased access and use of online dating websites, our process of narrowing by propinquity today looks much different than it did a few decades ago. For those involved in these sites, their dating pools remain much larger due to their contact with those around the globe.

The second level of filtering is based on the characteristics one finds attractive in a mate. For some, they're most drawn to tall and dark skinned people, for others it may be shorter people with curly hair and, for others yet, they may really have a thing for glasses. This not only varies from person to person; it also often changes and evolves overtime. In addition to physical characteristics, at this stage in the filtering process, individuals also consider what they find attractive in terms of style, dress, artifacts, and so on. Although this stage might initially sound or feel shallow or less important, we assure you that all of us, as humans, are naturally drawn to those we find attractive and have ingrained perceptions of what we consider to be "beauty." By considering the physical characteristics of those in close proximity to us, we can work to narrow our pool of potential mates further.

Up to this point in the filtering process, these stages have been pre-interaction; they are the way we filter down to those we want to initiate an interaction or conversation with. The third stage of filtering involves considering others' social backgrounds. *Did s/he come from a family with a high or low socioeconomic status? A rural or urban area? A culture that is similar to mine? Does s/he communicate like I do, and are we able to communicate well together? Do we live similar lifestyles?* For many, up to this stage in the filtering process, there is still a large pool of potential dating partners; however, this stage has arguably tighter parameters dictating who continues on as a potential mate. Said another way, you might find many people in close proximity to you as attractive, but there might be much fewer who have similar social backgrounds. We would imagine you might be wondering: *Why does it matter if they have a similar social background as me? I am interested in all kinds of people!* Yes, we believe that is true, yet the popular saying "birds of a feather flock together" rings true here. Although we might initially be interested in our *antitheses*—ones who are strikingly different from us—we tend to be more successfully matched in the long term with those who are similar to us (Burleson, Kunkel, & Szolwinski, 1997).

Working our way down the filter, the second to last stage involves considering how others are complementary to us. We look at the remaining pool of potential dating partners and ask ourselves: *Do they have similar attitudes and beliefs as me? Do our core values align?* If you value education, it is important that your partner values it too. If you want to have a large family, the best partner for you will be somebody who wants this too. The manners in which we live our daily lives are important to consider here, as well. If you are always on-time for social engagements, a person who is chronically late for everything is not a good match. If you are generally a clean and tidy person, somebody whose house or apartment is always messy and cluttered is similarly not such a good mate. Due to the intimate, personal nature of these questions, the strongest bonds are forged during this stage, as compared to the others. For most individuals walking through the Filter Theory very few individuals make it through these final stages.

The last stage of filtering down to the one or few potential dating partners is considering if they, too, are ready for commitment. If s/he is in close proximity to you, attractive to you, has a similar social background as you, and you are complementary, yet s/he is not looking for a commitment, it will likely not work out. According to Duck and Craig (1977), the result of going through the filtering process is that you arrive at one or a few potential mates that you are highly compatible with. The goal is that by filtering out individuals who do not possess some or all of the characteristics you are looking for, your likelihood for the relationship to survive and flourish is increased. However, humans are far from being mechanical creatures—we don't always set our parameters around filtering appropriately and may become too stringent or too loose with how we narrow down. Further, our criteria for what we are looking for in a partner might evolve over time, resulting in those that might have been filtered out previously to now become potential dating partners. Lastly, for many, the notion of "the one" is unrealistic, undesirable, and/or unattainable. Rather, you may view this theory as filtering down to a small number of mates who are compatible with you, as opposed to narrowing down to one single person.

WHEEL OF LOVE

Many approaches to love—especially within research and academic contexts—have worked to operationalize what love is and how it develops in an attempt to solidify what the *real, true* or *best* form of love is. Previous academic textbooks have portrayed love within the marital context as being preferred over other emotional experiences of love. Of course, it is understandable how previous researchers arrived at that conclusion when you also consider the predominant cultural beliefs in earlier time periods. Other types of love, such as the experience of infatuation, were less accepted as they are in today's culture. In response to previous conceptualizations of love that were quite limited and restricted, Ira Reiss developed the Wheel of Love Theory that in its es-

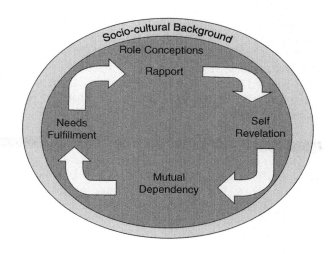

sence is a sociological approach (Reiss, 1960; Adams, 2012; Owens, 2007). Reiss (1960) set out to create a model that demonstrates the development of love and considers the psychological components as well as the social and cultural components that contribute to how couples join together and establish a relationship. As couples enter into the "wheel" or cycle of relationship development, these different components influence both partners' experiences and movement forward. This theory was originally proposed for heterosexual couples; however, it can be argued that it is equally applicable for all couples.

In today's society, couples meet in a variety of contexts. They meet through mutual friends, classes, work, or while attending a party or social event, to name a few. After meeting, the two individuals become aware of the presence of a feeling of rapport (Reiss, 1960), which is the first of four stages of this theory. *Rapport* is defined a sense of mutual understanding and comfort. The individuals might feel at ease talking with and being around one another, and may feel comfortable talking about themselves and learning about the other. Alternatively, those who have failed to establish a sense of rapport are likely to feel uncomfortable talking with one another for extended periods of time, and might look for ways to end the conversation early. As Reiss posited, developing rapport is not simply an indication of compatibility; rather, it provides information about the social and cultural backgrounds of the individuals and how their individual backgrounds are related to their personality needs. Hence, factors of our cultural and social backgrounds directly influence how we feel rapport for others.

The feeling of *rapport*, according to Reiss (1960), is the first stage in developing love relationships. The second stage is termed *self-revelation*, which is defined as sharing intimate aspects about one's self with the other. Revealing one's self might involve sharing hopes, dreams, desires, future plans, and fears. Additionally, it might involve sharing one's self physically through sexual activities. Here, too, we look to the social and cultural ties to determine what is appropriate to share with others. Particular cultures place certain restrictions on what is acceptable to share. For example, many Muslim women wear a *hijab*—a cloth head covering or scarf—to maintain modesty while in the presence of males outside of their immediate family. A person's social and cultural background will inform what is acceptable to reveal to others and at what point in developing rapport can it be revealed.

After developing rapport and sharing intimate aspects about oneself, the third stage of establishing love relationships is the development of mutual dependencies. The term *mutual dependencies* is defined as developing interdependent habit systems where partners become dependent on one another to fulfill one's own needs or wants (Reiss, 1960). As two people develop a rapport and begin to reveal intimate parts of their selves, they begin to develop habitual expectations for how they will be able to fulfill their needs or desires. For example, one partner may learn to look to the other to fulfill his/her need for comfort and a safe place to discuss one's feelings. When these expectations are not fulfilled, the individual might feel lonely and frustrated, unsure of why their partner was not available to them. Other habitual expectations that develop for couples include fulfilling sexual desires and telling jokes to and sharing ideas with one another.

In line with the previous two stages of love development, the development of mutual dependencies is also guided by one's social and cultural background. The type of habits one develops with regard to his or her partner is culturally determined, whether it is done consciously or unconsciously. Further, the habitual expectations are informed by and extend from the previous stage—self-revelation.

Finally, the fourth stage of the Wheel of Love Theory is termed *needs fulfillment*—defined as the basic personality needs that define and maintain a relationship between two partners. Table 1 displays several of the common personality needs considered in this stage (Reiss, 1960). Although the specific personality needs for each individual vary by social and cultural factors, as relationships become more established, the other processes are likely to contribute to meeting one's personality needs. As Reiss noted, "These four processes are in a sense really one process, for when one feels rapport, he reveals himself and becomes dependent, thereby fulfilling his personality needs" (1960, p. 143). These processes do not simply occur in a particular order and conclude when a couple reaches personality needs fulfillment. Rather, they are constantly occurring, developing a cyclical pattern similar to the motion of a wheel.

Of course, it is important to note that the "wheel" does not always move in a positive direction; rather, it can reverse and begin to rotate backward. For example, a couple might experience a particularly hurtful argument that weakens their sense of rapport, which in turn decreases the amount they are willing to reveal to one another, their dependency on one another, and their sense of fulfillment. The "wheel" can also continue to positively rotate, indefinitely, and at whatever level of intensity the couple and their social and cultural backgrounds allow. Lastly, these four processes are understood to be at the heart of all loving relationships, including friendships and parent–child relationships. It is argued that all types of love travel through the four stages, though their routes may look different. The romantic love hurries through the processes quickly in an excitement to establish the relationship; the sexual type focuses most on self-revelation; the rational type goes through the four processes slowly to establish an in-depth understanding of one another. Regardless of type of love, this theory is distinguished from other theoretical perspectives on the development of love due to its emphasis on the social and cultural influences at each stage.

TABLE 1 Personality Needs: For someone . . .

1. Who loves me
2. To confide in
3. Who shows me affection
4. Who respects my ideals
5. Who appreciates what I want to achieve
6. Who understands my moods
7. Who helps me in making important decisions
8. To stimulate my ambition
9. I can look up to
10. Who boosts my self-confidence in my relations with people

TRIANGULAR THEORY

Sternberg's Triangular Theory of love holds that love, like a triangle, is understood by three interacting components. The three main components are intimacy, passion, and commitment, which sit at the vertices of the triangle. Each of these components embraces different characteristics of relationships, so having a working understanding of how they are differentiated from one another is important. However, one should be cautioned to not lose sight of the whole when focusing solely on its parts. By focusing on only one or two of the parts, the complexity of the concept of love as a whole is partially or entirely lost.

MAIN COMPONENTS. *Intimacy* refers to feelings of closeness, connectedness, and being bonded with another. Couples with high levels of intimacy often enjoy spending quality time together, enjoying one another and reestablishing their connection. The specific factors as outlined by Sternberg that make up intimacy are identified in Table 2 (Madey & Rodgers, 2009; Owens, 2007; Sternberg, 1986). The term *liking* is associated with relationships where intimacy is the only component present for one or both members, and is most commonly seen in friendships.

Passion refers to the physical and psychological drives that guide romance, physical attraction, and sexual activities or other forms of arousal in relationships (Sternberg, 1986). You might notice these couples being highly physical or touchy, sitting close to one another and exuding a sense of lust and infatuation. The term *infatuate* (or infatuated) is associated with relationships where passion is the only component present for one or both members. Table 3 highlights several of the factors within this particular component, and is oftentimes connected with the experience of "love at first site" (Sternberg, 1986).

Commitment is partitioned into two factors (see Table 4): the decision that one loves another, and committing to the maintenance of that love (Sternberg, 1986). These relationships are often depicted as a slow burning love, protected so that the flame isn't extinguished. From an outsider's perspective, couples with high levels of commitment may appear more similar to a friendship than to a romantic relationship, though highly committed couples can certainly hold on to the romance. The term *empty love* refers to those who have made a decision to love another and have made a long-term commitment to the relationship, but do not possess any passion or intimacy for the other person.

To explain the differences between the three main components of the love triangle further, Sternberg likened each component to temperature:

TABLE 2 Factors within the Intimacy Component

a. Desire to promote the welfare of the loved one
b. Experience happiness with the loved one
c. High regard for the loved one
d. Being able to count on the loved one during times of need
e. Mutual understanding with the loved one
f. Sharing of one's self and one's possessions with the loved one
g. Receipt of emotional support from the loved one
h. Giving of emotional support to the loved one
i. Intimate communication with the loved one
j. Valuing the loved one in one's life

TABLE 3 Factors within the Passion Component

a. Sexual needs
b. Self-esteem
c. Dependence
d. Nurturance
e. Affiliation
f. Dominance
g. Submission
h. Self-actualization

TABLE 4 Factors within the Commitment Compenent

a. The decision that one loves another
b. The commitment to maintain that love

Intimacy as being a warm sensation, passion as hot, and commitment as feeling cool. Furthermore, different forces drive the three components: the intimacy component is primarily driven by an emotional investment, the passion component by a motivational investment, and the commitment component by a cognitive decision (Sternberg, 1986).

The three components also differ with respect to their properties. Specifically, the intimacy component and the commitment component share a sense of relative stability, whereas the passion component is often experienced as being unstable. The commitment component has a high degree of control over the decision to invest in the relationship, yet possesses little control over becoming aroused after looking at or interacting with an attractive person. There is usually high awareness when it comes to the passion component, as evidenced in the level of arousal experienced, whereas the intimacy and commitment components may be less obvious to a person. Sometimes the experience of feeling connected to or bonded with another person is more obvious to those around us, such as our close friends, than it is to us. Similarly, we may not realize how committed we are to a person or relationship until it is tested or threatened. The three components may also differ in the length and intensity of a relationship, the applicability to other relationship types (i.e., friendships, parent–child relationships), and other biological, psychological, and social influences. For example, the passion component will likely experience significantly more physiological influences or cues than will the commitment component.

SUBCOMPONENTS. So far, we've discussed the three main components—intimacy, passion, and commitment—that sit at the vertices of the triangle. There are also components that sit along each side of the triangle that are blends of the two main components surrounding it. *Nonlove* refers to the absence of all three main components of love. In short, these are simply casual interactions with strangers or acquaintances that do not possess any form of love. *Romantic love* is a combination of passion and intimacy and sits on the left side of the triangle. Couples with romantic love are drawn to one another and truly enjoy one another, yet they have not made the decision or commitment to the relationship. *Companionate love* is a combination of intimacy and commitment and is located on the right side of the triangle. Those with this type of love have a blend of intimacy and commitment without much passion. This is often seen in couples that have been together for several decades and have "lost their spark." *Fatuous love* refers to a combination of the passion and commitment components and sits at the foot of the triangle. These types of relationships quickly develop without providing adequate time to develop true liking and companionship between the partners. Due to the quick pace, these couples are at higher risk of divorce. Lastly, *Consummate love* refers to a combination of all three components of love. These are couples that have struck a healthy balance of intimacy, passion, and commitment, which is commonly seen as the gold standard of love types. However, it is important to note that not all couples seek to develop all three components in tandem, and therefore it cannot be claimed as the "best" type. Attaining consummate love can be an arduous process that requires attention both in the formation stages as well as in maintenance. For many, it is easier to arrive at the desired type of love than it is to maintain it over time.

GEOMETRY OF THE LOVE TRIANGLE. When considering the geometry of the triangle, both area and shape communicate important information about one's love type. With regard to area, the smaller the love triangle, the less intense the love is understood to be. In contrast, those with a large area within their triangles are understood to experience more love in their relationships. With regard to shape, the equilateral triangle represents love that is equally balanced in all three main components. Triangles that are unbalanced represent relationships where there is significantly more of one component than the others. For example, if an individual experiences significantly more passion in her relationship with little intimacy or commitment, her triangle would look like a scalene triangle pointing toward the left. When considering both the area and shape of the love triangle, a wide variety of relationship types are represented. In addition to exploring the geometry of one's own triangle, it is also important to consider the size and shape of your significant other, friend or family member's triangle. After all, love does not exist solely with one person. For example, a couple where one member has a very small sized triangle and the other member has a fairly large triangle are not likely to be compatible because they're unequally invested in their relationship. Moreover, a couple where one member has a scalene-shaped triangle pulled to the right (emphasizing the commitment component) and the other member with an equilateral triangle may experience difficulty due to their different areas of focus.

LOVE STYLES

Love styles—or the manners in which we tend to think, feel, and behave in love—were originally developed by John Lee (1973). Six major styles capture almost all of us, and while we might evidence characteristics of two or more in our everyday functioning, a dominant one is generally leading the way (Lee, 1973, 1978; Neto, 2007).

Six Love Styles

EROS. This love style is what we see in popular movies or read about in romance novels. Eros is a love based on beauty, physical attraction, and "chemistry." It's the love-at-first sight as you see her from across the room at the party. It's the "Oh my God, he is so amazing!" that we hear ourselves saying, often after only knowing each other for a very short time. People loving in this manner want to know everything about the other; they'll talk on the phone for hours, send each other "good morning," "goodnight," "I'm thinking about you," and "I love you" texts every day. They want to spend all of their time with their partners, and oftentimes do so even at the expense of losing contact with other friends or family. Eros lovers see marriage as an extended honeymoon, and they view sex as an ultimate aesthetic experience. They call each other pet names (like "Sexy" or "Sweet-pea") and tend to view each other in very idealized ways (like "She is the most beautiful woman in the world!"). They leave love notes for their partners to find, create play-lists of romantic songs, write poetry, and send "just because" cards. Every day is a day of romantic adoration.

To be sure, Eros love is a dynamic and fun way to love. And couples who are able to sustain it tend to report high levels of satisfaction. But they can also be perceived as hopeless romantics, and risk declines in said satisfaction (or even risk breaking up altogether) as the novelty of a new relationship naturally wears off, or as physical beauty and attraction declines with age and time. They are also very sensitive to others' criticism of a partner, and can take break ups very hard.

MANIA. Like Eros, Mania love can encompass a strong attraction and draw to partners, but in a considerably more obsessive way. Mania lovers tend to have very low self-esteem, and view a relationship as a way to feel worthy or good. They are thereby quickly consumed by thoughts about a new person, maintaining that they "need" him or her. Mania lovers function with an insatiable want for attention and signs of affection (read: approval). Sex is often viewed as reassurance that everything is okay. Mania lovers also tend to evidence considerable possessiveness, alongside high levels of jealousy and insecurity about the partner leaving, cheating, or otherwise not reciprocating love with equal intensity or commitment.

Some people seem to thrive on drama, and Mania no doubt delivers this kind of relational intensity (rollercoaster highs and lows). However, people who love this way are also good at score-keeping ("After all I've done for you . . .!"), and their insatiable needs for attention and regard can be exhausting to their partners. Mania lovers are also prone to violence (verbal, physical, or sexual), some right away and others later on as their insecurities and poor self-control are allowed to foster and grow.

LUDUS. People loving in a Ludus manner are carefree and casual in their approach to relationships. If it feels good, they do it. Love is often experienced as a "game" wherein seduction, getting-the-girl/boy, and the thrill or challenge of "the chase" drive a way of interrelating with others that is both fun and straightforwardly pleasure-seeking. They generally will not reveal personal thoughts or feelings, as the acquisition of their current conquest requires they do or say whatever is necessary. In marked contrast to Mania, Ludus lovers are not at all possessive. They prize relationships with "no strings attached" and tend to have many of them (either sequentially or simultaneously). Probably due to their extensive experience and comfort, Ludus lovers also tend to be excellent sexual partners (with considerable knowledge and skills in a variety of sexual methods and techniques).

People who love in a Ludus manner do not usually stay in any single union for very long, and they are generally not troubled by relationship break-ups (there are always other potential partners out there, and rebounds can happen very fast). In fact, they oftentimes see marriage as a trap because it would circumvent their ability to "play the field". They are the most likely of any love style to commit infidelity, and are thereby generally best-matched with others who love in the same way(s).

PRAGMA. Pragma lovers are rational, objective, and even strategic in their approach to love. This love style is defined by a careful appraisal of what potential partners offer before advancing into any type of union. Likely fueled by evolutionary dispositions that we discussed earlier in this chapter (i.e., heterosexual men seeking women who they see as readily able to reproduce, heterosexual women seeking men who can support them), Pragma lovers approach relationships with a "shopping list" of criteria. *Is she young, beautiful, and sexy? Is he educated? Does he have a good job? Does he make a lot of money?* Once a potential mate has passed such tests, then—and only then—can a relationship begin.

While many view Pragma lovers as shallow or otherwise taking the romance out of relationships, they are generally not too worried about what their critics think. They see themselves as realistic and sensible in the unions and life they are creating. They don't tend to get married until they are wholly ready to do so. They won't have any more children than they can afford. And if she's beautiful (which makes him happy) and he's rich (which makes her happy), everybody wins.

STORGE. This kind of love is based on—or even defined by—friendship. And in comparison to how romance can develop quickly (ask any Eros lover if you doubt this!), friendship takes considerably longer to take hold and grow. People who love in a Storge manner tend to take their time. Their love is "slow burning" and affectionate, oftentimes trading a strong sense of stability in exchange for the passion and romance evidenced in other styles. Like friends, Storge lovers enjoy each other's company, and their affection for each other grows over the years.

From the outside in, others can view people who love in this manner as "low key," almost plutonic or even boring. But for those loving this way, relationships are seen as contexts of stalwart commitment and safety. Think about it: Have you ever noticed how you can go through your life and have many boyfriends or girlfriends, husbands or wives, but your one or two closest friends are always there? What is different about those relationships—the ones that stand the test of time? Storge lovers argue that friendship is stronger than the passionate romance so many others seek. And instead of having different people be their best friend and lover, they combine the two within one person.

AGAPE. At almost every Christian wedding, it seems, couples have somebody read passages from Corinthians (verse 13: 4–7) about how love is patient, kind, never keeps score, and is always persevering. This type of love—Agape love—is altruistic, self-sacrificing, and never in pursuit or expectation of reciprocity. People who love in this way pride themselves for always putting their partners first and for loving "unconditionally".

In reality, however, Agape love is oftentimes difficult to maintain over the long haul. People who love this way tend to give to their partners considerably more than they receive. This can be measured in time, tasks, energy, or actions. And while appropriate between, say, an infant and a parent, the unbalanced nature of this exchange can eventually wear Agape lovers out. And if they continue loving in this manner (and it is not reciprocated), people loving in an Agape style can become difficult to differentiate from martyrdom or co-dependency. Even in light of how varied they can be in their respective viewpoints, most relationship experts agree that adults are more happy when their unions are balanced (give-and-take) and conditional (e.g., expecting respect, not accepting violence).

PUTTING IT ALL TOGETHER

It is clear that the theories presented here—trying to explain what we are looking for in a partner, how we court each other, the ways that we love one another, and whether we stay together or break up—overlap in a variety of ways. Remember that intimacy is a fuzzy concept, and one that can be looked at from any variety of personal, dyadic, familial, ethnic/cultural, and contextual angles. For example, biopsychosocial/spiritual theories of love are arguably the most broad (what individual or relational process could not fall under such a large umbrella?). Innate drives to propagate one's species certainly inform why men tend to be such visual creatures vis-à-vis women's tendencies to care more about men's material resources. This also is likely connected to how more men love in Ludus manners (i.e., spreading one's genes) and more women love in Pragma manners (i.e., ensuring stability and survival).

Then consider Storge; would someone not need to cycle through the Wheel Theory's series of rapport, self revelation, mutual dependency, and needs fulfillment in order to achieve the friendship so valued by lovers of this character? And would not the Consummate Love held up by the Triangular Theory equally combine Eros (passion), Storge (liking), and Agape (commitment)? And so on.

We thereby encourage you, the reader, to reflect about how these theories—and indeed, everything throughout this text—fit for you. There are some things that you will undoubtedly connect with (e.g., how you systematically traversed sequential layers of the Filter Theory to find the person you are with today). There are other things that you may not connect with, or even agree with (e.g., maybe you and your "opposite" partner are an exception to the "birds of a feather flock together" adage). Think about it. Take it in. Challenge it. And challenge yourself, especially as you identify things you want to change. You, and your relationships, will be better for it.

REFERENCES

Adams, W. J. (2012). A counselor's assessment of love development in mate selection and marriage. *Canadian Journal of Counselling and Psychotherapy/Revue canadienne de counseling et de psychothérapie, 13*, 93–97.

Burleson, B. R., Kunkel, A. W., & Szolwinski, J. B. (1997). Similarity in cognitive complexity and attraction to friends and lovers: Experimental and correlational studies. *Journal of Constructivist Psychology, 10*(3), 221–248. doi:10.1080/10720539708404624

Buss, D. M. (1988). The evolution of human intrasexual competition: Tactics of mate attraction. *Journal of Personality and Social Psychology, 54*, 616–628. doi:1988-20021-001

Duck, S., & Craig, G. (1977). The relative attractiveness of different types of information about another person. *British Journal of Social & Clinical Psychology, 16*, 229–233. doi:10.1111/j.2044-8260.1977.tb00223.x

Engel, G. (1977). The need for a new medical model: A challenge for biomedicine. *Science, 196*, 129–136. doi: 10.1126/science.847460

Grammer, K., Fink, B., Møller, A. P., & Thornhill, R. (2003). Darwinian aesthetics: Sexual selection and the biology of beauty. *Biological Reviews, 78*, 385–407. doi:10.1017/S1464793102006085

Kiecolt-Glaser, J. K., Loving, T. J., Stowell, J. R., Malarkey, W. B., Lemeshow, S., Dickinson, S. L., Glaser, R. (2005). Hostile marital interactions, proinflammatory cytokine production, and wound healing. *Archive of General Psychiatry, 62*, 1377–1384. Retrieved from: http://archpsyc.jamanetwork.com/

Lee, J. (1973). *Colours of love: An exploration of the ways of loving.* Toronto: New Press.

Lee, J. (1988). Love styles. In M. Barnes and R. Sternberg (Eds.), *The Psychology of Love* (pp. 38–67). New Haven, CT: Yale University Press.

Madey, S. F., & Rodgers, L. (2009). The effect of attachment and Sternberg's triangular theory of love on relationship satisfaction. *Individual Differences Research, 7*, 266–271. doi:1541-745X

Miller, G. F., & Todd, P. M. (1998). Mate choice turns cognitive. *Trends in Cognitive Sciences, 2*(5), 190–198. doi: 10.1016/S1364-6613(98)01169-3

Neto, F. (2007). Love styles: A cross-cultural study of British, Indian, and Portuguese college students. *Journal of Comparative Family Studies, 38*, 239–254. Retrieved from http://www.jstor.org.ezp1.lib.umn.edu/stable/41604144

Owens, E. (2007). The sociology of love, courtship, and dating. In C. Bryant and D. Peck (Eds.), *21st century sociology* (pp. 266–271). United Kingdom Look in edit book SAGE Publications.

Reiss, I. L. (1960). Toward a sociology of the heterosexual love relationship. *Marriage and Family Living, 22*, 139–145. doi:10.2307/347330

Sternberg, R. J. (1986). A triangular theory of love. *Psychological Review, 93*, 119–135. Retrieved from: http://psycnet.apa.org.ezp1.lib.umn.edu/journals/rev/93/2/119.html

2

Attachment: How Where We Have Been Influences What We do in Relationships

Kirsten Lind Seal, Ph.D., LMFT
Graduate School of Health and Human Services
Saint Mary's University of Minnesota

Jennifer L. Doty, Ph.D.
Department of Pediatrics
University of Minnesota

LEARNING OBJECTIVES

- Understand the key processes and assumptions of attachment theory
- Articulate how different attachment styles relate to views of the self and others
- Understand how early attachment styles follow us into adulthood
- Articulate ways to challenge and/or change attachment during adulthood

Lacy and Drew

STAGE 1: AT A PARTY

"That guy keeps looking at you!" Jessica loudly and drunkenly informed her friend.

"Which one?" Lacy grimaced. Jess was looking toward a large group of guys, some with greasy hair, some without hair at all, and many of whom seemed too old anyway.

"That green guy with blonde hair. Blondie. Blondie over there." Jess kept adding sentence fragments as she tried to make her face look increasingly concentrated, a thing she often did when she was so tipsy.

Lacy saw who Blondie was. The hot guy with the green shirt standing next to the keg. "He looks a bit old for a college party. Probably a weirdo."

"Pervy man from Australia likes you. Likes you likes you, for real, Lace."

"How do you know he's from Australia?" Lacy liked men with accents, and suddenly he looked less strange in this group of younger-looking people.

"He probably isn't. Who knows for sure? No one ever knows if a man is Australian, do they?"

Great, Lacy thought. *A hot guy who isn't from Australia likes me—which means either trouble or I'll be married within the year.* She pictured telling the story as an old woman. *I say, when I met your Grandfather he was wearing an* utterly despicable *green shirt and I was under the impression that he was from Australia. I was indeed.*

STAGE 2: THREE YEARS LATER

The couple was in the supermarket buying groceries for their in-home date night. A thriller was on Netflix and they thought they'd watch it at his house. Green-shirt-man had turned out to be Drew, who was only a year older than Lacy and neither a weirdo nor Australian. *Not a weirdo*, thought Lacy, *maybe he was someone who could be* the one. Sometimes, though, the concept of *just one* was no longer popular with her. They had a fight the night before about what to do after Drew's graduation in a month. She wanted

(continued)

Kirsten Lind Seal, Ph.D., LMFT; Saint Mary's University of Minnesota; Graduate School of Health and Human Services; Marriage and Family Therapy Program; 2500 Park Avenue South; Minneapolis, MN 55404. E-mail: klseal12@smumn.edu.

to move in with him but he insisted on staying in separate places until she finishes her undergraduate education. *Three years and he won't even move in with me*, she thought to herself as she scanned the peanut butter while Drew was most likely looking for vegetables. The thoughts she frequently pushed away came sliding through her mind like a dirty mop on the grocery store's floors. *He is going to leave me.* Lacy said it under her breath. *He is going to leave me. He will leave. Simple as that.*

She pictured herself calling her mother at 11 p.m. on a Friday night, but then what would that do? *I told you so Lacy*, she'd say. *They always leave. If you're really my daughter, and I think you are, you know it deep down. You don't need him. You don't need anyone.*

Shut up mom, you've never been much help, Lacy would say. *You've been a loser ever since the divorce, but I can hardly remember a time when you weren't a loser anyway. And now I'm in a lame-ass grocery store trying to call my mom because that's what 20-year-old girls do when bad things happen, and all I can get from you is, "suck it up, Lacy," and all I ever wanted was to be good enough. But I've never been good enough for anybody and now Drew is going to break up with me because of you and you know what? I don't need you. I don't need anyone.*

Deep breath. *No*, Lacy thought. *No one needs you.* Lacy stood in front of the peanut butter, forgetting where she was—and suddenly, she jumped at the sudden sound of his voice.

"Hey, I just got—I didn't mean to scare you. Jeez, Lacy, you're supposed to freak out *during* the movie." Drew was grinning and holding two full grocery baskets. "And by the way, choosing which peanut butter to get is not that hard."

Lacy realized that she had been staring at the creamy peanut butter as if she was turning it back to peanuts with her mind. She relaxed her expression and put on a smile. "I was just practicing my expression," she said sarcastically. "I know how scared you get during this kind of film. Don't want you to feel alone."

"How considerate of you."

Lacy shrugged. "I try."

"Did you get popcorn?"

Lacy looked at him. "You said 'no popcorn'. As in, *no popcorn.*"

"Actually I said, 'popcorn', as in, *popcorn.*" When Lacy made no response, Drew said, "Okay weirdo, *I* will get the popcorn and it's going to be that low calorie kind." He left. Lacy followed him shortly afterward, wondering how any film could be as scary as a relationship.

INTRODUCTION

How do our experiences in childhood relate to and/ or influence our thought patterns and behaviors in our adult relationships? Many scholars, therapists, and family researchers point to attachment theory (e.g., Main, Kaplan & Cassidy, 1985; Sroufe, 2005) as one of the major reasons we do what we do in relationships. In the story above, Lacy is clearly struggling with some serious anxiety over her relationship with Drew. She also seems to have some relationship issues with her mother; even when she wants to reach out for comfort, she talks herself out of it. Attachment theory can help us understand Lacy's strong reaction to her argument with Drew and why it stirs up so much anxiety for her. Lacy is not quite sure what is going on with her emotions or why she seems to be reacting so strongly to fairly innocuous statements. Attachment theory can help explain some of what was going on with Lacy during this particular interaction with her loved one.

In this chapter, we will discuss how attachment in childhood is related to adult experiences in intimate relationships. First, we examine the basics of attachment theory as it was originally conceptualized. Then, we review evidence that early attachment experiences affect adult functioning. In conclusion, we consider how attachment applies to romantic relationships in adulthood.

OVERVIEW OF ATTACHMENT THEORY

Attachment theory is considered by family scholars to be one of the most empirically supported theories in developmental literature (Murray, 1991; Palkovitz, 2006; Sroufe, 2005). The basic theory posits that attachment springs from the biologically-based necessity of an infant to be close to his or her caregiver for the sake of survival; thus attachment behavior can be seen as evolutionary in nature (Sroufe, 2005). Attachment is seen as an absolute necessity for human infants because of their complete state of physical helplessness at birth. Bowlby (1988) theorized that the attachment behavioral system was evolutionarily "designed" in order to ensure reproductive success and thus survival of the species.

Mary Ainsworth (1979, 1989) conducted the original research that created the empirical basis for attachment theory. Her original, groundbreaking work was built upon closely observing mother–infant interactions in both Africa (Uganda) and the United States. She developed a lab experiment called the *Strange Situation*. In this sequence, a mother and baby would enter a room filled with toys. Then a stranger would enter, and sit near the pair. After a minute or two the mother would leave the baby with the stranger in the room and, after a few minutes, return. The behavior of the baby upon the mother's leaving and upon the mother's return would determine

what Ainsworth termed the baby's *attachment style*. Secure babies would cry and protest when the mother left the room, rush to her upon her return, and then be soothed fairly quickly. Insecure babies, however, revealed a variety of behaviors. Some would not protest at all as the mother left the room, and then ignore her upon her return (*dismissive/avoidant*). Some would become inconsolable when she left and then continue to be inconsolable upon her return, oftentimes clinging to the mother long after she had come back (*anxious/preoccupied*). Thus, when distressed, secure babies sought out their "safe havens"—their mothers—and were able to be comforted within a few minutes. The insecurely attached babies, however, appeared to be unable to be comforted by their mothers, even upon the mothers' return, continuing to cry or ignore their mothers although their mothers were there. The inability of these babies to be comforted indicated that they do not have the same attachment security to their primary caregivers as the securely attached babies. They did not perceive their mothers as the same "safe base." Whereas dismissive/avoidant babies relied upon themselves for consolation (and potentially repressed their distress), the anxious/preoccupied babies were unable to be consoled. In both cases of insecure attachment, the babies sent signals indicating they did not rely upon their mothers to respond to their needs (see Chapter 2 Supplemental link).

Attachment theory rests upon four main assumptions (Levinger, 1994; Steele, 2006). The first states that a child must form an emotional bond with a caregiver to develop optimally. Second, how a child is cared for during his/her earliest years has a strong effect on his/her personality and future relationships. Third, this early attachment bond with caregivers forms an internal working model—a template—that guides future behavior and expectations in relationships. And fourth, although attachment bonds and patterns that are formed in infancy are fairly stable, they can be changed later in life based on later experiences. For example, our internal working models can change from insecure to secure if we forge strong, healthy relationships with intimate partners or invest effort in personal change (e.g., through therapy). Similarly, intimate relationships with neglectful or inconsistently responsive partners can undermine secure attachments. Central to all of these assumptions is the belief that it is the *perception* of the child that is most important for defining attachment styles; the idea of "felt security" is the linchpin of attachment theory.

In addition to the empirical evidence supporting attachment theory in early development, theoretical support exists, too. Many social scientists agree with the importance of Ainsworth's theory and build upon it in their own work. For example, object relations theory has helped explain why perceptions are so important in attachment experiences (Liu, 2006; Williams & Kelly, 2005). The main tenet of object relations theory is that the infant psychologically internalizes the love object (the primary caregiver) and it is this internalization that fosters feelings of self-worth, self-esteem, and understanding of place in the emotional world (Murray, 1991). Therefore, attachment processes result in internal working models of trust—or mistrust—that serve as a foundation for later exploration with others (Benson, 2005). For example, a child who feels loved, safe, and secure within the caregiving relationship will later feel free and able to explore what might otherwise be a terrifying and scary world.

How Attachment Works

Caregivers are hard-wired to find little babies with big heads and big eyes cute, and they are "programmed" biologically to respond to babies' cries. Similarly, when babies' needs are met with responsiveness and consistency, they become more securely attached to their caregivers because they assume they can rely upon them. In other words, humans—both babies and caregivers—are hard-wired to develop close relationships. When infants learn that their distress is met with love and care, they develop secure attachments (Waters & Cummings, 2000). But when attachment figures, usually parents, are not responsive and sensitive to babies' needs, or are inconsistent in responding, then children develop what theorists call *insecure* attachments (because they learn caregivers cannot be depended upon). These attachment patterns affect us in our childhood relationships, first, and then carry over into adolescence and adulthood when we form romantic relationships later on.

Attachment styles have a strong influence on how we think of and form relationships with intimate and significant others. If we feel secure, we will feel comfortable exploring the world around us as long as our attachment figure is nearby (Waters & Cummings, 2000). This is called *secure base behavior*. For example, at the library a toddler might wander around the play area, but when a strange adult comes into the room, she scurries back to her parents. According to Attachment Theory, this is because the parents are serving as a "secure base" from which the young child can explore. However, as soon as something that seems threatening or scary gets too near, the child will go rushing back to the safety of her secure base. Then, after having been comforted and rekindling her sense of safety, the toddler can venture out again, perhaps going a little farther next time. A secure base promotes autonomous behavior because children understand their needs are met even when they take risks. As we grow older and become more competent, we can practice our independence more easily and fully if we are secure in the knowledge that we have a safe haven to which we can return if needed.

Attachment: Does It Follow Us into Adulthood?

Many studies have shown early attachment styles to have long-term influence, affecting our relationships into adulthood (e.g., Englund, Sally, Peg, & Collins, 2012). Going back to our case study, we can now see that as a young adult, Lacy is exhibiting a desire for a secure base when she is in distress because she wants to talk to her mom. Although she may not have the best relationship with her mother, and even though she seems to know that her mother will not necessarily comfort her about her relationship, Lacy still feels pulled to reconnect with her mother for comfort. Perhaps Lacy is trying to preserve her sense of emotional security after fighting with her boyfriend; seeking our attachment figures is one way people attempt to minimize anxiety.

As we enter adulthood, our early attachment experiences can impact how we approach romantic relationships. We carry these "inner working models" about how

relationships work into adulthood and then apply them to our romantic unions (Hazan & Shaver, 1987). For example, if Lacy has developed an insecure attachment style because she was never quite sure if she could reliably depend on her mother, she may not be able to easily let go of her anxiety when she is worried about a troubling interaction with her boyfriend (who is her new desired "secure base"). As her anxiety builds, she may protect herself by trying to please Drew instead of doing what she would really like to do (in this case, eating popcorn instead of peanut butter, and smiling when she feels anxious). Or she might withdraw from the interaction entirely, disengaging with Drew because it is easier for her than risking being rejected. It would probably be pretty hard for Lacy to be straightforward with Drew about her own needs, given how anxious she is because he will not move in with her yet, for instance. And this anxiety has more than likely been stoked because of the inconsistency that Lacy learned from her mother when she was growing up. If her mother had been inconsistent or inadequate with her love and responsiveness, Lacy would not expect Drew to respond to her needs warmly. This insecure working model can explain Lacy's inability to speak out and ask for what she wants and needs in the relationship. Instead, she stays silent and imagines the worst, while simultaneously becoming more and more anxious about how things are going. And if she stops dating Drew and begins another relationship with a different partner, *chances are high that the same issues will arise.* Generally speaking, attachment patterns do not vary that much from one relationship to the next. It is important to note that we only have one attachment type at any given time. However, our attachment may display itself differently across our relationships, depending on who we are in a relationship with and our history with that person, among other factors. We carry our internal working models with us from one relationship to the next—especially if we do not reflect on them and make concerted efforts to do something different.

Can We Change Our Attachment Styles?

If someone has had a hard time in childhood and developed an insecure attachment style, is s/he stuck with this fate forever? Is s/he doomed to have poor relationships for his or her whole life? What about securely attached individuals? Can they just sit back, confident that every relationship they enter will be filled with unicorns, rainbows, and glitter? The *Adult Attachment Interview* was developed to measure attachment representations by inquiring about adults' childhood experiences and memories (Main, Kaplan, & Cassidy, 1985; Van IJzendoorn, 1995). Researchers have used it to better understand how childhood attachment correlates with adult attachment (Mikulincer & Shaver, 2007). Evidence using this tool and similar measures suggests that although attachment styles are fairly stable, they are not set in stone. Furthermore, it appears that early secure attachment continues to benefit most individuals into adulthood. But all is not lost if you have realized that you do not have a secure attachment style. People with insecure attachments are not destined to be this way forever. Working on oneself through self-reflection and, if necessary, through therapy, can be hard but extremely helpful for those who wish to develop more secure attachment.

The first studies to follow individuals from the time they were infants into adulthood were published around the turn of this century, and evidence was mixed. In a small sample of 30 children, Hamilton (2000) found that 77% of adolescents age 17 to 19 remained in the same attachment classification they had been in as infants, which is considerably more than would be expected by chance. Those who experienced stressful and negative life events (e.g., parental divorce, a parent's drug use) were more likely to maintain an insecure classification or move from secure to insecure. Waters, Merrick, Treboux, Crowell, & Albersheim (2000) also found stability in attachment from infancy to adulthood. A change to insecure attachment was associated with loss of a family member, life-threatening illness in a loved one, parental divorce, abuse by a family member, or the presence of a psychological disorder in the family. Other studies found little continuity between attachment in childhood and attachment in adolescence, though those who experienced stressful life events were more likely to be classified as insecurely attached (Aikins, Howes, & Hamilton, 2009; Lewis, Feiring, & Rosenthal, 2000; Weinfield, Sroufe, & Egeland, 2000). These studies suggest that during difficult times, especially those that affect parents' ability to provide care, an individual may experience temporary insecure attachment or a long-term shift to an insecure attachment style. Recent studies have also found that family risk (e.g., abuse) and depression may contribute, too, to insecure attachment in adolescence and adulthood (Allen, McElhaney, Kuperminc, & Jodi, 2004; McConnell & Moss, 2011).

Fewer studies have examined change from insecure attachment to secure attachment; however, the existing research provides some clues for what might help an individual develop secure attachment. Adolescents who reported that their parents were supportive during disagreements were more likely to change to secure attachment style over time (Allen et al., 2004). Even after controlling for initial levels of security, adolescents who perceived their mothers as supportive had gains in security over a two-year period. Adaptive and flexible coping styles may also promote developing a secure attachment style (Zhang & Labouvie-Vief, 2004). This finding underscores the importance of approaching life challenges with maturity, flexibility, and a perspective grounded in the different possibilities that comprise our realities. Individual or group therapy can help individuals navigate this terrain in a way that builds interpersonal skills and supports attachment relationships (Kinley & Reyno, 2013).

When romantic relationships develop in adulthood, intimate partners often displace parents as their primary attachment figures. However, parents remain an important attachment presence even in later years (McConnell & Moss, 2011). In fact, Bowlby (1977) asserted, "Whilst especially evident during early childhood, attachment behavior is held to characterize human beings from the cradle to the grave" (p. 129). When adults feel distressed they reach out to their loved ones for comfort and support. An intense example of this was during the 9/11 World Trade Center attacks: people on the planes reached out to loved ones in their final moments, and many gathered with loved ones in the aftermath of that horrible day (Collins & Feeney, 2013). Some evidence suggests women are more comfortable displaying attachment behaviors and are more likely to seek support and comfort than men when they are in distress (Heister, Nordstrom, & Swenson, 2009). Though parent–infant attachment patterns are equally distributed across genders, in adulthood, men tend to have higher avoidance and lower anxiety than females (Del Giudice, 2011).

Another example of secure base behavior in the life course is found during the transition to young adulthood. During freshman year of college, when a student is feeling lonely or is going through a hard time, s/he may call home or rely on parents for support (Kenny, 1987; Heister et al., 2009). Research has found that among first year college students, a secure attachment style was related to feeling competent and well-adjusted at school (Heister et al., 2009). Another study found that when college first-years talked with their parents during the weekend, they were less likely to abuse alcohol (Small, Morgan, Abar, & Maggs, 2011). These studies suggest the parent–child relationship remains important during the transition to adulthood and can protect young adults from risk. A recently published book, *Seven Letters That Will Bring You Closer to Your College Student*, outlines how parents can write letters that can improve parent–child relationships during this transition (Bean & Harris, 2012).

Furthermore, early attachment experiences have been shown to affect adult functioning later down the road. Englund and colleagues (2012) found that individuals who were securely attached as infants were more likely to develop close friendships in childhood and romantic relationships in young adulthood. In turn, these predicted a measure of global functioning in people during their late twenties (Englund et al., 2012). In other words, early secure attachment started a positive chain of events that resulted in individuals reporting social wellbeing in adulthood.

ATTACHMENT IN ROMANTIC RELATIONSHIPS

A key tenet of attachment theory is that we learn how to love and form relationships from our childhood experiences. As teenagers, we pull away from our parents, start hanging out with friends more, and find other sources of security, including our friends, cultural groups and identity, or even our own intelligence (Waters & Cummings, 2000). We develop crushes and hope that they will become our first boyfriends or girlfriends. Having a history of sensitive caregiving and supportive relationships makes establishing romantic relationships easier and supports the kind of emotional flexibility that is important for a healthy relationship (Collins et al., 2009). Rarely are individuals ready for a mature romantic love that balances attachment needs, caregiving, and sexuality until

FIGURE 1 Four Types of Attachment

	Positive View of Self	Negative View of Self
Positive View of Others	**Secure** Comfortable with intimacy & autonomy	**Preoccupied** Preoccupied with relationships
Negative View of Others	**Avoidant/Dismissive** Dismissing of intimacy; strongly independent	**Avoidant/Fearful** Want social contact, but fear rejection

their late adolescence or early adulthood (Collins et al., 2009; Waters & Cummings, 2000). We focus here on how romantic love can be viewed as an attachment process, and how attachment theory helps us understand different types of healthy and unhealthy unions (Hazan & Shaver, 1987).

Findings about attachment in early life and young adulthood are complex. It is widely supported that our relationships with our parents in childhood influence romantic relationships later in life, but researchers are still trying to figure out how this works. For example, when it comes to the development of adolescent and young adult relationships, it appears that our relationships with our parents (i.e., parent–child relationship) is more important than our parents' romantic relationships (Collins, Welsh, & Furman, 2009). Similarly, parent–child relationships in childhood and adolescence are related to reports of romantic love in adulthood (Solmeyer, Lam, & McHale, 2012). Another study found, though, that early attachment scores were not strongly related to romantic anxiety and avoidance in adulthood. However, an increase in maternal sensitivity over time was related to lower levels of avoidance in romantic relationships in adulthood (Fraley, Roisman, Booth-LaForce, & Owen, 2013). This finding is good news because it indicates that relationship patterns can change when there is a growth in sensitivity.

According to attachment theory, our attachment in different types of relationships (e.g., family vs. romantic) is controlled by the same biological system (Fraley & Shaver, 2000). We have internal working models of ourselves and others (Bartholomew & Horowitz, 1991; Mikulincer, Shaver, Bar-on, & Ein-Dor, 2010) that we learn in childhood and continue to apply in all of our relationships when we are older. When we consistently receive responsive care and love from our attachment figures, we gain a positive view of ourselves (i.e., we feel lovable) and a positive view of others (i.e., we see others as reliable, trustworthy, and kind) (Bartholomew & Horowitz, 1991; Mikulincer et al., 2010). Based on these internal working models, four types of attachment have been identified in romantic relationships: *secure, anxious preoccupied, dismissive avoidant, and fearful avoidant* (see Figure 1; Bartholomew & Horowitz, 1991).

The hopeful part about all this is that your attachment style can change. If, for example, you have a partner who is consistent and sensitive in terms of his or her responses to you, then in re-working the attachment relationship you can develop a more secure attachment style and override the old messages that you carry from childhood. One college student, Becky, reflected back on her relationship with her highschool boyfriend. He was emotionally abusive and obsessively jealous. Before they went out at night, he would criticize her outfit and make her change if he didn't like it. If she got a text, he would hover over her and read it to make sure it wasn't another guy, and if it was, he would blow up. After a while, she started feeling extremely anxious and tried to do anything she could so as to not upset him. It took some good friends to help her see how unhealthy this relationship was. When she got to college, Becky found herself being anxious around guys in general—that is, until Jake came along. He was so patient with her and reminded her over and over again that he was not like the jerk she dated in high school. With his support, Becky started to relax and develop a secure attachment style; she began seeing the value that both she and Jake brought to their relationship instead of constantly criticizing herself.

Contrast Becky's experience with Ben's; Ben could not shake his feeling that he was not worthy of being with Stacy, his new girlfriend. This avoidant/fearful attachment infiltrated his unconscious thought patterns, and he found himself messing around with other girls at a frat party more than once. In other words, his fears driven by avoidant attachment lead him to a self-fulfilling prophecy and he made no movement toward changing his insecure attachment style. He wanted to distance himself from the anxiety of not being good enough for Stacy by sabotaging the relationship. So, attachment patterns can be changed, but it is easier said than done. The first step is awareness of negative thought patterns and feelings driven by insecure attachment that threaten relationships.

What Does All This Really Mean for Me? The Four Attachment Styles

Upon learning about your attachment type, try to reflect on what you actually do in a relationship, and not on what you wish you did or what you hope to do. A clear awareness of and accountability for your own behavior is the crucial first step toward learning how to create better relationships in your life.

SECURE ATTACHMENT. As noted above, those who are securely attached in adulthood have a positive view of themselves and of other people. Because they have experienced warm, sensitive caregiving in the past, when they are stressed out they seek support and comfort from their partner (Hazan & Shaver, 1987). The researchers who developed this four-part classification came up with simple statements that describe how individuals might experience secure attachment, including: "It is relatively easy for me to become emotionally close to others. I am comfortable depending on others and having others depend on me. I don't worry about being alone or having others not accept me" (Bartholomew & Horowitz, 1991, p. 244). When you are securely attached, you tend to be less anxious about your romantic relationships in general.

On a day-to-day basis, secure individuals experience more intimacy and are more satisfied with their interactions than insecure individuals (Kafetsios & Nezlek, 2002). Research suggests that although individuals tend to find secure attachment attractive, couples who are similar in attachment tend to attract one another (Mikulincer & Shaver, 2007). Secure individuals are good at providing reassurance, comfort, and compassion to their partners (Sprecher & Fehr, 2011). Also, over the long run, securely attached individuals tend to have higher levels of commitment to their partners than their insecure counterparts (Mikulincer & Shaver, 2007). Broadly speaking, this body of research implies that when both partners are secure, they are more likely to have faith in the fact that their relationship is going well and this, in turn, can help a relationship actually go well. One way of looking at this is to say that secure individuals have an easier time being in relationships because a secure attachment does not provoke either anger or anxiety in and of itself. For example, someone who is securely attached to her boyfriend might be less likely to worry that he is out with other women if he forgets to call her when he comes home late. Because her internal working model tells her that she is consistently loved, she does not automatically leap to the worst-case scenario in her thinking.

Similarly, if Lacy, from our case study, had a secure attachment style, she would be much less likely to predict a negative outcome to the relationship in response to Drew's preference to live separately for now. A securely attached Lacy would be more likely to surmise that he is thinking about their future and that he is giving her room to grow as she matures into her postgraduate life. Because she is still in college while he has graduated, this slow-and-steady process in a relationship could be considered thoughtful and respectful, as opposed to anxiety producing. But everything in Lacy's past history of relationships with significant others (such as her mother) is pushing her to hold fast to the worst-case scenario.

INSECURE ATTACHMENT: ANXIOUS/PREOCCUPIED. The first of the three insecure attachment types is anxious/preoccupied. Individuals with anxious/preoccupied attachments have a negative view of self, but a positive view of others (Bartholomew & Horowitz, 1991). Someone who falls into this category might experience romantic relationships in the following ways: "I want to be completely emotionally intimate with others, but I often find that others are reluctant to get as close as I would like. I am uncomfortable being without close relationships, but I sometimes worry that others don't value me as much as I value them" (Bartholomew & Horowitz, 1991, p. 244). An example of insecure attachment can be seen in the early part of Lena Dunham's TV series *Girls* (Dunham, Konner, & Lipes, 2012), wherein the character of Hannah is always wondering what Adam thinks about her and whether they are boyfriend and girlfriend. Hannah is showing her insecure attachment by not actually dealing with Adam in a straightforward fashion, and spends the majority of her time worrying about what he thinks rather than dealing with the reality of the relationship. She worries that Adam values her less than she values him. Rather than trusting her own instincts about feeling taken advantage of by Adam, Hannah bends herself into a pretzel trying to second-guess the relationship. Her anxious/preoccupied attachment style pushes her to value Adam's needs and wants above her own. Interestingly, in the series, viewers also witness Hannah being cut-off from her parents' funding of her lifestyle in a rather abrupt fashion (particularly on the part of her mother, who seems quite cold, distant, and impatient; Dunham, 2012). From an attachment perspective, it makes sense that Hannah would be anxious and eager to please in a romantic relationship; she does not have a secure base, and she did not carry a secure internal working model with her from childhood.

Rather than enjoying their relationships, preoccupied individuals tend to feel on edge and experience nervous apprehension (Davis, Shaver, & Vernon, 2004). This anxiety may arise because preoccupied individuals tend to have little faith in the possibility of the relationship working out well for them (Mikulincer & Shaver, 2007). When their partner is in need, they typically offer a lot of help, but with the motivation that they will score points with their partner (Sprecher & Fehr, 2011). Anxious individuals are more likely to give in to their partners than secure or avoidant adults (Topham, Larson, & Holman, 2005). Over time, anxious/preoccupied individuals are more likely than others to break up and then get back together with their ex multiple times (Kirkpatrick & Hazan, 1994). Because they cannot manage being single for very long due to their high anxiety, these people are also the most likely to suffer from the "rebound" phenomenon: going from one relationship to another very quickly. Rebound relationships, however, are forged to prevent anxiety rather than out of other more durable needs and wants (e.g., true liking and compatibility), and therefore, tend to be less stable. In this way, the cycle of anxiety, break-up, anxiety, hook-up, anxiety, break-up continues, which does not support or lead to strong and functional relationships in most cases. Instead, individuals have experiences that reinforce their anxious/preoccupied fears, making it difficult to evolve toward a more secure attachment.

INSECURE ATTACHMENT: DISMISSIVE/AVOIDANT. Dismissive/avoidant individuals have an internal working model with a positive view of themselves, but a negative view of others (Bartholomew & Horowitz, 1991). This causes them to be fairly independent and choose to rely on themselves—and not others—for support. Dismissive/avoidant individuals may identify with the following statements: "I am comfortable without close emotional relationships. It is very important to me to feel independent and self-sufficient, and I prefer not to depend on others or have others depend on me" (Bartholomew & Horowitz, 1991, p. 244).

The insecurities dismissive/avoidant individuals possess feed a view of others that is filled with suspicion (Collins & Allard, 2001). Avoidant individuals see others as dishonest and untrustworthy. Therefore, they do not tend to share emotionally intimate experiences, feelings or desires (Feeney et al., 1999), which makes it hard to establish compassionate love (Sprecher & Fehr, 2011). Because they feel uncomfortable with intimate feelings or vulnerability, avoidant individuals may get angry when they are asked to comfort a partner who is upset (Campbell, Simpson, Kashy, & Rhodes, 2001). Returning to our example of various attachment styles in the show Girls (Perez & Dunham, 2012), we find that Marni is a good example of someone with a dismissive attachment style. Marni's boyfriend is extremely loving and kind, but this makes her nervous and irritable. In fact, the more loving he is, the angrier she gets. Something about the way he expresses his love so openly makes her cranky and suspicious; she states that she does not love him anymore and feels constricted by his behavior. Eventually, she breaks up with him. This is dismissive/avoidant attachment behavior at its most destructive level. Even though her boyfriend kept trying to figure out how to please her, Marni could not accept his love, pushing him away until finally she pushed him completely out of her life.

This type of mismatch of attachment styles among partners—secure (for her boyfriend) and dismissive/avoidant (for Marni)—is one example of how attachment can strongly influence relationships. If Marni had been able to perceive the loving attentions of her boyfriend as legitimate, then she might have had a chance to forge a more secure attachment. This connection would help her to find a new secure base with him, and the two of them might have been able to go forward as a team within a healthy relationship. But as it was, Marni was so turned off and dismissive of his efforts that she actually created the reality that she dreaded: such a negative relationship that it collapsed under its own weight. This outcome leaves Marni more lonely and unhappy, and still stuck in her unhelpful attachment style.

INSECURE ATTACHMENT: FEARFUL/AVOIDANT. Individuals in the fearful/avoidant category may be the most vulnerable of the four groups because they have a negative view of themselves and of others. Although they often wish they did not feel this way, avoiding relationships allows them to protect themselves from getting hurt (Bartholomew & Horowitz, 1991). Fearful avoidant individuals might describe themselves this way: "I am somewhat uncomfortable getting close to others. I want emotionally close relationships, but I find it difficult to trust others completely, or to depend on them. I sometimes worry that I will be hurt if I allow myself to become too close to others" (Bartholomew & Horowitz, 1991, p. 224).

Fearful/avoidant individuals scoring high in anxiety and avoidance are more likely than others to have highly distressed relationships and experience violence in their relationships (Mikulincer & Shaver, 2007). Individuals with a fearful/avoidant attachment style are also more likely to be single (Bookwala, 2003). Recent research shows, however, that as individuals work on their interpersonal skills in a therapy setting, positive gains in security can occur. This is especially true for those whose initial attachment style was avoidant (Kinley & Reyno, 2013). A safe and trustworthy setting allowed these individuals to work through their attachment issues. However, this setting can often be difficult to create for those people who struggle with fearful/avoidant attachments. Being suspicious of others' motives in the relationship as well as worried and fearful about your own abilities to be in a strong and healthy relationship can be difficult to overcome without a lot of support from a compassionate and understanding partner.

Sex and Attachment

Not surprisingly, secure individuals report having a more satisfying and passionate sex life than their insecure counterparts (Mikulincer & Shaver, 2007). More specifically, they tend to report more frequent sex, greater arousal, more intense pleasure, and more frequent orgasms (Mikulincer & Shaver, 2007). Secure individuals also tend to have fewer sexual partners and do not frequently have sex outside of a relationship (Paul, McManus, & Hayes, 2000), perhaps because they do not view sex as the only avenue for feeling loved or accepted (Mikulincer & Shaver, 2007). Because secure individuals are more relaxed and attentive to their partners during sex, these findings imply that a relationship comprised of two secure individuals will boast a more fulfilling sexual relationship than relationships where at least one partner is insecure.

A lack of emotional intimacy may translate into a lack of passion for insecurely attached individuals. Those young adults who report high anxiety in relationships may be less likely to turn away unwanted sex and are less likely to practice safe sex than securely attached young adults (Feeney, Peterson, Gallois, & Terry, 2000). Another study showed that these young adults may be more likely to try to please their partner or show love through sex (Impett, Gordon, & Strachman, 2008). This behavior may occur because those who do not have faith in their own worthiness try to give their partners whatever the partner seems to want without first considering what they, themselves, might want. Although individuals typically end up with someone with a similar attachment pattern, one exception is the tendency for avoidant and anxiously attached individuals to attract one another (Mikulincer & Shaver, 2007). Avoidant-preoccupied couples tend to have sex less frequently than other couples (Brassard, Shaver, & Lussier, 2007). Generally, those who are avoidant tend to avoid sex even in the context of a committed relationship.

Now let's go back to the case of our friend Lacy at the beginning of the chapter. If she was aware of her attachment style, then maybe she would not be quite so reactive with Drew. Although insight does not necessarily equal behavior change, it is often the first step. If she knew that her attachment style was anxious preoccupied, she might try to count to ten before erupting at him when he turns down a sexual advance because he wants to get to the gym. She might also need to remind herself that his desire to keep his New Year's resolution is not a reflection of her attractiveness or the quality of their relationship. Continuing along this path, if Lacy ultimately felt like she was not getting what she needed within the relationship, understanding her attachment tendency might help her to stand up for herself instead of pleasing him before meeting her own needs. The key idea here is that awareness can allow Lacy to consciously choose to fight her anxiety, knowing that the anxiety stems from earlier experiences and not the current situation. If Lacy is aware of her tendencies to respond from anxiety, she has the chance to try to create a different sort of relationship with Drew.

Lacy and Drew, Continued

STAGE 3: HAPPY HOLIDAYS

Holiday break was almost over, and Lacy was lounging in her footy pajamas when Drew's text popped up on the screen. *I'm stopping by to take you to the gym.* Lacy cringed, *What is he thinking? Am I too fat for Mr. Health Kick? It is so cold out there—I am not leaving this couch!* She texted back some lame excuse, but that didn't stop him from showing up on her door-step (well, apartment hallway).

"Come on, Lacy," Drew cajoled her, teasing slightly.

Usually Lacy tried to go along with his health nut stuff, but this time something just snapped. "Listen, I already told you I've got stuff to do."

"Hey, I just thought that if . . ."

"Well, you thought wrong!"

"What the f***, Lacy, I just wanted to hang out with you—All you ever do is mope around."

From there, things just got ugly. *Yes, mom. You can say I told you so. I think he's going to leave me this time. He's probably got three girls ogling his pecs under that tight spandex right now.* Another text interrupted her thoughts . . . *Lacy, this isn't working. Maybe we should see a therapist.*

THREE WEEKS LATER. Lacy gathered up her courage and told the voices in her head to shut up. She opened up her journal and remembered what Dr. Marin had said about attachment anxiety. And as she started to write, it all came pouring out. The men in and out of the house, her mom always too happy to arrange a sleepover to get Lacy out of the house . . . or the screaming, raging fights before her mom moved onto the next guy. Maybe she did just expect Drew to be walking out that revolving door too. . . . that wasn't exactly fair to him. . . . but it wasn't fair that he was always trying to get her to fit his mold. She glanced at the growing pile of tissues by the side of her bed, and thought. *Okay, something has to change, but this is only going to work if Drew does his part. But I have to be the one to start, so it is up to me.*

SO WHAT? WHAT NOW?

From our outsider perspectives, we can see that Lacy's anxious/avoidant attachment style is affecting her relationship with Drew. So, how could she change this? Now that Lacy understands, what could she actually *do* to break habitual patterns that are causing her to feel very stuck? Lacy has taken the first step to gain awareness that this is going on. This kind of awareness takes thought and self-questioning. Ask yourself—really ask yourself—which parts of your relationship are you or were you responsible for? Often, merely thinking about why you do the things you do can help begin changes in relationship patterns that are not working. Once we can see the patterns in our behaviors, we can then do something about it. After we reflect, we need to be accountable for our own actions. Understanding that we are the common denominators in our current and past relationships can help us try to change the patterns and habits that have been un-helpful before. Again, if you can understand why you are doing a certain behavior that is not helping in a relationship, then you have more control over what you are doing than if you do not understand the origins of your behavior. And remember, even though at-tachment styles are fairly firmly set in child-hood, the newest research shows us that we can change our attachment styles through awareness of what we are actually doing and working to change it (Kinley & Reyno, 2013).

Interestingly, although many cultures have different definitions of how to create family and how to treat children, attachment appears to hold true across cultures in terms of the importance of the parent–child relationship for children's wellbeing (Sroufe, 2005). Attachment can be considered a fairly universal way of understanding patterns of behavior in relationships. Patterns of healthy or unhealthy behaviors in relationships can be changed, but not without awareness and hard work. And the first and most important piece is awareness, which is where this chapter comes in.

As you can see by now, attachment theory has the power to help us understand some of the ways we behave in our intimate relationships. However, if we discover that we have an insecure attachment style, it does not mean that we are doomed to have poor relationships. What it does mean, though, is that we need to pay attention to our patterns and become aware of what our triggers. Understanding our attachment style can aid us in creating a deeper and richer way of being together with our intimates and loved ones: it helps us do our relationships on purpose.

REFERENCES

Aikins, J. W., Howes, C., & Hamilton, C. (2009). Attachment stability and the emergence of unresolved representations during adolescence. *Attachment and Human Development, 11*(5), 491–512. doi:10.1080/14616730903017019

Ainsworth, M. D. (1979). Infant-mother attachment. *American Psychologist, 34*(10), 932–937. doi:10.1037/0003-066X.34.10.932

Ainsworth, M. D. (1989). Attachments beyond infancy. *American Psychologist, 44*(4), 709–716. doi:10.1037/0003-066X.44.4.709

Allen, J. P., McElhaney, K. B., Kuperminc, G. P., & Jodi, K. M. (2004). Stability and change in attachment security across adolescence. *Child Development, 75*(6), 1792–1805. doi:10.1111/j.1467-8624.2004.00817.x

Bartholomew, K., & Horowitz, L. M. (1991). Attachment styles among young adults: A test of a four-category model. *Journal of Personality and Social Psychology, 61*(2), 226–244. doi:10.1037/0022-3514.61.2.226

Benson, M. (2005). Parent-adolescent relationships: Integrating attachment theory and Bowenian family systems theories. In V.I. Bengston et al. (Eds.) *Sourcebook of Family Theory and Research* (pp. 382–385). Thousand Oaks, CA: Sage.

Bookwala, J. (2003). Being "single and unattached": The role of adult attachment styles. *Journal of Applied Social Psychology, 33*(8), 1564–1570. doi:10.1111/j.1559-1816.2003.tb01963.x

Bowlby, J. (1977). *The making and breaking of affectional bonds*. London: Tavistock.

Bowlby, J. (1988). *A secure base: Parent-child attachment and healthy human development*. New York: Basic Books.

Brassard, A., Shaver, P. R., & Lussier, Y. (2007). Attachment, sexual experience, and sexual pressure in romantic relationships: A dyadic approach. *Personal Relationships, 14*(3), 475–493. doi:10.1111/j.1475-6811.2007.00166.x

Bretherton, I. (2004). Theoretical contributions from developmental psychology. In P.G. Boss et al. (Eds.) *Sourcebook of family theories and methods* (pp. 275–297). New York: Springer.

Campbell, L., Simpson, J. A., Kashy, D. A., & Rholes, W. S. (2001). Attachment orientations, dependence, and behavior in a stressful situation: An application of the actor-partner interdependence model. *Journal of Social and Personal Relationships, 18*(6), 821–843. doi:10.1177/0265407501186005

Collins, N. L., & Allard, L. M. (2001). Cognitive representations of attachment: The content and function of working models. *Blackwell Handbook of Social Psychology: Interpersonal Processes, 2*, 60–85. doi:10.1002/9780470998557.ch3

Collins, W. A., Welsh, D. P., & Furman, W. (2009). Adolescent romantic relationships. *Annual Review of Psychology, 60*, 631–652. doi:10.1146/annurev.psych.60.110707.163459

Collins, N. L., & Feeney, B. C. (2013). Attachment and caregiving in adult close relationships: Normative processes and individual differences. *Attachment and Human Development, 15*(3), 241–245. doi:10.1080/14616734.2013.782652

Davis, D., Shaver, P. R., & Vernon, M. L. (2004). Attachment style and subjective motivations for sex. *Personality and Social Psychology Bulletin, 30*(8), 1076–1090. doi:10.1177/0146167204264794

Del Giudice, M. (2011). Sex differences in romantic attachment: A meta-analysis. *Personality and Social Psychology Bulletin, 37*(2), 193–214. doi:10.1177/0146167210392789

Dunham, L. (Director & Writer). (2012). Pilot [Television series episode]. In Dunham L., Apatow, J., & Konner, J (Producers), *Girls*. New York: HBO.

Dunham, L (Writer), Konner, J. (Writer), & Lipes, J. L. (Director). (2012). Welcome to Bushwick [Television series episode]. In Dunham L., Apatow, J., & Konner, J (Producers), *Girls*. New York: HBO.

Englund, M. M., Sally, I., Kuo, C., Puig, J., & Collins, W. A. (2011). Early roots of adult competence: The significance of close relationships from infancy to early adulthood. *International Journal of Behavioral Development, 35*(6), 490–496. doi:10.1177/0165025411422994

Feeney, J. A. (1999). Adult attachment, emotional control, and marital satisfaction. *Personal Relationships, 6*(2), 169–185. doi:10.1111/j.1475-6811.1999.tb00185.x

Feeney, J. A., Peterson, C., Gallois, C., & Terry, D. J. (2000). Attachment style as a predictor of sexual attitudes and behavior in late adolescence. *Psychology and Health, 14*(6), 1105–1122. doi:10.1080/08870440008407370

Fraley, R. C., Roisman, G. I., Booth-LaForce, C., Owen, M. T., & Holland, A. S. (2013). Interpersonal and genetic origins of adult attachment styles: A longitudinal study from infancy to early adulthood. *Journal of Personality and Social Psychology, 104*(5), 817. doi:10.1037/a0031435

Fraley, R. C., & Shaver, P. R. (2000). Adult romantic attachment: Theoretical developments, emerging controversies, and unanswered questions. *Review of General Psychology, 4*(2), 132–154. doi:10.1037/1089-2680.4.2.132

Hamilton, C. E. (2000). Continuity and discontinuity of attachment from infancy through adolescence. *Child Development, 71*(3), 690–694. doi:10.1111/1467-8624.00177

Harris, S. M., & Bean, R. A. (2012). *Seven letters that will bring you closer to your college student*. Self Published.

Hazan, C., & Shaver, P. (1987). Romantic love conceptualized as an attachment process. *Journal of Personality and Social Psychology, 52*(3), 511–524. doi:10.1037/0022-3514.52.3.511

Hiester, M., Nordstrom, A., & Swenson, L. M. (2009). Stability and change in parental attachment and adjustment outcomes during the first semester transition to college life. *Journal of College Student Development, 50*(5), 521–538. doi:10.1353/csd.0.0089

Impett, E. A., Gordon, A. M., & Strachman, A. (2008). Attachment and daily sexual goals: A study of dating couples. *Personal Relationships, 15*(3), 375–390. doi:10.1111/j.1475-6811.2008.00204.x

Kafetsios, K., & Nezlek, J. B. (2002). Attachment styles in everyday social interaction. *European Journal of Social Psychology, 32*(5), 719–735. doi:10.1002/ejsp.130

Kinley, J. L., & Reyno, S. M. (2013). Attachment style changes following intensive short-term group psychotherapy. *International Journal of Group Psychotherapy, 63*(1), 53–75. doi:10.1521/ijgp.2013.63.1.53

Kirkpatrick, L. A., & Hazan, C. (1994). Attachment styles and close relationships: A four-year prospective study. *Personal Relationships, 1*(2), 123–142. doi:10.1111/j.1475-6811.1994.tb00058.x

Levinger, G. (1994). Attachment theory as a paradigm for studying close relationships. *Psychological Inquiry, 5*(1), 45–48. doi:10.1207/s15327965pli0501_8

Lewis, M., Feiring, C., & Rosenthal, S. (2000). Attachment over time. *Child Development, 71*(3), 707–720. doi:10.1111/1467-8624.00180

Liu, Y. (2006). Paternal/maternal attachment, peer support, social expectations of peer interactions and depressive symptoms. *Adolescence, 41*(164), 705–723. Retrieved from http://www.ncbi.nlm.nih.gov/pubmed/17240776

Main, M., Kaplan, N., & Cassidy, J. (1985). Security in infancy, childhood, and adulthood: A move to the level of representation. *Monographs of the Society for Research in Child Development, 50,* 66–104. doi:10.2307/3333827

Main, M., Hesse, E., & Kaplan, N. (2005). Predictability of attachment behavior and representational processes at 1, 6, and 19 years of age: The Berkeley longitudinal study. In K. E. Grossmann, K. Grossmann, E. Waters (Eds.), *Attachment from infancy to adulthood: The major longitudinal studies* (pp. 245–304). New York, Guilford Publications.

McConnell, M., & Moss, E. (2011). Attachment across the life span: Factors that contribute to stability and change. *Australian Journal of Educational & Developmental Psychology, 11*, 60–77. Retrieved from: www.newcastle.edu.au/journal/ajedp/

Mendenhall, T. M. (2013a, Spring). *Attachment Styles lecture*, University of Minnesota, Minneapolis, MN.

Mendenhall, T. M. (2013b, Spring). *Intimacy lecture*, University of Minnesota, Minneapolis, MN.

Mikulincer, M., & Shaver, P. R. (2010). *Attachment in adulthood: Structure, dynamics, and change*. New York: Guilford Press.

Mikulincer, M., Shaver, P. R., Bar-On, N., & Ein-Dor, T. (2010). The pushes and pulls of close relationships: Attachment insecurities and relational ambivalence. *Journal of Personality and Social Psychology, 98*(3), 450–468. doi:10.1037/a0017366

Olson, D., DeFrain, J. & Skogrand, L. (2011). *Marriages and families: Intimacy, diversity, and strengths*. New York: McGraw Hill.

Small, M. L., Morgan, N., Abar, C., & Maggs, J. L. (2011). Protective effects of parent-college student communication during the first semester of college. *Journal of American College Health, 59*(6), 547–554. doi:10.1080/07448481.2010.528099

Solmeyer. A. R., Lam, C. B., & McHale, S. M. (2012, March). *Sibling influences on the development of empathy in early adolescence.* Poster presented in the biennial meeting for the *Society for Research on Adolescence,* Vancouver, Canada.

Sprecher, S., & Fehr, B. (2011). Dispositional attachment and relationship-specific attachment as predictors of compassionate love for a partner. *Journal of Social and Personal Relationships, 28*(4), 558–574. doi:10.1177/0265407510386190

Steele, M. (2006). *The "added value" of attachment theory and research for clinical work in adoption and foster care.* England: Karnac Books.

Topham, G. L., Larson, J. H., & Holman, T. B. (2005). Family-of-origin predictors of hostile conflict in early marriage. *Contemporary Family Therapy, 27*(1), 101–121. doi:10.1007/s10591-004-1973-2

Van IJzendoorn, M. (1995). Adult attachment representations, parental responsiveness, and infant attachment: A meta-analysis on the predictive validity of the Adult Attachment Interview. *Psychological Bulletin, 117*(3), 387–403. doi:10.1037/0033-2909.117.3.387

Wallin, D. (2007). *Attachment in psychotherapy.* New York: Guilford Press.

Waters, E., Merrick, S., Treboux, D., Crowell, J., & Albersheim, L. (2000). Attachment security in infancy and early adulthood: A twenty-year longitudinal study. *Child Development, 71*(3), 684–689. doi:10.1111/1467-8624.00176

Weinfield, N. S., Sroufe, L. A., & Egeland, B. (2000). Attachment from infancy to early adulthood in a high-risk sample: Continuity, discontinuity, and their correlates. *Child Development, 71*(3), 695–702. doi:10.1111/1467-8624.00178

Williams, S. & Kelly, F. (2005). Relationships among involvement, attachment, and behavioral problems in adolescence: Examining father's influence. *Journal of Early Adolescence, 25*(2), 168–198. doi:10.1177/0272431604274178

Zhang, F., & Labouvie-Vief, G. (2004). Stability and fluctuation in adult attachment style over a 6-year period. *Attachment & Human Development, 6*(4), 419–437. doi:10.1080/1461673042000303127

3

Personality and Intimate Relationships

Noah E. Gagner, M.A., M.Ed.
Lisa J. Trump, M.S.
Department of Family Social Science
University of Minnesota

LEARNING OBJECTIVES

- Understand what personality is, why it is important, and how it is formed
- Identify popular measures of personality characteristics
- Understand how personality impacts our relationships
- Apply gained knowledge of about personality to intimate relationships

Vignette

ISAAC

From the time he was born, Isaac was called "Show Time." This nickname grew from his perpetual want to be the center of attention. Whether it was singing out loud, asking questions to other kids, or playing sports, Isaac made sure that others were aware of his presence. As he got older, he found that being social had many benefits. In high school, Isaac often planned and attended large social gatherings, was the first to raise his hand in class, and was a part of the group of students considered most popular. Isaac went on to play basketball in college, which brought with it increasing recognition and opportunities to socialize with peers. During the week, he often thought about when he would be able to hang out with friends, having long-found that being social brought him energy and a sense of feeling "alive."

RACHEL

From a very young age, Rachel loved to read. You name it, she reads it. Her parents liked to take credit for the veracity of Rachel's reading by saying that they used to read to her while she was still in her mom's womb! For the most part, her parents were happy with Rachel's love for reading; she was a "low maintenance child" who would keep herself occupied for hours. When Rachel got to middle school, she grew to have a few very close friends. She got straight "A's," and later began taking college classes during her junior year of high school. When she began applying to colleges, Rachel was offered several scholarships and—ultimately—chose a program close to home that was known for its engineering program. During the week, she often thought about the upcoming weekend and having time to relax with her books and/or watch her favorite shows.

RACHEL AND ISAAC

During Rachel's junior year of college, a good friend from summer camp came to visit. For dinner that night, they decided to visit a new restaurant on campus that was famous for its artisan foods. When they walked in, Isaac noticed Rachel right away. Isaac, never one to fear asking people out on dates, asked Rachel if she would be free the next weekend. And then it began: for the first few weeks, Rachel and Isaac were inseparable. Rachel had been telling herself that she wanted to enjoy campus more, and now felt like she was finally getting her chance. Two months later, though, she began to feel increasingly exhausted and distant from Isaac. Rachel suggested that they spend some

---

Corresponding Author: Noah E. Gagner, M.A., M.Ed.; University of Minnesota; Department of Family Social Science; 290 McNeal Hall; 1985 Buford Ave; Saint Paul, MN 55108. E-mail: gagn0060@umn.edu.

quiet time alone (vs. out-on-the-town) watching movies. At first Isaac said "yes," but soon began to resist. The couple began to argue a bit… and later on, a lot. Nowadays, Rachel and Isaac are finding themselves in a tough spot; Isaac feels cut-off from his friends, and Rachel feels detached from Isaac. Rachel is beginning to wonder whether they should just breakup, or maybe try the somewhat cliché road of just being "friends."

WHAT IS PERSONALITY?

"Who am I?," "Who do I want to be?," and *"Who I am looking for?"* are questions that we ask ourselves when looking for jobs, choosing which cities to live in, and/or embarking on our search for an intimate relationship. Have you ever heard someone say, *"The way you act reminds me a lot of your mother."*—as she or he highlights your similar taste in bad jokes, your high intelligence, or your shared passion for working with people in the helping professions? Or in contrast, have you ever had your partner notice that something is wrong with you, asking, *"What's going on? You're not acting like yourself."* These questions and comments highlight how we observe the ways that important people in our lives act, think, and feel. These observations give us information that may, at least partially, help us answer our own questions about who we are.

The question, *"Who am I?,"* taps into our unique and respective inner workings, and distinguishes us from (or aligns us with) others. This question also gets at what makes up our personalities. **Personality**, in a formal sense, encompasses the character that we enact through our distinct thoughts, feelings, and behaviors (American Psychological Association, 2016). Common assumptions about personality suggest that it is: (a) relatively stable over time, (b) distinguishable from others, and (c) influential on behavior (Engler, 2014). Trait or type theories of personality are primarily used to describe characteristics that are emblematic of our individuality. **Type** theories describe our personality as made up of dichotomous phenomena (e.g., introvert or extrovert). Similar to handedness, we are right-handed or left-handed, but not somewhere in-between. In contrast, **trait** theories describe our personality as made up of characteristics that vary across continua (e.g., introvert, ambivert, and extrovert). The term "ambivert," in this example, describes a blend of introvert and extrovert features. Instead of two categories (types), introverts and extroverts are conceptualized in degrees, with ambiverts residing somewhere in the middle. In this chapter, we will primarily discuss the Big Five personality factors, as trait views are the most researched and empirically supported characterizations of personality. Another popular view of personality, the Myers-Briggs Type Indicator, will also be briefly discussed.

Early Perspectives on Personality

Understanding personalities became popular among scientists in the beginning of the 20th century. During this time, changes across cultural, economic, social, and political structures in the United States and Europe mediated a social impetus to operationalize and hold up the importance of personality (Cain, 2013). The second industrial revolution (as it was effectively called), alongside mass immigration, forced a shift from farms to factories and offices (Hitschman & Mogford, 2009a). As a result, mass urbanization took place as millions of workers and their families migrated to cities. Carter (2006) described how, for example, urban populations in the United States expanded from less than 25% to more than 50% of the national population between 1880 and 1920. Cain (2013) states that "Americans found themselves no longer with neighbors, but with strangers" (p. 22). This shift meant that the manner in which strangers perceived you was becoming increasingly important. This represented a change from a society that valued character (e.g., hard work and family values) to one focused more on individual attributes and skillsets. Our public selves began to become more important than our private selves as we began to focus on how we marketed ourselves and how we were perceived by others. For example, Cain (2013) points out that popular words in books about personality shifted from terms like "honor," "integrity," and "morals" in the 19th century to terms like "fascinating," "attractive" and "energetic" in the beginning of the 20th century. The focus shifted toward how we can stand out from others in an increasingly competitive society.

Dating scripts regarding courtship and marriage were also starting to change. Increases in political, economic, and social power brought on by important social movements (e.g., feminism) beginning in the 1920s necessitated a shift from marriage being a purely economic decision to a choice informed by modern-day notions of love (Coontz, 2005). As decisions to marry became less dependent on economic proclivities, individuality (i.e., personality) and compatibility became more salient. Ansari (2015), in his comedic look at *Modern Romance*, foretold that we were no longer looking for "good enough" marriages; instead, we began looking for soul mates. Specifically, "We want something that's passionate, or boiling, from the get-go. In the past, people weren't looking for something boiling; they just needed some water. Once they found it and committed to a life together, they did their best to heat things up" (p. 24).

What Shapes Our Personality?

What forms our personality, changes it, and maintains it are essential questions. In the 1920s, as these questions took on greater importance, a number of theories developed. While a thorough discussion of these theories is outside of this chapter's scope, suffice it to say that many aspects of personality that we still regard most were already being articulated, for example, the interaction of nurture (e.g., family and friends) and nature (e.g., genetics). These interactions are classified as passive, evocative, and active. **Passive** interaction approaches suggest that our personality is shaped based on the interests of those in our immediate environment. For example, because our parents were in dance lessons when they were children, they might think that it is a great idea to enroll us in dance lessons, too. Our parents' traits (genetics and environment), therefore, provide a context wherein our personality is developed. An **evocative** interaction approach suggests that, as a child, we might show natural coordination and rhythm (genetics), which is positively reinforced by our parents (environment) through praise and sending us to dance classes. **Active** interaction approaches suggest that, even though our parents signed us up for a variety of activities, we eventually chose dance based on its fit with our personal interests (and these environments actively reinforced our personality traits). Each of these approaches demonstrates the variety of ways that nature and nurture can work to form, change, and maintain who we are. These and related assumptions of interaction, however, were not always accepted by scientists until later innovations in research regarding genetic (nature) and environmental (nurture) interactions took hold.

Our genes and the environment. As we reach for that fifth slice of pizza and proudly exclaim, "I can eat as much as I want and never gain a pound!," someone might wonder how we came to be blessed with such great genes. When we talk about genes, we often talk about their impact on our physical features (e.g., metabolism, height, and eye color). However, they also play a significant role in your or your partner's propensity to go to (or avoid) parties, how emphatic (or self-centered) you or your partner is, and how often you or your partner complement each other on a job well done. These characteristics are considered phenotypic, or observable, parts of our personality.

Genetics research has explored identical and fraternal twins, raised together and separately, to understand how genes and one's environment interact. Because identical twins share the same genetic makeup, researchers are able to control for individual variability in genetics and environment. Findings from Jang, Lively, and Vernon (1996) suggest that the genetic influence on agreeableness, conscientiousness, extraversion, neuroticism, and openness was 41, 44, 53, 41, and 61% respectively. In fact, research on twins has reported an estimated 42–46% genetic influence on an individual's personality (Bouchard, 1994). If genetics explain roughly half of the story, then, we must also consider the environmental factors at play to understand the rest.

There are two main schools of thought regarding environmental influences on personality development. The first is that environmental factors naturally surrounding an individual throughout his or her lifetime influence his or her personality. Using a set of twins reared apart as an example, one twin might have grown up living on a large farm and held several responsibilities, whereas the other twin might have grown up in an environment where she or he was sheltered from life's difficulties. It would be expected that different aspects of their personalities would be brought out due to their drastically different experiences. The first twin might be much more adventurous and organized, whereas the second twin might be more risk-averse and nervous about new experiences. The second school of thought is that each individual selects from a range of stimuli and events based on his or her genotype and creates his or her own set of experiences and environment (Bouchard, 1994). This view highlights the role of learning and views humans as creative and desirous of new experiences, things, and environments. In comparing the two schools of thought, the first is a much more passive view of environmental influences, whereas the second view is more active. While researchers and theorists differ with respect to their views on how genetic and environmental factors influence personality, the majority unite in the conclusion that the two are entwined together (i.e., that both play important roles).

ASSESSMENTS OF PERSONALITY

Personality assessments provide an opportunity for naming, reflecting, and evaluating our individuality through commonly accepted dimensions. You have probably already taken some sort of personality assessment, either through school (e.g., StrengthsFinder), work (e.g., Myers-Briggs), or via social media (e.g., Which Simpsons character are you?). It is important to remember that these personality assessments are not meant to be prescriptive; they identify facets of your complex individuality that are similar to (or different from) others. Two popular assessments, the **Big Five Factor Model** and the **Myers-Briggs Personality Type Indicator** are discussed below.

The Big Five

From early courtship to long-term intimate relationships, we commonly hear about how partners are a "good" or "bad" match. Some of us might have an uncanny ability to predict which of our friends' relationships are going to work out and which ones will fail. A prominent way that research has understood these "matches" between individuals and other people, workplace environments, and social contexts is through an examination of personality traits. The five-factor model, effectively known as the Big Five Personality Trait Factors (Costa & McCrae, 1992), categorizes individual differences across the following trait factor continuum: (a) Openness to Experience (ranging from inventive or curious to consistent or cautious); (b) Conscientiousness (ranging from efficient or organized to easygoing or careless); (c) Extraversion (ranging from outgoing or energetic to solitary or reserved); (d) Agreeableness (ranging friendly or compassionate to analytical or detached); and (e) Neuroticism (ranging sensitive or nervous to secure or confident). If you have not already done so, we suggest that you take an assessment that measures these markers in you (see http://personality-testing.info/tests/BIG5.php).

Scores on each factor are described on a continuum from low to high. For example, if you scored on the low end of the neuroticism scale, your score would suggest that you are more secure and confident in your social interactions than someone who scored high on neuroticism (i.e., more sensitive and nervous). Looking at the chart below, you can probably get a sense of how these personality traits impact our intimate relationships. Someone who is very sociable and active, like Isaac in our vignette, for example, may have a difficult time with someone who is more reserved and prefers to be in a quiet space.

Myers-Briggs Personality Type Indicator

The Myers-Briggs Personality Type Indicator (MBTI) is based of Carl Jung's early work; it was originally developed in the 1940s by Isabel Briggs Myers and Katharine Cook Briggs as an assessment to help women find jobs during World War II (Kaplan & Saccuzzo, 2001). The MBTI is still used in a

The "Big Five" Personality Traits		
Trait	Characteristics of a High Scorer	Characteristics of a Low Scorer
Neuroticism (N)	Worrying, nervous, emotional, insecure, inadequate, hypochondriacal	Calm, relaxed, unemotional, hardy, secure, self-satisfied
Extraversion (E)	Sociable, active, talkative, person-orientated, optimistic, fun-loving, affectionate	Reserved, sober, un-exuberant, aloof, task- orientated, retiring, quiet
Openness to Experience (O)	Curious, broad interests, creative, original, imaginative, untraditional	Conventional, down-to-earth, narrow interests, unartistic, unanalytical
Agreeableness (A)	Soft-hearted, good-natured, trusting, helpful, forgiving, gullible, straightforward	Cynical, rude, suspicious, uncooperative, vengeful, ruthless, irritable, manipulative
Conscientious (C)	Organized, reliable, hard-working, self-disciplined, punctual, scrupulous, neat, ambitious, persevering	Aimless, unreliable, lazy, careless, lax, negligent, weak-willed, hedonistic

Adapted from Perving (2003).

variety of settings (e.g., school, career counseling, work, and team building) to understand how our preferences shape our interests, motivations, needs, and values. For instance, if you are a *Perceiving* type, you prefer to see rules and deadlines as flexible compared to a *Judging* type who prefers to have rules and deadlines respected. Preferences based on a structured questionnaire are based on four categories (see image below), including where you get energy, how you take information in, how you make decisions, and how you organize your life. These four categories combine to describe **16 distinctive personality types** (e.g., ENFJ and ISFP). Unlike the Big Five personality traits, MBTI types are dichotomous, meaning that you would align with one descriptive or the other in

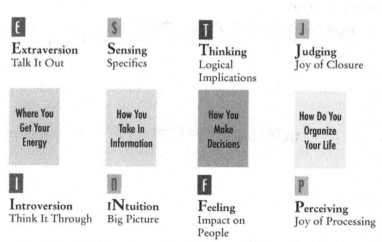

Source: http://www.trinitylc.org/page/show/231958-myers-briggs-type-indicator-mbti-

each of the four categories. Many university and college career counseling centers offer MBTI assessments; otherwise, you can take a MBTI-like assessment here: http://www.humanmetrics.com/cgi-win/jtypes2.asp.

PERSONALITY AND DATING

Throughout every phase of intimate relationships (e.g., courtship, dating, breaking up, and marriage), aspects of personality are discussed—explicitly or implicitly. We often talk about our intimate relationships and partners with comments like *"I really like his personality, "Our personalities are so similar," "It's like we can complete each other's sentences!,"* and *"I just could not stand the way he always wanted to go out."* as ways that imply either matches or mismatches in personality. In the vignette in the beginning of the chapter, we might have contemplated whether Isaac's outgoing personality was really a good fit with Rachel's quiet demeanor and preference to stay in on Friday nights. Underneath these comments are even bigger questions that many might wonder about, such as: *"What are the 'good' or preferred personality types?," "Do men and women desire different personality types in their partners?," "Is it important that my personality matches my partner's?," "Do opposites really attract, or do birds-of-a-feather flock together?," "How does the personality of my partner impact our relationship satisfaction and sex?"* These are important questions that are quite complicated to answer. Below we provide an initial discussion to get us started.

What if We Like the Same Things?

So far we have encountered theories such as Duck and Craig's filter theory of attraction and Reiss' wheel of love (see Chapter 1). These theories have shown us important processes that lead to selecting a partner and falling in love. Based on our discussion about gene-environment interactions, we can see how our individual personality shapes who we find complementary, the environments/contexts that we seek out, and whether we establish rapport with others. For example, Milfont and Sibley (2012) found that individuals who scored high in the traits of agreeableness, conscientiousness, and openness to experience endorsed high levels of environmental engagement and conservation. That being said, a couple who meets while at summer camp—as they both enjoyed outdoor environments —might be expected to have other beliefs and interests that are similar, too. For example, they may expect that their feelings toward water conservation, knowledge about local hiking trails, and attitudes toward pollution will be the same. These shared experiences and beliefs, then, might be expected to increase the rapport of the two individuals as they reminiscence about their first meeting while camping. The study of how individuals seek out partners who are similar and/or complementary to themselves and its impact on relationship satisfaction and outcomes is understood as **assortative mating**.

Assortative mating research looks to untangle the numerous ways that we make choices and what those choices say about social norms, expectations, and values. Its studies suggest that we seek out individuals who have similar to higher levels of traits that are similar to our own. To give an analogy from a classic Disney film, it is becoming less likely in today's age that Princess Jasmine would really still seek out and marry the impoverished Aladdin. Increasingly, we are finding and spending our life with individuals who are similar in income, education, and intelligence (to name just a few things). This practice has lent support to the "birds-of-a-feather flock together" phenomenon. So too, then, would we be drawn to others whose personalities are like our own.

Researchers Botwin, Buss, and Shackelford (1997) found that those individuals who scored high in agreeableness, conscientiousness, and intellect/openness were the most likely to prefer and find partners who were similar in these domains. For example, a highly conscientious person who is very organized and works ahead on assignments, keeps his or her home clean, and is always on time to appointments, is most likely to prefer and seek out others with the same traits. For a couple with mismatched (low vs. high conscientiousness), we could see why conflict or decreased relationship satisfaction could occur; one partner would always be waiting for the other to show up, telling him or her to pick up his or her stuff, or arguing about wanting to hang out when his or her homework is not yet complete. In a sample of college-aged and newlywed couples, research suggests that similarity at the beginning of the relationship and convergence over a year—meaning that some couples become more alike in personality over time—report higher relationship satisfaction compared to those who are less similar initially and/or become more different in personality during this time.

For the couple in the vignette at the beginning of the chapter, then: does this mean that they are doomed from the beginning? Is the relationship automatically on a path toward failure because Isaac is highly extroverted and Rachel is introverted? The answer is that it depends. While the "birds-of-a-feather flock together" pattern is common and may contribute to the demise of this relationship, other factors such as environment (e.g., high stress vs. low stress) and developmental benchmarks (e.g., job, age, and brain development) also impact the development and interaction of personalities within our relationships. For example, Rachel and Isaac might have more arguments in high stress times, like during finals-week and/or when Isaac is travelling for basketball games. In contrast, once Isaac graduates and is out of the social scene (i.e., college), he might find that he desires to be home more, and that their differences were not as vast as he initially perceived.

Gender Norms and Personality

Social and cultural norms regarding gender have a significant impact on our personality. Within Western culture there are distinct ways in which we are socialized to believe that we should act, feel, and think as a result of gender scripts and norms. Antiquated ideas about gender reinforce males who demonstrate stoicism, independence, and courage, and females who demonstrate nurturance, thoughtfulness, and emotional attunement (Knudson-Martin, 2013). For example, findings from Costa, Terraccino, and McCrae (2001) show that support for how our personality is affected by biology and social/cultural norms regarding gender. In their study, females reported higher neuroticism, warmth, extroversion, agreeableness, and conscientiousness in 49 out of 55 countries, whereas males scored higher in assertiveness and openness to new ideas. Further, the most prominent and consistent difference across all cultures was neuroticism. In Costa et al.'s (2001) discussion about these findings, they contend that gender norms (as socially/culturally informed phenomena) contributed most.

All of this suggests that self-reported personality traits are similar to the norms that we maintain regarding how each gender should act (see Chapter 4). And to be sure, when we do not act in conventionally "feminine" or "masculine" ways, there can be significant personal and/or professional consequences. The documentary called *The Mask You Live In*, for example, describes how ideas about masculinity lead young men to avoid expressing vulnerability (Newsom, Cogdon, & Anthony, 2015). This results in a higher likelihood to commit violent crimes, drink excessively, and even take one's own life. Traits of stoicism, independence, and courage in males are more likely to promote characteristics of being unemotional and insecure. Therefore, it is more likely that a male who is struggling will not speak up (e.g., ask for help) when he needs to. To do so would be to go against the messages he has received about what it means to be a man. For women, pressures to ascribe to traditional gender roles (and backlashes from deviating from the status quo) have been shown to contribute to fewer women presuming positions of power and leadership. For example, when Hilary Clinton campaigned to be the first female President of the United States in both the 2008 and 2016 Presidential elections, opponents often suggested through attributions of gender-scripted norms that she is too agreeable and "unstable" (neurotic) to hold a position in which one must be analytical, reasonably detached, and confident in decision making.

So why do scholars like Costa et al. (2001) find that women across numerous countries report higher neuroticism compared to men? Research has pointed to gender socialization for women to function as the "emotional barometer" of relationships; this explains their endorsement of more neurotic traits. Conversely, men are more likely to follow gender norms that abscond from signs of emotion and instability (Gottman & Gottman, 2015). Regardless, high levels of neuroticism in either partner can spell trouble for relationships. Characteristics of an individual with high neuroticism point to many of the intimacy killers that are discussed in Chapter 9. Put simply, individuals with high neuroticism are more likely to express criticism, defensiveness, and contempt in their relationships. You will learn that higher incidences of these intimacy killers, especially contempt, can lead to higher relationship dissatisfaction, relationship dissolution, and even poor physical health for both partners.

Characteristics of individuals with high levels of neuroticism also suggest a low tolerance for stress, frequent expressions of negative emotions (and for significant amounts of time), and increased incidences of depression and anxiety (Gottman & Gottman, 2015). Like the other Big Five personality traits, neuroticism can be impacted by both environmental and genetic factors. We know that environmental causes, such as trauma and abuse, are associated with individuals who score high on indicators of neuroticism (e.g., feelings of being inadequate and emotionally unstable). Twin studies have also found a genetic contribution to neuroticism, that is to say one's propensity for neuroticism might also run in the family. Remember that up to 48% of an individual's neuroticism may be accounted by genetics (Bouchard & McGue, 2003). Although this is similar to the percentage of other personality trait factors, neuroticism has become significant as emerging research points to environmental factors from historical events and intergenerational trauma that have preceded our birth (e.g., Transatlantic Slave Trade, Trail of Tears, Holocaust). These events can lead to our propensity to inherit and behave in ways that are characterized as neurotic. Therefore, from a relational perspective, understanding how environmental and genetic factors influence personality is important for better understanding our partners and ourselves.

Complementing Personalities

What happens when our partners do not match our preferred personality types, such as when they are lower (or higher) in the traits such as agreeableness, conscientiousness, extraversion, and openness to experience? Perhaps to no one's surprise, no matter who we end up with, our partners typically do not live up to our ideals. Just because our partner's personality style is not similar to ours, however, does not mean that we are destined to fail as a couple. It just may take more patience and attention to intimacy killers and applications of intimacy healers in our relationship (see Chapters 9 and 10). Somewhere in-between "birds-of-a-feather flock together" and "opposites attract" endpoints lay couples who complement each other. For instance, had Rachel and Isaac stayed together as they got older, their personality differences may have acted as a catalyst to relationship satisfaction—rather than as a barrier.

Research regarding our developmental needs and tasks as we age suggests that although initial matching may lead us to our partners, similarities can sometimes impact us negatively over time. Shiota and Levenson (2007) put forth that events such as dating, emotional intimacy, and shared political ideologies that may be more important at the beginning of our relationships are less important when we start to think more about finances, parenting decisions, and taking care of the house. As we get older, partners' personality differences may in fact fortify their relationship by building upon each other's respective strengths. Using Rachel as an example, when reflecting on what she looks for in a partner, she talked to her friends privately about wanting to find someone who was outgoing, got along well with her family, and was down-to-earth. Although "down-to-earth" would encompass a lower score on openness to experience, Rachel's idiosyncratic preferences of "low" versus "high" scores may matter more when it comes to romantic interests and attraction. For Rachel it meant that a lower score was more preferable compared to a higher score in openness to experience. Similarly, Isaac talked about wanting to find someone to settle down with, who could push him academically, and that enjoyed getting to know him and his family. In this example, Rachel and Isaac could see benefits to finding someone who was complementary.

What personality types are most likely to seek complementary rather than similar personality matches? Zentner (2005) suggests that openness is one of the most desired personality traits, while neuroticism is the least desired. He goes on to say that it is less likely that we would seek out someone with similar traits if our traits were less desirable (e.g., low openness and high neuroticism); we would instead be more likely to seek out someone who complements our personality (e.g., high openness and low neuroticism). For the individual with less desired traits, she or he would likely be happier with a partner who had complementary traits. However, this may not be the case for the partner. Think about your personality profile. What are your ideal traits when looking for a partner? Are they similar to yours or do they complement your personality?

Along the way, the dangers of looking for somebody to "complete you" should be noted. While looking for a partner with complementary personality traits can be beneficial, the understanding that we, as individuals, are somehow "lacking" should not drive this search. Rather, we must maintain self-focus and find completeness within ourselves. It is only at this point that we will be ready to enter into a relationship with another person without putting unrealistic expectations and pressures onto them.

What Our Room and Office Says About Our Personality

According to a study by Gosling et al. (2002), strangers are better at accurately predicting our conscientiousness, neuroticism, and openness to experience than our good friends after only 20 minutes of observing our living and/or office spaces.

Vignette, Continued

Isaac decides to try online dating after he and Rachel transitioned to just being "friends." Having never dated this way before, he quickly puts together a profile picture and summary. He thinks to himself, *"How do I portray my best self?,"* *"What information will I need to include so that I can attract people that I also find attractive?"* After asking friends, family, and even an ex-girlfriend what he should post in this profile, Isaac winds up even more confused. Ultimately, he just posts a photo.

PERSONALITY AND SOCIAL MEDIA

In Chapter 5, you will be introduced to how technology matters when it comes to meeting, dating, and maintaining relationships. The ways that we display our personality in cyberspace are becoming increasingly important. How we display our personality continues to be an exercise in perception of ourselves, others, and society as a whole. Others' perceptions of our personality may influence what schools accept our applications, which employers Google our names, the dates we get from posting funny profile photos, and the boosts in self-esteem we get from "likes" regarding our online photos and comments. Important questions we might ask ourselves include: *"Who am I?,"* *"How do I portray myself?,"* *"What does society say about what I should highlight versus leave in the periphery?,"* *"What type of personality characteristics will catch the attention of the people that I also find most attractive?."*

Online Dating and Personalities

The emergence of online dating is evident in the burgeoning number of online interactions that occur every day. Estimates suggest that about 38% of adults who are "single and looking" have used online dating sites (Smith & Duggan, 2013). Further, those in college and who live in urban and suburban areas are twice as likely to use dating apps compared to individuals not in college and/or who live in rural areas. If a person is not single or does not use dating apps, it is still likely that friends or family members might ask him or her for advice when creating their online profiles. This means that, at some point in our lives, it is likely we will have to think about how to present ourselves and/or others as to achieve what we/they are looking for, whether that be long-term romance or a weekend fling.

When it comes to meeting and dating, we all seem to have that one friend who is "braver" than the rest of us. She or he can go up to anybody and ask if they would be interested in going out on a date. For others of us, the prospect of going up to someone and asking them out can leave us frozen. We may think that *"If I weren't so shy, I would have a date by now!"* Television shows like the *Pick-up Artist* were in part so popular because they purported—often in misogynistic ways—the way we (stereotypically men) need to be more outgoing (high extroversion) and act like bad boys (low agreeableness), while at the same time seeming relaxed (lower conscientiousness). No wonder the pick-up game seems so hard! For those of us who are shy, the online environment can present an opportunity for meeting partners in a way that feels safe and comfortable. Interestingly, research findings tell us that our online personalities are a continuation of offline personalities. The rich-get-richer hypothesis posits that the Internet increases the dating opportunities for those with low dating anxiety and strong dating skills (Valkenburg & Peter, 2007). This contradicts the common assumption that online dating levels the playing field for people who are shy and have less confidence in their dating skills.

What can we understand from someone's online profile, anyway? Analyses from online environments (e.g., Facebook) find that we most often infer individual personality characteristics through text and pictures on a person's profile page (Hitsch, Hortacsu, & Ariely, 2010). Studies regarding personalities and Facebook pages have found strong correlations between our personality characteristics and online presences (see below).

What Your Facebook Use Reveals About Your Personality (Morin, 2014)	
Extroverts	Higher scorers are likely to upload photos and post statuses more often. They also use the like button more.
Conscientiousness	Higher scorers are more likely to organize their photos in neat and methodical ways using folders.
Openness	High scorers are more likely to fill out their personal profiles thoroughly.
Neurotic	High scorers post mostly photos and tend to have the most photos per album. Appearing happy and in socially acceptable ways is a priority in the posted photos.
Agreeableness	High scorers are featured (tagged) in other people's photos most often. Friends often enjoy taking photos with them and posting them on social media.

Your Best Self

The online environment, much like in-person, requires us think about how others perceive us. This means that, in order to present our best self, we must share ourselves in a way that those we are attracted to will reciprocate interest. In a popular TED talk, *How I Hacked Dating,* Amy Webb explains how relying on a traditional mathematical formula led her on countless dates and dead ends. Fed up, she tells us how she knew the type of person she wanted; the only problem was that those individuals were often paired up with people not like her. She then studied women and men by taking on different personas to understand what attracted the men she was attracted to. Ultimately her system "hacking"—learning what lead to better matches—resulted in a relationship that turned to marriage.

Webb's discovery of what lead to better matches is not a one-size-fits-all method, however. Rather, it was unique to her personality traits and what she deemed to be important qualities in a potential partner. We must, then, "hack" the system for ourselves by first determining what characteristics in a potential mate are non-negotiable for us. With that knowledge, we can then consider what personality traits we feel are important to be similar between partners, and in what ways we might be better off with a partner who is complementary. Of course, you cannot boil a complex experience down into a simple process and immediately find your perfect match. It instead requires taking an honest look at one's own self; work to understand your own strengths and weaknesses/difficulties. It also requires that you gain an understanding of what traits you are really looking for in a partner.

What this all illustrates is the struggle for how we present ourselves versus the way we might act in-person. Many people wonder, *"How much does this disconnect matter?"*, *"What if I lie in my profile to get a date?"* Surveys regarding how people represent themselves online show that over 50% of people have "seriously misrepresented" themselves while online. These surveys found that individuals who were further from the socially prescribed mean (average) were more likely to misrepresent themselves (Smith & Duggan, 2013). Often these deviations are regarding physical attributes (e.g., height, weight, and age) and physical attractiveness (e.g., using filtered or outdated photos). The outcomes of these discrepancies seem to depend on the severity of the misrepresentation. According to Ellison, Hancock, and Toma (2011), our online identities encompass aspects of our past, current, and future self as a promise to others of what we could become with them as a partner. It is when someone presents something fundamentally different—in a way that was not imaginable based on their profile and description—do we risk losing trust and alienation when we finally meet face-to-face. For example, it might be harder to have a second date if we portrayed ourselves as someone who is relaxed using words like "chill," "calm," and "confident" (along with a photo of us doing yoga) when we show up to our first date and question why they were late, complained about the temperature of the fries, and continually asked them why they were checking their phone. This scenario, however, speaks to the difficulties we may have when trying to present our true self versus what is looked upon favorably by societal standards.

Personality and Attractiveness

Peterson (2014) said that:

. . . maybe what we call the argument of one's genitals is, in truth, incredibly—and both consciously and subconsciously—influenced by the cultures in which we grow up as well as our distinct (and equally culturally influenced) ideas of what a "good couple" or "good relationship" would look like. Put differently, we swipe because someone's "hot," but we find someone "hot" based on unconscious codes of class, race, education level, religion, and corresponding interests embedded within the photos of their profile. (p. 1)

This passage alludes to the ways that attractiveness and unconscious codes are connected. Like class, race, education, and religion, for example, personality and physical attractiveness are inextricably linked as one one's preference in a "good partner." Think about (what you presume to be) the personality of the following people: What would you assume about them based on their photos?

What we know about personality is that we often include ideas about what we find attractive in how we perceive others' personality, and similarly what we find attractive is influenced by our own personality type. Findings regarding personality show that we are prone to attribute positive qualities to individuals who are considered within our society/culture as more attractive. For instance, attractive individuals are deemed more intelligent and competent in social and work settings, and are treated more positively by friends and family (Segal-Caspi, Roccas, & Sagiv, 2012). When it comes to personality traits, for people who are attractive, we tend to overestimate their agreeableness, conscientiousness, extroversion, and openness to experience (Segal et al., 2012). In contrast, when we meet individuals who deviate from cultural norms, like the pierced and tattooed gentleman in the image above, we tend to rate them as less intelligent, less attractive, and underestimate their agreeableness, conscientiousness, extroversion, and openness to experience. For individuals who find people with piercings attractive, a study found a significant association between attractiveness and openness to experience (Swami et al., 2012). In the same study, individuals with piercings were more likely to have higher levels of agreeableness, extroversion, higher thrill and adventure scores, and higher neuroticism. Simply put, our personality impacts what we find attractive in others.

What Happens if They Have a Great Personality but I Still Do Not Find Them Attractive?

Conversations with friends and advice columns in magazines often give recommendations based on the question *"What happens if they have a great personality, but I am not attracted to them?"* Given what we learned earlier regarding evolutionary theory and sociocultural expectations of men and women, it is not unexpected that attractiveness—beauty and/or resources—are important when partners are selecting who to date. Not surprisingly, personality is often found to be more important to women than men, as women place more value on "resources" that include personality. We also know from the section above that our personality (e.g., openness to experience) shapes who we find attractive, even if they deviate from societal standards. For example, a photo of couple at a wedding gained national notoriety recently based on the apparent mismatch in the attractiveness of the partners. Public comments about the photo ranged from "he must be rich" to "he is fat and disgusting." The bride's response, which went viral, spoke to the unfair and mean-spirited criticism by addressing how love and personality prevailed despite dominate sociocultural ideas about beauty. She said:

> . . . let me just tell you, I won the jackpot with Christopher . . . He may not have rock hard abs like the world tells girls to want in a guy, but really, why does that even matter when you are trying to really find someone to spend the rest of your life with?" (Burke, 2015, p. 1)

She goes on to describe how her husband is open to new experiences, thoughtful (i.e., conscientious), and outgoing (i.e., extroverted)—and that they make a great team (i.e. complementary). This couple's story exemplifies how attractiveness, while important, intersects with other important factors (e.g., personality of our partners and ourselves) that lead to the partners we chose.

APPLICATION

Maritain (1958) famously said that "We don't love qualities; we love persons; sometimes by reason of their defects as well as their qualities." This quote speaks to the totality and complexity of our intimate relationships, at to our attempts to answer the question: *Do birds-of-a-feather flock together, or do opposites attract, when it comes to personality?* While we know that being similar is beneficial for relationship success, researchers (along with a number of online dating sites) are still seeking to gain a better understanding about how couples with different personalities traits can successfully navigate and engage in intimate relationships.

When it comes to personality and intimate relationships, remembering that 1 + 1 = 2 (i.e., maintaining a self-focused rather than other-focused approach) is important whether we are just beginning to date, have been partners for several years, or are even divorcing. Assessments like the Big Five and the MBTI can help in establishing a basic understanding, and giving language to who we are, what we aspire to be, and what we are looking for in our partners. These will allow you to have deeper conversations about what you agreed with and what differed. For instance, you might not see yourself as someone who is outgoing (an introvert) and feel as though you worry all the time. However, someone you know might find that you are a fun-loving and that you appear calm and relaxed. Talking about our perceived and observed discrepancies with others can provide more holistic views of one's self.

What if Isaac and Rachel had been so similar that they, after a while, felt stuck and stagnant in their relationship? One thing we know about personality is that we often find niches (i.e., environments) that support our unique characteristics. These niches are often in line with our perceived selves, and likely strengthen their salience in our lives (Roberts, O'Donnell, & Robins, 2004). For example, if someone were to grow up in a family with parents and siblings who were doctors, lawyers, and business executives, she or he most likely grew up in an environment that stressed characteristics associated with high conscientiousness (e.g., organized, reliable, and self-disciplined). These are characteristics that we might expect to be internalized in an individual's identity due to the context. For individuals and couples who might not like some of the traits that developed in part as a result of their environment, one approach toward making change might be to seek out new environments for dates and activities that they may not have previously considered. For instance, if later this same person in the highly conscientious family goes to school in a surf-town where schedules are more relaxed and having fun is prioritized over deadlines, she or he might observe changes over time in how she or he acts, thinks, and feels. This is often the reason why when people move away to new environments (e.g., go to college), they say that they "found themselves" through adapting characteristics different from what they experienced previously. Similarly, for couples like Isaac and Rachel, who are both highly conscientious, seeking out different activities in environments that support characteristics associated with lower levels of conscientiousness may lead them to think about their relationship more positively.

Couples with different personalities (e.g., high vs. low extraversion) might also worry that they are just "too different." Gottman and Gottman (2015) contend that even though couples might be similar in a lot of ways, 69% of our arguments are a result of personality differences—and these problems are not easily resolved. For example, Rachel and Isaac often got into fights over Isaac wanting to go out with his friends on the weekend vis-à-vis Rachel wanting to stay in. Both felt that the other did not appreciate him/her and were often left feeling alone and defeated. For couples with different personality types, having self-awareness regarding personality can help us to explain and communicate our respective wants and desires. Gottman and Gottman (2015) suggest that soft start-ups, as opposed to harsh start-ups, alongside avoiding criticism, defensiveness, contempt, and stonewalling are imperative for relationship satisfaction and success. Further, they suggest that finding win-win outcomes in situations, instead of win-lose, is an important goal for couples.

Going back to our couple, Isaac might say in a sarcastic way to Rachel *"Why are you being so boring? You only think about yourself!"* This expression of both contempt and criticism would likely trigger a fight. Let us say that after reading this chapter and taking the personality assessments described herein, Isaac learns that he scores high on neuroticism (a characteristic of individuals more likely to use contempt). Knowing this, he may start his next conversation with Rachel by saying *"Rachel, I appreciate how you are so reflective and enjoy conversations and time to think about our relationship. I also find it enjoyable and relaxing to see my friends after a hard week of classes. What can we do to make sure that each of our styles are attended to?"* This speaks to both partners' personalities and needs, validating Rachel's feelings and searching for a win-win outcome that both can be satisfied with. When compromise and understanding by both partners are present, other options are more readily available. For instance, if Isaac and Rachel decided to hang out together on Fridays, and to go out with friends on Saturdays, they could attend to both personalities and their respective desires and needs.

Personality differences between partners, as reviewed earlier in this chapter, might also be important to achieving goals over the life-course. By changing one's perspective(s) about differences, we can see how to more effectively navigate life challenges and opportunities. For example, the partner who is highly conscientious might be tasked with paying bills and making sure their children's schedules are in order, whereas the more relaxed partner may decide what the family does on vacation and/or plan fun activities for the upcoming weekend. One of the problems many couples encounter is when society's gender roles and expectations do not fit with our personality, especially among heterosexual couples. This makes sense given that communities that traditionally abscond from gender roles, such as LGBTQ and gender non-conforming communities, engage more frequently in purposive communication about roles based on personality differences and strengths (Gottman, 2011; Knudson-Martin, 2013). Problem solving, such as how to divide roles within the family, guided by recognition of our strengths and differences, can produce outcomes that are a better fit for each individual, couple, and family over time.

What We Don't Know

When it comes to personality, there is a lot that we still do not know. Take the online dating industry, for example. When it comes to understanding matching personalities, billions of dollars are spent on measuring and trying to successfully understand the complexities of the interaction between individuals and their environments. Even with advancements in computing, the rise of experts on personality and psychology, and having more information available about personality than ever before, many of our online meetings do not happen or turn into dates, let alone commitment or marriage. With that being said, there are many factors regarding personality that are continuing to be examined.

The interaction between environment and genetics continues to be an emerging area of study. Science is just beginning to understand how our environments (e.g., trauma and in-utero stress) impact our development and personality based on changes to, and expressions of, genes. Further, researchers are attempting to understand more about how a couple's genetics may lead to greater or less relationship satisfaction. Based on desired personality traits, neuroticism and its associated difficulties (e.g., mental illness and decreased martial satisfaction) will continue to be studied to increase understanding of healthy development and interpersonal relationships.

With LGBTQ couples, there is still very little research regarding personality matches and types, and a lot of what is known is rooted in traditionally heterosexual and gendered scripts. This disparity was highlighted over recent years when a lawsuit alleged discrimination on the part of an online dating site because it did not match gay and lesbian individuals. Later, we learned that the company claimed it did not have enough information about personality fit and preferences, gender roles, and associated interests to understand and make significant guesses regarding matches (Cloud, 2007). Further research needs to explore how our cultures and communities shape preferences and perceived personality matches.

Current measures of personality also have limited predictive power when it comes to work, school, relationships, and a variety of social settings. For example, chances are that you have taken, or will take, a personality inventory for a job. What we have found, however, is that personality may only account for a small proportion of the success that you have in your career. For instance, even for an introvert, there are myriad of ways to be a successful and engaging speaker, fundraiser, or president of a company. Personality, in return, can be a starting point for further exploration. For others, personality's predictive power can be immense, as recognition of the important facets of one's self can be applied to school, work, and relationship contexts. Like many measures of social indicators (i.e., personality), increased understanding of humans' complexity can lead to further exploration and realization of self and the environments we seek out.

CONCLUSION

In the beginning of this chapter, we asked questions like: *"Who am I?," "Who do I want to be?," "Who am I looking for?,"* and *"Who is compatible with me?"* These are important questions to consider, as they shape how we experience and behave in a world full of different people. Characteristics associated with personality types, and the ways in which our similarities and differences interact and affect our intimate relationships, are important to consider. We encourage you to reflect and apply your insights here to your own life, and to your intimate relationships.

REFERENCES

Ansari, A., Klinenberg, E. (2015). *Modern romance.* New York: Penguin Press.

Botwin, M. D., Buss, D. M., & Shackelford, T. K. (1997). Personality and mate preferences: Five factors in mate selection and marital satisfaction. *Journal of Personality, 65*(1), 107–136. doi:10.1111/j.1467-6494.1997. tb00531.x.

Bouchard Jr., T. J. (1994). Genes, environment, and personality. *Science, 264*(5166), 1700–1701. doi:10.1126/ science.8209250.

Bouchard Jr., T. J., & McGue, M. (2003). Genetic and environmental influences on human psychological differences. *Journal of Neurobiology, 54*(1), 4–45. doi:10.1002/neu.10160.

Burke, D. (2015, July 11). *Girlfriend defends her man in the best possible way after bullies say he's punching above his weight.* Retrieved from: http://metro.co.uk/2015/07/11/girlfriend-defends-her-man-in-the-best-possible-way-after-bullies-say-hes-punching-above-his-weight-5290915/.

Cain, S. (2013). *Quiet: The Power of introverts in a World that can't stop talking.* New York: Crown Publishing.

Cloud, J. (2007, June 1). *Is eHarmony biased against gays?* Retrieved from: http://content.time.com/time/business/article/0,8599,1627585,00.html.

Coontz, S. (2005). *Marriage, a history: How love conquered marriage.* New York: Penguin Books.

Costa Jr., P. T., Terracciano, A., & McCrae, R. R. (2001). Gender differences in personality traits across cultures: Robust and surprsing findings. *Journal of Personality and Social Psychology, 81*(2), 322–331. doi:10.1037//0022-3514.81.2.322.

Costa, P., & McCrae, R. (1992). Normal personality assessment in clinical practice: The NEO personality inventory. *Psychological Assessment, 4*(1), 5–13. doi:10.1037//1040-3590.4.1.5.

Ellison, N. B., Hancock, J. T., & Toma, C. L. (2011). Profile as promise: A framework for conceptualizing veracity in online dating self-presentations. *New Media & Society, 14*(1), 45–62. doi:10.1177/1461444811410395.

Engler, B. (2014). *Personality theories: An introduction.* Belmont, CA: Wadsworth.

Gosling, S. D., Ko, S. J., Mannarelli, T., & Morris, M. E. (2002). A room with a cue: Personality judgments based on offices and bedrooms. *Journal of Personality and Social Psychology, 82*(3), 379–398. doi:10.1037//0022-3514.82.3.379.

Gottman, J. S., & Gottman, J. M. (2015). *10 principles for doing effective couples therapy.* New York: W. W. Norton & Company.

Gottman, J. M., Gottman, J. S., & Atkins, C. L. (2011). The comprehensive soldier fitness program: Family skills component. *The American Psychologist, 66*(1), 52–57. doi:10.1037/a0021706

Hitschman, C., & Mogford, E. (2009a). Immigration and the American industrial revolution from 1880 to 1920. *Social Science Research, 38*(4), 897–920. doi:10.1016/j.ssresearch.2009.04.001.

Hitsch, G. J., Hortacsu, A., & Ariely, D. (2010). What makes you click? Mate preferences in online dating. *Quantitative Marketing and Economics, 8*(4), 393–427. doi:10.1007/s11129-010-9088-6.

Jang, K. L., Livesley, W. J., & Vernon, P. A. (1996). Heritability of the Big Five personality dimensions and their facets: A twin study. *Journal of Personality, 64*(3), 577–591. doi:10.1111/j.1467-6494.1996.tb00522.x.

Knudson-Martin, C. (2013) Why power matters: Creating a foundation of mutual support in couple relationships. *Family Process, 52*(1), 5–18. doi:10.1111/famp.12011.

Martian, J. (1958). *Reflections on America.* New York: Scribner.

Milfont, T. L., & Sibley, C. G. (2012). The Big Five personality traits and environmental engagement: Associations at the individual and societal level. *Journal of Environmental Psychology, 32*(2), 187–195. doi:10.1016/j.jenvp.2011.12.006.

Morin, A. (2014, October 31). *What your Facebook use reveals about your personality and your self-esteem.* Retrieved from http://www.forbes.com/sites/amymorin/2014/10/31/what-your-facebook-use-reveals-about-your-personality-and-your-self-esteem/#2da04d4d5bda

Peterson, A. H. (2014, September 11). *How I rebuilt Tinder and discovered the shameful secret of attraction.* Retrieved from https://www.buzzfeed.com/annehelenpetersen/we-are-all-classists?utm_term=.ikd7mNrr#.lkpAbOyy

Roberts, B. W., O'Donnell, M., & Robins, R. W. (2004). Goal and personality trait development in emerging adulthood. *Journal of Personality and Social Psychology, 87*(4), 541–550. doi:10.1037/0022-3514.87.4.541.

Segal-Caspi, L., Roccas, S., & Sagiv, L. (2012). Don't judge a book by its cover, revisited: Perceived and reported traits and values of attractive women. *Psychological Science, 23*(10), 1112–1116. doi:10.1177/0956797612446349.

Shiota, M. N., & Levenson, R. W. (2007). Birds of a feather don't always fly farthest: Similarity in Big Five personality predicts more negative marital satisfaction trajectories in long-term marriages. *Psychology and Aging, 22*(4), 666–675. doi:10.1037/0882-7974.22.4.666.

Smith, A., Duggan, M. (2013, October 21). *Online dating and relationships.* Retrieved from http://www.pewinternet.org/2013/10/21/online-dating-relationships/

Swami, V., Stieger, S., Pietschnig, J., Voracek, M., Furnham, A., & Tovée, M. J. (2012). The influence of facial piercings and observer personality on perceptions of physical attractiveness and intelligence. *European Psychologist, 17*(3), 213–221. doi:10.1027/1016-9040/a000080.

Valkenburg, P. M., & Peter, J. (2007). Who visits online dating Sites? Exploring some characteristics of online daters. *CyberPsychology & Behavior, 10*(6), 849–852. doi:10.1089/cpb.2007.9941.

Zentner, M. R. (2005). Ideal mate personality concepts and compatibility in close relationships : A longitudinal analysis. *Journal of Personality and Social Psychology, 89*(2), 242–256. doi:10.1037/0022-3514.89.2.242.

Gender Socialization and Relationship Formation: What Is It and What Has It Got To Do with Me?

Jane E. Newell, Ph.D.
Department of Family Studies & Social Work
Miami University

Anna I. Bohlinger, M.S., LAMFT
Department of Family Social Science
University of Minnesota

LEARNING OBJECTIVES

- Articulate views of gender across traditional, modern, and postmodern perspectives
- Understand gender, gendered behavior, and dating scripts as social constructions
- Articulate ways that gender socialization has changed over time, especially for women
- Articulate ways that gender socialization intersects with culture and religion
- Understand classifications of masculinity, femininity, androgyny, and undifferentiated gender

GENDER SOCIALIZATION AND RELATIONSHIP FORMATION

Gender: you've heard the word before but you may be asking yourself, "What is it? And what has gender got to do with me?" Well, as it turns out—quite a lot! However, most of what we experience around gender seems to be "just the way it is," rather than it being something we can understand and impact ourselves. We hope to change that perspective in this chapter.

Our intention here is to provide relevant content on how gender influences the formation of your relationships and to give you opportunities to apply this information to your own lives in ways that are meaningful. We will take a look at how society contributes to the ways we think about our gender and believe we should behave (i.e., gender roles and gender role expectations). We will begin this discussion with a look at the changing role of gender over the last century and into the 21st century, and review the resultant changes in dating and mating rituals. We will examine the major contexts where gender is constructed, such as our family, our ethnic and cultural settings, and our religious institutions. We will explore the influence of mass media in today's society on gender, gender role expectations, and relationship formation. We will introduce you to the gender continuum, which conceptualizes gender as complex and multifaceted. This continuum is distinct from the more simplistic view held by many in society—that gender consists of only two options: male or female.

Finally, we invite you, after considering the information we present, to examine how you see yourself in the gender socialization process and how this affects your views and behavior in dating and mate selection. How did you come to hold the thoughts, expectations, and beliefs you have about gender and

Corresponding Author: Jane E. Newell, Ph.D.; Miami University; Family Studies & Social Work; 110C McGuffey Hall; Oxford, OH 45056. E-mail: newellj2@miamioh.edu.

The authors wish to acknowledge contributions to this article by Polina Levchenko, Michigan State University.

gender role expectations in your relationships? Do you consider your expectations for those you date to be influenced by gender socialization? Do you hold expectations for yourself about how you think you should behave in your intimate relationships? Did you know there is such a thing as dating scripts? And that you have them—that they guide you, without you knowing it, on every date and in every consideration about who to date or what to expect from them when you do? And that your potential date has them too—guiding his or her expectations of you? What, if anything, will you do with this new knowledge?

To begin, we'd like to introduce you to two college students, Courtney and Matt. In the scenario that follows, see if you recognize yourself and any of your own lived experiences in the descriptions they provide of their lives leading up to their chance meeting on campus. Does any of this sound familiar?

Courtney and Matt give us a glimpse into the challenges of relationship formation in the college years. There is so much more than attending classes, reading books, and writing papers going on in their new lives on campus. While focusing on the demands of academic life, students are smack in the middle of building new relationships! Relationships from high school may be gone or starting to fade and meeting new people from different cultures, family backgrounds, religions, and experiences make building relationships central to the college years. Erik Erickson (1950) called this developmental life stage young adulthood, and named the major task in this stage "Intimacy vs. Isolation". The central task of the young adult stage is to build relationships—so, take heart, you are right where you should be!

Courtney grew up in rural Wisconsin, the last child and first daughter in a family of six boys. From the second her mother walked out of the doctor's office at her 20 week ultrasound, family and friends began purchasing pink, purple, and princess-themed items to decorate her nursery. At her birth her parents ooo-ed and aww-ed over her "sweet little fingers" and "perfect little tummy." When she cried, she "whimpered" and everyone in the family took gentle, loving care of her. She grew up playing with Barbie Dolls and tiaras. As a little girl, she wanted to be a ballerina and a kindergarten teacher. All of these professions were encouraged as appropriate choices for her by her parents and loved ones.

As she became a teenager, she grew hips and breasts and often felt uncomfortable with her changing body. She and her girlfriends compared body shapes against the popular teen magazines at the time. "My hips are awful" her friends would complain. "Well, I see your hips and raise you one set of thunder-der thighs" she would respond. Together, she and her friends tried to achieve the beauty ideal: thin thighs, curvy (but-not-too-curvy) hips, small breasts and clear skin. Her freckles betrayed her and she worked to use concealer and powder to achieve the "flawless" complexion that she and her friends idealized.

Adolescence came with not only family life, school, first jobs, and puberty, but also dating. Together with her girlfriends, they pored over popular television shows, magazines, and celebrity gossip and compared those experiences of dating against the dating experiences that they saw their friends having. It seemed clear that there were many important rules for a young woman to follow to ensure dating success: dress sexy, but not too sexy; do not eat too much lest your date think that you are a pig; be funny; be smart; do not be too funny or smart; do not "give it all away." (Her parents scolded "Why would anyone buy the cow if you can get the milk for free?") While some of the rules were explicit, most of them were just the things that were expected and no one seemed to know why or where they came from.

Matt grew up in urban Chicago, Illinois. While his parents did not find out his sex until he was born, from the minute his mother's doctor announced "It's a boy!" his family began thinking about him in gendered terms. This meant that as a baby his gripping reflex was described as "strong." His cries were "wails" and his previously gender neutral room was quickly filled with fire engines, action figures, and Nerf guns. He was encouraged to run around and play and get dirty, and when he occasionally fell and cried at the sight of his own blood, he was quickly reprimanded "Save your tears for something important."

When he was a teenager he joined the football team with his friends. As an offensive lineman, his job was to protect the quarterback from being hurt. His protective instincts served him well in dating situations. When he went on dates, he walked on the outside of the sidewalk, between his date and cars. When other young men approached a woman he was dating, he would subtly position himself between them and her. Being protective was a big part of how he thought about himself as a person, and as a man.

One role he got flack for was his role of Romeo in his high school's production of Romeo and Juliet. In spite of being able to stage kiss one of the hottest girls in school, being in the drama club earned him the following epithets: "That is so gay!" "What a pussy!" and other taunts meant to minimize his manhood. This surprised him, because no one else was kissing that girl, and his rapidly broadening shoulders, deep voice and thickening facial hair as a 16 year old should have assured his masculinity.

Courtney and Matt ended up at the same Big 10 University and met each other in their freshman orientation. Courtney came to orientation wearing a pretty yellow sundress, her hair curled in loose waves and leather sandals. Matt arrived wearing skinny jeans and an NOFX t-shirt. Courtney took one look at Matt and decided that he was not the kind of man she would want to have anything to do with—he was wearing girl's pants! On the other hand, Matt took one look at Courtney and immediately decided that he was going to try to date her before the year was out. *The game was on.*

As in this story of Courtney and Matt, we all know that learning gained from reading a text book is one thing—whereas forming new relationships is quite another! You may be wondering, "How do we do this well?" "Why are people so different?" "In a world of more than 7 billion people, I just want to find ONE person to love and care about me. What could be so hard about that?" In this chapter we will explore some factors that you may not have yet considered that influence the building of relationships—even before we ever meet one another, and especially in the very beginning of relationship formation. What is the role of gender on our success or failure in forming our relationships? To begin, let's take a look at how all people are affected by the socialization process. Why it is that people tend to think about themselves as a "man" or a "woman"? How did you come to think about yourself as a "man" or a "woman"—and how does that influence what you expect from those around you—and, more importantly, from yourself?

Differing Views of Knowledge and Gender Roles

To understand gender roles, how they are created, and the purposes they serve, we begin with a description of how knowledge is viewed from three different perspectives: traditional, modern, and postmodern, and discuss how each of these perspectives affects the development of our gender role expectations.

When viewed from *traditional* ways of thinking about knowledge, what is known and believed to be true comes from experts and leaders we look to for guidance in how to live our lives. In this sense, knowledge is given to us by those we trust and we accept what is said as "the truth." This is most notable in our religious institutions. Examples of this are expectations that gender roles conform to what is described in religious texts such as the Torah, Bible, Koran, or other religious guidebooks.

Modern ways of thinking about knowledge consist of knowledge generated from scientific experiments about the roles of men and women in today's society. Knowledge is considered trustworthy if it emerges from research studies on the interactions between men and women in the midst of their relationships. John Gottman (Gottman & Silver, 2013) is an example of a current researcher from whom family studies scholars draw knowledge about couples. Having worked with more than 650 couples in his career by 1999 (and many more by now), Gottman provides us with scientific knowledge that informs our teaching today. He uses a number of empirical measures to determine levels of stress and arousal for each member of the couples who participate in his experiments.

Postmodern ways of thinking about knowledge reflect that knowledge is socially constructed, changes over time, and is personal in nature. For example, each of you as you read this chapter will come to your own conclusions about the influence of gender and gender role expectations on the formation of your relationships. This would be considered a postmodern view of knowledge generation—when you consider and determine for yourself how gender affects you and your relationships and what you will do with that knowledge.

Today, we know that gender roles are changing in our society and around the world, but we do not yet know much about how college students conceive of themselves as gendered human beings as they are developing intimate relationships in a changing world. This is important for family researchers and educators to know because as our society changes and students' experiences change, we need to hear directly from those having the experience for our texts and classrooms to remain relevant and current.

Historical Social Construction of Gender

Throughout history, at different historical times and in various social settings, expectations for the behavior of a society's citizens shaped beliefs not only about what was expected, but also what was forbidden. This is especially true when it comes to gender and gender role expectations and how this affects our dating and mating behavior. The term gender differs from the term sex, even though these terms are used interchangeably by most people. *Sex* refers to classification based upon the biological sex of male or female at birth. *Gender* is a term that refers to the expectations in a society for how men and women should behave in that society. Each society has its own expectations and those expectations are embedded so seamlessly in everyday living that they often go unnoticed and are rarely challenged. We invite you to discover for yourself the gender role expectations that have shaped how you think about yourself and what you think is acceptable or unacceptable when it comes to your dating and relationship behavior. The society you live in, your family of origin, race, ethnicity, culture, and/or religion all affect what you have come to believe is true about gender and gender roles; we call this *socialization*.

> Human beings are not born with any pre-existing knowledge of, or orientation to, their world. What we come to feel about life and about ourselves, we learn through socialization, the social mechanisms through which gender developments occur. (Bryjal, 1997)

We live in a world with 7 billion people in 230 countries, speaking somewhere between 6800 and 6900 languages, and in which eight out of every ten people identify with a religion. With this much diversity, it is no wonder that gender role expectations vary widely across the globe. For the purposes of this text and the course you are taking on intimate relationships, we will discuss major societal influences on gender role expectations as they have been identified primarily in the United States, and therefore can be considered as a Western model of relationship formation. If you are from a country other than the United States, we invite you to use the concepts and tools presented in this chapter to assess for yourself the influence of socialization in your country of origin upon your beliefs about how you believe you should behave when dating and forming intimate relationships. Do you see differences in the ways you are expected to behave while you are in the United States versus your country of origin? How do you decide for yourself what is acceptable?

Changing Gender Roles in the United States

Throughout European history, what was expected for men and women in society changed, on average, about every century. A notable example is the extreme difference between the Age of Romanticism in the late 1700s and the Victorian Age of the 1800s. In the Age of Romanticism, love and romance ruled the day: books, poetry, plays, and expected dating and mating behavior all celebrated the joys and sorrows of romantic love. By the Victorian Age, women were buttoned up and locked down—sending the societal message "no touching allowed"—the goal was to maintain social order in reaction to the explicit romantic love and sexual expression of the previous stage. As society shifts and changes, so also does the behavior of its citizens. Conversely, as citizens begin to challenge the status quo by their behavior change, changes at the societal level are seen over time. History has shown us that dating and mating is a bit like the weather: if you do not like what you see—wait another 50–100 years and you will see a change in the climate (provided you live that long!).

History is being made all the time. We are making it now. How we think about and act regarding our dating and mating behavior and the development of intimacy in relationships is unquestionably influenced by the societies in which we live our lives. Let's look at dating and mating behavior that is closer to us in historical time and see how society in the 20th and emerging 21st century have affected how we think about and act in our intimate relationships.

Changing Gender Roles for Women

In the early 20th century (1920) women gained the right to vote in the United States. The 19th Amendment to the Constitution stated that "The right of citizens of the United States to vote shall not be denied or abridged by the United States or by any State on account of sex" (US Const. amend. XIX). Here, the reference is made to biological sex—being born a male or a female. Prior to the 19th Amendment to the Constitution of the United States, the right to vote belonged exclusively to men. The right to vote affects behavior, which in turn, affects how our country operates. By obtaining the right to vote, women in the United States began to have a say about the society in which they lived. The right to vote, and therefore to take action politically, is an example of changing *gender role expectations*. Prior to this major change in the United States, women had little to no power to influence their society and were expected to maintain traditional gender roles, within and outside of the home, based solely on societal expectations for how women should behave at that time in the history of the United States.

Traditional gender roles means that women were expected to get married young, to a man, and to have children within the marriage. They were expected to not work outside of the home, nor was it acceptable to challenge the traditional view that men held power in the home and therefore, also in society. Like the traditional approach to knowledge, these gender roles are most often defined by authority figures and based on ideology, as opposed to personal experience (postmodern) or empirical evidence (modern). The 19th amendment was the beginning in a series of historical changes over the 20th century that affected gender role expectations for both women and men in the United States.

With World War II, change came not only across the globe, but also right here in the United States. While men were overseas fighting the war, women were here in factories supporting the war effort by building needed parts and keeping our economy moving. Women's behavior at this time could be seen as an extension of the "take care of the home front" story line that prevailed before wartime. Some believe that women of this era are responsible for the next big step in changing women's roles in America because after men returned from the war, women did not want to give up their newfound empowerment through work and their ability to contribute to society. This is a compelling example of how women's behavior changed (working in factories) based on the needs of society at the time. The unintended outcome was that some women, once they had experienced the empowerment from being a fully engaged member of society, could no longer return to traditional gendered role expectations. This is not to say that all women went into the work force, or that all women gave up traditional gender roles of marriage and family, but it did signal a macro-level (large societal level) change that was here to stay. Traditional gender roles continued to change over time as our society continued to shift and with those changes came new ways that relationships were formed and maintained.

THE FEMININE MYSTIQUE: CONSUMERISM AND THE POST-WAR ERA

After the troops' return in the late 1940s, and before the cultural and political upheaval of the mid-to-late1960s, feminist thought was beginning to expand with Betty Friedan's 1963 publication of *The Feminine Mystique.* In this book, considered to have helped launch the second-wave of feminism, Friedan, founder for the National Organization of Women (NOW), discussed the many contradictory messages that American housewives experienced through the media and how market forces seemed to coalesce to promote that "more is better." For instance, she talked about how advertisers appeared to be selling the image of an ideal family life, and promoting the notion of an "ideal woman" to the masses of American women, but no matter how much women bought the new appliances, furniture, and clothing, and brought into fulfilling the role of wife and mother, there was still a profound feeling of emptiness for many. She described the feminist mystique as "the problem with no name" and with the publication and wide reading of this text, many women and men began thinking more critically about the role popular media played in determining norms for family life. The following quote by Friedan depicts the silent crisis:

> Each suburban wife struggles with it alone. As she made the beds, shopped for groceries, matched slip-cover material, ate peanut butter sandwiches with her children, chauffeured Cub Scouts and Brownies, lay beside her husband at night—she was afraid to ask even of herself the silent question–"Is this all?" (Friedan, 1963, p. 57)

Friedan, a journalist, had come to understand something she had been hearing for years from the women she had interviewed across the nation: a profound feeling of emptiness and, for many, despair. After men returned from WWII, women returned to their homes. In the ensuing decade women were encouraged to find their fulfillment in being a housewife and mother, exclusively. Pursuing higher education was frowned upon, as the "ideal woman" was portrayed as the good wife of a good man with at least four children in a stylish home in the suburbs. At this time, many women lived lives that looked like they had everything they wanted but were still desperately unhappy and unfulfilled. During the 1950s and into early 1960, masses of women were conforming to society's *gender role expectations*: get married young, to a successful businessman, have and raise children with every new gadget marketed to you—and you will be happy—by conforming to society's *gender norms.* Another way to think about the "feminine mystique" was that there was some mystery around the fact that when women conformed to what society told them would make them happy, many were not. And no one could put their finger on exactly why. This silent suffering found a voice in Betty Friedan's writing. A new movement was afoot in the lives of women in the United States.

Women's Liberation Movement

By the 1960s major movements in social justice were bringing about change in many arenas of social life in the United States. Civil rights movements to end segregation based on race and protests to end the war in Vietnam set the stage for the women's liberation movement of the 1970s and with it, the fight for the rights of women to have power over reproductive rights, equal opportunity in the work force, and equal pay. Traditional stereotypical gender roles were challenged and a movement began that identified society itself to be at fault for the inequities in gender roles and rights. New awareness of the socialization process was bringing about demands for changes in the law as it pertained to equal rights for all U.S. citizens, and women were leading the charge. Women, and other disenfranchised groups, took to social action, in the form of protests, lobbying, and political action, to bring about changes that were made and maintained at the societal level. Equal access to reproductive rights, employment, and education, all once viewed as an individual issue, shifted to being viewed as the result of an imbalance of power between the sexes (both at the individual level and at the societal level) and played out politically on a large scale in our society.

By the 1970s the United States enacted significant legislation that forever shifted the balance of power between men and women and with it the role of women in society. Three major pieces of legislation were: (1) the Equal Employment Opportunity Act of 1972, (2) the Equal Opportunity in Science and Engineering Act of 1980 (targeting underrepresented groups in medicine, science, and engineering), and (3) in 1986, the Advisory Committee on Women's Health Issues was established by the National Institute of Health. A women's movement, which sourced new legislation, also helped to bring about changes in gender roles in the United States, and abroad. What did dating and mating, and the development of intimate relationships look like in the 1960s–1970s? Women were burning their bras in a statement of "liberation." Liberation from what? Consider that the bra may have represented a kind of conformity to what was expected for women at that time—and that burning it was a way of saying "This is my body . . ."—a way of claiming themselves and control over their own bodies—to begin to change stereotypical, gender role expectations.

Changing Gender Roles for Men in the 20th and 21st Centuries

Early in the 21st century, it was evident that with the changing role of women in the United States, men experienced changes in role expectations too. Greater equality for women in work and career aspirations meant men's dominance in the labor force decreased from 70% in 1945 to less than 50% in 2010, according to *Newsweek* magazine (Romano, A. & Dokoupil, T., 2010). While the numbers of men and women in the work force are about even today, the wages earned are not. Still in U.S. society, women earn 81 cents for every dollar a man earns (among men and women who worked full time) (U.S. Department of Labor, 2011). Changes in role expectations for men were outlined in Newsweek's "Man Up: The traditional male is an endangered species. It's time to rethink masculinity" (Romano & Dokoupil, 2010). The article highlights that men also have been socialized to believe that they, too, must fulfill societal expectations for how a man should behave, and that these gender role expectations have been noticeably changing over the last 50 years. Today, young men thinking about their future professions must consider the fact that the jobs that are in demand are those in the traditional helping fields (e.g., nursing, care-providing). A modern film depicting this challenge to traditional roles is seen in the movie *Meet the Parents* with actor, Ben Stiller. In the film Ben's character, who is engaged, travels with his fiancée to meet her parents. His fiancée's father is a retired CIA agent and Ben's character is a nurse. Taunts and challenges to his masculinity come from the father and his doctor friends—demonstrating stereotypical traditional male behavior such as being tough and playing rough sports. Men's roles are changing, but as you can see from the chart depicting male role models, it has taken some time (Kimmel, 1996). Just as with the changing roles of women, men's roles have shifted and changed as society has changed. Early in our country's history, men were viewed as good-hearted patriarchs, who worked to bring about good for everyone; women and children were expected to be grateful. The late 1800s and early 1900s brought industrialization, and men working outside of the home in factories to provide for their families, while women worked within the home. The 20th century saw incredible change in gender role expectations and behavior for women and, with it, considerable change in role models for men.

Men's role models in the United States have shifted and changed as society has shifted and changed over time—and ensuing gender role expectations have changed as well, thereby affecting men's behavior. Typical behavior for a male in 1890 to 1910, *The Blue Collar Hero* era, meant that men worked hard outside of the home in the factories of that day to bring home income to the wife and children who lived and worked inside the home. Today, according to the *Newsweek* article, the major role for men in U.S. popular culture is *The New Macho* and the role model is Brad Pitt (Romano, 2010). In today's society where both men and women have careers and families they are committed to, Brad Pitt epitomizes these new male gender role expectations for heterosexual couple relationships. Current marketing practices focus on the new male role model to sell their products.

Male Role Models in U.S. Society over Time
Pre-1776: The Genteel Patriarch—*George Washington*
1890–1910: The Blue Collar Hero
1920–1945: The Muscle Man
1945–1960: The Company Man
1960–1980: The Playboy
1980s: The Cutthroat Capitalist
1990s: The New Age Man
2000s—Present Day: The New Bacho—*Brad Pitt*

We have talked a lot in this chapter about the changing roles for women and how this has led to the changing roles for men as well. Stereotypical roles portrayed in movies have been challenged for the impact upon developing girls and we are now beginning to see some changes in cinema representation of the roles of girls (e.g., *Brave*). Recently, these same stereotypical images are being questioned by both women and men. Women and men seek to empower their daughters and to prepare their sons for their role in a new society where men and women work collaboratively. In more and more ways, we are being led by women in places of authority and power to help bring about change in society.

Changing Gender Roles and Marriage Equality in the U.S.

Recently in the United States (June, 2013), history was made when the Supreme Court upheld a lower court ruling that determined that the denial of federal benefits to same sex couples under the Defense of Marriage Act (DOMA) was unconstitutional. Enacted during the presidency of Bill Clinton (1993–2001) and signed into law in 1996, DOMA defined marriage as between one man and one woman, thereby creating unconstitutional discrimination by prohibiting same-sex couples from receiving the same benefits that heterosexual couples receive through marriage (visit http://www.hrc.org/resources/entry/an-overview-of-federal-rights-and-protections-granted-to-married-couples to learn more about legal benefits of marriage). These benefits number in the range of more than 1,000 legal benefits (e.g., social security, tax, family and medical leave). Years after his presidency ended, former president, Bill Clinton, applauded the ruling as he stated in the following:

> By overturning the Defense of Marriage Act, the Court recognized that discrimination towards any group holds us all back in our efforts to form a more perfect union. We are also encouraged that marriage equality may soon return to California. We applaud the hard work of the advocates who have fought so relentlessly for this day (Bill Clinton, 2013)

Early in 2013, historical change occurred at the state level as well, when Minnesota joined eleven other states to become the 12th state in the Union to legalize same-sex marriage paving the way for the Supreme Court decision. This legislative action signifies a major shift in gender socialization—what is considered acceptable relationship behavior—and is backed by the law of the land in several states in the Union, with more joining all the time. Nearly a century after women received the right to vote in 1920, all people in Minnesota, regardless of their gender and sexual orientation, have the right to marry the person they love and receive access to the same benefits that married heterosexual couples have received without challenge as long as marriage has been legal in the United States. This is a monumental shift in the movement for equal rights in the United States, and with it comes changes in gender socialization in our society, and new ways of thinking about gender roles in relationships. We have much to learn about what it means to be a "man" or a "woman" in our heterosexual and same-sex romantic relationships, as well as relationships of all kinds, with all people, regardless of where we may land on the sexuality and gender continuum.

Dissolving Gender Roles

As the power imbalance between men and women continues to shift, though we are not yet totally egalitarian, the goals of work and pay equality were embraced and supported when President Barack Obama signed into law the Lilly Ledbetter Fair Pay Act of 2009 (visit http://en.wikipedia.org/wiki/Lilly_Ledbetter_Fair_Pay_Act_of_2009).

With the changing demographics of our workforce, where more and more women with children are working outside the home (National Center for Policy Analysis, 2013), and pregnant women work longer during pregnancy while returning to work earlier than in the past (58% return within 3 months) (Benokraitis, 2012), both men and women in society in the early 21st century must rethink gender roles. Individuals, couples, and families, all are affected by changing gender roles in the United States. What does it mean to be a man or a woman, a female or a male in today's society? Are these terms even applicable any longer? *Newsweek* implored us to rethink "masculinity" (2010)—what if we also rethink gender role expectations broadly? What is the purpose of gender role expectations? How shall we now think about what it means to be a developing human being in today's society? Can we now say that we have had a women's liberation movement, an emerging men's liberation movement, and that something new—a gender role liberation movement is afoot in society today? To consider for yourself how this may be meaningful to you, let's discuss how gender roles and gender role expectations are created. Let's turn now to learning more about how our perceptions of how we should behave, and what we expect from others are formed in our families, cultures, and religious institutions.

Perceptions of Gender and Gender Role Expectations

Where do our own perceptions about gender come from? As it was described above, the sociopolitical processes that took place in the last century changed what contemporary U.S. society expects from men and women (*gender norms*), and how society generalizes its understanding of men and women (*gender stereotypes*). It is easy to see how both gender norms and gender stereotypes impact our relationship formation with intimate partners. But socialization does not only occur at the level of society at large, it happens every day in a myriad of unexamined ways, such as in our families and our cultural and religious affiliations. To have a better understanding of gender and gender socialization, it is important to explore how we develop our own personal perceptions about gender. How are we socialized into our gender roles? What does it mean to be male or female? To answer these questions one needs to reflect on his or her own gender socialization, which originates primarily within the family. The impact of peer groups, schools, and media is also important.

Numbers of Women in the Work Force have Dramatically Shifted Over Time
• In 1950, 34% of adult women were in the labor force
• In 2000, 60% of adult women were in the labor force
• The number of working women is projected to reach 92 million by 2050

Source: Toossi, M. (2002). A century of change: The U.S. labor force, 1950–2050. Monthly Labor Review, 125, 15–28.

FAMILY. It is where we learn about love. It is where we learn about relationships. Our first experiences of attachment usually occur with our parents, primarily with our mothers. And, in these early years we are forming mental models of how to be in relationships with others. The process of gender socialization within a family can take many forms. It is what children observe, hear, and see practiced in their homes. In a traditional family, a father and a mother exemplify the very first impression of what roles women and men take in the society in which they live. Although traditional gender role ideology is on decline, it remains more common in certain cultures in U.S. society (e.g., certain religious groups, Hispanic culture).

In recent years in U.S. society, more children have been raised by two same-sex parents than at any time before in our society (Lofquist, Lugailia, O'Connell, & Feliz, 2012). This is an example of changing gender roles and gender role expectations at the family level. Because of the emergence of families who consist of same-sex parents, or even single parent families groups who hold traditional ways of thinking about the composition of families have challenged the legitimacy of alternative family configurations. In fact, the health and well-being of children in same-sex families has been questioned. However, current research indicates that children raised by same sex parents do as well as children who are raised by traditional opposite sex parents (Crowl, Ahn, & Baker, 2008).

Some questions related to gender role socialization in families are: Who is responsible for what kind of chores? Who makes financial decisions in the family? Who stays home and who works outside? Everyday messages that parents and other family members say to a child can have a powerful lifelong impact. How many girls have heard during their childhood "good girls do what they are told" or "girls do not burp/fart out loud"? "Girls should make the meals, do the dishes, clean the house" are just a few of the messages many female (and male) children heard throughout their critical developmental years.

How many boys heard during their childhood "boys do not cry" or "boys do not play with dolls" or "boys do not wear . . ." pink, a dress, etc.? Boys should play sports, be aggressive, and grow up to be a doctor, lawyer, or president. That boys and men should keep all emotions inside? Or that the expression of emotions and creativity should not be an acceptable part of being a man and most definitely, should not be shown to the world? What male stereotypes do these comments perpetuate?

According to Rotheman (1987), gender socialization begins in pregnancy, during *in utero* development, and starts as early as 20 weeks. It is the period when the inner ear of the fetus is fully developed. Rotheman (1987) refers to this as pre-birth gender talk. When talking to their male babies, mothers changed the tone of their voice to a sharper and stronger one. They also described male babies as moving vigorously, being very active, and their female babies as quiet (Rotheman, 1987). The author suggests the pre-birth gender talk predetermines a child's personality and as it continues after birth it solidifies gender differences.

So, you might be asking, how much of behavior is socially constructed (belongs to gender) and how much is biologically defined (an attribute of sex)? Lise Eliot (2011) summarizes the current findings on physiological differences between males and females that later in life develop into a greater gender gap.

- Girls demonstrate toileting skills at earlier ages than boys (Schum et al., 2002)
- Baby boys are modestly more physically active than girls (Campbell & Eaton, 1999)
- Toddler girls talk one month earlier, on average, than boys (Fenson et al., 1994)
- Boys appear more spatially aware (Quinn & Liben, 2008)

These differences might impact boys' preferences for active toys and girls' preferences for verbal-relational toys. However, it does not mean that boys will never need verbal skills to express their emotions and be respectful in relationships, and that girls will never need skills for physical activities and spatial orientation. The differences described above can be attributed to one's biological sex. Gender socialization starts when society further encourages these differences in children and adolescence by stressing the importance of one type of activity over the other.

It is important to also note that during the socialization process there tend to be rewards and punishments for acceptable and unacceptable behavior. Think about a time in your childhood when you were rewarded with praise by your parents for acceptable "gendered" behavior. What happened? Did your parents say "You look just like a young lady should" or "You are such a good young man"? Or perhaps for you, it was more notable when you behaved in a way that was considered against the norm or expected behavior. What happened? Were you a girl who wore pants to church when the expectation was to wear dresses? What did your parents or religious leaders say to you? What were you expected to do?

MEDIA SOCIALIZATION, GENDER, AND THE FAMILY. Gender socialization in the family setting is not restricted to what parents and others in the family do, but is influenced by the presence of mass media within the family setting as well. With the penetration of mass culture into everyday life through the media, it is getting harder for parents to keep track of and filter the messages that overflow into their children's and families' lives. Contemporary businesses see young children as current and future consumers and tend to target them with their products at earlier and earlier ages (Bakir, Blodgett, & Rose, 2008; Calvert, 2008).

Commercials that target children reinforce those few physiological differences between boys and girls and reinforce them as *gender norms*. Messages in commercials for children's toys are strongly stereotypical. Boys' toys teach about: "warrior-like" roles, focus on respect for their physical ability, foster mental stimulation, and teach coordination and problem solving. Adventure and physical activity outside the home, role-play of high paying white-collar occupations (e.g., "Electronic Rescue Center," "Police Communication System," and "Emergency Action Set") toys encourage young boys to fulfill traditional gender role expectations.

Girls' toys, in contrast, are designed specifically to discourage participation in highly physical activities, encourage caution, and stress physical beauty and appearance. They encourage girls to sit and play quietly, and they stress roles inside the home: cooking, cleaning, and taking care of the young. Furthermore, children's toys have undergone a startling process of sexualization over time. Contemporary toys, such as My Little Pony and Tinker-Bell, once presented as child-like, are now scantily dressed and wearing high-heels!

A good example of the fact that gender and attributes related to it are socially constructed is the fact that the color pink has been inconsistently associated with both girls and boys (Paoletti, 2012) over time. For example, the *Ladies' Home Journal* in 1890 stated, "Pure white is used for all babies. Blue is for girls and pink is for boys, when a color is wished." It was in the 1950s when the societal norm was set to its current pattern (Paoletti, 2012). For decades in Western society, we have seen (and still see today) pink as a color associated with girls, especially in young children's toys and clothing (Paoletti, 2012).

In childhood and adolescence the impact of social institutions becomes more influential on what a young person thinks about gender. Broadly speaking, Hollywood films, and specifically, the plethora of Disney films (and associated toys, books, and clothing) have helped to shape every Western generation of young children since the 1950s, when the invention of the television meant that large level socialization about gender and gender role expectations would make its way into the homes of Americans without any questioning. The expected behavior of women was depicted for all to see on the big screen. Disney films, while being enjoyable for millions of young children, carry with them strong stereotypical messages about the roles of men and women that translate to expectations for boys and girls. Take for example, in many Disney films, such as Snow White, we can see how the female waits in expectation for her "prince charming" to rescue her. Ask yourself now; if you have not before, how this kind of socialization has informed the way you think about relationships and, therefore, your expectations for a partner?

A stereotypical way of thinking about the roles of men and women in relationships is to believe that women are weak and in need of being rescued by a stronger and (it is assumed) smarter, male. At the very least, these kinds of messages suggest that women are not whole and complete individuals alone and believe that being in a relationship with a man will make them so (Holz Ivory, Gibson, & Ivory, 2009). Rather, gendered messages permeate movies (and help to sell them) that there is always trouble in relationship formation. In most romantic films, at least part of the trouble is due to women who refuse to conform to traditional ways of thinking and behaving in relationships. According to stereotypical gendered expectations, relationship maintenance is the woman's responsibility (Metts, 2006). In addition to films, toys, and books, daily exposure to commercials on our television sets are filled with gender stereotypes that have influenced purchasing behavior for decades and, through continuous exposure have influenced what children and developing adolescents believe about how they should behave in the development of their relationships.

GENDER AND CULTURE

Ethnic minority children in the United States must learn to function within a pervasive, individualistic U.S. culture, while maintaining one's family ethnic culture with its interdependence and group focus (Coatsworth, Maldonado-Molina, Pantin, & Szapocznik, 2005; Harrison et al., 1990). Members of ethnic minorities growing up in the United States face challenges that the majority culture do not— learning to live within and be successful in one's education, career, societal, and relationship goals in the dominant culture, while still honoring one's ethnic and familial collectivist values at home.

The four major ethnic minority groups in the United States are African-American, American Indian/Alaskan Native, Asian Pacific Americans, and Hispanic Americans (U.S. Census Bureau, 2011). While each of these ethnic groups contains unique expressions of their culture, what they have in common is a worldview orientation that focuses upon family structures designed to provide support for all members, often through extended family, with highly interdependent roles. For many ethnic groups in the United States, religion, ethnicity, and culture are interwoven and it is difficult to provide a distinct definition of one without the other. For example, the purpose of "religiosity" (Harrison et al., 1990, p. 354) is described as follows:

> To refer to images, actions, and symbols that define the extent and character of the world for the people and provide the cosmic framework for which their lives find meaning, purpose, and fulfillment.

Ethnic origin and accompanying cultural experiences in families of origin, communities, and religious affiliations, all impact how gender and gender role expectations are perceived. While many ethnic and cultural groups are considered to be traditional in gender role expectations, Native American culture holds an exception in its acceptance of and even celebration of tribal members who identify as two-spirited. Contrary to traditional dichotomous gender roles forcing individuals to fall into one or another classification (male or female), within indigenous Native American culture being two-spirited is not only accepted, it is respected—as two-spirited members are said to have special powers to interact with the spiritual world (visit http://www.guardian.co.uk/music/2010/oct/11/two-spirit-people-north-america for more about "two-spirit" people). Here is an excerpt from the website by author, Walter L. Williams:

> Rather than emphasizing the homosexuality of these persons, however, many Native Americans focused on their spiritual gifts. .. androgynous or transgender persons are seen as doubly blessed, having both the spirit of a man and the spirit of a woman.

As with ethnicity, culture, and religion, sexuality in many indigenous cultures is viewed from multiple perspectives, and is not dichotomous or easily parceled out for examination. Rather, lived experience is messy, complex, and interrelated.

In addition to ethnic and religious influences on one's perception of gender and gender role expectations, additional influences can be seen in urban versus rural cultural differences; the influence of music culture on perceptions of gender and gender expectations; and in numerous other contexts that inform how men and women are expected to behave in society. What are some ways you can now see where you experienced gender role socialization due to race, ethnic, cultural, or geographic contexts? How might this socialization have affected (or currently affect) your dating and mating experiences as you seek to develop intimate relationships with others?

GENDER AND RELIGION

More than 80% of people in the world identify with a religious group (for more information, visit http://www.pewforum.org/global-religious-landscape-exec.aspx to learn more about the world's religions).

Like being raised in our families and our ethnic communities, religion has a pervasive impact upon our lives—what we think, believe, and how we behave. It is important to consider how religious socialization may also impact one's gender socialization. What are the pervasive messages you learned in your religious community about what it means to be a man or a woman and how to behave? The most common ways that gender is socialized in mainstream religions is typically related to taboos and expectations around sexuality. For instance, many women and girls in Christian congregations are encouraged to dress modestly in order to "not cause their brother to stumble" (Romans 14:21).

Christianity is not the only religion with specific expectations for men and women in relationships. Orthodox Judaism prohibits husbands from having sex with their wives during menstruation. Some Islamic practices encourage women to wear the *hijab*, a special head covering to practice modesty. As stated above, many of the exhortations and taboos for gender roles in religious settings are specifically related to sexual behaviors or family life, and often focus on heterosexual relationships.

While gender socialization in religious groups is frequently focused on taboos and restrictions on sexual behavior, admonitions in some religious texts helped to bring about change that led to greater respect for women in society. Writings in the Koran, the holy book of Islam, greatly improved conditions for women at the time it was written. Women, who were once considered little more than the property of their fathers or husbands, were now freely granted consent to marry. The Koran also sanctified marriage as the only appropriate place for sexual activity, thereby prohibiting rape (Smith, 1991).

Most studies examining religion and gender confirm a gender difference in religiosity—women are more religious than men (Collett & Lizardo, 2009; Miller & Stark, 2002). However, in recent research (Miller & Stark, 2002) the notion that religious gender socialization was the only explanation for this difference was challenged. Miller and Stark proposed that "risk preference" regarding perceived consequences of incompliance due to a belief in an after-life, instead explained the gender difference. Another possible explanation, could be physiological (recall we addressed biological differences between male and female infants earlier in this chapter), but they did not test this hypothesis in their study. Still, while this study may have revealed another important factor for our consideration, significant historical and empirical evidence abounds for the perspective that gender role differences exist within differing religious practices and that gender socialization plays an important part.

If you are a member of a religious group, the next time that you attend worship or are with your religious community, keep an eye out for the written or spoken expectations for behavior related to gender (how a man or a woman "should" behave) and be aware of the unwritten or unspoken expectations. What families in your community are considered upstanding families? What about these families makes them outstanding according to your religion? Does it have to do with stereotypical gendered behavior? If you are single, what traits are you encouraged to look for in a potential partner? What traits are you to avoid? What are some of the things that you, as a sexed and gendered being, are supposed to do to be "marriageable" according to your religious traditions? As with the other sections addressing gender socialization, take a moment to record your thoughts about how religious socialization has impacted your expectations for your romantic partner.

Thinking about Gender on a Continuum

In this chapter, we have discussed how gender development is influenced by a number of social, familial, and religious contexts and now we will highlight the impact of these socialization processes on one's sense of self and how this affects relationship formation. We have also discussed how the terms *sex* and *gender* mean different things, with sex referring to one's biological or chromosomal sex, and gender referring to one's identification as masculine or feminine. This section of the chapter will introduce you to the idea of gender as existing along a continuum, rather than the long-held notion of gender as dichotomous, with only two options: male or female.

The gender continuum describes a way to think about one's gender and sexuality as being constructed of multilayered and complex components—not as easily described by a dichotomous orientation of male or female, as has been employed for centuries. Many structures like the U.S. census (conducted once a decade to gather demographic information about U.S. citizens) and in most demographic questionnaires, participants are asked to place themselves into discrete categories (male or female). However, we invite you to think about gender as existing on a continuum because this gives more space for the multitude of ways that people actually experience themselves as gendered and how this influences the development of relationships with others (see Appendix A).

BIOLOGICAL OR ASSIGNED SEX. *Biological sex* refers to an individual's anatomy or chromosomal sex at birth (Gender Spectrum, 2013). Historical dichotomous classification upon birth forces doctors to make determinations about *sex* for newborn infants that sets a trajectory in only one of two directions—male or female. For individuals who are born with sexual characteristics of both males and females, the term *assigned sex* frequently refers to which sex they are labeled by a medical doctor at the time of birth (Gender Spectrum, 2013). Typically, an ensuing gender reassignment surgery is conducted while the infant is a newborn (Dreger, 1997). While assigning one sex at birth for children with male and female sexual characteristics is currently the most common medical practice among pediatricians, a burgeoning movement among parents and medical professionals has begun which forgoes this classification at birth, instead waiting until pre-pubescence to learn from the individual which biological sex the child identifies with (Dreger, 2008). Individuals who have sexual characteristics of both males and females are referred to in this model as *intersex*.

GENDER IDENTITY. *Gender identity* refers to an individual's sense of self as a gendered being. The two ends of this continuum are "man" and "woman." Terms in the middle of the continuum, "genderfluid" and "genderqueer," acknowledge individuals who identify somewhere along the continuum and not squarely within one or the other extremes. Gender identity exists at the core of how people see themselves, and like the rest of gender, the meanings of those identities are culturally and socially bound. People may identify in any number of ways along the continuum. In one example, Maria is a biological female and identifies as a "woman." Since Maria's biological sex (female) and gender identity (woman) match, she would be described as *cisgendered*. Cisgendered is a term that was developed as an antonym for the term *transgendered*, where an individual identifies with a sex different than that assigned at birth. In other words, being cisgendered or cissexual, signifies continuity between assigned sex and gender identity. The meaning of her womanhood might be a combination of the social expectations her family had for her as the oldest daughter in a Roman Catholic family, the societal expectations at a Big Ten research university, and her own thinking about what sorts of characteristics she admires or abhors in other women in her own life.

One distinct form of gender identity is the *transgender* identity. People who identify as transgender are born with the biological and/or chromosomal characteristics of one sex, but identify as a different sex. Transgender people have existed throughout history. For instance, many Native American tribes in the United States of America have had terms and traditions for the "two-spirited" for hundreds of years (American Psychological Association, 2013; National Aboriginal Health Organization, 2012). Numerous cultures throughout the world recognize individuals who identify as a different sex than the one that they were assigned at birth, whether that is what they identify as the "opposite" sex (a genetically and physically male person identifies as a female) or being born with male and female genitalia (Intersex Society of North America, 2008) and not being certain for some time about gender identity. Currently, an estimated 700,000 individuals identify as transgender in the United States (Gates, 2011). (For more information on this population, be sure to review Chapter 16.)

GENDER EXPRESSION. *Gender expression* refers to the ways individuals communicate their own gender identification. Three classifications are as follows: "masculine," "androgynous," and "feminine" (Bem, 1974). The ways that individuals express their gender might vary depending on their social context. For instance, Maria, discussed above, might wear only skirts or dresses to mass,

Bem Sex Role Inventory		
	Masculine	Not Masculine
Feminine	Androgynous	Highly Feminine
Not Feminine	Highly Masculine	Undifferentiated

which would communicate femininity, but wear jeans and a hooded sweatshirt to class, which may communicate a more masculine message. People who communicate gender in an *androgynous* way may communicate aspects of both masculinity and femininity. Compared to people who communicate most frequently in the extremes of masculinity or femininity, people who communicate with androgyny demonstrate better social and emotional health on multiple measures (Guastello & Guastello, 2003).

One of the earliest measures of gender expression was the Bem's Sex Role Inventory. Developed by Sandra Bem in 1971, the inventory measures an individual's endorsement of a number of adjectives to describe self, and then links those endorsements to typically feminine, masculine, androgynous, or undifferentiated categories (Bem, 1974). Individuals considered to be feminine scored high on stereotypical feminine traits, like "kind," "yielding," and "loves children." Individuals considered masculine scored high on stereotypical masculine traits, like "strong," "authoritative," and "loves to argue." Androgynous individuals scored high on both masculine and feminine traits. The final category, undifferentiated, was a psychometric artifact, designed to see if individuals endorse items that are not typically linked to femininity or masculinity. Androgyny in both men and women is associated with greater flexibility and functioning in relationships. The key seems to be the capacity to embrace cross gender characteristics. Both masculine and feminine behaviors are functional in relationships.

SEXUAL ORIENTATION. *Sexual orientation* refers to whom one is attracted. People may be attracted to men, or masculinity, or be attracted to women, or femininity (Johns Hopkins University, 2013). People might also be attracted to mostly men, but some women, or mostly women, but some men, or attracted to any gender expression or biological sex. People who land in the middle along that continuum most often refer to themselves as bisexual, queer, or pansexual. Individuals are generally born with their sexual orientation, but like other aspects of this continuum, it may be fluid throughout the lifespan (American Psychiatric Association, 2008; Moore & Rosenthal, 2006). For more details on sexual orientation, be sure to read Chapter 16 in this textbook.

Evidence for a broadening perspective on gender, sexuality, and gender role expectations is seen in the 1980s alternative rock song "Androgynous." It depicts a range of gender socialization, sexuality, and gender identity issues and was listed as one of the 25 Greatest Albums of All Time by *Spin* magazine. Another example of contemporary music in 2013 is a song celebrating equal rights for same sex partners as depicted in "Same Love" by Macklemore & Lewis.

Contemporary music and music videos are important artifacts of history. Through musical and theatrical expression, historical shifts and changes in gender role expectations and expressions can be captured, documented, and enjoyed over time.

SEXUAL BEHAVIOR. *Sexual behavior* is different than sexual orientation. Sexual behavior refers to with whom people have sexual contact (Gartrell, Bos, & Goldberg, 2011). They may have sexual contact with men or masculine people, women or feminine people, both, or none of the above. This construct will be examined more in Chapter 16.

How do you see yourself along the gender continuum? Take some time now, and identify for yourself where you think you fall in the areas of biological/assigned sex, gender identity, gender expression, sexual orientation, and sexual behavior. In what ways do your descriptions match or not match the way you have been socialized? How does this way of thinking about sexuality and gender affect your dating and mating practices as you develop intimate relationships with others?

Gender-Norm Differences in Pathways to Intimacy

In this chapter we have acknowledged that stereotypical gender roles are changing as society is changing, and with these changes come more complex ways of thinking about what it means to be a man or a woman in society. Still, there are a few areas where research acknowledges gender-norm differences between men and women—and that is in pathways to intimacy.

Research supports notable differences between men and women in patterns of disclosure. In general, women appear to engage in more intimate/emotional disclosures (e.g. family problems, personal development), whereas men tend to engage in non-intimate/factual disclosures, such as discussing what they did at work that day. Furthermore, women's satisfaction is linked to men's knowledge of the woman's intimate life (Troy & Lewis-Smith, 2006). Generally speaking, women distinguish relationships based on levels of self-disclosure—in other words, women tend to experience a greater sense of intimacy when they are able to be with a romantic partner with whom they can feel safe to reveal themselves in self-disclosures about things and experiences that are deeply meaningful. They appreciate a partner who is a good, non-judgmental listener and with whom they can be authentic. Women tend to place high value on this type of relationship.

Men, on the other hand, are noted to emphasize the strength of a relationship when they are able to both self-disclose and share activities with someone they care about. This may mean going for a bike ride, playing a game of basketball, going for a run, or attending a sports game together. In sharing the physical experience, communication about important thoughts and feelings are much more likely to occur. Another difference is that women are seen as more likely to evaluate the value of friendships based on the level of intimacy than are men. Women report higher levels of intimacy in their friendships than men (Johnson, 2004). Said another way, it is deeply meaningful to most women to be able to experience intimacy with others, and this is highly valued. For example, women are noted to value love, faithfulness, and lifelong commitment in their romantic relationships more than men (Meier, Hull, & Ortyl, 2009).

In Western cultures higher relationship satisfaction is associated with major decisions being made jointly, household tasks divided by interests, and both partners being satisfied with the division of housework chores. For the majority of contemporary young adults in committed, romantic intimate relationships, it is imperative that both partners' roles are perceived as egalitarian and of high-value (Taylor & Segrin, 2010; Pettifor, Macphail, Anderson, & Maman, 2012). For example, Sara is a financial analyst and Joey is a registered nurse. In their relationship it is Sara who handles the family budget and Joey makes sure the laundry is done. In this couple's relationship, they each contribute to the chores getting done but they also choose the chores they like and feel best qualified to do.

College life as a young/emerging adult is your time to explore who you are and what you want out of your life educationally, in your future careers and professions, and in all of your intimate relationships, from family, to friends, to romantic partners. This is your time to come to know many things about yourself and your preferences in life—understanding where you find yourself today on the gender/sexuality continuum will empower you in your life now and into the future.

Making it Real: Gender, Dating Scripts, and You

Our goals for this chapter were to help clarify what gender is, how it is constructed, and how it influences you. Now that you have a sense of the range of socialization processes occurring at varying levels of society (historical changes over time, the influence of race, ethnicity, culture, religion, and mass media, including being raised in your family) you may be quite a bit clearer about the initial questions you had about gender. Let's now talk about the development of your intimate relationships and what you can do about building your relationships on purpose. We want to introduce to you an important concept that will be helpful in the development of your relationships: *dating scripts*. We encourage you to think critically about this process because understanding how dating scripts are constructed and influence you will help you to form better relationships.

Dating Scripts

Dating scripts are made up of one's typically unexamined perceptions of his/her gender roles and the ensuing expectations held for the self and others in the development of relationships. Understanding what dating scripts are, how they are constructed, and to be able to recognize the impact of one's gender beliefs on relationship formation, will greatly empower you in the development of your relationships.

To begin our talk about dating scripts, let's recall Matt and Courtney's upbringings as they were described at the beginning of this chapter. If you would like to, go back and re-read their story and pick out the key differences in their gender socialization. Now, imagine that they are both students at (name your university here) and are getting ready for their first date.

After their coincidental meeting at freshman orientation, Courtney and Matt went their separate ways. What they did not know at the time, but learned on the first day of their first class, is that they were in the same major, Family Social Science. As different as they seemed to one another on the first day of orientation, they soon discovered that they had things in common: they both wanted to work with kids and families. Being in the same major meant that Courtney and Matt had several classes together and Matt could not have been happier. Courtney, on the other hand, was not as interested as Matt was but she was learning about him as they took classes together, and she liked what she was hearing. Finally, Matt's dream of dating Courtney became a reality; one day after class he simply said "Want to get something to eat tonight?" She quickly responded, "Yep, I'd like that!" Addresses and phone numbers were exchanged. The following timeline gives you a sense for how this "date" went for these first-time daters:

7:00PM: Matt arrives at Courtney's apartment. He buzzes to get let in, and she tells him that she's almost ready and buzzes him up.

7:05PM: Matt gets to Courtney's apartment door and she greets him with a towel around her hair, but otherwise ready to go. "It'll be just a second, make yourself at home" she shouts to him as she runs back to the bathroom. Having been on many other dates that started the same way, Matt settled in for at least 20 minutes of occupying his own time.

7:47PM: Matt finishes reading "How to Keep your Man Coming Back for More" for the third time in the *Cosmopolitan* on Courtney's coffee table. Exasperated, Courtney curses the humidity and puts her hair into a loose up-do. "It's awful, but it will have to do" she thinks to herself. Courtney comes out of the bathroom, finally ready to go, after changing her outfit three times.

8:30PM: At the restaurant prior to dinner, even though Courtney would love a Coke with her meal, she orders a Diet Coke. Matt asks if she would want an appetizer, but she declines. Courtney's stomach grumbles. She hopes Matt didn't hear it.

9:00PM: Food arrives: Steak and potatoes for Matt; Salad for Courtney. Matt is not actually that hungry, but he has heard rumors that Courtney thinks he's a wimp because of his skinny jeans. "I'll prove her wrong" he thinks, right before ordering a porterhouse that he cannot afford.

10:15PM: At the end of the date there is brief haggling over the bill. Ultimately, Matt pays for everything. Matt curses the porterhouse again.

10:30PM: Matt drives Courtney home. He leans in to kiss her, but she turns her head and he lands only a chaste kiss on the cheek (nothing more until at least the third date). Courtney heads up to her apartment—still hungry.

10:45PM: Matt drives away confused. "Did she even like me?" he thinks to himself. Convinced he blew the date and has no chance with Courtney because she would not kiss him, he heads off to find his buds and party, still a little nauseous from stuffing himself on the porterhouse.

11:00PM: After polishing off a peanut butter sandwich and chips, Courtney heads to bed.

In Courtney and Matt's first date, you saw a number of dating scripts that apply to gender. For instance, Matt followed the dating script that says that the male must initiate and ask for the date, is the one to drive over and pick up his date, wait for his date (regardless of what time was originally agreed upon), and pay for everything. Courtney followed the dating script that says that the female must play "hard-to-get", not appear too interested, can expect to be "waited on" in every regard, not display too large of an appetite (eating a salad vs. a steak), and fully expect that although she offers to pay, her male date will pick up the tab. Both of these scripts are gendered, which means that they have different expectations for Courtney as a woman, and Matt as a man. Another important thing to note is that dating scripts are most evident during the "in-between" parts of a relationship: the pick-ups and drop-offs, the ordering of meals, and the paying for events. What other gender role expectations/norms do you see in this scenario? Do you recognize some of your dates in this scenario?

Your dating scripts are impacted by your own perceptions of gender and gender roles. For instance, two feminine women might have very different expectations for their own behaviors and their partner's behaviors dependent on their own views on femininity. Perhaps one woman embraces the sexual components of her femininity and, with that, expects a male potential dating partner to hit on her. She can then make whatever decision she wants to from there, but as sexuality is a central part of her identity as a feminine woman, some flirtation is an expected part of the dating interplay. In contrast, another woman might embrace a more traditional perspective of her femininity. For that woman, purity and chastity might be highly valued and being flirtatious on a date might be completely taboo.

In general, dating scripts serve as an early filter through which potential dating partners must pass, as people look for others to fulfill their expectations for gender roles. Occasionally people are attracted to others with completely opposite expectations as far as gender in dating goes; however, over the long haul, these relationships rarely last. While the saying "opposites attract" is true (at least initially), the real idiom to remember here is that "birds of feather flock together" (in the long run). People are more likely to have long lasting relationships with others who are more like them.

Your Turn

Now that we have taken a look at macro-level (large societal influences), meso-level (family, religion, culture, and how these work together), and micro-level (this is you in your everyday life) socialization processes that influence our views of gender and the formation of our relationships, let's move to the applied level. In other words, "So what?" you may be thinking, "That is all great to know but what does that have to do with me?" That is exactly where we want this chapter to conclude—with you and what is important to you. Close this chapter by asking yourself the following questions and record your thoughts and feelings:

- What are my expectations for those I date?
- Are those expectations dichotomously "gendered"? In other words, do I expect my dates to behave in certain ways because of their sex (male or female)?
- What expectations do I hold for myself? Do I believe that I must behave in certain, expected ways in my dating and relationship life?
- Have I thought about my own gender socialization? Do I see myself fitting into one of two boxes (male or female) or do I see myself somewhere on a continuum?
- How was I socialized to think about gender roles in my family? My religion? My culture?
- How am I affected by mass media's messages about dating and gender role expectations?
- What are some actions I can purposefully take in my intimate relationships?

Key Learning Points

Now that you've had a chance to ask and answer the questions about gender, "What is it? And what has gender got to do with me?" for yourself, let's summarize what we've learned together and identify some of what we do not yet know about gender socialization.

- Gender is socially constructed at macro, exo, meso, and micro levels
- Gender is influenced by family, race, ethnicity, culture, religion, geographic location, and mass media, among other societal influences
- Gender socialization shifts and changes over historical time
- Gender and sexuality are better understood as existing on a continuum
- Dating scripts are constructed from one's typically unexamined perceptions of his/her gender roles and the ensuing expectations held for the self and others in the development of relationships
- Self-examination of one's socialization helps to bring dating scripts and other forms of socialization to light, giving you more personal power to act purposefully in the development of your intimate relationships

Things We Still Don't Know

While we have covered a great deal of information in this chapter on what gender is, how it is constructed, and how it influences the formation of your intimate relationships, there is still much we do not yet know. As a society we are always evolving and changing, so too, is the socialization process;

it stands to reason then, that as gender roles have changed over the years, they are changing even as we speak. Some things we do not know much about are:

- gender roles in same sex relationships
- gender roles in unconventional religious groups, such as neo-pagans
- the role of peers on changing gender roles
- traditional gender roles vis-a-vis more and more couples being dual-career couples
- what will the new gender role socialization look like?
- how do we do gender socialization on purpose?
- how much does the role of gender influence healthy, strongs relationships?

REFERENCES

American Psychiatric Association (2008). *Sexual orientation, homosexuality and bisexuality*. Retrieved from: http://www.apa.org/helpcenter/sexual-orientation.aspx

American Psychological Association (2012). *Answers to your questions about transgender people, gender identity, and gender expression*. Retrieved from http://www.apa.org/topics/sexuality/transgender.pdf

Bakir, A., Blodgett, J. G., & Rose, G. M. (2008). Children's responses to gender-role stereotyped advertisements. *Journal Of Advertising Research, 48*(2), 255–266. doi:10.2501/S002184990808029X

Bem, S. L. (1974). The measurement of psychological androgyny. *Journal of Consulting and Clinical Psychology, 42,* 155–162. doi:10.1037/h0036215

Benokraitis, N. (2012). *Marriages & families: Changes, choices, and constraints*. Boston, MA: Pearson Education.

Bronfenbrenner, U. (1994). Ecological models of human development. In T. Husen & T.N. Postlethwaite (Eds.), *International Encyclopedia of Education,* (2nd ed., vol. 3, pp. 1643–1647). Oxford, England: Pergamon Press.

Bryjak, G. J. &. Soroka, M. P. (1997). *Sociology: Cultural diversity in a changing world*. Boston, MA: Allyn & Bacon.

Calvert, S. L. (2008). Children as consumers: Advertising and marketing. *Future of Children, 18*(1), 205–234. doi:10.1353/foc.0.0001

Campbell, D. W., & Eaton. W. O. (1999). Sex differences in the activity level of infants. *Infant and Child Development, 8*(1), 1–17. doi:10.1002/(SICI)1522-7219(199903)8:1<1::AID-ICD186>3.0.CO;2-O

Coatsworth, J., Maldonado-Molina, M., Pantin, H., & Szapocznik, J. (2005). A person-centered and ecological investigation of acculturation strategies in Hispanic immigrant youth. *Journal of Community Psychology, 33*(2), 157–174. doi:10.1002/jcop.20046

Collett, J. L., & Lizardo, O. (2009). A power-control theory of gender and religiosity. *Journal for the Scientific Study of Religion, 48*(2), 213–231. doi:10.1111/j.1468-5906.2009.01441.x

Crowl, A., Ahn, S., & Baker, J. (2008). A meta-analysis of developmental outcomes for children of same-sex and heterosexual parents. *Journal of GLBT Family Studies, 4*(3), 385–407. doi:10.1080/15504280802177615

Dreger, A. (1997). Ethical problems in intersex treatment. *Medical Humanities Report, 19*(1), 1–9. Retrieved from http://www.bioethics.msu.edu/index.php?option=com_content&view=article&id=79&Itemid=122

Dreger, A. (2008). *Shifting the paradigm of intersex treatment*. Retrieved from http://www.isna.org/compare

Eliot, L. (2013). Single-sex education and the brain. *Sex Roles, 69,* 363–381. doi:10.1007/s11199-011-0037-y

Fenson, L., Dale, R., Reznick, J. S., Bates, E. E., Thai, D., & Pethick, S. (1994). Variability in early communicative development. *Monographs of the Society for Research in Child Development, 59*(5), 1–185. doi:10.2307/1166093

Friedan, B. (1963). *The feminine mystique*. New York: W.W. Norton and Company.

Gates, G. (2011). *How many people are gay, lesbian, bisexual and transgender?* Retrieved from http://williamsinstitute.law.ucla.edu/research/census-lgbt-demographics-studies/how-many-people-are-lesbian-gay-bisexual-and-transgender/

Gartrell, N., Bos, H., & Goldberg, N. (2011). Adolescents of the U.S. National Longitudinal Lesbian Family Study: Sexual orientation, sexual behavior, and sexual risk exposure. *Archives of Sexual Behavior, 40*(6), 1199–1209. doi:10.1007/s10508-010-9692-2

Gender Spectrum. (2013). *Understanding gender*. Retrieved from https://www.genderspectrum.org/understanding-gender

Gottman, J. M., & Silver, N. (2013). *What makes love last? How to build trust and avoid betrayal*. New York, NY: Simon & Schuster.

Guastello, D. D., & Guastello, S. J. (2003). Androgyny, gender role behavior, and emotional intelligence among college students and their parents. *Sex Roles, 49*(11/12), 663–673. doi:10.1023/B:SERS.0000003136.67714.04

Harrison, A. O., Wilson, M. N., Pine, C. J., Chan, S. Q., & Buriel, R. (1990). Family ecologies of ethnic minority children. *Child Development, 6*(2), 347–362. doi:10.2307/1131097

Holz Ivory, A., Gibson, R., & Ivory, J. D. (2009). Gendered relationships on television: Portrayals of same-sex and heterosexual couples. *Mass Communication & Society, 12*(2), 170–192. doi:10.1080/15205430802169607

Intersex Society of North America (2008). *Does ISNA think children with intersex should be raised without a gender, or in a third gender?* Retrieved from http://www.isna.org/faq/third-gender

Johns Hopkins University. (2013). *LGBT glossary.* Retrieved from http://web.jhu.edu/LGBTQ/glossary.html

Johnson, H. (2004). Gender, grade, and relationship differences in emotional closeness within adolescent friendships. *Adolescence, 39*(154), 243–245. Retrieved from http://web.ebscohost.com/abstract?direct=true&profil e=ehost&scope=site&authtype=crawler&jrnl=00018449&AN=14899019&h=Y535GVJzhf%2bRJ13fSbClaSD9 HgrfOLP0CrWIvmgS6OYtLQNeHSV00wj66prISxbmn51f8Rkl8fgmF99KKzeQZw%3d%3d&crl=f

Kimmel, M. (1996). *Manhood in America: A cultural history.* New York: Free Press.

Lofquist D., Lugailia, T., O'Connell, M., & Feliz, S. (2012). *Households and families.* Washington, DC: U.S. Bureaus of Census.

Meier, A., Hull, K. E., & Ortyl, T. A. (2009). Young adult relationship values at the intersection of gender and sexuality. *Journal of Marriage and Family, 71*(3), 510–525. doi:10.1111/j.1741-3737.2009.00616.x

Metts, S. (2006). Gendered communication in dating relationships. In B. J. Dow & J. T. Wood, Eds., *The SAGE handbook of gender and communication.* Thousand Oaks, CA: Sage Publications.

Miller, A. S., & Stark, R. (2002). Gender and religiousness: Can socialization explanations be saved? *American Journal of Sociology, 107*(6), 1399–1423. doi:10.1086/342557

Moore, S., & Rosenthal, D. (2006). Sexuality in adolescence: Current trends (2nd Ed). London, UK: Routledge.

National Aboriginal Health Organization (2012). *Suicide prevention and two-spirited people.* Retrieved from http://www.naho.ca/documents/fnc/english/2012_04_%20Guidebook_Suicide_Prevention.pdf

National Center for Policy Analysis (2013). *Women in the workforce.* Retrieved from: http://www.ncpa.org/sub/ dpd/index.php?Article_ID=3341

Paoletti, J. (2012). *Pink and blue: Telling the boys from the girls in America.* Bloomington, IN: Indiana University Press.

Pettifor, A., Macphail, C., Anderson, A., & Maman, S. (2012). "If I buy the Kellogg's then he should buy the milk": Young women's perspectives on relationship dynamics, gender power and HIV risk in Johannesburg, South Africa. *Culture, Health & Sexuality, 14*(5), 477–490. doi:10.1080/13691058.2012.667575

Quinn, P. C., & Liben, L. S. (2008). A sex difference in mental rotation in young infants. *Psychological Science, 19*(11), 1067–1070. doi:10.1111/j.1467-9280.2008.02201.x

Romano, A. (2010, September 20). Why we need to reimagine masculinity. *Newsweek.* Retrieved from http:// www.newsweek.com/why-we-need-reimagine-masculinity-71993

Rotheman, B. (1987). *The tentative pregnancy: Prenatal diagnosis and the future of motherhood.* New York: Penguin.

Schum, T., Kolb, T., McAuliffe, T., Simms, M., Underhill, R., & Lewis, M. (2001). Sequential acquisition of toilet-training skills: A descriptive study of gender and age differences in normal children. *Pediatrics 109*(3), 48–54. doi:10.1542/peds.109.3.e48

Smith, H. (1991). *The world's religions.* San Francisco, CA: HarperCollins.

Stacey, J., &. Biblarz, T. J. (2001). (How) Does sexual orientation of parents matter? *American Sociological Review,* 159–183. doi:10.2307/2657413

Taylor, M., & Segrin, C. (2010). Perceptions of parental gender roles and conflict styles and their association with young adults' relational and psychological well-being. *Communication Research Reports, 27*(3), 230–242. doi:10.1080/08824096.2010.496326

Troy, A. B., & Lewis-Smith, J. (2006). Preliminary findings on a brief self-disclosure intervention with young adult dating couples. *Journal of Couple & Relationship Therapy, 5*(2), 57–69. doi:10.1300/J398v05n02_04

U.S. Census Bureau. (2011). 2010 Census shows America's diversity. Retrieved from: http://www.census. gov/2010census/news/releases/operations/cb11-cn125.html

U.S. Const. amend. Retrieved from https://www.law.cornell.edu/constitution/amendmentxix.

U.S. Department of Labor. (2011). *Women in the labor force: A databook.* Retrieved from http://www.bls.gov/ cps/wlf-databook2011.htm

5

Social and Cultural Contexts of Meeting and Dating

Jennifer L. Doty, Ph.D.
Department of Pediatrics
University of Minnesota

Tai J. Mendenhall, Ph.D., LMFT
Jonathan J. Kleba
Department of Family Social Science
University of Minnesota

LEARNING OBJECTIVES

- Understand Bronfenbrenners' Ecological Systems Theory as a framework for social contexts
- Articulate how relationships are influences by contemporary Western culture and market economy
- Understand modern-day influences of technology in relationships

Case Vignette

Connor

For the past year, Connor has been working at a local designer clothing outlet in his town. He was recently promoted from a part-time sales associate to hiring manager. He is now in charge of conducting all hiring interviews and reviewing job applications. When Connor was promoted, his boss made it very clear that attractiveness should be a major qualifying factor for potential new hires. The company's image is that their clothes are for the hottest and coolest demographic of young people, so it is Connor's responsibility to uphold that image for this store.

After a year of working full-time in this atmosphere, the company values have begun to rub off on Connor. He has never really been one for long-term commitments or serious relationships, but the culture of his work environment has contributed to a "so many girls, so little time" dating outlook. He only chases after the physically beautiful ones, and grows bored of them relatively quickly. The constant messages he receives at work have altered Connor's ideas about the worth of women. In the store, attractiveness is emphasized as each person's most important trait. Other characteristics are secondary. Connor first accepted this philosophy exclusively in the context of retail, but over time, it has started to seep into his personal life.

Raquel

An incoming University of Minnesota freshman, Raquel has never had a boyfriend. Not even a fling. Her tastes are very specific and none of the guys she met in high school have shared her interests. She is nervous that college will just be more of the same. Raquel feels that she is ready to try a real relationship, but is unsure about how she can meet people who enjoy the same things that she does. Everyone talks about how many new friends she will meet in the dorms and in classes, but Raquel wants to take a more structured approach. A week or so before move-in day at the residence hall, she decides to try her hand at online dating.

From the start, Raquel is optimistic about the possibilities of her new quest. She loves the idea that she can filter out everyone but the best matches for her, saving a lot of time. And to be sure, the dating scene has never been appealing for Raquel. In her mind, it is a lot more hassle than it is worth. Plus, by dating online, she is free to browse through hundreds of profiles without worrying about being rejected or rejecting others. Rachel's only genuine concern is the validity of the profiles she is viewing. After all, it would be disappointing to set up a date with a guy she met on the Internet, only to find out that he was nothing like his profile!

Jennifer L. Doty, Ph.D.; University of Minnesota; Department of Pediatrics; 717 Delaware Street SE; Room 353 (3rd Floor West); Minneapolis, MN 55414. E-mail: dotyx093@umn.edu.

INTRODUCTION

The culture(s) we live in is like the water fish swim in—it encompasses us and informs how we experience the world. Surrounding us, like the air we breathe, we receive our social cues and norms from our environments. A **social norm** is an expectation or belief about how individuals should act that is held by a group of people. For example, ideas about when to have sex in relationships are influenced by social norms. The plots we see in movies, the stories our friends tell us the night after a party, and lyrics in the songs we hear give us ideas about what is considered "normal" in our society. Further complicating matters, we live in different cultures that influence us simultaneously. The cultures of your university might possess different norms than your family's ethnic culture or the religious culture that you were raised in.

Consider the ecological systems framework as a way to understand the social contexts that surround us. When Bronfenbrenner (1979) introduced this theory, he compared our social worlds to a set of Russian dolls, with each layer of context nested inside another layer (see Figure 1 below). At the individual level, or **microsystem** level, the people we see day to day, such as our roommates or our families, influence us. The **mesosystem** level describes connections between the people we are in contact with on a regular basis. For example, if a good friend of Joe's from high school meets all of his friends at the fraternity he joined in college, and they start comparing notes about how to meet girls, this is a mesosystem connection. Joe's high school friend may walk away with some mental notes on things he wants to try, and some of the fraternity brothers may have learned a thing or two as well.

FIGURE 1 *Bronfenbrenner's Ecological Systems*

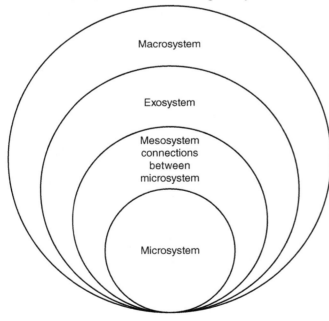

According to the ecological systems framework, other systemic layers of context include the exosystem and the macrosystem. The **exosystem** refers to the influence of institutions to which we belong. The university or college that a student attends would be considered part of his/her exosystem. Rules and norms about whether freshmen live in dorms their first year or whether dorms are coed could have a huge impact on who students meet and the relationships they form. The rules and norms that are part of a sorority or fraternity are more examples of cultural influence from an institution. An Individual's affiliation with groups on campus, such as the GLBT Ally program, Health Alliance, or Christian Student Fellowship, could influence both individuals and larger systems' social norms. At the **macrosystem**, even broader patterns of shared cultural influence occur. These include the Hollywood movies we see current fashion trends, and the social norms about dating and relationships that are generally shared on a cultural level. Although all levels within this theory are levels of social influence, the focus of this chapter is on the macrosystem and the ways that prevalent cultural ideologies, patterns, and beliefs impact individuals and couples today.

In many ways, culture is the foundation of relationships because it teaches us from a very young age how we should act. Think of preschool girls who play with princess dolls and kitchen sets, and preschool boys who play with trucks and Nerf guns. Children are learning how women and men act in our society. The **socialization process** is the process in which we learn the roles and social norms that are expected of us—how men and women should act in the context of dating; when is the right age to get married, if ever; what are the roles men and women should play in a marriage or as parents, and so on. Culture teaches us the meaning of something as simple as a diamond ring or a receiving a text message at 2 a.m. from a guy or girl that you just met.

Expectations in intimate relationships have changed in dramatic ways over the last five decades or so. This means that our parents' and grandparents' generations likely had different expectations than we do about how to approach love and commitment. As our society becomes increasingly culturally diverse, emerging adults face a wide variety of opinions and cultural differences in social norms surrounding relationships. Some gender norms and pressures remain from decades ago, while others have changed drastically. Technology, for example, has instigated cultural shifts regarding how people get to know one another and how they approach dating. Each of these aspects of cultural influence will be considered in this chapter.

A SHORT HISTORY LESSON: SOCIAL CONTEXTS AND RELATIONSHIPS

The ways in which our larger social contexts and their multiple systems' layers have influenced our relationships over millennia are myriad, and to provide a comprehensive account of these—even within a single culture or group—is outside of the scope of this chapter. What is most important to understand is that social contexts have been influencing relationships since the beginning of recorded history. For example, we know that even contemporary courtship and marriage traditions in Western cultures stem from social sequences originating long ago. Carrying one's bride "over the threshold" of her marital home is reminiscent of how women were captured from neighboring villages and clans, and forced into wedlock during the pre- and early- middle ages (circa 400–1000AD). The "honeymoon" of today also came from this era, wherein captured women were sequestered and hidden from their families until they became impregnated by their captor husbands and were no longer "valued" by their original clan. Thus, the primary societal concern during this era was survival and dominance.

In the high middle ages (circa 1000–1400AD), as marriages began to serve political functions uniting different regions and rule, traditions like the "bridal shower" (to make a woman more valuable to her suitor's family) and the father "giving away" his daughter during her wedding (as a transfer of property from himself to the groom) came into vogue. In contrast to the pre- and early- middle ages, this period was geared toward joining clans together for economic and political purposes. The Renaissance era's (circa 1400–1600AD) emphasis on love and romance brought us traditions of courtship defined by conspiring friends (best man, maid-of-honor) and high regard for women's choice and approval (so much so that a man proposed in deference on one knee, and later wore a boutineer showing the colors of his bride's clan to their wedding). Narratives focused on "wooing" and the courtship dance marked this particular era. As larger social establishments later tried to quell its youth's passion, the Age of Reason's (early 1700s) emphasis on logic in marital decisions brought legal documents, such as wedding announcements and guest books, alongside public displays of approval by marriage parties and proclamations to "speak now or forever hold your peace." The Age of Reason was marked by a cynical viewpoint on marriage and the return of males' control of females. The Romanticism era (late 1700s) celebrated the Individual Spirit (i.e., the expansion of

Self), and was characterized by dramatic love (think: Romeo and Juliet). Next, the Victorian era's (1800s) arguably phobic handling of sexuality, wherein profound proclamations of pathology were paired with normal human desires and responses, is still with us today as so many people struggle with guilt and shame instilled into them through baseless "science" and abusive "religious" teaching. The rise of "scientific" theories of matchmaking also contributed to the rigidity and formality of this era. For a detailed discussion regarding contextual influence on courtship and marriage, see Cott (1978), Garton (2013), Waggoner (2002), and Wood and Wood (2011). For a detailed discussion regarding how these phenomena vary around the world, see Hamon and Ingoldsby (2003) and Monger (2013).

RELATIONSHIPS IN TODAY'S MARKET ECONOMY

Like every culture around the world, the United States has dating customs and traditions that are shaped by the country's values and systems. The current U.S. culture is a market economy, where people and relationships have become targets of consumerism. In the context of relationships, this culture promotes a view of sex as being simply a transaction between two people (Baumeister & Vohs, 2004), and it is used to market almost everything that we buy. In this environment, women are perceived as objects of sexual desire rather than as complex human beings. Although men are increasingly objectified, too, women especially feel the pressure of impossibly high standards of beauty. Ironically, the marketplace then feeds on the insecurities it fosters, promoting products that promise beauty and love. Because we often don't recognize the cultural messages that surround us (like the air we breathe), these cultural themes warrant further examination and thought.

The Sexual Marketplace

According to Baumeister and Vohs (2004), relationships and sexual connections are often perceived as private, but in reality the larger culture has a huge impact on negotiations between partners. They argue relationships today take place in the sexual marketplace, "a cultural system where men and women play different roles resembling buyer and seller" (p. 339). From this view, men are consumers of sex and women are the gatekeepers, which makes female sexuality a valuable resource. These marketplace exchanges are often quite subtle. Under this perspective, while men value sex, women seek commitment, self-esteem, or economic resources. This perspective is closely related to the evolutionary theory, which suggests that men are more likely to value health and beauty, whereas women are more likely to value financial prospects (see Chapter 1). However, Baumeister and Vohs (2004) also emphasize the role of economics in relationships. Following laws of supply and demand, in a culture where sex is offered freely and without constraint, little is provided in return. Alternatively, resources might be more readily offered for those that withhold or limit sex.

Some evidence suggests that this theory explains sexual exchanges in relationships in our current culture well. In a study of gender differences, when young researchers approached college students and randomly asked if they would like to sleep with them tonight, 75% of the males said yes, whereas none of the women agreed (Clarke & Hatfield, 1989). Another study found that women were more likely than men to favorably rate an ad if sexuality was portrayed as part of a relationship (Dahl, Sengupta, & Vohs, 2009). These studies suggest that men may be more likely to value sex without commitment whereas women are more likely to value sex within the context of a relationship.

Assuming that there's some truth to these study results, what makes a relationship more valuable to women? Research and theory give us some clues. Using the website HotOrNot.com, one recent study found that women were more likely to rate men as attractive if they were standing next to an expensive car (Schuler & McCord, 2010). In the study, the same man posed three times in front of three different white cars; when he was next to a Mercedes, the women on the site rated him much more attractive than when he was next to a broken down Dodge Neon. Remember the evolutionary theory of attraction discussed in Chapter 1? These findings support the idea that, in general, men and women may value different things in relationships. However, caution should be taken in interpreting results or generalizing them to all men or all women, because many individual men and women do not follow such patterns.

The concept of the sexual marketplace is also supported by evidence suggesting that supply and demand influence partner selection. One influence on the timing of relationships is the pool of possible partners that is currently available. A couple of hundred years ago in a small village, the choice of partners was very limited, and competition between potential suitors was high. Today, if a person lives in a city with millions of others, choice and competition are exponentially different than they were in the past (Oliver, 2006). The Internet has further expanded possible partners to a global pool. HotOrNot.com, a dating website, had 1.6 million users in 2007 and 12 billion people had been rated (Lee, Loewenstein, Ariely, Hong, & Young, 2007). Facebook has over a billion users; this is three times the population of the United States (Scott, 2013). The vast number of possible partners may make it harder for emerging adults to believe they can commit to just one person.

Another way that the sexual marketplace influences relationships is through advertising and marketing strategies. Marketers are well aware that "sex sells". In her classic film series *Killing Us Softly*, Jean Kilbourne points out that sex is used to sell everything from beer to jeans to Oreo cookies. Images of women, and parts of women (e.g., their legs or abdomen), are the emphasis of hundreds of thousands of ads. In advertising, a picture is worth a thousand words, and as the sexual marketplace has expanded in a connected, mobile society, emphasis on visual cues has become increasingly important (Oliver, 2006). This means women are in competition not only with a larger pool of women, but also men may compare them to unrealistic images they see in advertising. The competition the sexual marketplace perpetuates has created an environment with a frighteningly intense pressure to be beautiful.

Female Objectification

The sociocultural pressure causing women to be viewed as objects of beauty and sex is known as *objectification*. Sexual Objectification Theory outlines the consequences of living in an environment where women's bodies, their body parts, and their sexuality are viewed as separate from their personhood (Frederickson & Roberts, 1997). In a culture that emphasizes heterosexuality, women are often objectified and treated as bodies that exist for men's pleasure. In 2007, the American Psychological Association reviewed media outlets, such as television, music, and magazines, and found that women are more likely than men to be portrayed as a body part cut off from the rest of the body, as sexually ready and willing, or as a decorative object dressed in provocative clothing. Although not all men view women in this way, most women have felt the gaze of objectification and the consequences of this accepted cultural practice. Recently, objectification theory has been extended to include male heterosexual experiences and LGBT experiences (Engeln-Maddox, Miller, & Doyle, 2011; Parent & Moredi, 2011).

What are the consequences of objectification in our society? Victims of sexual objectification are more vulnerable to anxiety and mental health disorders (Calogero, 2004; Calogero, Davis, & Thompson, 2005). This process can occur when women begin to **self-objectify**. In other words, as women begin to see themselves as objects, they start to evaluate themselves by their appearance rather than their talents and competencies (Fredrickson, Hendler, Nilson, O'Barr, & Roberts, 2011). In this environment, women are more likely to feel anxious about their bodies, which can inhibit their cognitive performance on tasks. To evaluate this idea, researchers first asked men and women to take a math test and then later to change into a bathing suit and take a math test (Frederickson, Roberts, Noll, Quinn, & Twenge, 1998; Fredrickson, Peplau, & Lever, 2006). When women were in a bathing suit, on average, their math performance was significantly poorer than when they were dressed in street clothes. This was not the case for men. This study suggests that when women feel self-conscious about their bodies, they are less likely to be able to perform well. These ideas extend to women's sexual performance as well (Fredrickson & Roberts, 1997). In one study, adolescent girls age 16 to 19 who reported inauthenticity in relationships and objectification of their bodies were less likely to feel competent acting on their own sexual needs and less likely to use protection for sexual safety (Impett, Schooler, & Tolman, 2006). Exposure to sexualized and objectified images of women in the media has been related to feelings of self-objectification, body shame, depression, and eating disorders (Fredrickson & Roberts, 1997; Moradi & Huang, 2007). Overall, research implies that sexual objectification can be harmful to women's sense of self and to their relationships.

Objectification theory also helps explain why women face oppression in the form of violence, marginalization of their accomplishments, and discrimination in the workplace. If women are seen as merely objects for sexual pleasure, it subtly becomes more socially acceptable to abuse or rape a woman (Berkowitz, Burkhart, & Bourg, 1994). Women are taken less seriously in politics, and the color of their lipstick or their latest haircut may receive more attention than their public speeches or policy agenda (Heldman & Wade, 2011). Discrimination in the workplace based on appearance has also been well documented, which explains why women's accomplishments are sometimes valued less than their appearance (Fredrickson & Roberts, 1997; Moffit & Szymanski, 2011). Moradi and Huang (2008) call for a more thorough examination of the social consequences of objectification.

Objectification of men, both heterosexual and homosexual, has also been increasing in our society. Although more studies are needed regarding the application of Objectification Theory to men (Moradi & Huang, 2008), evidence suggests that men who internalize cultural standards of attractiveness may be more likely to use steroids. One study of gay men's magazines found that emphasis on thinness and masculinity has significantly increased over the last 20 years (Schwartz & Andsager, 2011). In the film series *Killing Us Softly,* Kilbourne (2010) points out that with the exception of homosexual men, males are much less likely to experience negative consequences of objectification, such as violence or rape, when compared to females.

Objectification intersects with other forms of discrimination in our society, such as heterosexism and racism. Lesbian women have also been increasingly objectified in our society. Lesbian women who reported higher levels of internalized heterosexualism were more likely to report self-objectification, which in turn was related to higher levels of disordered eating and depression (Haines et al., 2008). Women of color who internalize a White standard of beauty may be more likely to obsess over body shape and size, monitor their skin color or undergo surgery to change the shape of their nose or eyes (Frederick & Roberts, 1997). In conclusion, objectification creates an environment where women become self-critical of their bodies, and an entire beauty industry has risen to profit from the insecurities that follow.

Cosmetics Market

The overemphasis on appearance has created a commercial market for beauty tools, dieting products, and surgical solutions. Not surprisingly, women who view television ads regarding beauty and fashion magazines with thin models are more likely to negatively compare themselves to other women and have a poor sense of body image (Groesz, Levine, & Murnen, 2002; Hargreaves & Tiggerman, 2003). Evidence suggests that during economic downturns, women are more willing to spend money on cosmetics, in part to compete for men with economic resources (Hill, Rodeheffer, Griskevicius, Durante, & White, 2012). Those who rate themselves as less attractive are more likely to engage in unhealthy dieting and opt in to cosmetic surgery (Brown et al., 2007; Neumark-Sztainer, Paxton, Hannan, Haines, & Story, 2006). In short, the beauty industry profits from a culture of sexual objectification.

Millard (2006) points out, "To be part of the beauty elite requires a carefully managed set of . . . resources, including long, shiny hair; clear, smooth skin; cosmetics; thin body; straight, white teeth; and trendy clothes" (p. 150). In the pressure to compete with other women for male attention, women spend much more time and money on restoring or improving their appearance than men (Hill et al., 2013). For example, in one study, college age women at a large state university were asked to rate the of men, and the results revealed that the women were more likely to use unhealthy products to increase attractiveness, such as tanning and diet pills, after being primed by rating attractive potential mates (Hill & Durante, 2011). Further, the Dove Campaign for Real Beauty launched their well-known marketing campaign for natural beauty after a report found that only 2% of women found themselves beautiful (Etcoff, Orbach, Scott, & D'Agostino, 2004). Although Dove has been praised for reimaging beauty, the company has also been criticized for being insincere and profit driven (Millard, 2011).

The dieting industry also benefits from unhealthy beauty standards, and more specifically, the idealization of extreme thinness. In his book, *Fat Politics*, Eric Oliver (2006) argues that the dieting industry profited handsomely when the recommended BMI levels were lowered and millions became "overweight" overnight. He points out that many of the scientists who supported that decision were also board members of companies selling dieting products. As objectification theory would predict, women are more likely than men to consume diet pills and diet programs (Neumark-Sztainer, Shenvood, French, & Jefsery, 1999). However, one study found both young men and women who had low body satisfaction as adolescents were more likely to engage in unhealthy dieting, binge eating, and lower levels of physical activity (Neumark-Stainer et al., 2006). For women, this relationship was found regardless of their physical size (BMI), implying that women may evaluate their bodies based on social cues rather their physical body type.

Cosmetic surgery has risen dramatically over the last several decades, fueled by a culture that has made objectification the rule rather than the exception. According to the American Association of Plastic Surgery (2013), 14.6 million cosmetic surgeries were performed in 2012. Breast augmentation has been the top surgery since 2006, while the number of underarm lifts has increased by over 4%. Among college women, those who have a high level of media exposure are more likely to be open to having plastic surgery (Henderson-King & Brooks, 2009).

TECHNOLOGY IN RELATIONSHIPS

Dan Slater, the author of *Love in the Time of Algorithms* (2013), points out that technology makes it easier to sift through the marketplace to find someone compatible to date on some levels. He also questions, "But what if online dating makes it too easy to meet someone new? What if it raises the bar for a good relationship too high? What if the prospect of finding an ever-more-compatible mate with the click of a mouse means a future of relationship instability, in which we keep chasing the elusive rabbit around the dating track?" (Slater, 2013, paragraph 11). In this section, we examine research on the role of technology in our culture when it comes to meeting, dating, and maintaining a relationship.

Meeting Online: A Visual Focus

Technology is powerful because it makes everything more visual. Between Facebook, Snapchat, Instagram, Match.com, and countless dating applications and platforms, visual marketing has become a mainstay of relationships in the new millennium. Branding one's self online to look attractive and interesting has become a first step in many relationships (Whitty & Joinson, 2009). Relationship researchers Hertlein and Blumer (2014) suggest that the main difference between meeting face-to-face and online is the ability to edit. Editing can introduce a level of mistrust in the information presented in online dating profiles. When potential partners discover between online presentation and face-to-face experiences, relationships can tank quickly!

In one example, Claire and Marty started dating after meeting through a dating site (Hertlein & Blumer, 2014). According to his profile, Marty was 25 and a local DJ. Claire later found out from his father that he was 28-years-old and an officer in the Armed Forces. (Ironically, she was also an officer, and she outranked him!). The take-away for Claire was that she could not trust Marty and the relationship ended. In another situation, a guy decided to completely

avoid online dating because he had started to become emotionally involved with a woman, only to find out that she was ten years older than she said on her profile (Heino, Ellison, & Gibbs, 2010). Perhaps this is one reason why the longest Internet relationships are between those who have never met one another in person (McKenna, 2008).

So, how many couples actually meet online? In the United States, a significant portion of couples connect online, especially after college years. Among 19- to 25-year-olds, about 16% met online (Dutton, Helsper, Whitty, Buckwalter, & Lee, 2010). That number jumped to 42% in the next age bracket including 26- to 35-year-olds. About 19% of those who were married said they had met online; the percent in the United States of couples meeting online is higher than other countries (e.g., Britain, Spain, and Australia) where only 6–9% of couples met online (Dutton et al., 2010). Although some couples report meeting through instant messaging or in chat rooms, by far the most common meeting places for romantic relationships are online dating sites. Some evidence suggests that same-sex couples are more likely to meet online than heterosexual couples, and that they tend to use a wider variety of tools for meeting online (Rosenfield & Thomas, 2012). Compared to couples who meet face-to-face, those who meet online are more likely to have differences in age and educational background. However, partners in online relationships tend to emphasize personality, emotional qualities, and physical attraction more than those who seek relationships via face-to-face methods.

© Syda Productions, 2014. Used under license from Shutterstock, Inc.

Technology: A Help or Hindrance for Couples?

Technology can serve as a double-edged sword when it comes to relationships. The ways that it can strengthen relationships can also undermine them; a lot depends on the partners as individuals, and how they use technology (Hertlein & Blumer, 2014). In a sense, the digital context of our society interacts with the microsystem of the couple.

EMOTIONAL INTIMACY. Technology can enhance emotional intimacy in several ways. When people communicate online, they may be less inhibited than they are in offline encounters (Hertlein, 2012). This promotes self-disclosure, and emotional sharing in particular creates a sense of intimacy. In addition, technology allows more frequent communication during the day, and people report that they often use a cell phone to text or call their partner to express affection (Coyne, Stockdale, Busby, Iverson, & Grant, 2011).

Although some research suggests that online interaction can strengthen the quality of a relationship (e.g., Kennedy, Smith, Wells, & Wellman, 2008; McKenna, Green, & Gleason, 2002), the quality of a relationship may also influence whether partners enjoy spending time online together or not (Hertlein & Blumer, 2014). On the positive side, playing video games together, for example, can promote a sense of togetherness, encourage partners to get to know each other without the pressure of physical aspects of attraction, and create an opportunity to grow through perspective taking using different avatars (Hertlein & Blumer, 2014). Also, some couples use technology to build on rituals that strengthen their relationships, or to practice rituals together when they are separated by distance.

On the negative side, technology can also undermine the strength of relationships. One potential challenge for virtual relationships is that people tend to project a favorable image onto the people they meet online (Hertlein, 2012); sometimes they see what they want to see and do not always see their online partner as they really are. Sometimes an online relationship is grounded in fantasy rather than reality.

Constant digital disruptions can also be a source of problems for couples in romantic relationships. Women, when compared to men, report more frustration at their partner's use of smartphones when they are spending time together (Hertlein, 2012). Ironically, other research has found that women are more likely than men to use technology to connect with other people when they are in the presence of their partners (Coyne et al., 2011). Hertlein and Blumer (2014) emphasize the importance of individual accountability; when it comes to the use of technology in relationships each partner should be responsible for his/her own behavior and conscious of the time he/she spends using technology at the expense of time spent with his/her partner. Often, people do not realize how much time is passing when they are online. Accountability also applies to behavior with others outside of the relationship, which leads to another potential challenge of technology: in fidelity.

Infidelity can be a challenge because the online world has expanded the sexual marketplace, and some worry that monogamy is a hard sell when there are so many fish in the sea. Slater (2012) poignantly reminds us that the CEOs of dating sites profit with every breakup and actively encourage customers to return to the online dating scene. Because infidelity has never been easier from an instrumental standpoint, many men and especially women report monitoring their partner's technology use (Helsper & Whitty, 2010). This monitoring may be nonthreatening, such as simply paying attention to a partner's Facebook activity, or more invasive, like breaking into a partner's account without his or her knowledge (Hertlein & Blumer, 2014). An invasive breach of trust can damage relationships, but ultimately each couple negotiate their own boundaries regarding netiquette (Helsper & Whitty, 2010). Although most couples agree that falling in love, having cybersex, and becoming emotionally intimate with others are out of the question, individuals and couples may differ in their agreement about the acceptability of other online behaviors such as viewing pornography, time spent gaming, and online flirting. Discussing these issues to find agreement before an issue arises can ensure that technology does not drive a wedge between couples later on.

SEXUAL INTIMACY.   When it comes to sexual intimacy, many couples find that technology offers tools for strengthening their sex life and satisfaction. Informational sites are tremendously helpful for many couples. For example, Tina Sellers is a sex therapist who has posted a series of online videos discussing sexual intimacy with a Christian woman who is about to be married. These conversations address the transition from restraint to openness regarding sexual activity for Christian couples. In one study, some men and women reported that viewing adult websites helps them express openness to trying new activities and encourages them to talk more with their partners, especially when couples view the sites together (Grov, Gillespie, Royce, & Lever, 2011). Those who visited adult sites together were also more likely to report increased frequency of sex and less boredom when compared to adults who viewed the sites alone (Grov et al., 2011). Another study in a laboratory setting found that partners who viewed an erotic film reported more general arousal and desire for their partners (when compared to non-erotic films), regardless of whether they watched the film together or independently (Staley & Prause, 2013). However, these couples also reported greater guilt and anxiety than others.

Many couples report enjoying cybersex, which is defined as sexual interaction involving at least two people using the Internet as a medium (Hertlein & Blumer, 2014). Cybersex might involve text messaging or webcams. Those who engage in cybersex outside of their primary relationship, though, may put that relationship at risk. Sexting is more common among college aged young adults than teens and is reported most frequently between "friends with benefits."

Technology can also present challenges to couple's relationships; for example, those who participate in online sexual activities report less desire to have physical sex (Albright, 2009; Grov et al., 2011). Women, in particular, reported feeling that their partners who viewed online sexual content were critical of their bodies and feeling pressured to try things their partner saw online (Grov et al., 2011). Regarding pornography, studies have shown that those viewing pornography, even when in a randomly assigned laboratory experiment, report lower levels of commitment (Lambert, Negash, Stillman, Olmstead, & Fincham, 2013). Viewing porn was found to increase online flirtation with a third person outside the couple, which was related to infidelity (Lambert et al., 2013). Among fraternity brothers, 83% viewed mainstream pornography, which was associated with greater behavioral intent to rape compared to non-viewers (Foubert, Brosi, & Bannon, 2011). Those who viewed more violent forms of pornography were more likely to believe rape myths and less likely to intervene.

Hertlein and Blumer (2014) point out that online sexual material may affect individuals in different ways. Some may become vulnerable for sexual addiction. Others may use technology to enhance sexual experiences recreationally without serious negative consequences. Some may become compulsive users of online sexual material, which could interfere with offline relationships. As researchers and therapists, Hertlein and Blumer (2014) caution that defining a problem as a sex addiction may undermine an individual's sense of accountability and personal responsibility for their relationship.

WHAT WE DON'T KNOW

What don't we know about the effects of a market-driven, consumer culture that emphasizes physical beauty, sexual objectification, and Internet dating? First, much of the research is cross-sectional, which means the data were gathered at one time point. We need longitudinal data to better understand the effects of these phenomena over time on individuals and their relationships (Moradi & Huang, 2008). For example, what does a lifetime of internalizing unrealistic beauty ideals do to relationship stability in the long run? Also, we are just beginning to understand how the objectification of men might affect relationships; more research is needed in this area (Moradi & Huang, 2008). Another promising area of research examines how queer theory might contribute understanding to LGBT experiences with objectification.

Another challenge with understanding relationships in the digital age is that technology is changing so rapidly. For example, more people are connecting to the Internet through mobile phones, especially African Americans and Hispanics. Social networking sites have exploded in the last several years, but research is just beginning to emerge that addresses the phenomenon of the online social network. Also, we do not know if technology is simply a tool to facilitate communication in relationships, or if it fundamentally changes relationships in some way. There is no question, however, that technology has impacted our culture profoundly.

DISCUSSION

Identifying the impact of shifting cultural trends within casual and intimate relationships is only the beginning. It is also crucial to evaluate how to take advantage of this knowledge in our daily lives and relationships. For example, simply being aware of the increasing sexualization in advertising is not as important as consciously choosing to resist the cycle of insecurity it creates. Knowing that nearly every face and body in the media has been digitally altered can serve as a defense for a battered self-esteem and prevent us from fruitlessly spending excessive amounts of money in order to live up to an unrealistic standard. Sex only sells because we allow ourselves to be manipulated by products' marketers. The sexual marketplace functions by the same basic economic principles as any other. If we aren't buying it, they won't sell it. By building self-confidence and working on maintaining a positive body image, we can loosen the hold of the sexualized marketplace.

Over-sexualization in the media is a troublesome reality, but to most people, it is hardly surprising anymore. This trend has been manifesting for years. In contrast, the growing influence of technology in personal relationships has only become apparent over the past several years. It will take some time to adapt to this ever-changing dating environment molded by our newfound reliance on networking technologies. The younger generations may have a relatively easier adjustment, because this is the world they know. Most teenagers and twenty-somethings are aware of the unwritten rules if dating in modern times. For example, the importance of a conversation relates to the medium over which you discuss it (unimportant = text/online chat; moderate importance/urgency = phone call; high importance = face-to-face conversation; exceptions may vary). Younger people also generally acknowledge that all online profiles should be considered with a grain of salt, whether it was created for a dating site or a more casual social hub.

Some of the recent changes that accompany this new technological environment are not understood as well. One significant consequence of the social networking era comes with our newfound ability to connect with millions of people, anywhere in the world. With so much potential in terms of a dating pool, it may be difficult to choose one person to see exclusively. There may be such a thing as "too many options." Adjusting to this new hurdle in relationships is about resisting the urge to find perfection. There may always be someone out there who is more compatible, but there is a balance that must be found between making peace with what one has and pursuing an ideal or "perfect" match. This problem is not brand new, but it has certainly been exacerbated by the Internet age.

REFERENCES

Albright, J. M. (2008). Sex in America online: An exploration of sex, marital status, and sexual identity in Internet sex seeking and its impacts. *Journal of Sex Research, 45*(2), 175–186. doi:10.1080/00224490801987481

American Association of Plastic Surgeons (2012). 14.6 million cosmetic plastic surgery procedures performed in 2012. Retrieved from http://www.plasticsurgery.org/news-and-resources/press-release-archives/2013/14-million-cosmetic-plastic-surgery-procedures-performed-in-2012.html

American Psychological Association, Task Force on the Sexualization of Girls. (2007). Report of the APA Task Force on the sexualization of girls. Retrieved from http://www.apa.org/pi/women/programs/girls/report-full.pdf

Baumeister, R. F., & Vohs, K. D. (2004). Sexual economics: Sex as female resource for social exchange in heterosexual interactions. *Personality and Social Psychology Review, 8*(4), 339–363. doi:10.1207/s15327957pspr0804_2

Berkowitz, A. D., Burkhart, B. R., & Bourg, S. E. (1994). Research on college men and rape. *New Directions for Student Services, 1994*(65), 3–19. doi:10.1002/ss.37119946508

Bronfenbrenner, U. (1979). *The ecology of human development: Experiments by nature and design.* Cambridge, MA: Harvard University Press.

Brown, A., Furnham, A., Glanville, L., & Swami, V. (2007). Factors that affect the likelihood of undergoing cosmetic surgery. *Aesthetic Surgery Journal, 27*, 501–508. doi:10.1016/j.asj.2007.06.004

Calogero, R. M. (2004). A test of objectification theory: The effect of the male gaze on appearance concerns in college women. *Psychology of Women Quarterly, 28*(1), 16–21. doi:10.1111/j.1471-6402.2004.00118.x

Calogero, R. M., Davis, W. N., & Thompson, J. K. (2005). The role of self-objectification in the experience of women with eating disorders. *Sex Roles, 52*(1-2), 43–50. doi:10.1007/s11199-005-1192-9

Clark, R. D., & Hatfield, E. (1989). Gender differences in receptivity to sexual offers. *Journal of Psychology & Human Sexuality, 2*(1), 39–55. doi:10.1300/J056v02n01_04

Cott, N. F. (1978). Passionlessness: An interpretation of Victorian sexual ideology, 1790-1850. *Signs, 4*, 219–236. doi:10.1086/493603

Coyne, S. M., Stockdale, L., Busby, D., Iverson, B., & Grant, D. M. (2011). "I luv u:)!": A descriptive study of the media use of individuals in romantic relationships. *Family Relations, 60*(2), 150–162. doi:10.1111/j.1741-3729.2010.00639.x

Dahl, D. W., Sengupta, J., & Vohs, K. D. (2009). Sex in advertising: Gender differences and the role of relationship commitment. *Journal of Consumer Research, 36*(2), 215–231. doi:10.1086/597158

Dutton, W. H., Helsper, E. J., Whitty, M. T., Li, N., Buckwalter, J. G., & Lee, E. (2009). The role of the internet in reconfiguring marriages: A cross-national study. *Interpersona, 3*, 3–18. doi:10.5964/ijpr.v3isupp2.73

Engeln-Maddox, R., Miller, S. A., & Doyle, D. M. (2011). Tests of objectification theory in gay, lesbian, and heterosexual community samples: Mixed evidence for proposed pathways. *Sex Roles, 65*(7–8), 518–532. doi:10.1007/s11199-011-9958-8

Etcoff, N., Orbach, S., Scott, J., & D'Agostino, H. (2004). The real truth about beauty: A global report. Retrieved from http://www.clubofamsterdam.com/contentarticles/52%20Beauty/dove_white_paper_final.pdf

Frederick, D. A., Peplau, L. A., & Lever, J. (2006). The swimsuit issue: Correlates of body image in a sample of 52,677 heterosexual adults. *Body Image, 3*(4), 413–419. doi:10.1016/j.bodyim.2006.08.002

Fredrickson, B. L., & Roberts, T. A. (1997). Objectification theory. *Psychology of Women Quarterly, 21*(2), 173–206. doi:10.1111/j.1471-6402.1997.tb00108.x

Fredrickson, B. L., Roberts, T. A., Noll, S. M., Quinn, D. M., & Twenge, J. M. (1998). That swimsuit becomes you: Sex differences in self-objectification, restrained eating, and math performance. *Journal of Personality and Social Psychology, 75*(1), 269. doi:10.1037/h0090332

Fredrickson, B. L., Hendler, L. M., Nilsen, S., O'Barr, J. F., & Roberts, T. A. (2011). Bringing back the body: A retrospective on the development of objectification theory. *Psychology of Women Quarterly, 35*(4), 689–696. doi:10.1177/0361684311426690

Foubert, J. D., Brosi, M. W., & Bannon, R. S. (2011). Pornography viewing among fraternity men: Effects on bystander intervention, rape myth acceptance and behavioral intent to commit sexual assault. *Sexual Addiction & Compulsivity, 18*(4), 212–231. doi:10.1080/10720162.2011.625552

Garton, S. (2013). *Histories of sexuality: Antiquity to sexual revolution.* New York: Routledge.

Groesz, L. M., Levine, M. P., & Murnen, S. K. (2002). The effect of experimental presentation of thin media images on body satisfaction: A meta-analytic review. *International Journal of Eating Disorders, 31*(1), 1–16. doi:10.1002/eat.10005

Grov, C., Gillespie, B. J., Royce, T., & Lever, J. (2011). Perceived consequences of casual online sexual activities on heterosexual relationships: A US online survey. *Archives of Sexual Behavior, 40*(2), 429–439. doi:10.1007/s10508-010-9598-z

Haines, M. E., Erchull, M. J., Liss, M., Turner, D. L., Nelson, J. A., Ramsey, L. R., & Hurt, M. M. (2008). Predictors and effects of self-objectification in lesbians. *Psychology of Women Quarterly, 32*(2), 181–187. doi:10.1111/j.1471-6402.2008.00422.x

Hargreaves, D., & Tiggemann, M. (2003). Longer-term implications of responsiveness to 'thin-ideal' television: Support for a cumulative hypothesis of body image disturbance? *European Eating Disorders Review, 11*(6), 465–477. doi:10.1002/erv.509

Heino, R. D., Ellison, N. B., & Gibbs, J. L. (2010). Relationshopping: Investigating the market metaphor in online dating. *Journal of Social and Personal Relationships, 27*(4), 427–447. doi:10.1177/0265407510361614

Heldman, C., & Wade, L. (2011). Sexualizing Sarah Palin. *Sex Roles, 65*(3-4), 156–164. doi:10.1007/s11199-011-9984-6

Helsper, E. J., & Whitty, M. T. (2010). Netiquette within married couples: Agreement about acceptable online behavior and surveillance between partners. *Computers in Human Behavior, 26*(5), 916–926. doi:10.1016/j.chb.2010.02.006

Henderson-King, D., & Brooks, K. D. (2009). Materialism, sociocultural appearance messages, and paternal attitudes predict college women's attitudes about cosmetic surgery. *Psychology of Women Quarterly, 33*(1), 133–142. doi:10.1111/j.1471-6402.2008.01480.x

Hertlein, K. M. (2012). Digital dwelling: Technology in couple and family relationships. *Family Relations, 61*(3), 374–387. doi:10.1111/j.1741-3729.2012.00702.x

Hertlein, K. M., & Blumer, M.L.C. (2014). *The couple and technology framework: Intimate relationships in a digital age.* New York: Routledge.

Hill, S. E., & Durante, K. M. (2011). Courtship, competition, and the pursuit of attractiveness: Mating goals facilitate health-related risk taking and strategic risk suppression in women. *Personality and Social Psychology Bulletin, 37*(3), 383–394. doi:10.1177/0146167210395603

Hill, S. E., Rodeheffer, C. D., Griskevicius, V., Durante, K., & White, A. E. (2012). Boosting beauty in an economic decline: Mating, spending, and the lipstick effect. *Journal of Personality and Social Psychology, 103*(2), 275–291. doi:10.1037/a0028657

Impett, E. A., Schooler, D., & Tolman, D. L. (2006). To be seen and not heard: Femininity ideology and adolescent girls' sexual health. *Archives of Sexual Behavior, 35*(2), 129–142. doi:10.1007/s10508-005-9016-0

Kennedy, T. L. M., Smith, A., Wells, A. M., & Wellman, B. (2008). Networked families. Retrieved from http://www.pewinternet.org/~/media//Files/Reports/2008/PIP_Networked_Family.pdf.pdf

Kilbourne, J. (2010). Killing us softly 4: Advertising's image of women [Video recording]. Available from Media Education Foundation, http://www.mediaed.org

Lambert, N. M., Negash, S., Stillman, T. F., Olmstead, S. B., & Fincham, F. D. (2012). A love that doesn't last: Pornography consumption and weakened commitment to one's romantic partner. *Journal of Social and Clinical Psychology, 31*(4), 410–438. doi:10.1521/jscp.2012.31.4.410

Lee, L., Loewenstein, G., Ariely, D., Hong, J., & Young, J. (2008). If I'm not hot, are you hot or not? Physical-attractiveness evaluations and dating preferences as a function of one's own attractiveness. *Psychological Science, 19*(7), 669–677. doi:10.1111/j.1467-9280.2008.02141.x

McKenna, K. Y. (2008). MySpace or your place: Relationship initiation and development in the wired and wireless world. In S. Sprecher, A. Wenzel, & J. Harvey (Eds.), *Handbook of Relationship Initiation,* 235–247. Mahweh, NJ: Lawrence Erlbaum.

McKenna, K. Y., Green, A. S., & Gleason, M. E. (2002). Relationship formation on the Internet: What's the big attraction? *Journal of Social Issues, 58*(1), 9–31. doi:10.1111/1540-4560.00246

Millard, J. (2009). Performing beauty: Dove's "Real Beauty" campaign. *Symbolic Interaction, 32*(2), 146–168. doi:10.1525/si.2009.32.2.146

Moffitt, L. B., & Szymanski, D. M. (2011). Experiencing sexually objectifying environments: A qualitative study. *Counseling Psychologist, 39*(1), 67–106. doi:10.1177/0011000010364551

Monger, G. (2013). *Marriage customs of the world: An encyclopedia of dating customs and wedding traditions* (Expanded 2nd ed.). Santa Barbara, Calif.: ABC-CLIO.

Moradi, B., & Huang, Y. P. (2008). Objectification theory and psychology of women: A decade of advances and future directions. *Psychology of Women Quarterly, 32*(4), 377–398. doi:10.1111/j.1471-6402.2008.00452.x

Neumark-Sztainer, D., Paxton, S. J., Hannan, P. J., Haines, J., & Story, M. (2006). Does body satisfaction matter? Five-year longitudinal associations between body satisfaction and health behaviors in adolescent females and males. *Journal of Adolescent Health, 39*(2), 244–251. doi:10.1016/j.jadohealth.2005.12.001

Neumark-Sztainer, D., Shenvood, N. E., French, S. A., & Jefsery, R. W. (1999). Weight control behaviors among adult men and women: Cause for concern? *Obesity Research, 7*(2), 179–188. doi:10.1002/j.1550-8528.1999.tb00700.x

Oliver, J. E. (2006). *Fat politics.* New York, Oxford University Press.

Parent, M. C., & Moradi, B. (2011). His biceps become him: A test of objectification theory's application to drive for muscularity and propensity for steroid use in college men. *Journal of Counseling Psychology, 58*(2), 246–256. doi:10.1037/a0021398

Rosenfeld, M. J., & Thomas, R. J. (2012). Searching for a mate: The rise of the internet as a social intermediary. *American Sociological Review, 77*(4), 523–547. doi:10.1177/0003122412448050

Schwartz, J., & Andsager, J. L. (2011). Four decades of images in gay male-targeted magazines. *Journalism & Mass Communication Quarterly, 88*(1), 76–98. doi:10.1177/107769901108800105

Scott, M. (2013). Five surprising social media statistics for 2013. Retrieved from http://socialmediatoday.com/docmarkting/1818611/five-surprising-social-media-statistics-2013

Slater, Dan. (2013). A million first dates. Retrieved from *The Atlantic:* http://www.theatlantic.com/magazine/archive/2013/01/a-million-first-dates/309195/

Staley, C., & Prause, N. (2013). Erotica viewing effects on intimate relationships and self/partner evaluations. *Archives of Sexual Behavior, 42,* 615–624. doi:10.1007/s10508-012-0034-4

Szymanski, D. M., Moffitt, L. B., & Carr, E. R. (2011). Sexual objectification of women: Advances to theory and research. *Counseling Psychologist, 39*(1), 6–38. doi:10.1177/0011000010378402

Waggoner, S. (2002). *I do! I do! The origins of 100 classic wedding traditions.* New York: Rizzoli.

Wood, J., & Wood, M. (2011*). Wedding traditions and customs throughout the centuries.* United Kingdom: M J Wood Digital Media.

Whitty, M. T., & Joinson, A. N. (2009). *Truth, lies and trust on the Internet.* New York: Routledge/Taylor & Francis Group.

6

Dances of Intimacy: Patterns of Communication, Boundaries, and Specific Barriers

Kirsten Lind Seal, Ph.D., LMFT
Graduate School of Health and Human Services
Saint Mary's University of Minnesota

Elizabeth J. Plowman, Ph.D.
Department of Family Social Science
University of Minnesota

Jaime E. Ballard, M.S.
Department of Family Social Science
University of Minnesota

LEARNING OBJECTIVES

- Understand key elements of communication in interpersonal relationships
- Articulate commonplace barriers to effective communication
- Articulate common relationship "dances" that couples get stuck in
- Outline strategies and ways that couples can alter negative dances

HOW DO WE DANCE?

Vignette

In the early episodes of the HBO TV series *Girls* (Perez & Dunham, 2012), Marnie and her boyfriend Charlie show us a great example of one of the most common intimacy dances: the pursuer–distancer. They begin as college sweethearts. Charlie appears endlessly devoted and constantly seeks closeness with Marnie. However, Marnie feels vaguely dissatisfied and increasingly less willing to be close to Charlie. As Charlie grows more and more anxious for Marnie to tell him "what she wants" and "how I should do things," Marnie becomes more and more distant and frustrated with the relationship. Finally, Charlie decides to break up with her after indirectly hearing some harsh realities about how Marnie really feels about him. At this point Marnie does a complete 180 degree turn, begging Charlie not to break up with her. After some time he finally agrees, and Marnie then breaks up with him again. What is

going on here? It is the classic intimacy dance of the pursuer and the distancer; one chases and the other runs away. When the one chasing stops chasing, then the other one often begins to chase, and the cycle begins again.

Intimate relationships are processes that are shaped and affected by each partner's behaviors, beliefs, thoughts, and feelings. Cycles of verbal and nonverbal communication that promote togetherness, mutual self-disclosure, and commitment are considered *dances of intimacy* (Lerner, 1998). We use the metaphor of a "dance" because the dualistic and systemic nature of relationship is very well suited to a dance. Each partner in a dance is responsible for his or her part and what each partner does affects what the other partner does in the dance (or relationship) as a whole. The phrase "It takes two to tango" is an extremely apt one for intimate relationships.

Corresponding Author: Kirsten Lind Seal, Ph.D., LMFT; Saint Mary's University of Minnesota; Graduate School of Health and Human Services; Marriage and Family Therapy Program; 2500 Park Ave. South; Minneapolis, MN 55404. E-mail: klseal12@smumn.edu.

This chapter will focus on the dances of intimacy that are most commonly found in romantic couple relationships. As in the rest of this book, we include all types of relationships, straight and LGBTQ, married and unmarried, deeply in love and newly dating, when we use the word "relationships." These dances of intimacy include the interplay of three components: communication, boundaries, and specific barriers. In this chapter, we will address all three components of the dance of intimacy, and then identify common patterns. We will begin by looking at communication.

COMMUNICATION

Communication is culture-bound; different cultures value different ways of communicating. In many Asian cultures, for example, straightforward verbal communication can be considered quite rude (Fox, 2008). In Native American cultures, people often do not look others in the eye when speaking because this, too, can be considered offensive (Chiang, 1993). Culturally speaking, it is important to understand that a person's background can strongly influence how s/he thinks about and communicates with his or her intimate partner. The idea of intimacy being a dance, however, transcends culture, and we hope that it is useful to you in your relationships going forward. For more information on culture and how it affects intimate relationships, please see Chapter 12. In this chapter, we will focus primarily on verbal communication.

Communication serves as a facilitating factor of cohesion and connection in relationships (e.g., Olson, 2000; Olson, Olson-Sigg, & Larson, 2008); couples can more easily overcome challenges as a united team when it is fluid and clear. Imagine a game of "telephone." When playing telephone, all participants sit in a circle, and one speaker shares a message with his neighbor by whispering in his ear (Bay & Ragan, 2000). The goal of the game is for the receiver to accurately translate the message despite the difficult conditions of communication. Having heard the message, the receiver then passes it on to his neighbor. Everyone in the circle waits to hear how the message might have been altered.

When the message is whispered from speaker to receiver, the clarity of the message's receipt is dependent on two variables: 1) the quality with which the speaker shared the message, and 2) the ability of the receiver to filter out distractions and accurately hear and translate the message. If the speaker delivers the message in a raspy, unclear voice, the receiver has little opportunity to understand the intended contents. Likewise, if the speaker clearly delivers the message, but the receiver is listening to his neighbor or interrupting the speaker, the message has less chance of an accurate delivery.

This example demonstrates three basic communication skills. In an intimate relationship, the quality with which the speaker transmits the message to his partner illustrates his *expressive skills*. Skillful expressive messages are honest, clear, and non-attacking. In order for partners to understand each other, messages must honestly convey how both are really thinking and feeling. An important aspect of honest communication is congruence: when our body language and verbal statements both match our true feelings. If one partner states that he is "fine" while his eyes are still puffy from crying, this sends a very confusing message, and the other partner will have difficulty knowing how to respond. Our body language alone can send conflicting messages. For example, if I reach out for my partner and then give him a very rigid hug, he will be confused about my expectations for closeness. Half-hearted kisses and communicating with crossed arms can have a similar effect. In the end, if the verbal message conflicts with the nonverbal message transmitted by our body language, then our partner will be unsure which message is the "real" one. This kind of confusion can lead to misunderstandings and eventual lack of trust within the couple relationship.

Messages should also be clear and non-attacking. Partners with strong expressive skills have little difficulty sharing clear messages in neutral, non-blaming dialogues. An important expressive skill is the use of "I" statements. "I" statements communicate a specific feeling about a specific incident, instead of commenting on a partner's character. For example, rather than saying, "You never do the dishes, you're such a slob," saying "I felt annoyed today when I came home and none of the dishes were done, because it is hard to cook without clean dishes." "I" statements and use of positive personal pronouns ("I," "we," "us") are correlated with more positive problem-solving outcomes and suggest an individual's ability to self-focus within the relationship. They are also related to stronger marital satisfaction in the longer term (Simmons, Gordon, & Chambless, 2005). Additional important skills for expressive communication are presented in Text box below.

Healthy Expressive Communication Skills

1. Start with "I" statements . . .
Example: "I feel frustrated when you do not call me after getting home from work.", "I feel disrespected when you don't put your things away at my apartment.", "I really felt loved when you planned our weekly date nights."
- Leads to self-awareness and greater clarity in communication
- Encourages curiosity from your partner because the issue is focused on you
- Decreases defensiveness from the partner

2. And avoid "You" statements
- "You" statements cause your partner to feel blamed
- "You" statements cause confusion about who is responsible for your feelings

3. Ask "what" and "how" questions
- These are usually focused on how to understand and solve the problem at hand

4. And avoid "why" questions (generally)
- Can lead to blaming; they feel attacked
- It is focused on the other person
- Can be productive, in calm conversations ("I'm interested in your thoughts, why did you . . .?")

5. Distinguish your thoughts, perceptions, and judgments from your feelings, because your expressed feelings are not disputable, but your perceptions and judgments are.

For thoughts, perceptions, and judgments, use these:
- "I wonder if you are listening to me"
- "I could be wrong, but it seems to me that you don't want to talk right now"
- "I think we might not have enough time to talk about this"
- "I think that wasn't a very sensitive thing to say"

Avoid these:
- "I feel like you're not listening to me"
- "I feel like you don't want to talk to me anymore"
- "I feel like we never have the time to talk"
- "You have the sensitivity of a doorknob"

For feelings, use these:
- "I feel accused"
- "I don't feel heard"
- "I'm feeling really angry"
- "I feel like _____" "I feel that _____"

Avoid these:
- "You're accusing me . . ."
- "You're not listening"
- "You're making me mad"
- "Why are you making me _____?"

6. Expand your emotional dictionary
- Instead of "I feel bad," "I feel (sad, discouraged, hurt, embarrassed, angry, frustrated, anxious, etc.)"

7. Use XYZ statements
- I felt X when you did Y in situation Z

Receptive skills demonstrate the receiver's abilities to listen, understand, and acknowledge her or her partner. Partners who possess strong receptive skills are able to listen actively, seeking to comprehend or "get" what they are hearing. A good receiver listens without interrupting and asks clarifying questions that further understanding (or attempts at understanding) instead of just waiting for an opening to defend oneself or launch an attack. A good receiver then validates his or her partner's emotions and acknowledges his or her own part in the process, in both the positive and the negative interactions. Additional elements of effective expressive skills are presented in Text box below.

Let's briefly return to the metaphor of the telephone game. If the pair continues to play the game with the intention of improving dyadic communication, it will require both participants to determine areas of improvement and fine-tune their expressive and receptive skills. A partner's abilities to be aware of his or her role in communication and use this awareness to improve relational communication are *reflective skills.* An instance of reflective skills might be when one person says that they are feeling very sleepy during a late-night argument over whose turn it is to take out the trash. Though it is possible that the other person might feel that this is a delaying tactic and become even more irritated, making the choice to reflect back to the first person what exactly they are hearing can be very helpful. Maybe the reflecting partner says something like, "It sounds like you are tired right now. Should we continue the discussion tomorrow instead so we can get some sleep?" In this way the reflecting partner is showing a deeper level of understanding of the actual situation rather than reacting automatically.

Reflective skills can be useful when both members of the couple can "rise above" the conflict or the disagreement to understand their respective parts in it. As with any system, each participant bears some of the responsibility for creating whatever moment or reality exists. By following six steps, partners can help one another to build strong communication patterns (Mendenhall, 2013). The six steps are: Stepping back; Debriefing; Self Reflecting; Owning Responsibility; Perspective-Taking/Switching; Contextualizing.

When we want to solve a tense disagreement, stepping back is the first step. We need to remove ourselves, just a little, from the stresses of the current situation. Sometimes, we can just close our eyes and take a deep breath. At other times, we may need to say, "I need a 5-minute break. Let's take

Healthy Receptive Communication Skills

1. Aim for understanding and put your own needs second
   - "Seek first to understand, then to be understood" (Covey, 2004, p. 235)
2. Paraphrase content
   - "What I hear you saying is that my coming home late put pressure on you because . . . ")
3. Paraphrase emotion
   - "So, if I understand you correctly, you're pretty angry right now"
4. Validate what your partner is feeling
   - "I can see why you feel angry if you thought I hurt you intentionally"
   - Note that validation is not the same as agreeing with their statements
5. Ask for more details
   - "Tell me more about that . . ."
6. Ask for clarification
   - "What I hear you saying is . . . did I get it or is there something I'm missing?"
   - "Help me understand . . . "
7. Edit out your own emotional response in an open way
   - "It's hard for me to hear you say this, but I'm trying to understand your experience of this"
8. Use empathy and put yourself in your partner's shoes
   - Receptive communication comes more naturally to people who have a desire to understand others

a 5-minute break, and then I can come back and talk about this." To debrief is to ask for information about an experience. For instance, we might ask our partner how they are feeling about the discussion so far—if they feel like they are being heard or bulldozed over as sometimes happens. Self-reflecting is thinking about what our own experience has been. Once we can actually note and pay attention to what is going on inside of us, we can think about how we would like it to be different. Owning responsibility is acknowledging that we are responsible for the current patterns, and that there are things we can each do to change the current situation. Perspective taking and switching is when we try to see from our partner's point of view, and they do the same. For example, we might say, "If I were you, and my partner was always late for our dates, I might feel like s/he didn't care about my time or being with me. Is that how you feel?" Finally, contextualizing is looking at outside factors that might be influencing the disagreement. For example, lack of sleep can often make arguments much more difficult to resolve. After completing these six steps, we will be better able to understand our partners' points of view and to communicate respectfully.

How might these steps have been applied to Charlie and Marnie? Here is a hypothetical example. During one particularly tense argument, Charlie is feeling frustrated, lost, and alone. He has been begging Marnie to tell him "what she wants" and how he should do things, but suddenly realizes this is not getting him anywhere. He decides to step back, and tells Marnie, "I need a 10-minute break. I'm going to step outside. I'll be back in ten." He listens to music, calming down. After a few minutes, he starts self-reflecting. He realizes that he has been feeling distant from Marnie, that he wants their relationship to be closer, and that he feels like he has been putting in all of the effort. He decides he wants to be direct about these feelings. When he comes back after ten minutes, Marnie still looks upset. Charlie debriefs, asking her what her experience of the disagreement has been so far. She says that she feels pestered and attacked by the way Charlie always asks her what to do, and feels like he should figure it out on his own. Charlie owns responsibility, and says that he has been a broken record in his requests. This throws Marnie off balance. She owns some responsibility, too, stating that she could think about what he is asking a little more. Charlie takes Marnie's perspective, stating, "If I were you, and my partner kept asking me what to do, I might feel like they didn't care enough to think of anything on their own. I might feel overwhelmed and suffocated. Is that how you feel?" Marnie adds some more thoughts, and Charlie does his best to listen. He asks her to think about how he might feel. Marnie is somewhat pained to realize that Charlie thinks she does not care enough about their relationship to invest any effort in it. Both Charlie and Marnie realize that they are hungry and tired, and this might be adding to the fire of the argument tonight. Charlie and Marnie are now in a good place to start brainstorming helpful actions and possible solutions.

All of these communication skills influence the development and maintenance of intimacy. When partners are unable to express their thoughts or feelings, their partners are much less likely to understand them and thus be able to meet them in a space of acknowledgement, validation, and empathy. When partners feel heard and understood, they are able to share their whole selves and feel safe to grow within the relationship. The three types of communication skills—receptive, expressive, and reflective—are important tools to have in your toolbox in order to build a good relationship with your loved one.

BARRIERS TO COMMUNICATION. Take a moment to think about your last argument with an intimate other. Although consistent healthy communication is the goal, chances are high that at least one individual behaved disrespectfully, immaturely, or inappropriately at some point during this argument. It tends to be easier for the person who has been offended to identify a moment when a conversation turned sour, so we may first remember a mistake made by our partner. Yet most of us are also aware of times that we have crossed a line. We may remember that a nasty comment slipped out, or that we rolled our eyes when a partner was finally becoming vulnerable. In those moments, whether when expressing or receiving, it is all too clear what disrespectful communication looks and feels like. But in many other moments before conflict escalates, it can be difficult to identify transgressions or subtle hostility.

Roadblocks to communication are behaviors that negatively influence the outcome and progress of a conversation or problem-solving discussion. Each time that one partner uses a negative behavior, such as sarcasm or ignoring, that partner puts up a STOP or DETOUR sign on the healthy communication road. A common list of roadblocks to communication is found in Text box above.

Roadblocks to Communication

1. **Focused on changing the other**: Failing to focus on your own internal process (feelings or thoughts) and using feeling words to describe your response or thinking words to describe your perceptions or intentions.

2. **Problem-solving:** Getting the facts (not feelings) and solving or fixing the problem without validating that the feelings of the other person first. The mindset is, "Your problem makes me anxious! If I can help you see a solution to the issue, then I'll feel less anxious and you should, too."

3. **Competing:** Assessing others in comparison to myself. Must be smarter, better . . .

4. **Computing:** Giving only super responsible, thoroughly accredited feedback, never dealing with feelings. "Let's be rational. Let's look at this logically . . ."

5. **Distracting:** Letting you talk only for so long, then changing the subject, interrupting.

6. **Dreaming:** Wandering off into a mental vacation.

7. **Silo listening:** Before conversation begins, I have already decided what I will listen to and what I will filter out. Maybe even saying, "I don't want to hear anymore about that . . ."

8. **Gunnysacking:** Having stored negative thoughts and feelings, you let go and dump them, that is, at some point you switch from calm and quiet to just exploding at your partner.

9. **Identifying:** "Yes, that's like the time when I . . ." Taking the center of conversation rather than hearing the other's story.

Your experience is really my opportunity to talk about my experience.

10. **Ignoring:** I hear you and act like I'm listening but rarely respond; just have a blank look.

11. **Name calling or labeling:** Putting someone into a category, "You're just a workaholic!" "Why are you so lazy?"

12. **Placating:** I want to be liked so I am always pleasant. Can't stand conflict or negative thoughts or feelings.

13. **Rehearsing my response:** Thinking of my response while you're still talking. Turning our talk into a debate.

14. **Sarcasm:** Someone who is uneasy with real emotions so always has some witty sarcasm to keep you from getting too close. A form of emotional distancing.

15. **Over-generalizing:** Using blanket statements like "you always" or "you never" are not only an exaggeration of reality, but they give your partner good reasons to defend themselves.

16. **Minimizing:** You tend to point out that complaints aren't that bad and don't warrant worrying about them. It's just energy spent uselessly, no matter what the other is feeling.

17. **Asking why (condescendingly):** "Why did you say/do that?" almost always leads to a defensive response from the other.

These behaviors can be used intentionally or unintentionally. Although it may seem counterintuitive to block communication, roadblocks are often strategic moves because they fulfill an individual's personal need to lessen anxiety. This commonly occurs with ignoring, sarcasm, and overgeneralization. For example, my decision to ignore you is my way of communicating that *I do not respect you and you cannot hurt me.* Being sarcastic keeps you from understanding my true feelings and allows me to protect myself from your intention to harm me. I overgeneralize and say you *always* drink too much at parties and *never* call me on time because I worry you will not believe me if the problem is not presented as a severe issue.

All three of these behaviors stem from an individual's desire to lessen the anxiety s/he is experiencing in a relationship (Lerner, 1998). Additionally, all three of these behaviors can lead to specific dances of intimacy. It is important to use reflective skills to examine our own communication patterns and roadblocks, be honest with ourselves about why we are blocking effective communication, and make the decision to move forward in a way that is consistent with our underlying emotions.

The second reason we might choose to use roadblocks in our communication is because we feel defensive when our partners are critical or hostile. Once one roadblock emerges, it is sometimes easier to put up more roadblocks rather than simply ask our frustrated partner in a mature way "What could we do better right now to limit the hostility I'm feeling?" it is often hard to realize and then to say, "I am really attacking you right now. Let me think of a different way to express what I've been thinking" or to suggest "I love you, and I really want to communicate this clearly. I think it might be best for me to take a timeout, gather my thoughts, and come back to the topic in the morning."

Ineffective communication skills within relationships influence individual wellbeing and also impact the couple unit as a system. When communication breaks down, individuals tend to: a) pull away from the relationship or b) cling to it desperately because they are too anxious to give it distance and focus on themselves. The tendency of partners to lessen or increase distance from one another or the relationship often stems from anxiety or fear (Fournier, Brassard, & Shaver, 2011; Lerner, 1998). Healthy communication can help individuals understand one another and to establish helpful boundaries.

Even couples who possess highly effective communication skills and display virtually no roadblocks can experience threats to intimacy. Although effective communication is a facilitating factor in relationships and can serve to protect couples from the impact of relationship problems (Lederman & Macho, 2009), even "perfect" communicators can experience betrayals to intimacy, such as control, jealousy, infidelity, and even violence.

Boundaries

In the physical world, we have many types of protective boundaries. We have lines to mark our property, we put up fences around cliffs, and we avoid unwanted visitors with "No solicitors" signs. These boundaries identify lines, protect us from threats, and identify who is welcome (Rosenberger, 2011).

Our interpersonal boundaries serve the same purposes. Discussed in detail in Chapter 7, boundaries can be defined as the rules that surround a relationship, establishing what behaviors are acceptable and how much information and resources will be exchanged (Wilson, 1998). These boundaries are based on our family norms, cultural norms, and past experiences. Boundaries can range from diffuse to rigid. With diffuse boundaries, I have few to no barriers, and I try to share all of my time, resources, and personal information with another person. With rigid boundaries, I keep many barriers and a lot of distance between myself and others. I may avoid sharing any personal information with others, and I may keep my schedule too busy to spend much time with any one person. This can have the effect of making me feel more safe because I am more isolated but it is ultimately a pretty lonely choice. The more diffuse my boundaries are, the more likely it is that my sense of self will come to depend on the other person (Rosenberger, 2011). The more rigid my boundaries are, the more distant I will feel from those around me.

Boundaries are specific to each relationship: for example, we generally have different boundaries with coworkers than we have with a close friend. Boundary crossings and violations are a common issue in families and other relationships (McKie & Cunningham-Burley, 2005). In healthy relationships, partners tend to have similar boundary expectations, so that what the other person wants is similar to what we are willing to give (Rosenberger, 2011). For example, I might expect that my boyfriend and I will talk openly about our backgrounds, dreams, and stresses, but that we still spend time with our friends separately and we keep our finances separate. If he has similar expectations, our relationship will operate more smoothly than if he expects to us to share all of our friends, debts, and assets.

DANCES OF INTIMACY

In healthy dances of intimacy, each partner is given the space and freedom to be their authentic selves, and partners act with one another's best interests at heart. Communication is healthy because each partner feels the freedom to express himself or herself openly, and does so while respecting his or her partner's boundaries and emotional space. Trust is upheld. Communication and conflict can promote intimacy by encouraging individuals to grow together within the relationship and establish lasting, respectful communication patterns.

Not all dances of intimacy are so healthy, however. Whether motivated from a place of fear, anger, or any known or unknown cause, some couples experience patterns of inappropriate control, power, and communication. Unhealthy intimacy dances, also known as "intimacy killers" (for more information see Chapter 9) can begin early in a relationship, years into a relationship, or even after a relationship has officially dissolved. They may last the entirety of a relationship, years, or only days. No matter when they begin or how long they last, cycles of unhealthy communication threaten individual partners' abilities to be themselves in the relationship, prevent individuals from experiencing freedom in commitment, and temporarily or permanently harm the potential for true intimacy. When unhealthy intimacy dances continue, couples can feel "stuck" in

the relationship—they experience either too much distance or too much intensity (Lerner, 1998). Intensity is not the same as intimacy; intensity refers to extreme feelings that lead to over-focusing on the other person, often in an angry or worried way (Lerner, 1998). Extreme levels of distance, intensity, or both, can paralyze couples and keep them from making the changes needed to get back on track in their relationship.

What Patterns Can Fuel Unhealthy Relationships Dances?

Patterns of control, jealousy, and triangulation are often involved in unhealthy dances, though they can appear different in different couples. Below, we will address each of these patterns and address common dances in relationships.

CONTROL. Perhaps one of the most commonly witnessed patterns involves an attempt by one partner to exert control over the other partner's behavior; the issue of control is, in many ways, inherent to all intimate relationships (Doherty, Colangelo, & Hovander, 1991). For example, Sally might passivel aggressively tell John that it is okay that he talks with his ex-girlfriend, Susan, but *she* certainly would never talk to her ex, Justin. Pat might exert control more directly, telling Richard that he simply will not engage in a relationship where his partner speaks with his past lover. Mary uses a different approach; she tells Jeremy that she forbids him seeing his ex-fiancé, Marlene. The common thread between Sally, Pat, and Mary's behaviors? They are all controlling their partners. Many family therapists would quickly point to insecurity of the controlling partner as the root cause. Whether the insecurity stems from the past (e.g., an anxious/preoccupied attachment with one's primary caregiver) or the present (e.g., body image issues, recent infidelity, stress), the controlling behavior indicates felt insecurity about oneself and/or about the relationship.

JEALOUSY. Jealousy has rightfully earned the reputation of being a monster; in close relationships, it can destroy trust and intimacy, and once it emerges, it can spiral out of control. Jealousy is the emotional and behavioral response to the perceived threat of losing one's romantic partner (e.g., Sharpsteen & Kirkpatrick, 1997). It is related to negative emotional states like suspicion, loneliness, insecurity, distrust, and fear (Buunk, 1997). As with control, insecurity and fear are typical sources of jealousy, and it can fall into three categories with varying outcomes and causes: anxious jealousy, possessive jealousy, and reactive jealousy. These types of jealousy are addressed in detail in Chapter 9. They are briefly addressed in Text box left side.

Types of Jealousy

1. **Anxious jealousy:** Rumination about the potential transgressions one's partner might commit.
   For example, "He hasn't called me . . ."
2. **Possessive jealousy:** Attempts to prevent partner from unfaithful behavior.
   For example, "Don't talk to other guys. It's not that I don't trust you; I don't trust them."
3. **Reactive jealousy:** Jealousy felt in response to a known occurrence of partner's infidelity or indiscretions.
   For example, "Please don't go to lunch with anyone from work without telling me. After you did that so often with Susan, it makes me uncomfortable."

Jealousy is a complex danger because it can seem to promote intimacy at times, especially the first few times it rears its ugly head. When a person behaves jealously, it often requires a reassuring response from his partner. Even if this response is conflict or anger, it reaffirms the value of the jealous partner and it temporarily decreases the anxiety the jealous partner is feeling. Unfortunately, this sense of relief and security is often short-lived and creates a negative cycle of communication. When left unchecked, jealousy is more likely than control and verbal abuse to spiral into aggressive, and potentially abusive, cycles of communication (Babcock, Costa, Green, & Eckhardt, 2004).

Interestingly, a recent study has suggested that, on average, different types of jealousy affect gay, lesbian, and straight relationships differently (Barelds & Dijkstra, 2008). For example, straight men and women and gay men report decreased relationship satisfaction when higher levels of anxious jealousy is present in their relationship; however, this was not true for lesbian women. In fact, for lesbian women, researchers found no significant association between jealousy and relationship satisfaction. For straight men and women, reactive jealousy was positively associated with relationship satisfaction, suggesting that when a threat is present, straight couples consider jealousy a protective effort to preserve the relationship. Gay men reported significantly lower levels of reactive jealousy than all other relationship types. The varying associations indicate that the association between jealousy and relationship satisfaction is influenced by relationship and jealousy type.

TRIANGULATION. Triangulation is a term for bringing another person into a dyadic (two-person) relationship to reduce the anxiety of one of the members of the couple (Bowen, 2004). Think about all of your relationships for a moment. Are there times when three seem better or more stable than two? This is the idea behind triangulation; a third person could provide extra support, just as a three-legged stool is more stable than even four- legged one. However, this often has dangerous implications in close relationships. Consider a young couple, Samantha and Janet. Janet is frustrated with Samantha's lack of attention and seeming inability to listen to her when she really needs her, but it is too difficult for her at this point in the relationship to bring it up to her and deal with it in a straightforward fashion (e.g., by using expressive and reflective skills). Instead, she goes to talk to her best friend Sara. Complaining to Sara about Samantha makes Janet feel a lot better, even though it does not help the relationship at all, except perhaps by lowering Janet's anxiety. Without speaking directly to Samantha, the core issue of communication and the couple dynamics will never be addressed. Eventually it is quite possible that Sara will become tired of listening to Janet complain about Samantha, which will put strain on their friendship as well. In this way triangulation becomes a solution that creates more problems than it solves (Bowen, 2004; Charles, 2001; Titelman, 2008).

A key problem caused by triangulation is the splitting of social support. If you complain to a family member about your partner, your family member will often have a lingering bad impression or resentment toward your partner. Family support of a relationship is related to relationship's success and satisfaction, and so triangulation can be damaging to both our partner's relationship with our family and our own partner relationship (Bryan, Fitzpatrick, Crawford, & Fischer, 2001).

Types of Intimacy Dances

There are some dances of intimacy that are common in couples, and so the steps of each partner can be described in detail. Below, we address four common intimacy dances which can be negative for the partners involved.

PURSUER–DISTANCER. This is the dance that we saw in Marnie and Charlie in the vignette at the beginning of the chapter. This particular combination usually begins when one member of the couple begins to feel the need for more attention or reassurance from the other. This leads to more bids for connection by the one member. They may begin to call and text frequently, consistently ask for reassurance, or nag their partner for more time together. The other partner counters by a corresponding lack of or lessening of attention. This greater distancing effort is then met by greater and more significant bids for connection by the first member. As the first partner texts more and more often, the second partner returns the texts less and less promptly or often. This continues the cycle, and so forth and so on in an endless dance.

This is also where the concept of the *Principle of Least Interest* comes into play (Waller, 1938). This principle states that within any given relationship, the person who is more emotionally invested in the relationship runs the risk of being exploited by the person who is less emotionally involved. For example, if the relationship is more important to Ted than it is to Zoey, he may pretend to be interested in her interests or spend time with her when he really should be at work. This imbalance of investment in relationship can cause distress within the couple, particularly if the imbalance is great. Waller posited that if this sort of imbalanced relationship continued on to become a marriage, then it would more than likely be an unhealthy one. Recent research (Sprecher, Meeckle, & Felmlee, 2006) shows that this principle is still germane; those who reported a lesser interest in their couple relationship reported feeling more control or power over the relationship. Furthermore, couples who reported a more even balance of interest and emotional investment reported higher relationship satisfaction (Sprecher, Meeckle, & Felmlee, 2006).

OVERFUNCTIONER–UNDERFUNCTIONER. This dance happens when one member of the couple begins to over function in the relationship. This is a reciprocal pattern. When one partner begins to do more than is their part in the relationship on a regular basis (such as initiating conversations or scheduling dates), it often encourages the other to do less. Similarly, if one partner begins to do less, the other one can start doing more, in order to maintain the balance. This can easily happen within an older sister-younger brother pairing, or a pairing where one member grew up in a substance abusing family. Alfred Adler first introduced Birth Order Theory (1927) into the social science arena. This theory posits that our birth order can affect how we do relationships throughout our lives. Though, of course, this is not true for every older sister and younger brother, in general older sisters tend to want to take charge of things and in general younger brothers will let them. This pattern in and of itself is not necessarily a recipe for overfunctioning–underfunctioning dances, but it can lay the groundwork. The trouble begins when the imbalance continues and becomes destructive to the relationship, with one partner feeling put upon and resentful and the other one feeling bossed around and powerless. This particular dance is also frequently found when one or both members of a couple either grew up in an alcoholic or substance abusing family or when one partner is abusing substances. If one partner begins to abuse substances, it will likely impair their participation in domestic, social, and occupational activities (Moos, Brennan, Schutte, & Moos, 2010; National Institute on Alcohol Abuse and Alcoholism, 2001). This partner's underfunctioning can lead to the other partner's overfunctioning. Taken to an extreme, overfunctioning can look very much like co-dependence, where one partner is preoccupied with meeting the other person's needs and controlling their behavior (Beatty, 1986).

POSITIVE PARTNER–NEGATIVE PARTNER. This dance has much in common with the two earlier mentioned dances, in that one partner's behavior is highly dependent on the other's behavior and reaction. However, this particular dance can lead to a more toxic relationship. In this dance one partner becomes more positive and optimistic about everything, perhaps most specifically about the relationship itself, while the other partner becomes more and more negative. In order to counteract this, the positive partner continues to try to cheer up the negative partner, which can have the effect of irritating the negative partner, who then reacts even more negatively, and so on. It is as though each holds firmly to the particular lens they started out with, and neither can give in or see the other person's side. This dance continues until one or the other simply gives up. Generally speaking, the more positive partner is the one who gives up, thus fulfilling the prophecy of the more negative partner.

CYCLES OF VIOLENCE: COMMON COUPLE VIOLENCE VS. INTIMATE TERRORISM. The most dangerous dances of intimacy are those that lead to violence. There are two types of Intimate Partner Violence (IPV): common couple violence and intimate terrorism (Johnson, 1995; Graham-Kevan & Archer, 2003). Though both involve the use of violence within the couple relationship, common couple violence is considered to occur more frequently and to be less dangerous than intimate terrorism. One example of a cycle of violence is given in Text box on the next page.

Common Couple Violence

BY ANONYMOUS

When my high school sweetheart and I were married, we were young and there were already signs of abusiveness in our three-year relationship. Our first months of marriage were spent in Biloxi while my husband completed his military training. This is when the physical abuse began. At 18 years old this was the first time I had been away from my family for any period of time. I was too frightened to leave our apartment by myself and the Air Force had warned the soldiers to stay off the Hurricane Camille buried debris-riddled Gulf coast just outside our window. We were still teenagers adjusting to life with one another on a daily basis and marriage was far different from dating. I truly expected a fairy-tale ending. With no place to go, being young, alone, and afraid, I remember sitting on the floor of the apartment closet sobbing after getting beaten.

The physical abuse would continue for the next five years about every couple of weeks to a month apart. The verbal abuse included yelling, blaming, name-calling, threats, and belittling while the physical abuse involved primarily hitting and pushing me. In addition, my husband would often go on a rampage breaking furniture and other household items. After he got out of the service we returned to the Midwest to try farming with my father. Once I was shoved into the gutter while we were milking the cows and had to be taken to the emergency room for stitches to my head. Cleaning me up before taking me to the ER was the only time I remember my husband apologizing for his actions. No doubt he did not want me to explain how I really got hurt, which I explained away to ER staff as slipping and falling in the barn. Later my parents were, also, shoved and knocked down by my husband as they tried to intervene on my behalf. It was at this point that I filed for divorce.

Early on when we were still in the service and living in Arizona, I sought out counseling. When needed most, I had a bad experience with a counselor who only wanted to talk about himself. It wasn't until several years into our marriage that I connected with a counselor who gave me the encouragement and confidence I needed. My parents and sisters were supportive but knew the decision to leave the marriage had to be my own. In my mind there were different levels of abuse and I could see improvements. Before the divorce was finalized, my husband and I met to discuss our relationship. As we still loved one another, my husband agreed to counseling for his temper as a stipulation to ending the divorce and for the most part it has been effective. Over six years after we were married we started our family with a joint commitment to stop the cycle of violence that had existed in both our families. Overall, we have been successful in this endeavor through our attendance in effective parenting courses, the positive support of professionals, family, and friends, and our continual struggle for improved communication.

With the domestic abuse in our relationship there were power and control issues my husband faced and we've danced the Abuser/Victim dance. I believe my husband learned violence, using his anger and temper to exert his way, plus poor, ineffective communications skills from his father. His parents, also, exemplified intimate relationships in a negative way with an abusive marriage. My husband has a very traditional image of what an intimate relationship involves and is most comfortable when he's the dominant partner. Although my husband is no longer physically violent, he often still possesses a quick temper, a low self-esteem, and occasionally uses verbal abuse. I used to be submissive, partially due to the cultural standards of my youth, my fear of being abused, and a history of violence in my mother's family of origin and a part of my childhood involving my mother's physical violence with two adopted brothers. By not challenging my husband, I avoided confrontation and possible abuse. Because I was shy in my younger years, I learned by not speaking up I felt safe and did not risk being incorrect or feeling embarrassment. As I have grown and become stronger, I am much more outspoken and independent. Because we love one another and because my parents modeled how our commitments should not be broken, we have remained a couple. I feel our relationship is not always totally equal, but we have come a long way in the past four decades.

Common couple violence, while not a mark of a healthy relationship, is defined as violence that occurs when stresses and conflict get out of hand; and which does not escalate in frequency or severity over time (Johnson, 1995; Graham-Kevan & Archer, 2003; Christensen, 2007). Both genders initiate common couple violence, and the other partner will frequently reciprocate (Whitaker, Haileyesus, Swahn, & Saltzman, 2007). In straight couples, women are more likely to initiate physical aggression in this context, but they are also more likely to sustain injuries (Archer, 2000), in part because they tend to be smaller in size and strength than their male partners. For couples in this cycle, tension and arguments are especially problematic. When there is less stress and during the space in between arguments, the couple may feel fulfilled in their relationship. When tensions build, the couple does not have the skills to address them in a healthy way. Feeling stressed and unheard, one partner may begin by damaging property, or breaking dishes or punching a wall. This can build up to hitting, slapping, punching, or throwing something at the other. The other may retaliate in kind.

Intimate terrorism, on the other hand, is violence that escalates over time, and results from a need to control the partner (Johnson, 1995). It is most often perpetrated by a man against a woman. Those who practice intimate terrorism need to feel in control and powerful, and will do almost anything to win back a partner who tries to leave. The partner may believe that violence is normal in a relationship and/or may believe there are no alternative ways to deal with conflict (Rondon, 2003). Intimate terrorism can lead to the death of the victimized partner, or to the victim killing the abuser in order to protect themselves (Roberts, 2006). If you suspect that you are in a relationship and your partner is terrorizing you, please call a Crisis Center or hotline (e.g., the national, confidential hotline: 1-800-799-7233) for help. Every state and most counties have specific resources to help you. This is the most dangerous type of IPV and you deserve help and support in order to get out safely. If you are concerned that your own behavior might be unhealthy, there are confidential hotlines where you can talk with someone about your concerns and possible ways to get help.

SO REALLY—HOW DO WE CHANGE?

It can be easy to fall into one of these dances, but we find ourselves wishing for a way to have more balance and connection. How do we change our patterns? Just as in a dance, each partner has a responsibility and what one partner does will affect the other partner. Although it may seem impossible sometimes, it is important to realize that we are the ones who are responsible for change (Jacobson, 1996). We cannot force our partner to change; therefore, it is up to us to take the

first steps. There are several concrete steps you can take to begin to make a change in your relationship if you find you are engaging in one or more of the dances that we have described thus far.

The first thing to do is to slow down and think. Consider what you want to get out of being in relationship. Is this relationship what you had hoped it could be? If not, why not? What is your part in the dance? When considering this issue, resist the tendency to polarize, for example: he "always" does this or she "never" does that. Using "I" language, even when thinking to yourself, will help you express your feelings in a straightforward and honest fashion. This will help clarify the dynamics in your relationship.

If it seems that it would be a good idea to change some of your behaviors, consider the fact that it might be a positive change for you individually as well as a good idea for your relationship. If we change our behaviors only to try to satisfy our partner or to try to encourage our partner to change, this can lead to resentments. If we change for our own good, then whether or not this particular relationship works out, we will be becoming more clear and intentional. These efforts at self-improvement will continue to help you with all of your relationships going forward.

Next, try out the change! Staying with our metaphor of the dance, we know that in order to change a dance pattern, we must start by learning a new step. You do not have to commit to this forever, just take it out for a test drive. For example, if you have been feeling resentful that you always plan the dates, you might decide to pull back for two weeks. You might decide to spend time together casually, but not plan any specific activities during this time. Remember your reflective and expressive skills; they can support your efforts. As we have already discussed, it is important to clearly communicate our intentions and motivations to our partner. For example, you might say, "I love you, and I am very invested in making this work. When I think about some of the patterns that are derailing us, one of these is that I am most often taking over in our planning and life-logistics. This week I am going to try pulling back from doing that so much . . ." For two weeks, you can see if this new pattern is more comfortable, and then decide if you want to continue it, add to it, or try something else.

Once we've initiated this new step, we must watch how our partners respond. Our partners can respond in a number of ways. For example, my partner may try to force me into the previous, known routine, or s/he may respond with a new step of his or her own. Usually our partners will push back at the beginning, but if you hold fast to your new behavior then the chances grow that your partner will change in response. Again, it is important that we clearly communicate our intentions and our motivations throughout this process. Our partners will then have an opportunity to be more involved in and understanding of the pattern changes within the relationship.

Eventually, our partner must also be open to change in order for our patterns to be coordinated. Sometimes, it can take just a few days for partners to initiate, respond to, and adjust their dance. In other cases, it may take weeks, months, or years. In some cases, it may never happen. We may find our partners are unwilling or unable to change their steps in the pattern no matter how long we have been trying to change the dance. We must then decide if the relationship is still desirable, knowing the current dance is going to continue. It can be hard to know how long to continue trying a new step, or how to judge our partners' reactions. It takes constant re-evaluation and, as will be explained below, communication.

And all the while, communicate directly. As much as we might like to be, we are not mind-readers. There is no way for someone to know what you need or wish for unless you speak up. For example, even if you feel that you are always more optimistic about the relationship than your partner, she may have no idea that you are discouraged by her comments. She may feel that she is doing her part to keep the relationship grounded. For example, state your feelings clearly: "I feel discouraged when you say 'nobody stays together for very long.' If there are times when you feel hopeful about our relationship, could you tell me?" Clear statements like these can help our partner know what we are looking for. We often think our partners know exactly what we are thinking, but they may have a very different idea. Communicating directly makes it more likely that we can create and nourish the patterns we hope for.

If you practice speaking up regularly and work on your communication together as a couple, you will be much more likely to create the relationship that you want than if you just wait quietly, or act in a passive-aggressive fashion. It is especially important to communicate about that which is good in the relationship. There is substantial research that tells us, for example, that we need to say five positive statements to our loved one for each negative statement in order to build a good relationship (Gottman, 1999). Begin by letting your partner know what you like about them and what they are doing in the relationship. Compliments like, "I really appreciate that you keep me company while I run my errands" or "I love the way you hold my hand when we're out together" are always recommended. This will both help them feel appreciated and help them know to keep doing those behaviors.

CONCLUSION: WHEN INTIMACY DANCES WORK

Intimacy dances work best when they support both people, and when this support is not at the expense of either person's sense of self. The unhealthy dances of intimacy, such as pursuer–distancer or overfunctioner–underfunctioner, exist because someone in the relationship is sacrificing self to the relationship. This is unsustainable in the end. It may work for a while, but just like Marnie and Charlie in the vignette that began this chapter, it is the mark of an unbalanced relationship. Each of the partners in a couple is important as an individual; because of this we need to bring and honor our whole selves within our relationships. Healthy dances of intimacy allow us to communicate our needs clearly and maintain boundaries that help us feel close to our partner and thrive within our relationship.

REFERENCES

Adler, A. (1927). *Understanding human nature*. Garden City, NY: Garden City Publishers.

Archer, J. (2000). Sex differences in aggression between heterosexual partners: A meta-analytic review. *Psychological Bulletin, 126*(5), 651–680. doi:10.1037/0033-2909.126.5.651

Babcock, J. C., Costa, D. M., Green, C. E., & Eckhardt, C. I. (2004). What situations induce intimate partner violence? A reliability and validity study of the Proximal Antecedents to Violent Episodes (PAVE) Scale. *Journal of Family Psychology, 18*, 433–442. doi:10.1037/0893-3200.18.3.433

Barelds, D. P., & Dijkstra, P. (2006). Reactive, anxious and possessive forms of jealousy and their relation to relationship quality among heterosexuals and homosexuals. *Journal of Homosexuality, 51*(3), 183–198. doi:10.1300/J082v51n03_09

Bay, J. M., & Ragan, G. A. (2000). Improving students' mathematical communication and connections using the classic game of "Telephone." *Mathematics Teaching In the Middle School, 5*(8), 486–489. Retrieved from http://www.nctm.org/publications/mtms.aspx

Bowen, M. (2004). *Family therapy in clinical practice.* Lanham, MD: Rowman and Littlefield.

Buunk, B. P. (1997). Personality, birth order and attachment styles as related to various types of jealousy. *Personality and Individual Differences, 23*(6), 997–1006. doi:10.1016/S0191-8869(97)00136-0

Beatty, M. (1986). *Codependent no more.* Center City, MN: Hazelden.

Bryan, L., Fitzpatrick, J., Crawford, D., & Fischer, J. (2001). The role of network support and interference in women's perception of romantic friend, and parental relationships. *Sex Roles, 45*(7), 481–499. doi:10.1023/A:1014858613924

Charles, R. (2001). Is there any empirical support for Bowen's concepts of differentiation of self. *American Journal of Family Therapy, 29(4),* 279–292. doi:10.1080/01926180126498

Chiang, L. H. (1993, October). Beyond the Language: Native Americans' Nonverbal Communication. Paper presented at the Annual Meeting of the *Midwest Association of Teachers of Educational Psychology,* Anderson, IN. (ERIC Document Reproduction Service No. ED 368540).

Collins, N. L., & Read, S. J. (1990). Adult attachment, working models, and relationship quality in dating couples. *Journal of Personality and Social Psychology, 58*(4), 644–663. doi:10.1037/0022-3514.58.4.644

Covey, S. (2004). 7 habits of highly effective people: Powerful lessons in personal change. New York: Simon & Schuster.

Doherty, W., Colangelo, N., & Hovander, D. (1991). The family FIRO model: A modest proposal for organizing family treatment. *Journal of Marital and Family Therapy, 10*(1), 19–29. doi:10.1111/j.1752-0606.1984.tb00562.x

Fournier, B., Brassard, A., & Shaver, P. R. (2011). Adult attachment and male aggression in couple relationships: The demand-withdraw communication pattern and relationship satisfaction as mediators. *Journal Of Interpersonal Violence, 26*(10), 1982–2003. doi:10.1177/0886260510372930

Fox, S. (2008). China's changing culture and etiquette. *China Business Review, 35*(4), 48–51.

Gottman, J. (1999). *The Marriage Clinic: A scientifically based marital therapy.* New York: W. W. Norton & Co.

Graham-Kevan, N., & Archer, J. (2003). Intimate terrorism and common couple violence: A test of Johnson's predictions in four British samples. *Journal of Interpersonal Violence, 18*(11), 1247–1270. doi:10.1177/0886260503256656

Jacobson, N. (1996). *Integrative couples therapy: Promoting acceptance and change.* New York: W.W. Norton.

Johnson, M. P. (1995). Intimate terrorism and common couple violence: Two forms of violence against women. *Journal of Marriage and the Family, 57,* 283–294. doi:10.2307/353683

Lerner, H. (1998). *The dance of intimacy.* New York: Harper & Row.

McKie, L. & Cunningham-Burley, S. (Eds.). (2005). *Families in society: Boundaries and relationships.* Bristol, UK: Policy Press.

Mendenhall, T. M. (2013, Spring). *Dances of Intimacy lecture,* University of Minnesota, Minneapolis, MN.

Moos, R. H., Brennan, P. L., Schutte, K. K., & Moos, B. S. (2010). Spouses of older adults with late-life drinking problems: Health, family, and social functioning. *Journal of Studies on Alcohol & Drugs, 71*(4), 506–514. Retrieved from: http://www.jsad.com/jsad/article/Spouses_of_Older_Adults_With_LateLife_Drinking_Problems_Health_Family_a/4466.html

National Institute on Alcohol Abuse and Alcoholism. (2001). Economic perspectives in alcoholism research. *Alcohol Alert, 51,* 1–4. Retrieved from: http://pubs.niaaa.nih.gov/publications/aa51.htm

Obst, L. (Producer). *How to lose a guy in ten days* [Motion picture]. Los Angeles: Paramount Pictures.

Olson, D. H. (2000). Circumplex Model of marital and family systems. *Journal of Family Therapy, 22*(2), 144–167. doi:10.1111/1467-6427.00144

Olson, D. H., Olson-Sigg, A., & Larson, P. J. (2008). *The couple checkup: Find your relationship strengths.* Nashville, TN: Thomas Nelson.

Perez, J. (Writer), & Dunham, L. (Director). (2012). Hard Being Easy [Television series episode]. In Dunham L., Apatow, J., & Konner, J (Producers), *Girls.* New York: HBO.

Roberts, A. (2006). Classification typology and assessment of five levels of woman battering. *Journal of Family Violence, 21*(8), 521–527. doi:10.1007/s10896-006-9044-0

Rondon, M. B. (2003). From Marianism to terrorism: The many faces of violence against women in Latin America. *Archives of Women's Mental Health, 6*(3), 157–163. doi:10.1007/s00737-003-0169-3

Rosenberger, E. W. (2011). Where I end and you begin: The role of boundaries in college student relationships. *About Campus, 16*(4), 11–19. doi:10.1002/abc.20069

Sharpsteen, D. J., & Kirkpatrick, L. A. (1997). Romantic jealousy and adult romantic attachment. *Journal of Personality and Social Psychology, 72*(3), 627–640. doi:10.1037/0022-3514.72.3.627

Simmons, R. A., Gordon, P. C., & Chambless, D. L. (2005). Pronouns in marital interaction: What do "You" and "I" say about marital health?. *Psychological Science, 16*(12), 932–936. doi:10.1111/j.1467-9280.2005.01639.x

Simpson, L. E., Doss, B. D., Wheeler, J. & Christensen, A. (2007). Relationship violence among couples seeking therapy: Common couple violence or battering? *Journal of Marital and Family Therapy, 3(2),* 270–283. doi:10.1111/j.1752-0606.2007.00021.x

Sprecher, S., Schmeeckle, M., & Felmlee, D. (2006). The principle of least interest. *Journal of Family Issues, 37(9),* 1255–1280. doi:10.1177/0192513X06289215

Titelman, P. (2008). *Triangles: Bowen family theories systems perspectives.* New York: Haworth Press.

Waller, W. (1938). *The family: A dynamic interpretation.* New York: Gordon.

Whitaker, D. J., Haileyesus, T., Swahn, M., & Saltzman, L. S. (2007). Differences in frequency of violence and reported injury between relationships with reciprocal and nonreciprocal intimate partner violence. *American Journal of Public Health, 97*(5), 941–947. doi:10.2105/AJPH.2005.079020.

Wilson, L. L., Roloff, M. E., & Carey, C. M. (1998). Boundary rules: Factors that inhibit expressing concerns about another's romantic relationship. *Communication Research, 25*(6), 618. doi:10.1177/009365098025006003

7

Boundaries: Where I End and You Begin

Elizabeth J. Plowman, Ph.D.
Damir Utrzan, M.S.
Department of Family Social Science
University of Minnesota

LEARNING OBJECTIVES

- Define what interpersonal boundaries are and how they function
- Articulate the differences between rigid, balanced, and enmeshed couples
- Articulate "basic rights" in intimate relationships
- Understand how leading theories and frameworks conceptualize boundaries and interpersonal change over time

Case Vignette

Kari's first yoga class was an adventure, to say the least. After two years of her best friend Laura begging her to come with, she finally bit the bullet and decided to give it a try. Before they went, she jokingly told Laura, "I'll be fine, but if they touch me, I am going to freak out!" Always a bit shy, Kari was nervous because she did not know what to expect and did not want to feel stupid doing the wrong thing. When she lay down in child's pose at the beginning of class, the friendly instructor asked students to raise their hands if they did not want hands-on adjustments. Kari peeked out from her mat and was surprised to see no hands in the air. She was too hesitant to be the only one in class with her hand raised, so she bravely returned her forehead to the mat and hoped for the best.

About 30 minutes passed and the class was half over. Although Kari was still getting used to seeing her classmates and reflection in the mirrors scattered around the room, she started feeling a bit more comfortable as she relaxed into the focus on her breath. She could even see why people started liking it! Then came the awkward pose. Kari sat down into her seated "chair" and followed the step-by-step instructions of the teacher. Out of nowhere, the instructor came behind

her and adjusted Kari's hips. Kari tensed immediately and felt her heart rate increase. She felt uncomfortable, especially because she didn't notice this happening to anyone else. She sat lower, trying to do the pose perfectly so the instructor would not come back to her. Luckily, she did not return. After one more sun salutation, however, the instructor was back. She not only repositioned Kari's hips, but pulled her own pelvis against Kari's backside and sat them both lower. Kari turned

© CREATISTA, 2014. Used under license from Shutterstock, Inc.

Corresponding Author: Elizabeth J. Plowman, Ph.D., University of Minnesota; Department of Family Social Science; 1985 Buford Ave.; 290 McNeal Hall; Saint Paul, MN 55108. E-mail: eplowman@umn.edu.

tomato red and held her breath. She felt completely upset. After less than a minute, it was over—but Kari did not find the story nearly as funny as Laura did when she told their girlfriends over dinner that night. Here she had opened herself up to a new experience, only to feel violated.

WHAT ARE BOUNDARIES?

Why didn't Laura feel the same way as Kari did when she was adjusted by the yoga instructor? Kari had a difficult time with yoga class for several reasons, but most of the underlying causes of her discomfort could be explained by personal boundaries. Boundaries are the invisible lines we draw to differentiate ourselves from others—they are the rules we set in social contexts to let others in or keep them out (Minuchin, 1974). Boundaries help us balance intimacy and autonomy in our relationships (Jacobvitz, Hazen, Curran, & Hitchens, 2004); they allow us to more easily differentiate between "I" and "We." Individuals can have closed boundaries (like Kari), which means they like to protect themselves from intimate others, acquaintances, and strangers—or they can have open boundaries (like Laura), which means they easily let people into to their inner physical and emotional worlds. Some researchers (e.g., Hartmann, Harrison, & Zborowski, 2001) also refer to boundaries as thick (i.e., well defined) or thin (i.e., permeable and poorly defined).

In Kari's first yoga class, boundaries about physical space are highlighted; however, boundaries also refer to psychological or emotional thresholds. In this chapter, we discuss why it is so important to understand one's own boundaries, consider the potential advantages and disadvantages of different boundary constellations, and evaluate the role of boundaries in promoting change in couple or family systems. After we develop a common understanding of what boundaries are and what they do, we'll take a glimpse at how couple and family therapists put concepts like boundaries into practice by learning about Family Systems Theory and the Circumplex Model of Marital and Family Systems.

Building and Maintaining Intimacy: A Balance of Setting Limits and Opening Up

Every individual and every relationship has boundaries, and boundaries vary across different relationships. For example, you might be very open with a sibling but closed with your coworkers. You might be open with strangers, but have a hard time opening up to your immediate family. "Intra" is equivalent to "within"—so, *intrapersonal boundaries* are the boundaries we have within ourselves. They represent self-directed thoughts that govern how we perceive and behave in the social world. Intrapersonal boundaries dictate how easily a person will open up to you, what s/he expects you to share about yourself, and how s/he decides to trust you. See Chapter 8 where we learn about the Johari's window to explore our authentic selves. How do you think the size of the four windowpanes might vary between individuals with open versus closed boundaries? If you guessed that people with open boundaries are more likely to have larger public selves, you're headed in the right direction.

> *Intrapersonal boundaries* determine how much an individual is willing to let others in and let others influence his or her own beliefs, feelings, or self-concept.

Interpersonal boundaries, or relational boundaries, are boundaries between people or groups of people. In couples and families, interpersonal boundaries determine where one person ends and the other begins. They dictate how and what individuals communicate with each other, which partner does what in the relationship, and the degree of connection between partners. Boundaries influence our ability to build and maintain intimacy with others, so it's important to understand how our ideas of self and other influence boundaries.

> *Interpersonal boundaries* are the boundaries that govern relationships. They allow individuals in couples or families to connect with one another by sharing their own thoughts and emotions.

In this chapter, we consider couples as possessing diffused (i.e., undifferentiated), balanced, or rigid (i.e., very distinguished) interpersonal boundaries. Kari's relationship with her boyfriend, Jeremy, is built upon balanced boundaries. She and Jeremy can easily shift between being alone and being together. They have some privacy as individuals, but they also share important private details with each other. They have invisible rules about what is okay and not okay when it comes to influencing each other. For example, Kari is okay with Jeremy staying out all night without calling as long as he sends her a text, and Jeremy feels comfortable texting Kari (no matter what his friends say) because he does not feel controlled by her. In relationships with balanced boundaries, couples are able to value and maintain independence and intimacy. They feel comfortable being apart, but they like being close, too. Kari is an "I" because she has her own sense of self, but she is also happy to be part of a "we" because an important aspect of her identity is her role as a partner.

Boundaries are important in intimate relationships for several reasons. First, they influence our communication patterns and support roles in a couple or family. Second, they define our potential for intimacy. When individuals are too open with one another, they can violate each other's sense of trust or make each other feel uncomfortable, which can ultimately limit a partner's willingness to share. When individuals are too closed with one another, an invisible wall is built, preventing people from opening up and being their authentic selves. Third, boundaries in our families-of-origin and cultures can influence our development as individuals and our expectations about intimate relationships (Jacobvitz et al., 2004). Finally, when it comes to understanding how couples and families can break unhealthy patterns when they are "stuck," boundaries and related concepts offer a great starting point for couples and therapists to promote positive change.

Before we begin exploring theories and therapeutic interventions, let's take another look at Kari's yoga experience and see why boundaries are essential for building and maintaining intimacy.

Crossing a Line: Boundary Violations

During yoga class, Kari experienced something known as a *boundary violation*. Boundary violations happen when other individuals, knowingly or unknowingly, trespass the limits of our personal space. Boundary violations are important keys to how we interact with others; a person can almost always tell (immediately) when his/her boundaries have been infringed upon. It might be the feeling of wanting to put up a wall or disengage from the interaction. Even boundary violators can usually understand what has happened when they go a bit too far. Have you (or someone you know) ever made a comment and thought, *"Oops! It was too soon to say that,"* or *"Wow, I really wish I had said something different"*? If you have been in this situation, chances are that you have violated someone's boundaries. The reason that boundary violations are typically so easy to identify is because boundaries have an important purpose for our selves and our relationships: they keep us safe.

© Edw., 2014. Used under license from Shutterstock, Inc.

Boundary violations are perceived as minor or severe based on the openness of our own interpersonal and intrapersonal boundaries. Have you ever met someone, and within the first hour of knowing him or her, s/he was sharing intimate details of their life? Your companion likely had open boundaries, and violating these boundaries would be more difficult than violating the boundaries of someone who thinks it's odd to talk about intimate personal details or relationships with others. Another example of how we perceive (and potentially violate) boundaries happens early in romantic relationships. Boundaries might come to the surface when a new potential partner asks you, *"When will you be home tonight? Will you call me as soon as you get home?"* and something about the question just feels off. When our boundaries are violated, we can feel uncomfortable or controlled. It feels like someone has intruded our personal space because the balance of connection and autonomy is threatened (Lavy, Mikulincer, Shaver, & Gillath, 2009). People with very open boundaries, on the other hand, might feel rejected and want to withdraw when someone does not respond to their questions or behavior with equal openness or intensity.

> ### Considering Boundaries in Your Relationships
>
> Think about your current or past intimate relationship or a relationship with a close friend:
>
> - How did you know when it was the right time to begin sharing private details about yourself?
> - Did you and your partner bring different ideas of what was "okay" and "not okay" in the relationship in terms of influencing one another?
> - If so, how did you negotiate these differences?
> - Did you ever feel like your boundaries were violated? If so, how did you become aware of this?
> - Were you and your partner able to talk about the boundary violation?

Boundary violations might occur when boundaries have not yet been negotiated in a relationship. Boundary negotiations can happen at any time in a relationship, but when a couple starts out, each partner brings their own boundaries to the relationship from his or her family of origin and early dating experiences, and the pair must determine what types of boundaries will work for both parties. In some relationships, boundary negotiations might be direct discussions, and in others, boundaries might be negotiated subtly and indirectly.

© oliveromg, 2014. Used under license from Shutterstock, Inc.

Black and White? Or Blurry and Gray?

Boundaries exist to keep us healthy in our relationships with others (Rosenberg, 2013). It might seem counterintuitive that a bit of distance from our love object is actually good for a relationship, but boundaries make it clear whose feelings belong to which partner. When you own your feelings and take responsibility for them, you have the maturity to take responsibility for your own emotional responses and behaviors. People with healthy boundaries have self-differentiation; it means that they are capable of being a partner in a relationship, but not being defined solely by that relationship. It is clear where "self" and "other" begins. See Figure 1 for an illustration of what boundaries might look like in a romantic relationship.

Boundaries are functional for individuals and relationships. They protect us from feeling intense loneliness when temporarily separated from our significant others (Rosenberg, 2013). For example, in healthy relationships, partners are able to spend time together *and* apart. Perhaps partners prefer to spend time together, but after the initial honeymoon phase has worn off, partners should feel comfortable and healthy doing some activities independently. Boundaries also protect us from feeling overly guilty when our partners' feelings are hurt. When individuals do not set boundaries, it is unclear whose behaviors and feelings belong to whom. Imagine the relationship of Jenna and Tanya:

> Although Jenna and Tanya have been dating for two years and still truly enjoy each other's company, they have spent every weekend together since they have met. Jenna can hardly even remember what it feels like to sleep alone in her bed. Last week, Tanya went out of town for a job interview and was gone for two days. Jenna was very supportive because she knew they would be moving together; she wanted Tanya to get the job so they could start planning. She decided to set aside their night apart for time with her best friend. When she and her friend, Matt, got together, they ended up talking the whole night about Tanya's and Jenna's future. Matt was so supportive! But Tanya tried calling Jenna a few times that night—the night before her big interview. When she could not get ahold of Jenna, Tanya became an emotional wreck. Where was she? How could she do this to her? Was she out with another girl? When Jenna finally called her back (after 15 calls), Tanya was so angry she could barely speak. She told her

FIGURE 1 Visual Comparison of the Boundaries of Rigid, Balanced, and Enmeshed Couples

A couple with rigid boundaries

When both partners have closed boundaries (left), self-differentiation is obvious, noted in this image by the thick borders of the colorful circles and the distance between the individuals. Each individual possesses his or her own thoughts, feelings, and behaviors and is influenced by the other's actions or emotions very little (or not at all).

When both partners have balanced boundaries (right), some mutual influence occurs as noted by a small degree of overlap between the circles. Partners with balanced boundaries let others in, but also maintain a sense of self. Notice how the circles remain distinct, but are slightly transparent. Both members of the pair are able to function, whether together or apart.

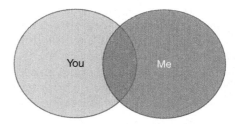

A couple with balanced boundaries

A couple with diffused boundaries

When both partners have diffused boundaries (left), the couple's connectedness is strong, but their sense of individuality is weak. Partners' feelings are shared rather than separate, and it is difficult for individuals to determine whose feelings belong to whom. The couple has a difficult time handling separateness.

she was rethinking their entire relationship because she was so hurt. She ended up sleeping only two hours that night, and completely underperformed at the interview. When Tanya came home, Jenna was waiting for her on the couch. She immediately asked how the interview went. Tanya did not want to be angry at Jenna anymore, but she told her exactly how she felt, "I'm sorry, Jenna, but I feel like it's all your fault. If you had just answered the phone or even texted me, I would have been able to fall asleep and concentrate better. I was sitting there all night thinking you were out with another girl, or partying with your friends without telling me. I can't believe you did that to me." Jenna felt terrible. Because she and Tanya were so inseparable, both emotionally and physically, she felt enormous guilt and responsibility for her failed interview and frustration. When she told Matt about it, he said, "Jenna, I know you love her, but this is not healthy. Of course it makes sense that Tanya is upset with you, but to blame you for the entire interview? The last time I checked, Tanya is an adult. She can *choose* how she responds to a missed phone call. Not to mention, you can choose to tell her to accept responsibility for making the assumptions she makes."

Matt had some great insight when it comes to the concept of boundaries. With boundaries comes responsibility for one's own self, emotions, and experience. If a person is responsible for his or her own well-being, it means that it is his or her own responsibility to share expectations about behavior in relationships. We cannot blame someone else for our feelings or make assumptions about what s/he might be doing without acknowledging our own role in the situation. And we cannot expect others to read our minds; we are accountable for communicating our needs and desires in our relationships. If those needs or desires are not fulfilled, it is our responsibility—and ours alone—to determine if we want to try to change the relationship, dissolve the relationship, or continue in a relationship where our needs are unmet. Tanya may have had good intentions, and Jenna may have rightfully felt bad about what happened—but in both cases, these individuals would have had an easier time using this argument as an opportunity to develop deeper intimacy if they could differentiate their feelings from one another's.

You might already be thinking to yourself, "*Great. So now I know why it's important to set boundaries, but what happens when both intimate partners have very open boundaries? Isn't that okay?*" or, "*What if my partner and I both want to have firm boundaries? We're more comfortable being apart— but we're still together. Is that bad?*" Like so many other situations in social science, the answer is, "it depends."

In Chapters 11 and 18, we highlight the importance of the $1 + 1 = 2$ equation when it comes to intimate relationships. This equation refers to two people bringing their whole selves to a relationship to create a healthy couple comprised of two individuals. Instead of two poles leaning against one another for stability as one unit (and sure to fall under pressure), two whole selves are like two pillars standing up straight—a strong foundation for a healthy relationship. When partners are so close that their selves become diffused, however, the equation is $1 + 1 = 1$, and their relationship is considered as *enmeshed* or *controlling* (Jacobvitz et al., 2004; Minuchin, 1974). Couples in enmeshed relationships often do not even recognize how unhealthy the relationship is or could become. On the other hand, when one or both partners have *very rigid* boundaries and the couple has a hard time connecting with one another, intimacy is prevented (or extinguished) because the connection is not there to fan the fire.

We noted above that boundary violations are usually easy for humans to identify. Sometimes, however, violations are more subtle or frequent. When boundary violations occur frequently in the same relationship or family, they are considered *boundary disturbances*. These disturbances might seem invisible to family member "insiders" because the family's identity is rooted in these patterns. Some examples of boundary disturbances include family alliances, parentification, psychological control, and neglect. *Family alliances* occur when two family members (often across generations) are so engaged with one another that they shut the remaining family members out (Jacobvitz et al., 2004); a common example of this is a parent being so close with a child that the other parent disengages emotionally because s/he feels disinvited from the family. *Coalitions* are similar to family alliances but are more often within a generation. *Parentification* occurs when a child is expected to act at the developmental level of his or her parent (Jacobvitz et al., 2004); the child's boundaries are violated because s/he is too young to understand what is happening while being forced to "grow up" and assume more responsibility than what is appropriate. *Psychological control* occurs when one or more family members manipulate other individuals by making decisions for them, undermining their autonomy or authority. *Neglect* occurs when individuals' basic needs (psychological or physical) are ignored by another, sending the message that the individual is not worthy of time or attention. In all of these cases, individuals' interpersonal boundaries and rights to emotional safety are violated. We conceptualize boundary disturbances as being longer-term boundary violations; because individuals are so "stuck" in the family relationship or for other potential reasons (e.g., child not being developmentally mature enough to understand), they often do not recognize how entrenched the family is in these unhealthy patterns. When individuals live and breathe these situations every day, it is difficult to understand how their individual well-being and family identity is affected by boundary disturbances.

So, let's revisit the question: are imbalanced boundaries okay if a couple is okay with them? Research and theory suggest that typically, boundary disturbances are not healthy (Jacobvitz et al., 2004; Jacobvitz, Riggs, & Johnson, 1999; Minuchin, 1974)—especially imbalances in parent–child relationships. However, this research has been conducted mostly on middle class, white families in the United States—which means it was nested in a Western culture that values independence above interdependence. Researchers' and participants' lenses matter when it comes to conducting culturally competent research, so the next generation of studies should include more diverse participants and use more culturally sensitive measures. However, even if a couple is accepting of its imbalanced boundary constellation, it is important to realize that there are also some universal rules for human needs that should never be crossed. See Table 1 for a list of basic human rights in a relationship that can help us—as partners or practitioners—identify appropriate and inappropriate behavior.

TABLE 1   Basic Rights in Intimate Relationships (adapted from Evans, 1992)

- The right to expect good will from the other
- The right to emotional support
- The right to be heard by the other and to be responded to with courtesy
- The right to have your own view, even if your partner has a different view
- The right to have your feelings and experience acknowledged as real
- The right to receive a sincere apology for any jokes you may find offensive
- The right to clear and informative answers to questions that concern what is legitimately your business
- The right to live free from accusation and blame
- The right to live free from criticism and judgment
- The right to have your work and your interests spoken of with respect
- The right to encouragement
- The right to live free from emotional and physical threats
- The right to live free from angry outbursts and rage
- The right to be called by no name that devalues you
- The right to be respectfully asked rather than ordered

As we continue in this chapter, we will discuss the role of culture in boundaries. In the meantime, it's important to know that every culture has different perspectives about boundaries. In some cultures, it's functional to have an enmeshed family unit—and in others, enmeshment is the first sign that something is wrong. It's all about finding what is right for your relationship and your family, but it's essential to realize that society's opinion of what is healthy or not healthy matters, too. In the next section, we'll examine how theories use the concept of boundaries to better understand families. Whether for therapists, researchers, or family members themselves, these theories can help promote positive change in couples and families by examining connectedness and distance in relationships.

THE RIPPLE EFFECT OF RELATIONSHIP PONDS: FAMILY SYSTEMS THEORY

Although therapists and researchers use many different models and theories in an attempt to better understand interpersonal relationships, Family Systems Theory (FST) (Whitchurch & Constantine, 2009) is perhaps the most widely recognized. The gentle bounce of a stone across the smooth surface of a pond creates seemingly endless waves that are analogous to FST, which examines how individuals' emotions, cognitions, and behaviors influence couple and

> *Family* is a place where children are raised and nurtured – but also where cultural values, roles, and rules are transmitted.

family dynamics. As an interdisciplinary domain of general systems theory, FST is unique because it views the family (or couple) as a complex emotional system with the primary function to join together each individual in the creation of one unit (Rosenblatt, 1994). In FST, boundaries help explain the psychological closeness or distance between individuals.

According the central tenant of FST, the family is a system in which each member has a role to play and rules to respect. This means that members of the family system are expected to respond to each other in specific ways according to the roles and rules they together have established (Whitchurch & Constantine, 2009). Remember how we mentioned above that boundaries are invisible rules that dictate how people interact? Family Systems Theory sees these rules and roles of individuals in the family as threads that keep a family connected. While you might be thinking that roles and rules sound boring and rigid, FST is actually one of the more dynamic and modern perspectives in the social sciences. The value of this theory lies in its two assumptions. First, a family must be understood as a whole rather than through individual members alone. Second, humans are unique from other species because of their capability to reflect on their own behaviors and thoughts; this is called *self-reflexivity*. These tenets lead FST to being one of the few perspectives that not only honors, but also embraces, the uniqueness of human life.

According to FST, families are made up *subsystems*, which are smaller groups of people within the larger system. In other words, a married couple is a subsystem within a family. The membership and roles within these smaller subsystems, in turn, influence individual behaviors and interactions among family members (Vetere, 2001). Over time, these behaviors eventually become patterns, and these patterns shape family identity and contribute to the formation of interpersonal boundaries. To illuminate the intricacies of boundaries, rules, and the ripple effects on individuals in the family, we will examine a case study about the Babić family.

CASE STUDY

Denis Babić is a 24-year-old man who currently lives with his Serbian-Orthodox father, Anto, who is 57 years old, and Bosnian-Muslim mother, Lejla, who is 50 years old. The Babić family lives in a small apartment on the South Side of Chicago and has faced many challenges over the years. Denis and Lejla fled the war in Bosnia and Herzegovina in 1992 while Anto remained behind for required service in the military. Denis and Lejla were granted temporary asylum in Germany and lived there with Lejla's oldest brother for two years. After two years of mandatory military service, Anto deserted his position without proper documentation and paid smugglers $5,000 to traffic him into Germany. The family was reunited and received extended asylum. They were deported shortly thereafter, and ultimately immigrated to the United States where they were granted permanent asylum and hoped to apply for citizenship. In the United States, the family did not have a regular income because neither Anto nor Lejla could speak English (which made securing and sustaining employment difficult). Their situation worsened as Anto began to drink every night and physically abused Denis while Lejla helplessly watched. The physical abuse affected Denis' behavior adversely. Although no formal psychiatric evaluation was made, it was obvious that Anto had developed posttraumatic stress disorder during the war. When confronted about his frequent drinking and child abuse, Anto became emotional, stating that alcohol dulled horrific memories of war. The abuse ended shortly after Anto began attending weekly support meetings with other men who had also developed posttraumatic stress disorder. Despite the frequent drinking and abuse, there was a strong family bond. As a result of the physical abuse, however, Denis struggled in forming and maintaining intimate relationships, and still does to this day.

The concept of boundaries is essential to FST because boundaries define who is included within and excluded from the family, and because they can promote family members' well-being in times of stress. It is easier for families to implement boundaries when individuals recognize that they influence others' behaviors and situations as much as others influence their behaviors and the situation. The Babić family's postwar adjustment, and subsequent attempts to maintain a semi-normal level of functioning amidst chaos, illustrates the importance of boundaries in times of stress. Aside from the typical stressors associated with fleeing an armed conflict, individuals and families are often unprepared for the impending culture shock of a new place. During stressful situations (e.g., war, natural disaster), parents set boundaries by imposing limits that clearly communicate to children, *"I care about you and I want you to feel safe and secure after what we just experienced."*

In the case of the Babićs, Lejla and Anto used self-reflexivity to set a boundary between their family and the outside world. This enabled them to make themselves and their own behaviors the focus of examination (Whitchurch & Constantine, 2009). Escaping an armed conflict is an example of setting boundaries around the family to better ensure the safety of its members and the future opportunities of its child(ren). This decision to flee is also an example of FST's notion of emergent properties. *Emergent properties* are behaviors that result from interactions between individuals within a family unit. As a whole, however, the couple was able to effectively organize and execute an escape plan by dividing responsibilities, such as gathering belongings, preparing their child, locating a destination, and planning a safe passage. Another example of emergent properties is Denis' inability to connect with others, which resulted from the violation of his personal boundaries through the abuse he sustained.

How Family Impacts Individual Development

There is little debate that family impacts individual development and, subsequently, functioning and well-being. Our families of origin are powerful in determining our ability to open ourselves to others. When families experience severe stress or atypical situations, their environments can influence rules and roles within the home. Stress can have lasting impact on individual and family well-being through its influence on boundaries.

Family is analogous to branches on a tree because all members grow in different directions while sharing the same roots.

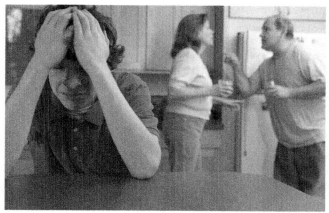

TRAUMA. Although traumatic experiences are not deterministic in the sense of painting a dark future as a result of a dark past, the aftermath of traumatic situations contribute to difficulties implementing or maintaining interpersonal boundaries in families or couples. For example, in the Babić family, Denis' exposure to family violence influenced the formation of his future interpersonal relationships. As a child, Denis was exposed to his father's binge drinking in response to stressful situations. When his father became frustrated with situations that he perceived to be outside of his control, he exerted control on his spouse and child through physical violence. Because children do not always understand the intricacies of family relationships and do not know that abusive behaviors are never justified, Denis felt personal responsibility for his father's drinking and abusive acts. This interaction began to disturb boundaries in the parent–child relationship; Denis was forced to grow up ahead of his developmental age and could not disentangle his father's feelings from his own. Although the situation gradually improved after Anto sought treatment and attended a psychotherapeutic support group, Denis could not understand the sudden change and continued to feel personally responsible. Denis' boundaries were generalized outside of abusive behaviors in the family to all interpersonal relationships.

As a shy adolescent, Denis became withdrawn and quiet. The situation at home improved and abusive behaviors ceased but the resulting anxiety remained. Denis longed for connection and an interpersonal relationship with others, but he felt anxious and incompetent. This was perhaps the first time in his life that the boundary confusion from childhood became apparent in his relationships with others. In instances where someone reached out in friendship, Denis felt overwhelmed and determined not to let that relationship deteriorate. Unfortunately, the very behaviors intended to maintain relationships led to their deterioration, because others felt overwhelmed and unable to cope. This led to a vicious cycle that reinforced Denis' withdrawn nature. His inherent belief that it was unsafe to trust others became a self-fulfilling prophecy, influencing how he interacted in social settings. Denis' behaviors within interpersonal relationships, however, are no fault of his own. Instead, they are a byproduct of atypical, stressful childhood experiences associated with fleeing, collapsed family boundaries, and an attempt to make the best of a seemingly hopeless situation. Denis' example illustrates the complexity of boundaries; in one instance, boundary disturbances have hurt him, but in another instance, too rigid boundaries promoted necessary distance between him and others.

DIVERSITY AND CULTURE. In order to better understand the impact of family and cultural values on individual development, it is important to present a cohesive definition of culture. *Culture* encompasses beliefs and traditions that unify a group of people through various means that are not limited to geographic location. In this sense, cultural connectedness can span as distant as a faraway country or as near as the neighborhood in which one presently lives.

As refugees and immigrants, the Babićs had to overcome seemingly insurmountable obstacles. Although their story is only one example of how obstacles can influence diverse families—and there are many others (e.g., urban gang violence, homelessness), it highlights the importance of understanding sociocultural factors' impact on families. It is difficult to clearly define identity because "humans draw theirs in part, from simultaneous membership in a multitude of contexts that include ethnicity, race, religion class, geographic region, economic status, education, sexual preference, and age" (Breunlin, Pinsof, & Russell, 2011, p. 304). This list of identity characteristics is not complete but it alludes to the complexity of family diversity.

Talking about diversity can provide insight into the lived experiences of individuals. The truth is that minorities, regardless of type, do not want to be pitied or empowered. The feat of empowering in and of itself implies that minorities hold a lower position on the social hierarchy. If helping professions do not recognize that, they will inadvertently perpetuate a self-feeding cycle in which clients do not feel safe and are unable to explore the meaning of their own authenticity. The safe environment provided by other men who developed posttraumatic stress disorder during the armed conflict is what allowed Anto Babić to come to terms with events that stole several years of his life. Feeling connected through others who share similar experiences is important because individuals and families find "strength, comfort, and guidance in adversity through connections with their cultural and religious traditions" (Walsh, 2003, p. 9). While no cultural perspectives or traditions are alike, the driving want to learn about sociocultural differences and similarities is essential to understanding and growing in relationships.

Clinical Applications

Equipped now with a stronger grasp of the importance of interpersonal boundaries in individual and family life, we will address the clinical applications of assessing interpersonal boundaries using specific relational tools.

GENOGRAMS. At its fundamental level, a genogram is similar to a family tree. However, it encompasses considerably more information by graphically representing emotional relationships, individual characteristics, boundaries, and patterns across generations. Initially developed by McGoldrick and Gerson (1980) and revised several times with the newest edition by McGoldrick, Gerson, and Petry (2008), this is a unique and helpful tool for assessing both individual and family functioning. A genogram of the Babić family is presented in Figure 2.

FIGURE 2 Genogram of the Babić Family

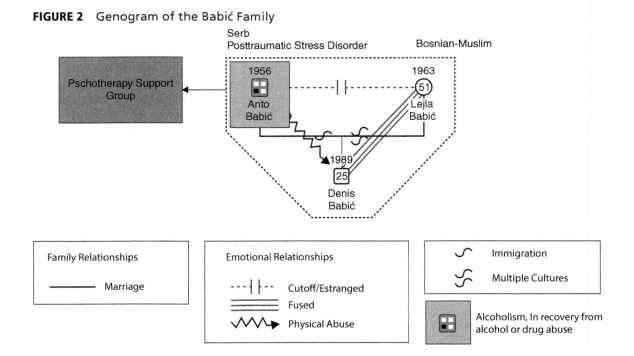

Systemic Therapy Inventory of Change

SYSTEMIC THERAPY INVENTORY OF CHANGE (STIC)
While therapists and scientists alike have traditionally utilized, and sometimes struggled with, tools such as the Genogram and the Couple and Family Map to graphically represent interpersonal relationships, empirically based measures such as the Systemic Therapy Inventory of Change (STIC) are changing how previously vague concepts are defined and evaluated. The Systemic Therapy Inventory of Change, or STIC, is part of the Dan J. Epstein Foundation Center for Psychotherapy Change at the Family Institute at Northwestern University. As a new tool in measuring change in the therapeutic context, the STIC is breaking down previously unimaginable barriers. The second author was trained in marriage and family therapy at the Family Institute and has direct experience with the clinical application of this measure and its scientific contribution. While the impact of past experiences on interpersonal relationships has been greatly discussed by the scientific community, the STIC is the first assessment tool of its kind that examines potential problems as a result of family of origin influences.

In an attempt to better understand the process of change in the therapeutic setting, the STIC was developed as an empirically validated and interactive measure to track clients' personal histories and emotional states (Pinsof et al., 2009). After measuring changes between therapy sessions in individual adult, couple, and child functioning, it analyzes the data and provides instant feedback to the therapist, graduate student, and his or her clinical supervisor. This, subsequently, allows the treatment team to make better-informed choices. As measures are collected from the clients, they are displayed on an easy to read graph before being made available for review. In an increasingly integrated healthcare setting, the STIC ensures that clients' well-being is the first priority of the treatment team and that graduate students in therapy receive the most innovative training available. These are some of the powerful tools that illuminate hidden emotional patterns and provide an opportunity to observe the previously unobservable.

Interpersonal or relationship problems are typically not attributed to any single individual, which was previously suggested in the discussion of FST. In a therapeutic context, however, interpersonal problems are referred to as *presenting problems* and the client is referred to as the *identified patient*. While it is outside of the scope of this chapter to address medical family therapy, the rapid integration of mental and emotional health within physical health services in the United States refers to clients as "patients." In the Babić family, Anto is considered the identified patient because his symptoms of posttraumatic stress disorder are resulting in the abuse of alcohol, and as a result, they impact the family's interpersonal functioning.

The square around Anto signifies his status as the identified patient. The dashed line denotes the nuclear family unit, which typically consists of members that are in contact with each other on a daily basis. It is important to note that cultural values, which play an important role in the Babić family, may suggest that extended family members live with the nuclear family. This should not be taken as a dysfunctional arrangement because contextual factors are subjective. It is also important to note that modern measures are being developed to replace the genogram in assessing interpersonal relationships.

Although emotional relationships are complex and may at times appear contradictory when individuals are face-to-face, examining the Babić family genogram simplifies the situation and makes it easier for clinicians to understand issues impacting the family members' relationships. It illustrates that Anto and Lejla have been estranged from one another, which is not atypical of couples who experience life-changing and traumatic events. As a result of this estrangement, Anto and Lejla formed a triangular relationship with their child. According to the concept of triangulation, couples will introduce a third individual to stabilize their relationship. This had an adverse effect on Denis because he felt trapped between parents whom he loved equally, despite suffering physical violence at his father's hands. It also illustrates another FST concept, *homeostasis*, because Denis is simultaneously fused, having an overly close relationship or friendship with his mother, and distance from his father. Homeostasis refers to a human desire to maintain an equilibrium or status quo; Denis' behavior and unhealthy pattern is an attempt to maintain homeostasis, stability of any sort, and a semi-normal level of functioning amidst chaos.

Circumplex Model of Marital and Family Systems

Often, larger theories pave the way to more specific frameworks that elaborate more specifically upon particular concepts. The Circumplex Model of Marital and Family Systems (Olson, Russell, &

Sprenkle, 1989) is a conceptual model grounded in FST that gives us a fresh way to think about how rules, roles, connection, and distance fit into our relationships. Although the Circumplex Model applies to either couples or larger family units, we will discuss intimate couple relationships in the following sections.

The Circumplex Model (also highlighted in Chapter 18) focuses specifically on three relational constructs: cohesion (closeness), flexibility (adaptability), and communication. *Cohesion* is highly related to the concept of boundaries. When couples are connected to one another, they feel emotional closeness and intimacy. Connection refers to the amount of emotional bonding in the relationship; it is the "glue" that holds the partners together in a couple. Partners can be disconnected, which means they are essentially living separate lives, or they can be overly connected, which means their energy in life is defined primarily by their relationship. Whereas disconnected couples may be more likely to have partners who possess closed boundaries, overly connected couples may be comprised of individuals with diffused boundaries. Somewhere in between, there are couples who balance being together with being apart (both in terms of time and emotion). Partners in these relationships have fulfilling parts of their lives that come from their individual identities, but they also find personal fulfillment in their relationships.

Flexibility refers to the couple's ability to adapt to changes in its environment or development. In some couples, there are strict roles and rules. These couples know exactly what is expected of each partner, and one partner tends to be in more control than the other. They know who makes the decisions, who the leader is, and who is responsible for which part of the relationship. In other couples, "rules" are absent. Life can sometimes seem chaotic and sometimes important things slip through the cracks. No one is the leader, and the couple tends to act on impulse. Somewhere in between, there are couples who share roles. They have some stability and structure, but also some fluidity. When they need to change, they can figure it out and adapt. This flexibility allows them to "roll with the punches."

The Circumplex Model suggests that clinicians, researchers, and individuals can consider cohesion and flexibility visually in a Couple and Family Map (see Figure 3). This map places cohesion

FIGURE 3 Circumplex Model of Marital and Family Systems

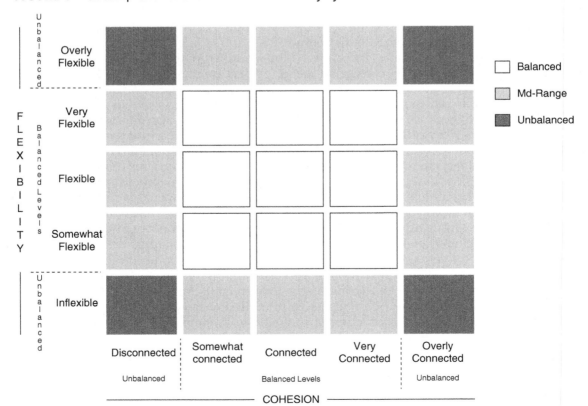

and flexibility on two opposing dimensions; it shows that couples can possess high, low, or balanced levels of closeness and flexibility. Olson and Gorall (2003) hypothesize that relationship systems in the balanced areas of the map tend to exhibit greater functioning. When partners are able to balance separateness and togetherness, they find energy within and outside the relationship. When they can maintain stable but flexible roles in their relationship, they are more likely to weather the storms and challenges that life throws at them. Although couples in the unbalanced regions are sometimes able to navigate their own paths and make the "extreme" area work for them (which is more likely when their imbalance is congruent with their culture's values), for the typical couple, balanced regions are predictive of more positive outcomes.

The third component of this model, *communication*, is considered a facilitating factor in relationships. This means that when interpersonal communication is clear and effective, couples are able to better navigate the (potentially stressful) developmental changes in their relationship by adapting levels of closeness and flexibility to their needs. In Chapter 6, we discuss communication more thoroughly, but for now, it is important to recognize that communication is not only about speaking. The Circumplex Model maintains that communication is such a positive force for couples because it involves expressive skills (e.g., speaking, sharing), receptive skills (e.g., listening, respect), and reflexive skills (e.g., ability to reflect and improve our communication clarity). Couples who are balanced in closeness and flexibility are more likely to evidence effective communication when compared to unbalanced couples.

USING THE COUPLE AND FAMILY MAP TO TRACK A COUPLE'S DEVELOPMENT. As a relationship develops, partners establish an initial particular amount of connection, flexibility, and communication; however, what a relationship looks like initially along these three domains is rarely the same as what it looks like later in time. Couples can move to different locations on the map in different stages of their relationship. For example, some couples may start out very connected as they court one another, but pull away a bit as the relationship evolves. Also, environmental stress (like financial issues, mental health struggles, caregiving, etc.) can push couples toward more unbalanced ways of functioning, at least temporarily.

© Blend Images, 2014. Used under license from Shutterstock, Inc.

Let's consider Angie and Rob. When they started dating, this couple was together all of the time. They scheduled their semesters so they could take electives together, spent every weekend night in one or the other's apartment, and even went on each other's family vacations—all of this, after only a few months of dating. They were very connected, and their relationship was flexible as they tested out different ways of interacting with one another (see "A" in Figure 4). Once they decided to move in together and Rob started graduate school, things changed. Angie started spending a little more time with her girlfriends because Rob had to study; she was ecstatic about finally being done with studying and wanted to enjoy her social life and her first regular paycheck. They still spent weekends together and called each other "honey" and "sweetie," but they had a little more personal privacy and did not share every intimate detail of their days with one another. Because of the stress associated with grad school, they had a bit more rigidity in their interactions. Angie was usually the one to check with Rob to see if he was available, and not the other way around. Rob became the decision-maker in the relationship, and when Angie made decisions about how they would spend their mutual time, little arguments came to the surface. At this point, Rob and Angie were in a somewhat flexible/somewhat connected relationship (see "B" in Figure 4).

After finishing his program, Rob was able to relax and share leadership in his relationship with Angie. Instead of following Rob's career opportunity across the country, Angie and Rob decided together that they would build a home in Chicago, where Angie had received a great job offer. Weekends once again became mutual decisions; one weekend they would do what Angie wanted, and the next, Rob would decide. Their relationship was more equitable when it came to roles and rules.

FIGURE 4 Angie and Rob's Couple and Family Map During Initial Courtship (A), Rob Attending Graduate School (B), and A New Beginning in Chicago (C) (Adapted from Olson & Gorall, 2003)

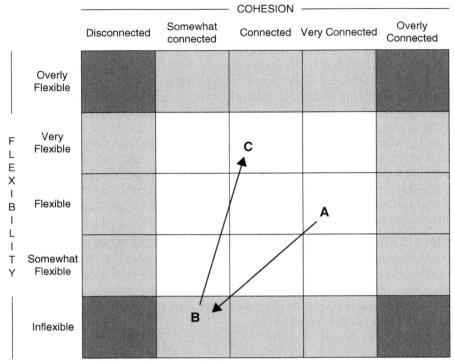

Because of their move to a new city, they simultaneously felt more and less connected. They felt more connected because they were able to lean on each other in a way they had not experienced before, but less connected because they were experiencing their own challenges as individuals. After a few months in Chicago, both Angie and Rob would have agreed their relationship could be classified as connected/very flexible (see "C" in Figure 4). Over time, they realized this was the sweet spot in their relationship—the type of balance that made them both feel they could function as individuals and as partners.

You may be wondering, "How did Rob and Angie navigate their way through the difficult times when they were less connected and more rigid in their interactions?" Like we noted earlier when discussing the Circumplex Model, communication was key. Angie was able to be patient with Rob being the decision-maker during his time in graduate school because they were able to talk about why they needed that kind of (temporary) structure in their relationship. Angie knew it was not a permanent change, and she was able to empathically put herself in Rob's shoes because he told her how stressed he was. She knew that it would only make him feel more anxious if she put up barriers around spending time together when he was balancing teaching two courses, taking three classes, and working part-time. Because Rob reminded her often that he appreciated her willingness to compromise, it was easier for Angie to be supportive; their relationship survived this visit to an unbalanced region of the map because they listened to each other and shared their honest feelings. Rob's ability to communicate clearly helped Angie maintain her balanced interpersonal boundaries with him, rather than closing herself off to Rob and becoming distant.

Boundaries and Therapeutic Change

Now that we understand why boundaries are so important for relationships, and can consider ways to use theoretical concepts to examine our own patterns, let's consider how we can put these ideas to work in our own lives.

Definitions of Change

It is difficult to define the concept of change because individual perspectives vary tremendously. Although there are multiple subjective truths—and we all certainly have our own individual ideas—Carl Rogers (1956) described change as a modification: "In the personality structure of the individual, at both surface and deeper levels, in a direction which therapists would agree means greater integration, less internal conflict, more energy utilizable for effective living; change in behavior away from behaviors generally regarded as immature and toward behaviors regarded as mature" (p. 95). This comprehensive definition provides an overarching framework for understanding change as a process.

Although Rogers and Murray Bowen (the "father" of FST) differed in their theoretical perspectives, it seems that their understandings of change were similar. Rogers' inference of change and integration is analogous to Bowen's (Harris, 1996) concept of differentiation, which he defined as the ability to think during an argument, instead of being emotional. Bowen was adamant that being undifferentiated leads to the formation of a false self, a lack of authenticity, and emotional reactivity. Rogers, on the other hand, emphasized the importance of developing a sense of self through a safe environment (Cepeda, Davenport, & Donna, 2006).

So, *how* do people change? How do we know *what* to change? And what *is* change, anyway? The definition of change is elusive because individual experiences and perspectives are so different. However, in order to facilitate change, it is important to understand its meaning and implications for individuals and families. The idea of change relates to the concept of boundaries because improving interpersonal relationships often consists of renegotiation preexisting boundaries, which may at times be very difficult.

According to noted Austrian psychiatrist and Holocaust survivor Viktor Frankl (2006), people are forced to change themselves when they are unable to change their situations. This may seem sentimental, but change is actually an incredibly ambiguous process on a linear continuum that spans from pre-contemplation to determination, and finally, action (Prochaska & DiClemente, 1983). Since Breunlin (1999) noted that individuals and families might experience a variety of constraints that prevent them from changing, we define *change* as a process that depends on recognizing problems, becoming determined to reach a goal, and acting upon it. Often, change occurs after multiple failed attempts at resolving the problem.

As one of the most influential figures in the development of FST, Murray Bowen (1994) proposed that anxiety is an inevitable part of life that stimulates togetherness, and as a result, promotes change. Whether the anxiety is physiological or psychological (and sometimes psychological anxiety can even evolve into physiological symptoms), the desire for reduction and elimination of discomfort is an evolutionary response to fear. When individuals experience discomfort, it is in their best interest to reduce it by any means possible. Humans desire and seek change in response to problems, but they do not always make adaptive choices about *how* to change, for a variety of reasons.

It would seem rational to assume that the act of changing is in fact the byproduct of a desire to improve one's situation. However, human beings have a unique ability to circumvent pain and suffering, preferring (consciously or subconsciously) to remain in their current, undesired situation. In addition, "pain and suffering" can take various definitions and must not be confined to extremes. For example, even the slightest discomfort of obsessively checking one's mobile device in anticipation of a text message can be attributed to a smaller degree of suffering. In this example, what keeps a person who obsessively holds and checks his/her mobile device from changing? We all know people who will continue obsess about their texts, and we also know those who can finally put their phones away (after they gain insights that connect suffering to mobile devices). It is up to us, as individuals, to use self-reflexivity to determine our needs, capacities, and readiness for change in a given situation.

Change is complex; there is no single method of assuring a successful transformation, and no single path towards a "right" answer. Sometimes change feels like our only available choice, and sometimes it feels impossible. Individuals can use the concepts of boundaries to determine what types of behaviors are adaptive or maladaptive. For individuals and couples hoping to make changes or improvements in their relationships, it might be most effective to start small. For example, if you can recognize that your own intrapersonal and interpersonal boundaries in your relationship are too open, it might help to set limits. Tell your partner what your goals are so s/he can get on board to support you (and also so s/he is not surprised by your behavior). Tell him or her, for example, that you want begin spending one night apart per week, or that you want to try only talking on the phone once per day instead of once per hour. Set a condition (e.g., if it does not feel right after five days, we will try something else) so you know there is a safety net if you need it. And refer occasionally to the basic rights of a relationship (see Table 1) to ensure you're not beginning to trespass on your partner's limits or freedoms.

If you're on the other side of the fence, and you are hoping your too open or too closed partner will be motivated to change, be sure to have an honest conversation with him or her regarding your needs. Engage in self-reflexivity as a couple and examine your respective boundaries as a pair. Keep in mind that your partner's "set point" is exactly how s/he is behaving, so phrases like, *"I need more space"* or *"I don't feel like I know you"* can come across as harsh. Try to put yourself in his or her shoes and think about what you would want to hear. Then, suggest small steps if your partner agrees to the goal; tell him or her that you are in this as a team and you want to make sure s/he feels safe, too. For example, if your partner's boundaries are so closed that it makes you feel uncomfortable, you might ask, *"When do you feel connected to me? How could we help you feel more comfortable being part of a 'we' while still maintaining your privacy?"* If your partner is more of the open type, you might say, *"I care about you a lot, but I think we might have a different perception about how to balance 'I' and 'we' in our relationship. I feel healthier—and more excited to share with you—when I have some of my own things going on. I want you to feel safe and loved by me, but I think we will have a stronger foundation if we also take time for ourselves as individuals."*

CONCLUSION

In this chapter, we explored why and how boundaries are crucial aspects of healthy intimate relationships. Whether open or closed, rigid or flexible, it is up to you to consider how your interpersonal and intrapersonal boundaries influence your intimate relationships and make a conscious decision to change them or maintain them. We also examined the theoretical contributions of FST, genograms, and the Circumplex Model. Our hope is that these perspectives can help guide you in making changes within your relationships that are both healthy and enriching.

As we close, we leave you with some final questions to help improve your awareness of your own interpersonal boundaries:

- How easy is it for me to let people in?
- Do I ever make others uncomfortable by sharing too much or not enough?
- Does this seem to be more about myself, or more about them?
- If I could draw a line of personal space around by body, how large would it be?
- What does this mean for how I interact with others?
- How much is too much for me to share?
- How do I know when I have shared too much?
- What does it mean for me to cross a line?
- How can I tell if I have trespassed someone's boundaries?

There are no right or wrong answers to these questions. Your answers may vary greatly from your partner's—and that is okay. Acknowledge that your boundaries impact your ability to develop and maintain intimacy. Set, and adjust, them intentionally. Be thoughtful about how you move forward with your partner and intimate others, knowing that your boundaries communicate to where you end and they begin.

REFERENCES

Bowen, M. (1994). *Family therapy in clinical practice.* Lanham, MD: Rowman & Littlefield.

Breunlin, D. C. (1999). Toward a theory of constraints. *Journal of Marital and Family Therapy, 25*(3), 365–382. doi:10.1111/j.1752-0606.1999.tb00254.x

Breunlin, D. C., Pinsof, W., & Russell, W. P. (2011). Integrative-problem centered metaframeworks therapy I: Core concepts and hypothesizing. *Family Process, 50*(3), 293–313. doi:10.1111/j.1545-5300.2011.01362.x

Cepeda, L., & Davenport, D. (2006). Person-centered therapy and solution-focused brief therapy: An integration of present and future awareness. *Psychotherapy: Theory, Research, Practice, Training, 43* (1), 1–12. doi:10.1037/0033-3204.43.1.1

Evans, P. (1992). *The verbally abusive relationship: How to recognize it and how to respond.* Holbrook, MA: Bob Adams.

Frankl, V. (2006). *Man's search for meaning.* Boston, MA: Beacon Press.

Harris, S. M. (1996). Bowen and symbolic experiential family therapy theories: Strange bedfellows or isomorphs of life? *Journal of Family Psychotherapy, 7*(3), 39–60. doi:10.1300/J085V07N03_04

Hartmann, E., Harrison, R., & Zborowski, M. (2001). Boundaries in the mind: Past research and future directions. *North American Journal of Psychology, 3*(3), 347–368. Retrieved from http://connection.ebscohost.com/c/articles/6542709/boundaries-mind-past-research-future-directions

Jacobvitz, D., Hazen, N., Curran, M., & Hitchens, K. (2004). Observations of early triadic family interactions: Boundary disturbances in the family predict symptoms of depression, anxiety, and attention-deficit/hyperactivity disorder in middle childhood. *Development and Psychopathology, 16* (3), 577–592. doi:10.1017/S0954579404004675

Jacobvitz, D., Riggs, S., & Johnson, E. (1999). Cross-sex and same-sex family alliances. In N.D. Chase (Ed.), *Burdened children: Theory, research, and treatment of parentification* (pp. 34–55). Thousand Oaks, CA: Sage.

Kerr, M.E. (1998). Bowen theory and evolutionary theory. *Family Systems, 4*(2), 119–179.

Lavy, S., Mikulincer, M., Shaver, P. R., & Gillath, O. (2009). Intrusiveness in romantic relationships: A cross-cultural perspective on imbalances between proximity and autonomy. *Journal of Social and Personal Relationships, 26,* 989–1008. doi:10.1177/0265407509347934

McGoldrick, M., & Gerson, R. (1986). *Genograms in family assessment.* New York: W.W. Norton & Co.

McGoldrick, M., Gerson, R., & Petry, S. (2008). *Genograms: Assessment and intervention.* New York: W.W. Norton & Co.

Minuchin, S. (1974). *Families and family therapy.* Cambridge, MA: Harvard University Press.

Olson, D. H., & Gorall, D. M. (2003). Circumplex model of marital and family systems. In F. Walsh (Ed.) *Normal Family Processes* (3rd Edition) (pp. 514–547). New York: Guilford Press.

Olson, D. H., Russell, C. S., & Sprenkle, D. H. (1989). *Circumplex model: Systemic assessment and treatment of families.* New York: Haworth Press.

Pinsof, W. M., Zinbarg, R. E., Lebow, J. L., Knobloch-Fedders, L. M., Durbin, E., Chambers, A., et al. (2009). Laying the foundation for progress research in family, couple, and individual therapy: The development and psychometric features of the initial systemic therapy inventory of change. *Psychotherapy Research, 19,* 143–156. doi:0.1080/10503300802669973

Prochaska, J. O., & DiClemente, C. C. (1983). Stages and processes of self-change of smoking: Toward an integrative model of change. *Journal of Consulting and Clinical Psychology, 51*(3), Retrieved from http://www.ncbi.nlm.nih.gov/pubmed/6863699.

Rogers, C. R. (1956). The necessary and sufficient conditions of therapeutic personality change. *Journal of Consulting Psychology, 21,* 95–103. Retrieved from http://psycnet.apa.org.ezp1.lib.umn.edu/journals/ccp/21/2/95.pdf

Rosenberg, R. (2013). *The human magnet syndrome: Why we love people who hurt us.* Eau Claire, WI: PESI Publishing & Media.

Rosenblatt, P.C. (1994). *Metaphors of family systems theory: Toward new constructions.* New York: Guilford Press.

Vetere, A. (2001). Structural family therapy. *Child and Adolescent Mental Health, 6*(3), 133–139.

Walsh, F. (2003). Family resilience: A framework for clinical practice. *Family Process, 42*(1), 1–18. doi:10.1111/j.1545-5300.2003.00001.x

Whitchurch, G. G., & Constantine, L. L. (2009). Systems theory. In P. G. Boss, W. J. Doherty, R. LaRossa, W. R. Schumm, & S. K. Steinments (Eds.). *Sourcebook of family theories and methods: A contextual approach* (pp. 325–352). New York: Springer.

8
Authenticity in Intimate Relationships

Anna I. Bohlinger, Ph.D., LAMFT
Elizabeth J. Plowman, Ph.D.,
Tai J. Mendenhall, Ph.D., LMFT
Department of Family Social Science
University of Minnesota

LEARNING OBJECTIVES

- Understand the complimentary roles that authenticity and vulnerability play in forming and maintaining relationships
- Understand the role of authenticity in creating social change
- Identify the risks of authenticity and vulnerability
- Apply the Johari Window to develop insight into how we can be more authentic with loved ones and each other

Case Vignette: Why Didn't You Call?

Justin and Anne were introduced to each other by mutual friends who thought they would be a great match. Anne had never been in a serious relationship before, but had begun talking about wanting one over the previous several months. Justin was on the heels of a painful breakup. He wasn't looking for anybody to date at the time, but found himself drawn to Anne as the two talked more and more at parties and other social events.

It wasn't long before Justin and Anne were an "item." They fell in love quickly (too quickly, some thought). Every morning, the two would send each other "good morning" texts, and every evening they would send "good night" texts (even if they had just finished talking on the phone). Within a couple of weeks' time, they were talking about getting married someday and what their kids' names would be. They talked about their school, their future career plans and steps, their hopes, and their dreams.

One day, Anne left town for a few days for her job. She told Justin that she'd call him that evening when she returned to her hotel, and estimated that this would likely be around 9:00 p.m. She didn't call. At 9:15 p.m., Justin called Anne and left her a message. At 9:20, he sent her a text. By 10:00 p.m., he

© Christian Draghici, 2014. Used under license from Shutterstock, Inc.

Corresponding Author: Anna I. Bohlinger, Ph.D., LAMFT; University of Minnesota; Department of Family Social Science; 1985 Buford Ave.; 290 McNeal Hall; Saint Paul, MN 55108. E-mail: abohling@umn.edu.

had left three more messages and sent half a dozen more texts, this time asking her to please call him because he was worried about her safety. By the time Anne got back to her hotel and checked her phone—around 10:30 p.m.—she had 27 missed calls and more than a dozen texts. When she called Justin, he was drunk and almost unintelligible. They spoke for less than a minute.

At 4:00 a.m., Justin woke up and immediately—desperately—checked his phone. He called Anne, and angrily asked her why she hadn't called him. Anne, also angry, countered that she had called. Justin could not remember this, which made Anne even angrier. They quickly escalated as Justin asked why she didn't call at 9:00 p.m., and as Anne tried to explain—again and again—that her 9:00 p.m. estimate was exactly that: an estimate. While she was sorry that she completed work later than the thought, she could not understand why all of this was such a big deal.

"But how could you possibly not call or text me when you knew you'd be late? Couldn't you just have said something like, 'I'm running late; I'll call you later.'?" Justin whined. "Am I really so unimportant to you that you couldn't do that? All you had to do was spend 30 seconds typing a text! If your boss didn't like it, you could have done it in the bathroom or something—unless your boss won't let you go to the bathroom!"

"Justin, I didn't understand that this was such an issue for you! You knew that I was working!" Anne countered. "And what the hell is wrong with you? 27 missed calls? A thousand texts? And what's up with being drunk? Is that something you do now? Drink all by yourself at home when your girlfriend is—apparently—ignoring you?"

"Are you really my girlfriend? It doesn't really feel like you love me, anyway!"

"Then I'm not," Anne said, and hung up.

INTRODUCTION

Intimacy in relationships requires authenticity. *Authenticity* is defined as consciously bringing your whole self into intimate relationships. It entails the willingness to listen to and consider feedback from others and incorporate feedback as appropriate. The feedback process is essential for intimate relationships because it is how individuals grow on their own and with each other. By the end of this chapter, you will become more familiar with authenticity and vulnerability, understand how authenticity can affect social change, and become familiar with the Johari Window, a tool that can help people understand more about themselves for increasing authenticity.

WHAT DO WE KNOW?

In order to be authentic with your own self, a working definition of the self is necessary. The concept of self is one that has been explored in philosophy, spiritual traditions, and psychology. Other traditions have defined the self as the object of consciousness (Butterworth, 1995; Gallagher, 2000; Reddy, 2003), the sum of the id, ego, and superego (Freud, 1961), and the combination of one's conscious and unconscious shadows (Jung, 1958). This textbook defines the *self* as the sum of all that you are and all that you can be; your total potential. The self is both known and unknown and we will examine that specifically in a later part of chapter. In addition to including what is known and unknown about ourselves, the self also encapsulates things we love, are proud of and enjoy about ourselves, and the things that we feel guilt or shame about, try to avoid, and sometimes even hate.

Part of being in an intimate relationship is being willing to openly and honestly share our whole selves with others. The process of being authentic with others can feel extremely vulnerable because it requires sharing not only the things that we like about ourselves, but also the things that we dislike. *Vulnerability* is defined as the state of being vulnerable or exposed. When we are vulnerable with others, we may risk rejection, sharing what we believe even when it is unpopular, or having others we care about change their opinions about us for the worse. When referencing authenticity, the metaphor of being exposed may be a powerful one. While we're not talking about literal nakedness here (although that may be a part of vulnerability in intimate relationships), when we take the risk to be emotionally exposed, we show our secret selves to others and in doing so, build connections that relationships are sustained by.

Authenticity and the Research

Perhaps you are wondering what research says about authenticity. Most of the research on authenticity has been at the associational level; we know that people who are more authentic tend to have better emotional health and relationships (Wenzel & Lucas-Thompson, 2012), but we don't necessarily know that authenticity causes improved relationships. As we will discuss below, individuals who are more authentic tend to also have stronger emotional health, be better able to cope with disappointment or failure, and be more proficient at setting achievable goals. Authentic individuals also tend to have longer lasting and happier intimate and platonic relationships.

To investigate these associations further, three researchers have examined authenticity and vulnerability in important and different ways: Brene Brown, Kirsten Neff, and Joseph Luft. These researchers have examined why vulnerability is necessary for relationships, how to enable our own vulnerability and finally, how to promote our own authenticity.

Brene Brown is a sociologist who studies vulnerability. As a qualitative researcher, she interviewed many women about their experiences with shame and vulnerability. She found that the main difference between people that experience vulnerability as being laden with shame and guilt, and those that experience vulnerability while still believing that they are worthy of love and support, was that the people that believe that they are worthy enter into life "wholeheartedly." They experienced the same discomfort about imperfection and exposure, but they approach their own imperfection with courage. As Dr. Brown described in a TED talk on the topic, people with a sense of worthiness "were willing to let go of who they should be, in order to be who they were" (2010). The thing that made them willing to experience the discomfort associated with vulnerability was that they believed that "what made them vulnerable, also made them beautiful" (Brown, 2010).

> "Vulnerability is not knowing victory or defeat, it's understanding the necessity of both; it's engaging. It's being all in."
>
> – *Brene Brown, Daring Greatly: How the Courage to Be Vulnerable Transforms the Way We Love (2012)*

In order to believe that what makes us vulnerable makes us beautiful, we also have to be willing to demonstrate compassion toward ourselves. Kirsten Neff is a psychologist who studies self-compassion (2003). Self-compassion consists of three important parts: self-kindness, common humanity, and mindfulness. Self-kindness is the degree to which we respond kindly to ourselves when we experience disappointment or failure instead of self-flagellation or self-criticism. Common humanity is the awareness that all of the failings, suffering, and other experiences we have as individuals are also experienced by other people across time and across the world. In short, discomfort is part of the human experience. Finally, mindfulness involves taking a balanced approach to our negative emotions through awareness to avoid over-identifying with or ignoring them. It requires taking a non-judgmental approach to our own feelings and simply experiencing them as they are (Neff, 2003). Self-compassion enables an individual to be authentic toward our own experiences of vulnerability and failure, and by doing so we are better able to be compassionate in interpersonal relationships. Neff and her colleagues found this by examining how college students' levels of self-compassion correlate with how they responded to academic failure and goal setting (Neff, Hsieh, & Dejitterat, 2005; Neff, Kirkpatrick, & Rude, 2007). Neff and colleagues suggest that people can increase their levels of self-compassion by thinking about how they would respond to a friend who was suffering, and then treating themselves the same way (instead of beating themselves up or minimizing their own suffering) (2005; 2007). Meditation practices can also increase individual's levels of self-compassion (Neff, 2003).

Finally, once we have the capacity to understand why vulnerability and authenticity are necessary, and utilize the resources, such as self-compassion, that make them possible, we are able to solicit and receive feedback from others that assist in making us more authentic. One of the tools that can help people become more aware of how authentic they are is the Johari Window. In the 1960s, Joseph Luft developed the Johari Window that examines the boundaries between what individuals and their loved ones know and do not know about themselves. You will practice applying the Johari Window to a case study later on in the chapter.

AUTHENTICITY AND SOCIAL CHANGE

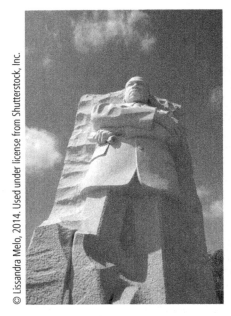

© Lissandra Melo, 2014. Used under license from Shutterstock, Inc.

Authenticity can have powerful effects not just in dyadic relationships, but also in creating social change in larger systems. Some significant examples of people who used their authentic selves and their own experiences to create social change are Martin Luther King, Jr. and Harvey Milk. Both civil rights leaders for different causes; they used their own experiences of oppression, both visible and invisible to affect change in the world around them. Dr. King said in his famous "I Have a Dream" speech, "I have a dream that my four little children will one day live in a nation where they will not be judged by the color of their skin, but by the content of their character." How powerful that he was speaking of his own experience, not describing an abstract other, but instead said "I have a dream that my children . . ." Dr. King was not talking about other people's children, or someone else's issue, but a problem that directly impacted both him and his children. His willingness to be authentic and vulnerable about his and his family's experiences contributed to the significant impact this speech had on the world.

Harvey Milk is another example of a civil rights leader who led from his authentic self. As the first openly gay person to be elected to public office, he was open about his sexuality during his campaign and then during his run in office. As sexuality is not visible, his choice to be authentic about that part of his life, as opposed to keeping it private, was even more courageous. He was a powerful advocate for creating social change for LGBT individuals in the United States. Now, a mere 50 years since his run in office, 37 states have passed marriage equality in the United States and more may be on their way. He described authenticity and its social and personal effects powerfully in his speech *That's What America Is*:

> Every gay person must come out. As difficult as it is, you must tell your immediate family. You must tell your relatives. You must tell your friends, if indeed they are your friends. You must tell the people you work with. You must tell the people in the stores you shop in. Once they realize that we are indeed their children, that we are indeed everywhere, every myth, every lie, every innuendo will be destroyed once and for all. And once you do, you will feel so much better.—Harvey Milk (as cited in Epstein, 2008)

While Dr. King and Mr. Milk lived 50 years ago and promoted authenticity for social change, social media has enabled an entirely new way to approach authenticity for social change. One significant example of this has been Dan Savage's "It Gets Better" campaign. Started after an epidemic of suicides among LGBT high school students, this campaign provided a way for adults and other people outside of adolescence to create YouTube videos to encourage teens and other LGBT people who were struggling to know that it gets better. Since its inception in 2010, over 50,000 user-generated videos have been uploaded to the project and those videos have been viewed over 50 million times (It Gets Better Project, 2010). This video project is a part of building authenticity and community for social change. For more information on the It Gets Better campaign, please visit: http://www. itgetsbetter.org.

On a smaller scale, Michael Kimber created a blog and series of videos on his experiences with anxiety and depression. His video on "coming out" with a mental illness has generated over 12,000 views and promotes the importance of people with disorders being the ones who lead the movement toward de-stigmatizing those same disorders. To view the video, please visit: http://www .youtube.com/watch?v=Z94xofA35Y4.

Taking Risks with Authenticity and Vulnerability: Encouragement and a Caveat

While authenticity is something to be admired and supported, there are also risks inherent in being authentic. Because authenticity requires vulnerability, you may find that people who you choose to disclose to may reject your disclosure, may disapprove or may even put your safety at risk, especially with more volatile disclosures, such as those around sexuality. These risks highlight the importance of being conscientious about who you share with and how much to share. Instead of dumping personal information on an acquaintance, we recommend that you get to know that person slowly and over time, disclose as desired, thoughtfully and with awareness. Appropriate boundaries are those in which each person takes responsibility for their own disclosures and allow others the freedom to respond as they see fit. Understand that you cannot control other people's reactions to your vulnerability because the only person you can control is yourself. This is particularly important with considering sharing personal information online, such as that described by Dan Savage and Michael Kimber. We encourage you to take safe risks in personal relationships, meaning that you understand your own role and responsibility in sharing yourself, and that you are emotionally prepared and healthy enough to be courageous. If you decide to share something publically with the goal of effecting social change, such as those examples provided by Michael Kimber and Dan Savage, we recommend that you first share what you want to in numerous personal relationships. By doing so, it not only provides you practice, but also provides the social support you will likely need if public sharing goes poorly. Authenticity requires risk. Without taking risks, it may be difficult for relationships to flourish.

> There is no safe investment. To love at all is to be vulnerable. Love anything, and your heart will certainly be wrung and possibly be broken. If you want to make sure of keeping it intact, you must give your heart to no one, not even to an animal. Wrap it carefully round with hobbies and little luxuries; avoid all entanglements; lock it up safe in the casket or coffin of your selfishness. But in that casket—safe, dark, motionless, airless—it will change. It will not be broken; it will become unbreakable, impenetrable, irredeemable. (C. S. Lewis, 1971)

THE JOHARI WINDOW

What if we could live more authentically—and be open to greater levels of intimacy—by sharing our secrets and seeing ourselves the way others see us? The Johari Window provides a framework for how we can uncover new dimensions of our authentic selves and others through self-awareness, other-awareness, and communication. Developed by John Luft and Harry Ingham in 1955 as a guide for understanding interpersonal communication, the Johari Window offers a guide for examining how we reveal our identities to the world—including ourselves—and how we can use feedback from others to live more authentically and embrace intimacy.

Imagine a window with four panes of glass. These four panes represent four selves that we carry with us throughout our lives and relationships. Though depicted equally in Figure 1, at different times in our lives, panes can shift sizes as different aspects of our identities shift or grow. The aspects of identity that are covered by the Johari window are broad, including attitudes, behaviors, beliefs, qualities, feelings, experiences, and anything else that a person considers as influential in shaping his or her self-concept (Luft, 1969; Luft & Ingham, 1955; Sutherland, 1995).

FIGURE 1 Johari Window

	Known to self	Not known to self
Known to others	(Open) Public Self	(Blind) Rejected Self
Not known to others	(Hidden) Private Self	(Unknown) Projected Self

The Four Selves

The **public self** refers to an identity that is shared in the open; it is the self that is seen by others and us. It is the parts of our selves that we display when we feel safe to share. For example, you and your friends may both consider you to be outgoing and a social butterfly. For Justin from our case example, the public self was a sensitive young man who was also charismatic; both he and Anne recognized his sensitivity and ability to charm others in social settings. When the public self is the largest pane of glass in the window, it indicates that we are living authentically because we are not hiding much from others or ourselves.

Although the extent to which a person shares his identity publicly is highly influenced by his own self-esteem, confidence, and security, it is also impacted by the quality of his environment. Parallel to the development and maintenance of intimacy, sharing the public self through self-disclosure and openness is dependent upon the quality of relational communication and individual preferences. Intimate relationships that possess safe, respectful communication patterns foster healthy self-disclosure and more opportunity to build a public self. When communication is positive and relational trust is present, partners are less likely to feel the need to hide aspects of their inner selves.

In addition to benefiting ourselves by living authentic lives, as seen when the public self is the largest of the four panes of our Johari Window, living authentically also benefits our partners and relationships. Typically, when others are able to witness our own sharing and self-disclosure, they are more likely to feel comfortable disclosing as well. Additionally, they gain more insight into why we behave in the ways that we do, and can more understand when our behaviors are confusing.

The **private self** is the part of ourselves that is known to us, but not revealed to others. It includes the aspects of our inner worlds that we prefer to keep safe from the attention of others. The private self tends to be related to doubts, fears, and insecurities, but it can also include positive parts of our identities that we choose to keep to ourselves for various reasons. Some examples of aspects of the private self might include: a sense of inadequacy or never feeling good enough, the perception that one's body just does not look the way it used to, a tendency to abuse alcohol, and so on. For some reason (whether conscious or not), we believe it serves us to keep these parts of ourselves hidden. At the beginning of relationships, the fear of rejection or anxiety regarding where the relationship will go may motivate us to keep certain parts of our selves private. For example, it may not be attractive to share with a new partner that one is insecure about relationship fidelity, or that one has a hard time telling the truth. In some cases, it may feel more comfortable to keep parts of us hidden than to open our selves up to sharing. This is particularly true when the pieces of our private selves are deeply rooted in longstanding fears, insecurities, or past traumas.

However, the private self may become public over time, with changing circumstances e.g., conflict, life events) or with increased intimacy. As individuals, when we feel safe and secure in our close relationships, we often begin to share aspects of our selves that were once kept hidden. The responses from partners as we begin to reveal our inner worlds will shape how much we choose to share in the future. If partners are supportive and embrace the newfound knowledge of our previously private selves, we will be more likely to share additional layers in the future. If they respond critically or punitively, we may be less likely to reveal more of our private selves.

It is important to note that an individual may have a different private self across different relationships or types of relationships. For example, Justin may keep his fear of rejection hidden from Anne, but his last girlfriend, brother, or best friend may be privy to this aspect of Justin's emotional world. Because our private selves are often formed through experience, we might have different private selves in our current relationships than we did in our past relationships. As individuals, we can reflect on the lack of congruence about what is hidden or shared across different relationships in our lives, and then use this information to consider new avenues for sharing with our partners.

The *rejected self* is the self that is known to others but is not known to us—it represents our blind spot when looking at our selves. For example, Justin's rejected self was his insecurity; he knew he was afraid of rejection, but he did not consider himself needy or insecure, however Anne was aware of his insecurity. It is possible to minimize the rejected self by welcoming and asking for feedback from our intimate others, friends, families, and coworkers. Open and honest conversations with our partners about who we are and who we want to become can provide partners reasons to share specific, safe, and constructive feedback. Both parties are free to set boundaries on how far the discussion will go; for feedback to encourage continued reflection and future openness, the individual seeking feedback must feel safe. Feeling vulnerable is an important piece of becoming authentic, but not at the expense of sharing raw emotional wounds or traumas before we are ready. Therefore, it is also important to seek this feedback from people who have our best interests in mind.

An additional avenue for discovering our rejected selves is to put ourselves in other people's shoes and replay particular social exchanges. An example of how to do this would be to first think about a break-up from your own perspective, and then to think about how your ex would tell the story of the break-up. Although challenging, with enough openness and attempted objectivity, we may see others' points of view and begin to see ourselves through their eyes. Through this aspect of the self, the risk of rejection is limited, but the possibility of missing important insights is present.

Finally, the *projected self* refers to the aspects of our selves unknown both to ourselves and others. The clearest version of the projected self is the future self. Because we are unable to tell the future, our future selves are unknown. We do not know what experiences we will have, how they will shape us or who we will become. Another more abstract version of the projected self refers to our unconscious. Humans often have motives, attitudes, and beliefs that are unbeknownst even to themselves. These parts of our selves can become known through self-reflection, interaction with others, or a combination of the two. In some situations, we may discover our projected selves when we project our own feelings onto others. For example, let's consider Justin and Anne. Justin argued with Anne because he was afraid of rejection by Anne, though neither he nor Anne knew this was at the root of their argument. Instead of being authentic with Anne about his worries, he projected them on to her: "I don't even feel like you're my girlfriend anymore." Other common examples are seeing others as being angry or insecure when in fact those feelings are really true for us.

Using the Johari Window to Promote Authenticity and Intimacy

In relationships, partners can use feedback processes to increase the open area of the public self and live more authentically. The ideal Johari Window is not proportionate, with all four panes being equal in size. Instead, as we strive for authenticity by sharing our private selves and discovering our rejected selves, the public self will increase in size and create a disproportionate window. By pulling back the shades to minimize the size of the rejected self and private self, we inevitably influence the size of the projected self and increase the extent of our public self (see Figure 2).

Individuals are responsible for the growth of their public selves. To decrease the extent of the rejected self, individuals can solicit feedback from loved ones, especially people who know a great portion of their public self. By doing so, they can gain insight into the areas that others see and that they cannot see.

Application: Justin and Anne

Take a few minutes to think about the story of Justin and Anne that was shared at the beginning of the chapter. Objectively, what happened? Anne went on a trip, was late calling Justin back, and Justin became upset which ended in Anne breaking up with him. However, as you are beginning to learn, what happens objectively rarely describes what happens subjectively. Now, we'll explore the subjective with Justin and Anne's story and use the Johari Window to find out more.

FIGURE 2 Re-sizing Our Selves

Public self	Rejected self
Private self	Projected self

WHY DIDN'T YOU CALL: THE SUBJECTIVE VERSION

Justin's selves (public, private, rejected, and projected) were all operating over the course of his and Anne's courtship—the latter two especially working against him on the night Anne broke things off. Justin's public self is what attracted Anne to him in the first place. His professional success and charismatic personality were very desirable, and his hopeless romantic nature and sensitive side separated him from other more "macho" or arrogant men that Anne had met.

It was Justin's private self, however, that began to break his and Anne's relationship down. While he had recently gone through a painful breakup (which was public), Justin attached this breakup to other breakups that he had endured. Over the course of his dating life, Justin was generally the one that was broken up with, and his sense of self as a "good catch" was waning. He had begun to fear rejection a great deal, and worked hard in relationships to avoid this. Justin knew he harbored this fear, but felt strongly that if he shared it with anybody that they (she) would see this as reason enough to leave. After all, who wants to be with somebody who is insecure with himself?

Justin knew from the beginning that he was battling these demons again when he met Anne. While, from her perspective, his sweet "good morning" and "good night" texts were endearing, they were agonizing for Justin. Every day, Justin would send these texts first, and then wait for Anne's reply. Sometimes she would reply right away. When she did, Justin could then—and only then—concentrate on his work and have a good day. Other times, Anne would not reply for several hours (and sometimes not at all). When this happened, Justin could not get any work done. He was tuned-out or irritable with colleagues, running through his mind the myriad of reasons that Anne was not texting him back—from the mundane (e.g., a dead cell phone battery) to the disastrous (e.g., Anne changed her mind about Justin and wants to break up). Mostly the disastrous.

In fact, almost everything Anne did (or did not do), Justin would analyze and over-think. "Why didn't she kiss me quite the same that time?" "Why did she just say 'When I have a child someday . . .' to her friend instead of "When Justin and I have a child someday . . .'?" "How come she closed her laptop when I came home? Is there something on there that she doesn't want me to see?"

And so, while Justin's public self with Anne was one of a happy partner in a young couple's courtship, his private self was that of a terrified young man who was downright miserable. On the night that they broke up, Justin's rejected self—that of a needy and insecure person—ultimately surfaced. After functioning so long to appear to Anne like he was okay, he could longer do it. His "concerns" about Anne's safety had nothing to do with Anne's safety. Justin needed to talk with Anne, or somehow hear from her, to be reassured (at least until the next day's "good morning" texts) that she was still interested in the relationship. His insecurities were obvious to her, but not to him. Justin's turning to alcohol to subdue his pain while waiting through each passing moment without a call or text further demonstrated his inability to tolerate feeling so helpless and unlovable.

Enter the projected self, stage left. Justin's desperate questions to Anne about why she couldn't just send him a quick text, and his wondering about whether she really loved him, anyway, were clearly driven by an unconscious dislike for himself. Seeing himself as unworthy, he accused Anne of not perceiving him to be important enough to call. Seeing himself as unlovable, he accused Anne of not loving him. And this ultimately drove her away, painfully confirming for Justin his self-deprecating views.

Epilogue

Justin knew well enough to not chase Anne anymore. Clearly he had chased her too hard, which ultimately made her run away. Not wanting to hurt in the ways that he was any longer, Justin connected with a therapist for help. He began to explore, articulate, and face his fears of being unlovable, of being rejected, and of being alone.

As he and Anne crossed paths again, Justin apologized for his role(s) in what had happened to them. He explained to her how his insecurities in relationships had grown out of his history with others that had failed, but did not frame this history as an excuse for his behavior. Justin took responsibility for making more of his private self public, thereby taking away its secrecy and power. He owned up to his rejected self, seeing how his needy and insecure behaviors were (are) off-putting and unattractive. He communicated understanding about how his questions regarding personal worth or being loved were driven by his own sense(s) of being unworthy and unlovable.

Ultimately, Justin and Anne did not work out. However, as he moved forward, Justin was inspired to live life on purpose—to be authentic to himself and to others about his strengths and his weakness. In his next relationship, he did this and things went better. In the one after that (which he is still in), Justin found himself living almost peacefully. And he doesn't wait for texts anymore.

SUMMARY

Let's return to the relationship of Anne and Justin and consider how use of the Johari Window feedback process may have benefited their couple relationship. When coming back together after their initial argument and 27 missed calls, Anne and Justin had the opportunity to reflect and disclose in a mutual feedback process. Perhaps Anne could have used the argument as a talking point to share her perspective of Justin's irrational insecurity—not by attacking Justin and blaming him for being insecure, but by patiently describing her perceptions and asking empathic questions to get to the root of the behavior. By rushing forward with complaints and criticism, Anne invited Justin's defensiveness to surface and made it difficult for Justin to see his behavior from her perspective. Alternatively, perhaps Justin could have disclosed his angst of unreturned phone calls and fear of rejection from previous relationships. By sharing this private belief, Justin's public self would have expanded and the couple could work through these fears together or make decisions maturely about if Justin was ready for the relationship. By keeping his private self hidden, however, Justin's behavior came across only as immature, impatient, and disrespectful—something that Anne could not understand and contributed to pushing Anne away.

In this example, we can see that the feedback process is more likely to be fruitful in a relationship where respectful, mature communication occurs. When partners remember and acknowledge that they are on the same team, the feedback process provides an opportunity for both partners to become the most authentic versions of their whole selves while in relationship. In this sense, self-awareness and identity development can occur within a relationship. Rather than embarking on a typically independent model of self-discovery, individuals can remain in relationship and flourish together as they work with their partners to support self- and other-awareness.

What Don't We Know

Although we have gathered a wealth of knowledge regarding authenticity from past efforts (e.g., research), there are still things to learn about authenticity, from both a research and personal perspective. As most of the research on authenticity and vulnerability has been correlational, we don't know if the positive outcomes that are associated with it are caused by it. Very few measures also exist for authenticity, so figuring out if someone had gained more authenticity in a systemic way is currently difficult. As it is difficult to measure authenticity, and because existing research is primarily correlational, we are not able to make causal claims that increasing your level of authenticity will prevent relationships from ending.

More personal to you, this textbook also cannot know what the right levels of authenticity are for you. We don't know when the right time to be authentic is for each of you, and we do not know how to tell you who your authentic self is, especially because who you are is constantly evolving. More to the point, we do not know how your life will be affected by authenticity, but we encourage you to attempt it, and step by step, become a little more real with the people you love.

REFERENCES

Brown, B. (2010, December 23). *The power of vulnerability* [Video File]. Retrieved from: http://www.ted.com/talks/brene_brown_on_vulnerability.html.

Brown, B. (2012). *Daring greatly: How the courage to be vulnerable transforms the way we live, love, parent, and lead.* New York: Penguin.

Butterworth, G. (1995). The self as an object of consciousness in infancy. In P. Rochat (Ed.), *The Self in infancy: Theory and research.* Philadelphia, PA: Elsevier.

Epstein, R. (2008). *What Harvey Milk tells us about proposition 8.* Huffington Post. Retrieved February 19, 2014 from http://www.huffingtonpost.com/rob-epstein/what-harvey-milk-tells-us_b_145288.html

Freud, S. (1961). *Civilization and its discontents.* New York: W. W. Norton & Company.

Lewis, C. S. (1971). *The four loves.* Orlando, FL: Houghton Mifflin Harcourt.

Gallagher, S. (2000). Philosophical conceptions of the self: Implications for cognitive science. *Trends in Cognitive Science, 4*(1), 14–21. doi:1364-6613/00

Jung, C. G. (1958). *The undiscovered self.* Oxford, England: Little, Brown.

Luft, J. (1969). *Of human interaction.* Palo Alto, CA: Mayfield.

Luft, J., & Ingram, H. (1955). *The Johari Window model.* Los Angeles, CA: Western Training Laboratory Group.

Neff, K. D. (2003). Self-compassion: An alternative conceptualization of a healthy attitude toward oneself. *Self and Identity, 2*, 85–101. doi:10.1080/15298860390129863.

Neff, K. D., Hsieh, Y., & Dejitterat, K. (2005). Self-compassion, achievement goals, and coping with academic failure. *Self and Identity, 4*, 263–287. doi:10.1080/13576500444000317.

Neff, K. D., Rude, S. S., Kirkpatrick, K. L. (2007). An examination of self-compassion in relation to positive psychological functioning and personality traits. *Journal of Research in Personality, 41*, 908–916. doi:10.1016/j.jrp.2006.08.002.

Oliver, M. (2004). *Wild geese.* Northumberland, UK: Bloodaxe.

Reddy, V. (2003). On being the object of attention: Implications for self-other consciousness. *Trends in Cognitive Science, 7*(9), 397–403. doi:10.1016/S1364-6613(03)00191-8

Sutherland, J. A. (1995). The johari window a strategy for teaching therapeutic confrontation. *Nurse Educator, 20*(3), 22–24. doi:10.1097/00006223-199505000-00016

Wenzel, A. J., & Lucas-Thompson, R. G. (2012). Authenticity in college-aged males and females, how close others are perceived, and mental health outcomes. *Sex Roles, 67*(5-6), 334–350. doi:10.1007/s11199-012-0182-y

9

Intimacy Killers

Jennifer L. Doty, Ph.D.
Department of Pediatrics
University of Minnesota

Carrie L. Hanson, Ph.D., LMFT
Matthew A. Witham, M.A., LMFT
Alejandra Ochoa
Tai J. Mendenhall, Ph.D., LMFT
Department of Family Social Science
University of Minnesota

LEARNING OBJECTIVES

- Identify the components of the Gottman Sound Relational House
- Apply the Sound Relational House to a case study
- Understand Chapman's Five Love Languages
- Articulate how the Sound Relational House and the Five Love Languages can improve intimate relationships

Case Vignette

Anne has been waiting two long years for her spouse's return from a deployment to Iraq; two years that felt almost like two decades. She fantasized about their picture-perfect reunion—Anne would run into Richard's waiting arms with reckless abandon as he would cry tears of joy at the sight of his beautiful bride and 2-year-old daughter whom he just met. Anne imagined they would continue with their relationship right where they left it.

The first days of his return were even better than she expected—relentless laughter, unending physical touch, frequent and passionate sex, and the sharing of two years' worth of happenings. Now, he has been home for 10 months and their relationship is far from perfect. In fact, it's like a painful contract they are required to maintain. Richard and Anne constantly hurl hateful, accusatory statements at each other in the midst of arguments—words that can never be taken back. Instead of being a team, they have become two strangers sharing a house and a child. They are constantly defending their own innocence, unwilling to compromise and always pointing fingers at the other. For the first few months, Anne avoided confronting her husband about their rocky marriage, hoping it was just a phase which would soon pass. After 10 months of verbal abuse and agony, though, she knows that she needs to address the topic. The tender Richard who was once head-over-heels for her and wanted to spend every second together is now hardhearted Richard who uses every opportunity to be far away from his spouse and daughter.

One night, Anne stays up waiting for her husband to return from work so that they can have the much needed talk. Like most nights since his return, he walks through the door at 2:30 a.m. tripping over everything due to his drunkenness. Anne, who has been waiting for hours in the living room, stands up and yells, "Richard, this is unacceptable! Your irresponsible partying is driving me crazy—why can't you just grow up already?!"

Corresponding Author: Jennifer L. Doty, Ph.D.; University of Minnesota; Department of Pediatrics; 717 Delaware Street SE; Room 353 (3rd Floor West); Minneapolis, MN 55414. E-mail: dotyx093@umn.edu.

"What do you mean my behavior? YOU are the one who is always moody and ready to fight!" screams Richard in defense.

This triggers Anne, who responds, "You are never home, and when you are home you are too drunk to spend time with me. You don't care about me and our own daughter! You never help me with chores. You spend all your money on alcohol. You are . . .."

Richard plays the victim and turns to accuse his wife, saying, "Hold on there, Little Miss Perfect. You are the one who stopped having sex with me months ago. When I left to Iraq, I left behind my affectionate, sweet and gentle pregnant wife. Now, I return only to find a self-governing, psychotic, and demanding woman with a 3-year-old girl I barely know!"

As soon as he is done talking, Richard turns his back to Anne (who is still talking) and storms toward the bedroom.

"Come back here and listen to me!" screams Anne in a desperate attempt to get her husband's attention. Intoxicated and furious, Richard turns around and looks at Anne straight in the eye. And then he hits her. His face drops, realizing what he's done. He leaves, slamming the door behind him.

INTRODUCTION

How does a couple go from head-over-heals in love to hurtful, bitter, and breaking apart? Although every couple is different, we know from research that there are some general "intimacy killers" that are toxic to most relationships. John Gottman is a researcher who has been studying what makes relationships thrive or fail for decades. He readily admits that he got into this line of work because he was not altogether sure about his own skills in relationships! He has since learned how to predict whether couples will stay together with over 91% accuracy from watching and listening to a five-minute conversation between them (Gottman & Levenson, 2002; Gottman & Silver, 1999). In his Love Lab in Seattle, couples were invited to discuss a "hot-button" issue, and researchers have carefully coded their body language and verbal interactions to better understand relationships. Gottman's team found that not only the content of *what* is said, but also how it is said, matters. Couples exhibiting a certain set of hostile behaviors are more likely to break up (Busby & Holman, 2009). Gottman labeled these behaviors the *Four Horsemen of the Apocalypse*: criticism, defensiveness, stonewalling, and contempt. In this chapter, we will cover these patterns of behavior in depth and discuss how these processes lead to larger destructive problems. You might recognize many of the patterns from Anne and Richard's story.

After discussing the Four Horsemen, we will address other intimacy killers, such as money, jealousy, infidelity, violence, and alcohol abuse. We start with money because struggles and arguments regarding finances are the most commonly cited reasons for rel ationship dissolution. Next, we will hen address jealousy so you can learn to recognize when this emotion and process becomes an intimacy killer. Then, we'll examine infidelity. The concept of infidelity has fuzzy boundaries. In other words, what is cheating to one person may not be defined as cheating to another person. We will discuss different types of infidelity and consider how technology has influenced the ways we think about it. We will also review research on abuse and violence. More than a quarter of couples experience a violent act in their relationships at one point or another (Black et al., 2011), and most abuse occurs within the context of romantic relationships. Why is this the case? We'll examine this phenomenon. Finally, we consider how and why alcohol and drug abuse contributes to relationship problems. Because alcohol binge drinking peaks in young adulthood, we'll pay careful attention to the drinking culture during college years. We examine each of these intimacy killers in the context of relationships.

When it comes to intimacy killers, there's one catch to keep in mind: problem solving alone cannot save relationships. Couples also need to focus on the positive things they enjoy together and make habits of seeing the good in each other (Busby & Holman, 2009; Gottman, 1999). From the start, we need to be working on preventative maintenance and need to consciously nurture our relationships. That's why Chapter 10 is entirely devoted to "intimacy healers" and what we can do to make our relationships better.

THE FOUR HORSEMEN

In his research, Gottman found that a "magic ratio" of positive to negative interactions between a couple makes a difference in their likelihood of staying together. This ratio is especially important when discussing conflict. Happy couples tend to have at least five positive interactions for every negative interaction (Gottman & Gottman, 2011; Gottman & Silver, 1999). Not all negative interactions are equal, though—some hostile actions are more damaging to relationships than others (Busby & Holman, 2009). Gottman calls the most corrosive behaviors the "Four Horsemen of the Apocalypse" because patterns of interaction that include criticism, defensiveness, stonewalling, and contempt can predict the end of relationships. This is a cycle that builds (see Figure 1), and by the time couples reach a level of contempt, the relationship is often beyond repair (Gottman, 1999; Gottman & Levenson, 2002).

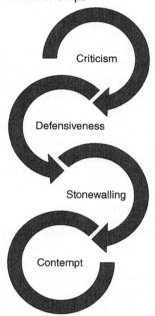

FIGURE 1 The Four Horsemen of the Apocalypse: A Pattern of Destruction in Relationships

Criticism

Criticism is the first horseman in Gottman's typology. Criticism includes general statements that attack the other partner's character or personality (Gottman & Silver, 1999; Kimberly & Werner-Wilson, 2013). Many criticisms begin with "you" and include the words "always" or "never." Criticisms are different than complaints. When someone complains, s/he brings up a specific behavior or problem. Complaints are not a problem for relationships in the same way that criticisms are; however, a huge laundry list of complaints can also come across as criticism of a person's character.

Let's say Alex moved in with Jake a few months ago, but Alex is getting aggravated because he is pretty tidy and his cleaning style is very different from Jake's. A criticism would look like this: "Jake, you are such a slob—why don't you ever do the dishes?!" A complaint, in contrast, would be less accusatory and more specific: "Jake, when the sink is full of dishes, it gets on my nerves. It would mean a lot to me if you could put them in the dishwasher." Notice that when Alex globally characterizes Jake in negative light (saying that he is a slob) and asks about "why" he doesn't "ever" do the dishes, there is little room to solve the problem (that Alex doesn't like dirty dishes). Being accused of being a slob is likely to elicit a defensive reaction from Jake, and saying that he never does the dishes is likely to elicit disagreements about times that he has.

...YOU MAY NOW GO FROM ADORING TO CRITICIZING EACH OTHER

REV. BOB, THE REALIST

Criticism is pretty common in relationships, but when it becomes a frequent habit, it leads the way to the other horsemen. In Gottman's research, women were more likely to exhibit criticism, whereas men were more likely to respond defensively. Rather than blaming women or men for relationship problems, however, a focus on couple interaction shines light on what both partners do to contribute to a crumbling relationship.

Defensiveness

The next horseman rides in when a person defends himself or herself from attack. Defensiveness is characterized by an unwillingness to accept responsibility and a tendency to blame the other partner. For example, a common defense is to exclaim, "I am only doing XYZ because you do ABC!" For example, Jake could yell back, "I don't clean the dishes because you always tell me that I don't clean them the right way; what's the point?" In effect, the defender is saying, "What are you picking on me for? I didn't do anything wrong. What about all the good things I do? I never get any appreciation. Poor me. I'm innocent." (Gottman, 1999, p. 45). Often, the defender throws in a counter-attack as part of the defense strategy.

If we continue with Alex and Jake's example, after an attack, Jake might respond, "Can't I just relax and enjoy myself after a long day?"

Alex attacks again: "Then, what? I'm supposed to be the maid around here? Can't you get off your butt every once in a while? "

"Whatever, you are the one who's a neat freak—not me!" Notice that Jake is counterattacking now by calling Alex a "neat freak" (a global characterization). Instead of calming the flames, defensive responses and labeling just fuel the fire, and the conflict continues and oftentimes escalates.

Stonewalling

Eventually, when this damaging pattern continues, one of the partners begins to shut the other out. Enter the third horseman: stonewalling. Stonewalling partners basically ignore their significant others, sitting there like stone walls rather than giving cues that they are listening. Stonewallers may cross their arms, clench their jaws, or physically turn away (Gottman, 1999; Gottman & Silver, 2012). Giving "a cold shoulder" or the "silent treatment" is a typical example of stonewalling (Carroll et al., 2010). In general, men are more likely to stonewall than women, and researchers believe that it may be a strategy for protection from stress arousal associated with conflict (Carroll et al., 2010; Gottman, 1999). Stonewalling is similar to the silent treatment but it also implies that the person is "shutting off" his/her partner. In response to stonewalling, women's heart rates usually spike dramatically. When women stonewall, typically in the midst of marital conflict, this relational aggression is a sign that the relationship is in very bad shape (Carroll et al., 2010; Gottman, 1999). This horseman usually does not show up until after a relationship has been unhealthy for some time.

Let's take a look at a couple letting this horseman ride into their relationship. Dave and Leigh have been married for several years. When she enters the room to complain about a credit card charge, Dave does not even look at her. She attacks, "You are so irresponsible—like you think we are made of money or something. I swear you are going to drive us into bankruptcy." Again, Dave does not respond, though a careful observer might notice that his jaw is tightening during the tirade. Leigh tries again to get through to him, "Hello, are you even listening?" and then walks out of the room. Obviously, this relationship is on the rocks.

Contempt

The fourth horseman is contempt, which is demarked by purposefully tearing down one's partner. This could include mockery, name-calling, sarcasm, and cynicism (Gottman & Silver, 1999; Kimberly & Werner-Wilson, 2013). In recordings, the Gottman lab found that nonverbal signals such as eye-rolling and sneering (literally lifting one side of the upper lip, usually on the right side) were powerful indicators of contempt. Contempt is considered the strongest predictor of a break up, and happy couples do not typically evidence signs of it. Furthermore, couples who behave contemptuously are physically affected; in multiple studies, contemptuous partners were more likely to get sick and have increased blood pressure than other people (Gottman, 1999; Newton & Sanford, 2003).

Here is another example of criticism, defensiveness, and contempt working together:

John noticed Phasoda on her phone again and could not hold back a comment, "Why are you always texting Sam?"

Phasoda responded with a sigh, "He's just a friend. You worry too much."

"You are the one who cheated on your ex!" John retorted, his voice rising.

Phasoda rolled her eyes, and sarcasm laced her reply. "I can't believe you are bringing that up again. Just a little paranoid? Can't let me out of your sight for a minute, can you?"

"Not when you are a cheating bitch."

Phasoda screamed back at him, "How many times do I have to tell you I am not cheating on you!! But at this rate, maybe I should!"

In Gottman's lab, individuals who were in relationships that possess frequent occurrences of these horsemen were more likely to have physiological reactions that indicated stress arousal of the autonomic nervous system (Gottman, 1999; Gottman, Gottman, & Atkins, 2011). In other words, when individuals feel threatened, their "flight, fight, or freeze" mechanisms are activated. Blood rushes to the heart and the brain starts to pay close attention to danger signals. As a result, partners become more combative, and this physiological reaction makes it harder for them to engage in productive activities, like listening and problem solving.

Recognizing the four horsemen in our relationships is the first step to changing communication habits because it allows us to evaluate our feelings and behaviors and take steps toward change. Mindfulness has also been recognized as a key tool for regulating intense emotions in relationships (Ben-Naim, Hirshberger, Ein-Dor, & Mikulincer, 2013). Mindfulness can include being aware of one's own feelings and accepting them as neither good nor bad. The most successful mindfulness strategy, though, is perspective taking (Ben-Naim et al., 2013). Perspective taking includes imagining one's self as an objective observer in a situation, or trying to imagine how one's partner feels. Ultimately, though, for relationships to heal and grow stronger, partners need to focus on positive aspects of each other. Chapter 10 covers intimacy healers in more depth and gives us tools to combat intimacy killers in our relationships.

© michaeljung, 2014. Used under license from Shutterstock, Inc.

COUPLES AND MONEY

As unromantic as it sounds, and as uncomfortable as it often is to bring up, it is essential for couples to talk about money (Burgoyne, Reibstein, Edmunds, & Dolman, 2007; Gigy & Kelly, 1993; Shapiro, 2007). This is not because money, per se, is an intimacy killer. It is because couples who cannot effectively communicate about it—those who engage in financial power struggles, live in fear of not having enough money, and/or cannot agree together about how to effectively save or manage it—are almost destined to fail.

Think about it. Everyone maintains a particular orientation to money and attaches meaning to it (Dean, Carroll, & Yang, 2007; Mitchell & Mickel, 1999). What does money mean to you? It is about status? Do you value it because it will impress other people? That the world will see you more positively if they see your designer clothes, sports car, or beautiful home in "best" part of town? Or is it about security? Does money bring a sense of security in an otherwise unpredictable world? Is it for enjoyment? Do you value money for the pleasure and fun that it can bring you and others? Or is about control? Is money your means of maintaining independence from others who might otherwise control you?

Whatever your orientation to money is, it is foolish to presume that your partner shares the same viewpoints. He or she could have grown up in a very different family or social context that taught dissimilar—or even conflicting—lessons to the ones you learned. If money is about enjoyment for you and it is about security for your partner, considerable conflict is coming (and soon!) unless you figure out a plan together. It's important to talk about whether and how you are a good match in terms of money management. Further, even if you share similar orientations, you still need to talk. If you both value status, for example, but do not have the education or income to support it—you might wind up mired in credit card debt with no easy way out. And couples living in poverty or overwhelming debt don't tend to fare very well in comparison to their financially stable counterparts.

Talking about Money

For many of us, talking about money is a very uncomfortable endeavor. Our families may have not talked about it (so we have had no previous practice), and may have instilled the sense that finances are an "off limits" topic. And it's so unromantic! Can you imagine being new into a relationship—say, dating for only a couple of months—and then talking about how much money you make, how much debt you are in, how much more financial aid you plan to take on before graduation, what your rent is like, and what your financial goals one, two, 10, or 20 years from now are?

Early on, we tend to intuit potential partners' financial orientations more than we ask about them (and vise versa). Does he drive an average car with $1000 rims while, at the same time, paying rent in a shoddy apartment? Does he drive a really nice car—which his parents paid for, alongside its maintenance and insurance? Does she spend money on $300 designer boots with a credit card or a debit card? Does she shop sales and discount stores with cash? Is she unimpressed—or very impressed—by your new car or the swanky restaurants you take her to? Is he great for a few days after each payday, and super-stressed for the last few days leading up to the next payday—or can you even tell when paydays are?

Later on in relationships, money comes up more explicitly. This oftentimes begins as couples' sense of commitment grows and is confirmed by events and processes that publically "prove" it. Moving in together, for example, can prompt conversations about how much rent a couple can collectively afford. Purchasing a car—even if it's seen as belonging to one member of the couple—can advance conversations about money. What can you (or we) afford? What is your (or my) credit score? And when considering these and related expenses, a couple's ability to afford fixed expenses (like rent or a car payment) is influenced by its ability to afford variable ones (like credit card payments, heating bills, or emergency house repairs). Talking about how to shoulder these expenses requires more conversations about credit card use and payment methods (e.g., all-at-once each month? minimum payments?), savings and saving strategies (e.g., all you can? a set amount?), and related topics that can feel very collaborative or extraordinarily awkward or conflictual.

Money Management Systems

As couples begin to talk about money, they must figure out together what kind of money management system works best for them. What fits their individual and collective orientations to money, and how can they best achieve their desired goals around it? The following five systems describe the most common ways that couples manage money (Pahl, 1989, 1995; Vogler & Pahl, 1994):

WHOLE WAGE. In this system, one partner manages all of the household finances (with the exception of the personal spending money of the partner). Whether the income comes from one or both partners, in this system it is only a single partner who pays the bills, puts money into savings, moves accounts around, and so forth. The other partner generally knows little about what the bills are, how much (or how little) the couple possesses, or where money is kept. When this systems works for couples, the money manager feels good about the control s/he has, while the partner is appreciative of not having to bother with the complexities of financial management.

ALLOWANCE. Partners in this system are usually in a situation wherein one is the primary breadwinner and the other does not bring financial resources to the household. The breadwinner provides an allowance of funds for household expenditures, while retaining the rest for himself or herself.

POOLING. In this system, household income is treated as a collective resource. Both partners play engaged and active roles in financial decision making, and work together in almost all money matters related to their daily lives. Checking and savings accounts are joint, credit cards carry both partners' names, and so on. While there is little personal financial privacy in this system, both partners are wholly aware of what money is coming in and what is going out.

PARTIAL POOLING. Partners in this type of system pool their resources for joint expenditures (e.g., mortgage or rent, household bills) while keeping the rest of their money separate to spend or save as they choose. These couples will often have both personal checking/savings accounts and joint ones. While both are generally aware of their collective financial standing at any given time, they also maintain some privacy and ability to spend personal money without the partner's knowledge.

INDEPENDENT MANAGEMENT. In this system, partners have individual control over their own money and maintain separate responsibility for expenditures. For example, while both live in the same house, one partner pays for the mortgage while the other covers all of the utilities or food expenses.

Choosing a Money Management System

The best money management system for one couple may not be the best one for another couple. Each couple must figure out a plan and method that best works for them. This is essential; doing so can help a relationship survive, and not doing so can break it down. And so, as unromantic as it might be, talk about it!

JEALOUSY

Jealousy is a combination of thoughts, emotions, and actions that follow a real or perceived threat to the existence or quality of a relationship (Buunk & Dijkstra, 2004; Fleishmann, Spitzberg, Andersen, & Roesch, 2005). It is often accompanied by its cousin, envy. Although similar, jealousy and envy are not the same. Jealousy is relationally-based while envy is object-based. *Envy* produces a strong desire to have something (an achievement, a possession, or a quality) that someone else possesses. Jealousy and envy can exist at the same time; for instance, a woman may be jealous of her boyfriend's female friend, and envious of the friend's beauty. Both jealousy and envy elicit affective responses. Affective responses to jealousy include fear of loss, anxiety, suspiciousness, betrayal, and anger; envy may produce feelings of inferiority, longing, resentment, and ill will (Haslam & Bornstein, 1996; Parrot & Smith, 1993; Smith & Kim, 2007).

> "It was just lunch, a look, a text message, two old friends getting together to catch up on old times. There's nothing to be jealous about."
>
> Maybe there is . . . maybe there isn't . . . but in the hollow of your stomach you can feel the churning combination of possessiveness, suspicion, rage, and humiliation start to boil. Its inky fingers slowly creep up your spine, infiltrate your thoughts and take possession of your mind. You find yourself looking through the eyes of "the green-eyed monster" (as Shakespeare called it), overwhelmed with feelings of fear, abandonment, anger, and betrayal. Hyper-vigilance moves in and suddenly every action, every statement, every move, is suspect. Your trust in your partner starts wavering. You become obsessed. You demand your partner cease all contact with the one who has become your rival. You sneak around, you argue, you accuse, you blame. In an attempt to gain control, you totally lose it.

Jealousy can spring from any relationship, but research shows that jealousy is more prevalent among individuals in committed relationships than in less-committed relationships (Aune & Comstock, 1991; Rydell, McConnell, & Bringle, 2004; Staske, 1999). In much of the literature, jealousy is associated with negative relational outcomes such as relationship dissatisfaction, relational conflict, relationship dissolution, aggression, and violence (Bareld & Barelds-Dijkstra, 2007; Fleishmann, Spitzberg, Andersen, & Roesch, 2005; Guerrero, Spitzberg, & Yoshimura, 2004). But some argue that jealousy can be positive, too (Barelds & Dijkstra, 2006; Buss, 2000; Staske, 1999). For instance, it may show partners that they care for one another and value their relationship. In this aspect, jealousy serves an evolutionary function by mate guarding, expressing commitment, and eliciting a response from one's partner (Guerrero et al., 2004).

Not all jealousies are created equal. Jealousy may be triggered by realistic or imagined threats, and it can manifest in many ways. Several typologies that distinguish between types of jealousy have been proposed. Buunk (1997) and Buunk and Dijkstra (2001, 2006) distinguish between three types: reactive, anxious, and possessive jealousy. *Reactive jealousy* is triggered by an actual event that leads to negative emotions such as anger. For instance, a man may witness his boyfriend kissing another man, immediately become angry and feel jealous. The second type, *possessive jealousy,* occurs when an individual purposefully works to prevent contact between his/her partner and those s/he considers as realistic or imagined threats. For instance, a wife forbids her husband to go to his best friend's bachelor party because she thinks there may be single girls at the party. In extreme cases, possessive jealousy can lead to isolation, violence, or stalking. Finally, *anxious jealousy* can come from real or imagined threats. It may stem from ruminating and daydreaming about potential threats; it can produce feelings such as worry, suspicion, and distrust. For example, a medical student in the midst of a busy residency becomes obsessed with worry that his wife sets up play dates for their children just so she can flirt and be around the neighborhood children's fathers.

The effects of jealousy are numerous. Jealousy can lead to communication insecurities, distrust, relational conflict, and can be used as rationale for breakups and affairs. It can also lead to internal conflict, insecurity, and low self-esteem (Buunk, 1997; Buunk & Dijkstra, 2004), irrational thinking (Lester, Deluca, Hellinghausen, & Scribner, 1985), and depression (Lavallee & Parker, 2009; Radecki-Bush, Farrell, & Bush, 1993). Put simply, jealousy does not feel good, and constant jealousy can impact how you feel about yourself.

So, what do you do when the green-eyed monster comes creeping into your relationship? First, let yourself experience the feeling. Sure, it's uncomfortable to feel the itchy-nag of jealousy, but the more you try to ignore it, the stronger it will become. So, become aware of your feelings, but then move toward understanding them. Second, ask yourself why you're jealous and do some self-reflection. Is an experience from the past coloring your current experience? Were you once a cheater? Were you cheated on? By examining past experiences, you can gain insight into your current reactions. For example, during high school Anna was in a relationship with Dan, a serial cheater. Several years later, she begins a relationship with Scott, a man she met in college. Although Scott is attentive and loyal, Anna finds herself consumed with feelings of jealousy. While talking with her roommate, Anna realizes that her earlier experience with Dan is coloring how she sees her relationship with Scott.

Third, ask yourself the tough question: what exactly are you jealous or envious of? Are your feelings based on a real or imagined threat? What is your biggest concern about: you, your partner, and/or your relationship? Answering these questions will help you know what exactly you're dealing with. Anna asked herself these questions and discovered that she was afraid that Scott would grow bored of her and cheat on her like Dan did.

Fourth, have a conversation. That's right, talk with your partner. Let him/her know what you're feeling, share your worries and concerns, and do it without being defensive or accusatory. Good conversations are the product of honesty, vulnerability, patience, and understanding. Anna decided to talk to Scott about the way she had been feeling. She told Scott about her experience with Dan. She explained how she had felt insecure in her relationship with Dan, like she was never quite good enough for him. Scott listened, but then asked questions and tried to understand why she felt this way. She expressed her fears, telling him that it was hard for her to trust men. She and Scott discussed how their relationship was different and what each could do to help squelch the unfounded feelings of jealousy.

Fifth, stop comparing yourself. It's easy to get caught up in comparing yourself with others, but this can lead to jealousy, diminished self-esteem, and a slew of other problems. When we get caught up in comparing ourselves, we fail to see what actually exists and who we really are. By reeling in the comparisons, you can start to see and appreciate the differences and qualities that make you uniquely you.

INFIDELITY

Come on, we all love a good scandal. We watch it, read about it, and talk about it. Who will this week's famous cheater be? A royal? A rock star? An athlete? How about the latest "it" couple of Hollywood? Arnold Schwarzenegger, Tiger Woods, and Kristen Stewart are just a few of the famous in the "Cheaters Hall of Shame." But infidelity is not unique to the rich and famous. Everyday men and women cheat, have affairs, step-out on their significant other, and engage in various acts of infidelity.

Infidelity, also referred to as cheating, adultery, or having an affair, is often categorized into three groups: sexual (e.g., kissing, fondling, oral sex, vaginal sex, anal sex), emotional (e.g., sharing thoughts and feelings, being vulnerable, falling in love), or a combination of the two. Wilson and colleagues (2011) define three alternative descriptors of infidelity: (1) ambiguous (e.g., going places, buying/receiving gifts, hugging, talking on the phone/internet); (2) deceptive (e.g., lying and with-holding information); and (3) explicit (e.g., heavy petting, dating, intercourse).

Although general definitions of infidelity exist, it is important for each couple to define infidelity on its own terms. For instance, one couple may consider pornography or going to a strip club as fantasy, agreeing that it's okay to "look but not touch," while another couple may feel that anything connected with the sex industry is inherently "bad" and a violation of the couple's relationship. Like-wise, some couples may believe having close friends of the opposite sex as being appropriate, but others feel it is a threat. Conversations about infidelity help define relationship boundaries and aid in the exploration of partner suitability.

Historically, men have been labeled as more likely to cheat than women (Smith, 2006; Wiederman, 1997), but recent research suggests the differing rates of infidelity may be decreas-ing between the sexes (Brand, Markey, Mills, & Hodges, 2007). Statistics drawn from a nationally representative sample of the U.S. population show that between 11 and 23% of married individu-als have committed at least one act of sexual infidelity during the course of their marriages (Smith, 2006). Various studies also indicate that infidelity is a common presenting problem in couple therapy (Doss, Simpson, & Christensen, 2004; Whisman, Dixon, & Johnson, 1997).

People engage in infidelity for a multitude of reasons, such as a lack of commitment, attraction to another person, revenge, dissatisfaction, neglect, or wanting more frequent—or more erotic, ad-venturous, kinky, and so on—sex (Atkins, Baucom, & Jacobson, 2001; Barta & Kiene, 2005; Drigotas, Safstrom, & Gentilia, 1999; Glass & Wright, 1985; Roscoe, Cavanaugh, & Kennedy, 1988). Research has shown that men and women engage in infidelity for different reasons. Women are more likely to engage in emotional infidelity, whereas men's infidelity is generally sexual (Barta & Kiene, 2005; Glass & Wright, 1985; Smith, 2006; Spanier & Margolis, 1983). Similarly, Buss, Larsen, Westen and Semmelroth's (1992) study showed that men are more distressed with sexual infidelity when com-pared to women, and women experience more distress in response to emotional transgressions than men.

Infidelity is hurtful. It damages trust and creates feelings of heartache. Leeker and Carlozzi (2012) found that sexual infidelity was more likely to elicit anger, anger while emotional infidelity is more likely to lead to anxiety and jealousy. Although the effects of infidelity transcend cultural groups and ethnicities (Druckerman, 2007), women and heterosexual men are prone to be more distressed by a partner's sexual or emotional infidelity than their male and lesbian and gay counterparts (Leeker & Carlozzi, 2012).

The detrimental effects of infidelity may extend beyond committed relationships to affect the immediate families, extended families, and careers of those involved (Blow & Hartnett, 2005). Al-though infidelity is often perceived as a severe relational betrayal, some also believe it is a deviant or immoral behavior (Previti & Amato, 2004). Infidelity often has social ramifications. For instance, a woman who cheats on her husband with her boss may be shunned by her religious group, ostra-cized by her coworkers, and viewed as a "slut." A male senator who is caught having an affair with another man may be forced to step down from his appointed office.

The landscape of infidelity has also changed with the advent of digital technology. Once upon a time, infidelity required the physical presence of another human being and pornography had to be purchased in a store or by mail. But with the introduction of the Internet, "internet infidelity" has become a modern phenomenon. Online pornography, social networking sites like Facebook, and pro-infidelity websites like Ashley Madison make it easier to connect with people in ways not previously possible—and it changes our ideas of what pornography and infidelity mean in our relationships. So, what exactly is Internet infidelity? Like other types of infidelity, research shows that its definition differs from person to person (Hertlein & Blumer, 2014). Pornography is no longer the classic printed photos of the past—now, a viewer can interact with the person in those images, blurring the lines between conventional pornography and infidelity. Individuals may enter a relationship with different definitions of what is acceptable or unacceptable for them, so partners need to share their definitions of Internet infidelity to ensure they feel respected in their relationship.

The increase in Internet infidelity has been partially explained by what Cooper (1998) referred to as the "Triple A" engine, driven by accessibility, affordability, and anonymity. First, the Internet is easily accessible for most through smart phones, tablets, and computers, and there are innumerous websites offering opportunities to peruse a wide variety of pornography, chat with strangers, and engage in various online activities. Second, the Internet is generally affordable. If one does not have access in their own home, it is easily obtained through coffee shops, universities and schools, libraries and other "hot spots." Third, people can be whoever they want to be online. One can choose to be anonymous and reveal as much or as little information as s/he chooses. This means that people can engage in emotional and sexual activities online that they would not normally. In the past, looking at magazines or videos was not necessarily considered infidelity, but because the Internet has introduced interactive, sometimes real-time pornography, partners are more likely to consider this a type of cheating (Hertlein & Blumer, 2014).

So whether it is pornography, chat rooms, reconnecting with an old friend on Facebook, or virtually getting married to an avatar, the jury is still out on what is and what is not Internet infidelity. But regardless of how it is defined, it can be just as damaging to relationships as offline infidelity (Cravens, Leckie, & Whiting, 2013). Online infidelity can lead to the same emotional damage as offline infidelity including anger, depression, shame, humiliation, and jealousy—all of which can lead to relationship dissolution, separation, and divorce (Bridges, Bergner, & Hesson-McInnis, 2003; Schneider, 2003). Couples need to work together to negotiate boundaries around all types of infidelity to prevent it from damaging their relationships.

VIOLENCE AND RELATIONSHIPS

Janice and Michael have been together for about seven months. They were introduced by a mutual friend. They immediately hit it off. They had so much in common; they liked to spend time outside and both of them enjoyed active lifestyles. They started to do everything together. Janice was nervous, but she and Michael quickly started talking about spending the rest of their lives together. It felt like their relationship was perfect—life was perfect.

Without noticing it, Janice started spending less time with her friends. Michael told her it was normal for them to spend all their time together. One day while she and Michael were out, she ran into a group of her friends. They encouraged her to plan to go to a movie with them sometime later in the month. Janice talked to Michael about it. He sounded hesitant. She didn't know why. She insisted it would be a good thing for her, but it seemed the more she asked, the more he didn't like the idea. He told her he needed her to stay with him. Was this normal? She wasn't sure, but her friends were concerned. From an outside perspective, it is easier to see that this type of controlling behavior is emotionally abusive, a possible precursor to partner violence. And indeed, violence often starts subtly in relationships.

Partner violence has many labels: intimate partner violence, domestic violence, marital assault, spouse abuse, intimate violence, and partner abuse. It can include physical violence, sexual abuse, emotional abuse, psychological abuse, economic abuse, and/or verbal harassment. Many times, it is hard to discern whether abuse is even happening. To outsiders, partner violence might seem like an obvious intimacy killer, but it occurs in a surprisingly large number of couples. More than one in three women and one in four men have experienced rape, violence, and/or stalking within a relationship (Black et al., 2011). Perhaps even more surprising, most violent partner relationships will continue despite violence occurring. In this section, we will explore the prevalence of violence in partner relationships, discuss the various types of relationship violence, and provide tools to help readers notice whether or not abuse is happening in their own relationship, or in the relationship of someone they love.

Prevalence

Partner violence occurs within both opposite-sex relationships and same-sex relationships. Moreover, it happens in relationships where the individuals are married, dating, divorced, separated, and living together. Partner violence is distinguished between other forms of violence by the nature of the relationship that exists between the two individuals involved; violence between relatives, acquaintances, and strangers are not the focus of this chapter. Assessing the prevalence of partner violence is a challenging task. The most obvious barrier to determining prevalence is that violence most often occurs in private domains—most frequently in the home—where individuals are concerned about the repercussions of their reports. Although legal ramifications may deter some victims from reporting abuse, it is often the affection victims feel for their perpetrators that keep them quiet. In fact, 40% of incidences of partner violence are never reported to authorities (Durose et al., 2005; Frieze & Browne, 1989).

Although partner violence in the United States has declined steadily since 1994, in 2010 there were nearly 1 million reported incidents of partner violence in this country (Catalano, 2012). Males are the most frequent perpetrators in partner violence and most victims in partner violence are women (Tjaden & Thoennes, 1998). However, this does not preclude men from being victims of violence in relationships. Male reports may be underrepresented because of the social stigma associated with male victimization. Partner violence occurs across race, ethnicity, culture, and socioeconomic status. All people have the potential to be affected by relational violence; there are probably people reading this chapter who are in a relationship where violence is present. You or a friend may be struggling to manage the complexity and weight of these circumstances. A website that helps young adults to think about where to draw the line and when to break up is www.loveisrespect.org.

Paradox of Partner Violence

One of the most puzzling things about partner violence is that it exists between two people who share intimacy. There is a strongly paradoxical nature to partner violence. How can violence and affection occur in the same relationships? Researchers have identified that abusive acts are more common in love relationships than in any other. The vast majority of violent acts occur between intimates and family. Strangely, the closer and more attached victims and perpetrators report to be, the more vicious the violence (World Health Organization, 2002).

Types of Partner Violence

As previously noted, partner violence comes in a variety of forms: physical violence, sexual abuse, emotional abuse, psychological abuse, economic abuse, and verbal harassment. These categories are not clearly delineated, and often individuals experience multiple forms of violence in varying degrees of intensity.

EMOTIONAL AND PSYCHOLOGICAL ABUSE. Emotional and psychological abuse includes a laundry list of behaviors used to make a victim feel threatened and powerless, including:

- humiliating or belittling the victim in private or public
- controlling the victim
- manipulating the victim
- isolating an individual by withholding information, possessions, or relationships from him or her
- taking advantage of the victim
- destroying property to threaten or scare the victim
- neglecting the victim

Like other forms of abuse, perpetrators use emotional and psychological abuse to control victims' spending, opinions, feelings, identity, and personal autonomy. Emotional and psychological abuse can also include verbal harassment, economic abuse, and religious/spiritual abuse.

In order to determine whether or not emotional or psychological abuse is occurring, here are some guiding questions:

- Are you ever put down or humiliated in front of others?
- Are you ever made to feel your opinions, feelings, thoughts, or suggestions are wrong or should be disregarded?
- Are you treated like a child or criticized to feel like your behaviors are always "inappropriate" or "inferior?"
- Is your spending controlled?
- Are you demeaned, reminded of your shortcomings, or made to feel always wrong?
- Is it hard for your partner to apologize or laugh at his/her mistakes?
- Do they blame you for his/her mistakes, problems, or negative emotions?
- Does s/he use pouting, withdrawal or withholding affection or attention?
- Does s/he neglect to pay attention to your emotions or thoughts?
- Does s/he refuse to take responsibility for his/her own actions?

Emotional and psychological abuse can be the most confusing form of abuse because it is not always visible. Victims can have difficulties recognizing it because it affects thoughts, emotions, and behaviors rather than the body. The effects are internal rather than external; the bruises are not physically visible, but they can be profoundly damaging. Further, psychological or emotional abuse is the most common form of partner violence because when other types of partner violence occur, psychological or emotional abuse is also likely taking place; nearly 90% of women who have been physically or sexually abused have also been emotionally abused (Yoshihama, Horrocks, & Kamano, 2009).

PHYSICAL AND SEXUAL ABUSE. The signs of physical or sexual abuse can be clearer than emotional and psychological abuse, but the effects can have lasting physical, social, emotional, and psychological enduring repercussions. Physical and sexual abuse exists in varying degrees. Physical abuse includes hitting, slapping, shoving, grabbing, biting, pinching, hair pulling, and other types of physical strikes and coercion. It also includes refusing to help a partner receive medical care or forcing alcohol or drug use upon him or her. Sexual abuse includes coercing or attempting to coerce any sexual contact without permission, or treating one's partner in a sexually demeaning manner.

To determine whether or not physical or sexual abuse is occurring, here are some guiding questions:

- Have you ever been pushed or shoved by your partner?
- Has your partner ever used his/her physical stature to intimidate or coerce?
- Have objects ever been thrown or property destroyed during an argument with your partner?
- Are you ever hit during arguments?
- Has a weapon (e.g., gun or knife) ever been used to control you or manipulate you?
- Does your partner use physical intimidation, like hitting walls?
- Are you ever pressured by your partner to drink alcohol or use drugs?
- Have you ever been pressured to engage in sexual contact?
- Has anyone ever had sex with you after you fell asleep, were unconscious, or blacked out?

The National Coalition Against Domestic Violence (2007) reported that U.S. women between the ages of 20–24 possess the greatest risk for partner violence. Many of these women attend colleges or universities. Despite having access to health centers, college students attempting to escape violent relationships face a number of obstacles. Smaller social networks on college campuses can make students feel trapped, isolated, and fearful. Also, college campuses limit students' ability to seek help outside of social circles. Even if students seek the help of administrators, the administration may not be educated enough on partner violence to recognize the scope of the problem and make appropriate referrals. Despite these challenges, help is accessible. Individuals who have questions about violence should seek professional help. There are numerous Internet and telephone resources available to assist individuals determine the scope of violence and connect them to services available in their geographical area. Please don't wait; no one deserves to be mistreated!

ALCOHOL AND RELATIONSHIPS

Alcohol use is not always an intimacy killer, but in many situations it can be, especially when addiction comes into the picture. What impact do personal relationships have on drinking habits? On the other hand, what impact does drinking have on relationships? How does addiction influence relationships? This section explores these issues.

In 2010, the Monitoring the Future study reported that, 78.6% of college students used alcohol in the past year, 35.0% used an illicit drug, and 37.0% participated in binge drinking (defined as using alcohol to the point of intoxication or blacking out episodically—as opposed to daily use) in the past two weeks (Johnston, O'Malley, Bachman, & Schulenberg, 2011). In fact, college students are more likely than non-college students to drink alcohol and participate in binge drinking. On a large Midwestern university campus, 80.0% of students reported using alcohol in the past year (Boynton Health Service, 2010). This survey also revealed that students reported high rates of negative consequences resulting from alcohol and drug use; 27.4% did something they later regretted, 22.8% missed a class, and 14.6% of students drove while under the influence (Boynton Health Service, 2010). This means that many students have woken up the morning after a party or a night at the bars to find that, in addition to a hangover, they have a tattoo they do not want, a criminal record, a sexually transmitted infection (STI), or memories of—or others' reports regarding—having sex with a complete stranger.

What factors influence how often and how much young adults drink? One key factor is our relationship with others. For example, having close relationships with parents may reduce the amount of an individual's drinking, perhaps because some parents offer emotional support to their children. When young adults have a positive family environment, they are more likely to have fewer peers and friends who drink, less perceived pressure from friends to drink, and increased self-efficacy for refusing alcohol and decreasing stress (Nash, McQueen, & Bray, 2005). One study of college freshmen found that when students talked with their parents before the weekend began, they consumed less alcohol and were less likely to binge drink (Small, Morgan, Abar, & Maggs, 2011). Parenting styles also influence young adults' drinking behavior; college athletes who had permissive or democratic parents were less likely to drink than athletes with authoritarian parents (Mallet et al., 2011). In other words, young adults' close relationships with parents may buffer them from heavy drinking patterns.

Romantic relationships also impact drinking patterns. Among young adults, a partner's use of alcohol influenced the individuals' own use (Meacham, Bailey, Hill, Epstein, & Hawkins, 2013). Also, those who reported poor relationship quality with a romantic partner were more likely to have an alcohol use disorder. In several studies, getting married predicted reductions in drinking behavior and drug use for both men and women (e.g., Merline, Schulenburg, O'Malley, Bachman, & Johnston, 2008); this decrease in risky behavior is sometimes referred to as the "marriage effect." Schulenberg and Schoon (2012) found that even getting engaged was related to a drop in drinking patterns. Together, the findings from these studies imply that there is a unique quality of relational commitment that can protect individuals from excessive alcohol use.

When alcohol abuse is reported in the context of an intimate or romantic relationship, it is typically associated with negative consequences. Using daily diaries and interviews, a series of studies established a causal relationship between drinking and intimate partner violence, suggesting that alcohol use increases the risk of violent interactions among couples (Stuart, O'Farrell, & Temple, 2009). In a sample of men who had previously perpetrated violence, Fals-Stewart (2003)

Resources are available for individuals and couples facing challenges with addiction. Alcoholics Anonymous is a 12-step program that offers support for staying sober or quitting a drug habit (www.aa.org). For partners whose loved ones struggle with addiction, a crucial realization is that no one can stop their partners from going back to the bottle. This is a personal decision that only the alcoholic can make, sometimes only after s/he hits bottom. Hitting bottom often means that a person can't hold a steady job, is failing classes, and/pr losing friends or a partner. The organization Al-Anon helps partners and family members of alcoholics to cope with the challenges of living with someone with problematic drinking. Their hotline number is 1-800-356-9996. Behavioral couples therapy has also been found to be effective in addressing alcohol abuse in a relationship (Ruff, McComb, Coker, & Sprenkle, 2010).

found that when male partners drank, they were 11 times more likely to hurt their partner. On 81% of the days when severe violence occurred, the men had consumed alcohol before the incident. According to college-aged patients who were admitted to an emergency room, dating abuse was significantly more likely to occur on a day that perpetrators or victims had been drinking (Rothman et al., 2012). Furthermore, when heterosexual date rape occurs, many times either the woman, the man, or both have been drinking (Littleton, Grills-Taquechel, & Axsom, 2009). When an individual is intoxicated, s/he cannot give consent, and when his/her partner takes advantage of this situation, it is considered rape.

The relationship between addiction and intimacy is even more complex. When addiction permeates a relationship, a pattern may emerge where the partner who struggles with alcohol becomes dependent on the other partner for support (Williams & Jimenez, 2012). This enables the alcoholic partner to "underfunction" and continue drinking because s/he is taken care of by the other partner. Underfunctioners may believe that they are in competent and adopt a passive role, shouldering little responsibility for the relationship. In turn, the nonalcoholic partner becomes an "overfunctioner," assuming responsibility and dominance in the relationship. Often, the overfunctioner takes on an attitude of a martyr who is overworked and underappreciated. In these relationships, control becomes a focal issue. Addiction may distract partners from the true underlying issues in their relationship, or encourage an atmosphere of avoidance.

WHAT WE DON'T KNOW

Relationships are changing in the new millennium, with fewer people getting married, marriage available to LGBT couples, and digital technology constantly adding new dynamics to relationships. We do not always know how intimacy killers like the Four Horsemen contribute to these circumstances, and researchers are continuing to investigate these areas. Another area of up-and-coming research focuses on how interventions, like mindfulness training or positive mindsets, might help couples avoid criticism, defensiveness, stonewalling, and contempt in conflicts (Ben-Naim et al., 2013; Webb, Miles, & Sheeran, 2012).

As it relates to finances, many of the struggles and challenges facing young people today are more complex than they were for generations preceding them. The increased costs of higher education (and concomitant debt); market economy pressures for lavish weddings at a time when most couples are just starting out; intergenerational stressors related to caring for elderly parents and grandparents while simultaneously starting or maintaining one's own family of procreation; longer life expectancies vis-à-vis social presumptions of when retirement should begin; and a myriad of other foci can be overwhelming for couples. Couples need awareness of what works when learning how to talk about money.

When it comes to jealousy and infidelity, research on the effects of technology use in couple relationships over time is lacking (Hertlein & Blumer, 2014). For example, are women jealous of the time their partners spend with Siri, or do dating websites destabilize relationships over time? Alternatively, perhaps couples find ways adjust to the ever-increasing presence of technology in their lives. Another area that we are just beginning to understand is how the role of sex and sexual orientation relates to jealousy and infidelity online and offline (Dijkstra, Barelds, & Groothof, 2013). Qualitative research has found that those in a same-sex partnership have less intense reactions to a partner's infidelity than heterosexual couples (Dijkstra et al., 2013), but we have little understanding about why that may be or how that difference may change as society increasingly recognizes same-sex couples.

Research in partner violence has helped to gain public recognition of violence in relationships, explain dynamics that cause and perpetuate it, and help victims and perpetrators to prevent it. Still, as the field advances and as theoretical movements change and develop, gaps remain in our understanding of this complex issue. For instance, most partner violence research has focused upon opposite-gender couples. McClennen (2005) is one of several researchers advocating for the advancement of same-gender research to paint a more accurate picture of prevalence, types of abuse, and interpersonal dynamics. This research has the potential to dismiss misconceptions and equip the next generation of helping professionals with knowledge and tools to address partner violence in same-sex relationships.

Partner violence does not only affect the adults involved. Children often witness adult violence. Partner violence research is still working to determine the neurological, psychological, and interpersonal effects of witnessing partner violence (Graham-Bermann & Edleson, 2001). Moreover, research continues to investigate factors related to children's resilience: why are some children affected more than others after witnessing partner violence?

Alcohol and drug use has been studied in couple relationships for years, and much of the future research focuses on more sophisticated prevention of addiction and understanding how policy changes can drive behavior. We do not know, for example, how to best harness technology and integrate it into prevention programs. Would evidence-based programs work in an online environment, so prevention programs could reach more people? Could device-based applications promoting mindfulness help individuals better regulate emotions and drinking habits and thereby help couple relationships? Another area where research is lacking is in understanding how new laws and policies, such as the acceptance of medical marijuana use in some states, may affect couple relationships. These questions and more remain central to the advancement of our understanding of intimacy killers in the future.

APPLICATION

As human beings, most of us have a built-in need and desire to be close to someone and receive affection, but sometimes we unconsciously sabotage our relationships. Intimacy is tough to navigate; it takes skills, intentionality, and commitment. So, why learn about intimacy killers? Why focus on the negative? Don't all relationships have their own struggles? Definitely! However, in order to build a strong, safe, and devoted relationship one must first destroy (or prevent) the weak, negative characteristics that can endanger our relationships. To build intimacy, trust and commitment in a relationship, one must destroy criticism, defensiveness, stonewalling, and contempt.

The most effective way to put an end to intimacy killers is by intentionally looking for them in your own and your partner's behavior. After you've identified these sneaky behaviors, it's time to stop them before they become patterns. If you do not recognize your enemy and fight it, you might find yourself wondering how you lost. If we return to the story of Richard and Anne at the beginning of this chapter, we can analyze how the scenario would have evolved differently if they had acted against these intimacy killers. When Anne asked Richard, "Your irresponsible partying is driving me crazy—why can't you just grow up already?" she doesn't really hope to understand why—rather, her intention is to attack. What if she had said, "It bothers me when you come home late. I want to spend more time with you; if you came home earlier, we could do this. It would mean a lot to me." Richard would not need to respond aggressively because Anne is specifically stating what bothers her and what she wants, instead of criticizing Richard as a whole. Although starting off the conversation on a positive note could prevent the whole conversation from escalating, though, Richard also has to take responsibility for his drinking and abusive behavior.

Sometimes defensiveness is our most natural reaction to receiving criticism. In this case, the best way to respond to criticism is to start sentences with I rather than with "you." As we learned in this chapter, contempt is the most poisonous of all intimacy killers—destroying psychological, emotional, and physical health. It expresses a complete absence of any respect towards one's partner and is toxic to intimacy. Even though Richard was attacked when he walked in the door, he could have diffused the situation by acknowledging that he and Anne need to talk, but asking if they could talk later. Instead, by the time Richard labels Anne "Little Miss Perfect," we know it is about to get sticky. Ultimately, problems do not just fade away; they need to be confronted and resolved in a constructive manner. Ignoring the problem, tuning out, or turning away won't solve the issue. Instead of building a stone wall, deal with the issue together and communicate your needs and feelings with "I" statements.

Some of the most effective tools we have in relationships are the actions we take to prevent intimacy killers from entering our relationship. Are criticism and defensiveness completely avoidable? No. Does avoiding them guarantee that you will never go through another breakup, or never get hurt in your relationship? No. But knowing how to recognize these patterns may save you some grief in the long run and maybe help prevent jealousy, abuse, and addiction. Hopefully, applying these positive principles will prepare you to relate to your partner in a way that more beautifully and intensely displays genuine love. And at times when self-awareness is not enough, a licensed professional can often help couples work through complex and painful issues.

CONCLUSION

When intimacy killers are lurking in our relationships, we may not notice them. We live with them daily, and they can become patterns that slowly undermine the strength of our relationships. Noticing these pernicious habits is the first step to changing. After reading this chapter, it will be harder to argue without realizing patterns of criticism, defensiveness, contempt, and stonewalling are sneaking into our relationship. When we are living life "on purpose," we will take time to self-reflect on our relationships, and we will examine how jealously, alcohol, infidelity, or abusiveness may be affecting our behaviors and feelings toward the people we love. Only then can we take steps toward healing.

REFERENCES

Atkins, D. C., Baucom, D. H., & Jacobson, N. S. (2001). Understanding infidelity: Correlates in a national random sample. *Journal of Family Psychology, 15,* 735–749. doi:10.1037/0893-3200.15.4.735

Aune, K., & Comstock, J. (1991). Experience and expression of jealousy: Comparison between friends and romantics. *Psychological Reports, 69,* 315–319. doi:10.2466/pr0.1991.69.1.315

Barelds, D., & Barelds-Dijkstra, P. (2007). Relations between different types of jealousy and self and partner perceptions of relationship quality. *Clinical Psychology and Psychotherapy, 114,* 176–188. doi:10.1002/cpp.532

Barelds, D., & Dijkstra, P. (2006). Reactive, anxious and possessive forms of jealousy and their relation to relationship quality among heterosexuals and homosexuals. *Journal of Homosexuality, 51*(3), 183–198. doi:10.1300/J082v51n03_09

Barta, W. D., & Kiene, S. M. (2005). Motivations for infidelity in heterosexual dating couples: The roles of gender, personality differences, and sociosexual orientation. *Journal of Social and Personal Relationships, 22,* 339–360. doi:10.1177/0265407505052440

Ben-Naim, S., Hirschberger, G., Ein-Dor, T., & Mikulincer, M. (2013). An experimental study of emotion regulation during relationship conflict interactions: The moderating role of attachment orientations. *Emotion, 13*(3), 506–519. doi:10.1037/a0031473

Black, M. C., Basile, K. C., Breiding, M. J., Smith, S. G., Walters, M. L., Merrick, M. T., Chen, J., & Stevens, M. R. (2011). *The National Intimate Partner and Sexual Violence Survey (NISVS): 2010 Summary Report.* Atlanta, GA: National.

Blow, A., & Hartnett, K. (2005). Infidelity in committed relationships I: A methodological review. *Journal of Marital and Family Therapy, 31,* 183–216. doi:10.1111/j.1752-0606.2005.tb01555.x

Boynton Health Service, University of Minnesota. (2010). *College Student Health Survey Report: Health and Health Related Behaviors.* Retrieved from https://www.bhs.umn.edu/surveys/

Brand, R. J., Markey, C. M., Mills, A., & Hodges, S. D. (2007). Sex differences in self-reported infidelity and its correlates. *Sex Roles, 57,* 101–109. doi:10.1007/s11199-007-9221-5

Bridges, A. J., Bergner, R. M., & Hesson-McInnis, M. (2003). Romantic partners' use of pornography: Its significance for women. *Journal of Sex & Marital Therapy, 29*(1), 1–14. doi:10.1080/713847097

Burgoyne, C. B., Reibstein, J., Edmunds, A., & Dolman, V. (2007). Money management systems in early marriage: Factors influencing change and stability. *Journal of Economic Psychology, 28,* 214–228.

Busby, D. M., & Holman, T. B. (2009). Perceived match or mismatch on the Gottman conflict styles: Associations with relationship outcome variables. *Family Process, 48*(4), 531–545. doi:10.1111/j.1545-5300.2009.01300.x

Buss, D. (2000). Prescription for passion. *Psychology Today, 32,* 54–61. Retrieved from http://www.psychologytoday.com/articles/200005/prescription-passion

Buss, D. M., Larsen, R. J., Westen, D., & Semmelroth, J. (1992). Sex differences in jealousy: Evolution, physiology, and psychology. *Psychological Science, 3,* 251–255. doi:10.1111/j.1467-9280.1992.tb00038.x

Buunk, B. P. (1997). Personality, birth order and attachment styles as related to various types of jealousy. *Personality and Individual Difference, 23,* 997–1006. doi:10.1016/S0191-8869(97)00136-0

Buunk, A. P. & Dijkstra, P. (2001). Extradyadic relationships and jealousy. In C. Hendrick, & S. S. Hendrick (Eds.), *Close relationships: A sourcebook* (pp. 316–329). London: Sage Publications.

Buunk, B., & Dijkstra, P. (2004). Jealousy as a function of rival characteristics and type of infidelity. *Personal Relationships, 11*(4), 395–409. Retrieved from http://onlinelibrary.wiley.com/doi/10.1111/j.1475-6811.2004.00089.x/abstract

Buunk, A. P., & Dijkstra, P. (2006). Temptations and threat: Extradyadic relationships and jealousy. In A.L. Vangeslisti & D. Perlman (Eds.), *The Cambridge handbook of personal relationships* (pp. 533–556). New York: Cambridge University Press.

Carroll, J. S., Nelson, D. A., Yorgason, J. B., Harper, J. M., Ashton, R. H., & Jensen, A. C. (2010). Relational aggression in marriage. *Aggressive Behavior, 36*(5), 315–329. doi:10.1002/ab.20349

Catalano, S. (2012). *Intimate Partner Violence, 1993-2010.* U.S. Department of Justice. Retrieved from http://www.bjs.gov/content/pub/pdf/ipv9310.pdf

Cooper, A. (1998). Surfing into the new millennium. *Cyperpsychology and Behavior, 1,* 187–193. doi:10.1089/cpb.1998.1.187

Cravens, J., Leckie, K., & Whiting, J. (2013). Facebook infidelity: When poking becomes problematic. *Contemporary Family Therapy, 35,* 74–90. doi:10.1007/s10591-012-9231-5

Dean, L. R., Carroll, J. S., & Yang, C. (2007). Materialism, perceived financial problems, and marital satisfaction. *Family and Consumer Sciences Research Journal, 35,* 260–281. doi:10.1177/1077727X06296625

Dijkstra, P., Barelds, D. P., & Groothof, H. A. (2013). Jealousy in response to online and offline infidelity: The role of sex and sexual orientation. *Scandinavian Journal of Psychology, 54*(4), 328–336. doi:10.1111/sjop.12055

Doss, B. D., Simpson, L. E., & Christensen, A. (2004). Why do couples seek marital therapy?. *Professional Psychology: Research and Practice, 35*(6), 608–614. doi:10.1037/0735-7028.35.6.608

Drigotas, S. M., Safstrom, C. A., & Gentilia, T. (1999). An investment model prediction of dating infidelity. *Journal of Personality and Social Psychology, 77,* 509–524. doi:10.1037/0022-3514.77.3.509

Druckerman, P. (2007). *Lust in translation: The rules of infidelity from Tokyo to Tennessee.* New York: Penguin Press.

Durose, M. R., Harlow, C. W., Langan, P. A., Motivans, M., Rantala, R. R., Smith, E. L. & Constantin, E. (2005). *Family violence statistics, including statistics on strangers and acquaintances.* Washington, DC: U.S. Department of Justice.

Fals-Stewart, W. (2003). The occurrence of partner physical aggression on days of alcohol consumption: A longitudinal diary study. *Journal of Consulting and Clinical Psychology, 71*(1), 41–52. doi:10.1037/0022-006X.71.1.41

Fleishmann, A., Spitzberg, B., Andersen, P. & Roesch, S. (2005). Tickling the monster: Jealousy induction in relationships. *Journal of Social and Personal Relationships,22*(1), 49–73. doi:10.1177/0265407505049321.

Frieze, I. H., & Browne, A. (1989). Violence in marriage. In L. E. Ohlin & M. H. Tonry (Eds.), *Family violence.* Chicago, IL: University of Chicago Press.

Gigy, L., & Kelly, J. B. (1993). Reasons for divorce: Perspectives of divorcing men and women. *Journal of Divorce & Remarriage, 18,* 169–188.

Glass, S. P., & Wright, T. L. (1985). Sex differences in types of extramarital involvement and marital dissatisfaction. *Sex Roles, 12,* 1101–1119. doi:10.1007/BF00288108

Gottman, J. M. (1999). *The marriage clinic: A scientifically-based marital therapy.* New York: W.W. Norton & Company.

Gottman, J., & Gottman, P. S. (2011). *The Art and Science of Love: Couples Workshop DVD Box Set.* Seattle, WA: Gottman Institute.

Gottman, J. M., Gottman, J. S., & Atkins, C. L. (2011). The Comprehensive Soldier Fitness program: Family skills component. *American Psychologist, 66*(1), 52. doi:10.1037/a0021706

Gottman, J. M., & Levenson, R. W. (2002). A two-factor model for predicting when a couple will divorce: Exploratory analyses using 14-year longitudinal data. *Family Process, 41*(1), 83–96. doi:10.1111/j.1545-5300.2002.40102000083

Gottman, J. M., & Silver, N. (1999). *The seven principles for making marriage work: A practical guide from the country's foremost relationship expert.* New York, NY: Random House Digital, Inc.

Gottman, J. M., & Silver, N. (2012). *What makes love last? How to build trust and avoid betrayal.* New York: Simon & Schuster.

Graham-Bermann, S. A., & Edleson, J. L. (2001). *Domestic violence in the lives of children: The future of research, intervention, and social policy.* Washington, D.C.: American Psychological Association. doi:10.1037/10408-000

Guerrero, L., Spitzberg, B., & Yoshimura, S. (2004). Sexual and emotional jealousy. In J. H. Harvey, A. Wenzel, & S. Sprecher (Eds.), *Handbook of sexuality in close relationships* (pp. 311–345). Mahwah, NJ: Erlbaum.

Haslam, N., & Bornstein, B. H. (1996). Envy and jealousy as discrete emotions: A taxometric analysis. *Motivation and Emotion, 20*(3), 255–272. doi:10.1007/BF02251889

Hertlein, K.M., & Blumer, M.L.C. (2014). *The couple and technology framework: Intimate relationships in a digital age.* New York: Routledge.

Johnston, L. D., O'Malley, P. M., Bachman, J. G., & Schulenberg, J. E. (2011). *Monitoring the Future national survey results on drug use, 1975-2010: Volume II, college students and adults ages 19-50*. Ann Arbor, MI: Institute for Social Research, University of Michigan.

Kimberly, C., & Werner-Wilson, R. (2013). From John Lee to John Gottman: Recognizing intra-and interpersonal differences to promote marital satisfaction. *Journal of Human Sciences and Extension Volume, 1*(2), 32–46. Retrieved from http://www.doaj.org.ezp2.lib.umn.edu/

Lavallee, K. L., & Parker, J. G. (2009). The role of inflexible friendship beliefs, rumination, and low self-worth in early adolescents' friendship jealousy and adjustment. *Journal of Abnormal Child Psychology, 37*(6), 873–885. doi:10.1007/s10802-009-9317-1

Leeker, O., & Carlozzi, A. (2012). Effects of sex, sexual orientation, infidelity expectations, and love on distress related to emotional and sexual infidelity. *Journal of Marital and Family Therapy, 40*, 68–91. doi:10.1111/j.1752-0606.2012.00331.x

Lester, D., Deluca, G., Hellinghausen, W., & Scribner, D. (1985). Jealousy and irrationality in love. *Psychological Reports, 56*, 210. doi:10.2466/pr0.1985.56.1.210

Littleton, H., Grills-Taquechel, A., & Axsom, D. (2009). Impaired and incapacitated rape victims: Assault characteristics and post-assault experiences. *Violence and Victims, 24*(4), 439–457. doi:10.1891/0886-6708.24.4.439

Mallett, K. A., Turrisi, R., Ray, A. E., Stapleton, J., Abar, C., Mastroleo, N. R., . . . & Larimer, M. E. (2011). Do parents know best? Examining the relationship between parenting profiles, prevention efforts, and peak drinking in college students. *Journal of Applied Social Psychology, 41*(12), 2904–2927. doi:10.1111/j.1559-1816.2011.00860.x

McClennen, J. C. (2005). Domestic violence between same-gender partners: Recent findings and future research. *Journal of Interpersonal Violence, 20*(2), 149–154. doi:10.1177/0886260504268762

Meacham, M. C., Bailey, J. A., Hill, K. G., Epstein, M., & Hawkins, J. D. (2013). Alcohol and tobacco use disorder comorbidity in young adults and the influence of romantic partner environments. *Drug and Alcohol Dependence, 132*, 149–157. doi:10.1016/j.drugalcdep.2013.01.017

Merline, A. C., Schulenberg, J. E., O'Malley, P. M., Bachman, J. G., & Johnston, L. D. (2008). Substance use in marital dyads: Premarital assortment and change over time. *Journal of Studies on Alcohol and Drugs, 69*(3), 352–361. Retrieved from http://www.jsad.com/jsad/article/Substance_Use_in_Marital_Dyads_Premarital_Assortment_and_Change_Over_Time/2236.html

Mitchell, T. R., & Mickel, A. E. (1999). The meaning of money: An individual-difference perspective. *Academy of Management Review, 24*, 568–578.

Nash, S. G., McQueen, A., & Bray, J. H. (2005). Pathways to adolescent alcohol use: Family environment, peer influence, and parental expectations. *Journal of Adolescent Health, 37*, 19–28. doi:10.1016/j.jadohealth.2004.06.004

National Coalition Against Domestic Violence. (2007). *Domestic violence facts*. Retrieved from http://www.ncadv.org/files/DomesticViolenceFactSheet(National).pdf

Newton, T., & Sanford, J. (2003). Conflict structure moderates associations between cardiovascular reactivity and negative marital interaction. *Health Psychology, 22*(3), 270–278. doi:10.1037/0278-6133.22.3.270

Pahl, J. (1989). *Money and marriage*. London: Macmillan.

Pahl, J. (1995). His money, her money: Recent research on financial organisation in marriage. *Journal of Economic Psychology, 16*, 361–376. doi:10.1016/0167-4870(95)00015-G

Parrott, W., & Smith, R. (1993). Distinguishing the experiences of envy and jealousy. *Journal of Personality and Social Psychology, 64*(6), 906–920. doi:10.1037/0022-3514.64.6.906

Previti, D., & Amato, P. R. (2004). Is infidelity a cause or a consequence of poor marital quality? *Journal of Social and Personal Relationships, 21*(2), 217–230. doi:10.1177/0265407504041384

Radecki-Bush, C., Farrell, A. D., & Bush, J. P. (1993). Predicting jealous responses: The influence of adult attachment and depression on threat appraisal. *Journal of Social and Personal Relationships, 10*, 569–588. doi:10.1177/0265407593104006

Roscoe, B., Cavanaugh, L. E., & Kennedy, D. R. (1988). Dating infidelity: Behaviors, reasons and consequences. *Adolescence, 23*, 34–43. Retrieved from http://www.ncbi.nlm.nih.gov/pubmed/3381685

Rothman, E. F., Stuart, G. L., Winter, M., Wang, N., Bowen, D. J., Bernstein, J., & Vinci, R. (2012). Youth alcohol use and dating abuse victimization and perpetration: A test of the relationships at the daily level in a sample of pediatric emergency department patients who use alcohol. *Journal of Interpersonal Violence, 27*(15), 2959–2979. doi:10.1177/0886260512441076

Ruff, S., McComb, J. L., Coker, C. J., & Sprenkle, D. H. (2010). Behavioral couples therapy for the treatment of substance abuse: A substantive and methodological review of O'Farrell, Fals-Stewart, and colleagues' program of research. *Family Process, 49*(4), 439–456. doi:10.1111/j.1545-5300.2010.01333.x

Rydell, R., McConnell, A., & Bringle, R. (2004). Jealousy and commitment: Perceived threat and the effect of relationship alternatives. *Personal Relationships, 11*(4), 451–469. doi:10.1111/j.1475-6811.2004.00092.x

Schneider, J. P. (2003). The impact of compulsive cybersex behaviours on the family. *Sexual and Relationship Therapy, 18*(3), 329–354. doi:10.1080/146819903100153946

Schulenburg, J., Maggs, J., Staff, J., Patrick, M., Martz, M. (2012). Role transitions and statuses during early adulthood: National panel data on their prevalence and effects on health and well-being. *Society for Research in Child Development 2012 Themed Meeting: Transitions from Adolescence to Adulthood.* Tampa, FL.

Schulenberg, J. E., & Schoon, I. (2012). The transition to adulthood across time and space: Overview of special issue. *Longitudinal and Life Course Studies, 3*(2), 164–172. doi:http://dx.doi.org/10.14301/llcs.v3i2.194

Shapiro, M. (2007). Money: A therapeutic tool for couples therapy. *Family Process, 46,* 279–291.

Small, M. L., Morgan, N., Abar, C., & Maggs, J. L. (2011). Protective effects of parent–college student communication during the first semester of college. *Journal of American College Health, 59*(6), 547–554. doi:10.1080/07448481.2010.528099

Smith, T. (2006). *American sexual behavior: Trends, socio-demographic differences, and risk behavior (GSS Topical Report No. 25).* Chicago, IL: National Opinion Research Center.

Smith, R. H., & Kim, S. H. (2007). Comprehending envy. *Psychological Bulletin, 133*(1), 46–64. doi:10.1037/0033-2909.133.1.46

Spanier, G. B., & Margolis, R. L. (1983). Marital separation and extramarital sexual behavior. *Journal of Sex Research, 19,* 23–48. doi:10.1080/00224498309551167

Staske, S. (1999). Creating relational ties in talk: The collaborative construction of relational jealousy. *Symbolic Interactions, 22*(3), 213–246. doi:10.1525/si.1999.22.3.213

Stuart, G. L., O'Farrell, T. J., & Temple, J. R. (2009). Review of the association between treatment for substance misuse and reductions in intimate partner violence. *Substance Use & Misuse, 44,* 1298–1317. doi:10.1080/10826080902961385

Tjaden, P. & Thoennes, N. (1998). *National Institute of Justice Center for Disease Control and Prevention.* U.S. Department of Justice. Retrieved from https://www.ncjrs.gov/pdffiles/172837.pdf

Vogler, C., & Pahl, J. (1994). Money, power and inequality within marriage. *Sociological Review, 42,* 263–288.

Webb, T. L., Miles, E., & Sheeran, P. (2012). Dealing with feeling: A meta-analysis of the effectiveness of strategies derived from the process model of emotion regulation. *Psychological Bulletin, 138*(4), 775. doi:10.1037/a0027600

Wiederman, M. W. (1997). Extramarital sex: Prevalence and correlates in a national survey. *Journal of Sex Research, 34*(2), 167–174. doi:10.1080/00224499709551881

Williams, L., & Jimenez, M. (2012). Treating the overfunctioning and underfunctioning couple. *American Journal of Family Therapy, 40*(2), 141–151. doi:10.1080/01926187.2012.650610

Whisman, M., Dixon, A., & Johnson, B. (1997). Therapists' perspectives of couple problems and treatment issues in couple therapy. *Journal of Family Psychology, 62,* 361–366. doi:10.1037/0893-3200.11.3.361

Wilson, K., Mattingly, B. A., Clark, E. M., Weidler, D. J., & Bequette, A. W. (2011). The gray area: Exploring attitudes toward infidelity and the development of the Perceptions of Dating Infidelity Scale. *The Journal of Social Psychology, 151*(1), 63–86. doi:10.1080/00224540903366750

World Health Organization (2002). Facts: Intimate partner violence. Retrieved from http://www.who.int/violence_injury_prevention/violence/world_report/factsheets/en/ipvfacts.pdf

Yoshihama, M., Horrocks, J., & Kamano, S. (2009). The role of emotional abuse in intimate partner violence and health among women in Yokohama, Japan. *American Journal of Public Health, 99*(4), 647–653. doi:10.2105/AJPH.2007.118976

10
Intimacy Healers

Christina J. Robert, Ph.D., LMFT
Robert Family Services

Holli M. Kelly Trombley, Ph.D., LMFT
U.S. Department of Veterans Affairs

Anna I. Bohlinger, Ph.D., LMFT
Department of Family Social Science
University of Minnesota

Lisa J. Trump, MS
Department of Family Social Science
University of Minnesota

LEARNING OBJECTIVES

- Identify the components of the Gottman Sound Relational House
- Apply the Sound Relational House to a case study
- Understand Chapman's Five Love Languages
- Articulate how the Sound Relational House and the Five Love Languages may improve intimate relationships

INTRODUCTION

Case Vignette

Lucy and Jim were in the same introductory Psychology 1001 class at the University of Minnesota. Lucy had a crush on Jim and, after getting up the courage, decided to ask him to hang out one night.

They decided to meet up at a local coffee shop. Before she left, Lucy's roommates asked her again and again whether or not she and Jim were going on a date. She shrugged, unsure and hopeful herself. Before leaving she decided to change out of the clothes that she wore that day and put on a cuter pair of jeans and a sweater that she bought the previous weekend. She patted down her hair and checked her outfit one more time before she headed out the door. She could barely contain her excitement to hang out with Jim.

Jim, meanwhile, was also feeling pretty excited to hang out with the cute girl from his Psychology class. He had noticed her a lot over the past few weeks, but was feeling too shy to do anything about it. Before leaving for coffee, he brushed his teeth for the third time that afternoon and changed his shirt. He hurried across campus. Upon arriving at the café, he saw Lucy sitting down and drinking a cup of chai. He ordered his coffee and sat down next to her. She smiled at him and started off by asking him the basic questions: What's your major? How did you get into studying that? The conversation expanded from there, and they sat in those two chairs for hours, talking about everything: their likes and dislikes, classes they were taking, why they decided to go to the university, their families and friends, and even politics and religion. They both left the café that night feeling like they made a really good friend, and maybe something more?

Corresponding Author: Holli M. Kelly-Trombley, Ph.D., LMFT; U.S. Department of Veterans Affairs; Atlanta, GA 30349. E-mail: htromble@umn.edu.

In Chapter 9, you learned about some of the most damaging practices couples can engage in intimate relationships. Although the experience of these intimacy killers often feels like a vicious cycle that entraps couples, there are specific ways that couples can respond to these violations of intimacy that work to preserve the relationship. This chapter will primarily focus on identifying and describing intimacy healers that may begin to restore the couple relationship. At the end of this chapter, you, the reader, will be prepared to discuss and apply the concepts of John Gottman's Sound Relational House and Gary Chapman's Five Love Languages to your own intimate relationships in order to improve them.

THE SOUND RELATIONAL HOUSE

John Gottman is a renowned marriage researcher who has studied dating and married couples for over twenty years. In contrast with many other marriage "experts" who give advice based on personal ideologies or speculation, Gottman is one of the most revered researchers in the

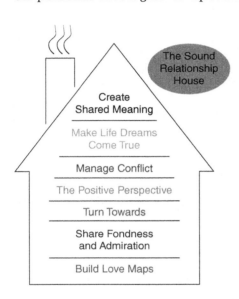

field. Specifically, by 1999, Gottman had worked with over 650 couples and studied them in such detail that he could predict with confidence the outcome of their relationship (i.e., stay together or dissolve the relationship) (Gottman & Silver, 2013). In Chapter 9, you learned about how his research has revealed common patterns of conflict (i.e., the Four Horsemen of the Apocalypse) that signify significant problems in couple relationships. However; Gottman did not stop after exposing common weaknesses in couples' relationships; he has also developed a framework for helping couples improve their relationships. This framework is called the Sound Relational House. Consider the process of building a house; one cannot install the roof or upper windows before first laying down a solid foundation to support the structure. Like a real house, strong relationships are built on a firm foundation of friendship. The first three levels of the house describe the strong friendship happily married couples experience, and the remaining four levels focus on the essential aspects of building a strong long-term relationship (e.g., a marriage). As the builder continues forward in the construction process, previous levels must be maintained to avoid the house from crumbling. Gottman's levels of the Sound Relational House are identified below, beginning with the foundation and working up.

Level 1: Building Love Maps

The first step to building a foundation of friendship for a strong relationship—romantic or otherwise—is getting to know each other. Gottman describes this first level of any relationship as *building love maps*. Each of us, knowingly or unknowingly, has established our own "maps" that contain the intimate details that make us who we are. These love maps include our dreams, hopes, and goals; our life philosophies and faith(s); our worries, fears, and doubts; our triumphs and strivings; our friends and families; and our past and current injuries and healings. Of course, the process of building love maps is an ongoing one, constantly informed by our new experiences and interactions. In the vignette shared at the beginning of this chapter, Lucy and Jim were beginning the process of learning about each other's inner-worlds by asking questions about one another, starting off with more surface-level topics (e.g., major in school) and slowly seeking to learn about more personal information (e.g., families). The key to building love maps is asking open-ended questions.

Level 2: Share Fondness and Admiration

The second level of a sound relational house is *sharing fondness and admiration*. This is in contrast with the intimacy killer, contempt, which was discussed in Chapter 9. The purpose of this level is to catch your partner doing something right and sharing your happiness with them. An example of this would be telling your partner, "Thank you for picking up the dry cleaning today. It really makes my life easier, and I appreciate when you do that." By doing so, you are building a couple-culture of appreciation, fondness, affection, and respect, and are increasing the likelihood that your partner will respond with fondness and admiration toward you. In addition, you are increasing the likelihood that positive events will be repeated in the future.

Level 3: Turn Towards

The purpose this next level of the house is to begin to know the ways that both you and your partner seek and give emotional connection. This is called making *bids for connection*. Said another way, a bid for connection is a way of reaching out to connect with your partner and forge an emotional bond. These bids can be verbal or nonverbal, and may take on a variety of different forms (e.g., high energy or attentiveness). Examples of turning toward (as opposed to away or against) a bid include, but are not limited to: sharing thoughts and feelings; invitations; playful or affectionate touches; and engaging facial expressions. Chapman's Love Languages, which are discussed later in this chapter, can be a powerful way to turn toward your partner. It is important to remember that everyone turns toward one another in different ways, and getting to know how your partner prefers to receive emotional engagement is a vital part to a successful and happy relationship.

© Zurijeta, 2014. Used under license from Shutterstock, Inc.

Level 4: The Positive Perspective

The positive perspective entails seeing the good in your partner, and expecting to see more good in your partner in the future. The process of seeking out the good/positive in your partner as opposed to his or her failings is known as *Positive Sentiment Override*. For example, a wife might actively focus on the positive aspects of her marriage by thinking *"He's so handsome," "He's such a good father to our kids," "He really shows me love when he. . . ,"* and so on. By thinking these types of thoughts regularly, the positive thoughts tend to supersede the negative thoughts, assumptions, or feelings she might have about her husband or marriage. In addition, this level supports mutual influence between partners and an equal distribution of power and work. This level is one that can only be achieved by maintaining the strong friendship described in the earlier three levels of the house. If they are lacking, the couple friendship is likely to also be lacking, making the fourth floor particularly challenging to achieve.

Level 5: Manage Conflict

One of Gottman's findings about relationships is that 69% of couple problems cannot be solved (Gottman & Silver, 1999). These problems stem from things that are at the core of who people are and reflect underlying and unchanging differences between individuals. Therefore, this level is **not** about not arguing with your partner or not having problems. Every couple is going to have arguments and disagreements. Rather, this level is about solving your *solvable problems* and continuing to talk about what is at the core of *unsolvable problems.*

Solvable problems are those problems that can be resolved. An example of this would be not spending enough time together because of conflicting work hours. Some of the ways a couple might approach this would be: asking a supervisor at work to switch shifts, staying up late or getting up early to spend time together, or initiating a date night to be sure to spend some time together during the week. By making specific changes to overcome the present obstacles, the couple is able to reach a solution.

In contrast, unsolvable problems are about the dreams that couples have that lie within the conflict. Said another way, the couple is not able to use their normal problem-solving techniques for these problems because their individual dreams are tied into the problem and conflict with each other. Simply rearranging one's schedule will not suffice. For example, Ana and Juan were recent newlyweds. They found themselves arguing constantly about who had to do the dishes. Ana grew up in a house where her mother did all of the chores and swore to herself upon growing up that she would live in a family with more gender equity. She also didn't really mind having dishes in the sink because one of the biggest compliments that someone could give her as a young woman was to have her over to their home without deep cleaning—it was a sign that you were more intimate when someone could see your house in its untidy state. She wanted to live in a family where gender equity and intimacy was highly and visibly valued.

In contrast, Juan grew up living on a cul-de-sac where most of his extended family lived on the same street. Consequently, family could come by anytime to visit. A rule in his house growing up was that the front rooms of the house (i.e., the living room, the kitchen, the dining room, and the bathroom) always had to be clean because you never knew when family would stop by. The way that you showed that you were ready to welcome guests was to keep those areas clean. It was important to him as a young man to live in a family where those same standards of welcoming others were maintained.

When Ana and Juan got married, they found themselves experiencing a lot of conflict over this issue, specifically with who did the dishes and when the dishes should be done. While on the surface, this may appear to be a solvable problem, the meanings that Ana and Juan put to the dishes contributed to the development of an unsolvable problem. More so, the meanings that they attached to the dishes were about deeply held values and dreams: gender equity, hospitality, and family. In the end, they decided that the next apartment they moved into had to have a dishwasher as an included appliance so that the dishes could be placed away, but did not have to be washed immediately. While they still fight about cleanliness, especially before having company over, knowing the meaning of those dreams enables them to talk about it without becoming contemptuous or gridlocked.

There are several techniques that couples can utilize in an effort to better manage conflict in their relationship. First, by softening your start-ups, the conversation begins with complaints as opposed to blame statements. Specifically, making "I" statements ("I felt ___ when you said. . .") as opposed to "you" statements ("You always. . .") and talking with clarity, politeness, and providing descriptions, as opposed to making critiques and judgments, can help. As you can imagine, this sets the stage for a more effective, respectful conversation. In addition to soft start-ups, making and receiving repair attempts can also help manage conflict. Examples of repair attempts include: admitting to your partner when you are wrong; maintaining confidence that you can solve the problem together; taking breaks when necessary; offering and accepting apologies; and communicating love and commitment throughout the discussion. Another conflict management technique involves the individuals' ability to soothe him or her self and each other. Taking the example of Ana and Juan, if they were in the midst of a particularly troublesome argument about how to handle the dishes, an individual soothing technique might be Ana doing deep-breathing to relax herself, and she might try to soothe Juan by inviting him to talk about what is hurting for him.

Next, seeking a win/win outcome, as opposed to a win/lose outcome where one member is forced to sacrifice his or her position in the argument, is another way to manage conflict. To do so, couples are encouraged to accept influence from one another, find common ground, consider multiple options and solutions, and identify "shared enemies" and work together against them. These steps strategically place the two partners on the same side, as opposed to fighting against one another to get what they need or want. Lastly, healthy conflict management involves being tolerant of each other's faults. If, when upset, Ana always resorted to thinking or saying, "If only Juan wasn't . . ." or "If only Juan was . . . ," her tolerance for her partner's flaws would plummet. Until you can accept your partner's flaws, you will not be able to achieve a win/win outcome because you will always remain pitted against your partner. By utilizing several or all of these techniques, couples will be able to develop better skills for managing their conflict in gentle and effective ways.

Level 6: Make Life Dreams and Aspirations Come True

As most, if not all, of us have experienced, managing conflict in relationships occurs in the day-to-day grind of any long-term relationship. As couples develop techniques within the previous floors to help build, support, and maintain the relationship, they must also begin to consider how they can enhance their relationship with dreams, fun, adventure, and play. This level of the house is about identifying the dreams and goals of partners, and working to make them possible, through physical, emotional, financial, and/or social support. Returning to the example of Ana and Juan, in this level of the Sound Relational House, Juan might share with Ana that his personal dream is to write a book, and Ana might share with Juan that her personal dream is to learn how to cook. The couple might also develop a shared dream of traveling to different parts of the world. By making these dreams known, the couple is better able to work together toward aspirations and support one another in both personal and shared dreams.

Level 7: Create Shared Meaning

One of the easiest ways to think about the final level of the Sound Relational House is the story that the couple will tell about themselves. As the relationship forms, develops, and deepens, what storylines and themes predominate in their narrative? Imagining the couple as grandparents, what values will they want to impress on their grandchildren as important things to look for in a partner, and ways to be a good partner? How do couples see the world and their role in it? A couple's shared meaning include: rituals of connection (e.g., a kiss goodnight); roles as husband, wife, and so on; couple and family rituals; personal and shared goals; personal and shared symbols; and personal and shared legacies. This level of the house is best created intentionally. How will you create meaning with your partner?

Gottman's concept of the Sound Relationship House uses the metaphor of building a house to illustrate the process of building a solid relationship. A relationship is most successful when it is built on a solid foundation of knowing one another's inner-worlds, and is slowly constructed while simultaneously reinforcing the levels below. Therefore, a couple's process of constructing their relationship house never reaches a true end, but continues to adjust and evolve.

© spotmatik, 2014. Used under license from Shutterstock, Inc.

LOVE LANGUAGES

Case Vignette

Raul wakes up early. It is his wife's birthday. He gets out of bed quietly so as not to wake her. He goes out to her car, cleans off the snow, and makes sure she has enough gas to get to work and to do her errands. He goes back in the house and makes breakfast for the children and puts on a pot of coffee. He lays out the clothes for the kids. He then goes back upstairs and sits on the bed next to his wife, who is now awake. He says, "Happy Birthday, Maria!" and gives her a big kiss. Then he says, "I have to go to work now. Everything is ready for the kids. I hope you have a great day." She looks at him in disbelief. "What? Don't you even LOVE me?" She closes her eyes and turns away. Raul's shoulders drop. What has he done wrong? He did everything he could to make it a great day for her. He picks up his coat off the bed and leaves for work. He'll call her later after she has calmed down.

In the scenario above, Raul is trying to show his wife that he loves her. It is her birthday and he cares about her and wants to try and please her. He is doing this in the best way that he knows how: by engaging in acts of service. Maria, however, is looking for something different. She is looking to be told that she is loved. She had hoped to be wished a happy birthday through Raul's words and actions, and to be reminded of how happy he is to spend her special day together. In short, Maria is seeking out words of affirmation. Maria and Raul are speaking two different languages. It would be like someone speaking French to a German and expecting to be understood.

No love language is the right or the correct love language. They are all just different ways of saying the same things: I love you; I care about you; you are special to me. When we speak the same love language as our partner, our messages communicating love are often easily heard and received. The love tank that we have inside us is slowly filled up as we hear and experience from our partner the love that we desire. Dr. Chapman says, "I like to picture [that] inside of us there's an emotional love tank. If the tank is full—that is we genuinely feel loved—then life is beautiful" (Chapman, 2013). However, when couples do not speak the same love language, as was the case for Maria and Raul, messages often get lost and partners may end up feeling less connected and cared for by one another. Having a working understanding of the different languages of love is essential to be able to identify the languages that you and your partner primarily speak, and to work toward becoming bilingual in the context of your relationship.

What are the Five Love Languages?

Based on Chapman's (1992) work, there are five main love languages. They include:

1. **Words of Affirmation**
2. **Quality Time**
3. **Receiving Gifts**
4. **Acts of Service**
5. **Physical Touch**

Chapman posits that each person has preferences for how s/he gives and receives love. For some, the way that they feel most loved is when they get a gift from their partner. For others, they feel most loved when they get a hug, a kiss, or a massage. Usually, when you feel most loved in a certain way, you tend to think that other people also feel loved in the same way. For instance, if a young woman feels most loved when she hears the words, "I love you," she may be sure to tell her partner every day that she loves him. However, for her partner, those special words may have less meaning for him than getting a hug or a kiss.

You may be thinking, ". . . but everyone likes all of those things!" Sure, that may be the case, but we would guess that if you dig deeply enough, you will probably discover that you feel most loved when your friend or partner does one of the five. One way to investigate what your love language might be is to consider how you typically provide love for those around you. Do you find yourself giving gifts often or are you more likely to provide compliments and affirmations? We often provide love to others in the same way that we would prefer to receive love. One more way that might be helpful is to ask yourself, "If someone were to withhold or reject a particular action, such as touch or acts of service, what would hurt most?"

Words of Affirmation

"I can live for two months on a good compliment."—Mark Twain (Kemp, 2012)

Mark Twain's love language must have been words of affirmation. If words of affirmation are the way that you feel most loved, then a good compliment, a sweet nothing whispered in your ear, or an encouraging word will fill up your emotional tank. Examples of compliments might include:

- "You look great in that suit"
- "You're the best mama in the wholllleee wide worrrllld!"
- "I just love the way you cook. The neighbors have got to be jealous of the smells coming out of our kitchen!"

Words of encouragement are also a type of affirmation. A spouse might offer moral support for an upcoming job interview or a boss might call attention to the great work you did on a project. A single mother might be told she's doing a great job balancing working and raising a child. Words of affirmation might also include the following: reinforcing a difficult decision; providing words of kindness and encouragement; providing words of humility; writing affirming notes; acknowledging a person's unique perspective; and providing indirect words of affirmation. In general, words of affirmation help us to overcome insecurities and instill confidence.

Quality Time

Quality time is more than just being around your friend or partner. It is not considered to be *quality* time if one or both partners are surfing the web on their computers or engaging in ongoing texting conversations with others. In contrast, the love language of quality time includes feeling close to your partner and focusing all of your energy on your mate for awhile. It can include either:

© Deklofenak, 2014. Used under license from Shutterstock, Inc.

Quality conversation

- Sharing experiences, thoughts, feelings, and desires in a friendly, uninterrupted context
- Listening and offering advice and responding
- Self-revealing—understanding your own emotions and inner feelings and revealing these aspects of your self to your mate

or

Quality activities

- Sharing physical time doing activities that they both love to do
- Intentionally creating memories that the couple will be able to reminisce about in the future

Individuals that love through this particular language would generally prefer to spend uninterrupted time with the people they love. These individuals feel most loved when their partner and others close to them dedicate this time to spend with them. These lovers are not as likely to respond to tangible things, such as gifts or touch, but feel closest to others when they are able to have quality conversation or engage in quality activities.

Receiving Gifts

Everyone likes to receive gifts, but for some, holding that special gift or small symbol of love in their hands means more than anything in the world—the item may even represent a part of the giver to that person receiving the item. It may serve as an expression of love and devotion. A special someone can show up with a piece of candy in their coat pocket intended for his or her loved one, and that can mean more than all the kisses in the world. A card in the mail may be better than all of the "I love you's" that person has to say.

© stefanolunardi, 2014. Used under license from Shutterstock, Inc.

Receiving gifts (and giving them) is one of the easiest languages to learn because it is often clear what the person wants. The gift can come in any form. It can be free, frequent, expensive, or rare. The cost is not what the person desires. The person desires a visual *symbol* of love. In the lack of these tangible expressions the person may feel that they are not loved. Receiving a tangible item can help to create happiness and security.

You may initially be tempted to consider this particular love language as the least desirable of the group. After all, would a person really want to admit that s/he would prefer receiving a gift to spending quality time with his or her partner? For many, this love language feels selfish and materialistic. We would like to gently challenge you on this initial assumption. Although this may not be your particular love language, it is certainly as accepted and valuable as any other. It is important to note that these gifts may be store bought, homemade or even a gift of the self. Thus, for those with this love language, they respond most to being given a token that symbolizes their partner's love for them.

Acts of Service

Both men and women often show their partners and friends they care about them by performing acts of service. For Raul, the acts of service were his way of showing his wife he loved her. Raul provided service after service to help Maria have an easier day, and then was let down when his efforts were not recognized or appreciated. Unfortunately, Raul was not aware that Maria's primary love language is words of affirmation.

© oliveromg, 2014. Used under license from Shutterstock, Inc.

Acts of service can come in the form of chores around the house, taking care of business, or doing something as simple as filling up the gas tank. A partner working to speak to the needs of this love language does these acts out of love, not obligation, and to promote happiness. Further, these acts of service are done sans expectation(s) for reciprocity. If your partner appreciates acts of service, it might be important to ask some questions to clarify what acts of service are most important. Does s/he like to have the laundry folded? Does s/he like it when you make coffee in the morning? Defining the act of service is an important step in getting one's needs met (if this is your primary language) and in meeting the needs of your partner (if this is his or her love language). It is important to understand what acts of service your mate appreciates most.

For some couples, this might involve a reversal of traditional gender roles as it might mean helping out with those tasks that one does not normally engage in. For example, if a wife's primary love language was acts of service, her husband might try to speak to her love language by washing the laundry, cooking dinners, and getting the children ready for bed. These acts are not connected to be traditional roles for males, yet they communicate messages of love to his wife. The division of roles within the relationship is unique to each couple, and for many with this love style, their roles might deviate slightly or substantially from traditional gender roles.

Physical Touch

Physical touch, like several other of the love languages, can make or break a relationship if one person desires this form of love and does not receive it. Sexual intercourse is one expression of physical touch and, for some, it promotes security and the sense of feeling loved. However, sex is only one form of physical touch. Other examples of physical touch include, but are not limited to: hand holding; massages; hugs; cuddles; sitting close together; and casual, romantic, or sexual caresses. For those with a partner with this love language, it will be important to pay attention to your partner's physical and psychological responses to the touch to find out what type(s) of touch is most valued, and in what circumstances. For example, a husband's desire for touch would likely look different in social settings versus in the privacy of the home. In a crisis, physical touch for these lovers can be very important as the need for physical proximity may provide the calm, safe base they need, whereas during interpersonal conflict, one's desire for physical touch might be very different. Figuring out how and when physical touch is appropriate and appreciated is an important task in your relationship.

The love language of physical touch, more so than the others, provides a potential challenge for couples with different love languages. It may be the case that one partner feels most loved through intimate touches from his or her partner, whereas the partner feels uncomfortable with touch. Especially in crisis situations for these couples, the need for and resistance to touch is likely to be heightened, creating a potentially damaging scenario. Before these situations arise, it is important for these couples to openly discuss their needs and wants, and to set agreed upon boundaries that do not sacrifice one partner's needs to fulfill the other partner's needs. These couples might benefit from discussing the type of touch that feels comfortable for both in different situations, and may create a code word to easily communicate when it becomes too uncomfortable. Open and effective communication here is key.

COMMUNICATING YOUR LOVE LANGUAGE

Now that you have an initial sense of what your primary love languages are, what do you do with that information? Do you keep it to yourself? Do you share it with all of your friends and family? Do you share it with your partner? Being in an intimate relationship requires ongoing communication. Every individual has his or her own needs and desires, and it is important to make them known to increase the likelihood that they will be met. Consider, if your partner has no way of knowing what your needs and desires are in your relationship because you are not able or willing to express them, how is s/he expected to be able to meet your needs and desires fully and consistently? Instead, it will become a guessing game for your partner, sometimes fulfilling your needs and other times not. In the vignette above, Raul was stuck in this guessing game. He had no idea what his wife was wanting or needing from him, and few opportunities to figure it out. Because Maria had not communicated what she desired on her birthday to make her feel most loved, Raul was unable to meet those needs and resorted to providing love in the way that he best knows how: through his love language.

Activity 1

Have you ever knowingly or unknowingly blamed a friend or partner for not speaking the love language you wanted? Write out a statement you might make to a partner or friend when your needs or wants for that relationship are going unmet.

Although common for many couples, failing to engage in an open dialogue regarding each partner's preferred ways of receiving love may eventually take its toll. For some couples, repeatedly having their needs and desires not met might leave them feeling disconnected and unloved and they may respond by becoming resentful and withholding demonstrations of their love to their partner. Thus, a cycle of disconnection between partners threatens to begin, leading the couple down a path they had not intended or wanted to go down. As previously stated, open communication is key to having one's needs met.

Activity 2

WHAT IS YOUR PREFERRED LOVE LANGUAGE?

Pick one of the following:

I feel most loved when my partner:

1. Expresses how much s/he cares about me; both who I am and what I do for him or her
2. Gives me undivided attention and spends time alone with me
3. Brings me gifts and other tangible expressions of love
4. Pitches in to help me, perhaps by running errands or taking on household chores
5. Expresses feelings for me through physical contact

Now that you have a better idea of what the five love languages are, let's put it all together. Rank your love languages in your order of preference (1-most preferred, 5-least preferred). Then, write specific examples of how you like to be loved the most and the least by those close to you.

Now look at the chart below and fill it in for the relationships that are most important in your life. Think of two people in your life with whom you have a close relationship. Write their names down. Under their names, write down how they typically show you that they love you. Do they both show love in the same way, or do they show love in different ways? Do they speak your language, or are they speaking their love language? Keep in mind, for the majority of people, we tend to speak the love language that we know best: our own preferred language. In the column entitled "Preferred Love Language Spoken," We encourage you to consider not what your love language is, but what your significant other, past relationship partner, and close friend's love languages are, and how you spoke those languages.

Activity 3

Name	Preferred Love Language Spoken	Preferred Love Language Received
You		
Significant Other		
Previous Relationship		
Close Friend		

After filling out the chart above, consider the following:
- Do the languages that you speak correspond to how the person likes to receive love?
- Do you know what love language your partner prefers to speak or to hear/receive?
- Knowing your love language, as well as that of your partner, can be transformative in your relationship.

Closing Thoughts

So what do I do if my partner shows love in a way that I don't prefer to receive? Shouldn't s/he just accept that this is the way I like for others to show me that they love me? Shouldn't s/he change the way s/he shows love? Good questions. However, these are not easily answered. On the one hand, it is important for your partner to know how you like to receive love so that s/he can try to meet your needs. At the same time, understanding the language that your partner speaks is equally as important. The first step in getting your and your partner's needs met is to make them known. Sit down with your partner and talk about your love languages. Talk about how you like to have someone show you love, and provide specific examples of things your partner has already done for you that resonated with you and made you feel especially loved. Ask your partner if s/he has additional ideas for how s/he would like to speak your love language, and how you could meet your partner's needs and desires. Are there ways you can change? What ideas do you have for how you can try to speak your partner's language better? Keep in mind, nobody learns a foreign language in a day. It may take some time to remember that your partner likes to hear words of affirmation when your tendency is to provide acts of service. If your partner is a touchy person and his or her way of showing you love is to give hugs, then accept them and understand that is his or her language even if you aren't an overly affectionate person. Continue to tell your partner that you value expressions of love, but also recognize and value his or her efforts in their own right. You will likely have to start small and practice until you get it right.

If we think back to Maria and Raul, we can understand their situation a little bit better now. If Raul knew that all Maria wanted was to be affirmed that she is loved and valued, he could have held off on helping out with the kids and pour his energy into speaking Maria's love language via words of affirmation. If Maria knew that Raul's way of showing her affection was to help out via around the house, she may have been less disappointed and less likely to jump to the conclusion that Raul simply doesn't love her. Giving and receiving love is a complex process that requires communication and patience. Try exploring your needs and desires with your partner and making adjustments to more effectively speak one another's love languages. After some time, ask yourself, *"Do I notice a change? Do I feel more loved? Does s/he feel more loved?"* If so, great job! Keep it up. If not, what other adjustments might you make to continue the process of learning each other's love language needs?

REFERENCES

Chapman, G. (1992). *The five love languages.* Chicago, IL: Northfield Publishing.

Chapman, G. D., & Campbell, R. (1997). *The five love languages of children.* Chicago, IL: Northfield Publishing.

Chapman, G. D. (2013, March 26). To feel loved. *In The Five Love Languages.* Retrieved from http://www.5lovelanguages.com/category/bible/

Chapman, G. D. (2000). *The five love languages of teenagers.* Chicago, IL: Northfield Publishing.

Chapman, G. (n.d.). *The five love languages.* Retrieved from http://www.5lovelanguages.com/

Gottman, J. M., & Silver, N. (1999). *The seven principles for making marriage work.* New York: Three Rivers Press.

Gottman, J. M., & Silver, N. (2013). *What makes love last? How to build trust and avoid betrayal.* New York: Simon & Schuster.

Gottman, J. M. (2009). *The scientific basis for the orcas island couples' retreat: The sound relational house.* Retrieved from http://www.gottmancouplesretreats.com/about/sound-relationship-house-theory.aspx

Kemp, J. (2012, February 28). Living two months on a compliment. [Web log comment]. Retrieved from http://www.strongerfamilies.org/living-two-months-on-a-compliment/

Start Marriage Right. (2014). *Gary Chapman: Preparing for marriage.* Retrieved from http://www.startmarriageright.com/videos/

Winfrey, O., & Chapman, G. (2013). *Sneak peek: Oprah and Dr. Gary Chapman—The five love languages.* Retrieved from www.oprah.com/oprahs-lifeclass/First-Look-Oprah-and-Dr-Gary-Chapman-Five-Love-Languages-Video#ixzz2KPfDWNe2

11

Uncharted Territory: Long Distance Relationships in College-Age Commuters

Polina N. Levchenko, Ph.D.
*Department of Human Development
and Family Studies
Michigan State University*

Cigdem Yumbul, M.S.
*Department of Family Social Science
University of Minnesota*

Tai J. Mendenhall, Ph.D., LMFT
*Department of Family Social Science
University of Minnesota*

LEARNING OBJECTIVES

- Become aware of how common long distance relationships (LDRs) are
- Understand who is more likely to be in a LDR during his or her lifetime
- Recognize strengths and weaknesses of couples in LDRs
- Become familiar with commonplace stressors/strains that LDR couples face
- Understand coping mechanisms for couples in LDRs

Vignettes

A College/University LDR

Brian and Aubree are high school sweethearts. They had been dating for 18 months when they started their new life chapter in college in the fall. The problem is that they got accepted to two different colleges that are a two-hour flight apart from each other. Initially, both their friends and families were not supportive of Brian and Aubree continuing their relationship. They told them stories about how long distance relationships (LDRs) did not work for other couples that they knew or had heard about, and how ugly the break-ups turned out to be. There were stories about cheating and betrayal.

Some of their friends began to change their minds, though, as Aubree and Brian continued to show how determined they were to make things work. To be sure, even without being in a LDR, freshman year for college students is difficult (e.g., new classes, new requirements, new people to meet and connect with, new places to see). Finding time to talk on the phone when one's partner is so far away—or even send a quick text message—is challenging. But Aubree and Brian are committed

to not being another "LDRs don't survive" story. They looked forward to seeing each other for a weekend every couple of months, and planned (and talked a lot about) to reunite during the summers (each year) and forever (after graduation in four years). So far, so good.

A Military LDR

Nick and Denise met in their senior year in college through mutual friends, instantly felt chemistry, and started dating. As months went by and graduation approached, they began talking about their future plans. Denise, a marine biologist, was applying for jobs in California (where she had always wanted to live) while Nick aimed to join the Navy. After graduation, Denise accepted a great offer in San Francisco and Nick enlisted, which required him to move to New York. Both Nick and Denise knew it would be difficult to maintain their relationship as they moved apart, but they believed their love and commitment would overcome the challenges a LDR would bring.

Corresponding Author: Polina N. Levchenko, Ph.D.; Department of Human Development and Family Studies; Michigan State University; 13C Human Ecology Building; 552 W. Circle Drive; East Lansing, MI 48824; E-mail: levchenk@hdfs.msu.edu.

At first, both Nick and Denise were busy adjusting to their new environments, cities, and work. Nick was undergoing an intense training and did not have much time, even for himself. Denise was adjusting to corporate life, but at the same time making new friends and enjoying the social scenes of San Francisco. As months went by, the couple started to worry about how they would maintain and manage their union, but left these concerns unspoken. Denise was anxious about Nick being deployed to war. Nick was uneasy about Denise's new friends, whom she seemed to spend most of her free time with. Both complained about limited phone calls and emails, alongside not seeing each other often. They could not plan reunions ahead of time due to Nick's ambiguous work and deployment schedule. The couple could not set a deadline for when to reunite.

An International LDR

After all the hard work she had put in over the years, finally Safak was accepted to her dream Ph.D. program in the United States. She was very excited for this opportunity, except that it meant she had to separate from her country (Turkey), her family and friends, and Ege (her boyfriend of five years). Ege had just started his medical residency in Turkey. After Safak moved to the United States and started the program, it became very difficult to arrange a time to talk over the phone or via Internet due to the couple's 10-hour time difference. When Ege was done with his work at the hospital and called Safak to talk about his day, Safak would be just starting the day (and, therefore, could not talk for very long). Safak also went through a difficult period when she first moved to the United States trying to restructure her life, from finding a house to making new friends, coping with the heavy responsibilities of a Ph.D. program, and adapting to the rules, expectations and social relationships of a foreign country.

The couple could only meet each other once a year (when Safak went back home for three weeks over the summer). They could not see each other over the Holiday/Christmas vacation or Spring Break due to the expensive plane tickets, and Ege could not come and visit her due to his demanding work schedule. When they reunited in Turkey the following summer, they wanted to spend as much time possible with each other. However, Safak's family and friends also wanted to spend time with her, and complained about Safak choosing Ege over them.

INTRODUCTION

Can you relate to any of the experiences shared above? Are you in a LDR, or do you have a friend who is in one? Are you the one who believes that LDRs are doomed to fail, or do you believe that couples living across a distance can still survive and grow?

Even if you have never been in a LDR, chances are—down the road—you might find yourself in one. They are becoming increasingly common, especially within the middle classes of the United States and Europe. As high school sweethearts go to different colleges, as strangers meet online, and as different career paths—professional or military—proceed in different zip codes, couples are choosing to stay together anyway. And it's not just intimate or romantic couples; LDRs happen among childhood friends whose later education and work ultimately separate them (physically) and they can happen among young adults after they meet during work- or study- abroad sequences.

Regardless of where you stand, this chapter will help you to learn more about common challenges and stressors of being in an LDR, alongside strategies and resources that LDR partners often implement to make their unions survive. And even if you are a strong opponent of LDRs—or if you are convinced that you will never engage in one—the information we present here is still relevant. LDR relationships succeed or fail for many of the same reasons that geographically proximate relationships do; the wisdom we have gained from them can thereby help all of us.

Historical Perspective on LDRs

LDRs are not a new phenomenon. For centuries, certain professions required husbands (usually) to be away from their families for weeks, months, and sometimes years at a time. Merchants, shepherds, sailors, fishermen, and others had to travel long and short distances for their work, often leaving their families behind. During times of war, governments (broadly defined) sent soldiers into unknown and dangerous places with limited opportunities for correspondence or connection with loved ones. Until recently, handwritten letters were the only way to communicate, and these oftentimes took weeks or months to reach home (if at all).

It is during the last two decades, however, that the visibility and prevalence of LDRs in the United States has noticeably—and exponentially—increased. Current estimates are that more than 14 million couples are in LDR arrangements (Center for the Study of Long Distance Relationships, 2013; Sahlstein, 2004). This drastic rise can be explained by a number of changes across social, technological, educational, and professional and job market foci.

CHANGES IN THE SOCIAL ENVIRONMENT. Gradual ideological changes and the feminist movement over the 20th century served to legitimize women's equality vis-à-vis men. Families in which both partners work outside home and pursue their respective career goals (vs. women sacrificing their goals in support of men) became more common. College education is now a desirable norm for both genders. The number of women pursuing higher education, in fact, has outnumbered those of men since the 1980s. With education comes a broader range of professional and *career* (not job) opportunities. In turn, we are seeing a shift away from conventional gender role divisions, both inside and outside of the home. It is no longer presumed that women will follow men wherever their academic interests and/or careers take them (Gilbert, 1993; Holmes, 2010; Sahlstein, 2004; Stafford, 2004).

CHANGES IN THE JOB MARKET. Once unique to those in aforementioned professions like merchant shipping or the military, LDRs are quickly gaining ground as a lifestyle arrangement. Nowadays, too, it is quite common when professionally oriented partners who are unable (or unwilling) to follow each other geographically at the expense of academic or professional achievement choose the LDR (Gerstel & Gross, 1984; Holmes, 2010). This relates back to the notion that middle class couple are functioning with increasing equality; both members' success is seen as valuable, and thereby pursued (Estrella, 2012; Mietzner & Li-Wen, 2005; Stafford, 2004).

CHANGES IN TECHNOLOGY. Healthy communication is core to any relationship, and it is even more crucial for partners in LDRs because nonverbal modes of communication (e.g., facial expression, body language, touch, gaze, etc.) are often not available for them. The development of new modes of communication like cell phones, email, text messaging, Skype video conversations, and social networking (e.g., Facebook, Twitter) has created new opportunities for an instant contact between partners. New technologies provide not only the opportunity for sharing via written text, but also create a sense of presence by allowing partners to see, hear, and actively interact with each other (Smith, 2011). These innovations have made LDRs more manageable (Aguila, 2011; Boase & Wellman, 2006).

LONG-DISTANCE RELATIONSHIPS AMONG YOUNG ADULTS

As you might have already noticed, there is considerable variety in what LDRs can look like. One type includes older couples who have been married for several years before they began the "long distance" characteristic of their union. They are referred to as *established commuters*. These couples are more likely to have developed strong relationship foundation prior to commuting. They also tend to have completed their education, and their concomitant financial stability allows them to be more flexible in how (and how often) they can see each other. Then there are the young couples, *adjusting commuters*, who are still building their relationships and developing a sense of "we-ness." Because of the novelty of their union, adjusting commuters have a smaller reserve of shared experiences and relationship foundation. They also have considerably less money and related resources, such as reliable cars and flexible work schedules. And while these are crucial elements for any relationship's success, they are of especial import when loving across a distance (Helgeson, 1994; Mietzner & Li-Wen, 2005).

Nowhere is the trend for LDRs more evident today than in college-age cohorts pursuing higher education (Center for the Study of Long Distance Relationships, 2013; Guldner, 2001; Kauffman, 2000). In fact, it is estimated that up to 80% of undergraduate college students have had personal experiences with an LDR. The percentage of LDRs is highest among first-year students as they transition from high school to college (i.e., having only recently separated geographically from their romantic partners, families, and friends). At any given time, about one-third of college students (30–43%) are currently involved in an LDR with their romantic partner (Guldner, 1996, 2001; Sahlstein, 2004; Statistic Brain, 2012).

University students report that romantic relationships in general (both proximal and long distance) play an extremely important role in their lives; however, they also represent one of the greatest areas of concern and stress. Unlike what their parents did, many young adults today postpone marriage by prioritizing educational, professional, and financial stability. Therefore, they date for a considerably longer time than previous generations. This stage of life, called *emerging adulthood* (Arnett, 1994), is unique because of its personal, relational, and professional uncertainties. Balancing a romantic relationship in the context of higher education is difficult in and of itself, and negotiating this balance within an LDR is often perceived as even more difficult (Guldner, 2001; Lydon, Pierce, & O'Regan, 1997).

As is already evident from the experiences of the three couples presented in this chapter's opening vignettes, LDRs can be a hard relationship challenge for adjusting commuters. And the experience can get more complicated if the LDR couple's families and friends are not supportive. In the next section we take a closer look at some of the myths that people share about LDRs.

COMMON MYTHS ABOUT LONG DISTANCE RELATIONSHIPS

Despite the growing trend of LDRs, society still has a strong belief that these relationships are destined to fail. Young couples who are entering a realm of love at a distance might hear a lot of criticism from family or friends about it. However, empirical research suggests that these myths are not true. The *Long Distance Relationships Center* (2014) was established to gather research-based information about LDRs and gain a better understanding of what makes those couples vulnerable and what makes them strong. Let's take a look at what the Center says about common myths regarding LDR couples in the United States:

MYTH #1: LDRS ARE MORE LIKELY TO FAIL THAN OTHER KINDS OF RELATIONSHIPS. Despite existing pessimism, LDRs do not break up at any greater rate than more traditional couples who live together.

MYTH #2: PARTNERS IN LDRS ARE MORE LIKELY TO CHEAT ON EACH OTHER. This is a common worry, as if proximate relationships did not require everyday surveillance. Again, evidence from research on cheating among LDRs and geographically close couples provides support that it is not the geographical proximity or distance that helps the couple to remain faithful, but instead the quality of the union between partners.

FIGURE 1 Rates of Breakup for LDRs versus Proximal (Close) Relationships (PR)

> 30% PR and 27% LDR over 6 months
>
> 21% PR vs. 37% LDR over 3 months*
>
> 35% PR vs. 42% LDR over 6 months*
>
> 23% PR vs. 11% LDR over 6 months
>
> 25% PR vs. 8% LDR over 1 year

Note. *Not a statistically significant difference (i.e., rates are statistically equal)
Source: Long Distance Relationships http://www.longdistancerelationships.net/faqs.htm

MYTH #3: COUPLES IN LDRS HAVE LESS SATISFYING RELATIONSHIPS. When asked about their relationships satisfaction, both LDR couples and couples living in geographical proximity demonstrate identical levels of relationship satisfaction, intimacy, trust, and commitment.

Aubree and Brian from the first vignette experienced a lot of pressure from their family and friends who shared those myths or mythologized the experience of others by focusing only on negative outcomes. It takes courage for a couple to give their relationship a chance despite this pressure. In next sections we share more about stressors and strains that make LDRs vulnerable, along with coping strategies and resources that facilitate their success.

REVIEW OF WHAT WE KNOW ABOUT LDRS

"If you don't like something, change it. If you can't change it, change your attitude."

—Maya Angelou

The ABC-X Model of Family Stress was developed by Reuben Hill (1958) to explain what predicts crises situations—or adaptive sequences—in families. The model can be summarized by a formula, which explains how stressors and strains (A), interacting with resources and coping strategies (B), viewed through the lens of one's perceptions (C), impact families mal- or bon- adaptation (X) (See Figure 2). The model can be applied to many couple or family situations, but here we will use it as a guideline to identify and understand the stressors and coping strategies that influence LDR couples—across individual, dyadic, and social (family and friends) levels—and their adaptation processes to commuting.

Stressors and Strains in LDRs (A)

INDIVIDUAL LEVEL STRESSORS AND STRAINS. If the couple started their relationship as proximate (dating, spending time face-to-face), they might have already developed certain couple routines. Initial stages of dating, rituals, and routines aid in the development of a couple creating a unique "culture" of their own (Pearson, Child, & Carmon, 2010). At some point, interactions across verbal and nonverbal means become routinized and habitual (Sillars & Wilmot, 1989). Seeing each other on a daily basis, having an opportunity for intimacy expression (e.g., shared silence, touching, gazing), spending time with mutual friends and having recreational activities together—a lot of what previously was taken for granted, now is lost once a couple moves into the LDR realm.

Consequently, *initial adjustment* to living apart is often a very difficult experience. Whether they knew they would be apart with plenty of advanced notice (e.g., next year when graduate school begins) or not (e.g., an immediate deployment through the National Guard), getting used to an LDR is almost always hard. As one drives by the movie theater that the couple used to go to (now knowing that this is not possible), gets ready for bed (now knowing that old routines of watching the late-show together or snuggling under the covers are being replaced by routines carried out by one's self), the reminders that one's loved-one is not there are constant. The concomitant loneliness that this can bring (especially for men) can be marked, alongside feelings of guilt (especially for women) for pursuing professional choices that make the couple have to choose an LDR in the first place (Byers, 2005; Helgeson, 1994).

Fears of growing apart are also quite typical for LDR couples, which is understandable since most relationships naturally develop through face-to-face contact. LDR partners may express concern that loss or absence of face-to-face contact could lead to a reduction in their intimacy (and then, consequently, relationship deterioration). A fear of growing apart also has to do with the fact that both partners might have different circles of friends that quite possibly never overlap. One female student shared:

> He has good friends out there . . . and I get a little jealous, because they spend every day with him, hanging out, and I get to see him maybe once every couple of months. I have friends here that I've made that

FIGURE 2 ABCX Model of Family Stress (Hill, 1958)

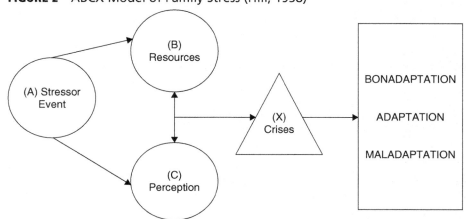

he doesn't know since he has left and he has made friends that I don't know, so in a way, because we don't know these people mutually, it makes us feel farther apart from each other. (Mendenhall, 1999)

Fear of infidelity is also a serious concern for many. Some perceive infidelity as only when a partner is physically intimate with another person (physical infidelity), but other people also consider cheating to be when their partner engages in and fosters emotional intimacy with another person (emotional infidelity). Additionally, there is notable evidence that men and women view infidelity differently. More women (88%) than men (55%) find emotional infidelity more distressing (Harris & Christenfeld, 1996). Because the social circles of friends do not overlap in LDRs, there is a limited opportunity to know people with whom another partner is regularly spending time and there are multiple opportunities to suspect infidelity if either of partners (or both) are insecure.

Commuting "gets old". Although not all LDR couples can financially manage frequent visits (e.g., partners residing in different countries or military couples), many of them have opportunities to see each other. And while this is helpful in fostering reconnection, after a short time partners have to say good-bye for yet another week or month. Doing this over and over again, alongside the everyday phone calls, missing each other, etc., can be emotionally draining over time. For some LDR partners, even just the desire to experience the relationship on a day-to-day basis without the pile-up of stressors and strains related to commuting can become formidable.

> It's just getting harder and harder to say goodbye on Sunday when the weekend's up. And it's just getting where I know I'm going to be his wife and I know that, that means a daily life together, and I want it now! I don't like to wait for it! I don't! . . . I'm sick of this. I'm fed up with it. I don't want to do it anymore. (Mendenhall, 1999)

DYADIC LEVEL STRESSORS AND STRAINS. Connected to individual partners' struggle with initial adjustment, described above, LDR couples report stress connected to their *loss of day-to-day intimacy*. These are the things that we take for granted when we live together, like sharing comfortable silences as we get ready for our days in the morning, study together in the library after class, drive in the car while listening to the radio. And these "little things" are not well reclaimed through modern technologies like the telephone or Skype because these mediums require a constant exchange of talking and interacting. Imagine, for example, calling one's partner and asking to share intimate silence while getting ready for one's day. Could you really just put the phone down (while still turned on) and feel the same sense of closeness as you could if your partner was actually there?

Another struggle that LDR couples face is called *spoiled time* (Long Distance Relationships Center, 2014; Rhodes, 2002). What this means is that because time spent together is not taken for granted anymore (and indeed, often held as precious), couples work very hard to have this time be perfect. Sometime for weeks, they will plan a weekend's dinner reservations, hotel accommodations, coordinating with work/school/roommates, and so on so that there are not any interruptions, and so forth—only to be heartbroken when something unexpected "messes up" the visit. An unplanned migraine or common cold, a roommate whose plans to be gone for the weekend fell through, a flight delay, or similar issues, can be catastrophized as ruining the weekend. Couples are thereby vulnerable to a sense of let-down, and having to wait another month or more to try again (i.e., during their next visit) to have the romantic and special union they anticipated.

Sometimes exacerbating this sense of spoiled time is a phenomenon called the *stranger effect* (Elite, 2012; Stafford & Merolla, 2007). This refers to a very normal couple process wherein some time to readjust to being together and comfortable in-person is necessary—but not well-understood or expected. And so, a couple can anxiously and excitedly wait to see each other, only to feel awkward and a bit "weird" when they initially do. Not knowing that this is normal, couples sometimes presume that something must be wrong, question each other why they are acting "strange" (or wondering why they, themselves, feel strange), and so forth. When a couple only has, for example, a weekend to visit each other, not realizing that the stranger effect is normal can cause arguments that could ultimately spoil the weekend.

FAMILY AND SOCIAL LEVEL STRESSORS AND STRAINS. A lot of couples have to deal with disapproval of their LDR relationships by family and friends (Maki & Dillow, 2009; Stafford, 2004). And while this tends to wane once the couple demonstrates that they are coping with distance and maintaining their relationship, many report that they are continually pressured to either live together in the same place or break up. For most, however, this is not an option since it would require one member (at least) to sacrifice his or her career or academic potential.

Pressure from friends can be no less complicated and influential. Friends may be under the perception that LDRs—per se—do not work. They may perceive that effort put into the LDR relationship is not mutual or balanced. They might see only part of the whole LDR picture (e.g., the stress and anxiety of their friend), and thereby work to better the "side" of the relationship they are more biased to support.

> When I was coming home to [city] every weekend . . . they were like, 'This has got to stop . . . We don't like that you're doing it for a boy, and you need to establish your life here in [town] where you're going to school for the next 2–3 years.' (Mendenhall, 1999)

Because commuting can be time-consuming (e.g., driving over the weekend, taking days off from school or work), it impacts one's social availability. This pressure is an indication that friends are dissatisfied with how much together time they lose because of LDRs. This concern expressed from friends adds yet another burden to LDR partners because they feel like they need to find a healthy balance between time with their partner, friends, and school/work.

> The stressful part was my friends were angry with me for going away every weekend. But I felt like I was obligated to do it for him, because at the time he didn't have a way to get to [town]. And it was kind of like, I'm stressed all the time because I felt like I wasn't balancing my time very well among the people that I'm close to that care about me. (Mendenhall, 1999)

OTHER STRESSFUL CHARACTERISTICS OF LDRS. *Expenses* related to traveling—from gasoline, to airfare, to hotel accommodations—can be particularly difficult for those who have had to rely on college-student budget. Telephone expenses for long-distance charges and cell phone minutes can easily pile up. One LDR partner exclaimed, *"It was overarching, I have to pay the phone bill!"* Another said, *"I probably win the university award for the highest phone bill. I'm serious! My first phone bill . . . was $500."* (Mendenhall, 1999).

Other stressors include having an *ambiguous deadline* as to when the couple will finally be able to live together, or—similarly—having to live with ambiguity regarding when future visits will occur. It is psychologically better to know the answers to these things (e.g., *"We will live together after graduation in two years."*, *"We will see each other on the first weekend of next month."*) than it is to not know (eHarmony, 2014; Vida, 2012).

Coping Strategies and Resources (B)

INDIVIDUAL LEVEL STRATEGIES AND RESOURCES. Adjusting to living in a LDR, handling fears of growing apart or worries about infidelity, and otherwise coping with a LDR on one's own are all facilitated by fostering (or developing) an *independent personality, being busy,* and maintaining a *positive and optimistic attitude* (Center for Long Distance Relationships, 2014; Mendenhall, 1999). An *independent personality* promotes non-dependence on ones' partner (or any partner) for happiness and includes being autonomous and goal-oriented. These individual qualities help LDRs not to focus on absence of a partner during time apart, but rather on pursuing academic and/or professional goals that eventually can bring partners closer. A participant in Mendenhall's (1999) study noted that: *"It would be nice for him to either be here or for me to be there, but I am not going to sacrifice [and] I don't want him to sacrifice his dreams and what he wants to do for me."*

Intentionally organizing one's days to be busy with school and/or work is helpful in keeping one's self distracted and reducing worries about the LDR.

> When he left, it was really hard . . . like at night I spent a lot of time with him. Well, I started doing more things. Like I coached a softball team, you know . . . I was busy in the evenings so I wasn't sitting at home thinking about him. Doing other things, like work things and stuff like that. (Mendenhall, 1999)

A *positive and optimistic attitude* helps commuters to cope with fears of growing apart and infidelity—and, it is a helpful resource regardless of one's marital or dating status. As related to intimate relationships specifically, individuals tend to be happier when their partner has high positive emotionality (i.e., more positive and optimistic; Robins et al., 2000). Individuals' temperament is also related to marital satisfaction; the more pleasant one is as a person, the more satisfied s/he is in marriage (Blum & Mehrabian, 1999).

DYADIC LEVEL STRATEGIES AND RESOURCES. In order to compensate for the lack of nonverbal cues in LDR communication, to foster the novelty of relationships at a distance, and cope with the inability to see each other regularly, *strong communication* between LDR partners is essential (eHarmony, 2014; Stafford, 2004). As one woman noted, learning how to communicate was a veritable survival skill for her.

> We learned how to talk about difficult things—talk about things that maybe some couples don't even share in the relationship. We talked about past things and family things, and, you know, when you see someone every day, you sometimes just don't get to those things. (Mendenhall, 1999)

From updating each other regarding daily activities to immediately discussing problematic issues and feelings, strong and clear communication is highly facilitative to couples' success. A recent study even suggests that compared to geographically close couples, LDRs try harder to communicate affection and intimacy, and their efforts do pay back (Jiang & Hancock, 2013). It is not only communication frequency that matters for LDRs; partners tend to also adapt their messages in terms of quality, the love "languages" they employ (see Chapter 10), and the more relationally intense topics they talk about.

Many partners in LDRs regard their boyfriend, girlfriend, or spouse as a *friend*. According to Davis (1985), romantic relationships are stronger when they contain both friendship (e.g., enjoyment, acceptance, trust, respect, mutual assistance, confiding, understanding, spontaneity) and passion and caring characteristics. According to this love-friendship model, maintaining a friendship in romantic relationships helps to build solid foundation in the relationship. When one's partner is perceived as a friend, communication is easier compared to if a friendship did not coexist with the romance (Mendenhall, 2000; Olson, Defrian, & Skogrand, 2011).

> He is my absolute best friend. I can tell him anything. My mom and I have been close since, I can't even remember how long. And mom and I can talk about almost anything. [Partner's name] and I can talk about everything. (Mendenhall, 1999)

Another important resource for LDR couples is that they have a *relationship foundation* and *shared history* (Center for the Study of Long Distance Relationships, 2013). What this means is that they have been together for an appreciable period of time before engaging in a relationship across distance. In contrast to a couple who meets online or over spring break (i.e., who has not yet built a reserve of shared experiences, memories, stories, and sense of "togetherness"), couples who have an established identity as a couple are better equipped to survive living apart.

> I think it's important that if you're going long distance with your relationship, that you have a firm foundation, because our foundation was extremely firm. We've had two and a half years together, and it was still hard. So make sure that if you really want to continue the relationship, that you have enough time invested in it, that you can do it without it totally pulling your life apart. (Mendenhall, 1999)

Teamwork. Couples who have a strong foundation with each other and view their union as one encompassing both love and friendship are better able to work collaboratively as a team. For example, partners can trade off who travels to see who when visiting (vs. one person always doing the traveling), who calls the other (vs. one doing all of the calling), and equitably contribute to the expenses of commuting (e.g., airline tickets, hotel rooms, cell phone minutes). Teamwork, too, is an indication that both partners are committed to succeed in their LDR, and that they co-own the work and outcome of this commitment (Hartwell-Walker, 2008; Livius, 2014).

FAMILY AND SOCIAL LEVEL STRATEGIES AND RESOURCES. While family and friends can be very influential in discouraging LDRs, they can be equally powerful in supporting them. This support can look different ways, depending on who is doing the supporting and the resources possessed by that person(s). For example, parents are often able to support their children's participation in LDRs through tangible means like money for visits, whereas friends are able to offer social and emotional support (Maki & Dillow, 2009; Stafford, 2004). One student said, "*I realized that there are other people* *that go through this. At first I felt like I was the only one going through this. I knew I wasn't, but it felt that way and now I have someone to talk to"* (Mendenhall, 1999).

OTHER RESOURCEFUL CHARACTERISTICS OF LDRS. Most LDR partners use the telephone to maintain *frequent contacts*, which for many of them is a daily practice. The accessibility of this technology is a vehicle for the very communication that is so essential to maintaining a sense of connection. As one LDR partner shared, *"We have a good relationship and we talk every day. The main thing that helps to get through is knowing I can talk to him every day, even if I can't see him"* (Mendenhall, 1999).

Although maybe least accessible for LDR couples, frequent visits are helpful in making commuting arrangements tolerable. Like with the telephone contact discussed above, visits were reported by many as helpful in staying "connected," as well as a driving force to "hang in there" for the much-awaited "light at the end of the tunnel." As one commuter explained, *"I think our relationship was kind of sustained on the visit part . . . it was the visits, I think, that kind of kept us going"* (Mendenhall, 1999).

Having a plan and/or clear deadline is something that helps many LDR partners to endure present hardships associated with commuting, something to look forward (Center for Long Distance Relationships, 2014; Stafford, 2004; Mendenhall, 1999). This can be likened to running a marathon: imagine running such a long distance while having mile-markers and a clear finish line to guide you versus running the same distance knowing that as soon as you have finished it, somebody would let you know. Mile-markers and finish lines offer extraordinary psychological support to keep going. One commuter said,

> You're always sad to see them go and you're always sad a few days, you know, afterwards, 'cause you had fun when they were here. But then, I don't know, it's just almost routine now. You know, they'll come back and you'll have fun again (Mendenhall, 1999).

Perceptions (C)

As the ABC-X model suggests, it is not the stressors and strains per se that define whether LDRs succeed. It's not the resources and coping strategies, per se, either. Rather, it is how partners perceive these stressors and resources, and what their attitudes are toward them. As participants of the Mendenhall (1999) study shared, there might be few common perceptions among LDRs. These perceptions can range from truly negative ones like LDRs never work to middle-ground ones like seeing commuting is a necessary evil en route to the accomplishment of professional aspirations.

Positive and optimistic attitudes, in general, also help. If you generally see the glass as half full, you can more easily see how an LDR can work. And if you do not begin with this perception, many LDRs eventually get there. After working on their LDR arrangement individually and as a couple, it is not uncommon for initial doubts to change.

> My feelings now have changed. I think if you want it to work, it can work. [If] two people together want it to work and can keep open communication lines between each other, [then] I think it can work. (Mendenhall, 1999)

Many LDR partners hold even stronger perceptions that *commuting improves the relationship*. Commuting can facilitate the development of individual and dyadic resources important to a strong relationship. Some say that they no longer took each other for granted and had an increased appreciation for time together:

> You have to use every minute that you're with each other . . . It's almost as if you're given an allotted amount of time and that each moment has to be savored a little bit more. (Mendenhall, 1999)

Others reported their communication skills having been improved as a beneficial consequence of an LDR. While working as a team and overcoming the challenges together LDR partners can create the feeling for the relationship to be stronger and more solid.

> I think everybody needs some distance, because, you know, once you're around each other [and] you know that you can get along together, you need to be able to know that you can get along apart. (Mendenhall, 1999)

This—and others like it—is an example of positive perceptions, and ultimately adaptation, to a type of relationship situation that can be very challenging.

SPECIFIC CASES OF LDRS

Military Couples

Military deployments present additional challenges to what those in everyday (e.g., educational, professional) LDR situations face. Geographic distance and limited or sporadic communication can cause elevated levels of uncertainty (regarding a partner's safety, the relationship's well-being, etc.), which can increase personal and dyadic distress. As presented in the second introductory vignette at the beginning of this chapter, Nick and Denise's relationship illustrates this.

Research demonstrates several factors that may put military couples at elevated risk for breakup or divorce. According to Negrusa, Negrusa, and Hosek (2013), more cumulative months of deployment in general, and deployment to hostile zones, such as war contexts, increment the risk of divorce in military marriages. When combined with deployments that are unexpected or unpredictable, this risk is exacerbated further.

Merolla (2010) conducted a study with the wives of deployed soldiers to explore how military couples maintain their relationships during deployment-based separations. Several relationship maintenance strategies were found to be effective in sustaining couples' bonds. First, materials that evoke sensory experiences of the away-partner, such as photos, special songs, and clothing were cited as helpful (along with purposeful positive thinking and reminiscing about happy memories). Focusing on one's own needs, than worrying about the deployed or left-behind partner—also facilitates beneficent adaptation.

Spiritual practices like praying or meditation can help military spouses cope with the separation due to deployment. Additionally, when partners appreciate (and act on) every opportunity to communicate during deployments, they find that doing so strengthens their emotional intimacy and allays their worries/fears. Future thinking and future-oriented cognition with regard to post-deployment reunions, reassuring safety, and accessing family, peer, and community support represent other resources that military partners can draw from to cope (Merolla, 2010).

International Couples

Over the last decade, education and work markets have become increasingly international, offering variety of opportunities across the globe, especially for young adults. This shift leads to a prominent increase in international LDR couples, in which partners live in different countries, mostly in geographically far away locations. An example of this LDR type is one person leaving to study/work abroad, while the partner stays in his or her home country. There is also a growing number of couples who meet while one or both partners are studying/working abroad and decide to go back home afterward.

As demonstrated in the third vignette at this chapter's first pages, international LDR couples face unique challenges. What are some of these challenges? Consider the information presented in Figure 3, and compare these to your thoughts about what an LDR across international distance(s) could be like.

To be sure, there are some stressors and strains that are more common for couples commuting overseas. Fears of growing apart may be intensified due to the increased geographic distance and fewer (and less frequent) opportunities for face-to-face contact. As demonstrated in Figure 3, the average number of times LDR couples visit each other is 18 times per year (which is approximately every two to three weeks), whereas Safak and Ege in the vignette above had only one chance per year to reunite. The cost of traveling overseas and the length of travel time clearly reduce the frequency and duration of face-to-face contact of international LDRs. Extended periods of time without physical contact may elevate partners' stress levels and make it more challenging for couples to sustain their bonds and intimacy.

FIGURE 3 Some Characteristics of LDRs

Average number of visits per year (times)	18
Average cost of travel per visit ($)	270
Average distance between partners (miles)	125

Source: Long Distance Relationships http://www.longdistancerelationships.net/faqs.htm

The initial adjustment period for a partner who moves abroad may be an additional stressor for international LDR couples. Moving to another country and coping/adjusting with a different culture, language, set of norms, and expectations may be unsettling for both the partner who moved away and the one staying home. The struggles during the adjustment period may demoralize both partners, which may in turn negatively impact the relationship.

Sustaining good communication may also be more challenging internationally compared to LDR couples living in the same country. It is known that for LDR couples, more frequent and extended communication mitigates the impact of being physically separated. Time-zone differences can be a major factor determining the frequency and length of overseas couples' communication. For example, in the vignette presented above, Safak and Ege needed to put an extra effort to adjust their schedules to fit times to talk. When Ege comes back home from work, and is longing for a decent conversation and an undivided time from Safak, she would just be starting her day in the United States, trying to get out of the door for classes and meetings. When she is finished with her school-related responsibilities, Ege would already be sleeping. For couples who are compelled to adapt and survive similar circumstances, extra effort and coordination is (obviously) indicated.

APPLICATION: SUCCEEDING IN AN LDR

So what makes LDR couples strong? What do they do to succeed, despite so many of the social perceptions that they cannot?

Individual Adaption in LDRs

For LDR partners on an *individual level*, it is important to achieve and maintain a clear sense of autonomy and independence. While maintaining a sense of togetherness—or "we"-ness—is obviously important, LDR partners must be able to function without their counterparts' ready presence. Remember that $1 + 1 = 2$. In any relationship (LDR or proximal), it is crucial to not lose one's individuality or ability to function on one's own. And while couples in proximal relationships can traverse (oftentimes without happiness) day-to-day life "needing" each other to survive, couples in an LDR cannot. Whether they had it to begin with, or learned how along the way, partners in LDRs are comfortable being alone and/or busy with individual work, interests, hobbies, or passions. And alongside this—regardless of one's gender—individual partners are able to fix leaky pipes, change the oil in their cars, cook food, clean the house, and do laundry without mixing whites with reds or darks.

Dyadic Adaption in LDRs

Within their relationship, itself, LDR partners can be very creative in finding ways to keep in touch. Maintaining a connection everyday over the telephone or other means of communication technologies requires more than simply dialing a number or typing an email. Commuters learn and practice communication skills and teamwork, share feelings and encourage each other across a distance, and avoid getting into routines like simply reporting each other's respective daily activities. Working together through ongoing communication, coordinating and planning visits as a team, and similar other activities, facilitate a sense of joint ownership and responsibility to the relationship's survival.

FIGURE 4 Statistics on Frequency of Communication among LDR Couples

> 1.5 times—the average number of times couples visited each other (per month)
>
> 3 letters—the average number of letters couples write each other (per month)
>
> 2.7 days—the average number of days between couples calling each other
>
> 14 month—the average number of months before couples expect to move back together

Center for the Study of Long Distance Relationships http://www.longdistancerelationships.net/faqs.htm

On *a family and social level,* it is helpful if commuters identify family members and friends who are supportive of their LDR and utilize this support in whatever manner(s) is appropriate to each respective relationship. Social support and encouragement from other LDR or former LDR couples can be empowering. Commuters may seek others who are experiencing similar challenges among their real life or virtual social circles (forums, via social networking, etc.).

Does the story end once partners overcome the distance and move in together (or at least move into the same zip code)? Do they live happily ever after? It depends. As a former LDR partner shared his experience in a recent online (anonymous) discussion forum:

> Long distance relationships do work . . . But when the long distance gap closes and you move in together, get married, etc., then (at least in my case) that changes completely. Now that your companion is there with you, the euphoria fades and then it becomes a lot of work. I'm still euphoric over my wife. But she's now, "used to" me and I feel taken for granted. I so, SO desperately want that passion back that we had when we were in that long distance relationship. In a way, it was almost better than what we have now . . . and we've been married for 8 ½ years now. Be sure when you take your relationship to the next level that you and your partner have a clear understanding of the others wants and needs when that long distance gap closes and you are now with each other.

Partners in any type of relationship need to be able to adjust to transitions to new situations (e.g., become parents, taking care of elderly parents, relocating). For most LDR couples, the transition they want is to move in together. Once former LDR partners do this, it is important that they continue to use the adaptive skills they learned during the LDR period. Adjustment processes are normal, while partners explore unknown territory of permanently living together, recreating daily routines, and making simple decisions like grocery shopping or meal preparation for two persons. To make this go easier, it is best for partners to be able to maintain a healthy balance of individuality and connectedness.

It is important to highlight here, too, that it *is best for couples to move in together to a place that is new to both partners.* While it might be easier for one partner to move into another's apartment or house, the metaphor connecting a "new chapter" in a couple's relationship is well-aligned with finding a "new place" to live (Moveline, 2014; Voo, 2011). The experiences and process of talking about how much space the couple needs, figuring out how much they can afford, touring possible apartments and homes, and deciding as a couple which one to choose—can be powerfully bonding. Then, couples can decorate a new space together (vs. modifying—or not—the existing space that one partner has already been living in), decide which one of the two coffee pots to keep, buying new furniture that is "ours," and begin their new chapter together—finally aligning their emotional "togetherness" with their geography.

WHAT WE DON'T KNOW

Research regarding what happens to LDR couples after they reunite is still limited. We do not know if or how the individual and relationship strengths that helped them to survive living apart are things that couples consistently maintain once they live together. We hope so, because successful LDR couples evidence a balance of individuality and connectedness, alongside communication and relationship maintenance skills, that would serve any union well.

Most research regarding LDRs has drawn upon samples that are heterosexual; we do not know if there are unique resources or stressors for young LBGT adults. In a similar way, it is not clear how or whether affiliation(s) to different faith, cultural, or ethnic groups impacts the viability of LDR relationships, and/or how inter-faith, inter-cultural, or inter-ethnic unions fare under these circumstances. With widespread social emphases on education and career success for both genders, will we see commonplace myths about LDR instability change? Will the disapproval and lack of support so often communicated by families and friends wane as LDRs are increasingly seen as a means to have a relationship without sacrificing school or work? To these—and other—questions, we ultimately do not know. Yet.

Questions for Self-Reflection

1. Did you share common myths presented in this chapter about LDRs? From your own experience or the experiences of your peers, do these myths have any grounds?
2. Do you have more chances of being in LDR compared to your parents (grandparents) when they were your age? Why? How does being in an LDR today differ from those trying it 20, 30, or 50 years ago?
3. How might individuals with different attachment styles cope differently with LDRs?
4. If you were (or are) in an LDR, which stressors would be (or are) most challenging for you?
5. How are some of the LDR coping strategies presented in this chapter relevant / applicable to couples who are in proximal relationships?

REFERENCES

Aguila, A. P. N. (2011). Living long-distance relationships through computer-mediated communication. *Social Science Diliman, 5*, 83–106. Retrieved from http://journals.upd.edu.ph/index.php/socialsciencediliman/article/view/2045/1955

Arnett, J. J. (1994). Are college students adults? Their conceptions of the transition to adulthood. *Journal of Adult Development, 1*, 154–168. doi:10.1007/BF02277582

Blum, J. S., & Mehrabian, A. (1999). Personality and temperament correlates of marital satisfaction. *Journal of Personality, 67*, 93–125. doi:10.1111/1467-6494.00049

Boase, J., & Wellman, B. (2006). Personal relationships: On and off the Internet. In A. Vangelisti & D. Perlman (Eds.), *The Cambridge handbook of personal relationships* (pp. 709–723). Cambridge, UK: Cambridge University Press.

Boss, P. (2002). *Family stress management: A contextual approach* (2nd ed.). Thousand Oaks, CA: Sage.

Buss, D. M., Larsen, R. J., Westen, D., & Semmelroth, J. (1992). Sex differences in jealousy: Evolution, physiology, and psychology. *Psychological Science, 3*, 251–255. doi:10.1111/j.1467-9280.1992.tb00038.x

Byers, E. S. (2005). Relationship satisfaction and sexual satisfaction: A longitudinal study of individuals in long-term relationships. *Journal of Sex Research, 42*, 113–118. doi:10.1080/00224490509552264

Center for the Study of Long Distance Relationships (2013). *Long distance relationship statistics.* Retrieved from: http://www.longdistancerelationshipstatistics.com/

Davis, K. E., & Todd, M. J. (1985). Assessing friendships: Prototypes, paradigm cases, and relationship description. In S. Duck, and D. Perlman (Eds.), *Understanding personal relationships: Sage series in personal relationships* (Vol. 1; pp. 17–37). Beverly Hills: Sage.

eHarmony (2014). Long distance relationship survival guide. *eHarmony Advice.* Retrieved from http://intimaterelationshipsproject.blogspot.com/2012/12/week-10-long-distance-relationships.html

Elite (2012). *Hardships of long distance relationships.* Retrieved from: http://elitedaily.com/dating/gentlemen/hardships-long-distance-relationships/

Estrella, J. (2012). *Equal couples: Facilitating mutual support in relationships.* Retrieved from http://equalcouples.com/?tag=long-distance-relationships

Gerstel, N., & Gross, H. E. (1984). *Commuter marriage: A study of work and family.* New York: Guilford Press.

Gilbert, L. A. (1993). *Two careers/one family: The promise of gender equality.* Newbury Park: Sage.

Guldner, G. T. (1996). Long-distance romantic relationships: Prevalence and separation-related symptoms in college students. *Journal of College Student Development, 37*, 289–295. Retrieved from http://www.safetylit.org/citations/index.php?fuseaction=citations.viewdetails&citationIds%5B%5D=citjournalarticle_268433_38

Guldner, G. T. (2001). Long-distance relationships and emergency medicine residency. *Annals of Emergency Medicine, 37*, 103–106. doi:10.1067/mem.2001.371103

Harris, C., & Christenfeld, N. (1996). Gender, jealousy, and reason. *Psychological Science, 7*, 364–366. doi:10.1111/j.1467-9280.1996.tb00390.x

Hartwell-Walker, M. (2008). Teamwork for two-career couples. *Psych Central.* Retrieved from http://psychcentral.com/lib/teamwork-for-two-career-couples/0001352

Helgeson, V. S. (1994). Long-distance romantic relationships: Sex differences in adjustment and breakup. *Personality and Social Psychology Bulletin, 20*, 254–265. doi:10.1177/0146167294203003

Hill, R. (1958). Generic features of families under stress. *Social Casework, 49*, 139–150. Retrieved from http://psycnet.apa.org.ezp3.lib.umn.edu/psycinfo/1959-08206-001

Holmes, M. (2010). Intimacy, distance relationships and emotional care. *Recherches sociologiques et anthropologiques* [En ligne], 41. Retrieved from http://rsa.revues.org/191

Jiang, L. C., & Hancock, J. T. (2013). Absence makes the communication grow fonder: Geographic separation, interpersonal media, and intimacy in dating relationships. *Journal of Communication, 63*(3), 556–577. doi:10.1111/jcom.12029

Kauffman, M. (2000). *Relational maintenance in long-distance dating relationships: Staying close.* Unpublished thesis. Virginia Polytechnic Institute and State University.

Livius, B. (2014). *Long distance lover.* Retrieved from: http://www.long-distance-lover.com/page/11/

Long Distance Relationships Center. (2014). *FAQs about long distance relationships.* Retrieved from: http://www.longdistancerelationships.net/faqs.htm

Lydon, J., Pierce, T., & O'Regan, S. (1997). Coping with moral commitment to long-distance dating relationships. *Journal of Personality and Social Psychology, 73,* 104–113. doi:10.1037/0022-3514.73.1.104

Maguire, K. C. (2007). "Will It Ever End?": A (re) examination of uncertainty in college student long-distance dating relationships. *Communication Quarterly, 55*(4), 415–432. doi:10.1080/01463370701658002

Maki, S., & Dillow, M. (2009). *Long-distance romantic relationships, social support, and the buffering hypothesis.* Paper presented at the annual meeting of the NCA 95th Annual Convention, Chicago Hilton & Towers, Chicago, IL. Retrieved from http://citation.allacademic.com/meta/p367136_index.html

Mendenhall, T. (1999). *A qualitative investigation of college-age commuters: Stressors and strains, resources and coping strategies, and perceptions of long distance relationships.* Unpublished Master's Degree Thesis. Kansas State University: Manhattan, KS.

Merolla, A. J. (2010). Relational maintenance and noncopresence reconsidered: Conceptualizing geographic separation in close relationships. *Communication Theory, 20,* 169–193. doi:10.1111/j.1468-2885.2010.01359.x

Merolla, A. J. (2010). Relational maintenance during military deployment: Perspectives of wives of deployed US soldiers. *Journal of Applied Communication Research, 38*(1), 4–26. doi:10.1080/00909880903483557

Mietzner, S., & Li-Wen, L. (2005). Would you do it again? Relationship skills gained in a long-distance relationship. *College Student Journal, 39,* 192–200. Retrieved from http://www.freepatentsonline.com/article/College-Student-Journal/131318259.html

Moveline. (2014). *The ultimate guide for couples moving in together.* Retrieved from: https://www.moveline.com/couples

Negrusa, S., Negrusa, B., & Hosek, J. (2013). Gone to war: Have deployments increased divorces? *Journal of Population Economics, 27*(2), 473–496. doi:10.1007/s00148-013-0485-5

Olson, D., DeFrain, J., and Skogrand, L. (2011). *Marriages and families: Intimacy, diversity, and strengths* (7th Edition). Boston, MA: McGraw Hill.

Pearson, J. C., Child, J. T., & Carmon, A. F. (2011). Rituals in dating relationships: The development and validation of a measure. *Communication Quarterly, 59,* 359–379. doi:10.1080/01463373.2011.583502

Robins, R. W., Caspi, A., & Moffitt, T. E. (2000). Two personalities, one relationship: Both partners' personality traits shape the quality of their relationship. *Journal of Personality and Social Psychology, 79,* 251–259. doi:10.1037//0022-3514.79.2.251

Rhodes, A. (2002). Long-distance relationships in dual-career commuter couples: A review of counseling issues. *The Family Journal, 10,* 398–404. doi:10.1177/106648002236758

Sahlstein, E. (2004). Relating at a distance: Negotiating being together and being apart in long-distance relationships. *Journal of Social and Personal Relationships, 21,* 689–710. doi:10.1177/0265407504046115

Sillars, A. L., & Wilmot, W. W. (1989). Marital communication across the life span. In J. F. Nussbaum (Ed.), *Lifespan communication: Normative issues* (pp. 225–253). Hillsdale, NJ: Erlbaum.

Smith, A. (2011). *Why Americans use social media.* Washington, D.C.: Pew Internet & American Life Project. Retrieved from http://pewinternet.org/~/media//Files/Reports/2011/Why%20Americans%20Use%20Social%20Media.pdf

Stafford, L. (2004). *Maintaining long-distance and cross-residential relationships.* London: Routledge.

Stafford, L., & Merolla, A. J. (2007). Idealization, reunions, and stability in long-distance dating relationships. *Journal of Social and Personal Relationships, 24,* 37–54. doi:10.1177/0265407507072578

Statistic Brain (2012). *Long distance relationship statistics.* Retrieved from: http://www.statisticbrain.com/long-distance-relationship-statistics/

Vida, M. (2012). *Long distance relationships.* Retrieved from: http://intimaterelationshipsproject.blogspot.com/2012/12/week-10-long-distance-relationships.html

Voo, J. (2011). Moving in together: What to do first and how to make it work. *Huffington Post.* Retrieved from: http://www.huffingtonpost.com/2008/08/18/moving-in-together-what-t_n_119641.html

12
The Influence of Culture on Relationships

Tisa A. Thomas, M.A.
Dung M. Mao, M.A.
Department of Family Social Science
University of Minnesota

Meghan N. Mao, RN
College of Biological Sciences
University of Minnesota

LEARNING OBJECTIVES

- Articulate the respective definitions of race, culture, and ethnicity
- Outline the most prevalent minority groups in the United States, alongside key characteristics of each
- Understand historical and modern-day challenges in intermarriage
- Articulate key challenges for minority families integrating into the United States
- Understand what Cultural Competence is, and how to apply it

The authors of this chapter come from very diverse backgrounds. Dung was born to parents of Vietnamese and Chinese descent and grew up in rural Cambodia, Meghan was born to parents of Norwegian and German descent and grew up in Texas, and Tisa was born to parents of Native American, African American, Puerto Rican, and European descent and grew up in the inner city of Minneapolis.

With this wealth of cultural knowledge and diversity, you would think the three of us would have all the answers when it comes to culture. But we do not. The biggest question that boggled us for weeks as we wrote this chapter, and will probably continue to haunt us in our dreams is, *How can we (really) define these concepts, and how can we predict how they affect intimate relationships?* To be sure, phenomena like race and culture are not easy to define. And it is not possible for us, the authors, to comprehensively capture their essence(s) without discussing personal and social values, beliefs, habitudes, pasts, and presents. Race and culture are not just labels; they are an essential and integrated part of an(y) individual's unique identity. So, if you are looking for clear, direct, and unambiguous answers about culture in relationships, you will not find them here. What you will find are ideas and concepts to use as a metacognitive tool for your own knowledge. As our world becomes more saturated with humans of different cultures and backgrounds, answers to tough questions about race and culture in relationships will become increasingly individualized—for each person, and for each unique relationship that each person forms. Growth in understanding of your own feelings and thoughts about these foci will ultimately lead to healthier relationships.

RACE, CULTURE, AND ETHNICITY

Some citizens of the United States of America have the background of coming from families that are considered by many as "typical" or "normal." In the United States, "typical" families are often-times framed as those that have two parents in the home, make incomes that are considered "middle class" (or higher), have adult members who are high school- or college- educated, and may or

Corresponding Author: Tisa A. Thomas, M.A.; University of Minnesota; Department of Family Social Science; 1985 Buford Ave; 290 McNeal Hall; Saint Paul, MN 55108. E-mail: tisa@umn.edu.

may not experience some type of prejudice or social injustice on a regular basis (Pyke, 2000; Smith, 1993). Other families, then, are compared to these "normal" families and don't come out looking so well (Pyke, 2004). And yet, a majority of families living here don't fit these definitions of normalcy. Factors such as poverty, prejudice, education, and life experiences affect the ability to maintain intimate family relationships such as extended family connections, parent–child relationships, and couple unions (Bent-Goodley, 2005; Perreira, Chapman, & Stein, 2006; Sarkisian, Gerena, & Gerstel, 2006). The historical experiences of some groups of people have had long-term effects on their ability to achieve and maintain what is considered to be the norm in intimate family lives today. For example, American Indians in this country historically have had land, language, and culture taken from them (Caldwell et al., 2005), which made passing on beliefs, traditions, and values to younger generations difficult. Missing out on learning certain lessons and gaining certain values could impact how a person identifies as an individual and, furthermore, how s/he behaves with and around others.

Many people feel comfortable when they are able to label give names for, or categorize people, places, and things we come in contact with (Rowntree, 2000). Categories give order to life, and every day we create classifications within our environments. We group our food (e.g., meats, fruits, vegetables), clothing (e.g., shirts, pants, dresses), schools (e.g., elementary, middle school, high school, college), and neighborhoods (e.g., the "bad" parts of down, the "good" parts of town), and so forth. Why would we treat people—or even ourselves—any differently?

Historically, we have separated groups of people by their race, culture, and ethnicity. *Race*, which is generally paired with common physical characteristics of a group, is a problematic concept that is gradually being used less frequently in scientific and popular language. The concept of race started as a way to explain the diversity of human populations internationally because it was efficient in dividing people into large and distinct groups. Cameron and Wycoff (1998) described race as a social, cultural, and political creation. Unfortunately, it has often been used as a psychologically and emotionally divisive tool, such as when the colonial United States used skin color to dehumanize (and justify) African captives for slavery, when the Nazi regime during WWII identified Jews as racial scapegoats who needed to be eliminated from society, or when the Apartheid was employed to divide groups in South Africa from 1948 to 1994.

When people talk about a race, they create a social reality through which social categorization begins. In this sense, the phenomenon is a social construct. Social constructs develop within various legal, economic, and sociopolitical contexts, and may be the effect, rather than the cause, of major social situations. And although race is considered a social construct, most scholars agree that it has real material effects in the lives of people through institutionalized practices of preference and discrimination (Lee, 1994).

Scientifically, racial characteristics are nonexistent. Variance in skin color, for example, can be defined on a continuum. Dark brown tones blend to light brown, that then blend to reds and yellows that blend even further to shades of pink, making it difficult to separate one color from the other. When color is considered as a spectrum, classifying people by the color of their skin becomes illogical. For example, consider the child with a Scandinavian American mother and a Chinese father. The child could very well have the same skin tone as his mother and the same eyes as his father. Genetically and aesthetically, the child is a mixture of both parents, but society will want this child to select a single racial group to belong to for identification purposes. Many Americans are faced with this dilemma and question the helpfulness of being labeled as a part of a particular group. Toni Morrison, the Nobel Prize-winning author of such novels as *Song of Solomon, Beloved,* and *Tar Baby,* puts it this way: "Race is the least reliable information you can have about someone. It's real information but it tells you next to nothing" (Morrison, 1998, p. 67).

With such a diverse population in the United States, a visitor could expect to see several different types of residents that could possibly belong to several different groups. One of the most important factors in determining ethnic or cultural distinctions is whether or not someone *believes* they belong to that group. Yet the social classifications of ethnicity most commonly used cannot be solely based on physical characteristics, religion, language, or lineage. Because of our society's growing diversity, opportunities for meeting, dating, and marrying someone from another racial, cultural, or ethnic group have greatly increased. Currently, there are more multiethnic marriages today than ever before—about one in every three marriages (U.S. Census, 2010). So what does that mean for the future? According to Olson (2001), more intermarriage will make it harder to determine an individual's ancestry, but it can only hasten the voyage to a color-blind society. Because intermarriage makes it more difficult to categorize people into racial groups, the use of the term "race" will likely decrease further over time.

To respond to this shift in terminology, the terms *culture* and *ethnicity* have been used in place of *race*. Culture, or cultural group, refers to people of the same nationality who share the same beliefs, values, goals, practices and (potentially) speak a common language. When people share *ethnicity*, they possess similar ancestral, cultural, social, or national experiences. Culture and ethnicity better describe different groups of people than race; however, even these more meaningful terms can be confusing and misrepresentative. Think about the Jewish population, for example. This group is often categorized as a an ethnic group, but that is not entirely accurate for a few reasons: (1) Jews hold a wide variety of religious views, from very conservative to very liberal; (2) They speak a variety of languages, and most do not speak the traditional language of Hebrew; (3) They hold several different nationalities; (4) Their physical characteristics range from dark-skinned, black-haired African Jews to light-skinned, blue-eyed, blond European Jews. When you think about it, a nomadic Jewish sheep farmer in Ethiopia has much more in common with other Africans than he would with a Jewish lawyer in Minneapolis (Olson, DeFrain, & Skogrand, 2010).

Both racial and ethnic groups can be considered as *minority groups*, depending on the social experience of their members. Belonging to a minority group can be a strong influence in how we interact with others in relationships because it is within these groups we learn to socialize with others. Having different perceptions of what is considered "healthy," "normal," "common," and so on, can sometimes lead to miscommunications and confrontations within intimate relationships if a couple is not prepared to deal with these differences.

MINORITY GROUPS IN THE UNITED STATES

Although the United States is made up of several unique ethnic and cultural groups, there are four prevalent minority groups that we will focus on in this chapter: American Indian/Native Alaskan; Asian and Pacific Islander; Black/African American; and Hispanic. As you will learn later, having cultural knowledge is the first step in becoming culturally competent.

American Indians and Alaska Natives

Over 560 tribes make up the American Indian and Alaska Native (AI/AN) population in the United States (Caldwell et al., 2005), and with this number of tribes come a wide range of tribal cultures. This group has experienced a rapid growth increase since 2000, but the exact reason for this growth is unknown. Many sociologists attribute the growth to changes made by the Census in 2000 which allowed people who have (or believe they have) Native American ancestry to designate themselves as being of more than one race, or to recent developments in genealogy research. This new

© Rob Marmion, 2014. Used under license from Shutterstock, Inc.

development has given rise to what we call "ethnic shifting" or "ethnic shopping." Sociologists believe that this phenomenon reflects a willingness of people to question their birth identities and adopt new ethnicities that they find more compatible (Hitt, 2005). The most populous tribes include the Cherokee nation and Navajo (U.S. Census, 2011). One of the unique characteristics of the AI/AN population is that their communities are sovereign political entities, which means most tribes have their own forms of government, culture, and history (Caldwell et al., 2005). Unfortunately, this group also has a stigma of poor physical health, short lifespans, and alcoholism (Brave

FIGURE 1   Overview of Median Income, Poverty and Marital Status by Minority Group

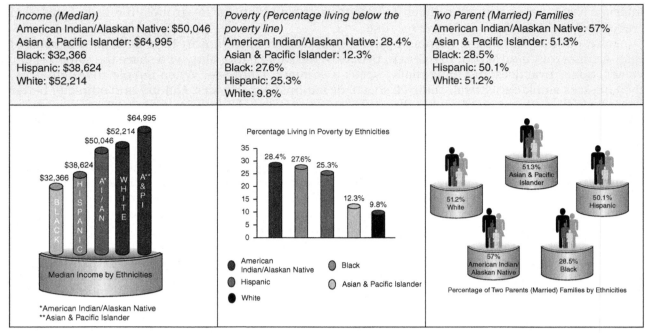

Income (Median)	Poverty (Percentage living below the poverty line)	Two Parent (Married) Families
American Indian/Alaskan Native: $50,046	American Indian/Alaskan Native: 28.4%	American Indian/Alaskan Native: 57%
Asian & Pacific Islander: $64,995	Asian & Pacific Islander: 12.3%	Asian & Pacific Islander: 51.3%
Black: $32,366	Black: 27.6%	Black: 28.5%
Hispanic: $38,624	Hispanic: 25.3%	Hispanic: 50.1%
White: $52,214	White: 9.8%	White: 51.2%

Source: U.S. Census Fact Finder, 2010

Heart & DeBruyn, 1998). The median age for American Indians and Alaskan Natives is 29 years, which is the lowest of the other U.S. minority groups (U.S. Census, 2011).

Spirituality is one of the most pervasive themes in the American Indian culture (Olson, DeFrain, & Skogrand, 2010). Personal health and wellness are centered around creating balance and harmony within one's self. Elders are highly valued and possess the responsibility of passing along the knowledge, cultural values, and beliefs to grandchildren and other youth in the community (Deloria, 1973). Tribal groups tend to function independently, with groups relying on each other within tribal systems before looking outside for help.

Asian Americans

Asian American people encompass the third largest minority group in the United States. This group consists of individuals who have roots in continental Asia. Countries represented herein include, but are not limited to: India, China, the Philippines, Japan, Korea, Vietnam, Cambodia, and Laos. The majority of contemporary Asian Americans are descendants of immigrant groups who immigrated to the United States in the early to late 1800s and in the late 1900s during the two large waves of Asian immigration (Hune, 2002).

The first large wave of Asian immigrants was comprised of Chinese laborers who came to the United States in the 1840s. Between 1840 and the 1880s, approximately 370,000 Chinese immigrants made their way to the United States. By 1920, another 400,000 Japanese immigrants had arrived in America looking for employment, and between 1900 and 1930 the United States saw the arrival of 180,000 Pilipino, 7,000 Koreans, and 7,000 Asian Indians (Chan, 1991; Hune, 2002).

The second large wave of Asian immigration occurred from the early 1940s to late 1970s with the passing of the Immigration Act of 1965, which promoted family unification, and the Indochina War. The Immigration Act of 1965 made it possible for a larger number of Chinese, Korean, and Asian Indian immigrants to enter the United States. In 1975, the United States Congress enacted the Indochina Migration and Refugee Assistance Act, allowing approximately one million Southeast Asian refugees (e.g., Vietnamese, Cambodian, Laotian) to resettle in the United States (Hune, 2002).

In the 1960s, the Hmong people joined the United States and took up arms against the Communist Lao government (Hamilton-Merritt, 1993). The eventual seizure of Laos by the Communist regime in the 1970s turned the Hmong people into a target of prosecution by the newly formed Lao government (Xiong, 2000). Fearing for their lives, the Hmong people undertook the dangerous journey to escape Laos and immigrated to other countries. In 1976, the United States welcomed the first wave of Hmong refugees (Olney, 1986).

Resettling in the United States was no easy task for the Hmong community. During the resettlement period, they faced many challenges, including economic in stability, language barriers, crime, and various religious and cultural differences (Fass, 1986; Detzner, 1992; Gross, 1986). According to the U.S. Census Bureau (2012), the United States is home to over 260,000 Hmong individuals. Additionally, 25% (66,181) of the Hmong population resides in Minnesota, making Minnesota the second largest home to the Hmong community (U.S. Census Bureau, 2012).

In 1970, there was an estimated 1.5 million Asian Americans residing in the United States. This number increased to over 7 million in 1990 (Paisano, 1993). The 2010 Census reports that the Asian population comprises 4.8% (15 million) of total U.S. population (Humes, Jones, & Ramirez, 2010).

Among the most common minority groups, Asian Americans have the highest educational achievements. According to Chen (2012), director of the Asian American Studies Program at Northwestern University, as of December 2012, Asian Americans comprised 12 to 18 percent of the student population at Ivy League schools, larger than their respective share of the nation's population. This statistic, however, is not generalizable to all Asian American groups living in the United States. Asian American subgroups like the Cambodian, Vietnamese, Hmong, Laotian, Burmese, and Thai do not have the high academic achievement records that their Japanese and Chinese counterparts possess. One factor that has contributed to this gap relates to the nature of their respective immigration journeys.

Unlike individuals from China and Japan, who tend to immigrate to the United States by choice (Hune, 2002), individuals from Cambodia, Vietnam, Laos (including Hmong), Burma, and Thailand tend to immigrate to the United States as refugees. Refugees are individuals who are forced out of their home country out of the fear of death or persecution (UNHCR, 2014); they tend to have lower professional skills and education attainment, alongside concomitant lower incomes or income potential (Hune, 2002). The combination of living in poverty and the traumatic past experiences create extra challenges for these immigrant groups.

Furthermore, differences in cultural values, traditions, and lifestyles between parents and their children often lead to misunderstandings (Lee & Liu, 2001) and stress. Although social support was found to buffer negative effects of family conflicts for Hmong American college students, self-blame for said conflicts often leads to higher levels of distress (Su, Lee, & Vang, 2005).

In 2012, 61% of Asian American adult immigrants reported having a college level education or advanced degree (Wang, 2012). Many Asian Americans share a cultural heritage that values discipline, family, commitment, hard work, and education. Much of the success of Asian American youngsters stems from the support of parents and grandparents within close, motivated family units. Common values of all Asian groups include filial piety (great respect for elders, alongside a presumption that younger generations will take care of older ones in senescence), a strong adherence to family privacy, and/or attention to public views and reputation. Conflict between parents and children can occur, though, within families where parents do not value academic success (e.g., instead seeing more value in youth joining the workforce so that they can take care of elders) (Xiong & Lee, 2011). Sometimes, even if parents do encourage their children to obtain higher education, they lack the knowledge to provide adequate support (Vang, 2004–05).

Hispanics / Latino Americans

Hispanics, or Latino Americans, currently comprise the largest minority group in the United States (est. 16% of population), passing Blacks for this position in the past few years. In 2000, there were 35.3 million members of the Hispanic community residing in the United States. Over the following 10 years, the Hispanic population increased by more than 15 million (Humes, Jones, & Ramirez, 2010). Today, there are over 50 million individuals residing in the United States who self-identify as Hispanic or Latino (Taylor, Lopez, Martínez, & Velasco, 2012). Because of the higher number of people belonging to this demographic, there has been a rapid increase in the amount of research, literature, and marketing that targets and surrounds this group.

Latino Americans maintain Mexican, Cuban, Puerto Rican, or other Spanish descent. Identification has recently been a topic of conflict and contingency for members of this group. Most people of Hispanic or Latin American descent dismiss the terms "Hispanic" or "Latino" when it comes to describing their identity. Instead, they prefer to be identified by their country of origin. When asked if they have a preference for either being identified as "Hispanic" or "Latino," the Pew Research study found a majority (51%) say they most often identify themselves by their family's country of origin, while 24% say they prefer a pan-ethnic label such as Hispanic or Latino.

Hispanic families place strong value on family support and loyalty. Members will provide financial, social, and emotional support for those in need, even at the expense of their own personal needs (Olson et al., 2010). This group also highly values religion, with a large majority (70%) identifying as Catholic (Ellison, Wolfinger, & Ramos-Wada, 2013). In many cases, religion influences ideals, decisions, and beliefs about marriage, family size, and divorce (Humes et al., 2010).

Black/African Americans

Black or African American people make up the second largest minority group in the United States (U.S. Census, 2010). The majority of the Black/African American population has ancestors that were brought to America during the time of slavery starting in the early 1600s. Unfortunately, because slaves were treated as property, tracing individuals' genealogy can be difficult. Common characteristics found in these group(s) include extended kinship networks (of support and household residence), out-of-wedlock childbirth, and religiosity. African Americans are also more likely than other minority groups to experience poverty.

In recent years, there has been an influx of African and Caribbean immigrants relocating to the U.S. (Thomas, 2011). Oftentimes, these immigrant groups are considered in combination with Blacks as one larger group. Bashi and McDaniel (1997), for example, argued that black immigrants are assimilated into a U.S. racial hierarchy that significantly constrains their levels of attainment relative to nonblack immigrants. Thus, immigrants that have a more similar physical appearance to U.S.-born blacks will have nuanced patterns of incorporation into a U.S. society in which skin color can be a barrier to social mobility (Thomas, 2011). However, despite others' tendencies to categorize them in the same racial group, many deeply entrenched cultural values and beliefs vary among these subgroups. For example, religious celebrations, choices in music, and dress can vary depending on which subgroup a person belongs to. Because of this increasing diversity within the African American population, researchers and educators need to be more aware of the diversity of cultural values and beliefs in what was previously perceived as a homogenous cultural group (Batson et al., 2006; Olson et al., 2010).

INTERMARRIAGE: HISTORY TO PRESENT DAY

Historically, it was illegal in the United States to be in an intimate relationship with—or to marry—someone who was not of the same ethnic background as you. Loving *v.* Virginia was a landmark civil rights case and a defining moment for the history of intermarriage. In this case, the United States Supreme Court unanimously declared the state of Virginia's anti-miscegenation statute, the "Racial Integrity Act of 1924," unconstitutional. This overturned the Pace *v.* Alabama (1883) decision, and served to end all race-based legal restrictions on marriage in the country.

Intermarriage refers to the marital union of individuals from differing ethnic, racial, and national origins (Bratter & Eschbach, 2006; Breger & Hill, 1998a; Jang, 2013; Kalmijn & van Tubergen, 2010). Intermarriage in the United States is a fairly new trend with increasing occurrence. For instance, in 2000, approximately 7% of new marriages in the United States were intermarriages (Lee & Edmonston, 2005). This rate increased to 14.4% in 2008 (Passel, Wang, & Taylor, 2010), and 15% in 2010 (Wang, 2012). Among those who intermarried in 2000, 2.7% identified as non-Hispanic Whites, 7% identified as Blacks, 14% identified as Hispanics, and 16% identified as Asian (Lee & Edmonston, 2005). In 2008, these rates increased to 9% non-Hispanic Whites, 16% Blacks, 26% Hispanics, and 31% Asian (Passel, Wang, & Taylor, 2010). These percentages illustrate that not all ethnic groups are increasing their rates of intermarriage. Statistics like these provide researchers and social service providers an opportunity to reexamine family structures and values (see Figure 2).

Research examining the support and rejection of intermarried couples is conflicting. On one hand, investigators have suggested intermarried couples experience negative reactions and rejection from family, friends, and society (Khatib-Chahidi, Hill, & Paton, 1998; Killian, 2001; Hibbler & Shinew, 2002; Chito Childs, 2005; Jang, 2013; Rosenblatt & Stewart, 2004; Yancey, 2007). Although the anti-miscegenation laws have been revoked, the social stigma related to Blacks marrying anyone other than another Black person persists in today's society. Research by Tucker and Mitchell-Kerman (1990) has shown that Blacks intermarry far less frequently than any other non-White group, and in 2010, only 17.1% of Blacks married interracially. This rate is far lower than rates for Hispanics and Asians (Yen, 2012). Black interracial marriages, in particular, engender problems associated with racist attitudes and perceived relational inappropriateness because of the history of slavery in the United States (Hibbler & Shinew, 2002). There is also a sharp gender imbalance to Black interracial marriages. In 2008, 22% of all black male newlyweds married interracially while only 9% of black female newlyweds married outside their race, making them the least likely of any race or gender to marry outside their race—and the least likely to get married at all (Hamner, 2011).

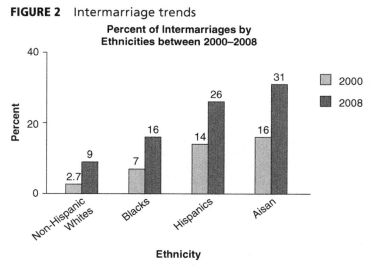

FIGURE 2   Intermarriage trends

Percent of Intermarriages by Ethnicities between 2000–2008

Source: Lee & Edmonston, 2005; Passel, Wang, & Taylor, 2010

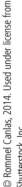

In support of the other side of this debate, a study conducted by the Pew Research Center (2010) found that 43% of participants believed that intermarriages will positively impact our society. Additionally, 63% indicated that they would accept one of their family members marrying outside of their race or ethnic group (Wang, 2012). The millennial generation, including people born between 1980 and 2000, are more accepting of interracial relationships and marriages than any other cohort before them. It is assumed that generation cohorts following the millennials will adopt and continue the social trend of intermarriage acceptance.

ETHNICITY AND INTERMARRIAGE

Although intermarriages represent a wide variety of different racial and ethnic groups, four groups (Whites, Hispanics, Blacks, and Asians) gain more attention in the intermarriage literature than others (Bratter & King, 2008; Kalmijn & Van Tubergen, 2000; Qian, 1997; Qian, Blair, & Ruf, 2001; Zhang & van Hook, 2009). The historical conflict between Blacks and Whites is one of the factors fueling research in marriages between these two ethnic groups (Batson, Qian, & Lichter, 2006; Chito Childs, 2005; Yancey, 2007). Intermarriages within Asian and Hispanic ethnic groups has gained attention from researchers of late due to the groups' increase in population and participation in intermarriages (Bratter & King, 2008; Zhang & van Hook, 2009).

Although recent poll research showed a general public support for intermarriages, research examining family relationships between the intermarried couples and their extended families tell a different story. Multiple studies have reported conflict between the intermarried couples and their relatives (Bustamante, Nelson, Henricksen, & Monakes, 2011; Hibbler & Shinew, 2002; Joanides, Mayhew, & Mamalakis, 2002; Khatib-Chahidi et al., 1998; Killian, 2001; Molina, Estrada, & Burnett, 2004; Roer-Strier & Ben Ezra, 2006; Rosenblatt & Stewart, 2004).

In-law Relationships

In-law interactions can be both a challenging experience and a growth opportunity for intermarried couples. Interactions with in-laws provide the partners in intermarried couples an opportunity to share their own cultural values, beliefs, and traditions—and also learn about the cultural values, beliefs, and traditions of their spouse. When partners are able to discuss, compare-and-contrast, and reflect upon the similarities and differences of values and beliefs of both cultures, they have the opportunity to grow both individually and as a couple. In this case, in-law interactions provide a fertile and fostering environment for the couple to grow, which is invaluable for the well-being of the couple, both individually and as a family unit.

However, in-law interactions are also a source of challenges and conflicts for many intermarried couples. Research shows that, more often than not, there is an overall disapproval of the intermarried couple's relationship by the couple's relatives (Hibbler & Shinew, 2002; Joanides et al., 2002). Indeed, there tends to be an initial disapproval from the individuals' relatives at the first announcement of their decision to marry outside of their own racial or ethnic group (Khatib-Chahidi et al., 1998; Killian, 2001; Joanides et al., 2002; Molina et al., 2004; Rosenblatt & Stewart, 2004). Some research does show that the intensity of relatives' disapproval tends to subside after the marriage (Joanides et al., 2002; Rosenblatt & Stewart, 2004), but only in some cases.

Although research indicates that interactions with in-laws could be stressful to the intermarried couple (e.g., Bustamante et al., 2011; Hohmann-Marriot & Amato, 2008), there is limited research examining the areas of interaction that tend to cause the most conflict. In the sections to follow, we will discuss values, boundaries, and roles, all of which have been found to differ between cultures and can cause friction for interracial couples and their extended families.

Values

Values can be tricky to express, explain, and tease out because they are so integrated into an individual's sense of self. Sometimes we do not fully understand or realize what we hold dear until our values are challenged or violated by another person. Adding to that complexity, the violations of these values can come in a variety of forms: verbal, nonverbal, or both.

Cultural values are traditions and beliefs that are integral to one's identity and dictate how we should live (Williams, 1970). Cultural values have been examined in the literature through different sets of opposing axes. They include individualism vs. collectivism, conservatism vs. autonomy, hierarchy vs. egalitarianism, and mastery vs. harmony (Schwartz, 1999).

INDIVIDUALISM VS. COLLECTIVISM. People from *individualist* (usually from Western parts of the world) cultures are more likely to identify themselves according to their personal attributes, whereas *collectivist* (usually from Eastern parts of the world) cultures are more likely to identify themselves as their role in a family or group (Triandis, 1995). This means that a person in an interracial relationship may suddenly find him or herself introduced to an unfamiliar role in his/her partner's family. When individualist persons marry into a collectivist culture, for example, there may be an expectation to prescribe to specific family norms that are not compatible with their original values.

Collectivist families tend to promote living arrangements that share the home with extended family members. This is especially true for sons, who are charged with the responsibility of caring for parents during their elder years. Living arrangements are also considered a part of family hierarchy, wherein the parents may maintain a position of authority over the married couple they reside with. Western cultures typically value a separation of the married couple from their parents in terms of living arrangements and authority; a new nuclear family is formed upon marriage, and the family unit includes the married couple and its children. These differing values could cause tensions between the intermarried couples and their relatives when planning for the future.

CONSERVATISM VS. AUTONOMY. Conservative cultures promote the status quo, restraint, and tradition, whereas autonomous cultures promote the expressions of feelings and ideas and independence (Schwartz, 1999). Let's consider a potential area of conflict between Sakiya and Andrew. Sakiya is from a conservative Vietnamese culture and may have difficulty with the expectation of conversational openness among her partner's older family members, or across genders. She may unintentionally send a message of disinterest, distance, or fear by not readily volunteering her personal viewpoints or experiences. From Sakiya's perspective, not volunteering such information is a sign of respect. However, this ideal might not be shared by Andrew or his family.

Childbirth and childrearing can also be a sensitive topic for the intermarried couples and their extended families. Each side of the family might have values they would like to instill in the children, and these values might not match. In the worst case, these values might clash. For example, one side of the family might encourage children to express their thoughts and opinions, while the other side does not embrace such values—even viewing such expression as disrespectful to elders. Autonomy and conservatism tend be associated with authoritative and authoritarian parenting, respectively. Disagreement regarding parenting values will often produce relationship stress for intermarried couples. This stress tends to compound when the couples also experience pressure from their extended families to conform to their family's values in childrearing. Although it is important for all couples, whether intermarried or not, to discuss childrearing approaches before extending their families, intermarried couples face unique challenges and should take time to determine a parenting strategy that works for both partners and their growing family.

HIERARCHY VS. EGALITARIANISM. Hierarchical cultures designate certain members of the family to have power, resources, or duties according to gender, age, or birth order; egalitarian cultures emphasize equality between persons within a group or family, and therefore, define roles loosely (Schwartz, 1999). Recall the story of Sakiya, who is from a hierarchical culture and is dating Andrew, who is not. Andrew may have difficulty adjusting to the concept of hierarchy in Sakiya's culture.

In Sakiya's culture, for example, there is a clear family hierarchy; older siblings and their spouses are referred to by their birth order (such as "sister five") and never by name. The order of birth often determines who will make decisions for the family.

Cultural practices, such as mealtimes, can be influenced by the family's position as hierarchical or egalitarian. In some hierarchical families, men and women do not sit together at mealtime—instead, they are divided by gender and age. For example, in a study examining the home environment of low-income Hmong youth, Mao, Deenanath, and Xiong (2012) found both gender and generation separation within the household. That is, males and females tend to socialize within their own gender, and younger and older individuals tend to socialize within their age groups. The researchers observed less interaction *between* these groups (e.g., male–female interaction, young–elder interaction) than within them. In egalitarian families, we would be less likely to see mealtime interactions determined by positions in the family or characteristics of its members.

MASTERY VS. HARMONY. Cultures that value mastery place value on ambition, as opposed to cultures that place precedence upon harmony or acceptance (Schwartz, 1999). For example, those who grew up in a culture under the mastery umbrella tend to believe in promoting independence in children at a very young age. Those who grew up with a harmonious philosophy, however, may believe in allowing their very young child to take steps toward independence, such as potty training, when s/he is ready (regardless of age). This may also include bathing and spoon-feeding the child years after the child is able to perform the task on his/her own. This anticipation of the child's needs eases as the child grows older. After a certain age, most likely during elementary school, parents shift from doing everything for the child to training the child to perform tasks and behaviors that are promoted by their society; more often than not, these tasks are gender specific.

INTERPERSONAL BOUNDARIES. Negotiating boundaries between the intermarried couples and their extended families often requires careful thought on the part of the couple because it can be a strong source of conflict. Misunderstandings in expectations surrounding household roles, personal space, and family hierarchy, for instance, can generate conflict for the intermarried couple. This is especially true if one spouse comes from a family that tends to embrace a more collective and hierarchical philosophy, like Sakiya, while the other spouse comes from a family that adopts a more individualistic philosophy, like Andrew.

Regarding household boundaries, Sakiya and Andrew have gotten married and moved in with one another. Remember, Sakiya's family embraces a collective philosophy and believes space (such as one's home) is to be viewed by the family as "community space." Thus, family members tend to freely utilize the space inside and outside of Sakiya and Andrew's home without invitation, often coming into the home unannounced. Sakiya's family members take up residence in the living room. They are utilizing the kitchen and using household items like pots, cleaning supplies, and appliances at their leisure. Sakiya's in-laws will often plan activities in the couple's backyard without acquiring prior approval from Sakiya and Andrew with the mindset that there was no approval needed. These actions often trigger stress and conflict between Sakiya and Andrew. Furthermore, attempts to address this boundary issue with the extended family place the couple at the risk of causing misunderstandings and conflict between themselves and their relatives. Due to reverence of older family members, it may be seen as inappropriate to openly question family members' actions.

Personal space is another high-potential source of conflict between couples and their relatives. Personal space refers to both physical proximity and inquiry of personal information. For example, when it comes to food and feeding, some will think being spoon-fed is a signal of tremendous dependency between the person doing the spoon feeding and the person accepting the food, and that spoon feeding an adult is only done if the individual is too sick or old to feed himself. Authors Tisa and Meghan's experiences have been within families that embrace a more individualistic philosophy where autonomy is highly valued. Children in these families are encouraged to be independent at a young age. Author Meghan shared that her parents stopped spoon-feeding her as soon as she was able to reach for food and/or grasp it while sitting in a high chair. On the contrary, author Dung shared that when he was younger, being spoon-fed was viewed as a sign of love and trust. Adults usually spoon-fed their children or older siblings would spoon-feed their younger siblings because they wanted to show their love for them. It is worthwhile to note that Dung grew up in a small town where most of the residents live in extreme poverty and food is scarce. Thus, the act of giving up food for another person comes at a great sacrifice for the giver for s/he will not have enough food for himself/herself.

It is also important to note that Dung (collectivist roots) and Meghan (individualistic roots) are married to each other. It is not hard to imagine, then, the conflict and misunderstanding that occurred once when the relative of the collectivist individual, Dung, in an attempt to express love and endearment, spoon-fed his spouse, Meghan, who grew up in an individualistic household. To Meghan, the act signaled a physical proximity violation and was received as an insult. As Meghan reacted in reply to the message perceived, her reaction triggered a negative response from Dung's relative, who interpreted Meghan's reaction as a sign of disrespect and rejection of Dung's love.

Last, but certainly not least, family hierarchy also tends to be an area of conflict for intermarried couples. This is especially true if one spouse grew up in a family that embraced in the Eastern philosophy of filial piety (respecting one's elders), and the other grew up believing in the Western philosophy of equal and open dialogue. Often, filial piety is taken to such length that individuals are not allowed to question the decisions and actions of one's elders. Differences in beliefs about family hierarchy can be a great barrier if intermarried partners want to engage in conversation with their relatives to work through misunderstandings.

ROLES. Negotiating roles is another challenge for intermarried couples and their relatives. Individuals growing up with an individualistic philosophy tend to desire a nuclear family home consisting of the couple and their children, where the household is run by two partners. One partner might play a stereotypically "feminine" role while the other might play a "masculine" role in the home. There are different roles and expectations that each gender is expected to perform, but each gender has dominion over its own area. Roles work a little differently in families who prescribe to a collectivist philosophy. In these families, the couples are expected to live with their extended family. In a Chinese household, for example, a daughter-in-law is expected to live with her husband's family (Shih & Pyke, 2009). Due to this living arrangement, the role of the "lady of the house" is shared by daughter-in-law and mother in-law. Because filial piety is highly valued, the daughter-in-law is expected to let her mother-in-law take lead role as "woman of the house" while she serves as the backup. The mother-in-law is then entrusted to train the daughter-in-law on how to be a wife (Shih & Pyke, 2009).

The living arrangement and the shared power between the mother-in-law and daughter-in-law is a potential area of conflict for intermarried couples wherein one is from an Eastern philosophy and another is Western. First, one spouse in the intermarried relationship may not agree with the living arrangement. Second, the lack of absolute dominion as the "woman of the house" might provide some confusion and stress. Finally, unless both mother in-law and daughter in-law can communicate effectively, the negotiation of roles and transfer of knowledge can be Communication issues have the potential to contribute to strain that could already be happening in the relationship.

CHALLENGES FOR MINORITY FAMILIES INTEGRATING INTO THE UNITED STATES

One of the biggest challenges facing ethnically diverse families is navigating how to interact in a place where they may be the only source of "diversity." Whether that source is you or someone you know, many families are faced with choosing a process when making the transition to a new place where they are not a part of the dominant culture. In the United States, people and families who have emigrated must balance how much *Americanization* (to make or become "American" in character; to assimilate to the customs and institutions of the United States) they want to undergo. For example, it is common to hear about children of first-generation immigrants and their parents having arguments about clothing choices (traditional clothing of their culture versus new "cool" American clothing), how much time is spent with family, and how much time is spent with new friends.

Assimilation is the process of replacing "old" cultural values with those of the dominant culture. Assimilation is a challenging process for new immigrants because it is difficult to completely let go of everything someone has learned from his/her culture. Assimilation would be comparable to an American going to Zambia and completely enmeshing into the culture of that country, abandoning his/her American identity (e.g., clothes, music, food, interpersonal manners, entertainment, dance). That is not an easy task, nor the most logical transition to take.

Today, *acculturation* is a more common and acceptable process for integrating into a new culture. Acculturation is the blending of both "old" and "new" cultures. Acculturation is becoming a more acceptable transition in society with the recent wave of "fusion" style restaurants and clothing fashions. Acculturation allows the person to pick and choose what parts of his/her new world s/he wants to add to his/her life without diminishing his/her own cultural beliefs and values.

Lastly, *segregation* is the process in which an ethnic group isolates itself, or is forced into isolation. A glance at the history of the United States will give multiple examples of segregation at its finest moments. The Pilgrims, slavery, women not having the right to vote, Native Americans being forced onto reservations, Asian Americans being sequestered after Pearl Harbor—all are strong examples of how segregation has played a part in the history of the United States.

People that have primarily experienced living in the majority culture have never had to make the choice to assimilate, acculturate, or segregate themselves—so it can sometimes be difficult for them to understand why new immigrants are hesitant to venture outside their comfort zones. This lack of understanding is where *stereotypes* (i.e., generalizations) and *prejudices* (i.e., pre-judgments) begin to show themselves. If these thoughts are left uninformed, *racism* (i.e., hatred or intolerance of another race or races) or racist ideals and values set in. Racism is the perception that one's own race is superior to and has the right to dominate others.

Those of us who live in the majority or dominant culture are frequently unaware of the advantages we enjoy by nature of our status. Life can feel very smooth when everyone speaks your language, understands the same cultural norms as you (e.g., timeliness, personal hygiene and grooming, acceptable interpersonal interactions), thinks in similar ways as you, holds your spiritual values, and celebrates your religious holidays. Rules of communication (both verbal and nonverbal), behavioral and cultural norms, and values are some of the issues that need to be considered before beginning a relationship with anyone, especially someone that comes from a different background. Each new ethnic or cultural group that comes to the United States will face issues of assimilation and acculturation it's up to all individuals—whether members of the dominant or minority group—to exercise empathy and understanding when interacting with others.

Culture and the Healthcare Experience

The healthcare field has a long way to go in its quest to understand and create harmony between those who believe in Eastern traditions and those who believe in Western ones. Physicians trained in the Western world prescribe to a healthcare system that is sometimes incompatible with the beliefs of the Eastern world. For instance, the Western view of health is based on germ theory, which means sicknesses are caused by bacteria and mycobacteria. When an individual is ill, physicians are trained to search for the infection and prescribe drugs to eliminate it. The Eastern view of health, on the other hand, is based on the idea of balance and energy flow. When an individual is ill, an Eastern physician searches for the interruption of energy flow within the person's body and figures out a way to correct the interruption.

Author Dung explained that his family, adopting an Eastern perspective, believes bad air is the cause of some illnesses. When someone is ill, his family believes the person has inhaled bad air into his/her body. One way to get rid of the bad air is to perform procedures known as "coining" or "cupping." In coining, a coin is used to scrape against the body, breaking the surface blood vessels and allowing the bad air to escape. Similarly, cupping involves placing a small cup on top of the skin and sucking all of the air out of it so that a vacuum is created. The resulting bruise (i.e., caused by breaking the surface blood vessels) allows bad air to escape from the body.

In Western medicine, physicians often view bruised skin as a sign of damage. In the past, Eastern and Western worlds would intersect each time author Dung would take his mother to the doctor after a coining procedure. Since the doctor was unfamiliar with these procedures, the doctor would often looked at him questioningly, as if he had abused his mother, and would thoroughly search his mother's body for more bruising. Today, physicians receive more training on cultural competence and have gained awareness of Eastern medicinal practices. Most are open to working with patients to combine – or at least accommodate – Western and Eastern methods of healing.

CULTURAL COMPETENCE

Cultural competence is defined as the capacity to draw effectively upon cultural knowledge, awareness, sensitivity, and skillful actions in order to relate appropriately to, and work effectively with, others from different cultural backgrounds (Sperry, 2012). Culturally competent individuals are able to apply these skills in difficult and/or awkward circumstances. A low level of cultural competence is evident when an individual demonstrates deficits in one or all of the four components of cultural competency, is unable to perceive the need to apply them, or is unable to do apply them for another reason. In contrast, a high level of cultural competence is evident when an individual knows, recognizes, respects, accepts, welcomes, and takes effective and appropriate skillful action with regard to another's culture.

Cultural Knowledge

The *cultural knowledge* dimension is cognitive, and it requires familiarity with a specific culture and facts and/or insights about that culture. There are two ways of achieving cultural knowledge. One way is through firsthand knowledge, derived from directly and personally spending time with, working alongside, visiting with, or talking to members of the cultural group. The second way is secondhand knowledge. This can be indirect and comes from reading about, talking about, or seeing documentaries about the cultural group.

Cultural Awareness

The *cultural awareness* dimension of cultural competence is also largely cognitive. Cultural awareness is the recognition of the impact of specific thoughts, attitudes, and feelings on a culture—as well as the recognition that awareness could be negatively affected by these factors. This awareness requires recognition and anticipation of the likely consequences of *your* specific thoughts, attitudes, and feelings. Whereas cultural knowledge involves data or observations that are largely impartial, cultural awareness involves subjectivity.

Cultural Sensitivity

The *cultural sensitivity* dimension of cultural competence is its attitudinal dimension. Culturally sensitivity individuals demonstrate an attitude of respect, welcoming, and/or acceptance. Genuine cultural sensitivity can be distinguished from "practiced" cultural sensitivity. Genuine cultural sensitivity requires an individual to become aware of the other's worldview and perspective, and then to respond in an empathic, caring, and/or helpful manner based on that understanding.

FIGURE 3 Cultural Competence

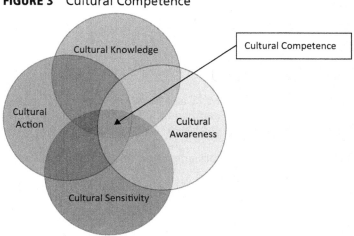

Cultural Action

The *action* dimension of cultural competence is behavioral. Whereas cultural sensitivity is largely about intentions, cultural action refers to decisions and actions that can affect the other. Individuals who demonstrate cultural action respond with decisions and actions that foster the well-being of others.

Reaching a high level of cultural competence takes hard work. It requires intention. It is not something that will happen overnight even for the smartest, most determined people. Working toward it can begin with something as simple as picking up a book or watching a movie that you otherwise would not. Joining clubs in your local community, or volunteering your time in places outside your normal environment, can help you make an even bigger stride toward cultural competency.

FUTURE RESEARCH ON CULTURE IN RELATIONSHIPS

One concept we know to be certain about culture is that it is ever changing. The influence of culture on relationships evolves daily, affecting families and researchers alike. What remains unknown for now is how and what influence immigrants to the United States will have on both the American mainstream culture, and how the mainstream culture will continue to influence the cultures recent immigrants bring. We are learning more, for example, about how new views of academic achievement affect elder members of West Asian groups now living in the United States. We are also beginning to learn more about how the debate and issues surrounding female genital mutilation in the African immigrant community will affect the dating culture and mate selection process for second generation immigrant women. Researchers are also just scraping the surface on how advertising, media, and politics geared toward Hispanic populations will shape American social media and government. These are just a few of the many unique areas of daily American life culture can play a role in.

CONCLUSION

The goal of this chapter was to celebrate, understand, and appreciate the diversity that surrounds us on a daily basis. This is important to do for a variety of reasons, but most importantly, because inter-racial/ethnic/culture relationships are more common today than ever before. Thus, it is essential that we come together and work toward cultural respect and competence within this social evolution. Doing so will equip us with the skills to navigate differences across group viewpoints and beliefs, practices and rituals, family relationships, gender roles, and interpersonal behaviors and habitudes. Furthermore, evolving will also allow us to integrate old and existing (and to create novel) ways of "doing" all of these things together in new dyadic and family unions. As a reminder, these skills will not and should not be attained overnight. Cultural competency and understanding requires time, trial and error, and patience. Luckily, these are also elements of healthy relationships.

REFERENCES

Bashi, V., & McDaniel, A. (1997). A theory of immigration and racial stratification. *Journal of Black Studies, 27,* 668–682. doi:http://www.jstor.org/stable/2784874

Batson, C. D., Qian, Z., & Lichter, D. T. (2006). Interracial and intraracial patterns of mate selection among America's diverse black populations. *Journal of Marriage and Family, 68*(3), 658–672. doi:10.1111/j.1741-3737.2006.00281.x

Bent-Goodley, T. B. (2005). An African-centered approach to domestic violence. *Families in Society, 86,* 197–206. doi:10.1606104438942455

Breger, R., & Hill, R. (1998). Introducing mixed marriages. In R. Breger & R. Hill (Eds.), *Cross-cultural marriage: Identity and choice* (pp. 1–32). New York: Berg.

Bratter, J., & Eschbach, K. (2006). "What about the couple?" Interracial marriage and psychological distress. *Social Science Research, 35*(4), 1025–1047. doi:10.1016/j.ssresearch.2005.09.001

Bratter, J. L., & King, R. B. (2008). "But will it last?": Marital instability among interracial and same-race couples. *Family Relations, 57,* 160–171. doi:10.1111/j.1741-3729.2008.00491.x

Brave Heart, M. Y. H., & DeBruyn, L. M. (1998). The American Indian holocaust: Healing historical and unresolved grief. *American Indian and Alaska Native Mental Health Research Journal, 8*(2), 60–82.

Bustamante, R. M., Nelson, J. A., Henriksen, R. C., & Monakes, S. (2011). Intercultural couples: Coping with culture-related stressors. *Family Journal, 19* (2), 154–164. doi:10.1177/1066480711399723

Caldwell, J. Y., Davis, J. D., Du Bois, B., Echo Hawk, H., Erickson, J. S., Goins, R. T., Hill, C., Hillabrant, W., Johnson, S. R., Kendall, E., Keemer, K., Manson, S. P., Marshall, C. A., Running Wolf, P., Santiago, R. L., Schacht, R., & Stone, J. B. (2005). Culturally competent research with American Indians and Alaska Natives: Findings and recommendations of the first symposium of the work group on American Indian research and program evaluation methodology. *Journal of the National Centre, 12*(1), 1–21.

Cameron, S. C. & Wycoff, S. M. (1998) The destructive nature of the term race: Growing beyond a false paradigm. *Journal of Counseling and Development, 76,* 277–285. doi:10.1002/j.1556-6676.1998.tb02543.x

Chan, S. (1991). *Asian Americans: An interpretive history* (p. 145). Boston, MA: Twayne.

Chao, R. K. (1994). Beyond parental control and authoritarian parenting style: Understanding Chinese parenting through the cultural notion of training. *Child Development, 65*(4), 1111–1119. doi:10.1111/j.1467-8624.1994.tb00806.x

Chen, C. (December, 2012). Asians: Too smart for their own good? *New York Times Magazine,* 43–45.

Chito Childs, E. (2005). Looking behind the stereotypes of the "angry black woman": An exploration of black women's responses to interracial relationships. *Gender and Society, 19*(4), 544–561. doi:10.1177/0891243205276755

Deloria, V. Jr. (1973). *God is red.* New York: Grosset and Dunlap.

Detzner, D. F. (1992). Life history: Conflict in Southeast Asian refugee families. In J. F. Gilgun, K. Daly, & G. Handel (Eds.), *Qualitative methods in family research* (pp. 85–102). Thousand Oaks, CA: Sage.

Ellison, C. G., Wolfinger, N. H., & Ramos-Wada, A. I. (2013). Attitudes toward marriage, divorce, cohabitation, and casual sex among working-age Latinos: Does religion matter? *Journal of Family Issues, 34*(3), 295–322. doi:10.1177/0192513X12445458

Fass, S. M. (1986). Economic development and employment projects. In G. L. Hendricks, B. T. Downing, & A. S. Deinard (Eds.), *The Hmong in transition* (pp. 202–209). Staten Island, NY: The Center for Migration Studies of New York, Inc.

Goldstein, J. R. (1999). Kinship networks that cross racial lines: The exception or the rule? *Demography, 36*(3), 399–407. doi:10.2307/2648062

Gross, C.G. (1986). The Hmong in Isla Vista: Obstacles and enhancements to adjustment. In G. Hendricks, B. Dowing, & A. Deinard (Eds.), *The Hmong in transition* (pp. 145–158). New York, NY: Center for Migration Studies.

Hamilton-Merritt, J. (1993). *Tragic mountains: The Hmong, the Americans, and the secret wars for Laos, 1942–1992.* Bloomington, IN: Indiana University Press.

Hamner, B. M. (2011). A cultural relative analysis of Black women and marriage. Proceedings of the National Conference on Undergraduate Research (NCUR), Ithaca College, NY.

Hibbler, D., K., & Shinew, K. J. (2002). Interracial couples' experience of leisure: A social network approach. *Journal of Leisure Research, 34* (2), 135–156. Retrieved from http://search.proquest.com.ezp1.lib.umn.edu/openview/424cd181210ae4e473e8f6d3a36e38b6/1?pq-origsite=gscholar

Hitt, J. (2005). The newest Indians. *New York Times Magazine,* 36–41. Retrieved from http://www.nytimes.com/2005/08/21/magazine/21NATIVE.html

Hixson, L., Helper, B., & Myoung, O. K. U.S.Census, (2011). *The White population: 2010* (c20108R-05). Retrieved from: http://www.census.gov/prod/cen2010/briefs/c2010br-05.pdf

Hohmann-Marriott, B. E., & Amato, P. (2008). Relationship quality in interethnic marriages and cohabitations. *Social Forces, 87*(2), 825–855. doi:10.1353/sof.0.0151

Humes, K. R., Jones, N. A., & Ramirez, R. R. (2010). *Overview of race and Hispanic origin: 2010 Census Briefs* (C2010BR-02). Retrieved from http://www.census.gov/prod/cen2010/briefs/c2010br-02.pdf

Hune, S. (2002). Demographics and diversity of Asian American college students. *New Directions for Student Services, 2002*(97), 11–20. doi:10.1002/ss.35

Jang, J. (2013). Potential social capital and psychological distress for intermarried persons. (Doctoral dissertation, University of Minnesota).

Joanides, C., Mayhew, M., & Mamalakis, P. M. (2002). Investigating inter-Christian and intercultural couples associated with the Greek Orthodox archdiocese of America: A qualitative research project. *American Journal of Family Therapy, 30*(4), 373–383. doi:10.1080/01926180290033484

Kalmijn, M., & van Tubergen, F. (2010). A comparative perspective on intermarriage: Explaining differences among national-origin groups in the United States. *Demography, 47*(2), 459–479. doi:10.1353/dem.0.0103

Khatib-Chahidi, J., Hill, R., & Paton, R. (1998). Chance, choice and circumstance: A study of women in cross-cultural marriages. In R. Breger, & R. Hill (Eds.), *Cross-cultural marriage: Identity and choice* (pp. 49–66). New York: Berg.

Killian, K. D. (2001). Crossing borders: Race, gender, and their intersections in interracial couples. *Journal of Feminist Family Therapy, 13*(1), 1-31. doi:10.1300/J086v13n01_01

Lee, J. C. S. (1994). Navigating the topology of race. *Stanford Law Review,* 747-780.

Lee, S. M., & Edmonston, B. (2005). New marriages, new families: U.S. racial and Hispanic intermarriage. *Population Bulletin, 60* (2), 1–36. Retrieved from http://www.prb.org/pdf05/60.2newmarriages.pdf

Lee, R. M., & Liu, H. T. (2001). Coping with intergenerational family conflict: Comparison of Asian American, Hispanic, and European American college students. *Journal of Counseling Psychology, 48,* 410–419. doi:10J037//0022-0167.48.4.410

Mao, D., Deenanath, V., & Xiong, Z. B. (2012). Hmong students' perceptions of their family environment: A consensual qualitative analysis of family photos. *Hmong Studies Journal, 13*(1), 1–27. Retrieved from http://hmongstudies.org/MaoDeenanathXiongHSJ13.pdf

Molina, B., Estrada, D., & Burnett, J. A. (2004). Cultural communities: Challenges and opportunities in the creation of "happily ever after" stories of intercultural couplehood. *The Family Journal, 12* (2), 139–147. doi:10.1177/1066480703261962

Morrison, T. (1998). *Paradise.* New York: A. A. Knopf.

Olney, D. (1986). Population trends. In G. L. Hendricks, B. T. Downing, & A. S. Deinard (Eds.), *The Hmong in transition* (pp. 179–184). Staten Island, NY: Center for Migration Studies of New York, Inc.

Olson, D., DeFrain, J., & Skogrand, L. (2010). *Marriages and families: Intimacy, diversity, and strengths,* 4th edition. Boston, MA: McGraw Hill.

Olson, S. (2001). The genetic archaeology of race. *Atlantic Monthly,* (4) 69–80.

Paisano, E. L. (1993). *We the American—: Asians.* U.S. Department of Commerce, Economics and Statistics Administration, Bureau of the Census.

Paisano, E. L. (1993). *We the American—: Pacific Islanders.* U.S. Department of Commerce, Economics and Statistics Administration, Bureau of the Census.

Passel, J., Wang, W., & Taylor, P. (2010). Marrying out. Pew Research Social & Demographic Trends. Retrieved from http://www.pewsocialtrends.org/2010/06/04/marrying-out/

Perreira, K., Chapman., M., & Stein, G. (2006). Becoming an American parent; Overcoming challenges and finding strength in a new immigrant Latino community. *Journal of Family Issues, 27,* 1383–1414. doi:10.1177/0192513X06290041

Pyke, K. (2000). "The Normal American Family" as an interpretive structure of family life among grown children of Korean and Vietnamese immigrants. *Journal of Marriage and Family, 62*(1), 240–255. doi:10.1111/j.1741-3737.2000.00240.x

Qian, Z. (1997). Breaking the racial barriers: Variations in interracial marriage between 1980 and 1990. *Demography, 34*(2), 263–276. doi:10.2307/2061704

Qian, Z., Blair, S. L., & Ruf, S. D. (2001). Asian American interracial and interethnic marriages: Differences by education and nativity. *International Migration Review, 35*(2), 557–586. doi:10.2307/2061704

Roer-Strier, D., & Ben Ezra, D. (2006). Intermarriages between Western women and Palestinian men: Multidirectional adaptation processes. *Journal of Marriage and Family, 68*(1), 41–55. doi:10.1111/j.1741-3737.2006.00232.x

Rosenblatt, P. C., & Stewart, C. C. (2004). Challenges in cross-cultural marriage: When she is Chinese and he Euro-American. *Sociological Focus, 37*(1), 43-58. doi:10.1080/00380237.2004.10571233

Rowntree, D. (2000). *Statistics without tears: An introduction for non-mathematicians.* London, England: Penguin.

Sarkisian, N. Gerena, M., & Gerstel, N. (2006). Extended family ties among Mexican, Puerto Rican,and Whites: Superinteration or disintegration? *Family Relations, 55,* 331–344. doi:10.1111/j.1741-3729.2006.00408.x

Schwartz, S. H. (1999). A theory of cultural values and some implications for work. *Applied Psychology, 48*(1), 23–47. doi:10.1111/j.1464-0597.1999.tb00047.x

Shih, K., & Pyke, K. (2010). Power, resistance, and emotional economics in women's relationships with mothers-in-law in Chinese immigrant families. *Journal of Family Issues, 21,* 333–357. doi:10.1177/0192513X09350875

Smith, D. E. (1993). The Standard North American Family (SNAF) as an ideological code. *Journal of Family Issues, 14*(50), 50–65. doi:10.1177/0192513X93014001005

Sperry, L. (2012). Cultural competence: A primer. *Journal of Individual Psychology, 68*(4), 310–320.

Su, J., Lee, R. M., & Vang, S. (2005). Intergenerational family conflict and coping among Hmong American college students. *Journal of Counseling Psychology, 52*, 482–489. doi:10.1037/0022-0167.52.4.482

Taylor, P., Lopez, M. H., Martínez, J. H., & Velasco, G. (2012). When labels don't fit: Hispanics and their views of identity. Retrieved from http://www.pewhispanic.org/2012/04/04/when-labels-dont-fit-hispanics-and-their-views-of-identity/

Thomas, K. J. (2011). Familial influences on poverty among young children in black immigrant, US-born black, and nonblack immigrant families. *Demography, 48*(2), 437–460. doi:10.1007/s13524-011-0018-3

Triandis, H. (1995). *Individualism & collectivism: New directions in social psychology.* Boulder, CO: Westview Press.

Tucker, M. B., & Mitchell-Kernan, C. (1990). "New trends in black American interracial marriage: The social structural context". *Journal of Marriage and Family, 52*(1), 209–218. doi:10.2307/352851.JSTOR 352851

United Nations High Commissioner for Refugees (UNHCR). (2014). *UNHCR - Refugees.* Retrieved March 8, 2014, from http://www.unhcr.org/pages/49c3646c125.html

U.S. Census Bureau. (2010). U.S. Census 2010. Retrieved from http://factfinder2.census.gov/

U.S. Census Bureau. (2011). U.S. Census 2011. Retrieved from http://www.census.gov/newsroom/releases/archives/facts_for_features_special_editions/cb11-ff22.html

U.S. Census Bureau (2012). *2010 Census Briefs—The Asian Population: 2010.* Retrieved from https://www.census.gov/prod/cen2010/briefs/c2010br-11.pdf

Vang, C. T. (2004-05). Hmong American K-12 students and the academic skills needed for a college education: A review of the existing literature and suggestions for future research. *Hmong Studies Journal, 5*, 1–31. Retrieved from http://login.ezproxy.lib.umn.edu/login?url=http://search.proquest.com.ezp2.lib.umn.edu/docview/220387409?accountid=14586

Wang, W. (2012). The rise of intermarriage: Rates, characteristics vary by race and gender. *Social and Demographic Trends.* Washington, D.C.: Pew Research Center.

Williams, R. M. Jr. (1970). *American society: A sociological interpretation.* New York, NY: Knopf Doubleday Publishing Group.

Xiong, S., & Lee, S. E. (2011). Hmong students in higher education and academic support programs. *Hmong Studies Journal, 12*, 1–20. Retrieved from http://hmongstudies.org/XiongandLeeHSJ12.pdf

Xiong, Z. B. (2000). Hmong-American family problem-solving interactions: Conceptualizations, communications, and problem-solving processes. Unpublished doctoral dissertation, University of Minnesota, St. Paul, Minnesota.

Yancey, G. (2007). Experiencing racism: Differences in the experiences of whites married to blacks and non-black minorities. *Journal of Comparative Family Studies, 38*(2), 197–213. doi:http://www.jstor.org/stable/41604142

Yen, H. (2012). Interracial marriage climbs to a new high, study finds. *Huffington Post.* http://www.huffingtonpost.com/2012/02/16/interracial-marriage-in-us_n_1281229.html

Zhang, Y., & Van Hook, J. (2009). Marital dissolution among interracial couples. *Journal of Marriage and Family, 71*(1), 95–107. doi:10.1111/j.1741-3737.2008.00582.x

13
Religion and Spirituality in Intimate Relationships

Julie A. Zaloudek, Ph.D.
*Department of Human Development
and Family Studies
University of Wisconsin - Stout*

Gregg T. Schacher, Ph.D., LMFT
The Relationship Therapy Center

Elizabeth Plowman, Ph.D.
*Department of Family Social Science
University of Minnesota*

LEARNING OBJECTIVES

- Articulate the differences between religion and spirituality
- Understand how religion and spirituality influence fidelity in relationships
- Understand how religion and spirituality influence cohabitation, marriage, and divorce

INTRODUCTION

Greg and Candace are both active Lutherans and come from Lutheran families. They met at a Christian college and immediately appreciated the fact that they share similar values and beliefs. They plan to marry when Candace finishes graduate school next year and start a family of their own. How might Greg's and Candace's shared religion and activities impact their relational quality, chances for staying together, and ways of behaving and making meaning out of their shared life?

Lacey and Anne are in a long-term cohabiting love relationship. Lacey is a Jewish atheist, and Anne is an agnostic who practices daily meditation to feel more connected to the universe. Lacey enjoys practicing traditional Jewish rituals to stay connected to her family, past, and culture. Anne is a supportive participant in these practices. Lacey does not join Anne in her meditation, though, nor does she share Anne's belief that all living things in the universe are connected in a mystical way. Lacey and Anne hope to have children in the next few years and provide them with the foundation they need to develop a healthy sense of identity and connection to family. How might their lack of religiosity and Anne's spirituality impact them as a couple and a family? How might they use their practices and beliefs to make meaning of and strengthen their relationships and family?

In this chapter, we will explore these questions in light of what social scientists have learned from research and practice about the roles of religion and spirituality in families and romantic couple relationships.

Corresponding Author: Elizabeth J. Plowman, Ph.D., University of Minnesota; Department of Family Social Science; 1985 Buford Ave.; 290 McNeal Hall; Saint Paul, MN 55108. E-mail: eplowman@umn.edu.

> An individual's spiritual or religious identity is influenced by many factors, including family of origin, society and community, and individual experiences. How and where we grow up, what we learn, and the type of exposure we have to religion and spiritual ways of living influence how we live our lives and identify ourselves. What generation we grew up in also makes a difference. In recent decades there has been a trend away from people thinking of themselves as "religious" and toward identifying as "spiritual" (Pew Research, 2010). The chart below shows that the younger you are, the less likely you are to be religiously affiliated.
>
> *– Pew Research Center, 2012, p. 10*

Religious Affiliation by Age

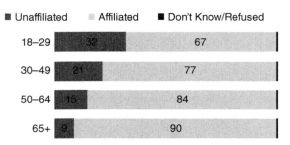

■ Unaffiliated   ▨ Affiliated   ■ Don't Know/Refused

18–29	32	67
30–49	21	77
50–64	15	84
65+	9	90

Source: Pew Research Center for the People & the Press, January–July 2012.
PEW RESEARCH CENTER (2012, p. 7)

For interactive information about religious life in the U.S., check out the Religious Landscape Study from the Pew Research Center at http://www.pewforum.org/religious-landscape-study/

RELIGION AND SPIRITUALITY

A person's religious and spiritual orientation (or lack of one) can impact how couples relate and connect. Like family of origin or culture, religion and spirituality have the potential to both challenge and enrich a couple's relationship. For example, religion and spirituality might affect Greg and Candace's relationship differently than it affects Lacey and Anne's relationship.

There has been much debate about how to define religion and spirituality (Ammerman, 2013; Gall, Malette, & Guirguis-Younger, 2011), and this debate is outside of the chapter's scope. We define *spirituality* as a personal, inner experience of, or relation to, the sacred aspects of life, as perceived and experienced by an individual. We define *religion* as organized and collective practices, rituals, doctrines, rules, teachings and structures for and of groups of people around a particular approach to understanding sacred aspects of life. Individuals can be religious and spiritual, religious but not spiritual, spiritual but not religious, or neither spiritual nor religious.

One key factor that influences our religious and spiritual identification is the generation to which we belong. Despite differences between generations in religious affiliation, the Millennials (i.e., birth years from the early 1980s to the early 2000s) are very similar to older generations in their beliefs (e.g., life after death, existence of miracles) and practices (Pew Research, 2010). For example, about 45% of Millennials report praying daily, a response similar to people their age over the past few decades, though lower than the rate that older people pray. Younger people are more open to same-sex couples and evolution as the best explanation for human existence than older generations, yet they are very similar in their beliefs about morality. For example, 76% of adults ages 18–29, and 78% of adults aged 65+ report that they "completely agree" or "mostly agree" that there are absolute standards of right and wrong (Pew Research, 2010).

Despite the trends moving away from identifying as religious, 39% of Americans attend services weekly and 46% are religiously affiliated, 35% read religious scriptures weekly, 58% pray daily, and 39% meditate weekly (Pew Research, 2010). Fifty-six percent of Americans say that religion is "very important" and 71% claim to believe in God.

Decades of research suggest that people's religious involvement and spirituality can influence intimate relationships in important ways such as attitudes about premarital sex, relationship satisfaction, likelihood to marry, likelihood to engage in extramarital sex, likelihood to divorce, and others. People also use religious and spiritual ideas to help them interpret their relationships and make meaning out of their lives together. These influences make religion and spirituality important to consider when studying intimate relationships and working with couples and families.

What We Know

Conducting research on how religion and spirituality impacts couples is challenging. Depending on how we measure what is "religious," we might get different outcomes for how it impacts couples' unions. For example, when measuring religiosity by affiliation, we do not see any difference in divorce rates, but when measuring it by frequency of joint church attendance, we find that religious couples are less likely to divorce (Myers, 2006; Vaaler, Ellison, & Powers, 2009; Woods & Emery, 2002). Complicating the issue further is the increasing diversity of religious—and now spiritual—orientations within the United States. Researchers have continued to meet these challenges, and we have learned a lot about how religiosity and spirituality can impact intimate relationships and family life. In the next few sections, we'll review what researchers understand, and have yet to understand, about religion, spirituality, and intimacy.

Sexuality and Fidelity

Much discussion surrounds the intersection between religiosity and fidelity. Are religious couples more likely to remain faithful? Higher religiosity—especially in a religion with taboos against sex outside of marriage—has been linked to later age for first sex, fewer sexual partners, lower rates of premarital sexual activity, and less permissive attitudes toward sex outside of marriage (Helm, McBride, Knox, & Zusman, 2009; Lefkowitz, Gillen, Shearer, & Boone, 2004; McMillen, Helm, & McBride, 2011). (Find more information about the intersection between spirituality and sexuality in Chapter 15). Some potential explanations for this are that these young people have a large network of people who support their attitudes about waiting for sex, fear of stigma within their community if they engage in sex outside of marriage, and the belief that sex is "sacred" or "blessed" if it takes place within marriage (or at least between committed partners).

Religiously affiliated couples show less risk for marital infidelity on average, but this finding is especially strong when they frequently attend religious services together (Atkins, Baucom, & Jacobson, 2001; Atkins & Kessel, 2008; Burdette, Ellison, Sherkat, & Gore, 2007). This is one of the more consistent findings regarding couple infidelity and religiosity. Other interesting findings are about prayer. Atkins and Kessel (2008) did not find any difference in rates of infidelity between people who prayed compared to people who did not. The only significant protection from infidelity was frequently attending religious services together. However, Fincham, Lambert, and Beach (2010) found that individuals who prayed for their partners daily participated in less infidelity than did the control group who engaged in daily positive thoughts about their partners. It also appears that jointly attending religious services is especially helpful in protecting against infidelity when marital satisfaction is low. It appears that nonreligious couples rely more on satisfaction to protect them against the risks of infidelity than religious people for whom satisfaction did not make much of a difference in whether they remained faithful (Atkins et al., 2001).

Authors have theorized about why being more religious appears to reduce the likelihood of infidelity. It may be that religious communities reinforce fidelity by providing opportunities for marital enrichment, a group of peers that are supportive of marriage, and the threat of ostracism or stigma if a partner is unfaithful (Burdette et al., 2007). Religious services may also reinforce beliefs about the "sacredness" of marriage or the importance of staying in the marriage regardless of satisfaction or personal fulfillment. These beliefs are not without criticism. Family historian Stephanie Coontz (2005) reminds readers that marriages are less stable than they were in the past because people expect more from them, such as sexual fulfillment and emotional intimacy. People have more choices than they once did, too, and although it may change how willing people are to remain faithful in an unsatisfying marriage, fidelity and staying together are not the only way to measure the health of couple relationships. In other words, although religion appears to protect unsatisfying marriages from infidelity, people may argue if staying faithful and committed to an unsatisfying relationship is a helpful goal for individuals, couples, and families.

One other consideration of the impact of religion on fidelity is that the vast majority of available research is on Christian populations, many of which tend to assume *dualism*, or an inherent incongruence between the body and the spirit (Bloom, 2007; Dualism, 2011). The spirit is viewed as superior to the body, and people are advised to constrain their physical desires for the purpose of spiritual purity. Another approach is a *non-dualistic* one, presuming that sexuality and spirituality complement each other. This belief is present across many different religions, although it may not always be emphasized. When we examine meaning making later in this chapter, we consider ways that people attach spiritual meaning to sexual activity and how that matters for their sexual

behavior. *How do you think dualistic or non-dualistic beliefs might influence individual's perspectives on physical intimacy?*

Cohabitation, Marriage, and Divorce

Religion and spirituality have important impacts on social trends like cohabitation, marriage, and divorce. Less religious couples are more likely to cohabit before marriage (Fincham & Beach, 2010). They are also less likely to marry at all. Remember how couples who frequently attended religious services were expected to experience less infidelity? This also appears true for divorce. Although attending religious services regularly predicts lower rates of divorce, people who simply report a religious affiliation are about as likely to be divorced as those that report no religious affiliation (Association of Religion Data Archives, 2013).

What is it about attending religious services that increases the chances of staying married? It may be that couples who have a strong commitment to marriage also have a strong commitment to their religions and so attend regularly. It may also be that these couples are surrounded by a religious community that is supportive of marriage, or that more highly religious couples tend to seek counseling more often than less religious couples. There is growing evidence that it is the meaning that these couples attach to their marriages that may result in higher investment in the relationship (Goodman & Dollahite, 2006). This suggests that religious beliefs are one way in which couples communicate the significance and meaning of their relationship. Religion can provide a "ready" explanation of what marriage means and why it is important. Nonreligious couples may also make meaning of their relationships through shared experiences, symbols, and rituals. If those meanings are not already developed for them, as they may be through religion, they may need to be more creative and intentional about strengthening their relationship through meaningful activities and rituals.

Marital Quality and Satisfaction

According to recent research, general religiousness (e.g., claiming to be a member of a certain religion), as opposed to religious involvement (e.g., regularly attending religious services), is only weakly related to marital satisfaction (Ellison, Henderson, Glenn, & Harkrider, 2011). In contrast, religious involvement is positively related to marital relationship quality (Wolfinger & Wilcox, 2008). Interestingly, this effect is different for husbands and wives in heterosexual couples. Wives mostly benefit from participating in religious activities if their husbands take part in the experience, whereas husbands benefit and perceive their relationship more positively after attending activities, even if they are the only participants (Wolfinger & Wilcox, 2008). Ellison et al. (2011) found that couples who viewed their marriages as sacred or believed that God was present in their relationship had higher levels of marital satisfaction. It is likely that these couples tend to have more positive and less negative emotions toward their partners. Mahoney et al. (1999) also found that couples with sacred beliefs about their marriages were more likely to be collaborative in their problem solving and less likely to engage in unproductive conflicts.

These findings suggest that the meanings people make of their relationships—especially spiritually infused meanings—may be the mechanism by which they achieve higher levels of satisfaction and healthy approaches to communication and conflict. Researchers are still learning about how spiritual and religious differences in relationships can influence relationship satisfaction and individual well-being, but they do know some ways religion influences couple interaction and family roles.

Marital Equality

Previous research has concluded that highly religious individuals are the most likely to uphold traditional gender roles in marriage. This is especially clear when considering the decisions that highly religious, heterosexual couples make about economics. For example, between 2000 and 2010, white married fathers aged 25 to 54 who regularly attended church earned almost $20,000 more per year than similar single men of the same age (Association of Religion Data Archives, 2013). Conversely, devout married white women earned about $7,000 less per year than similarly religious single women of the same age, suggesting that these religious couples are espousing traditional gender roles with husbands as primary wage earners and wives who sacrifice career and earning power for traditionally gendered and unpaid family work.

Religion affects how couples make daily decisions in their relationships, too, and much of the research to date has focused on Christian religions. For example, when it comes to decision-making in religious relationships, many conservative and liberal Protestants fail to practice what they preach. Although conservative Protestants are more likely to support the ideology that the husband is the "head" of the family, they do not significantly differ from other groups in the structure and process of decision-making (Denton, 2004). Conversely, liberal Protestants claim a very egalitarian ideology, but their reports of marital decision-making are often not as equal as their beliefs would suggest.

When it comes to housework, conservative Evangelical Protestants are quite different than non-Evangelical groups. Ellison and Bartkowski (2002) used the National Survey of Families and Households to compare amount and type of household labor completed by religion. The researchers found that Evangelical women spent four to five more hours per week on housework than non-Evangelical women, and that the majority of that housework was traditionally "women's work" like doing laundry or household cleaning (Ellison & Bartkowski, 2002). An intriguing finding was that Evangelical men did not differ from non-Evangelical men in the amount or type of housework they did. In a different comprehensive study, Wilcox (2004) found that conservative Christian men did more housework and childcare than mainstream Christian men in response to a changing construction of manhood that kept his position of "head" intact while defining her role of "leader" as someone who serves and is highly involved in family life.

Additional analysis from Ellison and Bartkowski (2002) suggested that there are two main reasons for this gender inequality for Evangelical women. One is that theologically conservative women tend to be less educated than less conservative women, decreasing their ability to reduce their domestic workload by engaging in outside work. Second, Evangelical gender ideology tends to value women's domestic contributions while minimizing contributions in the public sphere which may discourage Evangelical women from trying to lighten their domestic load. It is likely that there are gender implications for other religious traditions as well. However, there is little research on gender equality as it connects to non-Christian religions in the United States. Rather, much of the research on gender equality for other religious groups has been framed in ethnicity, culture, and immigration issues.

Religious Heterogamy

What happens when partners of different religions have long-term, committed relationships? *Religious heterogamy*—defined as people of different religions who marry each other—is increasing among couples in the United States (Fincham & Beach, 2010). This shift occurs in spite of ongoing findings that women and men prefer partners who are similarly religious—a trend that can be seen in repeated surveys of mate preference among college students over the past 50 years (Mahoney, 2010). *Why might this be?* Although society is opening up to supporting differences on broad levels, individuals may still have desires about being similar to their mates in fundamental beliefs and religious approaches. For some couples, religious similarity can impact couple satisfaction. For example, similar ratings of personal religiousness are related to greater marital satisfaction among older married couples, but not among younger married couples (Myers, 2006). In addition, Dudley and Kosinski (1990) found that the strongest links between religion and marital quality were associated with couples who shared high levels of agreement about religious beliefs and high levels of church attendance. Furthermore, couples who share aspects of religiosity are not only less likely to get divorced, but are also less likely to consider divorce as an option if their relationships are in trouble.

Shared religious beliefs or viewpoints, in particular, seem foundational to how many couples think about or approach their marriages. Mahoney, Pargament, and DeMaris (2009) found that a majority of their sample of married and pregnant couples agreed with the statement "God played a role in how I ended up being married to my spouse"; 86% of wives and 79% of husbands reported some level of agreement. Stanley and Markman (1992) have suggested that sharing deeply held religious values may help couples form a couple identity—a sense of "we-ness"—which is associated with greater sacrifice and harmony. In a study of 57 older married couples, Kaslow and Robinson (1996) found that two-thirds of the couples indicated that having similar religious beliefs was a critical contributor to their marital satisfaction. Similarly, Mahoney et al. (1999) found that greater global marital satisfaction, less marital conflict, and a greater sense of partner collaboration was associated with spouses who shared a view of marriage as having sacred characteristics and significance.

In contrast, religious heterogamy has been shown to be a potential source of stress for both individuals and their intimate relationships (Curtis & Ellison, 2002). For example, disagreement or dissent over religious beliefs or practices has been shown to impact psychological health (Trenholm, Trent, & Compton, 1998). Trenholm et al. (1998) found that conflicts related to religious issues are associated with perceptions of moral transgression and are predictive of guilt, anxiety, and even panic symptoms. This means that when individuals come together with different religious beliefs and values, many struggle to reconcile that their partner is different than them, and may even feel guilty about this difference. It also can impact how couples interact with one another. More conflict is present among couples with different levels of church attendance and differences in theological beliefs (Curtis & Ellison, 2002).

Given the unique challenges faced by interfaith couples, Furlong and Ata (2006) studied Muslim–Christian married couples in order to identify how they adapted to the significant differences represented by their faith backgrounds. They found that couples adopted six different ways of adapting to an interfaith union. Two types of adaptation were rigid and either involved the conversion of one spouse to the faith of the other or the couple maintained distinctly separate religious practices and rigid rules prohibiting religious discussions. The other four types of adaptation involved some degree of respect for, or participating in, the other spouse's religion. The expression of their faith in different domains—public and private—seemed to be a contributing factor in how these couples integrated their dual identities.

Overall, research suggests general support for the notion that couples experience greater marital quality and stability when aspects of religiosity are shared, and lower marital quality when these critical aspects of religiosity are not shared. However, it is important to remember that religiosity and spirituality are just two of many important predictors of relationship satisfaction and, like any stressor, satisfaction is determined by how the couple manages this situation rather than the situation itself.

So, what are some ways interfaith couples can develop respect for the spiritual beliefs and practices of their partners and their families? Partners can garner respect by helping each other learn to appreciate the meaning of their personal and historical ties to their spirituality. Because open and direct communication is a strong predictor of relationship satisfaction (Byers, 2005), it follows that communicating openly about the meaning of one's spiritual beliefs or practices can nurture mutual tolerance and respect. Many religious traditions esteem behaviors that promote relationship stability and quality, which is why interfaith couples may benefit from exploring the shared virtues that underlay their diverse religious or spiritual beliefs, such as love, selflessness, commitment, and ethical behavior (Onedera, 2008).

How Religion Influences Relationships

What is it about being religious that results in correlations with positive relational qualities? One hypothesis is that religion promotes many positive marital qualities, such as commitment and investment in family life, while discouraging negative behaviors, such as infidelity and drug use (Wolfinger & Wilcox, 2008). It may be about the promotion of family norms and rituals, gaining supportive social networks through religious groups, or a sense of well-being associated with religious beliefs. A promising potential mechanism for how religion and spirituality may translate into positive relationship outcomes is the meaning that it can give to close relationships and family commitments.

Changing Spirituality in "Emerging Adulthood"

Late adolescence and young adulthood is a time of transitions for individuals. Transitions in personal-family identity (including physical and emotional separation from home and family members), vocational changes (greater participation in the workforce), economic changes (with increasing income or struggles with unemployment), and educational changes (intensity and focus of higher education) are rampant in the landscape of emerging adulthood. Re-examining one's spirituality or religiosity is another significant transition linked to becoming an adult (Smith & Snell, 2009).

Spiritual questing involves "openly facing complex, existential questions (questions of life's meaning, of death, and of relations with others) and resisting clear-cut, pat answers" (Batson & Shoenrade, 1991, p. 430). Spiritual questing can cause questioning because more doors may be left open rather than closed. In a sample of college students who reported a diversity of religious affiliations (or were at least moderately religious,

though unaffiliated), higher levels of spiritual questing were associated with lower spiritual well-being (Genia, 2001); this indicates that spiritual questing is challenging and can leave some stones unturned.

One area that has received attention limited attention in research about couples and spirituality is the impact of a shift in spiritual or religious beliefs on a couple's relationship. Studies of individuals who undergo personal shift from one religious paradigm to another have been characterized as a spiritual conversion (Mahoney & Pargament, 2004) or spiritual transformation (Sandage & Shults, 2007). These shifts may occur across the life course, but are most common during late adolescence or young adulthood and are associated with the developmental process of individuation.

Given the challenges already identified with religious heterogamy, any differences—especially changes—may be problematic in how both partners adapt to these changes.

Meaning Making and Intimate Relationships

People use religion and spirituality to make meaning out of their lives, to understand situations beyond their control, and to shape and interpret their own behaviors. Have you ever relied upon spiritual beliefs to guide your decision-making and behavior? One way people make meaning through religion is called *sanctification*, which is a psychological way of assigning qualities representing God/s or a Deity directly to an object or experience—such as viewing a cross or a wedding ceremony as "holy" or a reflection of divine will. This way of assigning sacred qualities may even apply to nontheistic processes, such as viewing natural events like the lifecycle or the universe as miraculous or mysterious (Mahoney, Pargament, Murray-Swank, & Murray-Swank, 2003; Pargament & Mahoney, 2005). This is done by believing that God or another divine power is being manifested through natural means (e.g., a person's marriage) or believing that something natural is "blessed" or "sacred" (e.g., a pregnancy). Sanctification allows intimate relationships to be experienced as spiritual.

One example of sanctification in the Christian tradition is *Covenant Marriage*. This practice arose from the belief of conservative Christians that marriages are a promise—not only between the couple, but also with God—and should not be easily broken (Baker, Sanchez, Nock, & Wright, 2009). In some states, covenant marriages are a different type of legal union that makes it much more difficult to obtain a legal divorce. In this way, inscribing marriage with spiritual qualities resulted in both policy change and a different kind of public commitment. Another example is the Jewish *Ketubah* or marriage contract which is no longer a legal contract but a documentation of the spiritual significance of the vows the couple make to each other in marriage (Interfaith Family, 2012).

Earlier, we examined how being religious (at least attending religious services regularly) was linked to delaying onset of sexual activity and having less permissive attitudes about sex outside of marriage. While investigating the relationship between spirituality and sex (but not religiosity), researchers have revealed several different outcomes and associated factors (Murray-Swank, Pargament, & Mahoney, 2005). For example, college students who reported viewing sex as a spiritual experience or manifestation of God were more likely to report positive feelings about sexual activity, and also more likely to have had premarital sex (Murray-Swank et al., 2005). This is one example of how religion and spirituality may influence intimate relationships differently. However, similar to the findings on religious involvement, newlyweds who perceived their sexual relationships as spiritual were more likely to report greater feelings of satisfaction, marital intimacy, and spiritual intimacy than those who did not (Hernandez, Mahoney, & Pargament, 2011).

There is even evidence that marital inequality can have different meaning if couples perceived their marriages as "sanctified." DeMaris, Mahoney, and Pargament (2010) found that couples who thought of God being manifest in their marriage or their marriage as sacred were less likely to experience marital dissatisfaction and conflict in the face of marital inequality than those who did not view their marriages as "sanctified."

A growing body of research on the construct of sanctification suggests that experiencing intimate relationships as spiritual or "sacred" has benefits for couples and individuals (Pargament & Mahoney, 2005). One hypothesis is that individuals are willing to invest more in their relationships if they view them as spiritually significant, resulting in healthier and more satisfying unions. However, there are also risks in placing spiritual meaning on relationships. It may present psychological dangers to couples who fall outside of what is viewed as "sacred" or a "manifestation of God"—such as a household where the wife is the spiritual leader or if the marriage dissolves (Mahoney et al., 2003). Krumrei, Mahoney, and Pargament (2009) found that viewing divorce as a sacred loss was linked to higher rates of depression, but spiritual coping mediated the relationship between sacred loss and depression. It is clear that both religion and spirituality can be powerful tools for creating meaning and identity within intimate relationships.

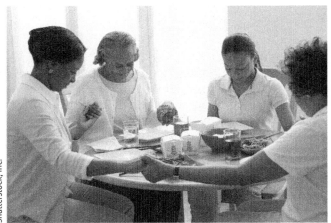

Meaning Making through Rituals

Spirituality and religion in relationships can illustrate what couples or individuals hold sacred. Yet, couples who consider spirituality and religion to be absent from their lives and relationships participate in psychologically and emotionally meaningful experiences. Regardless of the quality of a couple's spiritual connectedness or religiosity, all couples and intimate relationships share one thing in common that communicates their values: the practice of rituals. Rituals are patterned events that connect couples to their pasts and futures through behavior and practice (Wolin & Bennett, 1984). Symbolically and experientially, they communicate investment in the couple or family relationship because they require effort to develop and maintain.

Religiously involved couples who participate in religious family rituals together (e.g., family scripture reading, praying together, welcoming in of the Shabbat in Jewish families) also report family satisfaction, closeness, and spousal spiritual connection (Lee, Rice, & Gillespie, 1997; Marks, 2004). Mahoney et al. (2001) suggest that joint participation in religious activities contribute to couple intimacy and commitment. Not all partners experience religious rituals in the same way, however. Fiese and Tomcho (2001) examined married couples and found differences in how rituals contributed to spouses' marital satisfaction when celebrating one another's religious holidays. Husbands' marital satisfaction was associated with the meaning of the ritual whereas wives' marital satisfaction was associated with the roles and routines of the rituals and with how much meaning husbands assigned to the rituals.

Prayer is a spiritual activity that many couples practice as a relationship ritual. The ritual of praying during times of conflict has been found to de-escalate emotionality, serve as a coping mechanism, and give each partner time to self-soothe (Gardner, Butler, & Seedall, 2008). In a qualitative study, Butler, Stout, and Gardener (2002) found evidence for positive effects of prayer, including: diffused hostility, decreased reactivity or "softening," greater understanding or their partner's perspective, movement toward examining the self-change that they could focus on apart from their partner. These qualitative findings suggested that prayer created meaningful perceptions of being emotionally supported by

God/s or a Deity during couple conflicts and through mindfulness and accountability. The spiritual practice of prayer has received growing attention from family researchers.

Conversely, prayer also has the potential to harm couples if it is used in ways that promote conflict avoidance or maintain attitudes of blame. Gardner et al. (2008) sampled religious couples and found evidence of three avenues wherein respondents sometimes used prayer as part of a negative coping process, including: aligning with God or a Deity against one's spouse, commiserating with a Deity (but avoiding relationship conflict) or avoiding ownership of one's role in conflict through deferring responsibility for resolution of the conflict to a Deity. Therefore, just like how religiosity and spirituality vary among couples and individuals, so do the effects of their religious involvement. It is up to us as individuals and couples to use these behaviors and beliefs to protect, rather than harm, our relationships.

WHAT WE DON'T KNOW

It is important to consider that much research on the influence of religion on couples and families focuses on Christians, and especially Protestants. This certainly influences the ways that being highly religious impact family life. For example, if a person were "highly religious" in a congregation that emphasized marital equality and embraced social justice ideals in their theology, couples' frequent church attendance would surely impact them in different ways than demonstrated in the research we examined. More research is needed on highly religious people in diverse religions in the United States.

There is also a lack of research on how spirituality in the absence of religion can influence couple and family relationships. You may recall that defining "religiosity" defined by attendance to religious services, was a better predictor of marital satisfaction and likelihood of divorce than other ways of measuring (like how "important" religion is to the person, if they are affiliated with a religious group, frequency of prayer, etc.). This does not shed any light on how spirituality may influence intimate relationships and marriage. The idea of "sanctification" or viewing and experiencing couple relationships and structures as "sacred" or opportunities for Divine expression has strong potential to help us understand how spiritual meaning can strengthen these bonds and influence relationships and outcomes.

It is also important to consider the implications of the research findings we have. Some outcomes may act as a double-edged sword and warrant careful consideration by individuals, couples, clergy, and family professionals. First, being highly religious may strengthen marital commitments and protect against infidelity and divorce, but might they keep people in miserable or even dangerous marital relationships? Structures that may be very supportive and helpful of some people and families may be very oppressive to those who do not fit the group expectations (e.g., divorce). If wedlock is "sacred," it may be particularly distressing for couples when their marriages fail. Additionally, if a couple is highly involved in a religious group that values traditional family roles, it may provide assistance and support for those families who are structured traditionally, but be stigmatizing for families with nontraditional divisions of roles. For example, gay and lesbian people and other sexual minorities may struggle within religious theologies that are unaccepting or render them invisible. We need to better examine, interpret, and theorize on existing and future research to fully address these complexities.

CONCLUSION

Religion and spiritual beliefs continue to be reported as important to the vast majority of Americans with a shift in younger generations toward identifying as spiritual but not religious (Pew Research, 2012). There are conflicting and/or weak findings about how identifying with a religious affiliation or claiming that religion is "important" impacts couple relationships. Active participation in religion—especially joint participation of the couple in religious services—predicts later age of first sex, fewer sexual partners, decreased chance of infidelity, and less likelihood to divorce. Being less religious also predicts increased likelihood of cohabiting and decreased likelihood of marrying. There is some debate on how to interpret these findings with regard to how they impact couples.

Remaining in an unsatisfying relationship may be interpreted as a sign of a strong commitment and/or relationship and be perceived as positive, especially if the relationship quality improves over time. Others may argue that staying in an unsatisfying relationship, especially over the long term or if they involve abuse, is a risk, rather than strength for highly religious couples.

Religiousness alone does not strongly relate to marital quality, but perceiving a relationship as meaningful and significant has been shown to result in higher couple satisfaction. Many couples use their religion and/or spirituality to make meaning of their relationships, although secular beliefs can also create such meanings. There is a lack of research on how gender roles are impacted by non-Christian religiousness, but being conservative Christian does appear to support more traditional gender roles with regard to housework and earnings for married couples. Sharing religious beliefs is a potential strength for couples, while being very different in terms of how religious partners are or what religion each partner ascribes to is associated with relationship challenges. It is important to keep this in perspective as being religiously different is just one potential stressor in a constellation of strengths and stressors within a couple relationship. How a couple handles these differences is key to their success in resolving conflicts.

There is a strong body of evidence that the impact of religion and spirituality on couples often works through the significance and meaning the couples place on their relationship and family. This can be a benefit as couples may invest more when they view their relationships as spiritually meaningful. It can also be harmful when relationships do not fit the "meaning" ascribed to them by an individual's religion (e.g., getting divorced when marriage is viewed as a sacred union). Creating spiritual or secular meanings within the relationship can be adaptive if the potential meanings are flexible enough to fit the individual and couple. A community supportive of the couple relationship may also be a strength for religious couples, whereas the risk of stigma or ostracizing may create distress. More research is needed to better understand the nuances of how religion and spirituality impact couples, to better understand the impact of the shift to more spiritual and less religious and to investigate diverse forms of religion and spirituality within the United States.

REFERENCES

Ammerman, N. T. (2013). Spiritual but not religious? Beyond binary choices in the study of religion. *Journal for the Scientific Study of Religion, 52,* 258–278. doi:10.1111/jssr.12024

Association of Religion Data Archives. (2013). General Social Survey 2010 Cross Section and Panel Combined. Retrieved from http://www.thearda.com/Archive/Files/Analysis/GSS10PAN/GSS10PAN_Var12_1.asp.

Atkins, D. C., Baucom, D. H., & Jacobson, N. S. (2001). Understanding infidelity: Correlates in a national random sample. *Journal of Family Psychology, 15,* 735–749. doi:10.1037/0893-3200.15.4.735

Atkins, D. C., & Kessel, D. (2008). Religiousness and infidelity: Attendance, but not faith and prayer, predict marital fidelity. *Journal of Marriage and Family, 70,* 407–418. doi:10.1111/j.1741-3737.2008.00490.x

Baker, E. H., Sanchez, L. A., Nock, S. L., and Wright, J. D. (2009). Covenant Marriage and the sanctification of gendered marital roles. *Journal of Family Issues, 30*(2), 147–178. doi:10.1177/0192513X08324109

Batson, D. C., & Schoenrade, P. A. (1991). Measuring religion as quest. *Journal for the Scientific Study of Religion, 30*(4), 430–447. doi:10.2307/1387278

Bloom, P. (2007). Religion is natural. *Developmental Science, 10*(1), 147–151. doi:10.1111/j.1467-7687.2007.00577.x

Burdette, A. M., Ellison, C. G., Sherkat, D. E., & Gore, K. A. (2007). Are there religious variations in marital infidelity? *Journal of Family Issues, 28,* 1553–1581. doi:10.1177/0192513X07304269

Butler, M. H., Stout, J. A., & Gardner, B. C. (2002). Prayer as conflict resolution ritual: Clinical implications of religious couples' report of relationship softening, healing, perspective, and change responsibility. *American Journal of Family Therapy, 30*(19), 19–37. doi:http://dx.doi.org/10.1080/019261802753455624

Byers, E. S. (2005). Relationship satisfaction and sexual satisfaction: A longitudinal study of individuals in long-term relationships. *Journal of Sex Research, 42*(2), 113–118. *doi:10.1080/00224490509552264*

Coontz, S. (2005). *Marriage, a history: From obedience to intimacy, or how love conquered marriage.* New York: Viking.

Curtis, K. T., & Ellison, C. G. (2002). Religious heterogamy and martial conflict: Findings from the national survey of families and households. *Journal of Family Issues, 23,* 551–576. doi:10.1177/0192513X02023004005

DeMaris, A., Mahoney, A., & Pargament, K. I. (2010). Sanctification of marriage and general religiousness as buffers of the effects of marital inequity. *Journal of Family Issues, 31*(10), 1255–1278. doi:10.1177/019253X10363888178

Denton, M. L. (2004). Gender and marital decision making: Negotiating religious ideology and practice. *Social Forces, 82,* 1151–1180. doi:10.1353/sof.2004.0034

Dualism (2011, Nov. 3). In *Stanford Encyclopedia of Philosophy.* Retrieved from http://plato.stanford.edu/entries/dualism/

Dudley, M. G., & Kosinski, F. A. Jr. (1990). Religiosity and marital satisfaction: A research note. *Review of Religious Research, 32,* 78–86. doi:10.2307/3511329

Ellison, C. G., & Bartkowski, J. P. (2002). Conservative Protestantism and the division of household labor among married couples. *Journal of Family Issues, 23,* 950–985. doi:10.1177/019251302237299

Ellison, C. G., Henderson, A. K., Glenn, N. D., & Harkrider, K. E. (2011). Sanctification, stress, and marital quality. *Family Relations, 60*(4), 404–420. doi:10.1111/j.1741-3729.2011.00658.x

Fiese, B. H., & Tomcho, T. J. (2001). Finding meaning in religious practices: The relation between religious holiday rituals and marital satisfaction. *Journal of Family Psychology, 15*(4), 597. doi:10.1037/0893-3200.15.4.597

Fiese, B. H., Tomcho, T. J., Douglas, M., Josephs, K., Poltrock, S., & Baker, T. (2002). A review of 50 years of research on naturally occurring family routines and rituals: Cause for celebration? *Journal of Family Psychology, 16,* 379–380. doi:10.1037/0893-3200.16.4.381

Fincham, F. D., & Beach, S. R. H. (2010). Marriage in the new millennium: A decade in review. *Journal of Marriage and Family, 72,* 630–649. doi:10.1111/j.1741-3737.2010.0072.x

Fincham, F. D., Lambert, N. M., & Beach, S. R. H. (2010). Faith and unfaithfulness: Can praying for your partner reduce infidelity? *Journal of Personality and Social Psychology, 99,* 649–659. doi:10.1037/a0019628

Furlong, M., & Ata, A. W. (2006). Observing different faiths, learning about ourselves: Practice with intermarried Muslims and Christians. *Australian Social Work, 59*(3), 250–264. doi:10.1080/03124070600833048

Gall, T. L., Malette, J., & Guirguis-Younger, M. (2011). Spirituality and religiousness: A diversity of definitions. *Journal of Spirituality and Mental Health, 13,* 158–181. doi:10.1080/19349637.2011.593404

Gardner, B. C., & Butler, M. H., & Seedall, R. B. (2008). En-gendering the couple-deity relationship: Clinical implications of power and process. *Contemporary Family Therapy, 30,* 152–166. doi:10.1007/s10591-008-9063-5

Genia, V. (2001). Evaluation of the Spiritual Well-Being Scale in a sample of college students. *International Journal for the Psychology of Religion, 11*(1), 25–33. doi:10.1207/S15327582IJPR1101_03

Goodman, M. A., & Dollahite, D. C. (2006). How religious couples perceive the influence of God in their marriage. *Review of Religious Research, 48,* 141–155. Retrieved from http://www.jstor.org/stable/20058129?seq=1#page_scan_tab_contents

Helm, H. W., McBride, D. C., Knox, D., & Zusman, M. (2009). The influence of conservative religion on premarital sexual behavior of university students. *North American Journal of Psychology, 11*(2), 231–245. doi:10/1207/S15327582IJPR1101_03

Hernandez, K. M., Mahoney, A., & Pargament, K. I. (2011). Sanctification of sexuality: Implications for newlyweds' marital and sexual quality. *Journal of Family Psychology, 25*(5), 775–780. doi:10.1037/a0025103

Interfaith Family (2012). The Jewish marriage contract (Ketubah). Retrieved from http://www.interfaithfamily.com/life_cycle/weddings/The_Jewish_Marriage_Contract_(Ketubah).shtml

Kaslow, R., & Robinson, J. (1996). Long-term satisfying marriages: Perceptions of contributing factors. *American Journal of Family Therapy, 24,* 69–78. doi:10.1080/10926189608251028

Krumrei, E. J., Mahoney, A., & Pargament, K. I. (2009). Divorce and the divine: The role of spirituality in adjustment to divorce. *Journal of Marriage and Family, 71,* 373–383. doi:10.1111/j.1741-3737.2009.00605.x

Lee, J. W., Rice, G. T., & Gillespie, V. B. (1997). Family worship patterns and their correlations with adolescent behavior and beliefs. *Journal for the Scientific Study of Religion, 21,* 48–58. doi:10.2307/1387855

Lefkowitz, E. S., Gillen, M. M., Shearer, C. L., & Boone, T. L. (2004). Religiosity, sexual behaviors, and sexual attitudes during emerging adulthood. *Journal of Sex Research, 41*(2), 150–159. doi:10.1080/00224490409552223

Mahoney, A. (2010). Religion in families, 1999–2009: A relational spirituality framework. *Journal of Marriage and Family, 72*(4), 805–827. doi:10.1111/j.1741-3737.2010.00732.x

Mahoney, A., Pargament, K. K., Jewell, T., Swank, A. B., Scott, E., Emery, E., & Rye, M. (1999). Marriage and the spiritual realm: The role of proximal and distal religious constructs in marital functioning. *Journal of Family Psychology, 13,* 321–338. doi:10.1037/0893-3200.13.3.321

Mahoney, A., Pargament, K. I., Murray-Swank, A., & Murray-Swank, N. (2003). Religion and the sanctification of family relationships. *Review of Religious Research, 44*(3), 220–236. doi:10.2307/3512384

Mahoney, A., & Pargament, K. I. (2004). Sacred changes: Spiritual conversion and transformation. *Journal of Clinical Psychology, 60*(5), 481–492. doi:10.1002/jclp.20007

Mahoney, A., Pargament, K. I., & DeMaris, A. (2009). Couples viewing marriage and pregnancy through the lens of the Sacred: A descriptive study. *Research in the Social Scientific Study of Religion, 20,* 1–45. doi:10.1163/ej.9789004175624.i-334.7

Mahoney, A. (2010). Religion in families, 1999-2009: A relational spirituality framework. *Journal of Marriage and Family, 72*(4), 805–827. doi:10.1111/j.1741-3737.2010.00732.x

Marks, L. (2004). Sacred practices in highly religious families: Christian, Jewish, Mormon, and Muslim perspectives. *Family Process, 43*(2), 217–231. doi:10.1111/j.1545-5300.2004.04302007.x

Myers, S. M. (2006). Religious homogamy and marital quality: Historical and generational patterns, 1980-1997. *Journal of Marriage and Family, 68*, 292–304. doi:10.1111/j.1741-3737.2006.00253.x

McMillen, E. K., Helm, H. W., & McBride, D. C. (2011). Religious orientation and sexual attitudes and behaviors. *Journal of Research on Christian Education, 20*, 195–206. doi:10.1080/10656219.2011.590755

Murray-Swank, N. A., Pargament, K. I., & Mahoney, A. (2005). At the crossroads of sexuality and spirituality: The sanctification of sex by college students. *International Journal for the Psychology of Religion, 15*(3), 199–219. doi:10.1207/s15327582ijpr1503_2

Onedera, J. D. (Ed.). (2008). *The role of religion in marriage and family counseling.* New York: Routledge.

Pargament, K. I., & Mahoney, A. (2005). Sacred matters: Sanctification as a vital topic for the psychology of religion. *Journal for the Psychology of Religion, 15*, 179–198. doi:10.1207/s15327582ijpr1503_1

Pew Research Center. (2012, Oct. 9). "Nones" on the rise: One-in-Five adults have no religious affiliation. Retrieved from: http://www.pewforum.org/files/2012/10/NonesOnTheRise-full.pdf

Pew Research Center. (2010, Feb.). *Religion among the Millennials: Less religiously active than older Americans, but fairly traditional in other ways.* Retrieved from http://www.pewforum.org/files/2010/02/millennials-report.pdf

Sandage, S. J., & Shults, F. L. (2007). Relational spirituality and transformation: A relational integration model. *Journal of Psychology & Christianity, 26*(3), 261-269. Retrieved from http://eds.a.ebscohost.com.ezp3.lib.umn.edu/abstract?site=eds&scope=site&jrnl=07334273&AN=27213781&h=uGO%2bcRtuZzEVCn84kES5Zf06lEm3S%2bNQa%2bkcJm2i%2beDzmRRPgfC3hACEfukcoWPageghdj4IuA9BTuvrIRP%2bTw%3d%3d&crl=f&resultLocal=ErrCrlNoResults&resultNs=Ehost&crlhashurl=login.aspx%3fdirect%3dtrue%26profile%3dehost%26scope%3dsite%26authtype%3dcrawler%26jrnl%3d07334273%26AN%3d27213781

Sanders, G. (2003) Systemic rituals in sexual therapy. In E. Imber-Black, J. Roberts, & R. Whiting (Eds.). *Rituals in families and family therapy,* (pp. 280–299) (2nd ed.). New York: Norton.

Smith, C., & Snell, P. (2009). *Souls in Transition: The Religious & Spiritual Lives of Emerging Adults* New York, New York: Oxford University Press.

Stanley, S. M., & Markman, H. J. (1992). Assessing commitment in personal relationships. *Journal of Marriage and the Family, 54*, 595–608. doi:10.2307/353245

Trenholm, P., Trent, J., & Compton, W. C. (1998). Negative religious conflict as a predictor of panic disorder. *Journal of Clinical Psychology, 54*, 59–65. doi:10.1002/(SICI)1097-4679(199801)54:1<59::AID-JCLP7>3.0.CO;2-P

Vaaler, M. L., Ellison, C. G., & Powers, D. A. (2009). Religious influences on the risk of marital dissolution. *Journal of Marriage and Family, 71*(4), 917–934. doi:10.1111/j.1741-3737.2009.00644.x

Wilcox, W. B. (2004). *Soft patriarchs, new men: How Christianity shapes fathers and husbands.* Chicago, IL: University of Chicago Press.

Wolfinger, N. H., & Wilcox, W. B. (2008). Happily ever after? Religion, marital status, gender, and relationship quality in urban families. *Social Forces, 86*, 1311–1337. doi:http://dx.doi.org/10.1353/sof.0.0023

Wolin, S. J., & Bennett, L. A. (1984). Family rituals. *Family Process, 23*, 401–420. doi:10.1111=j.1545-5300.1984.00401.x

Woods, L. N., & Emery, R. E. (2002). The cohabitation effects on divorce: Causation or selection? *Journal of Divorce and Remarriage, 37*, 101–119. doi:10.1300/J087v37n03_06

14

The Role of Ritual in Relationships

Elizabeth J. Plowman, Ph.D.
Department of Family Social Science
University of Minnesota

Gregg T. Schacher, Ph.D., LMFT
The Relationship Therapy Center

LEARNING OBJECTIVES

- Understand key roles that rituals play in intimacy for couples and families
- Articulate principal categories of rituals, based on their level of organization and degree of affective meaning
- Understand the ways that rituals may promote healing in relationships
- Understand the ways that rituals may promote stress in relationships

VIGNETTE 1: SAY "CHEESE"

Sam can easily recall the first time he knew it was no longer a fling and that he had serious feelings for Patrick. It was his family's annual Thanksgiving dinner; he and Patrick had been seeing each other for almost a year. All of his family members had accepted Patrick right away because he was so kind and genuinely interested in their lives. Patrick did everything right; he brought a homemade pie for Sam's mom, he asked Sam's sister about her new boyfriend at college, and he even made it through an entire football viewing session with Sam's dad. Patrick made it easy for Sam's family to welcome him. Sam also appreciated how open his family was being with Patrick, inviting him to play turkey bingo to see who would get to break the wishbone. But after the turkey was carved and the Thanksgiving blessing was said, it came time to take the annual family photo. Everyone stood by the fireplace, ready to say "cheese" and Sam noticed Patrick was standing behind the lens, instead of in front of it. *"Patrick, come join us,"* he said, waving him over, *"there's a spot right here."* Patrick shook his head, blushing. Sam's dad declared, "Maybe next year, Sam. These photos are for family only." Sam looked to his mom, who nodded and smiled. Sam stared blankly, the moment happening so quickly that he just agreed to go with it. But it was then, he knew: he considered Patrick part of his family. Why didn't his own family feel the same way?

VIGNETTE 2: CHRISTMAKKUH COMES TOO SOON

Audrey had just started dating Derek at the beginning of fall semester. At winter break, Derek invited her to fly home to celebrate Hanukkah with his family.

"It will be perfect," Derek said, "you can meet my family and see all of our fun traditions. After a few nights, we can head to see your family so you don't have to miss any time with them and I can meet your parents."

Audrey was shocked. She was falling in love with Derek—his cute dimples, sense of humor, and motivation in school—but she did not realize they were at the point of celebrating holidays together. She wanted to move in with him in spring semester, but holidays? It seemed a little intense. Christmas was her favorite time of year with her family. Time just seemed to stand still when they played games together, wore pajamas all day, and decorated the tree. She started thinking . . . *Would I bring him to church service? How would we exchange gifts with my family? Would he get a stocking? I mean, it definitely would not have his name sewn on it. Where would he sleep? What would my mom say? How would we make our annual meal? He was a vegetarian. I don't want him to think I'm not into him. . .* to say the least, she was caught a bit off guard. *"Derek, are you sure? I mean, I want you to meet my family, but Christmas with my family is pretty serious. I don't even know if my parents would be okay with it. It's always just the five of us, my parents and sisters."*

Corresponding Author: Elizabeth J. Plowman, Ph.D., University of Minnesota; Department of Family Social Science; 1985 Buford Ave.; 290 McNeal Hall; Saint Paul, MN 55108. E-mail: eplowman@umn.edu.

Derek leaned back in his chair, silent for a minute. *"Well, it was just an idea,"* he said. *"At my house, anything goes. It's not a big deal for guests to join in the festivities, and it's not a problem if I leave early. It doesn't mean it is any less special. In fact, that's why I love it so much. Maybe our families just feel differently about the holidays."*

Audrey felt relieved, and also mystified that they could feel so similarly about some things and different about others. She appreciated Derek's attempt to understand her. She leaned over, grabbing his hand. *"Maybe they do. Thanks so much for understanding, sweetie."*

VIGNETTE 3: TWO WEDDINGS AND A BREAK UP

Gary got back from his best friend's bachelor party, excited to call Amber and tell her how it went: *"It was unbelievable. We went to the casino, and then John's dad surprised all of us by having a limo pick us up and bring us to a club where he had reserved a VIP table! It was free food and drinks all night!"*

Amber shifted uncomfortably, trying not to let her assumptions about bachelor parties get in the way of being supportive to her boyfriend. *"That's great, honey. Is John excited about the wedding?"*

Gary grinned, *"Well, of course. Except here's the thing. They had to change the date. I guess John's grandpa is not doing very well, so they are getting married earlier so he can definitely be at the wedding. It's going to be June 6th now."*

Amber froze. *"June 6th?"* she asked. *"You've got to be kidding me. That's my sister's wedding day!"*

Gary responded, *"I know. It's not the best situation, but there is nothing we can do about it. Maybe I can fly out the day after."*

Amber felt sick to her stomach. *"You mean you're going to go to his wedding when my sister's was already planned?"* she asked. *"We've already booked our tickets to Mexico!"*

"Amber, what do you expect me to do? I'm his best man!" Gary braced himself for her reaction.

Amber felt like she couldn't breathe. *"I don't know, Gary, but if you don't show up to my sister's wedding, it's like broadcasting to my family that you are not committed to our relationship. And after missing my birthday to go to a dumb football game, it's telling me the same thing."*

"Amber, don't you think you're overreacting a little? You're the maid of honor. You won't see me most of the day, anyhow."

Amber felt a million questions run through her mind. How could he do this to her after missing her twenty-first birthday party? Was he right—was she overreacting? Or was he just not that into her and now it was finally becoming clear? *"You know how important this was to me, Gary. I told you from the beginning it was important, and you promised. This is just like last time. I think its time we call this what it is and just go our separate ways."*

Gary sat, stunned. How could Amber expect him to miss his best friend's wedding? They had known each other for almost 18 years, much longer than the two years he and Amber had been together. *"You know what, Amber?"* Gary said, getting angry, *"I never would have thought you would be so immature about something I can't control. If you're going to act like this about one stupid day, you're not the person I thought you were."*

Amber stiffened, *"One stupid day, Gary? One stupid day? If it's such a stupid day, why can't you miss it? Just forget it anyway. I never expected you to actually come."* She hung up the call, tears already falling down her face.

Gary sat, dumbfounded. What had just happened?

THE ROLE OF RITUAL IN RELATIONSHIPS

Every couple and every family—no matter what religion, culture, or socioeconomic status they come from—celebrates rituals. Rituals instantly communicate a family's values and identity to the outside world; for example, Sam's family Thanksgiving was open to others, but certain parts were reserved only for family. In Audrey's family, Christmas was together time for her parents and siblings; it was the only time of year that was just for the five of them. Derek's family, valuing flexibility and openness, welcomed any and all to celebrate Hanukkah with them. In each case, it was clear who was part of the family and who was not; and more importantly, it was clear that these rituals were magical and special for all of the individuals in these vignettes.

As patterned, recurring events that hold special meaning to individuals within a system, rituals connect couples to their pasts and futures through behavior and practice (Wolin & Bennett, 1984). Symbolically and experientially, they communicate investment in the couple or family relationship because they require effort to develop and maintain. In this chapter, we will define three types of family rituals so you can recognize them in your own relationships. Then, we will explore how and why rituals are so valuable for promoting intimacy. Toward the end of the chapter, we will consider how couples and helping professionals can use or adapt rituals to help couples navigate difficult periods in their relationships.

WHAT WE KNOW ABOUT FAMILY AND COUPLE RITUALS

Family rituals are pivotal for establishing a couple's identity and tell the world this is who we "are," and this is what we "do" (Fiese et al., 2002). As practitioners and observers, learning about couple and family rituals provides important insights into relationship functioning and satisfaction. When couples describe their rituals to clinicians, clinicians learn about family roles, flexibility and adaptability of the couple, and more. Here, we define *rituals* as patterned events or activities that hold special meaning to individuals (Wolin & Bennett, 1984). Whereas routines are patterned activities that generally occur in the same sequence or manner, rituals are patterned activities that are more meaningful and important for defining family or couple identities (Fiese et al., 2002).

Wolin and Bennett's (1984) conceptualizations defining family celebrations, family traditions, and patterned family interactions were the first to distinguish ritual from routine. Fiese et al. (2002) elaborated on the definitions by expanding the concepts on polarities of communication, commitment, and continuity. According to this idea, routines are instrumental (i.e., they are useful), happen frequently, and can be witnessed by outsiders to the family. Although similar, rituals are different in that they are symbolic; they define group identity, require commitment, and are understood most fully by family members or insiders (Dickstein, 2002; Fiese et al., 2002; Friedman & Weissbrod, 2004). For example, in Sam's family, Sam's parents just knew who was considered "in" or "out" in the family photo.

Rituals are important to individuals on emotional or psychological levels. Also, they transmit family rules, norms, and roles. For example, when Grandpa cuts the turkey at Thanksgiving, it is likely communicating more than who is cutting the turkey. It could be a demonstration of who is leading the family, or perhaps the role(s) of gender in that family system.

Although routines can be empty of meaning and significance, rituals are meaningful and special. Routines can turn into rituals. For example, John and his partner may have an exercise routine and meet after work every Friday to go on a long distance run. They might run on the same path and in the same direction, and perhaps even listen to the same playlist on their mp3 players. This routine becomes a ritual when it becomes meaningful and symbolic. Perhaps tying up their shoes and stretching out together before a run is associated with an emotionally freeing experience of leaving behind work for the day and closing the couple relationship to the pressures of work for the weekend. Hearing that same special song as they find their pace becomes a signal for "together time." For John, inviting his partner to set the pace of the run might represent John's willingness to share decision-making in the relationship. Routines become rituals when activities become psychologically and symbolically meaningful for individuals, couples, and families. They tell us who is a member of our family or identify our partners. Inclusion or invitation in ritual indicates family or couple membership (Oswald, 2002). In addition, family rituals often strengthen family relationships and provide a sense of continuity across generations (Fiese et al., 2002).

Family rituals are divided into three categories based on their level of organization and degree of affective meaning: patterned family interactions, family traditions, and family celebrations (Wolin & Bennett, 1984). *Patterned family interactions*, such as greeting rituals or date night activities, tend to occur with the most frequency but are the least deliberately organized and most diverse across families and couples. They are the most idiosyncratic of the family rituals (which means they are the most unique across couples) and emerge either intentionally or spontaneously. Early in relationships, couples tend to begin forming patterned interactions that subtly communicate what is important to them and their relationship. For example, couples may have weekly Sunday evening movie marathons, greet each other with the same special kiss and squeeze upon seeing each other or stop for a breakfast at their favorite café after their weekly attendance at a religious service. Creating these

Couples establish or adopt rituals that maintain or shape individual roles in the relationship. It is no coincidence that Jenny and Frank consciously take turns planning and paying for date night every Friday, whereas Alison and Doug's date night always consists of Doug picking up Alison at half past seven to bring her to the latest trendy restaurant that she picked out.

patterned interactions solidifies the sense of belonging in the relationship and the status as part of a couple. Individuals may have their own rituals as well, such as starting every day with a signature cup of coffee from a special cup or ending every day with a gratitude meditation.

Family traditions are more structured and meaningful than patterned interactions. They require moderate organization and are highly valued by family members and partners because of their increased meaningfulness. Family traditions include birthdays, anniversary customs, and family vacations. Couples establish or implement traditions in their relationship based on timing, level of commitment, families of origin, and individual preferences. Family traditions tend to be idiosyncratic, varying from family to family or couple to couple based on the unique family's values, beliefs, and interests. Based on their attitudes and experiences in their families of origin, individual partners will choose to bring their own family traditions to an intimate relationship, adapt the traditions to fit both partners' lifestyles and values or abandon traditions from the past and start afresh. Consider the following:

- How important was it in your family to eat dinner together?
- How important were birthday celebrations and what were the key ingredients of a birthday that made someone feel loved or special?
- What was the pattern of conflicts in your family and how did most conflicts resolve? Was there a ritual in how the resolution was communicated (e.g., apology, changing topics, shifting to a positive focus)?
- What roles did family members play for holiday celebrations or social events?
- What were the recurring inside jokes or humorous mannerisms that could be counted on to create a laugh?
- How were work and play activities balanced and what was negotiable to changing this pattern?
- Did family rituals change over time and, if so, who contributed to making these changes (directly or indirectly)?

The most highly organized family rituals are *family celebrations,* including religious and secular holidays and rites of passage celebrations. Holidays and celebrations are observed across cultures, social classes, religions, and income levels. These rituals typically elicit the most expectations from individuals about roles and behavior. Although family celebrations require the most effort and planning when compared to other family rituals, they also hold the most symbolic meaning and emotional significance for family members. Additionally, they are more likely to be subject to social norms and references than traditions and patterned interactions. They often mark a rite of passage in the life cycle, such as weddings or baptisms.

Rituals and Intimacy

Knowing that rituals shape a couple's identity and require togetherness, it is no surprise that rituals promote a couple's shared intimacy. Inherently, family rituals promote belonging and companionship, and fulfill multiple roles, such as:

- Boundary markers: Rituals are often a first signal that a couple is becoming a "we"
- Foundations of couple identities: Rituals say "This is who we are" and "This is what we do"
- Relationship indexes: When rituals change, it tells us something in the relationship is changing
- Meaning makers: Rituals give us a feeling of being part of something larger than ourselves
- Mirrors: Our feelings about rituals are reflections of how we feel about our partner and relationship
- Insight givers: Learning about how couples practice rituals sheds light on relationship functioning for practitioners and outsiders
- Protectors: When flexible and meaningful, rituals can offer a layer of protection to the couple relationship

Rituals are not as hard to establish as it may seem. Gottman (2001) gives some suggestions for how to create rituals of connection out of the informal and formal activities of our relationships, including the following types of rituals: waking up; mealtimes; affectionate partings or greetings; bedtime; hosting others in your home; handling finances; taking care of partners when they're sick; vacations; dates;

errands; chores; celebrations; rituals around failure or fatigue; rituals around initiating or refusing sex; apologizing or making repairs after conflicts; and rituals to mark emotional life transitions. For example, Ashley and Heidi, a newly cohabiting couple, may decide to light candles when they entertain to indicate the warmth they want to show to welcome their guests. Although their guests would never know that it had taken time and energy to light the "good" candlesticks meant for company, the night feels a little more special for Ashley and Heidi because of this practice. Or perhaps a recently married couple might schedule a monthly brunch for reviewing and paying their bills together online to bring joy to an otherwise challenging activity.

Rituals are most effective when they serve the growth of each individual in a relationship, helping to preserve value for both the individual and the relationship by sharing the roles and responsibilities across partners and reducing anxiety about what to expect from the other. The longer a couple has been together, the greater the likelihood that they will have adapted their rituals to uniquely reflect their deepening knowledge of each other, which, in turn, signals a deepening of the meaning symbolized in their shared activities (e.g., daily rituals may symbolize their level of relationship commitment). Married and unmarried couples, however, often practice the same types of rituals. For example, an exploratory study (Campbell, Silva, & Wright, 2011) illustrated that unmarried couples also reported the same 12 categories of rituals as married couples, including:

- Leisure activities
- Intimacy expressions
- Communication rituals
- Patterns/habits/mannerisms
- Daily routines and tasks
- Play rituals
- Togetherness rituals
- Couple favorites
- Private codes rituals
- Celebration rituals
- Escape episodes
- Spiritual rituals

In addition to these 12 ritual types, unmarried couples reported four unique categories including gift-giving, family involvement, future planning, and being supportive. *Why do you think the exploratory study uncovered four different types of rituals for unmarried couples?* One explanation could be the method of research: perhaps the researchers actually uncovered themes relevant to both types of couples, but they were not reported in earlier articles. Alternatively, maybe unmarried couples, potentially in earlier stages of their relationships, are still in the "honeymoon" phase and consider rituals like gift-giving and future planning as special, whereas married couples may perceive them as routines. As numbers of long-term unmarried couples continue to increase, more research needs to focus on differences between married and unmarried couples.

RITUALS AS INTIMACY HEALERS. Rituals can also help repair threats to intimacy, but only when couples use them this way. Psychologist and marriage researcher, John Gottman (2001), describes how rituals can promote intimacy by infusing relationships with natural opportunities to help couples maintain their connection in spite of their conflicts. For example, imagine a couple who had a heated argument just prior to going their separate ways in the morning. If they had an informal daily ritual of calling each other midday to "check in" about the events of their day, there would be an opportunity for one or the other partner to initiate what Gottman calls "repair attempts"—brief acknowledgments of the hurt experienced by the other or one's contribution to a conflict (e.g., "I guess I was pretty crabby

earlier," or "Will you let me try my part of the conversation over again?"). These statements shift the focus from conflicts to solutions. It may be that the couple has a ritual about using this time—when needed—to acknowledge their contribution to conflicts and to apologize. For some couples, this might spur the healing in their relationship, but for other couples where partners avoid mention of their conflicts during informal connection rituals, it might delay or prolong their healing process. The protective effect of rituals is not automatic—couples have to work to benefit from it.

Recently, researchers have begun exploring the relationships between individual personality characteristics and family ritual quality. What do we as individuals bring to our relationships that affect how we establish and maintain rituals with our partners and families? Adult attachment styles, for example, are related to individual's reports of ritualization (i.e., flexibility and meaning). Leon and Jacobvitz (2003) investigated the connection between attachment models in partners and family ritual quality, focusing particularly on family ritual quality dimensions of creating routines and meaning. On average, mothers and fathers possessed different attachment types and levels of ritual quality, suggesting that in heterosexual relationships, interactions between gender and attachment influences couple's ritualization (Leon & Jacobvitz, 2003). More specifically, insecure attachment in mothers was positively correlated with higher routinization and less flexibility of family rituals (Leon & Jacobvitz, 2003).

Knowing what we do from Chapter 2 about insecure attachment styles, *why do you think insecure attachment might cause people to be more set in their ways when it comes to rituals*? The high level of routinization may be a reaction to the anxiety associated with their insecure attachment styles. Leon and Jacobvitz (2003) suggest that for couples with insecurely attached individuals, intervention with family rituals should center on increasing emotional expressiveness (both positive and negative) and working to increase comfort with flexibility. When partners have different attachment styles from one another (i.e., mixed attachment couples), they were more likely to report less meaningful and less flexible family rituals. Recent research has shown that for avoidant attachment individuals, greater investment in family rituals can relate to greater relationship satisfaction. For people who have more avoidant attachments, family ritual investment had a protective effect for their feelings toward their marriages (Crespo, Davide, Costa, & Fletcher, 2008). More and more research is being done on how attachment might interact with other factors to influence ritual quality, and how these relationships influence couples' relationship satisfaction.

Rituals and Stress

Although family holidays and celebrations can strengthen familial bonds and togetherness, they also can be a source of tension or conflict (Leach & Braithwaite, 1996). Let's consider Amber and Gary's vignette in the chapter's introduction. For this young couple, finding a way to attend two weddings ultimately caused a rift in (or end to) their relationship. Unfortunately, even though celebrations like weddings are extremely important for individuals and couples, it is simply impossible to be in two places at once. Couples must learn how to negotiate ritual attendance early on in relationships. Finding a compromise that works for both individuals is important so that a couple can minimize stress associated with scheduling or attendance.

Attendance and organization of family rituals does not necessarily become less stressful in longer-term relationship. Coordinating family holidays and celebrations is one of the most frequently occurring unresolved issues in marital relationships affected by intergenerational relationships (Beaton, Norris, & Pratt, 2003). The pressure of not disappointing mom and dad by missing the family's annual New Year's celebration can really add up! Partners often experience difficulty balancing time and commitments between their families of origin and extended families. This is especially true early in a relationship's development because couples have not yet adapted their rituals to their family of procreation. Also, women are more likely than men to feel stressed from family rituals, likely because on average, women expend more time and energy in coordinating and preparing for family gatherings (Beaton et al., 2003). This may be one explanation for men reporting greater satisfaction than women in holiday family rituals (Fiese & Tomcho, 2001).

When we think of family rituals, a Norman Rockwell frame of reference often emerges. Holidays and celebrations are depicted as peaceful, magical, and special family time. It is not surprising that family rituals are perceived in a positive light because this affective value is paired with important stabilizing factors (Fiese et al., 2002). Yet despite the protective qualities and nostalgic connotations paired with family holidays and traditions, legitimate stressors accompany them. The preparation and effort required to organize family gatherings can be time-intensive and even exhaustive for particular family members (Meske, Sanders, Meredith, & Abbott, 1994). Also, traditions and celebrations provide a forum for couples and family members to communicate about family changes, such as changes in family membership (e.g., introducing a new romantic partner) or in values of a family member (e.g., disclosing one's sexual orientation for the first time). Some changes may not be welcome because they disrupt shared family norms and can cause distress for family members (Schuck & Bucy, 1997). Communication about difficult family issues surrounding health problems, family conflict, or financial problems can cause additional stress and conflict during a family holiday, especially when rituals are overly rigid and unaccommodating for the inevitably difficult conversations that ensue.

Families and couples may respond in different ways in attempt to minimize the stress associated with rituals. Some will avoid rituals or abandon them altogether, whereas others will tighten ritualization so no flexibility exists. *Underritualized* families display a low amount of ritual meaning and a large amount of flexibility (e.g., Wolin & Bennett, 1984). Sam and Jaime, an underritualized couple, might hold their Sunday breakfast in bed so infrequently that they eventually begin to lose its value and meaning. What once was sacred became less special because Sam was trying to be so understanding of Jaime's commitment to train for a marathon with long distance runs each Sunday. Eventually both Sam and Jaime wondered why they were even doing breakfast in bed anymore; the once meaningful rituals now felt empty and hollow.

Rigid ritualization couples have the opposite problem: rituals are highly valued and meaningful, but the lack of flexibility threatens their adaptation over time. Even though Anne's family of origin was not religious, she always loved celebrating Christmas with her parents. Looking back on her childhood, a smile would come across her face as she explained her family's holiday. Each year, Anne would open the last frame of her Advent calendar and find a special gift from her father inside. She and her mother would bake cookies and leave them out for Santa. Now that Anne is engaged to Jason, she struggles to understand why her family cannot celebrate Christmas Eve two days later so she could attend church service with his family. Her frustration at the inflexibility afforded by her parents makes the tradition seem less special to her. Rigid ritualization families struggle to adapt their rituals with changing times, likely because family members fear that any amount of change will threaten the sanctity of the ritual. A high degree of flexibility and meaning is optimal for the continuation of rituals—and the well-being of individual family members—within and across generations (Fiese et al., 2002).

Rituals as Opportunities for Intervention

Research demonstrates that rituals are important for examining individual development, family functioning, and family transitions. Family therapy research supports the creation of routine and rituals as significant therapeutic interventions with families and couples (Bennett, Wolin, & McAvity, 1988; Cheal, 1988; Rogers & Holloway, 1991; Selvini-Palazzoli, Boscolo, Cecchin, & Prata, 1977; Whiteside, 1989). Rituals can be used to help couples resolve conflicts, negotiate roles and boundaries, develop shared meanings, and mobilize resources for healing and growth (Bright, 1990). Also, by taking advantage of the unique capacity that rituals offer to examine individual and family identity and functioning, family rituals can provide a refreshing lens for practitioners who are examining intimacy in couple relationships. Due to their pervasiveness across a number of contexts including cultures, socioeconomic statuses, and geographic locations, couple and family rituals offer a broad opportunity for intervention. Family practitioners can use rituals to strengthen families in several ways, such as ritual creation and ritual adaptation.

RITUAL CREATION. When couples or families are underritualized, clinicians can help them build this core aspect of family culture by working with couples to develop meaningful rituals that fit their unique relationship. Importantly, clinicians must be aware that one-of-a-kind solutions are needed. Because rituals are idiosyncratic across families and couples, prescribing the same ritual to two couples will defeat the purpose of rituals in establishing a couple's identity (Imber-Black, 2002). The practitioner needs to work with the couple to cocreate rituals that are meaningful for the couple as a whole, or help couples adapt their rituals based on changing family needs.

One strategy for working with couples is to modify rituals based on quality of ritualization (Leon & Jacobvitz, 2003). Underritualized families, who have highly flexible rituals with relatively low meaningfulness, are more likely to avoid celebrations because they are afraid of conflict and disagreement. Underritualized families benefit from working on developing positive meanings through the use of group rituals. Unlike underritualized families, rigid ritualization families use a rigid structure and enforce rules through rituals to sway attention from family issues. Rigid ritualization families benefit from increasing ritual flexibility and understanding potential negative emotions resulting from spontaneity and freedom (Leon & Jacobvitz). In both cases, emphasis is focused on increasing meaningfulness and flexibility to encourage the development of effective family rituals.

Consider the following:

- Based on the definitions of family ritual types provided, which type is your family-of-origin? Why do you think this to be true? What are the strengths and weaknesses of this family type?
- If you are in a relationship, what is your partner's family type? If you are not in a relationship, imagine your future or past partner.
- Do you and your partner have the same family types? How does your family type influence your expectations of how rituals are practiced or celebrated?
- What impact does your family ritual classification have on your relationship? What can you do to understand your partner's situation better?
- What can you bring to your current or future relationship to benefit from the protective factors associated with meaningful, flexible family rituals?

HEALING RITUALS TO IMPROVE COUPLE AND FAMILY COPING. Cocreating rituals together is one way that therapists routinely intervene with couples, especially when the therapy process calls for facilitating experiences within which heighten couples' sense of meaning in their interactions. One illustration is the case presented by Sanders (2003), who treated a couple in which the female partner presented with vaginismus, a pain disorder during intercourse. It is often sufficient in similar cases to prescribe "sensate focus" or behavioral interventions intended to gradually progress from mildly pleasurable touch (e.g., light caressing or gentle massage) to more intensely arousing interactions with the goal of reducing the sensitivity to physical pain. However, in this case there was an impasse, in spite of the couple's efforts to comply with treatment. Sanders refocused treatment from prescribed and directive approaches to nondirective, systemic ones. Asking questions and making observations about the context and subsystems related to the impasse, such as dynamics of the couple–therapist subsystem and the context of the shared pain, helped to shift therapy's attention to the couple's emotional intimacy. These new and unique relationship rituals promoted greater flexibility and attunement, which had heretofore been a missing prerequisite for the sensate focus interventions.

Therapist Marcia Perlstein (2001) describes prescribing a memory-making ritual to a couple in which the female partner had retreated into a dark depression following her diagnosis of AIDS. The woman gradually engaged in sharing simple but pleasant activities with her partner and then bringing pictures of those events to their therapy sessions in order to explore their purposeful connection

Family Ritual Types

Underritualized families have highly flexible rituals with little or no meaning
Balanced families practice flexible and meaningful rituals
Rigidly ritualized families have inflexible rituals with varying levels of meaning

together in the face of illness. Some time later they decided to get married, a decision that marked an astonishing commitment to create shared memories that lent meaning to their relationship. Two weeks after the wedding the woman died, but left behind a precious legacy. This example illustrates how ritual brought them together while empowering them to tolerate the grief of their eventual separation.

RITUAL ADAPTATION. Diverse family types experience family rituals in different ways. Some couples find holidays and celebrations a natural opportunity to increase familial functioning, and others encounter difficulty in finding or adapting family rituals to accommodate their families' developmental needs. For example, changes in family structure or the disruption in the ritual process may lead to adaptations, such as who participates or how rituals are conducted. For a family experiencing transitions such as marriage, cohabitation, divorce, or the birth or loss of a family member, ritual adaptation may be difficult but it can provide much needed stability and a sense of familial belonging (see text box, below).

When families and couples are able to adapt their rituals to changing life trajectories, their rituals will be more likely to survive the developmental changes in the family over time (Wolin & Bennett, 1984). The role of practitioners may involve helping family members identify the underlying meaning associated with their rituals in order to redefine those rituals in more flexible and accommodating ways while retaining their meaning. Therapists often work with couples preparing for the transition to parenthood to adjust social rituals. For example, therapists may help one partner adapt his or her activities outside the home to creating social activities in the home that, once established, will create a smoother transition to more convenient infant care and may lead to support network as both partners make the significant shift from a "couple identity" to a "family identity."

Ritual disruption may occur when a family encounters structural change, such as divorce or remarriage. Stepfamilies and remarried families have an experience unique from other families for all three types of family rituals (Whiteside, 1989). Daily rituals, traditions, and celebrations provide opportunities for creating or recreating definitions of family identity at the stage of remarriage. Family therapy literature suggests that practitioners encourage and guide families to develop family rituals even if there is initial resistance from individual members (Imber-Black, 2002). The regularity and daily occurrence of patterned family interactions helps to communicate new roles to each family member. Stepfamily struggles can become acute without regularity and constancy; patterned family interactions reinforce role messages on a daily basis, defining a family structure for confused members. Traditions, on the other hand, provide the family with an opportunity to create their "stepfamily rituals" and generate a feeling of closeness (Whiteside). Over time, the stepfamily or remarried family becomes a family of its own with its own idiosyncrasies and identity.

Celebrations may lead to both tension and reward. Family celebrations can be difficult to negotiate among members and in-laws, yet they allow in-laws to establish relationships with all family members, new and old. As families employ strategies to surpass initial awkwardness surrounding these events, they grow closer and develop a sense of familial pride and group identity. Practitioners can support stepfamilies by encouraging clients to blend important past traditions and discover daily interactions that are meaningful for all members.

WHAT WE DON'T KNOW

Although family rituals are a hot topic in family studies literature because of their protective effects for families, we still have much to learn about the intricacies of how rituals develop, and how they develop differently for different types of families. For example, as noted earlier, researchers are still learning about how married and unmarried couples celebrate differently—if they do! The same could be said for understanding the rituals of heterosexual and homosexual couples. Also, how exactly do couples coming from different cultures, religions, and families-of-origin negotiate family rituals? What are successful methods for negotiating stressful aspects of rituals (e.g, attendance, organization) early in a relationship?

The field is also learning about how our environments influence couple and family rituals. For example, how does socioeconomic status influence how family rituals are practiced? We know that across socioeconomic status, all families celebrate rituals (Fiese et al., 2002), but do families with access to financial resources celebrate differently than families who are financially stressed? Or, alternatively, what happens to rituals when couples separate or divorce? Are rituals impacted by divorce similarly across separating couples, or are separating couples with children more likely to maintain rituals? Research has provided insights into how couples might blend family rituals during remarriage (e.g., Whiteside, 1989), but more specific research into exactly how rituals are impacted by a larger variety of family changes could help practitioners advise families on how to use rituals to protect their families in times of transition and stress. Furthermore, much ritual research that does examine how events or environments impact rituals focuses on the family level, rather than focusing explicitly on the couple unit.

CONCLUSION

Let's take a moment and return to the vignettes at the beginning of the chapter. After reading this material, you now may realize that all three vignettes focused on family celebrations, the most meaningful type of family rituals. Sam gained a unique insight into his relationship with Patrick—and his family-of-origin—during a seemingly harmless family photo. Derek and Audrey managed to find a point of understanding in a potentially tense moment when discussing how they might spend their winter breaks. The intensity of Gary and Amber's conflict about two important weddings ultimately drove them apart. The strong symbolic meaning and value of family celebrations makes them "high stakes" topics for most individuals and couples. Even if you disagreed with them at first, it might be just a little easier to put yourself into Sam, Audrey, or Amber's shoes. Because rituals are laden with emotions and meaning, they can help us open up to intimacy—but when disrespected or miscommunicated, they can be barriers to intimacy as well. In your current or future relationship, we hope you openly communicate the value of your family-of-origin rituals with your partner, listen as he/she shares about his/her own, negotiate fairly and maturely, and develop rituals that you both value and cherish. Keep in mind that rituals are your way of telling the world, and each other, this is who we "are," and this is what we "do" (Fiese at al., 2002).

REFERENCES

Beaton, J. M., Norris, J. E., & Pratt, M. W. (2003). Unresolved issues in adult children's marital relationships involving intergenerational problems. *Family Relations, 52,* 143–154. doi:10.1111/j.1741-3729.2003.00143.x

Bennett, L. A., Wolin, S. J., & McAvity, K. J. (1988). Family identity, ritual, and myth: A cultural perspective on life cycle transition. In C. J. Falicov (Ed.), *Family transitions: Continuity and change over the life cycle* (pp. 211–234). New York: Guilford Press.

Bright, M. A. (1990). Therapeutic ritual: Helping families grow. *Journal of Psychosocial Nursing & Mental Health Services, 28,* 24–29. doi:10.3928/0279-3695-19901201-08

Campbell, K., Silva, L. C., & Wright, D. W. (2011). Rituals in unmarried couple relationships: An exploratory study. *Family and Consumer Sciences Research Journal, 40*(1), 45–57. doi:10.1111/j.1552-3934.2011.02087.x

Cheal, D. (1988). The ritualization of family ties. *American Behavioral Scientist, 31,* 632–643. doi:10.1177/0002764288031006003

Crespo, C., Davide, I. N., Costa, M. E., & Fletcher, G. J. (2008). Family rituals in married couples: Links with attachment, relationship quality, and closeness. *Personal Relationships, 15*(2): 191–203. doi:10.1111/j.1475-6811.2008.00193.x

Dickstein, S. (2002). Family routines and rituals: The importance of family functioning. Comment on the special section. *Journal of Family Psychology, 16,* 441–444. doi:10.1037//0893-3200.16.4.441

Fiese, B. H., Tomcho, T. J., Douglas, M., Josephs, K., Poltrock, S., & Baker, T. (2002). A review of 50 years of research on naturally occurring family routines and rituals: Cause for celebration? *Journal of Family Psychology, 16,* 379–380. doi:10.1037/0893-3200.16.4.381

Friedman, S. R., & Weissbrod, C. S. (2004). Gender differences in the continuation of family rituals. *Sex Roles, 50,* 277–284. doi:1-.1-23/B:SERS.0000015558.21334.6b

Gottman, J. M., & DeClaire, J. (2001). *The relationship cure.* New York: Three Rivers Press.

Imber-Black, E. (2002). Family rituals—from research on the consulting room and back again: Comment on the special section. *Journal of Family Psychology, 16,* 445–446. doi:http://dx.doi.org/10.1037/0893-3200.16.4.445

Leach, M. S., & Braithwaite, D. O. (1996). A binding tie: Supportive communication of family kinkeepers. *Journal of Applied Communication Research, 24,* 200–216. doi:10.1080/00909889609365451

Leon, K., & Jacobvitz, D. (2003). Relationships between adult attachment representations and family ritual quality: A prospective, longitudinal study. *Family Process, 42,* 419–435. doi:10.1111/j.1545-5300.2003.00419.x

Meske, S., Sanders, G., Meredith, W., & Abbott, D. (1994). Perceptions of rituals and traditions among elderly persons. *Activities, Adaptation and Aging: The Journal of Activities Management, 18,* 13–26. doi:10.1300/j016v18n02_02

Oswald, R. F. (2002). Inclusion and belonging in the family rituals of gay and lesbian people. *Journal of Family Psychology, 16,* 428–436. doi:10.1037/0893-3200.16.4.428

Rogers, J. C., & Holloway, R. L. (1991). Family rituals and the care of individual patients. *Family Systems Medicine, 9*(3), 249–259. doi:10.1037/h0089223

Sanders, G. (2003) Systemic rituals in sexual therapy. In E. Imber-Black, J. Roberts, & R. Whiting (Eds.). *Rituals in families and family therapy,* (pp. 280–299) (2nd ed.). New York: Norton.

Schuck, L., & Bucy, J. (1997). Family rituals: Implications for early intervention. *Topics in Early Childhood Special Education, 17,* 477–493. doi:10.1177/027112149701700407

Selvini-Palazzoli, M. S., Boscolo, L., Cecchin, G., & Pratta, G. (1977). Family rituals as a powerful tool in family therapy. *Family Process, 16,* 445–453. doi:10.1111/j.1545-5300.1977.00445.x

Whiteside, M. (1989). Family rituals as a key to kinship connections in remarried families. *Family Relations, 38,* 34–39. doi:10.2307/583607

Wolin, S. J., & Bennett, L. A. (1984). Family rituals. *Family Process, 23,* 401–420. doi:10.1111=j.1545-5300.1984.00401.x

15
Sexual Intimacy

Lisa J. Trump, M.S.,
Department of Family Social Science
University of Minnesota

Tai J. Mendenhall, Ph.D., LMFT
Department of Family Social Science
University of Minnesota

Polina Levchenko, Ph.D.
Human Development and Family Studies
Michigan State University

Brian J. Willoughby, Ph.D.
School of Family Life
Brigham Young University

LEARNING OBJECTIVES

- Discuss sexuality along a biopsychosocial/spiritual continuum, and how it differs across culture and gender
- Understand the importance of effective communication about sexuality
- Understand the focus of Sex Therapy and how it addresses a variety of sexual problems
- Gain knowledge about sexual techniques across both individual and couple levels

Case Vignette: In the Same Place, But in Two Different Worlds

After returning home from an exhaustingly busy day at work, Ava walks in her front door and meets her boyfriend, Michael, in the kitchen. The two have been living together for about four months and are still getting used to their new patterns and ways of interacting in their shared space. Michael immediately notices Ava's sour mood, asks about her day, and receives short, blunt answers. "It was alright. I'm fine. No, nothing's wrong." Even as Ava gets settled in, her mind continues to return to the issues that she is dealing with at work. Michael, on the other hand, has had a very relaxed, uneventful day and has been waiting for Ava to get home so they can spend the evening together and reconnect. He had been replaying a collection of their most recent intimate moments in his mind, and had gotten increasingly excited to reenact them. As the evening progresses, Michael continues trying to get Ava to unwind, but gets nowhere. Michael's subtle hints and touches go unnoticed, even as they become more obvious. As Ava unknowingly and unintentionally fails to respond to him, Michael becomes more disappointed and hurt,

© michaeljung, 2014. Used under license from Shutterstock, Inc.

Corresponding Author: Lisa J. Trump, MS, University of Minnesota; Department of Family Social Science; 1985 Buford Ave.; 290 McNeal Hall; Saint Paul, MN 55108. E-mail: buch0245@umn.edu.

and finally begins to withdraw. Michael perceives Ava's actions as indicators of not wanting to be intimate. After losing all hope for the evening he had imagined, Michael stalks off to bed after making a comment under his breath about how he shouldn't be the only one in the relationship who ever wants to be sexual. Ava, taken off guard, did not have a chance to respond before Michael slammed the door, leaving both partners feeling hurt and alone.

SEXUALITY: PHYSIOLOGY OR PSYCHOLOGY?

The majority of sex education to date has focused primarily on physiology, while leaving the emotional, psychological, relational, and spiritual components of sexuality untouched. The first messages delivered to children and young adults are often fear-based, communicating that self-exploration and sexual experiences with others are both bad and forbidden. These direct and/or indirect messages communicate to children and young adults that they are not allowed to be sexually curious or ask their parents or those close to them questions about their bodies and their sexuality, so they turn to other sources like popular media for information about who they are and how they are supposed to act as sexual beings. However, for many, the information they find is inaccurate or incomplete, increasing the chance of participating in risky sexual behaviors later (Hadley et al., 2009; Whitaker & Miller, 2000).

Today, adolescent boys, in particular, are receiving less information about sex from their parents than their peers or the media. Further (and a bit more troublesome), much of the information that parents believe and do share with their children is erroneous (Epstein & Ward, 2008). For example, a recent study about parents' views regarding birth control found that many parents underestimated the effectiveness of condoms for preventing pregnancy and sexually transmitted diseases (Eisenberg, Bearinger, Sieving, Swain, & Resnick, 2004). Parents who hold more conservative ideologies were less likely than liberals to have accurate data; so, how can they provide safe sex information to their children?

Furthermore, many romantic couples struggle with the transition to sexual intimacy within their relationship. When is the right time to become sexual? What are the ramifications of taking things to the "next level"? Cultural and family messages about these questions are often contradictory and confusing. Thus, early messages focused solely on physiology and/or those communicated through scare tactics fail to tap into how we psychologically and emotionally experience sexuality. These messages drastically miss the mark and, in some cases, can leave us vulnerable to being mislead or hurt.

Cultural Implications

Beyond the potential complications met at the family level, culture(s) also presents many challenges for young adults seeking to understand themselves with regard to sexuality. The society of the United States is plagued by a sense of ambivalence and contradiction surrounding sexuality. On one hand, society's common feelings of discomfort with discussions about sex are reflected in the lack of conversation between parents and children and/or between romantic partners (Elliott, 2010; Jerman & Constantine, 2010). On the other hand, there is an intense obsession with sex, as displayed by the media. For example, Cope-Farrar and Kunkel (2002) posited that approximately 62–67% of television programs commonly viewed by adolescents contain sexual content, and Brown and L'Engle (2009) reported that approximately 53% of males and 28% of females reported using the Internet to view sexually explicit material.

Scare Tactics Some Choose to Talk about Sex

If you masturbate, you'll go blind.
Good girls save sex for marriage.
If you have premarital sex, you'll go to hell.
If you don't save your first time for your wedding night, it will be less special.
You are dirty if you watch pornography.

Cultural messages about sexual intimacy and relationships also tend to focus on the importance of "sexual chemistry" and how the lack of such chemistry may be detrimental to relationship success (Busby, Carroll, & Willoughby, 2010). From this perspective, being sexually experienced with multiple partners is portrayed as an asset while being a virgin is portrayed as naive and unsociable. However, our culture is also saturated with messages that high levels of sexual activity, especially for women, can leave one with the label of a "slut" and give people negative perceptions of her personal value. This negative perception of female sexual behavior is often labeled the *sexual double standard* and evidence of its existence continues to be documented among today's young adults (Crawford & Popp, 2003). For individuals who live within a religious culture, larger messages about the importance of sexual chemistry and sexual experience may run counter to devout teachings of abstinence and a focus toward a "higher-level" connection during intimacy. In these traditions, sex may be perceived as extending beyond physical gratification to also include symbolic commitment and spirituality within the relationship.

The experience, then, of learning about sexuality while growing up in the United States is confusing and difficult for many because the majority of what individuals are feeling regarding their sexuality is acknowledged by the media, yet rejected by those around them. Due to the culture of silence around sexuality and the inconsistent messages being received, one's emotions, histories, and experiences—good or bad—are often not addressed and openly talked about (even though they directly influence an individual's experiences of his/her sexual self in relationship with others). Using the metaphor of a personal light switch, after being accepted as a child and adolescent only when our switch is fully off (i.e., refraining from all sexual activity), it is very difficult to flip our switch to fully on (i.e., engaging in sexual activity), even when it becomes socially acceptable to do so. The process is much more comfortable with the use of a dimmer switch that allows for a slow transition. We become, in a sense, victims to our guilt and shame when our personal decisions regarding our sexuality do not align with what has been deemed acceptable by society's standards. In the context of relationships that we want to be beautiful, we have a difficult time feeling like beautiful sexual beings.

WHAT DOES THE RESEARCH SAY? In addition to the ambiguity within the U.S. culture, messages and attitudes regarding sexuality differ significantly across gender and cultures. Several studies have found that men tend to have more permissive sexual attitudes whereas women tend to be more conservative (Alexander & Fisher, 2003; Fugére, Escoto, Cousins, Riggs, and Haerich, 2008). For example, men tend to desire more sexual partners and are more likely to agree to casual sex without commitment than women (Fugére et al., 2008). Although some literature suggests a developing trend in that women's sexual attitudes are becoming increasingly more permissive, research suggests that sexual attitudes are not yet equivalent across gender.

In consideration of cultural differences, the literature to date has revealed that African Americans oftentimes have the most permissive attitudes, followed by White Americans, then Hispanic Americans, and lastly Asian Americans with the most conservative attitudes (Browning & Burrington, 2006; Feldman, Turner, & Araujo, 1999; Fugére et al., 2008). More specifically, Asian Americans often endorse a standard of abstinence within intimate relationships prior to marriage, while African American men, in particular, are more likely to hold attitudes that encourage early, casual sexual encounters. White Americans and Hispanic Americans of both genders did not significantly differ from one another in terms of their attitudes about sex (Browning & Burrington, 2006; Fugére et al., 2008). It is important to note that within each ethnic group, a continuum exists that encompasses the varying degrees of individuals' unique sexual attitudes. For example, although the Asian American ethnic group as a whole fosters more conservative attitudes, not every individual holds the same degree of conservatism within their personal attitudes. Additionally, other factors, such as socioeconomic status, early familial experiences, and education levels, are likely to influence an individual's personal sexual attitudes. For example, within the broader American culture, individuals who pursue higher education often initiate sexual activity later; however, due to variations in sex practices, families that refrain from talking about sex and sexuality often have children who have sex earlier.

International differences are also important when investigating the intersection of culture and sexual attitudes and behaviors. Researchers de Jong, Pieters, and Stremersch (2012) examined cross-country variation in the prevalence of permissive sexual behavior, and noted that the United States and Denmark reported the highest and Singapore and India reported the lowest prevalence of permissive sexual behavior. In a comparison of sexual attitudes for Pakistanis and Indians, data from Britain's National Probability Sex Survey revealed more conservative attitudes (e.g., viewing premarital sex as wrong), later first sexual intercourse, and lower rates of contraception use for

Pakistani participants than for Indian participants (Griffiths et al., 2011). Further, Cruz, Vinsonneau, Le Gall, Riviere, and Mullet (2010) found higher sexual permissiveness in European countries (e.g., Sweden, France) than for the United States, and higher permissive attitudes in the United States than in the Middle East or in other Asian countries.

Ahrold and Meston (2010) focused specifically on the unique differences in sexual attitudes of college students from different cultural backgrounds and noted that for all three groups studied (Asian, Hispanic, and Euro-American), a positive relationship was found between conservatism and religiosity/spirituality. So, individuals who placed more importance on their religious/spiritual identities held more conservative attitudes regarding sex. When looking at differences between groups, and in line with the findings noted above by Fugére et al. (2008), Asians reported more conservative attitudes (e.g., regarding casual sex and homosexuality), whereas Hispanic and Euro-American students held similar, more liberal, sexual attitudes (Ahrold & Meston, 2010). As an example, for Hispanic men, the cultural value of *machismo*—masculine power, strength, and pride—is associated with liberal attitudes about extramarital sex, whereas Asian men's attitudes on this topic are driven by their roles related to familial duties (Ahrold & Meston, 2010). In contrast with Hispanic men, Hispanic women are expected to be sexually inexperienced and to defer to their partners for all decisions regarding sex so as to avoid being viewed as promiscuous (Beaulaurier, Craig, & De La Rosa, 2008). Thus, differences regarding sexual attitudes occur both between and within cultures. Although this is not an exhaustive review of the research on cultural differences, it suggests that significant cultural differences exist with regard to sexual attitudes and behaviors.

A Holistic Perspective of Sexuality

At the same time that many are communicating messages to children and young adults that act to conceal or pathologize sexuality, our bodies are saying something very different. Our bodies are suggesting that we, as humans, are sexual creatures by nature (and we are). When we're taught that everything that has to do with sexuality is about avoiding sex, pregnancy, or diseases, we miss the larger reality of what our sexuality encompasses. Most of our sexuality happens above the neck—within the mind and its emotions, excitement, desire for connection and love, hypersensitivity to personal space, and so on. Our sexuality has less to do with our physiology and so much more to do with our psychology. Sex brings with it some of the most extraordinary things that we can experience, yet it can also bring with it some of the most damaging ones.

Sex, too, is not just about an individual person's emotional, spiritual, and physical experiences. It provides a platform for deeply connecting with another person. Much of our sexual interactions are, by definition, relational experiences. Sex can change the nature of relationships by deepening emotional bonds between partners. The hormones released during sex, particularly oxytocin, are related to bonding and feelings of interpersonal connection (Carter, 1992). In other words, when we decide to engage in sexual intimacy, we are inherently changing the nature of our relationships. In this way, the introduction of sex into a romantic relationship is a key turning point in the union.

When this point occurs is vital to relationship success. If intense emotional and physical connections are introduced before developing adequate foundations such as commitment to one's partner, healthy interpersonal communication, or a desire to nurture a long-term relationship, individuals may find themselves staying with partners they may have otherwise have left. Research has validated this assumption, showing that couples who try to begin their relationship after a sexual hook-up, or too soon after they begin dating, often experience negative relationship dynamics and a higher risk of break-up later on (Busby et al., 2010; Willoughby, Carroll, & Busby, 2014).

Therefore, sexuality functions as a biopsychosocial/spiritual phenomenon. Said another way, our physical selves, our mental and emotional selves, our social selves, and our spiritual selves all join together to inform how we experience sex, both individually and with our partners. Our sexuality is constantly evolving on an individual level, and then is further complicated by bringing in another person's experiences and beliefs. When sexuality is viewed as a multisystemic phenomenon, it is understood that everything that we experience on an individual level is going to manifest in our couple relationships, family and social relationships, and cultural and ethnic contexts. As a result, each individual's understanding of his/her sexuality must be considered across the domains

what's "normal" or acceptable with self, friends, strangers, and in the context of his/her intimate relationship itself.

Sexuality with the Self

As it relates to sexuality, ethnocentrism reigns. Ethnocentrism maintains that *my way is the best way*. It involves evaluating others based on our own personal standards or culture. Think about the experience of driving on the highway; as you see others speed past you, you might proclaim, "What a maniac!" Continuing on your drive, you later come up to a car driving 10 miles per hour slower than you, and you think to yourself, "What an idiot!" In this scenario, you are considering your speed to be the best speed to drive at, and anyone driving at any other speed is automatically bad, disadvantaged, or somehow "wrong." When you think about your sexuality—what you like, what you don't like, what you're excited about, what turns you on, what you look for on the Internet or in magazines—an ethnocentric perspective would lead you to consider your way as being the right or "best" way. Any other approach to sexuality is wrong, sick, prudent, disgusting, gross, weird, lame, too-much, or too-little.

However, there are innumerable ways to experience sexuality, and unless it is nonconsensual or abusive, it can't be considered "wrong." Perhaps different, but not wrong. Sexuality, then, is best considered along a continuum that encompasses all possible expressions, as opposed to clearly defined categories of acceptable or right and unacceptable or bad. As one shifts his/her ethnocentric thinking about sexuality as *"the best way"* to thinking about it as *"a way,"* space for future growth and possibility is carved out that did not previously exist. Until you can see yourself within a larger mosaic of attitudes, feelings, beliefs, and practices, you are unable to recognize and understand the boundaries of your perspective and, therefore, unable to accept influence from others regarding your sexuality. In this section we outline several domains of sexuality with the self, including masturbation, pornography, and spirituality, as well as different perspectives individuals might hold regarding these domains.

Masturbation

The very first person one typically has sex with is his/her self. This is done through self-exploration, such as self-touching and masturbation. As normal as this is, messages many of us received early on regarding masturbation were (are) guilt- and shame-based, and often gender-dependent (Hust, Brown, & L'Engle, 2008). Although first stated more than two decades ago, the observation by Oliver and Hyde (1993) still rings true today, noting:

> Perhaps of most concern are the mixed messages that young men and women receive in the media about sexual health decision making. By reinforcing traditional gender stereotypes of males as sexually obsessed and females as responsible for access and consequences, such content may reinforce the cross purposes at which many young men and women approach their romantic and sexual relationships, especially for those adolescents who model their behavior on such media portrayals. (p. 19)

For example, a young male might receive messages communicating that masturbation is unavoidable, socially acceptable, and healthy, whereas a young female might be told that she must cling to her purity and that it is not appropriate or necessary to learn about her body through self-exploration. Many young adults struggle with these conflicting messages about masturbation (Kaestle & Allen, 2011). As you can imagine, then, if these two individuals were to join together in young adulthood, their preconceived notions regarding their sexuality could make for a confusing first sexual experience. Where one partner has thoroughly explored his body and learned about his personal preferences, interests, responses, physiological control, and has increased his comfort with himself, the other partner has formed deep-rooted connections between self-exploration and a sense of shame, learning that her sexuality is something that is only valuable if it remains untouched, and has no idea about her preferences, interests, and responses—and may be quite uncomfortable with her body. Masturbation may begin as a solitary behavior but often progresses to a sexual act that involves romantic partners (Robbins et al., 2011). This may not be the case for every individual and couple; however, the messages that society provides us about masturbation and self-touch play an essential role in being able to share our bodies with other people in a comfortable way.

Although less extreme today than several decades ago, gender differences still exist within the recent literature on masturbation (Matthiesen & Hauch, 2004; Yuxin & Ying, 2009). Males report greater average masturbation frequency than females (Peplau, 2003; Pinkerton, Bogart, Cecil, & Abramson, 2002). Men, and especially women, report earlier experiences with masturbation today as compared to the 1960s (Dekker & Schmidt, 2002). Further, there is evidence that young women today are following a pattern of sexual socialization that was typical for males in previous decades (Dekker & Schmidt, 2002). To expand on this, Matthiesen and Hauch (2004) noted, "the liberalization of sexuality has opened up a wider area for experimentation with a variety of sexual experiences, for women in particular" (p. 491). Although gender differences in the occurrence and frequency of masturbation still exist, significant changes have been made regarding the global perception of masturbation for both genders.

Pornography

With regard to the sexual self, pornography is another means for exploring one's body and sexuality. Oftentimes people have very strong feelings about pornography—they thoroughly enjoy it or they reject all aspects of it. However, it is practically impossible to include all aspects of this media under a single umbrella-term or definition. As a result, people tend to resort to simply recognizing pornography when they see it, based off of their own definitions. For some, a lingerie catalogue from *Victoria's Secret* is "pornographic." For others, it's books with vivid descriptions of sex scenes, and for others still it's only "pornography" if it comes in a video format displaying explicit sexual acts. Brown and L'Engle (2009) suggested, "The mass media can be a private and comfortable way to learn more about sex and sexual norms" (p. 129).

Brown and L'Engle (2009) noted that within their diverse sample of early adolescents (around 13 years of age), roughly two-thirds of males and over one-third of females reported seeing at least one form of pornography within the past year. Further, predictor variables of exposure to pornography for early adolescents included, but were not limited to: being Black, being older, having less-educated parents, having lower socioeconomic status, and having a higher need for sensation (Brown & L'Engle, 2009). Another study with a sample of young adults reported that roughly half of women approved of pornography, and that nearly 90% of men use pornography to some degree (Carroll et al., 2008). Recent research has examined pornography consumption by males in the United States and concluded that there is a significant link between increased pornography consumption and having more positive attitudes toward and/or engagement in early sexual experiences, sex prior to marriage, and extramarital sex (Wright, 2013). Additionally, though demographic variables (e.g., age, religiosity, ethnicity, education) are related to U.S. males' pornography consumption, they do not significantly predict or influence it.

Hald and Malamuth (2008) conducted a study to examine pornography use by Danish men and women and to explore the relational effects of such use. They found that both genders reported small, if any, negative effects of pornography use, and moderate positive pornography consumption effects on sex life, attitudes toward sex, sexual knowledge, perceptions of attitudes toward the opposite gender, and life satisfaction in general. Interestingly, Danish men, as opposed to Danish women, reported slightly more negative effects, but also significantly more positive effects of pornography. Thus, Danish young adults (aged 18–30) reported primarily a positive effect of pornography use on their lives. Although the researchers note that there could be a cultural effect contributing to the study's findings, results indicate that for this representative sample, pornography use was viewed as a sexual enhancement tool (i.e., provided excitement) and provided significant pleasure for both the individual and the couple (Hald & Malamuth, 2008).

Other research, however, has suggested that pornography use may have negative effects for couples. Poulsen and colleagues (2012) found among a national sample in the United States that pornography use was related to lower sexual quality for both married and cohabiting couples. Likewise, several other studies have suggested that although individual well-being may not be altered by the use of pornography, many couples experience negative couple outcomes when one partner regularly consumes it (Bridges & Morokoff, 2011; Maddox, Rhoades, & Markman,

2011; Yucel & Gassanov, 2010). This result may be related to many factors, but is likely tied to one partner—often female—experiencing feelings of inadequacy and hurt when a romantic partner—often male—uses pornography for sexual arousal.

Research by Carroll et al. (2008) focused specifically on pornography and couple formation, and noted that pornography was not significantly related to young people's goals for marriage; rather, pornography was linked with sexual permissiveness and nonmarital cohabitation for couples. Another study by Daneback, Traeen, and Axel-Mansson (2009) concluded that the use of pornography in a relationship necessitates an active decision process; it is a topic that needs to be openly talked about and negotiated, which can be very difficult for some couples. Within their sample, 15% of the couples reported that the use of pornography enhanced their sexual relationship; these couples reported experiencing openness in discussing their sexual desires and fantasies, and a willingness to experiment and try new things (Daneback et al., 2009). However, the opposite can also be true—pornography may be used to overcome or compensate for problems, or it may become a source of conflict in the relationship over time (Daneback et al., 2009). In sum, the use of pornography within a relational context can provide additional opportunities for connection and shared pleasure—but it can also be a source of conflict, pressure, and/or disagreement.

So then, is pornography considered to be "bad" or unhealthy? Again, we return to our ethnocentric lenses. Each person's perspective on the intimacy level of masturbation, pornography, kissing, oral, anal, and vaginal sex, fetishes, or any other way of intimately connecting with another is filtered through his or her personal viewpoints about what is "okay." It is also important to note that what one partner considers a normal and healthy use of pornography may be considered unhealthy, immoral or simply unacceptable to his or her partner. Many consider kissing on the mouth to be the most intimate of all sexual acts, whereas others may consider it to be anal sex due to the increased need for trust and communication. In a sense, everybody is right—and at the same time, everybody is wrong. It simply depends on the viewpoints of you and your partner.

Spirituality

Although spirituality may be perceived as an unrelated or taboo topic in the context of sexuality, for many, the intersection between our sexuality and spirituality has a significant guiding influence on our thoughts, perceptions, behaviors, and interactions with intimate partners. Our sexuality lies at the core of who we are as humans, and it consciously and/or unconsciously impacts how we interact with the world around us. Yet for many, spirituality, too, is woven into the fabric of life. One's spirituality may be outwardly displayed through particular behaviors and/or language or it may remain a

personal experience that is hidden from others. Further, spirituality may be connected to a particular religion (e.g., Christianity, Buddhism, Islam) or it may be experienced outside of the existing religious structures. For the purposes of this chapter, we conceptualize "spirituality" as a personal, inner experience of, or relation to, the sacred aspects of life, as perceived and experienced by an individual. The experience of spirituality is unique to everyone and, as a result, it is unlikely that any single definition will capture all possible experiences. Therefore, we refer to spirituality based on this broad understanding, while recognizing that it may be understood differently from one person to the next.

The connection between sexuality and spirituality has been an area of focus in research for several decades and remains a heavily debated topic today. Previous research has described the link between the two as revolving around a sense of connectedness. Anderson and Morgan (1994) noted, "Spiritual connectedness is, in essence, the same connectedness that we are striving for when we express ourselves sexually. It involves the same somatic and

Photograph by William Dellenback. Courtesy of The Kinsey Institute for Research in Sex, Gender, and Reproduction.

visceral senses, the same altered states of consciousness, and is accompanied by the same feelings of ecstasy, peace, and contentment" (p. 118). Similarly, Horn, Piedmont, Fialkowski, Wicks, and Hunt (2005) posited, "It [sexuality] is the source of our capacity for relationship, for emotional and erotic connection, for intimacy, for passion and for transcendence" (p. 81). Thus, seeking connection is at the root of both our sexual and spiritual drives—a unique link among the biopsychosocial/spiritual dimensions of health.

Yet the intersection between sexuality and spirituality does not remain solely on the psychological and emotional level. Neurological researchers have suggested that changes in the brain that occur during deep meditation and prayer are similar to the changes that take place during sexual activity (Newberg & D'Aquili, 2008). It has also been suggested that one's level of awareness may act as the link between spirituality and health-related outcomes (e.g., health confidence, health behaviors, and health management) (Horn et al., 2005). Furthermore, new research on newlywed couples has suggested that couples who view their sexuality through a spiritual lens may place symbolic importance on such intimacy, a process called "sanctification." Such sanctification is linked to greater sexual satisfaction and better marital quality (Hernandez, Mahoney, & Pargament, 2011). Although this research is relatively new and requires further exploration to truly understand how the body and spirit influence one another, it provides support for the interacting relationship between our sexual and spiritual selves.

For some, the spiritual self takes precedence over the sexual self because the two cannot exist together. For example, Buddhist monks commonly believe that sexual pleasure is short-lived and is likely to draw one's attention away from his/her spiritual focus and desires. Buddhists often view marriage and sexual activity as unnecessary complications or attachments that get in the way of maintaining a peace of mind. For others, the sexual and spiritual selves cannot fully exist without the other. The book *Song of Solomon* in the Christian Bible provides an example of how one's spiritual beliefs are expected to guide his or her expressions of sexuality in and outside of the context of marriage. Christian author Rob Bell discussed the link between sexuality and spirituality in his book *Sex God*, stating, and "You can't talk about sexuality without talking about how we were made. And that will inevitably lead you to who made us. At some point you have to talk about God. Sex. God. They're connected. And they can't be separated. Where the one is, you will always find the other" (2007, p. 15). Later in his book, Bell noted, "Our sexuality is all of the ways we strive to reconnect with our world, with each other, and with God" (p. 42). The experience of the sexual self joined together with the spiritual self is felt by many to be a very powerful, dynamic relationship.

SEXUALITY WITH FRIENDS AND STRANGERS

As our personal perspectives drive our understanding of what we consider to be intimate and acceptable with our selves, they also determine our understandings of our sexuality with friends and strangers. As sex infiltrates the media and individuals are pushed to consider the physical elements of sex, alternative messages pushing for increased education and delayed marriage are also being emphasized. Understandably, many experience these messages as contradicting one another. As a natural response, what is known as the *hook-up culture* has developed as a compromise between the two demands (i.e., adhering to one's sexual demands as well as following society's scripted timeline).

The Hook-up Culture

The hook-up culture for young adults is influenced by both physiology (e.g., ability to have sexual encounters) and social structures (e.g., encouraging later marriages) (Garcia & Reiber, 2008). It is understood as an increasingly normal part of the young adult sexual culture and has been defined within the literature as casual sex between two consenting individuals who have not expressed any expectation to enter into a committed relationship with one another (Hamilton & Armstrong, 2009; Heldman & Wade, 2010). Garcia and colleagues (2012) found that approximately 60–80% of college students engaged in a hook-up and, of those, a large percentage did so more than once.

This casual arrangement is understood to considerably differ from dating relationships due to the lack of commitment between partners that is present in traditional romantic unions. As a result of this implicit or explicit agreement, both people's physical demands and the demands from their social structure(s) can be met. For those entering into the hook-up culture, our ethnocentric lenses must again be pondered. Several questions should be explored and discussed, including, but not limited to: *How are these arrangements negotiated? How do both partners remain on the same page and communicate their expectations? What is acceptable and not acceptable sexually?* And so on.

Sexuality With Friends and Strangers

FRIENDS. In addition to the hook-up culture influencing sexuality between friends or acquaintances, cultural phenomena also impact the expression of sex within friendships. For example, in Asian cultures women are often seen walking closely together, linked by the elbow. Those outside of this culture may interpret their physical display of connection as representing a sexual relationship, whereas those within this culture may understand it as an outward expression of their close nonsexual friendship. Scholars have termed these physically intimate friendships as *romantic* or *passionate friendships* (Faderman, 1993; Diamond, 2000)—they contain many of the emotional and behavioral characteristics of romantic relationships, such as inseparability, cuddling, and handholding (Diamond, 2000). These friendships are more common for women than men—Diamond (2000) stated that passionate friendships between men may be more common or more openly expressed in cultures that are more accepting of physical displays of affection between men. Within the predominant culture in the United States, intimate displays of friendship are typically not as obvious (e.g., spending time with one another, but not touching) for both males and females—and this is especially the case for males (Schmidt & Bagwell, 2007).

STRANGERS. The boundaries jointly constructed by us and our cultures that outline what demonstrations of sexuality are deemed acceptable between strangers are slightly different than the boundaries around friendships, and in many cases, they may overlap. For some, especially young adults, kissing can be an acceptable intimate activity between strangers in various contexts (e.g., at a party). Many experience casual sexual behavior with strangers as differing from sexual encounters with friends—previously formed relationships often bring with them histories, expectations, and pressures that entangle individuals (Grello, Welsh, & Harper, 2006), whereas sexual encounters with strangers may provide a sense of pleasure and connection without the complications of extant relationship ties.

Strangers might also become sexual with one another through venues connected to the sex industry. Different states and countries have developed different cultures surrounding the sex industry. For example, several countries, such as Argentina, Belgium, Brazil, and Costa Rica, have assumed the position that the government should not control the private actions of adults (e.g., prostitution) as long as it does not violate other policies or harm another person. Other countries have placed significant limits on prostitution, or even made it illegal. Although legalization of prostitution has its own challenges and/or downfalls, in many cases, those working in the sex industry are more protected through this process. Those who support the legalization of prostitution believe that by doing so, the occurrences of violence toward prostitutes will decline and there will be less stigma attached to this type of work.

With regard to an individual's experience of sexuality with friends and strangers, each person has to determine for him- or her- self what appropriate and comfortable boundaries might look like. As we continue to evolve, interact with, and define ourselves in relation to others, defining and redefining our boundaries with friends and strangers is a recursive process with no concrete end.

CASE VIGNETTE PART II: DIFFERING HISTORIES

Michael had been raised in a family that openly discussed sexuality and encouraged him to begin to explore who he is as a sexual being early on in adolescence. Rather than having one big sit-down "talk" with his parents, Michael had grown accustomed to having regular casual conversations with both of his parents about any and all aspects of sexuality. These conversations had been comfortable, informative, and most importantly, encouraged him to learn about his beliefs about himself, his body, and his sexuality. Michael had explored masturbation and pornography in his adolescence and has developed his own boundaries regarding sexuality that he feels most comfortable with.

In contrast, Ava, looking back, never remembers explicitly discussing sexuality with her parents. One distinct memory that has stuck with her over the years dates back to when Ava was about 10 years old and asked her mother a question about her anatomy, whereupon her mother immediately shut the conversation down and said that "Private parts are 'private' for a reason." In that moment, Ava felt ashamed about asking the question and vowed never to do it again. She had learned that questions regarding sexuality were unacceptable to talk about, and never pushed the subject with anyone again.

As Ava and Michael first began to be sexual with one another, Michael became frustrated because Ava would say that she wanted to be sexually intimate with him, yet when they got to a certain point, she would quickly end it without providing a reason. She would use excuses like "I'm tired" or "I don't feel well," and Michael got to the point where he could practically predict when these comments would come. When Michael tried to talk to Ava about it later, Ava would refuse to participate in the conversations. As Michael was receiving messages that Ava did not want to be intimate with him and wondering what it was that he had done, Ava was feeling conflicting emotions—wanting to be intimate with Michael, but feeling as though she was doing something that was unacceptable and shameful.

On an individual level, each one of us needs to consider what we think, feel, and believe around our sexuality. Is sexuality something that you were taught to cherish, respect, and feel positively about? Alternatively, were guilt, shame, and humiliation instilled in you at a very young age regarding your sexual self? Individuals must be in touch with (or get in touch with) their own sexuality and beliefs about sex to set the stage for understanding sexuality in relationship with another. This process is often done automatically—we learn about our preferences and boundaries through trial and error and what we are naturally exposed to—yet we don't push ourselves to be intentional in investigating what we like or don't like and what we feel comfortable exploring or thinking about. For Ava and Michael, their early experiences within their respective families of origin acted as foundations for how they experienced themselves and others as sexual beings. Michael developed a solid basis of comfort, which did not align with Ava's insecurities and deeply ingrained sense of shame. Understandably, this led to later difficulties. We must think about where we each came from in order to grow in the context of a relationship.

SEXUALITY WITHIN INTIMATE RELATIONSHIPS

Sexual experiences act as a barometer for how the couple relationship is doing. For those who feel fulfilled with their sexual life, for whatever they have constructed it to look like, they are likely to also be very happy in their intimate relationship. For those who begin to experience less fulfilling sexual experiences and are sexually intimate less often or less intensely (e.g., sexual contact has become routine and predictable), this is likely to be an indication of something else that's wrong in the relationship. Therefore, looking at a couple's sexual relationship is quite informative of the quality of their intimate relationship overall.

Recent research has revealed significant positive correlations between the quality of sex and the quality of the relationship for both men and women (Byers, 2005; Sprecher, 2002). Interestingly, the highest rating of the quality of sexual experiences takes place in the context of intimate relationships, not in casual hook-ups or flings (Montesi, Fauber, Gordon, & Heimberg, 2011). Great sex is driven by great intimacy (Sprecher, 2002). The sexual satisfaction of romantic partners is often intertwined and strongly correlated with couples' relationship satisfaction (Butzer & Campbell, 2008). Among married couples, the frequency of sexual activity is tied to the very stability of the marriage (Yabiku & Gager, 2009). Virtually any strong relationship will involve two partners who have a strong sexual connection to each other. The frequency of sexual behaviors and couples' sexual satisfaction remains a vital part of relationship health, even among couples well into their seventies and among couples who can no longer engage in intercourse (Delamater, Hyde, & Fong,

2008). However, sexual intimacy can be one of the most difficult things for couples to talk about, so as a result, we tend to look to social scripts to guide our behavior. The most commonly adopted social script directs the man to take up the role as the aggressor and the woman as the defender.

Social Scripts

As it relates to gender differences, men tend to have less trouble separating sex per se from sex in the context of an intimate relationship. This does not imply that they are shallow and unable to get their minds off of sex; rather, the evolutionary theory outlined by Buss and Schmitt (1993) suggests that men are designed to propagate their genes, and to be sure: intimacy and love are not fundamental to keeping the species going (refer to Chapter 1 to review this theory). As a result of the disconnect between sex and love, men, as compared to women, are more likely to be visually oriented, use pornography, and do not connect masturbation and/or pornography with their feelings about intimate partner. Men are often framed as the ones initiating and pushing for sex, hence the "aggressor" stereotype. Alternatively, women are less likely to separate sex and their intimate relationships. Returning to Buss and Schmitt's (1993) evolutionary theory, women are designed to conceive and care for a child, so their primary focus when seeking out a man is to find one who will help provide for the child over the long-term. Women assume the "defender" role to ward off undesirable men while they search for a partner who will provide resources and commitment. As this relates to the hook-up culture, this theoretical lens suggests that women are ultimately at a disadvantage in these arrangements due to their tendencies to bridge sex and intimacy.

As partners entering into an intimate relationship look primarily to social scripts for guidance early on, they tend to rely on said scripts as the relationship develops. However, if the couple begins to learn the intimate details about one another and begins to define the specifics of their relationship, the transition from relying on existing social scripts to writing their own unique scripts can be quite challenging. For many, the aggressor-defender roles become familiar and comfortable, which decreases the likelihood for later role adjustments. Although potentially less desirable in the long-term, these roles are known and safe (at least in a predictable sense), and do not provide the same ambiguity that accompanies the process(es) of change. This is the crossroads that many couples come to—do they proceed with what's familiar and comfortable so as to not change the "rules" of their relationship, or do they seek to redefine their roles with the hope that their new ways of interacting will allow them to be more intimate and authentic in their union?

For those who have utilized common social scripts to guide the development of their sense of self and sexuality, the process of developing true authenticity with both themselves and their partners presents challenges across both individual and relational levels. If you do not know and understand your own body, for example, it will be difficult for your partner to begin to understand your body with you. For example, if a woman has defined her sexual self through social messages that a woman should be "pure" and untouched, her lack of self-exploration may make it more difficult for her to communicate to her partner how s/he can pleasure her. Talking about sex, and more specifically, personal histories, likes and dislikes, fantasies, insecurities, or concerns should not happen solely in the bedroom while a couple is (or is becoming) sexually intimate. Rather, couples who are able to comfortably communicate about these intimate details over time are better positioned to have their needs and deepest desires met.

Talk with your partner about the messages you received early on about your sexuality. Talk about the language and vocabulary that you're comfortable with and that excites you. Talk about what you fantasize about. Teach your partner about what connects with you most. By discussing these things, it creates a sense of "we" that is unique to "us," and arguably more importantly, it creates a culture of comfort of being able to talk about and share vulnerable pieces of ourselves with our partners. This reciprocal sharing communicates, *"I can trust you to tell you what I've always fantasized about and want to try," "I can tell you what I like and what I don't like without worrying about how you will respond," "I am open to learning about your needs and desires, too."* Gottman (1999) termed this reciprocal sharing as *acceptance of influence*, and noted that this process requires significant trust within the couple relationship.

Interpersonal Experiences

Relationship challenges, such as poor communication between partners, poor compartmentalization or vicious relationship dances, often bleed into a couple's sexual relationship. Challenges in communication or compartmentalization often can be depicted as a cycle that sweeps both partners into it; each person's move being defined by their partner's previous move. For example, as a female harshly critiques her partner, he then takes up a position to defend himself and retorts with his own critique of her. As this cycle progresses and intensifies, the couple becomes entrapped in this cycle and often ends up in the same place—the partners are on opposing sides feeling disconnected from the other, having said things that have hurt the other, and feeling too hurt themselves to risk reaching out again. Poor compartmentalization, such as allowing work to take over one's focus, only adds to fueling this repeating cycle. It is understandable, then, how poor communication and compartmentalization have the capacity to interrupt a couple's ability to be sexually intimate.

Further, the experience of engaging in a pursuer–distancer dance, as discussed in prior chapters, will often elicit a sense of anger between partners, whereas over-functioner/under-functioner dances often elicit a sense of disgust. Think for a moment: Can you imagine having a fulfilling sexual relationship with your partner if you are experiencing significant anger or disgust toward him or her? We imagine not.

In addition to the negative implications of hostile relationship dances, physical attraction plays a role in the quality of sexual experiences within a relational context. As individuals gain weight, grow older, or otherwise change physically, partners may become less drawn to one another. This is potentially perceived as shallow, yet it is often a reality that couples face at different points throughout the duration of their relationships. Alternatively, attraction and connection between partners may grow stronger over time—and, indeed, it does for many older couples. In addition to perceptions of one's partner's physical attractiveness, perceptions of one's own attractiveness can influence the sexual relationship. A study by Koch, Mansfield, Thurau, and Carey (2005) found that the less attractive a woman perceived herself to be, the more likely she was to report a decline in her sexual desire and sexual activity. This can become quite distressing for one or both partners due to its sense of being semi-automatic and potentially uncontrollable.

Effective communication between partners is essential to predicting both sexual and relational satisfaction. Sexual communication is especially sensitive for couples due to the increased vulnerability required to discuss these intimate, personal topics (Montesi et al., 2013). Talking about needs and desires and maintaining self-focus, asking yourself, *"What is one thing that I could do to better communicate with my partner?"* all contribute to the development of the relationship—both sexually and otherwise. For many, one way to develop effective sexual communication is through sex therapy.

Sex Therapy

Sex therapy at its core is biopsychosocial and spiritual work. It engages all parts of our being—from our physical bodies and our minds, to the social, religious, cultural, and ethnic contexts in which we reside and function. It considers our physiology and hard wiring, alongside the intricate details of our hearts. The specific focus of sex therapy is unique to each couple and is dependent upon the presenting problems they come to therapy with. Much of the work of a sex therapist is to create a space that feels safe, comfortable, and open to discuss sexual issues and concerns. Oftentimes sex therapy is a mode for delivering information to present new perspectives or techniques regarding a particular issue. For example, medications are often understood to cause problems as they relate to sex. For men, taking antidepressants may result in difficulties becoming and/or remaining erect, and it may take longer to reach orgasm. Additionally, alcohol or drug abuse, health issues, and senescence (i.e., growing older) have also been paired with the inhibition of one's sexual desire or ability to perform. In these scenarios, the sex therapist may work with clients to explore alternative medication options or to take realistic steps toward improving physical health. However, as noted by Leiblum (2002), simply taking a medication is not sufficient: "Without an exploration of each partner's beliefs about using a pharmacologic adjunct during sex and without an exploration of desires and fears about resuming sexual intimacy, treatment may fail to bring about mutually satisfying sexual activity" (p. 18). By addressing multiple and/or all domains along the biopsychosocial/spiritual continuum, the likelihood for improvements within the sexual relationship is increased.

Oftentimes when couples present with sexual problems, said difficulties can be connected to experiences of depression, anxiety, or previous shameful experiences in one or both partners' sexual histories. For example, if one partner had been sexually abused as a child, her lack of comfort with exposing her body to a partner may be misunderstood as lack of trust within the relationship, and this may create significant trouble for the couple. By creating a space that feels safe to talk about the woman's painful early experiences, the couple can reach a place where both partners feel comfortable and fulfilled. The role of the sex therapist is to provide both general and specific pieces of information, leading to simple facts or suggestions for how to avoid or solve large issues for couples. One facet that sex therapists are recognized most for is the provision of sexual techniques.

Sexual Techniques

Sexual techniques, meant to provide pleasure and connection across the biopsychosocial continuum, can fall both within individual and couple domains. There are specific techniques that can be most helpful when utilized privately, as well as ones that are intended for the couple. These techniques are to be utilized in contexts wherein there is full consent from both partners and open communication about what is and is not acceptable. Sex therapists often suggest multiple techniques because couples differ from one to the next in terms of their respective comfort-levels, previous sexual experiences, and willingness to experiment. Additionally, if the couple does not appreciate or like one technique, there are several others for them to try. Dempsey (2008) proposed a variety of techniques as being particularly enjoyable for many couples; see Tables 1 (individual techniques) and 2 (couple techniques).

TABLE 1 Individual Techniques

Technique	Brief Description
Take a Yoga Class	Yoga offers benefits across one's physical, mental, and spiritual health, which can easily translate to feeling more fulfilled and satisfied when sexually intimate with a lover. Women, in particular, often experience a direct link between feeling good about their bodies and having relaxed minds and their desire to be sexually intimate.
Get a Close-up Look	Use a hand mirror to get a close look at your intimate parts. Get familiar with what you look like, and feel free to explore yourself through touch. Watch how your body changes as you become excited and see it through to orgasm. It can be a very interesting and exciting thing!
Do PC/Kegel Exercises	Women: Doing PC/Kegel exercises can help strengthen the pelvic muscles used during sexual intercourse. To do these exercises, squeeze your pelvic muscles tightly, similar to how you would stop the flow of urine during urination.
Shake It For Your Honey	Let your partner sit back while you perform a sexy dance and/or strip tease for him/her. Be playful and really get into it.
Add Pineapple Into His Diet	Men: If your partner complains that your semen tastes bitter, an easy fix is to add pineapple—or pineapple juice—into your diet. The unique ingredients in this tropical fruit work within the body to create a more pleasant taste.

TABLE 2 Couple Techniques

Technique	Brief Description
Positive Feedback	Provision of positive feedback to guide and encourage one's partner and communicates that s/he is doing it right. Examples: "Oh, I like that!"; "That's good!"; "I really like when you do it *that* way!".
Be Vocal	Usually quiet in bed? Time to make a change. Say your partner's name. Announce your intentions for what you plan to do to him/her next. Make sounds to communicate when it feels particularly good. Examples: "Next, I'm going to do _____ to you."
ABC's	When performing oral sex on a female, using your tongue to spell out the letters of the alphabet increases pleasure for the woman.
Write a Steamy Letter	Write a steamy love letter to your lover using hot adjectives and descriptions about what you love most about your partner, and suggest a time and place to act out your descriptions.
Focus on Foreplay	For one night, make foreplay the main attraction. Have both you and your partner take your time exploring each other's bodies, bringing in new activities and learning about how each other responds. Increasing foreplay in your routine can make for more satisfying sex.
Make One Change to Your Routine	Do you find that you and your partner tend to go in a particular sequence when being sexually intimate? Try to shake things up by making one small change, such as time of day or location.
Role Play	Have you and your lover take on various roles to simulate the classic "opposites-attract" pairings. Examples include: cowboy and city girl; cop and criminal; prison guard and inmate; doctor (or nurse) and patient; teacher and student, boss and assistant, strangers (like pizza delivery person and customer).
Use Your Tongue	Lick your partner's neck, nibble his/her ear, give your partner a hickey, blow in his/her ear (gently), kiss your partner's eyelids, and so on. Feel free to explore your lover's body with your tongue.
Sensual Touch	Be intimate with your partner by providing him/her with a back massage or provide more erotic attention to other sensitive areas.
Play Truth Ideas	Truth Idea #1: What's one sex trick you've always wanted to try but never had the nerve? Truth Idea #2: What's your secret turn-on? Truth Idea #3: What kinky things have you done in the past? . . . And so on. Feel free to make up your own truth ideas, too.
Play Dare Ideas	Dare Idea #1: "I dare you to let me watch you masturbate." Dare Idea #2: "I dare you to lick whipped cream (non-dairy) off of my _____." Dare Idea #3: "I dare you to let me blindfold you for 10 minutes and I can do whatever I want to you (within the agreed upon boundaries)." . . . And so on.

Technique	Brief Description
Ice Exploration	Carefully touch ice cubes to different areas of your partner's body. Especially in highly sensitive areas, this can be a very pleasurable experience. Be careful, though. Make sure the ice cubes are wet (such as in a glass of water) before placing them on your partner's body, and don't let the ice linger on one spot for too long.
Get Out of the Bedroom	To shake things up, be bold and consider other locations beyond the bedroom for you and your lover to get it on. For many, this could be in the bathroom, on the kitchen table or sun porch, and for even braver couples, this could even be in certain public places (think: car, office, beach, etc.). Be careful when taking your passion out into the public and select your place carefully so as to not get caught or charged with something illegal.
Hot and Cold	Alternate between blowing hot air (with an wider opened mouth) and cold air (with a narrow opened mouth) on different areas of your partner's body.
Hum Job	Vibrate your vocal chords while providing oral sex to your partner to create a very pleasant vibration for him/her. Play around with different vibrations and ask your partner what s/he enjoys most.
Eye Contact	Maintaining eye contact with your partner during oral sex or intercourse increases many partners' sense of connection and can be a very intimate experience. Keep the light on, or be intimate during the day, to increase your ability to see your partner well.

UTILIZING SEXUAL TECHNIQUES. Talk. Share your fantasies. Be willing and able to accept influence from your partner as you go. Clearly communicate what you are and are not comfortable with. Take a chance and try something new. Don't limit yourself to one or a few techniques in the evening; rather, utilize different techniques throughout the day as foreplay. Take your time. Enjoy one another. In the context of your relationship, you can evolve and grow in ways that you never thought possible if you can open yourself up to one another, and you can create a couple culture that is unique to your and your partner's relationship.

Resources for Couples

1. **Thank God for Sex**
   www.thankgodforsex.org
   www.tinaschermersellers.com
2. **Understanding Orgasm**
   http://www.apa.org/monitor/2011/04/orgasm.aspx
3. **Rituals for Initiating and Refusing Sex**
   http://www.gottmanblog.com/2011/08/creating-ritual-for-initiating-and.hrml

AREAS FOR FURTHER DEVELOPMENT

While this chapter has presented a great deal of information across multiple topics regarding our sexuality, including biopschosocial/spiritual influences, similarities and differences across gender and ethnic backgrounds, experiences of sexuality with the self, friends, strangers, and an intimate partner, and sex therapy, there is still much that necessitates further exploration. As one's experience of sexuality is predominantly an individual experience that evolves over time, and as the larger culture around sexuality has changed dramatically over the past decade, it is understandable that research investigating sexual intimacy must also continue to evolve. Some of the things we do not know much about include:

- Differences within ethnic groups regarding sexual attitudes and behaviors
- Long-term implications of the legalization of prostitution
- Long-term implications of the development of the hook-up culture, both on an individual- and cultural-level, as well as cross-culturally
- Long-term implications of pornography consumption across gender, culture, and type of pornography used

CONCLUSION

It is in our human nature to be sexual creatures, and to have sexual wants and needs. However, we receive contradicting messages from society and those around us (e.g., family) regarding how we ought to experience our sexual selves. From a young age, children and adolescents are tasked to sort through these contradicting messages to determine what is appropriate, accepted, and "normal" regarding themselves, friends, strangers, and within an intimate relationship. Society has developed a culture of silence around sexuality, so individuals often look to traditional social scripts for guidance. Each individual has his/her own personal histories, early experiences, and messages that s/he received about sex, and s/he brings these into the context(s) of an intimate relationship. The utilization of sex therapy is one means for addressing the difficulties that may arise from this joining process and transfer onto the sexual relationship. A number of specific sexual techniques are outlined in this chapter for both the individual and couple to utilize in an attempt to rekindle and/or improve the sexual union. Effective communication is essential in the process of opening one's self up to a partner in a vulnerable way with the hope of growing and evolving together.

REFERENCES

Ahrold, T. K., & Meston, C. M. (2010). Ethnic differences in sexual attitudes of U.S. college students: Gender, acculturation, and religiosity factors. *Archives of Sexual Behavior, 39,* 190–202. doi:10.1007/s10508-008-9406-1

Alexander, M. G., & Fisher, T. D. (2003). Truth and consequences: Using the bogus pipeline to examine sex differences in self-reported sexuality. *The Journal of Sex Research, 40,* 27–35. doi:10.1080/00224490309552164

Anderson, P. B., & Morgan, M. (1994). Spirituality and sexuality: The healthy connection. *Journal of Religion and Health, 33,* 115–121. doi:10.1007/BF02354531

Beaulaurier, R. L., Craig, S. L., & De La Rosa, M. (2008). Older Latina women and HIV/AIDS: An examination of sexuality and culture as they relate to risk and protective factors. *Journal of Gerontological Social Work, 52,* 48–63. doi:10.1080/01634370802561950

Bell, R. (2007). *Sex God: Exploring the endless connections between sexuality and spirituality.* Grand Rapids, MI: Zondervan.

Bridges, A., & Morokoff, P. (2011), Sexual media use and relational satisfaction in heterosexual couples. *Personal Relationships, 18,* 562–585. doi:10.1111/j.1475-6811.2010.01328.x

Brown, J. D., & L'Engle, K. L. (2009). X-rated: Sexual attitudes and behaviors associated with U.S. early adolescents' exposure to sexually explicit media. *Communication Research, 36,* 129–151. doi:10.1177/0093650208326465

Browning, C. R., & Burrington, L. A. (2006). Racial differences in sexual and fertility attitudes in an urban setting. *Journal of Marriage and Family, 68,* 236–251. doi:10.1111/j.1741-3737.2006.00244.x

Busby, D. M., Carroll, J. S., & Willoughby, B. J. (2010). Compatibility or restraint?: The effects of sexual timing on marriage relationships. *Journal of Family Psychology, 24,* 766–774. doi:10.1037/a0021690

Buss, D. M., & Schmitt, D. P. (1993). Sexual strategies theory: An evolutionary perspective on human mating. *Psychological Review, 100,* 204–232. doi:10.1037/0033-295x.100.2.204

Butzer, B., & Campbell, L. (2008). Adult attachment, sexual satisfaction, and relationship satisfaction: A study of married couples. *Personal Relationships, 15,* 141–154. doi:10.1111/j.1475-6811.2007.00189.x

Byers, E. S. (2005). Relationship satisfaction and sexual satisfaction: A longitudinal study of individuals in long-term relationships. *Journal of Sex Research, 42*(2), 113–118. doi:10.1080/00224490509552264

Carroll, J. S., Padilla-Walker, L. M., Nelson, L. J., Olson, C. D., Barry, C. M., Madsen, S. D. (2008). Generation XXX: Pornography acceptance and use among emerging adults. *Journal of Adolescent Research, 23,* 6–30. doi:10.1177/0743558407306348

Carter, C. S. (1992). Oxytocin and sexual behavior. *Neuroscience & Biobehavioral Reviews, 16,* 131–144. doi:10.1016/S0149-7634(05)80176-9

Cope-Farrar, K. M., & Kunkel, D. (2002). Sexual messages in teens' favorite prime-time television programs. In J. Brown, J. Steele, and K Walsh-Childers (eds.), *Sexual Teens, Sexual Media* (pp. 59–78). Mahwah, NJ: Lawrence Erlbaum.

Crawford, M., & Popp, D. (2003). Sexual double standards: A review and method critique of two decades of research. *The Journal of Sex Research, 40,* 13–26. doi:10.1080/00224490309552163

Cruz, G. V., Vinsonneau, G., Le Gall, A., Riviere, S., & Mullet, E. (2010). Sexual permissiveness: A Mozambique-France comparison. *Journal of Applied Social Psychology, 40,* 2488–2499. doi:10.1111/j.1559-1816.2010.00667.x

Daneback, K., Traeen, B., & Axel-Mansson, S. A. (2009). Use of pornography in a random sample of Norwegian heterosexual couples. *Archives of Sexual Behavior, 38,* 746–753.

de Jong, M. G., Pieters, R., & Stremersch, S. (2012). Analysis of sensitive questions across cultures: An application of multigroup item randomized response theory to sexual attitudes and behavior. *Journal of Personality and Social Psychology, 103,* 543–564. doi:10.1037/a0029394

Dekker, A., & Schmidt, G. (2002). Patterns of masturbatory behaviour: Changes between the sixties and the nineties. *Journal of Psychology & Human Sexuality, 14,* 35–48.

Delamater, J., Hyde, J. S., & Fong, M. (2008). Sexual satisfaction in the seventh decade of life. *Journal of Sex & Marital Therapy, 34,* 439–454. doi:10.1080/00926230802156251

Dempsey, B. (2008). *1001 sexcapades to do if you dare.* Avon, MA: Adams Media.

Diamond, L. M. (2000). Passionate friendships among adolescent sexual-minority women. *Journal of Research on Adolescence, 10,* 191–209. doi:10.1207/SJRA1002_4

Eisenberg, M.E., Bearinger, L.H., Sieving, R.E., Swain, C., & Resnick, M.D. (2004). Parents' beliefs about condom and oral contraceptives: Are they medically accurate? *Perspectives on Sexual Reproductive Health, 36*(2), 50–57. doi:10.1111/j.1931-2393.2004.tb00008.x

Elliott, S. (2010). Talking to teens about sex: Mothers negotiate resistance, discomfort, and ambivalence. *Sex Research and Social Policy, 7,* 310–322. doi:10.1007/s13178-010-0023-0

Epstein, M., & Ward, L. M. (2008). "Always use protection": Communication boys receive about sex from parents, peers, and the media. *Journal of Youth Adolescence, 37,* 113–126. doi:10.1007/s10964-007-9187-1

Faderman, L. (1993). Nineteenth-century Boston marriage as a possible lesson for today. In E. D. Rothblum & K. A. Brehony (Eds.), *Boston marriages: Romantic but asexual relationships among contemporary lesbians* (pp. 29–42). Amherst, MA: University of Massachusetts Press.

Farley, M. (2004). "Bad for the body, bad for the heart": Prostitution harms women even if legalized or decriminalized. *Violence Against Women, 10,* 1087–1125. doi:10.1177/1077801204268607

Feldman, S., Turner, R., & Araujo, K. (1999). Interpersonal context as an influence on sexual timetables of youths: Gender and ethnic effects. *Journal of Research on Adolescence, 9,* 25–52. doi:10.1207/s15327795jra0901_2

Fugére, M. A., Escoto, C., Cousins, A. J., Riggs, M. L., & Haerich, P. (2008). Sexual attitudes and double standards: A literature review focusing on participant gender and ethnic background. *Sexuality & Culture, 12,* 169–182. doi:10.1007/s12119-008-9029-7

Garcia, J. R., & Reiber, C. (2008). Hook-up behavior: A biopsychosocial perspective. *Journal of Social, Evolutionary, and Cultural Psychology, 2,* 192–208. Retrieved from http://psycnet.apa.org.ezp2.lib.umn.edu/journals/ebs/2/4/192.pdf

Garcia, J. R., Reiber, C., Massey, S. G., & Merriwether, A. M. (2012).Sexual hookup culture: A review. *Review of General Psychology, 16,* 161–176. doi:10.1037/a0027911

Gottman, J. M. (1999). *The marriage clinic: A scientifically based marital therapy.* New York: Norton.

Grello, C. M., Welsh, D. P., & Harper, M. S. (2006). No strings attached: The nature of casual sex in college students. *Journal of Sex Research, 43,* 255–267. doi:10.1080/00224490609552324

Griffiths, C., Johnson, A. M., Fenton, K. A., Erens, B., Hart, G. J., Wellings, K., & Mercer, C. H. (2011). Attitudes and first heterosexual experiences among Indians and Pakistanis in Britain: Evidence from a national probability survey. *International Journal of STD & Aids, 22,* 131–139. doi:10.1258/ijsa.2009.009496

Griffiths, M. (2003). Sex on the internet: Issues, concerns, and implications. *The wired homestead: An MIT Press sourcebook on the Internet and the family, 261.*

Hadley, W., Brown, L. K., Lescano, C. M., Kell, H., Spalding, K., DiClemente, R., Donenberg, G., & Project Style Group (2009). Parent-adolescent sexual communication: Associations of condom use with condom discussions. *AIDS Behavior, 13,* 997–1004. doi:10.1007/s10461-008-9468-z

Hald, G. M. & Malamuth, N. M. (2008). Self-perceived effects of pornography consumption. *Archives of Sexual Behavior, 37,* 614–625. doi:10.1007/s10508-007-9212-1

Hamilton, L., & Armstrong, E. A. (2009). Gendered sexuality in young adulthood: Double binds and flawed options. *Gender & Society, 23,* 589–616. doi:10.1177/0891243209345829

Heldman, C., & Wade, L. (2010). Hook-up culture: Setting a new research agenda. *Sex Research & Social Policy, 7,* 323–333. doi:10.1007/s13178-010-0024-z

Henderson-King, D. H., & Veroff, J. (1994). Sexual satisfaction and marital well-being in the first years of marriage. *Journal of Social and Personal Relationships, 11,* 509–534. doi:10.1177/0265407594114002

Hernandez, K. M., Mahoney, A., & Pargament, K. I. (2011). Sanctification of sexuality: Implications for newlyweds' marital and sexual quality. *Journal of Family Psychology, 25,* 775–780. doi:10.1037/a0025103

Horn, M. J., Piedmont, R. L., Fialkowski, G. M., Wicks, R. J., & Hunt, M. E. (2005). Sexuality and spirituality: The embodied spirituality scale. *Theology and Sexuality, 12,* 81–101. doi:10.1177/1355835805057788

Hust, S. J. T., Brown, J. D., & L'Engle, K. L. (2008). Boys will be boys and girls better be prepared: An analysis of the rare sexual health messages in young adolescents' media. *Mass Communication & Society, 11,* 3–23. doi:10.1080/15205430701668139

Jerman, P., & Constantine, N. A. (2010). Demographic and psychological predictors of parent–adolescent communication about sex: A representative statewide analysis. *Journal of Youth and Adolescence, 39,* 1164–1174. doi:10.1007/s10964-010-9546-1

Kaestle, C. E., & Allen, K. R. (2011). The role of masturbation in healthy sexual development: Perceptions of young adults. *Archives of Sexual Behavior, 40,* 983–994. doi:10.1007/s10508-010-9722-0

Koch, P. B., Mansfield, P. K., Thurau, D., & Carey, M. (2005). "Feeling frumpy": The relationships between body image and sexual response changes in midlife women. *Journal of Sex Research, 42,* 215–223. doi:10.1080/00224490509552276

Leiblum, S. R. (2002). After sildenafil: Bridging the gap between pharmacologic treatment and satisfying sexual relationships. *Journal of Clinical Psychiatry, 63,* 17–22. Retrieved from http://www-psychiatrist-com.ezp3.lib. umn.edu/JCP/article/Pages/2002/v63s05/v63s0504.aspx

Maddox, A. M., Rhoades, G. K., & Markman, H. J. (2011). Viewing sexually-explicit materials alone or together: Associations with relationship quality. *Archives of Sexual Behavior, 40,* 441–448. doi:10.1007/s10508-009-9585-4

Matthiesen, S., & Hauch, M. (2004). Will gender differences disappear? Dissolution, reversal, or continuity of traditional gender differences in sexual behavior: An empirical study with three generations. *Verhaltenstherapie & Psychosoziale Praxis, 36,* 491–508.

Montesi, J. L., Conner, B. T., Gordon, E. A., Fauber, R. L., Kin, K. H., & Hiemberg, R. G. (2013). On the relationship among social anxiety, intimacy, sexual communication, and sexual satisfaction in young couples. *Archives of Sexual Behavior, 42,* 81–91. doi:10.1007/s10508-012-9929-3

Montesi, J. L., Fauber, R. L., Gordon, E. A., & Heimberg, R. G. (2011). The specific importance of communicating about sex to couples' sexual and overall relationship satisfaction. *Journal of Social and Personal Relationships, 28(5),* 591–609. doi:10.1177/0265407510386833

Newberg, A., & D'Aquili, E. G. (2008). *Why God won't go away: Brain science and the biology of belief.* New York: Random House Publishing.

Oliver, M. B., & Hyde, J. S. (1993). Gender differences in sexuality: A meta-analysis. *Psychological Bulletin, 114,* 29–51. doi:10.1037//0033-2909.114.1.29

Peplau, L. A. (2003). Human sexuality: How do men and women differ? *Current Directions in Psychological Science, 12,* 37–40. doi:10.1111/1467-8721.01221

Pinkerton, S. D., Bogart, L. M., Cecil, H., & Abramson, P. R. (2002). Factors associated with masturbation in collegiate sample. *Journal of Psychology and Human Sexuality, 14,* 103–121. doi:10.1300/J056v14n02_07

Poulsen, F. O., Busby, D. M., & Galovan, A. M. (2013). Pornography use: Who uses it and how it is associated with couple outcomes. *Journal of Sex Research, 50,* 72–83. doi:10.1080/00224499.2011.648027

Robbins, C. L., Schick, V., Reece, M., Herbenick, D., Sanders, S. A., Dodge, B., & Fortenberry, J. D. (2011). Prevalence, frequency, and associations of masturbation with partnered sexual behaviors among U.S. adolescents. *Archives of Pediatrics & Adolescent Medicine, 165,* 1087–1093. doi:10.1001/archpediatrics.2011.142

Schmidt, M. E., & Bagwell, C. L. (2007). The protective role of friendships in overtly and relationally victimized boys and girls. *Merrill-Palmer Quarterly, 53,* 439–460. Retrieved from http://muse.jhu.edu.ezp3.lib.umn.edu/journals/merrill-palmer_quarterly/v053/53.3schmidt.html

Sprecher, S. (2002). Sexual satisfaction in premarital relationships: Associations with satisfaction, love, commitment, and stability. *Journal of Sex Research, 39(3),* 190–196. doi:10.1080/00224490209552141

Whitaker, D., & Miller, K. S. (2000). Parent-adolescent discussions about sex and condoms: Impact on peer influences of sexual risk behavior. *Journal of Adolescent Research, 15,* 251–273. doi:10.1177/0743558400152004

Willoughby, B. J., Busby, D. M., & Carroll, J. S. (2014). Differing relationship outcomes when sex happens before, on, or after first dates. *Journal of Sex Research, 51,* 52–61. doi:10.1080/00224499.2012.714012

Wright, P. J. (2013). U.S. males and pornography, 1973-2010: Consumption, predictors, correlates. *Journal of Sex Research, 50,* 60–71. doi:10.1080/00224499.2011.628132

Yabiku, S. T., & Gager, C. T. (2009). Sexual frequency and stability of marital and cohabiting unions. *Journal of Marriage and Family, 71,* 983–1000. doi:10.1111/j.1741-3737.2009.00648.x

Yucel, D., & Gassanov, M. A. (2010). Exploring actor and partner correlates of sexual satisfaction among married couples. *Social Science Research, 39,* 725–738. doi:10.1016/j.ssresearch.2009.09.002

Yuxin, P., & Ying, P. H. S. (2009). Gender, self and pleasure: Young women's discourse on masturbation in contemporary Shanghai. *Culture, Health, & Sexuality, 15,* 515–528. doi:10.1080/13691050902912775

16

Queering the Family

Kyle Zrenchik, Ph.D., ACT, LMFT
Department of Family Social Science
University of Minnesota

Jeni L. Whalig, M.S.
Applied Psychology Department Antioch
University New England

Anna I. Bohlinger, Ph.D., LMFT
Department of Family Social Science
University of Minnesota

G. Carnes
University of Minnesota

LEARNING OBJECTIVES

- Understand key elements of Queer Theory
- Articulate common acronyms and initials referring to different groups by sexual orientation and identity
- Understand common sequences and experiences paired with "coming out"
- Articulate key challenges and strengths within same-sex couples
- Outline some strategies that couples can use to foster resilience in their union
- Articulate common experiences, challenges, and strengths within the transgendered and asexual communities

INTRODUCTION

As a University of Minnesota student, you join a long history of people fighting for the rights of those who are Lesbian, Gay, Bisexual, and Transgender. In fact, did you know that the very first attempt at getting marriage rights for same-sex couples happened right here in Minnesota . . . by fellow Golden Gophers?

On May 18, 1970, Richard Baker and James Michael McConnell (two University of Minnesota students) went into the Hennepin County clerk's office and applied for a marriage license. At the time there were no laws that explicitly outlawed same-sex marriage. When the county clerk, Gerald Nelson, denied the couple a marriage license because they were a Gay couple, Baker and McConnell filed a lawsuit with the district court. The legal battle made it all the way to the Supreme Court of the United States. Unfortunately, the court dismissed the case because they argued that marital rights do not extend to same-sex couples. While they had lost their battle, this event was one of the first legal fights for marriage equality in the United States (*Baker v. Nelson*, 1971).

But, there is good news! On May 14, 2013 Minnesota extended marriage equality to same-sex couples, and in July of 2013, The US Supreme Court had ruled it unconstitutional for the Federal Government to deny same-sex married couples the same rights as male/female married couples. On the same day, the court also ruled that California's *Proposition 8* was unconstitutional. Proposition 8 was the state's constitutional amendment banning same-sex marriage (after it had already been ruled legal in Minnesota). While the court did not explicitly rule that every state must recognize same-sex marriages, until 2015 these monumental victories are signaling the end of the fight started over 40 years ago by fellow Golden Gophers!

Corresponding Author: Kyle Zrenchik, Ph.D., ACS, LMFT; University of Minnesota; Department of Family Social Science; 1985 Buford Ave.; 290 McNeal Hall; Saint Paul, MN 55108. E-mail: zrenc001@umn.edu.

The Gay rights movement has been garnering both increased support and fervent opposition in recent years. However, the history of those who are not exclusively Heterosexual or whose gender presentation does not mimic the mainstream is a history of struggle, discrimination, and pride. In this chapter, we will delve into an overview of all the identities covered herein. Next, we will explore the unique *Coming Out* experience from both the individual and family perspectives. After that, we will look into coupling and parenting within Lesbian, Gay, and Bisexual couples, as well as the Transgender experience for individuals, couples, and families. Lastly, we will introduce asexuality, before reflecting on what we don't know yet about the families and experiences covered in this chapter.

Before delving into the content outlined above, however, it is helpful to have a basic understanding of Queer Theory, which we encourage readers to keep in mind throughout the rest of the chapter.

QUEER THEORY

You may have heard the word "Queer" used as a derogatory term for those who are not Heterosexual or who are not *Cisgendered*. However, there has been a movement to reclaim the word and use it as an empowering term. To be **Queer** is to live uniquely, rejecting the restrictions that exist in larger society regarding gender, sexuality, romance, identity, and family. *Queer Theory*, deeply rooted in Feminism, is a response to the normalizing of Heterosexuality and seeks to destabilize norms and allow for inventiveness, ingenuity, and personal connection to the world without disrupting it. In other words, Queer Theory is a critique of what is considered "normal" and the way our society considers what "should" be. It seeks to move us beyond the socially defined norm of what it means to be a man, a woman, a couple, a family, and so on. Queer Theory focused on what Stone Fish and Harvey (2005) call "the borderlands of the margins...that new possibilities for love, commitment, and family structure emerge" (p. 31).

Queer Theory says that there are more ways to be oneself than exclusively heterosexual, than to act according to rigid gender norms, and that there is a plethora of ways to be a man, a woman, a husband, a mother, and so forth. Queer Theory encourages everyone to appreciate differences, to see how those that are different than you (in their gender expression and in their sexual/romantic orientation) have inherent value, worth, and bring great contributions and qualities to our community just as you do. Queer Theory does focus on those sexual and gender identities that fall in the "borderlands" rather than in the mainstream status quo, but does not argue for the superiority of any identity. Instead, it invites others to understand the complexity of the world around them, and the people in the world around them. In that complexity, we see the most wonderful parts of human experience.

So, when we think of the idea of *Queering the Family*, we think of expanding the idea of what a family looks like, and the evolving understanding of what constitutes family roles (sister, grandfather, wife, child, etc.). We also think of a growing number of couples and families that do not fit the conventional 1950s nuclear family model that has served as a model of perfection ever since (Bengtson, 2001; Widmer & Jallinoja, 2008). Contemporary couples and families are discovering new ways to be a family, redefining what it means to be in a family, what family values are, and expanding the concepts of love and acceptance that all families strive for. The idea of "family" is changing and being more representative of what real families are, what real families look like, and what real families do. Our understanding of "family" or "marriage" or "parent" is becoming *Queered*; it is finding room for more people to get to participate in whatever family, marriage, and parenting is to them.

A quick caveat about the use of the word "Queer" in this chapter. As authors, we chose to use the term *"Queer"* instead of consistently saying Lesbian, Gay, Bisexual, and Transgender, acronyms such as "LGBT", "LGBTTQQAAPKIO" (which includes identities such as Questioning, Asexual, and Intersex), or another term. This choice is both a pragmatic and political one. We believe that the term Queer is both a more accepting and inclusive term for the entire community, and we want to support the growing movement that chooses to reclaim the term as an empowering moniker. Also, we use it to encourage readers to explore what benefits and unique contributions Queering identity and Queering the family has on everyone's life. However, we are aware (and you should be, too) that not everyone agrees with the use of this term. Many people experience the term Queer, not as an empowering word, but as a negative, hurtful label. We respect this viewpoint as valid and appropriate. We choose to use the term both because it being often seen as an umbrella term, incorporating many other terms and identities under it. Thus, we encourage readers to use the term "Queer" cautiously and only when the person or family you are describing has deemed it appropriate or acceptable.

ALPHABET SOUP: WHAT DO ALL OF THOSE LETTERS MEAN?

The list of acronyms to capture the entire non-Heterosexual, gender divergent community can be so long and difficult to say, that it is often lovingly called *alphabet soup*. While the list is always changing, the acronyms are made up of, in no particular order, the Lesbian, Gay, Bisexual, Transgender, Queer, Questioning, Asexual, Polyamorous, Pansexual, Kink, Intersex, and Other communities. These communities are not mutually exclusive. Someone may identify as Transgender and Bisexual, someone else may identify as Heterosexual, Queer, and Pansexual. There are as many identities as there are people on this planet. So, what does each one mean? Let us briefly (and we do mean *briefly*) give some definition to each one.

Lesbian: A woman who is sexually/romantically attracted to other women.

Gay: A man who is sexually/romantically attracted to other men.

Bisexual: A person of any gender who is sexually/romantically attracted to men and women (equally or not).

Transgender: An umbrella term to encompass variations and subcategories of identities and behaviors that do not fit the norms of the traditional male/female gender binary.

Transsexual: A person whose biological sex they were assigned at birth does not match the sex they know themselves to be.

Two-Spirit: A Native-American term describing a revered person who has both a feminine and masculine aspect to their identity and gender performance.

Questioning: A person whom may currently identify as one sexual/romantic orientation but is exploring the possibility of identifying as another. This can include someone considering whether or not that they are Gay, Bisexual, Transgender, Heterosexual, and so on.

Queer: A person who does not identify as a specific gender and/or sexual/romantic orientation, but lives and presents in a manner unique unto themselves.

Androgynous: A person whose gender is a unique combination of masculinity and femininity.

Asexual: A person who does not have any strong sexual/romantic interest in any gender. Many also do not enjoy self-pleasure or masturbation.

Polyamorous: A person who engages in simultaneous sexual/romantic relationships with more than one partner, with the consent of all partners.

Pansexual: A person who is sexually/romantically attracted to people without consideration of their gender. This differs from Bisexual in that Bisexuals are typically attracted to males and females, and Pansexuals may also be attracted to persons who present themselves as genders outside of the traditional male/female gender binary (Queer, Two-Spirit, those who identify as having no gender, etc.).

Kink: A person who expresses their sexual/romantic feelings in nonconventional ways, often involving role-playing and sex toys.

Intersex: A person with sex characteristics, such as genitalia or secondary sex characteristics, of more than one gender. A common medical term for Intersex is someone who is born with *ambiguous genitalia*, but this term focuses mostly on the genitals.

Other: A term reserved for those who do not choose to identify as any term above but still elect to participate in the greater community.

Cisgender*: Someone whose gender identity, and the way they enact it, and the sex they were assigned at birth, are aligned with social expectations. For example, a person who was assigned at birth to be a Male, believes that they truly are Male, and present their maleness in ways that the general public expects (walks, talks and behaves like a traditional male, wears "male" clothes, enjoys activities that are largely associated with masculinity). This does not mean that one is only Cisgender if they are a stereotypical male/female. Instead, a Cigender male would have their sex (Male), their gender (Man), and their gender performance (how they enact their maleness) all align and the average person on the street would also consider that person a Man. *This is not a Queer identity. This term was included in the list for your reference when gender is discussed in greater detail later.*

You may notice that not every identity listed above is concerned with one's sexual or romantic orientation. In fact, many of them have to do with the way that one expresses his or her gender, or the gender they elect to live by. Confusing, huh? Well, who said describing individual identities should be easy?

COMING OUT

A unique experience for Queer families is the "coming out" experience. This term refers to the popular phrase "coming out of the closet," where the closet refers to the place of hiding, shame, and fear Queer individuals often find themselves when they keep their identity private (Adams, 2012). As the phrase "coming out" is historically reserved to Lesbian, Gay, Bisexual and Transgender folk, we will focus on their experiences here.

Many LGBT folk recall their time being *in the closet* as painful and feeling as if they were living a lie. Many things encourage LGBT folk to stay in the closet, including religious oppression, family pressure, fear of harassment from peers or the government, and concerns over losing employment or parental rights (Adams, 2012; Sedgwick; 1990). While coming out is a large obstacle that not all LGBT folk have, it is seen as a worldwide accomplishment and story of strength and resilience in the LGBT community. In fact, on October 11, 1988, an American Psychologist, Robert Eichberg, created the first annual National Coming Out Day which celebrates those who publicly identify as LGBT. Coming out is seen as a ceremonious rite of passage, and yet it is important to realize that sometimes the consequences of coming out are too great for a person to do it. Those who stay "in the closet" should not be shamed or *outted,* but instead understood as protecting themselves from a world that is still too-often full of hate, rejection, and violence.

> "I would like to see every Gay doctor come out, every Gay architect come out, stand up and let the world know. That would do more to end prejudice overnight than anybody would imagine."
>
> *–Harvey Milk*
> *First openly Gay elected U.S. official*

Stage 1: Identity Confusion
In this stage, people develop their awareness that they may be LGBT. This stage is commonly one of experimentation, reflection, denial, and repression of thoughts/behaviors.

Stage 2: Identity Comparison
After accepting the potentiality of being LGBT, the person may feel alienated. The difference between themselves and their Heterosexual or Cisgendered peers grows clearer. The individual may seek to meet other LGBT folk or explore the LGBT community.

Stage 3: Identity Tolerance
The individual, now more comfortable and committed to the LGBT identity, seeks friendships or relationships with other LGBT folk. They may not be entirely satisfied with being LGBT, but they see the need to be satisfied and are actively working toward it.

Stage 4: Identity Acceptance
Development of a more positive view of their LGBT identity, and a greater and more positive sense of self. This stage includes disclosure of their LGBT identity to more friends and relatives.

Stage 5: Identity Pride
In this stage, a deep sense of pride and feeling part of the community is achieved. Loyalty to the greater LGBT community is developed, and awareness of social stigmatization and oppression is achieved. This may often lead to LGBT folk confronting non-LGBT folk directly to assert validity and equality.

Stage 6: Identity Synthesis
Anger and pride in the earlier stage is less extreme, and a focus on cooperation and coexistence is sought and promoted to both the LGBT and non-LGBT community.

In the early 1980s, Vivienne Cass introduced a groundbreaking article in the *Journal of Sex Research* that described the linear stages of one's LGBT identity development. Though her article focused specifically on homosexuality, it has been expanded to the entire LGBT community (Cass, 1984).

While no identity development model is perfect, and other researchers have produced other respectable models (e.g., Coleman, 1982; Troiden, 1988), all models share similarities. These include the unique struggle LGBT folk have with their identity, negotiating how to incorporate this new identity and the characteristics that come with this identity into their lives, and how to maintain relationships with friends and family during and after this Transition.

WHAT ABOUT THE FAMILY?

The face of the American family is changing. Whereas in the early 20th century, there was virtually no data on Queer Americans, we now know many things about the lives of Queer Americans and their families.

The average age that youth formally identify as Lesbian, Gay, or Bisexual is about 13 years old for males, and about 16 for females (Allen, Glicken, Beach, & Naylor, 1998; Graham, 2011). Ignorance and hate result in queer youth (or those expected to be queer) being victimized by those around them, often including their family members. Further, parents are so commonly without affirmative and honest information regarding Queer identity that the mere act of having a Queer-identified family member can be a great struggle. At a time when Queer youth need family support the most, families are sometimes a prominent source of pain, shame, and anger (D'Augelli, Hershberger, & Pilkin, 1998). Queer youth are more likely to be victims of violence, run away from home, drop out of school, develop psychological disorders, become alienated from their families, and attempt or commit suicide (Coker, Austin, & Schuster, 2010; Grossman et al., 2009; Hatzenbuehler, 2011; Mutanski, Garfalo, & Emerson, 2010).

When parents are given sound, reliable, and affirmative resources concerning how to better parent a Queer child, then they are more likely to provide that youth the support they need to be happier, healthier, and more well-adjusted (Mutanski, Newcomb, & Garofalo, 2011). We know that having a Queer family member can be a great struggle in some families, especially those with religious fundamentalist or conservative family values. However, having a family member who is Queer can also be an incredibly transformative and wonderful experience that can help the family bond and grow in a unique and special way. Some parents or family members may struggle with having a Queer family member at first, but it is also very common that as the family grows more tolerant and accepting, family members will reflect with great joy and pride that they have a daughter who is Lesbian, a brother who is Transgender, or two parents who are both Gay men. Also, many families do not see it as a struggle at all, but rather something else that makes their family special (Hill & Menvielle, 2009; LaSala, 2010).

Sexual Conversion Therapy

Simply the act of being known as Gay or Lesbian can put one in a dangerous and vulnerable position (Setoodeh, Murr, & Ordonez, 2008). When they are really struggling, sometimes both parents and Queer folks themselves strive to find a "cure" and seek the services of those that perform *reparative therapy* or *sexual conversion therapy*. Such treatment involves subjecting already depressed and struggling youth or adults to dangerous, often traumatic treatments. In some instances, patients are subjected to chemical or electrical torture (Bright, 2004; Haldeman, 2002; Schroeder, & Shidlo, 2002). This practice has been prohibited by most major professional organizations, such as the American Medical Association and the American Psychiatric Association. In some states, including California and New Jersey, subjecting someone under the age of 18 to such treatment is illegal.

Family Planning

Like any Heterosexual person or couple might, many Queer individuals and couples want to have children. A report by the Williams Institute (Gates, Badgett, Macomber, & Chambers, 2007) estimated that roughly half of all Gays and Lesbians desire to have a child. One of the benefits that come from being in a same-sex relationship is that there are no "surprise" babies, or unintended pregnancies. However, creating larger families within a same-sex relationship is also more difficult. Same-sex individuals and couples who choose to rear children typically do so via *in-vitro* fertilization or adoption. Donor insemination, fostering, adoption, and surrogacy are potential options, but each of these comes with its own set of costs, risks, and difficult decisions that the couple must negotiate (Goldberg, 2010). Access to all of these options is largely dependent on resources, including access to donors, sperm banks, or surrogates, geographical location, insurance benefits, and finances.

For female/female relationships who elect to create a child through *in-vitro* fertilization, choosing who will become pregnant, whose eggs will be used, whether they will use an anonymous or known sperm donor, whether to use fertility drugs, and how many attempts will be made if the first one is unsuccessful complicate the issue of creating children. In addition, the average cost of such procedure is thousands of dollars per attempt (Goldberg, 2010). This can be prohibitive for many parents, especially low-income couples or single parents. For male/male couples, the process of finding a *surrogate mother* can also be both challenging and expensive. On top of the already expensive and exhausting process of surrogacy, the legal fees and processes to protect the interests of the adopting parents is something that must be discussed and explored.

> Check out the Williams Institute, a research and advocacy organization, for more information on Queer individuals, couples, and families at http://williamsinstitute.law.ucla.edu/

Adoption is also a tricky process, regardless of what type of person or couple is adopting. However, it is especially difficult for Queer folk to adopt because they are facing social stigma and political discrimination that those who are not Queer do not necessarily face. Some states explicitly prohibit same-sex adoption, or *second-parent adoptions* for same-sex couples (i.e., the non-biological parent legally adopts the child so that both partners would then have legal rights to the child). Many states have ambiguous language concerning whether same-sex couples can adopt. Because there is not a universal protection for same-sex parental adoptions, scary and tragic situations arise for interstate travel.

Even if states recognize same-sex adoptions or marriages, parents still face unjust hardship and discrimination from adoption agencies which may discriminate against Queer parents. Furthermore, international adoptions are also made difficult for same-sex parents. Many countries, including Russia, Iran, and Bolivia have expressly prohibited same-sex adoptions, regardless if by an individual or couple. South Africa is the only African nation that allows same-sex couples to adopt.

> Gay Parent Magazine offers the personal parenting stories of LGB folks and a whole lot more. You can subscribe or pay to view digital downloads at http://www.gayparentmag.com

PARENTING. In addition to the challenges that all couples face in transitioning to parenthood, Lesbian, Gay, and Bisexual couples face a number of unique issues related to being parents. First, they must choose to become parents, which is often made difficult by internalized homophobic beliefs that, for example, their relationship is wrong, their children will suffer, or that kids need a mother and a father (Goldberg, 2010). Of course, these internalized beliefs reflect cultural myths about the "dangers" to children of being raised by Queer parents. Some couples may also struggle with differences in motivation for becoming parents; one partner may want to become a parent, and the other may not (Goldberg, 2010). Once the decision has been made to become parents, couples must figure out how to bring children into their family. Finally, after becoming parents, couples must then cope with and respond to the challenges of parenting in a homophobic and heterosexist culture (Goldberg, 2010).

> One prominent myth about Queer parenting is that, either by effort on the part of the parents or simply by exposure, children will also turn out to be Queer. There has been so scientific evidence to support this claim (Schlatter & Steinback, 2010), and in fact Queer parents may experience great societal pressure to raise Heterosexual and gender-normative kids (Lev, 2010)!

Even given these challenges, there has been no evidence that children raised by same-sex parents are worse off than children raised by opposite-sex parents (American Psychological Association, 2004). In a 2004 policy statement, the American Psychological Association noted that "there is no scientific evidence that parenting effectiveness is related to parental sexual orientation [and that] the adjustment, development, and psychological well-being of children is unrelated to parental sexual orientation" (n.p.). Furthermore, same-sex couples can bring a number of unique strengths and qualities to their roles as parents. First, many parents are able to push the boundaries of what it typically means to be a mother or a father, such that they become blended, no longer based on gender (Goldberg, 2010). Additionally, same-sex couples may be less conventional in their parenting and may be more tolerant of their child's noncon-forming behaviors or self-expressions. Finally, Queer parents may be motivated to explicitly teach their children to have greater toler-ance for and acceptance of all differences (Goldberg, 2010; Goldberg, Downing, & Moyer, 2012).

> For a list of books, movies, and resources concerning same-sex adoptions, parenting, or family planning, see the end of this chapter.

SAME-SEX COUPLES

Recent research has legitimized same-sex couple relationships as being more similar than different from Heterosexual relationships in many aspects, including challenges, areas of conflict, and overall relationship satisfaction (Gotta et al., 2011; Kurdek, 1994; 1998; 2000; Otis, Rostosky, Riggle, & Hamrin, 2006) . Still, to assume that a same-sex couple relationship is "just like any other (Heterosexual) relationship" would be incorrect, if not harmful. It is important for us to recognize the contexts, experiences, and qualities that are a part of and unique to same-sex couple relationships, the sources of strength and resiliency, and the factors that contribute to satisfying, long-term relationships. We will begin by reviewing some of what we know about the challenges and strengths unique to same-sex couple relationships, followed by a brief overview of factors that contribute to relationship longevity and satisfaction. We conclude with a discussion of what we still don't know.

As we review what we "know," keep in mind that there is a great deal of diversity in Queer couple experiences both between and within couples. Social locations such as race, class, education, age, geographical location, and gender socialization interact to affect each partner and each couple system differently. Furthermore, it is important to consider *mixed orientation* relationships—relationships in which one partner identifies as Lesbian, Gay, or Bisexual and the other does not—in our conversation about same-sex relationships. Mixed orientation relationships can occur for a variety of reasons, perhaps most commonly because one partner identifies as Bisexual and is currently in a relationship with a Heterosexual partner of the opposite sex. However, an LGB partner might also enter into a relationship, or even marriage, with an opposite-sex Heterosexual partner because they do not know they are Lesbian, Gay, or Bisexual, or because of shame about their sexual attractions, external pres-sures, or too great a risk to be out (Grever, 2012). Often, the LGB partner's sexual orientation will be revealed, either by choice or otherwise. Although this disclosure can be devastating to the Het-erosexual partner, and the majority of these relationships end in divorce, some couples choose to remain together (Grever, 2012).

> Lesbian, Gay and Bisexual couple relationships are more similar to, than different from, Heterosexual relationships

Challenges and Strengths

For all couples, "making it," or staying together and happy in one's relationship, is no easy feat. Lesbian, Gay, and Bisexual couples face all of the same kinds of challenges that Heterosexual couples face, plus others, including finding one's partner, managing societal oppression and visibility of their identities, establishing a relationship without a roadmap or role model, finding support and community, negotiating sexuality, parenting, and "making it" without legal recog-nition or protection. Many of these challenges, as you will see, are a result of living in a culture and context that has not yet made space for affirming same-sex relationships as equal to male/ female ones. Yet in spite of this, or perhaps because of it, many same-sex couples experience long-term, healthy, and satisfying relationships. These relationships speak to great strength and resiliency.

FINDING ONE'S PARTNER. Until recently, Lesbians, Gay men, and Bisexual individuals had few places through which to find partners (Goldberg, 2010). With increasing tolerance and visibility, Queer folks are finding opportunities to meet partners in a variety of Queer-focused contexts, such as political groups, support groups, church groups, social events, and Internet dating sites, as well as the traditional avenues of Gay bars and friendship networks. Still, finding partners can be a challenge, perhaps especially in rural areas or more conservative communities. Becoming a couple brings risks, as it makes one's identity as a sexual minority more visible. Despite the cultural shift toward tolerance of Queer identities and relationships, oppression and discrimination are still very real (Goldberg, 2010).

MANAGING OPPRESSION AND NEGOTIATING VISIBILITY. Societal oppression for LGB folks is often understood as *homophobia* and *heterosexism*. Homophobia refers to the discrimination, violence, and a lack of legal protection. Heterosexism, on the other hand, is the dominant discourse that Heterosexuality is the normal, correct, or preferred way of being (Connolly, 2004). Societal oppression creates an experience of what has been called *minority stress*. Meyer (1995) proposes three processes of minority stress: *internalized homophobia* (taking on society's negative beliefs about one's sexual orientation and directing them to one's self) *perceived stigma* (maintaining constant vigilance in anticipation of discrimination or harm) and *prejudice events* (the actual experiences of discrimination, oppression, violence, etc.). Research has suggested that minority stress is related not only to perceived relationship quality, but also increased risk for domestic violence, mental illness, and lower life satisfaction (Balsam & Szymanski, 2005; Otis et al., 2006). Each of these processes takes energy to maintain, adds to the every-day stressors of life, and can negatively impact the same-sex couple relationship.

> Coming out is a continual process, not a one-time event.

Same-sex couples must manage minority stress both individually and, as a couple, are challenged with the additional stress of managing the visibility of their LGB individual and couple identities (Connolly, 2004; Otis et al., 2006). Coming out is a continual process, not a one-time event. *Visibility management* means making choices about when, how much, and to whom to disclose about one's identity and relationship. It involves things like how the couple behaves together in public places, how each partner manages inquiries about their family life, or whether to display pictures of the couple at work, or even in their home. Sometimes couples do not agree on their level of visibility, and partners who are at different stages of identity development or coming out may be particularly vulnerable to experiencing conflict around visibility management (Connolly, 2004).

LACK OF ROADMAPS OR ROLE-MODELS. Most Queer folks do not grow up with Queer parents; there is comparatively little representation of Queer relationships in the media, and the dominant culture is only beginning to make space for same-sex couples to be openly visible. In a world where Heterosexuality is the norm, Queer couples are tasked with the challenge of creating a relationship without a clear picture of how their relationship could be (Connolly, 2004) and what a "successful" same-sex or mixed-orientation relationship looks like (Shurts, 2008). Premarital counseling with heterosexual couples has been discussed with frequency in the counseling literature; however, little has been written about strategies and practices to serve same-sex couples planning to enter life partnerships. A review of the premarital counseling and same-sex couples counseling literature serves as a foundation for pre-union counseling recommendations (content areas, goals, and format. Men and women are socialized into complementary gender roles and expectations. These get incorporated into *Heterosexual scripts*, which are cultural norms that guide behavior, feelings, and perceptions, which are often the starting point for non-Heterosexual couples (Goldberg, 2010). For example, a common Heterosexual script is that when a man reaches his mid-to-late twenties, he should start thinking about creating his own family which includes finding a woman to marry and create their biological children. Of course, these scripts do not always apply so well to Queer couples. As couples attempt to figure out what will work for them, they can experience a stressful sense of ambiguity, uncertainty, lack of clarity, and even unconscious doubts about the likelihood of maintaining a long-term LGB relationship (Shurts, 2008).

At the same time, with few models or scripts dictating what their relationship "should" look like (Connolly, 2004), same-sex couples have the opportunity to create their relationship in a way that uniquely fits them; they can chart their own path, so to speak. In doing so, many Queer couples demonstrate creativity and flexibility in shifting away from the holds of patriarchy and traditional gender roles. Queer couple relationships tend to be more egalitarian than Heterosexual relationships, and partners are able to express, display, and identify with more flexible gender roles (Goldberg, 2010).

> Many same-sex couples demonstrate creativity and flexibility in shifting away from the holds of patriarchy and traditional gender roles.

FINDING SUPPORT AND COMMUNITY. Finding social support is an important challenge for Queer couple relationships (Connolly, 2004; Dziengel, 2012; Shurts, 2008), as it can greatly impact the success and well-being of the couple relationship (Connolly, 2004). In the dominant culture, there is often little validity, recognition, legal protection, or supportive services available to Queer couples (Connolly, 2004; Goldberg, 2010). Furthermore, same-sex couples may perceive less support from their families of origin (Connolly, 2004; Shurts, 2008), and often this perception is accurate. Additionally, some families invalidate the couple as not "real," either by directly refusing to acknowledge the couple as a couple or by excluding one partner in family expectations or events. These kinds of responses might also be experienced from other sources of support, like church groups, friends, or other social memberships. Racially and ethnically diverse Queer couples are particularly vulnerable to a lack of family and community support, including support from the Queer community itself (Goldberg, 2010), as racial discrimination may still be present (Lehavot, Balsam, & Ibrahim-Wells, 2009).

In response to a lack of support from their family of origin and other community groups, however, LGB couples often create a *family of choice*—a support network of people whom the couple has chosen as their family (Blumer & Murphy, 2011). This is an important source of strength, coping, and protection for the couple relationship; it is also another demonstration of the creativity, flexibility, and resiliency of LGB couples (Oswald, 2002).

SEXUAL RELATIONSHIPS. Sexual relationships in Lesbian, Gay, and Bisexual partnerships sometimes present partners with a challenge. As mentioned previously, men and women are socialized to complement each other in many ways, including their sexual relationship. For example: men are socialized to initiate sex, and women are socialized to be passive participants. Men are socialized to be primarily concerned with their own pleasure, and women are also socialized to privilege the sexual needs and desires of men. Thus, negotiating sexual intimacy as a couple as it relates to gender roles and expectations may be a challenge for some Queer couples who reject this Heterosexual script (Spitalnick & McNair, 2005). Yet, again, it may also be an opportunity for greater flexibility and authenticity in sexual exploration and expression. Two women in a sexual relationship may have greater room to explore their own eroticism, and share in the erotic experience, in a space where there are not men. A Bisexual man may enjoy when female partners initiate sex, but may prefer to initiate sex when being intimate with other men. One of the strengths of the Queer movement, and sexual revolution of the 1960s and beyond, is the greater freedom and flexibility to explore and practice a sexuality that is more individually authentic and satisfying.

Another potential area of challenge/creativity for Queer couples is in negotiating monogamy. Not all Queer relationships are monogamous. This may be especially true for Gay men (Goldberg, 2010) and can be a particularly salient issue for Bisexual folks (Rust, 2003). Mixed orientation couples also likely face this challenge. Of course, nonmonogamy does not imply infidelity. Rather, some Queer couples negotiate an open relationship, or *Polyamory*, with rules, boundaries, and agreements that feel right to them as a couple. Polyamory, from the Greek for "multiple loves," is similar to the idea of having open relationships, in that it leaves open a space for engaging in more than one sexual, intimate, and/or romantic relationship, and some couples may use the term interchangeably. A Polyamorous relationship can look many ways: one person who is intimate with multiple people but lives as a single person, a couple who is intimate with other individuals or couples, a family of three or more adults who live as one intimate relationship, and so on. There are endless

> Not all Queer couples are monogamous, but non-monogamy does not imply infidelity.

combinations and expressions of Polyamory. However, Polyamory is also a set of values and beliefs about love, intimacy, and relationships (Anapol, 2010). Although negotiating an open or Polyamorous relationship may be challenging, it can also be a creative avenue toward greater fulfillment of diverse needs, social support, and even stability. Polyamory is also not a new. Some evolutionary scholars argued that early humans lived in large, Polyamorous clans and that Polyamory has been the main expression of sexual and intimacy for the majority of human history (Ryan & Jethá, 2010). They argue that the concept of Monogamy is more of a cultural construct endorsed by early religions, governments, and societal groups and has continued since.

LACK OF LEGAL RECOGNITION AND PROTECTION. When a couple gets married, they are recognized as a legitimate family unit not only by their own family members, friends, and community, but also by the government. Along with this legal recognition come a number of legal protections and privileges that affect rights to property and estates, finances, children, and even access to one another (Polikoff, 2008). In the event of a partner's death, for example, not having legal recognition and protection of their relationship can be devastating to a same-sex couple; the surviving partner could lose everything that is legally recognized as belonging to the deceased, and may even lose the ability to make end-of-life decisions on behalf of their loved-one. Furthermore, marriage has been found to act as a barrier to relationship dissolution, and the lack of this barrier leaves same-sex couples at greater risk of breaking up (Kurdek, 1998, 2000).

The National Conference on State Legislature (www .ncsl) offers a US map of states that allow same-sex marriage as well as an updated history of the development of same-sex marriage legislation at the state level.

Historically, same-sex couples did not have access to legal protection or recognition of any kind. It was not until 2000 that Vermont initiated the first form of legal recognition and protection, a civil union, to same-sex couples (Solomon, Rothblum, & Balsam, 2004). This gave couples nearly all of the state benefits available by marriage. Still, none of these were available outside of Vermont, and none were available federally (as they would be in a traditional marriage). In 2004, Massachusetts became the first state in the United States to offer same-sex marriage, and prior to the U.S. Supreme Court's landmark ruling in 2015, 37 states and the District of Columbia had legalized it.

Clearly, many same-sex couples still live in places in which they have little or no legal recognition or protection. Yet even for those who have the option to marry, the choice is not necessarily an easy one. Although the state may recognize a same-sex relationship as equal to a Heterosexual one, many communities, church groups, and families may not. Partners themselves may struggle with internalized beliefs that it is wrong to marry someone of the same sex. Furthermore, parts of the Queer community advocate that getting married is an attempt to assimilate to heteronormative ideals of what it means to be family (Van Eeden-Moorefield, Martell, Williams, & Preston, 2011) This is *homonormativity,* or the idea that some LGB folks attempt to create their lives and relationships to become the same as Heterosexual ones. Thus, same-sex couples who desire to become married might even encounter disapproval from within their own Queer community (Van Eeden-Moorefield, Martell, Williams, & Preston, 2011).

Maintaining successful long-term relationships without legal protection is further testament to same-sex couples' strength and resiliency. Couples who cannot or do not get married have found creative ways to recognize, honor, and celebrate their relationships. They may perform their own non-marital commitment ceremony. Some may demonstrate commitment by taking on other legally binding arrangements, such as owning a house, taking advantage of partnership benefits at work, having children together (Porche & Purvin, 2008). For many couples, celebrating couple-relevant anniversaries becomes another important way of honoring their relationship (Degges-White & Marszalek, 2006).

OTHER IMPORTANT FACTORS. So far, we have discussed some of the unique challenges and contexts that LGB couples face, as well as some of the internal and external resources and strengths that couples use to get through these challenges, often with flying colors (so to speak). The combination of these challenges and resources in addition to the couple's other unique qualities can affect each couple relationship in numerous ways. It is helpful, then, to have a sense of some of the factors that seem to be particularly important to Queer couple longevity and satisfaction.

Qualities of Queer couples who maintain their relationship for the long term are not often studied, so what we know about factors that contribute to longevity is still limited. Recent studies have identified factors related to relationship resiliency and longevity for same-sex couples who had been together for ten or more years (Connolly, 2005; Dziengel, 2012; Porche & Purvin, 2008). Emerging trends from these studies suggest at least four important factors: a high level of commitment to and openness about their identity, the ability to protect the relationship and overcome factors contributing to minority stress, developing a strong couple identity, and utilizing external supports (such as developing other Queer friends or participating in Queer community groups). Thinking about the challenges presented above, it is easy to see how these relationship qualities are likely to serve as protective factors to the couple relationship.

More frequently studied than influences to couple longevity are influences to relationship quality and satisfaction. These inquiries are often done in comparison to Heterosexual couples and, as mentioned previously, suggest that there are no significant differences between relationship satisfaction of, say, Gay couples and that of Heterosexual couples (e.g., Gottman et al., 2003; Kurdek, 1998). Previous research has demonstrated that while the debates themselves have had largely negative impacts on same sex couples, the resulting legalization of same-sex marriage is widely associated with better mental, physical, and relational health among same-sex couples and families (Buffie, 2011). While the debates are occurring, couples in same-sex relationships frequently report feeling as though their lives are under scrutiny and suddenly in the public domain (Lannutti, 2005). For the over eight million (Gates, 2011) individuals in the US with same-sex attractions, and over 125,000 same-sex couples who are raising children, same-sex marriage builds the space for same-sex couples to experience the same family life trajectory made popular in the children's adage *first comes love, then comes marriage, then comes a baby in a baby carriage* (Gates, 2013; Herdt & Kertzner, 2006).

Also, same sex individuals, couples, and families who live in states that allow for same-sex marriage demonstrate significantly lower levels of depression, greater relational satisfaction, decreased rates of heart disease, diabetes and other stress related illnesses, and lower rates of anxiety (Buffie, 2011; Hatzenbuehler et al., 2009; Rostosky, Dekhtyar, Cupp, & Anderman, 2008).

INTIMATE RELATIONSHIPS FOR OUR TRANSGENDERED LOVED ONES

Cultural ideals about what it means for a person to be a man or a woman, a girl or a boy, influence our behaviors, perceptions, and identities. These influences are perhaps clearest in our most intimate relationships: with our partners and families. The very labels we use to name family relationships, such as husband/wife, mother/father, daughter/son, brother/sister, aunt/uncle, grandfather/grandmother are defined by the sex of the person (e.g., a male parent is a "father," a female sibling is a "sister"), and the roles and expectations for behavior within these relationships are based on gender (e.g., daughters are expected to take ballet classes and sons are expected to take karate, grandfathers are to dress in cardigans and have ear hair, and grandmothers are supposed to dress in floral blouses and give the best hugs).

There are endless cultural norms, which change constantly, that dictate how people who were assigned as "male" at birth are supposed to act throughout their lives. These norms are different than those who influence people that were assigned as female at birth are to act. Those that venture too far away from those norms stand out as odd, weird, or freakish. Not every person, however, fits neatly into the "male" or "female" box. Further, their behaviors, values, and self-expressions (their gender) are not exclusively masculine or feminine, but can be somewhere in the middle or outside of this *gender binary*. For some people, the roles and expectations placed on them simply because of their physical sex are too limiting and do not make space for their authentic expression of self. For others, their physical (birth) sex simply does not fit the gender they know themselves to be. For example, while a person's body may physically appear as female, *he* knows that *he* is male. Although it is improving, the current cultural climate makes little space for divergence from the gender norm. "Gender issues can often shake the foundation of the basic notions of intimacy, security, and stability" (Lev, 2004, p. 248). Thus, in many family relationships, identifying and/or expressing one's self outside of the gender binary can create significant challenges. There is probably no one who acts *exclusively* masculine or feminine at all times with all things; even the most masculine man may enjoy watching a "chick flick", and the most feminine woman may also enjoy boxing. However, when someone feels a great discrepancy between their sex and gender, so much that it is hard to feel authentic to both, then a person may be Transgender or Transsexual.

The term *Transgender* is used as an umbrella term to encompass variations and sub-categories of identities and behaviors that do not fit the norms of the traditional gender binary. Transgender often gets confused with *Transsexuality*, which is a sub-category under the Transgender umbrella. Transsexuality refers to individuals who believe their biological sex (the sex they were assigned at birth) does not match their true sex (the sex they deeply believe themselves to be). This struggle often causes a great deal of stress. Some, but not all, who identify as Transsexual choose to undergo medical procedures such as hormones, surgery, hair removal, etc., in order to live more authentically (Lev, 2010). Thus, identifying as Transgender does not mean one wants to transition genders; Transgender-identified folks have many life-affirming choices, of which gender transitioning is just one. At the same time, many Transgender folks express a strong desire for gender reassignment, but, for some, this may be influenced by cultural pressures, as it is much easier to fit the gender binary than to try to find authentic ways to live outside of these boxes (Raj, 2008).

> Identifying as Transgender does not mean one wants to Transition genders; it is just one of many life-affirming choices.

Transgender (or *Trans*) identities and experiences are often lumped together under the Queer umbrella. This may be, in part, because gender and sexual orientation are so closely connected, or that they experience very similar (yet not identical) struggles, discriminations, and successes. Indeed, the Transgender community shares many similar experiences with the sexual minority community such as discrimination, intolerance, lack of legal recognition, rejection, fear, violence, and limited resources. This is because both are Queer minorities in a cultural climate that is largely heterosexist, and oppressive. Certainly, Trans folks struggle with the three-fold burdens of minority stress (internalized homophobia, perceived stigma, and prejudice events) as discussed above (Hendricks & Testa, 2012). Yet it is essential to recognize that many gender minority (Transgender) experiences are importantly different from sexual minority (such as Lesbian, Gay, Bisexual, and Polyamorous) experiences, both on individual and relational levels.

> Transgender folks experience a mixed-bag of emotions and reactions, many of which change over time.

TRANSGENDER FOLKS. In a world where so much of whom we are is defined by gender, existing outside of gendered expectations can be, at worst, devastating, and at best, liberating. Most often, the experience for Transgender folks involves a mixed bag of emotions and reactions, many of which change over time. Lev (2010) offers a developmental model for understanding a Transgender person's *stages of emergence*. The six stages of Transgender emergence include: (1) Awareness— the Trans person recognizes and acknowledges that they are different, which often brings on a flood of overwhelming feelings such as frustration, distress, dysphoria, and terror; (2) Seeking information and reaching out—the Trans person begins to seek support for and education about what it means to be Transgendered and what their options are; (3) Disclosure to significant others— as they become more comfortable and liberated in their gender divergences, Trans folks long to share their authentic selves with their loved ones, yet they are also aware of the real risk of losing their partners and family members in response to their disclosure. Thus, they begin to disclose their Transgendered identity to loved ones cautiously: (4) Exploring identity and Transition—at this point, the Trans person has come to terms with their gender variance and begins to search for the most authentic way to understand, express, and label this part of their identity; (5) Exploring Transition and possible body modification—in this stage, the Trans person has figured out how they want to express gender, which for some includes making decisions about modifying their physical body, medically or otherwise; (6) Integration and pride—in the last stage of Transgender emergence, a person has fully integrated their Trans identity with their sense of who they are and how they live; many in this stage experience a sense of pride over their identity and the journey that they have taken in getting there.

PARTNERS, PARENTS, CHILDREN, AND OTHER LOVED ONES. When a Transgendered person discloses his or her identity to their loved ones, the response is often intense (Lev, 2010). Loved ones experience a range of emotions, including shock, confusion, grief, loss, anger, and fear. They are likely to experience a change in their relationship with their Trans-loved one and even a shift in their own identity within that relationship (Raj, 2008). For example, a father's sense of identity and relationship with a son is likely very different than his sense of identity and relationship with a daughter. Family members might even experience shifts in cultural status, rejection or discrimination from their communities, and struggles with religious or cultural beliefs. Particularly when their Transgendered loved one transitions genders, family members struggle to make sense of and find meaning in the change within their family system (Norwood, 2013). Many experience a sense of ambiguous loss—their loved one is here and yet gone, the same and yet different. Because Transgenderism is rarely understood or accepted, many family members feel isolated and struggle to find much-needed social support.

Like the Transgendered person, family members also undergo a process of emergence. Briefly, the four stages of family emergence, as proposed by Lev (2004), are: (1) Discovery and disclosure—the family finds out; (2) Turmoil—the family is characterized by chaos, turmoil, stress, and conflict as loved-ones struggle to come to terms; (3) Negotiation—the family realizes that this is not going to change and attempts to find compromise; (4) Finding balance—in the final stage, the family is no longer in turmoil and the Trans person is re-integrated. Thus, when a person comes out and lives a Transgender life, they do not do so in a vacuum, but this Transition affects the family just as the family affects the individual. The family adjusts and goes through a process of change as well. When done so with love, trust, and honesty, the family can come out of this Transition stronger, closer, and more satisfied than ever (LaSala, 2010).

Importantly, it is not just partners and immediate family who learn about and must adjust to the Transgender identity; it is also extended family and in-laws, employers and co-workers, friends and neighbors, teachers and students (Raj, 2008). Some families and loved ones may be able to Transition at the same time as the Trans-identified member by shifting roles, rules, interactions, and identities so that the family can remain intact. Other families may not be able to adjust and adapt and may, instead, break apart or experience significant distress. If the Trans person is a parent and their partnership ends, both the partners and the children are at risk of custody battles and parenting issues. Fortunately, there is no evidence that simply being raised by a Transgender parent or parents negatively affects children (American Academy of Child & Adolescent Psychiatry [AACAP], 2013), although conflict and discord certainly can.

> It is not just partners and immediate family who learn about and adjust to the Transgender identity; it is also extended family and in-laws, employers and co-workers, friends and neighbors, teachers and students.

There are a few additional considerations for partners of Transgendered folks. Partners in a relationship with a Trans person before they transition share the above-mentioned experiences and a few others. More so than other family members, partners have the choice of whether to remain in the relationship. Although many couple relationships end after the disclosure of a Trans identity, not all do (Malpas, 2006). If their loved one Transitions genders or sexes, one of the issues faced by partners who choose to stay in the relationship may be of a shift in their perceived sexual orientation. This might also bring a shift in status and privilege. Transgender partners may experience shifts in their own sexual desires, which presents further challenges to the couple relationship, although this may be less so when both partners identify as Bisexual (AACAP, 2013). Partners who knowingly enter into a relationship with a Transgendered person may also be considered a sexual minority, even if the relationship is Heterosexual, simply because they have an interest in Transgendered bodies (Malpas, 2006). Finally, couples in which one member is Transgender, and particularly if that partner has undergone a hormonal or surgical gender Transition, may face challenges in becoming parents. These challenges, and their solutions, are likely to be similar to those encountered by same-sex parents.

> Visit http://www.transequality.org/federal_gov.html for more information on Trans issues and what you and your local and federal government can do to help.

SOCIETAL AND POLITICAL CHALLENGES. As a whole, our society's attention to Transgender issues, needs, and civil rights lags far behind even the Lesbian, Gay, and Bisexual movement. The National Counsel for Transgender Equality (2011) has outlined 13 critical issues that negatively affect Transgendered individuals and their loved ones, and until addressed, prevent them from participating as equals in our society.

1. *Discrimination:* Transgender folks are discriminated against, particularly in healthcare and employment, at rates disproportionate to other minority groups.
2. *Economic opportunity:* Many workplaces refuse to hire Transgendered people, and many states still allow employers to fire Trans employees because of their Transgendered identities. Moreover, Trans folks often experience harassment and even physical or sexual violence in the workplace. As a result, Transgendered individuals have a higher rate of unemployment than their non-Transgendered counterparts.
3. *Identification documents and privacy:* For the majority of Transsexual individuals, updating all of their personal and legal documentation to reflect their authentic gender is prohibitive due to strict and difficult requirements that the Transsexual person may not meet, may not be able to afford, or may not have the resources to pursue. Identification that continues to display a previous gender status discloses the Trans person's Transgendered status and puts them at risk for discrimination, denial of employment and housing benefits, and even physical violence.
4. *Health:* Transgender folks are less likely to have insurance, and even if they do, it is unlikely that their plans cover Transgender-related healthcare needs. Furthermore, Trans folks face a number of high risk of health concerns including HIV/AIDS, depression and suicide risk, and substance abuse, and few health care professionals are trained on either Transgender issues or how to work sensitively with Transgendered patients.
5. *Homelessness:* It is estimated that one in five Transgendered people has experienced homelessness in their lives. Combined with frequent housing and employment discrimination, remaining homeless becomes a reality for many Trans folk.
6. *Safe and supportive schools:* An alarming number of Trans youth report being bullied in school, and many experience physical assaults. This affects not only the Trans youth's success in school, but also puts them at high risk for attempting suicide.
7. *Veterans and military issues:* Currently Transgendered people are not allowed to enter into military service. Veterans who have served and then later Transitioned often lose access to health care, and inflexible documentation rules often restrict access to other benefits, such as education.
8. *Improving the lives of Transgender older adults:* Folks in their senior years have a great need for comprehensive health care services and, as previously discussed, these are often inaccessible or unavailable to Trans folks. Additionally, Transgender seniors have reported experiencing discrimination and outright abuse in their long-term care facilities.
9. *Immigration:* Transgender immigrants face all of the challenges that gender-typical immigrants face, with the additional challenges of unclear documentation, difficulty getting recognition for their marital status to a U.S. citizen, and overt discrimination.
10. *Federal prisons:* Transgender folks in federal prisons often do not receive necessary health care, recognition of their authentic gender identity, or protection from harassment, violence and rape, and they are often placed with prisoners of the same birth sex, but not the Trans person's "true" sex (e.g., a male-to-female Trans woman would be placed in a men's prison because she still has male genitals).
11. *Family and partnership recognition:* Transgendered folks and their loved ones are often denied recognition as a legitimate family. This prevents them from having equal access to rights such as adoption and fostering, Family and Medical Leave Act benefits, and even marital rights.
12. *Hate crimes:* Transgendered people experience an extremely high level of intentional and brutal violence, so much so that an average of over one Trans-person is murdered every month. Additional minority identities (race, class, etc.) increase the risk, putting young low-income Trans women of color at the highest risk.
13. *Travel:* Although this has recently been improving, Trans folks who wish to travel by plane face a number of challenges, including documentation issues and harassment by security and airline personnel.

Clearly, there is much work to be done, socially and politically, to provide a safe, supportive, and equal society for our Transgendered loved ones.

On top of these critical social and political considerations, Transgendered folks face the everyday challenges of negotiating life in a gender-normative world. Our cultural discourse about sex and gender suggests that sex is biological and dichotomous and that gender is a natural, essential byproduct of our sex (Norwood, 2013). Much of our life and our world is classified by this gender dichotomy—bathrooms, social groups, sports, roles in relationships, and so on. Let's consider this as it might apply to using public restrooms. If one is born male, for example, one is a male, even if one dresses like and believes one's self to be a female. Therefore, one must use the men's restroom. For a Transgendered woman, however, using the men's bathroom would likely feel wrong, shameful, or even scary.

Furthermore, everything we "do" gets assessed in terms of our performance in our gender (West & Zimmerman, 1990). For example, how we walk, how we talk, and even how we throw a baseball are assessed in terms of whether they demonstrate ourselves as a male or a female. In her memoir, *She's not there: A life in two genders,* Jennifer Finney Boylan (2003) discusses the challenges she faced in trying to learn and demonstrate all of these social rules as a female when she had spent her entire life as a male. To change these experiences for our Transgendered loved ones, then, we must change some of our fundamental ideas about what it means to be male or female and whether all of the separations between genders are truly necessary.

ASEXUALITY

Alongside Heterosexuality, Homosexuality, and Bisexuality, Asexuality is a sexual identity. Unlike the others, Asexuality is often misunderstood or highly rejected to even exist. *Asexuality* is defined as the absence of interest in sexual contact or sexual intimacy. Although asexual people are still interested in having close relationships, they have little or no interest in sexual activity. Asexuality should not be confused with celibacy, which is the conscious choice to abstain from sexual activities, despite desire or attraction. A study conducted in 1994 found that 1 percent of the population may be Asexual; however, 30 percent of people initially contacted by the researchers declined to participate in the study, indicating that Asexuals may have been under-represented. Less sexually experienced individuals are more likely to refuse to participate in studies about sexuality, and asexual individuals are more likely to be less sexually experienced. It is therefore estimated that this number is actually higher.

Although it is still rarely discussed in public discourse or seen in popular culture, the movement to recognize Asexuality as being a legitimate sexual orientation is growing. Because researchers and clinicians are still at an initial stage of understanding Asexuality, we do not really know what causes it (or, conversely, what causes one to desire sexual contact). In fact, society-at-large is just beginning to learn about how to support people who identify as Asexual in their close relationships. Problems arise when Asexuality is mistaken with problems with intimacy or low sex drive. Scherrer (2008) argues that Asexuality presents an array of options for intimate relationships, including *heteroromantic* (romantic attraction toward persons of a different gender), *homoromantic* (romantic attraction toward someone of the same gender), *and aromantic* (lack of romantic attraction toward anyone). There is also significant variation among people who identify as asexual. Some, for instance, participate in sexual activity out of curiosity or for the sake of their partner; some report that they feel sexual attraction but have no desire to act on it; and some are averse to some sexual acts (such as intercourse) but not to others, such as kissing or cuddling. A person who is Asexual may masturbate or self-pleasure, but this is not universal (Brotto, Knudson, Inskip, Rhodes, & Erskine, 2008).

So, what if you are thinking that you might be Asexual? Because of the lack of research in this area, most of the really helpful resources are grassroots organizations. The Asexual Visibility and Education Network (AVEN) is a website and online community that was founded by David Jay in 2001 to increase resources and community among people like himself who identify as asexual (Hills, 2012). You can find their webpage online at: http://www.asexuality.org. Multiple resources exist on this page, including a number of community forums. You might also find it helpful to visit your college's LGBT/Ally office and get more local support.

If you have a friend who lets you know that they identify as Asexual, the best thing you can do is listen, support them, and appreciate the vulnerability that they showed in coming out to you. Part of what makes it so difficult to come out as an Asexual person is the fact that sexuality permeates American society; to not feel a drive toward sex with another person is often viewed as deviant or even pathological (Leiblum, 2002). Realizing that your sexuality does not fit into an easy box can be a really difficult and confusing experience. Asexual individuals face "coming out" just as individuals from other sexual orientations do and need just as much support and understanding.

> Even though I can't fully grasp it or understand the desire, it makes a little more sense to me how people feel sexual attraction . . . I'll see someone and think, 'they're cute, they have a nice personality.' But then my brain goes 'Look at their butt.' Maybe their butt is aesthetically pleasing. But I don't have a sexual urge to touch it. —RhaposodyinRed, AVEN Online Forum.

WHAT WE DON'T KNOW

ABOUT QUEER YOUTH, ADULTS, AND FAMILIES. While Queer people have always existed, we are entering a time in American history where the number of legally-recognized same-sex marriages and parents is greater than ever. Also, the amount of "out" Americans continues to climb as fears of rejection, discrimination, or harassment dissipate. The long-term impacts that homophobia has on our nation's well-being are still unknown, as it is still very present and palpable. However, nations that are Queer-affirmative also tend to report a greater quality of life in general (Rodriquez, 2008). While there is some interest among family researchers regarding the Queer experience, there is still a lack of information about topics such as immigration, aging, and homelessness in the Queer community. In fact, Queer research has been largely ignored by the field of family science and family therapy (La Sala, 2013). Also, some sexual identities are rarely researched and overwhelmingly misunderstood, such as Polyamory, Asexuality, and Kink.

ABOUT SAME-SEX RELATIONSHIPS. It has only been within the past couple of decades, a relatively short amount of time, that we have turned our attention to same-sex couple relationships. Thus, it may be fair to say that what we do not know is a whole lot more than what we *think* we do know. For one, we do not yet have an accurate picture of how many same-sex couple relationships there are; we have not historically had a way of acknowledging or recording them, and it has been and often continues to be unsafe for same-sex couples disclose their relationships (Van Eeden-Moorefield et al., 2011). We also do not know a whole lot about diversity within LGB couple relationships. Much of what we know comes from research samples of easily accessible, visible, and research participation-inclined people. These tend to be White, educated, middle-class Lesbian and Gay people who are largely "out" and active in the Queer community. We know much less about other Queer couples whose various additional identities (race, ethnicity, class, age, etc.) are also minority identities, or about mixed-orientation (e.g. Bisexual-Lesbian, or Gay-Heterosexual) couples.

> What we do not know is a whole lot more than what we think we do know.

Although we are starting to learn what factors predict relationship success and satisfaction, we have a long way to go. As mentioned previously, Queer couples who have been together for a very long time have hardly been studied. Additionally, while increasing legal rights and recognition is a welcomed trend, it is too new to have a real sense of how it will affect same-sex couple relationships. As Lyness (2012) describes it, the legal landscape for same-sex couples is "often confusing and contradictory, and saddled with heterosexist norms, beliefs, and laws that result in continued oppression and discrimination" (p. 389). Relatedly, we currently know very little about Queer relationship dissolution, and there has been no research on same-sex divorce (Lyness, 2012). We also do not know whether premarital programs, which have shown success in increasing satisfaction and decreasing the risk for divorce in Heterosexual couples, will have similar benefits for LGB couples.

ABOUT TRANSGENDERED IDENTITIES. Although awareness is growing, it is important to keep in mind that we currently know very little about the issues, experiences, needs, and intimate relationships of Transgender folks and their families. Much of what we know comes from clinical and personal experiences with Transgendered folks, as opposed to research that could add validity to our assertions. The few research studies that are conducted typically use limited samples. Greater attention to Trans folks from diverse backgrounds is even more sorely needed. Male partners and spouses of Transgender men and women have been studied far less than female partners and spouses, and Transgender men have been studied far less than Transgender women (Malpas, 2012). As a whole, we know relatively little about Transgendered couple relationships, and even less about Transgender families or Transgender parenting practices. Some attention is now being directed to understanding Transgender children, which is beyond the scope of this chapter, but nevertheless continues to be an area worth greater exploration and attention. To put it simply, our understanding of Transgender individuals and their intimate relationships is in its infancy; we have a lot more to learn on all accounts.

> Our understanding of Transgender individuals and their intimate relationships is in its infancy.

CONCLUSION

You may have had various feelings while reading this chapter: anger, sorrow, joy, empathy, confusion, maybe even hope. Believe that we, as authors, experienced a plethora of feelings as well. That, in itself, is the beauty of the Queer movement. The movement encourages dialogue, understanding, reflection, change, and to *do* and *be* what we *feel* is authentic to ourselves. Harvey Milk, a dynamic and passionate leader in the Queer community in the 1970s, stated that "all young people, regardless of sexual orientation or identity, deserve a safe and supporting environment in which to achieve their full potential." Thanks to the brave work of many Queer figures, including fellow Gopher Alumni Richard Baker and James Michael McConnell (first couple to petition for marriage equality in the United States), and Brian Coyle (one of the first openly gay U.S. politicians), the lives of all families have improved. However, there is much more left to do to increase equity and the quality of life for Queer individuals and families. We have some big shoes to fill. Let us rally together and unite for the rights of all families. Ski-U-Mah!

REFERENCES

Adams, T. E. (2012). *Narrating the closet: An autoethnography of same-sex attraction*. Walnut Creek, CA: Left Coast Press.

Allen, L. B., Glicken, A. D., Beach, R. K., & Naylor, K. E. (1998). Adolescent health care experience of gay, lesbian, and bisexual young adults. *Journal of Adolescent Health, 23*(4), 212–220. doi:10.1016/S1054-139X(98)00022-6

American Academy of Child & Adolescent Psychiatry (2013). *Facts for families: Children with lesbian, gay, bisexual and transgender parents*. American Academy of Child & Adolescent Psychiatry. Retrieved from http://www.aacap.org/App_Themes/AACAP/docs/facts_for_families/92_children_with_lesbian_gay_bisexual_transgender_parents.pdf

American Psychological Association (2004). *Sexual orientation, parents, & children: Research summary*. Retrieved from http://www.apa.org/about/policy/parenting.aspx

Anapol, D. (2010). *Polyamory in the 21st century: Love and intimacy with multiple partners*. Lanham, MD: Rowman & Littlefield Publishers, Inc.

Balsam, K. F., & Szymanski, D. M. (2005). Relationship quality and domestic violence in women's same-sex relationships: The role of minority stress. *Psychology of Women Quarterly, 29*(3), 258–269. doi:10.1111/j.1471-6402.2005.00220.x

Baker v. Nelson, 191 NW 2d 185 - Minn: Supreme Court 1971

Bengtson, V.L. (2001). Beyond the nuclear family: The increasing importance of multigenerational bonds. *Journal of Marriage and Family, 63*, 1–16. doi:10.1111/j.1741-3737.2001.00001.x

Blumer, M., & Murphy, M. (2011). Alaskan gay males' couple experiences of societal non-support: Coping through families of choice and therapeutic means. *Contemporary Family Therapy: 33*(3), 273–290. doi:10.1007/s10591-011-9147-5

Bright, C. (2004). Deconstructing reparative therapy: An examination of the processes involved when attempting to change sexual orientation. *Clinical Social Work Journal, 32*(4), 471–481. doi:10.1007/s10615-012-0418-x

Brotto, L. A., Knudson, G., Inskip, J., Rhodes, K., & Erskine, Y. (2010). Asexuality: A mixed-methods approach. *Archives of Sexual Behavior, 39,* 599-618. doi:10.1007/s10508-008-9434-x.

Buffie, W. C. (2011). Public health implications of same-sex marriage. *Journal Information, 101*(6), 986–990. doi:10.2105/AJPH.2010.300112

Cass, V. C. (1984). Homosexual identity formation: Testing a theoretical model. *Journal of Sex Research, 20*(2), 143–167. doi:10.1080/00224498409551214

Coker, T. R., Austin, S. B., & Schuster, M. A. (2010). The health and health care of lesbian, gay, and bisexual adolescents. *Annual Review of Public Health, 31,* 457–477. doi:10.1146/annurev.publhealth.012809.103636

Coleman, E. (1982). Developmental stages of the coming out process. *Journal of Homosexuality, 7*(2), 31–43. doi:10.1300/J082v07n02_06

Connolly, C. (2004). Clinical issues with same-sex couples: A review of the literature. *Journal of Couple & Relationship Therapy, 3*(2/3), 3–12. doi:10.1300/J398v03n02_02

Connolly, C. (2005). A qualitative exploration of resilience in long-term lesbian couples. *Family Journal, 13*(3), 266–280. doi:10.1177/1066480704273681

D'Augelli, A., Hershberger, S., & Pilkin, N. (1998). Lesbian, gay, and bisexual youth and their families: Disclosure of sexual orientation and its consequences. *American Journal of Orthopsychiatry, 68*(3), 361–371. doi:10.1037/h0080345

Degges-White, S., & Marszalek, J. (2006). An exploration of long-term, same-sex relationships: Benchmarks, perceptions, and challenges. *Journal of LGBT Issues in Counseling, 1*(4), 99–119. doi:10.1300/J462v01n04_07

Dziengel, L. (2012). Resilience, ambiguous loss, and older same-sex couples: The resilience constellation model. *Journal of Social Service Research, 38*(1), 74–88. doi:10.1080/01488376.2011.626354

Finney Boylan, J. (2003). *She's not there: A life in two genders.* New York: Broadway Books.

Frost, D. M., & Meyer, I. H. (2009). Internalized homophobia and relationship quality among lesbians, gay men, and bisexuals. *Journal of Counseling Psychology, 56*(1), 97–109. doi:10.1037/a0012844

Gates, G. J. (2013). Same Sex and Different Sex Couples in the American Community Survey: 2005-2011. *Williams Institute.* Retrieved from: http://escholarship.org/uc/item/8dk71277

Gates, G. J. (2011). How many people are lesbian, gay, bisexual and transgender?. *Williams Institute.* Retrieved from: https://escholarship.org/uc/item/09h684x2

Gates, G. J., Badgett, M. L., Macomber, J. E., & Chambers, K. (2007). *Adoption and foster care by gay and lesbian parents in the United States.* Los Angeles, CA: Williams Institute.

Goldberg, A. E. (2010). *Lesbian and gay parents and their children: Research on the family life cycle.* Washington, DC: American Psychological Association.

Goldberg, A. E., Downing, J. B., & Moyer, A. M. (2012). Why parenthood? Why now? Gay men's motivation for pursuing parenthood. *Family Relations 61*(1), 157–174. doi:10.1111/j.1741-3729.2011.00687.x

Gotta, G., GREEN, R. J., Rothblum, E., Solomon, S., Balsam, K., & Schwartz, P. (2011). Heterosexual, lesbian, and gay male relationships: A comparison of couples in 1975 and 2000. *Family Process, 50*(3), 353–376. doi:10.1111/j.1545-5300.2011.01365.x.

Gottman, J. M., Levenson, R. W., Gross, J., Fredrickson, B. L., McCoy, K., Rosenthal, L., Yoshimoto, D. (2003). Correlates of gay and lesbian couples' relationship satisfaction and relationship dissolution. *Journal of Homosexuality, 45*(1), 23–43. doi:10.1300/J082v45n01_02

Grever, C. (2012). Helping heterosexual spouses cope when their husbands or wives come out. In J. J. Bigner & J. L. Wetchler (Eds.), *Handbook of LGBT-affirmative couple and family therapy* (pp. 265–282). New York: Routledge.

Grossman, A. H., Haney, A. P., Edwards, P., Alessi, E. J., Ardon, M., & Howell, T. J. (2009). Lesbian, gay, bisexual and transgender youth talk about experiencing and coping with school violence: A qualitative study. *Journal of LGBT Youth, 6*(1), 24–46. doi:10.1080/19361650802379748

Haldeman, D. C. (2002). Gay rights, patient rights: The implications of sexual orientation conversion therapy. *Professional Psychology: Research and Practice, 33*(3), 260–264. doi:10.1037/0735-7028.33.3.260

Hatzenbuehler, M. L. (2011). The social environment and suicide attempts in lesbian, gay, and bisexual youth. *Pediatrics, 127,* 896–903. Retrieved from http://pediatrics.aappublications.org/content/127/5/896.short

Hatzenbuehler, M. L. (2009). How does sexual minority stigma "get under the skin"? A psychological mediation framework. *Psychological Bulletin, 135,* 707–730. doi:10.1037/a0016441

Hatzenbuehler, M. L., McLaughlin, K. A., Keyes, K. M., & Hasin, D. S. (2010). The Impact of institutional discrimination on psychiatric disorders in lesbian, gay, and bisexual populations: A prospective study. *American Journal of Public Health, 100*(3), 452–459. doi:10.2105/AJPH.2009.168815

Hendricks, M., & Testa, R. (2012). A conceptual framework for clinical work with transgender and gender nonconforming clients: An adaptation of the Minority Stress Model. *Professional Psychology: Research & Practice, 43*(5), 460–467. doi:10.1037/a0029597

Herdt, G., & Kertzner, R. (2006). I do, but I can't: The impact of marriage denial on the mental health and sexual citizenship of lesbians and gay men in the United States. *Sexuality Research and Social Policy Journal of NSRC, 3*(1), 33–49. Retrieved from http://download.springer.com/static/pdf/802/art%253A10 .1525%252Fsrsp.2006.3.1.33.pdf?originUrl=http%3A%2F%2Flink.springer.com%2Farticle%2F10.1525% 2Fsrsp.2006.3.1.33&token2=exp=1457817114~acl=%2Fstatic%2Fpdf%2F802%2Fart%25253A10.1525%25 252Fsrsp.2006.3.1.33.pdf%3ForiginUrl%3Dhttp%253A%252F%252Flink.springer.com%252Farticle%25 2F10.1525%252Fsrsp.2006.3.1.33*~hmac=c32b9eb24b8a71f68a66566075e13f2579b2a449389b579909d0a4 7f0be8fe54

Hill, D. B., & Menvielle, E. (2009). "You have to give them a place where they feel protected and safe and loved": The views of parents who have gender-variant children and adolescents. *Journal of LGBT Youth, 6*(2-3), 243–271. doi:10.1080/19361650903013527

Hills, R. (2012). Life without sex: The third phase of the asexuality movement. *The Atlantic*. Retrieved from: http://www.theatlantic.com/health/archive/2012/04/life-without-sex-the-third-phase-of-the-asexuality-movement/254880/

Joslin, C. (2010). Travel insurance: Protecting lesbian and gay parent families across state lines. *Harvard Law & Policy Review, 4*(1), 31-48. Retrieved from http://papers.ssrn.com/sol3/papers.cfm?abstract_id=1623861

Kurdek, L. A. (1994). Areas of conflict for gay, lesbian, and heterosexual couples: What couples argue about influences relationship satisfaction. *Journal of Marriage & Family, 56*(4), 923–934. doi:10.2307/353603

Kurdek, L. A. (1998). Relationship outcomes and their predictors: Longitudinal evidence from heterosexual married, gay cohabiting, and lesbian cohabiting couples. *Journal of Marriage and Family, 60*(3), 553–568. doi:10.2307/353528

Kurdek, L. A. (2000). Attractions and constraints as determinants of relationship commitment: Longitudinal evidence from gay, lesbian, and heterosexual couples. *Personal Relationships, 7*(3), 245–262. doi:10.1111/j.1475-6811.2000.tb00015.x

Lannutti, P. J. (2005). For better or worse: Exploring the meanings of same-sex marriage within the lesbian, gay, bisexual and transgendered community. *Journal of Social and Personal Relationships, 22*(1), 5–18. doi:10.1177/0265407505049319

LaSala, M. C. (2010). *Coming out, coming home: Helping families adjust to a gay or lesbian child*. New York: Columbia University Press.

LaSala, M. (2013). Out of the Darkness: Three waves of family research and the emergency of family therapy for Lesbian and Gay People. *Clinical Social Work Journal, 41*(3), 267–276. doi:10.1007/s10615-012-0434-x

Lehavot, K., Balsam, K. F., & Ibrahim-Wells, G. D. (2009). Redefining the American quilt: Definitions and experiences of community among ethnically diverse lesbian and bisexual women. *Journal of Community Psychology, 37*(4), 439–458. doi:10.1002/jcop.20305

Leiblum, S. R. (2002). Reconsidering gender differences in sexual desire: An update. *Sexual and Relationship Therapy, 17*(1), 57–68. doi:10.1080/14681990220108027

Lev, A. I. (2010). How queer!—The development of gender identity and sexual orientation in LGBTQ-headed families. *Family Process, 49*(3), 268–290. doi:10.1111/j.1545-5300.2010.01323.x

Lyness, K.P. (2012). Therapeutic considerations in same-sex divorce. In J. J. Bigner & J. L. Wetchler (Eds.), *Handbook of LGBT-affirmative couple and family therapy* (pp. 377–391). New York: Routledge.

Mackey, R. A., Diemer, M. A., & O'Brien, B. A. (2004). Relational factors in understanding satisfaction in the lasting relationships of same-sex and heterosexual couples. *Journal of Homosexuality, 47*(1), 111–136. doi:10.1300/J082v47n01_07

Malpas, J. (2006). From otherness to alliance: Transgender couples in therapy. *Journal of GLBT Family Studies, 2*(3-4), 183–206. doi:10.1300/J461v02n03_10

Malpas, J. (2011). Between pink and blue: A multi-dimensional family approach to gender nonconforming children and their families. *Family Process, 50*(4), 453–470. doi:10.1111/j.1545-5300.2011.01371.x

Meyer, I. H. (1995). Minority stress and mental health in gay men. *Journal of Health & Social Behavior, 36*(1), 38–56. Retrieved from: http://www.jstor.org/stable/2137286

Mutanski, B., Garofalo, R., Emerson, E. (2010). Mental health disorders, psychological distress, and suicidality in a diverse sample of lesbian, gay, bisexual, and transgender youths. *American Journal of Public Health, 100*, 2426–2432. doi:10.2105/AJPH.2009.178319

Mutanski, B., Newcomb, M. E., & Garofalo, R. (2011). Mental health of lesbian, gay, and bisexual youths: A developmental resiliency perspective. *Journal of Gay & Lesbian Social Services, 23*(2), 204–225. doi:10.1080/10538720.2011.561474

Norwood, K. (2013). Grieving gender: Trans-identities, transition, and ambiguous loss. *Communication Monographs, 80*(1), 24–45. doi:10.1080/03637751.2012.739705

Olson, C. L. (2009). Second-class families: Interstate recognition of queer adoption. *Family Law Quarterly, 43*, 161–180. Retrieved from http://www.jstor.org/stable/25740695

Oswald, R. F. (2002). Resilience within the family networks of lesbians and gay men: Intentionality and redefinition. *Journal of Marriage & Family, 64*(2), 374–383. doi:10.1111/j.1741-3737.2002.00374.x

Otis, M., Rostosky, S., Riggle, E., & Hamrin, R. (2006). Stress and relationship quality in same-sex couples. *Journal of Social & Personal Relationships, 23*(1), 81–99. doi:10.1177/0265407506060179

Otis, M., Riggle, E. D. B., & Rostosky, S. S. (2006). Impact of mental health on perceptions of relationship satisfaction and quality among female same-sex couples. *Journal of Lesbian Studies, 10*(1/2), 267–283. doi:10.1300/J155v10n01_14

Otis, M., Rostosky, S., Riggle, E., & Hamrin, R. (2006). Stress and relationship quality in same-sex couples. *Journal of Social & Personal Relationships, 23*(1), 81–99. doi:10.1177/0265407506060179

Polikoff, N. D. (2008). *Beyond (straight and gay) marriage: Valuing all families under the law*. Boston: Beacon.

Porche, M. V., & Purvin, D. M. (2008). "Never in Our Lifetime": Legal marriage for same-sex couples in long-term relationships. *Family Relations, 57*(2), 144–159. doi:10.1111/j.1741-3729.2008.00490.x

Prause, N., & Graham, C. A. (2007). Asexuality: Classification and characterization. *Archives of Sexual Behavior, 36*(3), 341–356. doi:10.1007/s10508-006-9142-3

Raj, R. (2008). Transforming couples and families: A trans-formative therapeutic model for working with the loved-ones of gender-divergent youth and trans-identified adults. *Journal of GLBT Family Studies, 4*, 133–163. doi:10.1080/15504280802096765

RhapsodyInRed (2013). *Feeling pressured by society, and has it gotten in my head?* Asexuality Visibility & Education Network. Retrieved from: http://www.asexuality.org/en/topic/87758-feeling-pressured-by-society-and-it-has-gotten-in-my-head/

Rostosky, S. S., Dekhtyar, O., Cupp, P. K., & Anderman, E. M. (2008). Sexual self-concept and sexual self-efficacy in adolescents: A possible clue to promoting sexual health? *Journal of Sex Research, 45*(3), 277–286. doi:10.1080/00224490802204480

Rust, P. C. (2003). Monogamy and polyamory: Relationship issues for bisexuals. In L. Garnets & D. Kimmel, *Psychological perspectives on lesbian, gay, and bisexual experiences* (pp. 475–496). New York: Columbia University Press.

Ryan, C., & Jethá, C. (2010). *Sex at dawn: The prehistoric origins of modern sexuality*. New York: HarperCollins.

Scherrer, K. S. (2008). Coming to an asexual identity: Negotiating identity, negotiating desire. *Sexualities, 11*(5), 621–641. doi:10.1177/1363460708094269

Schlatter, E., & Steinback, R. (2010). 10 Anti-gay myths debunked. *Intelligence Report* (140). Retrieved from http://www.splcenter.org/get-informed/intelligence-report/browse-all-issues/2010/winter/10-myths

Schroeder, M., & Shidlo, A. (2002). Ethical issues in sexual orientation conversion therapies: An empirical study of consumers. *Journal of Gay & Lesbian Psychotherapy, 5*(3-4), 131–166. doi:10.1300/J236v05n03_09

Sedgwick, E. K. (2008). *Epistemology of the closet: Updated with a new preface* (1990) Berkeley, CA: University of California Press.

Setoodeh, R., Murr, A., & Ordoñez, J. (2008). Young, gay and murdered. (Cover story). *Newsweek, 152*(4), 40–46. Retrieved from: http://uselectionatlas.org/FORUM/index.php?topic=79777.0;wap2

Shurts, W. M. (2008). Pre-union counseling: A call to action. *Journal of LGBT Issues in Counseling, 2*(3), 216–242. doi:10.1080/15538600802120093

Solomon, S. E., Rothblum, E. D., & Balsam, K. F. (2004). Pioneers in partnership: Lesbian and gay male couples in civil unions compared with those not in civil unions and married heterosexual siblings. *Journal of Family Psychology, 18*(2), 275–286. doi:10.1037/0893-3200.18.2.275

Spitalnick, J., & McNair, L. (2005). Couples therapy with gay and lesbian clients: An analysis of important clinical issues. *Journal of Sex & Marital Therapy, 31*(1), 43–56. doi:10.1080/00926230590475260

Stone Fish, L., & Harvey, R. G. (2005). *Nurturing queer youth: Family therapy transformed*. New York: W.W. Norton.

The Asexuality Visibility & Education Network. (2012). Retrieved from http://www.asexuality.org/home/ May 28, 2013

Todosijevic, J., Rothblum, E. D., & Solomon, S. E. (2005). Relationship satisfaction, affectivity, and gay-specific stressors in same-sex couples joined in civil unions. *Psychology of Women Quarterly, 29*(2), 158–166. doi:10.1111/j.1471-6402.2005.00178.x

Troiden, R. R. (1988). Homosexual identity development. *Journal of Adolescent Health Care, 9*, 105–113. doi:10.1016/0197-0070(88)90056-3

Van Eeden-Moorefield, B., Martell, C. R., Williams, M., & Preston, M. (2011). Same-sex relationships and dissolution: The connection between heteronormativity and homonormativity. *Family Relations: An Interdisciplinary Journal of Applied Family Studies, 60*(5), 562–571. doi:10.1111/j.1741-3729.2011.00669.x

West, C. & Zimmerman, D. H. (1990). Doing gender. In S. A. Farrell & J. Lorber (Eds.) *The social construction of gender* (pp. 13–35). Newbury Park, CA: SAGE Publications.

Widmer, E. D., & Jallinoja, R. (Eds.). (2008). *Beyond the nuclear family: Families in configurational perspective* (Vol. 9). New York: Peter Lang.

17

Compassion and Forgiveness in Intimate Relationships

Mary T. Kelleher, MA, LMFT
Department of Family Social Science
University of Minnesota

Kirsten Lind Seal, Ph.D., LMFT
Graduate School of Health and Human Sciences
Saint Mary's University of Minnesota

Jaime E. Ballard, MS
Tai J. Mendenhall, Ph.D., LMFT
Department of Family Social Science

LEARNING OBJECTIVES

- Understand principal processes and elements of compassion
- Differentiate empathy from sympathy
- Articulate the impact that compassion has on intimate relationships
- Define the respective phases of the forgiveness process

Vignette

It's Sunday afternoon. Padma is sitting on the living room couch with her laptop, concentrating on finishing a report for work. Gerald is standing a few feet away, bouncing a ball to his dog Roscoe. He's been bouncing the ball for a while now, and they're having a great time. Padma has glared at him a couple of times, hoping that he'll stop, but he's ignored her and keeps playing with Roscoe.

"Knock it off, Gerald! I'm trying to work in here. Take it outside," she says irritably. "Okay, okay. In a minute, huh?" Gerald snaps back.

Gerald throws the ball again; this time it bounces wide. Roscoe jumps for it, overbalances, and hits the bookcase as he comes down with the ball in his mouth. The impact on the bookcase causes a delicate blue glass vase that Padma inherited from her favorite aunt to tip over; it begins to roll toward the edge of the shelf. Both Padma and Gerald freeze as they watch it.

"Oh, no! Not the vase! Her Auntie Meera's vase!" thinks Gerald.

Padma holds her hand to her mouth in horror, her eyes wide. She feels sick. "No! Chachi Meera, it's the only thing of yours I have left!"

The vase rolls over the edge and smashes on the floor.

For a moment, no one moves—not even Roscoe. Both Gerald and Padma feel stunned and overwhelmed. Then they turn and meet each other's eyes.

"She looks heartbroken. She's missed her auntie so much and now the vase is ruined. What have I done? This is terrible. I've hurt her," he thinks.

"There are no words . . . no words for this. It hurts so much. I feel so angry and so sad. It was such a stupid thing to do! But he looks sad, too. So sad. Oh, Meera. Oh, Gerald," she thinks.

They move toward each other. "I'm sorry, Pad. I'm so sorry," he whispers as he puts his arms around her. She takes a shaky breath, and then rests her forehead against his shoulder and begins to cry wordlessly as she reaches up and softly rubs his back.

Corresponding Author: Mary T. Kelleher, M.S., LMFT; University of Minnesota; Department of Family Social Science; 1985 Buford Ave.; 290 McNeal Hall; Saint Paul, MN 55108. E-mail: mary@marykelleherlmft.com.

Conflicts, misunderstandings, stressors, tragedies, separations, hurt feelings, untruthfulness, betrayals; these are some of the things that couples deal with during the life of their relationship. Even the best of relationships will experience some of these misgivings. The difference between a healthy and unhealthy relationship is often not in what the couple experiences, but in how the two handle it. For example, there are many ways this scene with Padma and Gerald could have played out. Padma could have assumed Gerald threw the ball toward the bookcase on purpose (*How could you do this to me?*); she could have lost her temper when the vase broke and verbally attacked Gerald (*You stupid jerk!*), or shut down and refused to talk to him for days (the *"silent treatment"*). She might have broken something he loved to get revenge (*How does THAT feel, Gerald?*), or been so uncertain of her connection with Gerald that she minimized her own pain to keep the relationship safe (*It's okay… Never mind; it didn't mean that much…*). And Gerald could have panicked and blamed Padma (*You put it up there. It was just waiting to get knocked over!*), minimized what he had done (*No a big deal; it's just a piece of glass!*), or tried to defend himself without acknowledging the importance of this to Padma (*Hey, I said I'm sorry, okay?*). The outcome of any of these responses by Padma or Gerald could have damaged their relationship.

So, what made this situation end in the way it did? Why were the partners not only able to comfort each other, but also make choices that may lead to actually strengthening their relationship and even increase their intimacy? At an intense and potentially damaging moment, Padma and Gerald chose to act with compassion and forgiveness. Although they could have been overwhelmed by their own pain and anxieties, instead they were able to move past these and be aware of their partner's feelings. Rather than striking out at each other in reaction to the situation, they took action to reach out and comfort their partner.

Compassion means opening one's self to the suffering of others (and one's own) without judgment or defensiveness, and desiring to take action to relieve the suffering that has been observed (Armstrong, 2010; Gilbert, 2005a; Neff & Beretvas, 2013). It encompasses aspects of kindness, caring, warmth, acceptance, awareness of and the ability to tolerate our own and others' feelings, generosity, forgiveness, and the intent to lessen or end the suffering that we have observed. *Forgiveness* is making the decision to let go of anger, hurt, fear, and resentment when someone has wronged us in some way (McCullough, 2000).

Compassion and forgiveness are skills—not states or feelings—that we bring with us into our relationships. Humans need to exercise these skills to have healthy, warm, caring, and lasting relationships *and* to have healthy, happy, meaningful, and satisfying lives. Compassion and forgiveness allow us to reduce anxiety, make connections with others, comfort ourselves and others, attain awareness beyond our own limited existence, and heal the hurts in others and ourselves that are part of the human experience. Research shows that compassion and forgiveness improve the quality of our lives and our relationships (Fishbane, 2013); being compassionate and forgiving can improve our own mental and physical health and strengthen our relationship bonds. If we lack the ability to forgive, we inhabit an existence of bitterness and recrimination that sucks the pleasure out of life and isolates us. Our lives become deeply neurotic and self-involved as we focus on the wrongdoings of others. If we lack the ability to be compassionate, we cannot meaningfully connect with others—and we can experience difficulties with connecting to our own inner selves. Compassion is so fundamentally important to humans that those who are incapable of it are often diagnosed as having lifelong mental problems (e.g., Antisocial Personality Disorder). Individuals affected by these conditions are at high risk of spending their lives unhappy, and even in the criminal justice system (Fallon, 2013).

In this chapter, we will examine the following questions:

- What comprises compassion and forgiveness?
- Are you born compassionate and/or forgiving, or do you develop these skills?
- Can you have one, but not the other?
- Why do compassion and forgiveness seem to come easily to some people, while others struggle?
- What differences do compassion and forgiveness make for you and your relationships?
- Are there times when compassion or forgiveness can hurt you or your relationships?
- How can you improve these skills?

COMPASSION

Let's start our discussion on compassion with a mystery. Roughly 3000 years ago, something shifted in human cultures throughout the globe in a way that has baffled many historians—the birth of the Axial Age. This time was marked by a 1500-year period during which the Golden Rule in its many forms (e.g., *Do unto others as you would have them do unto you; Do not do to others what you would not have done to you*) began to spontaneously appear in the teachings of peoples separated by great stretches of distance, including the East (Confucianism, Daoism, Buddhism, and Hinduism), the Middle East (Zoastrianism, Rabbinical Judaism, Christianity, and Islam), and the West (the philosophical traditions of ancient Greece). The Golden Rule was the first appearance of a formalized definition and practice of modern compassion (Armstrong, 2006).

Aspects of compassion exist in all mammals and predated the appearance of human life. For example, elements of what we now know as compassion were present among mammal mothers who nursed their offspring (de Waal, 2009). Archaeological records have shown us that early humans carefully cared for tribal members who were so severely disabled that they could not have survived without assistance, but nonetheless lived to an old age and were lovingly buried (covered with flowers and other gifts). However, outside of family and tribal groups, there was little indication of compassion as a practice, and no record of any formal codification of compassion prior to the start of the Axial Age (Armstrong, 2006). From archaeological findings, ancient literature, and folk tales, we know that warriors were rarely concerned about the suffering of their victims. When a population was attacked, it was not just conquered. Often, it was completely wiped out. Whole families, including the youngest and most helpless members, were slaughtered or sent into slavery. Before the Axial Age, there was little sense of a shared and common humanity.

This first began to change with the Aryans, one of the premier warrior cultures of the ancient world (Armstrong, 2006). Prior to the first millennium BCE, historical documents and the archeological record paint a picture of these conquerors glorifying warfare and violence in religious practices and teachings. The themes of their teachings changed significantly by 900 BCE as Aryan priests began to extol the importance of peace, kindness, mercy, and a universal sense of concern for all people. Over time, these ideas would begin to appear in other cultures. As other Axial wisdoms, traditions, religions, and philosophies evolved, compassion grew to be a cornerstone for the promotion of the well-being of all members of society. Many of our most profound and far-reaching philosophers and teachers (such as Confucius, Rabbis Akiba and Hillel the Elder, Jesus, Socrates, Muhammad, the Buddha, Laozi, Francis of Assisi, Gandhi, Mother Teresa, and Martin Luther King, Jr.) based their teachings on this concept—a concept which has continued to be studied and practiced to this day.

But why did this idea of caring for outsiders as we do for ourselves mysteriously appear? Historians are not completely certain. As we discuss below, many of the elements of compassion already existed in humans prior to Axial Age thinkers; the building blocks of compassion are part of our basic neuropsychology. These building blocks are found in the areas of the brain that develop based on relational interactions between an infant and its caretakers, and they result in the infant attaining conscious awareness of him or herself, others, and the world at large. However, at about the time the concept of compassion appeared in Aryan culture, priests and philosophers had begun to conduct psychological experiments on ways to improve the human experience (Armstrong, 2010). One of the consistent findings of these experiments was that caring about others, including those outside of your family or tribe, created a sense of well-being and serenity within the practitioner. Compassion was (is) good for people.

Processes in the Mind and the Elements of Compassion

As straightforward as compassion can seem, it is actually a complex system of interrelated feelings, thoughts, and behaviors (Gilbert, 2005b), the mechanisms of which can be found in our brain and hormones. Some components of this system appear to be coded in our genes via millions of years of evolution, some are taught to us in our earliest relationships in infancy, and some are learned from ongoing interactions with our environment. Compassion is complex and dynamic; no two people are compassionate in exactly the same way and no single person will exhibit exactly the same amount of compassion in every instance. Further, people can gain or lose compassion over their lifetime dependent upon their genetic propensity, early experiences, environments, and thoughts or beliefs about compassion (Gilbert, 2005b). For example, a person who initially had low levels of compassion can increase his or her compassion by being exposed to compassionate treatment by others (Baer, 2010; Gilbert & Tirch, 2009; Johnson, 2002). A person could also read literature about the value of compassion, or join an organization that promotes compassionate behaviors, and ultimately choose to become more compassionate (Hoffman, 2001). Compassion exists on an internal continuum which can change throughout our lives. This continuum is based on three processes of the mind: *attachment, cognition,* and *motivation* (Gilbert, 2005a).

As described more fully elsewhere in this book (see Chapter 2), *attachment* is the name that English psychiatrist and developmental theoretician John Bowlby (1969) and colleague Mary Ainsworth gave to a relational process that starts in infancy and early childhood, and continues throughout our lives. Attachment styles shape how we relate to ourselves, the outside world, and others (especially significant others). The process of attachment takes place in both the emotional (limbic system) and rational (prefrontal cortex) areas of our brains, and attachment is strongly connected to how we experience feelings of danger and safety (Gilleth, Shaver, & Mikulincer, 2005). As infants, we are totally dependent upon others to feed, comfort, care, and protect us. Unlike other animals that are self-dependent from birth (e.g., most reptiles or fish), humans and other mammals will die if adult caregivers do not offer that care. As infants, establishing a close, safe, and secure relationship with older humans (usually parental figures) is what keeps us alive, aids in brain formation, and promotes the development of an internal working model of ourselves and the world. Through the process of attachment, we learn to soothe ourselves, regulate our emotions, attune to the feeling states of others, and maintain relationships (Main, Kaplan, & Cassidy, 1985; Sroufe, Egeland, Carlson & Collins, 2005).

COGNITION is the practice of processing information as abstract ideas and understanding how those abstractions interact (Siegel, 2012). Cognition takes place primarily in the outer layers of the brain, particularly the prefrontal cortex. As you read, interpret, and consider the written symbols you are reading on this page that represent abstract ideas about compassion, you are using your cognitive abilities. Cognition is also the basis for ethical and moral development in the individual, which is a process that can exist separately from the emotional underpinnings of compassion. One can seek to acquire a compassionate stance because of highly held ethical or moral beliefs that others should be treated with kindness and fairness, and that their suffering should be alleviated (Hoffman, 2001).

MOTIVATION is goal-directed behavior (Gilbert, 2005b). Although it can be unconscious (such as shifting in your chair to make yourself more comfortable or turning to look at an attractive person) or conscious (such as choosing to study hard enough to earn an "A" in a class), compassion-directed motivation is usually deliberate. When you mentally examine the abstract premises and make a decision to attempt compassion based on it seeming like a good idea, you are using cognition to direct your behavior. When you pursue that decision and attempt to act compassionately, you are using motivation.

Researchers have identified elements of compassion that engage both attachment and cognitive processes; these include kindness, common humanity (i.e., seeing a person's experiences as part of the process of living, rather than as shameful or isolating), understanding, forgiveness, acceptance, and warmth. One of the most thorough descriptions was presented by British psychologist Paul Gilbert (Gilbert, 2005b; Gilbert & Tirsch, 2009); he identified factors of sensitivity/attunement, distress tolerance, empathy, sympathy, non-judgment, and motivation toward compassionate action as essential elements of compassion (see Figure 1). Each of these elements can separately enhance intrapersonal (i.e., within ourselves) and interpersonal (i.e., between us and another) relationships.

FIGURE 1 Elements of Compassion

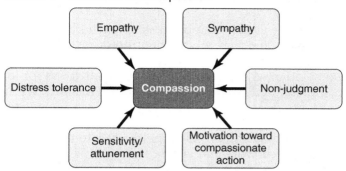

Adapted from: Gilbert, P. (Ed.). (2005). *Compassion: Conceptualizations, Research, and Use in Therapy.* London: Routledge.

SENSITIVITY/ATTUNEMENT. Compassion requires awareness and sensitivity. To be compassionate, we must increase our awareness of our own feeling states and needs, as well as sense others' feelings and needs. Another word for describing this sensitivity is *attunement.* We learn attunement in infancy during the formation of attachment bonds with our caretakers. The more present, attentive, and responsive caregivers are to an infant's feelings and needs (demonstrating just the right amount of stroking, soothing, distracting, and attention), the more the infant learns over time how to be sensitive to its own feelings and, ultimately, to those of others. Daniel Siegel (2001) calls this *mental state resonance.* When this resonance is present, there is a flow of energy and information in non-verbal communication patterns. Imagine a dance where two people do not know how to read each other's cues, step on each other's toes, bump into each other, move in opposite directions—you wince when you just think about it! Now imagine the same dance when two people are good dancers and are sensitive to each other's body language; they dip and twirl with grace and style; they are sensitive to both their own movements and the slightest changes in their partner's. They are attuned to one another.

Sensitivity plays out in intimate relationships in important ways. For example, imagine two couples: Sharon and Rick and Caleb and Allyson:

When Sharon gets home exhausted from a 15-hour flight from Bolivia, Rick can tell just how tired she is by the way she walks, her facial expression, and the tone of her voice. He adjusts his actions toward her (gearing down from celebratory, so-happy-you're-home high energy to something softer and more soothing) and his expectations about how she is going to respond. Caleb loves Allyson just as much as Rick loves Sharon, but he is not as attuned to the energy and feelings of his significant other. When Allyson walks in the door after the same long flight, Caleb is excited, very affectionate, and ready to talk for hours about her trip—but she is more interested in vegging-out with a glass of wine and Netflix.

DISTRESS TOLERANCE. It is logical that to be compassionate you would want to be sensitive to others, but why would you want to increase sensitivity to yourself? It's simple: being sensitive to another's pain and suffering can trigger feelings of pain in *yourself.* If you doubt this, notice the next time you watch a movie character that you identify with when she or he goes through something painful; your heart rate goes up, you breathe faster (or hold your breath), or your eyes may tear up. Humans (and other mammals) come hardwired from birth to sense the feelings of others at a basic level and respond as if they, too, are feeling those emotions. When two newborn babies are gathered in the same room, if one of them begins to cry, it will usually trigger crying in the other newborn (Gilleth et al., 2005). This is a form of emotional contagion known as *reactive empathic distress,* and it exists at the earliest stage of the attunement response in the attachment process. When a baby experiences another child crying, she or he mirrors the emotion because she or he cannot differentiate between his or her and another child's feelings. The baby will respond with increasing anxiety because she or he has no ability to affect those feelings. If this inability to differentiate one's own and others' feelings continued unabated throughout our lives, we would end up paralyzed by overwhelming negative emotions.

However, nature has designed the attachment process to teach humans to soothe themselves by mirroring how their adult caretakers soothed them when they were infants in distress; this ability to internalize soothing is called *distress tolerance* (Gilbert, 2005b). As an infant ages, the combined experiences of being soothed by others allow the child to tolerate distress for longer periods of time because the experience of being soothed has been internalized. The more we are able to internalize the ability to soothe (via secure attachment to our caretakers), the easier it is to tolerate uncomfortable feelings (whether our own or others') and avoid the escalation of negative emotions (Fruzzetti & Iverson, 2006). Internalization of soothing is essential to tolerate the distress of others and ourselves. Without it, we may become overwhelmed and flooded with anxiety; our ability to engage in meaningful relationships with others is limited. A lack of distress tolerance can underlie a person turning away from the sight of another's suffering; it is not cruelty, uncaring, or lack of empathy, but instead an inability to tolerate anxiety and soothe oneself.

EMPATHY. Empathy is comparable to attunement hitting the big leagues. In empathy, both visceral feelings and cognitive attempts at understanding are combined to deepen our understanding of another (de Waal, 2009). When we are empathic, we are able to stand in another person's shoes, to experience the subtleties of what she or he is experiencing and feeling while gaining insight into what it is like to be him or her. We *feel another's feelings* while understanding that these feelings are not our own (Hoffman, 2001). Empathy contributes to morality, emotions, motivations, and behaviors in relationships, and it is so essential to the compassionate response that many writers do not differentiate between empathy and compassion. However, as Sprecher and Fehr (2005) have pointed out, compassion is more encompassing and enduring than empathy. While an empathic response may last only a moment, a compassionate response includes shared feelings *and* actions to alleviate the suffering of another.

Similar to sensitivity and distress tolerance, empathy exists in other mammals besides humans. It is essential for the survival of all animals to be able to gage correctly the type and intensity of another animal's emotions. For example, prairie dogs must correctly gage if the chattering of another prairie dog is an attempt to alert the entire colony of danger from a predator; if they fail in this empathic test, they might be eaten (de Waal, 2009). Researchers observed that mice are more sensitive to pain when a familiar cage mate is in pain (Langford et al., 2006). When one mouse experiences a low dose of pain while in the presence of a mouse given a higher dose of pain, the low-dose mouse increases the amount of licking to its body (a signal of distress in mice). At the same time (and interestingly), the mouse that receives a higher dose of pain experiences a lowered pain response (less licking) in the presence of its cage mate. Also, many humans who own pets are well aware of how empathy crosses species; our pets often come to us to lick, paw, rub against, or snuggle us (even a usually aloof cat!) when we feel upset, while we in turn will sense our pet's changing emotions and respond in kind.

Each of the previous examples is the result of a developmental course that is guided by secure attachment processes. In humans, empathy starts when a toddler attempts to comfort another person in distress in the same ways the toddler would like to be soothed. For example, co-author Mary Kelleher's 14-month-old daughter brought her treasured blue blanket to her one day when Mary had the flu because that was how the toddler soothed herself. As a child grows and becomes increasingly aware of the difference oneself and others, she or he will seek to soothe the other person in a way that reflects that difference. For example, a three-year-old in a playgroup will bring the playmate's mother to a crying playmate rather than bring her own mother. As we age, we gain greater accuracy in our empathy; we interpret others' feelings more correctly, and improve at gauging how to comfort others (Hoffman, 2001). We begin to project how we would feel if we were in someone else's situation by the age of seven. By age nine, we understand that others could feel differently from us based on their personalities, histories, situations, and how long or intensely they have been in distress. Imagination also comes into play, and empathic individuals can imagine the experience of a person they have never met or who appears to be very different from them. They also can imagine what someone's experience might be to a situation that has not yet happened (Hoffman, 2001).

On average, males and females differ in how they experience, convey, and act on empathy (Fishbane, 2013). Multiple studies have shown that women are more reliant on a visceral, felt sense of another's suffering, whereas men are more reliant on cognitive attempts to understand another's suffering. These general differences in empathy can sometimes cause confusion between men and women. For example, imagine a couple that is on the brink of breaking up (in part) because the wife perceives her husband's attempts at empathy as fake. Her husband does not display the depth of feeling that she is familiar with from her female friends. When he is observed by their therapist, the therapist notices that he is concentrating very hard on what his wife is saying. The husband tries to understand her before offering comfort, asking many questions and suggesting different solutions. The wife does not understand that her husband simply has a different, more cerebral strategy than she does, so she has perceived him as cold and uncaring. It was a breakthrough for her when she realized that he does empathize with her, but in a different way than she had learned to expect from growing up in an all-female household.

When empathy is healthy, we combine our empathic response with distress tolerance so that we can internally explore what it must feel like for another person without becoming emotionally overwhelmed (Mikulciner & Shaver, 2005). We are also able to stay rational and make thoughtful decisions that value our own needs along with the needs of those who are suffering. People who balance empathy with distress tolerance are better able to experience another's feelings while staying steady and relatively calm. They are able to engage thoughtfully and make good choices on how to help—or not help—another. When people exhibit empathy without distress tolerance, they may become overwhelmed by anxiety at another's pain and rush headlong into action. They might act with the unconscious purpose of ending their own suffering rather than that of the other person.

Without the ability to engage thoughtfully in an empathic response, poor choices might actually worsen the other person's situation. For example, imagine a person sees a strange child crying over a dropped ice cream cone. Feeling the child's sadness and disappointment, the empathic adult becomes anxious and rushes to the child's side to give him or her a hug without slowing down to consider that a strange adult rushing over like that could terrify the child. Another equally empathic person with better distress tolerance might see the child, feel the sadness and disappointment, tolerate it without anxiety, and consider what might be the best route to lessen the child's distress: Would it best to find the child's parent? To slowly approach the child and ask what happened? Or would it be better to stay still, make eye contact and sadly smile to show the child that his or her loss is understood and shared?

SYMPATHY. Sympathy is the ability to appreciate or be moved by another's feelings, distress, or needs. It is different from empathy in that one is focused on the well-being of others, but does not actually experience their emotions (Gilbert, 2005b). Generally, it is easier for individuals to sympathize than to empathize because they experience less intense emotional upset. Consider the example of Camille, Sofie, and Lena:

As they shared a beer after a seminar, Lena began to relay the latest argument with her boyfriend to her friends. Camille listened thoughtfully, nodding at the right spots, giving feedback, all the while feeling sad for what Lena was going through. She was sympathetic, but not empathic. As Lena talked, Camille was not experiencing Lena's feelings. However, as Sofie listened, it was as if she were going through the fight herself. She felt Lena's frustration and hurt, and her eyes filled with tears as her heart beat faster and her fists clenched. Sofie responded to Lena with empathy.

NON-JUDGMENT. Non-judgment is defined as the avoidance of accusation or condemnation of self or others (Gilbert, 2005b). It is essential for the practice of compassion. If a deep empathic understanding of feelings is not paired with non-judgment, any compassionate response will lack warmth and caring. It is important to note that non-judgment does not mean abandoning one's own beliefs about right or wrong. One can see that another's actions are wrong (e.g., someone who hit and killed a person while driving drunk), yet have compassion for the driver's inner pain and seek to alleviate that suffering (e.g., expressing caring for the driver, helping him or her to get substance abuse treatment).

Although a person can learn non-judgment through reading or storytelling, it is a cognitive practice that is adopted primarily by observing others and patterning ourselves after them. While non-judgment may be enhanced by elements resulting from secure attachment (e.g., distress tolerance and empathy), it does not spontaneously arise from secure attachment as the other compassion elements do. Instead, it is more closely related to social learning and to the development of ethics and morality.

MOTIVATION TOWARD COMPASSIONATE ACTION. Compassion is not only about sensing or perceiving others' feelings. Compassion is about action—the action it requires to understand the experience of others, enhance their welfare, and lessen their suffering (Armstrong, 2010). People are internally directed toward the goal of compassionate behavior. Furthermore, to be able to demonstrate compassion toward others, it is necessary that one is motivated to also show self-compassion for oneself (Neff, 2003; Neff, Kirkpatrick, & Rude, 2007).

The majority of the elements of compassion (sensitivity, distress tolerance, sympathy, and empathy) are reflective of the strength of the attachment process (Gilleth et al., 2005), which means that they can be considered attachment derived. A series of three research studies by Sprecher and Fehr (2005) found that compassion is more strongly correlated to an individual's attachment security than to other factors like personality, self-esteem, happiness, or self-confidence. In a different study, Mikulincer and Shaver (2005) found that a person's level of compassion could be altered by inducing or reducing attachment security experimentally. They accomplished this by priming subjects with stories that invoke feelings of attachment security, happiness, or sadness. Then, they asked the subjects to read a story of a boy whose parents were accidentally killed. They tested the subjects' level of compassionate response toward the boy alongside their distress responses; attachment-primed subjects scored approximately 50% higher on compassion than positively and negatively primed subjects, and reported 30% less emotional distress than negatively primed subjects.

Independent of one's original quality of childhood attachment, all of the elements of compassion can be strengthened or weakened during the life course (Armstrong, 2010; Gilbert, 2005a). A person can *learn* to be more sensitive/attuned, distress tolerant, empathic, and non-judgmental through conscious decision and motivated practice (Gilbert & Tirch, 2009). Motivation to become compassionate—whether gained through the experience of being the object of compassion, witnessing the impact of compassion on others, or consciously deciding that compassion is an attractive quality that the individual wants to exhibit—can overcome childhood-based insecure attachment and limitations in the attachment-derived core elements. The motivation to become compassionate can act as the impetus for changing later attachment style or strengthening attunement, empathy, and distress tolerance. Developing these skills can enhance the quality of our intimate relationships. Individuals in intimate relationships are more likely to be compassionate than those who are not, likely due to the support and encouragement that they receive from others (Sprecher & Fehr, 2005).

Impact of Compassion on Intimate Relationships

Compassion in an intimate relationship is like warm scented oil between two bodies; things move more smoothly between them, and the partners are more relaxed and happy. They feel closer to each other. Their mutual trust deepens. When one lover listens to the other's suffering with compassion, the listener often unconsciously will make tiny gentle sighs (Fishbane, 2013). These sighs lower the anxiety of *both* partners in measurable ways; adrenaline and cortisol (two stress response hormones) will begin to drop as the fight, flight, or freeze response lessens in the speaker's and listener's bodies. Heart rates slow and oxytocin (the "cuddle" hormone) may be released into the brain. Both people feel soothed, calmer, and more connected. Interestingly, these empathetic non-verbal sounds differ across cultures but perform the same function; they work to reduce anxiety and signal understanding (Fishbane, 2013). For instance, an Icelandic woman listening to her friend's tale of woe might take short sharp intakes of breath in order to display her feelings of empathy. This practice extends throughout the Scandinavian countries. In the United States, however, such sounds are most often perceived as expressions of alarm or fright. Still, while types of empathetic sounds are culturally specific, the underlying function is the same: sounds express empathy and empathy soothes.

Compassionate couples demonstrate greater support, helping, and understanding between one another. Compassion increases the internal "cushion" of good feelings that can help them get through difficult times. If you have had the experience of your beloved reaching out to share your suffering and comfort you, you are more likely to be non-judgmental and more forgiving when your beloved does something that hurts you later (Fredrickson, 2013). In this way, compassion can contribute to a positive cycle in a relationship.

When a couple is upset or fighting, a display of compassion by one partner may reverse and calm the agitation that both partners feel. A compassionate display could be as simple as a light touch to communicate caring, understanding, and soothing from one partner to the other. Compassionate touch is a powerful intervention between partners during conflict. Coan, Schaefer, and Davidson (2006) found that holding the hand of your beloved actually reduces your perception of pain—something that did not occur when the individual held a stranger's hand or no one's hand at all. Compassionate touch from a lover releases oxytocin and endorphins (the body's natural pain-killer) in ways that sexual touch does not; this is one of the reasons that we feel so good when we are gently and lovingly held or touched—to our synapses, it is similar to a shot of morphine.

Displays of compassion between two partners can also heal deep emotional traumas and attachment wounds (i.e., attachment-based insecurities) reaching back into childhood (Solomon, 2003). A history of trauma, particularly trauma such as childhood emotional neglect, can make self-soothing very difficult in adulthood. A traumatized individual can experience memories associated with the trauma, hyper-awareness of potential danger, emotional numbing, and avoidance of people, places, sensations, or experiences that recall the trauma. Although it may seem counterintuitive, an intimate relationship can actually intensify the feeling of potential or imminent danger in a traumatized person, and the loved one can be sensed as potentially threatening (especially if the trauma was connected to a caretaker or previous partner, or was sexually abusive in nature). In this situation, intimacy can be filled with fear and shame, and as a result, loving partners can feel alienated and withdraw from the relationship. Drs. Susan Johnson's and Les Greenberg's *Emotionally Focused Couple Therapy* (Johnson, 2002) relies upon empathy and compassion from a partner to heal these traumas and wounds in the course of therapy. They found that a partner's compassionate response to his or her loved one's suffering can create feelings of secure attachment, even in those who have no history of secure attachment. The partner's compassionate response helps to calm and soothe, reduce anxiety, and increase feelings of safety and security in the loved one. Through the power of a partner's compassion, a traumatized individual can heal, increase his or her ability to tolerate distress, and find peace.

Learning Compassion: The Importance of Self-Compassion

Leslie is in her early 30s, attractive, and a successful author and educator. She has, however, never allowed herself to enjoy success. From the time she was little, Leslie has kept up a non-stop litany of why she is lazy, talentless, and a failure. If you asked her, she would tell you that she needs to tell herself these things because if she talked to herself with kindness, she would become a spineless blob without motivation. She believes that if she doesn't assault herself verbally, she would never succeed. Does she talk to her students in the same ways that she talks to herself? "Of course not!" Leslie would say. "That would be cruel. How would they ever learn to believe in themselves?

Leslie would never consider talking to her friends, students, family, or even strangers like she talks to herself. She does what a lot of us do to ourselves: we beat ourselves up with the belief that self-compassion encourages narcissism, laziness, self-centeredness, self-pity, or a whole host of other unwanted behaviors. These beliefs about the dangers of self-compassion saturate Western culture (Baer, 2010).

But does self-condemnation help us to be better, more successful, healthier, more honest, more mature, or more loving? The short answer is "no." In fact, self-condemnation usually does the opposite (Neff, 2003; Neff, Rude, & Kirkpatrick, 2007). When Leslie criticizes herself, her negative self-talk increases her anxiety, causes her muscles to tense, her blood pressure to rise, and her body to flood with adrenaline and cortisol. She feels helplessness and hopelessness. In response to her negative self-talk, she procrastinates on her writing because thinking about it makes her feel lousy. She makes up excuses for missing her faculty meetings and then feels dishonest and worthless. She avoids her husband after she snaps at him because she is sure she is a bad wife. And it is harder for her to be honest with herself about her real and human failings, because by admitting them, she will feel even more ashamed. The internal price of self-honesty, she believes, is too high. She would rather continue avoiding her husband, even when her marriage suffers as a consequence. All of this occurs because Leslie has never learned *self-compassion*.

A core aspect of being compassionate is the ability to be self-compassionate. If you carefully follow the original cultural statement of compassion, the Golden Rule, it suggests you should treat others based on how you want to be treated yourself. If you do not know how to treat yourself kindly, it is difficult to imagine how to treat others kindly. Although it may seem counterintuitive, the practice of caring for others needs to start with us caring for ourselves.

Kristin Neff, a researcher at the University of Texas, has spent most of her career researching self-compassion (Neff, 2003; Neff, Kirkpatrick, & Rude, 2007; Neff, Rude, & Kirkpatrick, 2007). She has defined it as "self-kindness versus self-judgment, common humanity versus isolation, and mindfulness versus over-identification" (Neff & Beretvas, 2013, p. 79). When one is self-compassionate, she or he is less self-absorbed and more aware of the emotions and feelings of others. There is less over-identification with one's own troubles. The greater the self-compassion, the more emotional regulation there is; tempers are not lost as easily and hurtful things are less likely to be said because you would not say them to yourself. A person exhibits greater acceptance, more warmth, and less internal criticism toward the aspects of self she or he dislikes. When a person experiences suffering, failure, or inadequacy, she or he is more likely to see himself or herself as "simply human." As a result, it becomes easier to be honest with oneself, be satisfied with one's life, and feel connected to others. There is less perfectionism, anxiety, and rumination. A person has stronger psychological well-being and a lower risk of mood and anxiety disorders (Segal, Williams, & Teasdale, 2002).

With reduced anxiety and greater distress tolerance, the body experiences less harmful physical stress and better immune functioning and tissue repair (Fredrickson, 2013; Gilbert, 2009; Pace et al., 2009). People who are self-compassionate are healthier and less prone to stress-related chronic illness—and they may even live longer and function better than those who are not self-compassionate. Self-compassion results in less judgment of and more tolerance and caring for others, and this in turn results in healthier intimate relationships (Neff & Beretvas, 2013). There are also strong connections between parents' self-compassion and their abilities to attune and foster secure attachment bonds with their children. In short, the benefits of self-compassion extend well beyond how you feel about yourself.

Learning Compassion: Skill Building

When Dr. Barbara Fredrickson (2013) was investigating ways of promoting and sustaining positive emotions in people, she first used methods that other researchers had relied upon to evoke these emotions—like beautiful music, film clips of a happy people, or unexpected gifts—but she found that the positive emotions were fleeting. So she switched to using a simple set of phrases, or meditations, that her subjects repeated to themselves for a few minutes each day. Although the phrases originated in ancient Buddhist meditation practices, they were not religious- or spiritually- oriented. They were simply short phrases that wished for kind outcomes for one's self and others. The phrases were meant to promote a compassionate state, and Fredrickson assumed that they might promote a more sustained period of happiness in her subjects. Unexpectedly, what she found was significant improvements in every aspect of her subjects' emotional states, especially in the ability to become more *loving*. The subjects began to report that their relationships improved, too. Finally, even measurements of the subjects' physical health showed improvement after daily repetitions of the phrases.

The exercises that Fredrickson used in her experiments are part of a lineage of compassion practices that can be traced back to the original psychological experiments of the Aryans 3000 years ago (Fredrickson, 2013). However, there are many other ways to learn compassion (e.g., reading, spiritual practices, and modeling a person who is compassionate); each major faith and wisdom tradition has its own methods of practicing compassion. We encourage you to explore them. A variety of different methods can be found in the accompanying text box, including two methods used in

Fredrickson's original study. No matter what you do, regular practice is the key needed to develop skills of compassion, just as repetitions with weights can strengthen muscles.

Compassion: The Downside

Are there any instances when compassion, either self-compassion or other compassion, can hurt us? In the case of self-compassion, probably not (Neff, 2011). Our review of current research did not bring to light a single mention of negative effects of the practice of self-compassion. The treatment of self with empathy and loving kindness seems to have a generally positive effect on humans. However, there are times when other compassion can be harmful. Even with a healthy distress tolerance and a secure attachment style, there are times of extreme stress when an individual becomes overwhelmed and cannot manage to be compassionate without potentially hurting the self. People begin to experience compassion burnout, or *compassion fatigue*, especially in intense situations where there is no break or when they are unable to sufficiently care for themselves (Figley, 1995). Compassion fatigue most often occurs during catastrophic situations (e.g., severe, prolonged, or life-threatening illnesses; natural catastrophes; and wars or terrorist attacks), when even the strongest people cannot cope with the intensity of their own or others' suffering. This can happen to anyone, but is frequently seen in first responders (police, firefighters, emergency medical technicians, and hospital personnel), mental health providers, and family caregivers (Mendenhall & Berge, 2010).

Exercises in Compassion

The following simple exercises can help strengthen your abilities to be compassionate and some of its constituent elements (attunement, empathy, and non-judgment):

Reflective Listening. Most of the time when we talk with someone, we aren't really present when they speak. We are thinking about other things, like what we are going to say next. Instead, *invite yourself* to be curious about the person speaking; imagine she or he is the most fascinating person in the world. Listen carefully to what she or he is saying, and if your mind wanders away, gently bring it back to the present moment. Place yourself in his or her shoes, imagining how she or he feels. When there is a natural break in the conversation, say in a friendly, thoughtful manner, "What I heard you say was . . . Did I understand you right?" Allow him or her time to correct your impression. Let him or her continue talking until she or he has said everything she or he wants to say.

Loving-Kindness Exercise. Like a tiny nitroglycerin pill that can relieve painful symptoms of cardiac angina, these simple phrases can precipitate major positive changes in your experience with yourself and others.

> *May I feel safe.*
> *May I feel happy.*
> *May I feel healthy.*
> *May I live with ease.*

Sit in a quiet place with your spine comfortably straight, eyes closed, and breathing gently. Start by focusing the meditation on yourself (the "I"). Slowly repeat each of the phrases silently ("May I feel safe. . . "), letting yourself feel the safety, happiness, well-being, or ease as you say each phrase in your mind. If your mind wanders, return it gently and kindly to the start of the sequence—there is no place for self-criticism or judgment here. After several minutes, gently move on to focus on a loved one or ones (or to yourself and your partner). Picture him or her in your mind as you repeat the phrases. Picture yourself radiating feelings of safety, happiness, well-being, and ease to him or her. Stay present and aware of how your emotions feel as you continue for several minutes. Finally, as you end, explore your own feelings at this moment. Remind yourself that you can return to these feelings anytime you wish by returning to the exercise (Frederickson, 2013).

Compassionate Love. This is another exercise used in the Fredrickson studies:

> *May you find safety, even in the midst of suffering.*
> *May you find peace, even in the midst of suffering.*
> *May you find strength, even in the midst of suffering.*
> *May you find ease, even in the midst of suffering.*

Repeat these phrases silently as you gently breathe. Envision the person or persons you are directing your compassionate wishes toward; tenderly hold them in your mind's eye as you say the words. Feel yourself radiating an unending source of love and strength to them with each outward breath, one that fills and soothes and strengthens you at the same time. Continue for several minutes. Feel your heart growing larger and stronger and more filled with love, warmth, and understanding. While the suffering individual(s) is the primary focus of the Compassionate Love exercise, by expanding the exercise to include yourself, you reinforce healthy empathy and enhance your ability to be compassionate. You also learn to care more deeply for others because it is anchored in your ability to care for yourself.

FORGIVENESS

Compassion's sister concept is forgiveness. But first, what is it? Sometimes it is easier to start defining a concept by noting what it is *not*. Forgiveness is not excusing, condoning, denying, or pardoning an action. It does not mean forgetting, either. In this chapter, we define forgiveness as "a process involving the reduction of negative feelings and the giving out of undeserved compassion" (Meneses & Greenberg, 2011, p. 491). Other researchers define the act of forgiving as letting go of our right to be resentful, judgmental, or angry toward a person who has hurt us, while coming to a positive view comprised of compassion, understanding, and love toward the wrongdoer (Enright, 1991; Lin, Enright, & Klatt, 2011).

Spiritual and Religious Dimensions of Forgiveness

The concept of forgiveness extends across a broad range of spiritual and philosophical traditions in human cultures. It is a practice that can be found in all of the major religions, including Buddhism, Christianity, Confucianism, Hinduism, Jainism, and Judaism (McCullough, 2000). Different faith traditions view forgiveness in different ways; however, all of them include the idea that forgiveness is virtuous. In general, religious traditions view forgiveness as that which we must do because God—however, He or She is defined—is forgiving. Therefore, in order to be like God, we should be forgiving as well (Rye et al., 2000).

Hinduism combines the word for forgiveness most often with the word for compassion, but the different traditions and viewpoints found within Hinduism make it difficult to define a single theological basis for forgiveness. However, the way of *dharma* (righteousness) includes forgiveness, forbearance, duty, and compassion, and the concept of *karma*, which pervades Hindu thought, is also germane. Through karma, individuals must face the consequences of their actions, and those who are unforgiving bring negative feelings into their future lives.

Buddhism embraces the idea of forbearance and acceptance; one must endure the wrong done to him or her and simultaneously renounce any right to be resentful or vengeful. The Jatakamala, a medieval Indian narrative, tells us how "a raging heart grows calm if one inclines to forbearance, that mainstay in this life and the next" (Arya & Khoroche, 1989, p. 197). In the Jewish tradition, perpetrators are directed to explicitly ask for forgiveness in order to be forgiven. But once the perpetrator has done so, the victim is bound to forgive and, in fact, if she or he does not, is considered to be a sinner. This is not necessarily the case in Christian theology, however, where the act of spontaneous forgiveness is considered to be "Christ-like," (although some modern Biblical scholars disagree about how passive the historical Jesus actually was). Still, the very last words attributed to Jesus were a plea for God to forgive those who were killing him (Luke 23:34 King James Version). Islamic tradition notes the example of the Prophet Muhammad forgiving the entire army and population of Mecca who had fought against him for years; instead of destroying the offenders when he triumphed, the Prophet declared amnesty. According to Haykal (2005), "Muhammad chose to forgive, thereby giving to all mankind and all the generations the most perfect example of goodness, of truthfulness, of nobility, and magnanimity" (p. 408).

How Does Forgiveness Work?

Forgiveness is one of the necessary ingredients in a healthy and functional intimate relationship. It is comprised of two aspects; the first is intrapersonal, and occurs when a person who has been wronged decides to let go of resentments toward the person who has done him or her wrong. The second aspect is interpersonal. In this part of forgiveness, the apologies or confessions of the wrongdoer can help to heal the wound and spur the wronged person to forgive, thereby hastening the repair of the relationship.

Is it possible to forgive without receiving an apology? The short answer is "yes." In the case of intrapersonal forgiveness, one forgives for one's own benefit, and not necessarily the good of the relationship. If the repair of the relationship is of importance, then the transgressor generally needs to repent, apologize, or explain. As we will examine later in this chapter, when the transgressor acknowledges his or her role in the hurtful act, the person who has sustained the injury can move toward forgiving and the healing can begin. In the chapter's opening example, Padma had already begun to release her hurt feelings when she saw how sad Gerald looked. She had begun the intrapersonal process of forgiveness. However, Gerald's apology helped heal the wound. It let her know that he understood he had hurt her, felt regret, and wanted to comfort her.

Forgiveness depends on the type of relationship between the transgressor and the wronged person. In other words, the act of forgiveness can be quite different depending on if the wronged person is in a close relationship with the transgressor, and if she or he has intentions to continue the relationship. For example, a stranger who wrongs someone during a rude incident on the street may not be a good candidate for forgiveness because a continuing relationship is unlikely. But the calculation changes when thinking about friends and family members; these are our close others. Whether, how, and why we decide to forgive them will matter a great deal to our personal well-being and that of the relationship.

Self-forgiveness can be an integral part of the entire process of forgiving in relationship; people who have a hard time with self-forgiveness tend to have a harder time forgiving others (Macaskill, 2012). For instance, consider an adult child who grew up in a household with her alcoholic mother. She might need to spend some time seriously considering whether and how to forgive her mom. Part of the "work" of forgiveness might also include forgiving herself for not being able to fix her mother or their relationship in the ways she wishes she could. Similar to self-compassion, self-forgiveness is something we need to give ourselves if we are to be able to extend it to others.

The dimension of time is another important part of forgiveness (Enright, 1991; Worthington, 2005). We have a harder time forgiving someone the closer we are to the actual instance of the offense. The passage of time, commitment to the relationship with the transgressor, and empathic response are all predictors of forgiveness (McCullough, Fincham & Tsang, 2003; McCullough, Luna, Berry, Tabak, & Bono, 2010). The lighter the transgression, the easier it is for the hurt individual to forgive the transgressor—and the more time that passes, the easier it is to forgive.

Enright (1991) developed a model of forgiveness based on the premise that forgiveness is a multidimensional construct combining the processes of cognition, affect (emotion), and behavior. Specifically, we traverse four phases:

1. The *uncovering phase* occurs when the person gets in touch with the pain, hurt, anger, and fear that she or he is suffering as a result of the injury by exploring the injustice that has been done to him or her.
2. The *decision phase* occurs when the person decides to forgive (even though emotionally she or he may not be ready to actually do the forgiving).
3. The *work phase* encompasses a new frame of seeing the offender through different eyes. Being able to see things through the lens of the offender and deal with the acceptance of the injury is at the heart of forgiveness. In this phase, the injured person accepts his or her own pain instead of hurling it back at the offender or taking it out on innocent others.
4. The *outcome phase* involves the impact that the act of forgiveness has had on the injured person. During this phase, the injured person realizes that the act of forgiveness precipitates healing in both parties.

When we forgive, we do for others and for ourselves. In doing so, we reap the benefits of improved psychological health and increased happiness (Freedman, Enright & Knudson, 2005; Worthington, 2005).

Forgiveness in Intimate Relationships

All relationships are fraught with the inevitability that we will eventually do harm to one another. It is the paradox of close intimate relationships; the ones who we are the closest to have the greatest capacity to hurt us, and vice versa. These emotional injuries can mar connections between people and significantly disrupt relationships (Allemand, Amberg, Zimprich, & Fincham, 2007; Meneses & Greenberg, 2011). Many forgiveness researchers maintain that the responses that victims have toward transgressors (such as holding grudges and rehearsing memories of the hurt) have significant consequences for their physical, emotional, and mental health (Witvliet, Ludwig, & Laan, 2001). Many point to actions such as rehearsing the hurt and holding grudges as the primary ways that individuals resist forgiveness (Witvliet et al., 2001). However, researchers have also found evidence that forgiveness in romantic relationships is linked to an increase in relationship satisfaction and intimacy because it rebuilds trust and balances relational power (Fincham, Beach, & Davila, 2004; Friesen, Fletcher, & Overall, 2005; Greenberg, Warwar, & Malcom, 2010).

Merolla (2008) examined three separate types of forgiveness: direct, indirect, and conditional. *Direct forgiveness* is when the person who has been wronged explicitly and authentically states the forgiving, "I forgive you" or "That's okay." *Indirect forgiveness* happens when the wronged person lets it be known that the relationship is back on solid ground by means of humor or other indirect means. In this case, forgiveness is simply understood between the two individuals in the relationship; the non-verbal behaviors and indirect communication signal that all is well and the negative effects of the transgression are past. For example, one partner may say, "It's no big deal" with a smile to indicate that the event is over (Merolla, 2008). Finally, *conditional forgiveness* occurs when forgiveness is communicated, but exists only under clear conditions. An example of this might be when the transgressor is verbally abusive when drunk, and the victim forgives with an agreement that the drinking will be controlled from now on. This third type of forgiveness often accompanies ongoing negative actions on the part of the transgressor.

Forgiveness and Reconciliation

Forgiveness and reconciliation are distinct from one another and constitute two separate actions. Forgiveness is the letting go of our right to be resentful, while reconciliation follows forgiveness and results in the "restoration of violated trust" (Fincham, 2000, p. 7).

There are times when reconciliation may not be appropriate, like when the damage to trust is irreparable, when the victim has become emotionally apathetic to the transgressor after a history of emotional injuries, or where there is chronic intimate partner violence (IPV) (Gottman, 2011). In the case of IPV, forgiveness might be based on rationalizations by the victim that she or he deserved the abuse (Lamb, 2002; Tsang & Stanford, 2007). When such rationalizations result in forgiveness *and* reconciliation, the IPV can continue.

Other situations that may require deeper consideration include survivors of genocide, such as the Holocaust and the massacres in Rwanda and Bosnia, to name only a few awful societal wounds in great need of repair (Brudholm & Gron, 2011). However, former South African President Nelson Mandela was a major example of using the power of forgiveness (Vandevelde, 2013). The Truth and Reconciliation Project in South Africa did a great deal of good in its attempts to bind the wounds of the two peoples, oppressors and oppressed, in order to knit the nation together going forward (Gathogo, 2012).

But How Do We Actually Do This?

Researcher Les Greenberg and his associates have observed couples who have suffered a serious emotional injury (such as infidelity by one partner) and identified a process that couples go through during therapy to successfully forgive and reconcile (Meneses & Greenberg, 2011). In their research, the couples who were able to repair their relationship (50% of them) were observed to follow certain steps in a specific order. Those couples who failed to follow these steps failed to repair their relationships (see Figure 2).

Consider how the process would look between Katherine and Max: Katherine had been deeply hurt when she discovered Max "sexting" with another woman. Max stopped sexting immediately, but that was not enough for Katherine. During therapy, Katherine was able to speak fully about what Max did and her feelings about it, while Max listened quietly and non-defensively. He did not attempt to shorten the process because he was uncomfortable, but sat it out, witnessing his wife's pain while owning his actions. Katherine could see in Max's facial responses and body language that he felt her pain (empathy) *and* felt shame that his actions had caused her pain. Seeing one's partner show empathy toward one's self and shame for his or her own actions seems to be the necessary step to open the victim up to forgiveness. As this happened, Katherine stopped seeing Max as the enemy. Without that first step, the forgiveness and reconciliation process would have stalled and failed.

FIGURE 2   Processes of Couple Forgiveness

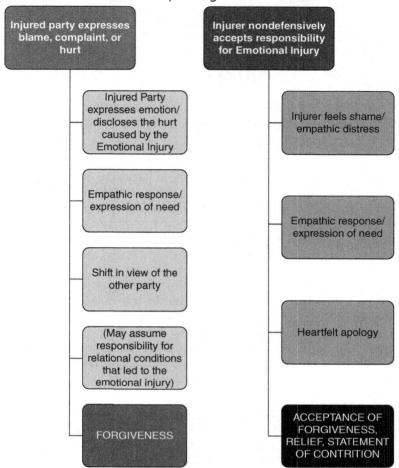

Adapted from: Meneses, C. W., & Greenberg, L. S. (2011). Construction of a model of the process of couples' forgiveness in Emotion-Focused Therapy for couples. *Journal of Marital and Family Therapy, 37*(4), 491–502. doi:10.1111/j.1752-0606.2011.00234.x.

The second half of the process took place when Max made a heartfelt apology for his actions (including a *realistic* promise to not repeat the hurtful act). This gave Katherine the emotional freedom to explore any possible part she may have had in the conditions that preceded the betrayal. By viewing herself as a participant in the occurrence, Katherine may have reduced her fear and felt less like a victim; she also could take steps in the future to recognize and prevent another betrayal. This is the point when forgiveness actually takes place. The process was incomplete, however, until Max acknowledged her forgiveness and responded with relief and contrition.

Reconciliation constitutes more than just forgiveness because it accommodates a movement toward greater intimacy and the rebuilding of trust. The researchers observed that for couples who did not reconcile, reconciliation was sidetracked by pressuring the victim to forgive the transgressor, the transgressor failing to show empathy or distress/shame, the couple entering into a competition of hurts, or the failure of the transgressor to apologize or offer reasonable assurances that the hurt would not be repeated.

While daunting at times, the act of forgiving those who have injured us may lead to better mental and physical health. It is necessary for sustaining (and deepening) loving relationships. Even though forgiving others can seem terribly difficult (and is considered appropriate or inappropriate based on the situation at hand), the outcome is generally worth the effort. Forgiving is not condoning or supporting injurious behavior, but instead recognizing that we need to forgive in order to receive forgiveness when we injure or do wrong to a loved one. And this is one of the core ideas within the forgiveness literature that brings us back to the Golden Rule: *Do unto others as you would have them do unto you, and forgive others so that you yourself might be forgiven.*

COMPASSION AND FORGIVENESS TOGETHER

Let's return to the story of Padma and Gerald, who we started this chapter with. What was going on inside of each of them that allowed them to recover from a painful interaction and move closer?

- When Gerald saw the vase begin to fall, his sense of empathy surged to the forefront. He remembered Padma's pain at losing her beloved aunt and he knew how the vase was a concrete representation of this person. In that split second, he stood in her shoes and *felt* loss and grief, and sensed that the destruction of the vase would bring that pain back. His awareness of her feelings was so strongly anchored in the moment that he had no thought of protecting himself from any anger she might feel. He moved toward her physically, attempting to comfort and soothe her. He also felt guilt for contributing to her pain—even if it was accidental—and sadness. The guilt and sadness showed in his face and his body, and in his words as he attempted to apologize.

- As the vase fell, Padma was flooded with grief and loss—just as Gerald had foreseen. In that moment, she was aware of her pain and was able to tolerate it in a state of self-compassion. Yet, even in the experience of her pain, as she turned to face Gerald, she became aware of how closely attuned his feelings were to hers. She *knew* in her deepest heart that he felt her pain; she was no longer suffering alone, and that comforted her. Her awareness of his empathy allowed her to observe his sadness and guilt and feel how he was suffering as the result of his actions. She was able to forgive him and make space within her grief to reach out to comfort him, just as he reached to comfort her.

Padma and Gerald stayed present and observant of their own pain, yet were comfortable enough to accommodate and honor the other. In doing so, they moved closer together in emotional intimacy. Each was a source of comfort, safety, and warmth for the other, and the memory of that would stay with them, both cushioning them in future adversity and strengthening their bond of love.

One plus one makes two. Ultimately, the most important thing we bring into our relationships are ourselves. Who we are and how we choose to interact with others is what makes or breaks relationships. The more compassionate and forgiving we can become, the richer and more resilient our relationships will be. The key to becoming a compassionate and forgiving lover is in being compassionate and forgiving to one's self. The greater the effort you put into growing yourself, the greater the return for both you and your relationship. And while some aspects of compassion normally develop in childhood, with effort they can be developed or enhanced at any time in our lives. The abilities to be compassionate and to forgive are a foundation for learning to be with others in ways that lead to healthy and functional relationships.

REFERENCES

Allemand, M., Amberg, I., Zimprich, D. & Fincham, F. (2007). The role of trait forgiveness and relationship satisfaction in episodic forgiveness. *Journal of Social and Clinical Psychology, 26*(2), 199–217. doi:10.1521/jscp.2007.26.2.199.

Armstrong, K. (2006). *The great transformation: The beginning of our religious traditions.* New York: Alfred A. Knopf.

Armstrong, K. (2010). *Twelve steps to a compassionate life.* New York: Alfred A. Knopf.

Arya, S., & Khoroche, P. (1989). *Once the Buddha was a monkey: Arya Sura's Jatakamala.* Chicago, IL: University of Chicago Press.

Baer, R. A. (2010). Self-compassion as a mechanism of change in mindfulness- and acceptance-based treatments. In R. Baer (Ed.), *Assessing mindfulness and acceptance processes in clients* (pp. 135–164). Oakland, CA: New Harbinger Publication, Inc.

Bowlby, J. (1969). *Attachment and loss. Volume I: Attachment.* New York: Basic Books.

Brudholm, T., & Grøn, A. (2011). Picturing forgiveness after atrocity. *Studies in Christian Ethics, 24*(2), 159–170. doi:10.1177/0953946810397441

Coan, J. A., Schaefer, H. S., & Davidson, R. J. (2006). Lending a hand: Social regulation of the neural response to threat. *Psychological Science, 17,* 1032–1039. doi:10.1111/j.1467-9280.2006.01832.x.

de Waal, F. (2009). *The age of empathy: Nature's lessons for a kinder society.* New York: Harmony Books.

Enright, R. D. (1991). The moral development of forgiveness. In W. Kurtines and J. Gewirtz (Eds.), The Handbook of Moral Behavior and Development, (Vol. 1, p. 123–151). Hillsdale, NJ: Erlbaum.

Fallon, J. (2013). *The psychopath inside: A neuroscientist's personal journey into the dark side of the brain.* New York: Current.

Figley, C. R. (1995). Compassion fatigue as secondary traumatic stress disorder: An overview. In C. R. Figley (Ed.), *Compassion fatigue: Coping with secondary traumatic stress in those who treat the traumatized* (pp. 1–20). London: Brunner-Routledge.

Fincham, F. D. (2000). The kiss of the porcupines: From attributing responsibility to forgiving. *Personal Relationships, 7*(1), 1–23. doi:10.1111/j.1475-6811.2000.tb00001.x.

Fincham, F. D, Beach, S. R. H., & Davila, J. (2004). Forgiveness & conflict resolution in marriage. *Journal of Family Psychology, 18,* 72–81. doi:10.1037/0893-2300.18.1.72.

Fishbane, M. D. (2013). *Loving with the brain in mind: Neurobiology & couple therapy.* New York: W. W. Norton & Company.

Fredrickson, B. L. (2013). *Love 2.0: How our supreme emotion affects everything we think feel, do and become.* London: Hudson Street Press.

Freedman, S. R., Enright, R. D., & Knutson, J. (2005). A progress report on the process model of forgiveness. In E. L. Worthington, Jr. (Ed.), *Handbook of Forgiveness* (pp. 393–406). New York: Brunner-Routledge.

Friesen, M. D., Fletcher, G. J. O., & Overall, N. C. (2005). A dyadic assessment of forgiveness in intimate relationships. *Personal Relationships, 12,* 61–77. doi:10.1111/j.1350-4126.2005.00102.x.

Fruzzetti, A. E., & Iverson, K. M. (2006). Intervening with couples and families to treat emotion dysregulation and psychopathology. In D. Synder and J. Simpson (Eds.), *Emotion Regulation in Couples and Families: Pathways to Dysfunction and Health* (pp. 249–267). Washington, DC: American Psychological Association.

Gathogo, J. (2012). Reconciliation paradigm in the post colonial Africa: A critical analysis. *Religion & Theology, 19*(1/2), 74–91. doi:10.1163/15743012-12341235

Gilbert, P. (2005a). Introduction and outline. In P. Gilbert (Ed.), *Compassion: Conceptualizations, research, and use in therapy* (pp. 1–9). London: Routledge.

Gilbert, P. (2005b). Compassion and cruelty: A biopsychosocial approach. In P. Gilbert (Ed.), *Compassion: Conceptualizations, research, and use in therapy* (pp. 9–74). London: Routledge.

Gilbert, P. (2009). Introducing compassion-focused therapy. *Advances in Psychiatric Treatment, 15*(3), 199–208.

Gilbert, P., & Tirch, D. (2009). Emotional memory, mindfulness, and compassion. In F. Didonna (Ed.), *Clinical Handbook of Mindfulness* (pp. 99–110). New York: Springer.

Gilleth, O., Shaver, P. R., & Mikulincer, M. (2005). An attachment-theoretical approach to compassion and altruism. In P. Gilbert (Ed.), *Compassion: Conceptualizations, research, and use in therapy* (pp. 121–147). London: Routledge.

Gottman, J. M. (2011). *The science of trust: Emotional attunement for couples.* New York: W.W. Norton & Company.

Greenberg, L. S., Warwar, S., & Malcom, W. (2010). Emotion-focused couples therapy and the facilitation of forgiveness. *Journal of Marital and Family Therapy, 36*(1), 28–42. doi:10.1111/j.1752-0606.2009.00185.x.

Haykal, M. H. (2005). *The Life of Muhammad.* Oak Brook, IL: American Trust Publications.

Hoffman, M. L. (2001). Toward a comprehensive prosocial moral development. In A. C. Bohart, & D. J. Stipek (Eds.), *Constructive & Destructive Behaviors: Implications for Family, School, & Society,* (pp. 61–86). Washington, DC: American Psychological Association. doi:10/1037/10433-003.

Johnson, S. M. (2002). *Emotionally focused couple therapy with trauma survivors: Strengthening attachment bonds.* New York: Guilford Press.

Lamb, S. (2002). Women, abuse, and forgiveness: A special case. In J. G. Murphy and S. Lamb (Eds.), *Before forgiving: Cautionary views of forgiveness in psychotherapy,* pp. 155–171. London: Oxford University Press.

Langford, D., Crager, S., Shehzad, Z., Smith, S., Sotocinal, S., Levenstadt, J., . . . Mogil, J. (2006). Social modulation of pain as evidence for empathy in mice. *Science, 312,* 1967–1970. doi:10.1126/science.1128322.

Lin, W. E., Enright, R., & Klatt, J. (2011). Forgiveness as character education for children and adolescents. *Journal of Moral Education, 40*(2), 237–253. doi:10.1080/03057240.2011.568106.

Macaskill, A. (2012). Differentiating dispositional self-forgiveness from other-forgiveness: Associations with mental health and life satisfaction. *Journal of Social & Clinical Psychology, 31*(1), 28–50. doi:10.1521/jscp.2012.31.1.28.

Main, M., Kaplan, N., & Cassidy, J. (1985). Security in infancy, childhood, and adulthood: A move to the level of representation. *Monographs of the Society for Research in Child Development, 50*(1/2), 66–104.

McCullough, M. (2000). Forgiveness as human strength: Theory, measurement and links to well-being. *Journal of Clinical and Social Psychology, 19*(1), 43–55. doi:10.1521/jscp.2000.19.1.43.

McCullough, M, Fincham, F. & Tsang, J. (2003). Forgiveness, forbearance, and time: The temporal unfolding of transgression-related interpersonal motivations. *Journal of Personality and Social Psychology, 84*(3), 540–557. doi:10.1037/0022-3514.84.3.540.

McCullough, M. E., L., Berry, J. W., Tabak, B. A., & Bono, G. (2010). On the form and function of forgiving: Modeling the time-forgiveness relationship and testing the valuable relationships hypothesis. *Emotion, 10*(3), 358–376. doi:10.1037/a0019349.

Mendenhall, T., & Berge, J. (2010). Family therapists in trauma-response teams: Bringing systems thinking into interdisciplinary fieldwork. *Journal of Family Therapy, 32,* 40–54. doi:10.1111/j.1467-6427.2009.00482.x

Meneses, C. W., & Greenberg, L. S. (2011). Construction of a model of the process of couples' forgiveness in Emotion-Focused Therapy for couples. *Journal of Marital and Family Therapy, 37*(4), 491–502. doi:10.1111/j.1752-0606.2011.00234.x.

Merolla, A. (2008). Communicating forgiveness in friendships and dating relationships. *Communication Studies, 59*(2), 114–131. doi:10.1080/10510970802062428.

Mikulincer, M., & Shaver, P. R. (2005). Attachment security, compassion, and altruism. *Current Directions in Psychological Science, 14*(1), 34–38. doi:10.1111/j.0963-7214.2005.00330.x.

Neff, K. D. (2003). The development and validation of a scale to measure self-compassion. *Self and Identity, 2,* 223–250. doi:10/1080/15298860390209035.

Neff, K. D. (2011). Self-compassion, self-esteem and well-being. *Social and Personality Psychology Compass, 5*(1), 1–12. doi:10.1111/j.1751-9004.2010.00330.x.

Neff, K. D., & Beretvas, S. N. (2013). The role of self-compassion in romantic relationships. *Self and Identity, 12*(1), 78–98. doi:10.1080/15298868.2011.639548.

Neff, K. D., Kirkpatrick, K. L., & Rude, S. S. (2007). Self-compassion and adaptive psychological functioning. *Journal of Research in Personality, 41,* 139–154. doi:10.1016/j.jrp.2006.03.004.

Neff, K. D., Rude, S. S., & Kirkpatrick, K. L. (2007). An examination of self-compassion in relation to positive psychological functioning and personality traits. *Journal of Research in Personality, 41,* 908–916. doi:10.1016/j.jrp.2006.08.002.

Pace, T. W., Negi, L. T., Adame, D. D., Cole, S. P., Sivilli, T. I., Brown, T. D., . . . & Raison, C. L. (2009). Effect of compassion meditation on neuroendocrine, innate immune and behavioral responses to psycholosocial stress. *Psychoneuroendocrinology, 34*(1), 87–98. doi:10.1016/j.psyneuen.2008.08.011.

Rye, M. S., Pargament, K. I., Ali, M. A., Beck, G. L., Dorff,E. N., Hallisey, C., Narayanan, V. & Williams, J. G. (2000). Religious perspectives on forgiveness. In M. E. McCullough, K. I. Pargament, & C. E. Thoresen (Eds.), *Forgiveness: Theory, Research and Practice* (pp. 17–40). London: Guilford Press.

Segal, Z. V., Williams, L. M., & Teasdale, J. D. (2002). *Mindfulness-based cognitive therapy for depression: A new approach to preventing relapse.* New York: Guilford Press.

Siegel, D. J. (2001). Toward an interpersonal neurobiology of the developing mind: Attachment relationships, "mindsight," and neural integration. *Infant Mental Health Journal, 22*(1–2), 67–94. doi:10.1002/1097-0355(200101/04)22:1<67::AID-IMHJ3>3.0.CO;2-G.

Siegel, D. (2012). *The developing mind: How relationships and the brain interact to share who we are* (2nd ed.). New York: Guilford Press.

Solomon, M. F. (2003). Connection, disruption, repair: Treating the effects of attachment trauma on intimate relationships. In M. F. Solomon & D. J. Siegel (Eds.), *Healing trauma: Attachment, mind, body, and brain* (pp. 322–346). New York W. W. Norton & Company.

Sprecher, S., & Fehr, B. (2005). Compassionate love for close others and humanity. *Journal of Social and Personal Relationships, 22,* 629–651. doi:10.1177/0265407505056439.

Sroufe, L., Egeland, B., Carlson, E., & Collins, W. (2005). *The development of the person: The Minnesota study of risk and adaptation from birth to adulthood.* New York: Guilford Press.

Tsang, J., & Stanford, M. S. (2007). Forgiveness for intimate partner violence: The influence of victim and offender variables. *Personality and Individual Differences, 42,* 653–664. doi:10.1016/j.paid.2006.08.017.

Vandevelde, P. (2013). Forgiveness in a political context: The challenge and the potential. *Philosophy & Social Criticism, 39*(3), 263–276. doi:10.1177/0191453712473079.

Witvliet, C. v. O., Ludwig, T. E., & Laan, K. v. L. (2001). Granting forgiveness or harboring grudges: Implications for emotion, physiology, and health. *Psychological Science, 12*(2), 117–123. doi:10.1111/1467-9280.00320.

Worthington, E., Jr. (2005). Initial questions about the art and science of forgiving. In E. L. Worthington, Jr. (Ed.), *Handbook of Forgiveness* (pp. 1–14). New York: Taylor & Francis Group/Routledge.

18
Relationships Across the Lifespan

J. Max Zubatsky, Ph.D., LMFT
*Department of Family and Community
Medicine
Saint Louis University*

Stephanie Trudeau, M.S.
*Department of Family Social Science
University of Minnesota*

LEARNING OBJECTIVES

- Understand key elements to sustaining a relationship over time
- Articulate the manners in which leading theories conceptualize change and growth within couples over the life course
- Understand contemporary trends in partnership (without marriage) and singlehood

INTRODUCTION

© Blend Images, 2014. Used under license from Shutterstock, Inc.

© Rommel Canlas, 2014. Used under license from Shutterstock, Inc.

© Andy Dean Photography, 2014. Used under license from Shutterstock, Inc.

"Having been married for 35 years, we have gone through numerous ups and downs. My husband, Don, was diagnosed with Alzheimer's Disease four years ago. To say that this has been a stressor on our relationship is putting it mildly. I try to find perspective through the most difficult times. It started as occasional forgetfulness, where he began to misplace his keys or forgot what to buy from the grocery store. I could see the pain on his face when he forgot even the smallest of things. He's a stubborn but proud man, a quality that I was surprisingly attracted to when we first met. Now, Don has to be reminded 15–20 times a day about routine things. His memory has gotten to the point where he can no longer drive and he can't be left alone. When Don worked in the financial industry, I remember both of us going to fine dining restaurants with his colleagues and clients. Now, I have to remind him what goes into a BLT for lunch.

My role as a wife has changed as well. I'm in an ongoing tug-of-war between spouse and caregiver. It's a role that I've accepted, but was not something I imagined years back. You always picture growing old with someone who can enjoy sharing those golden memories in life together. You reminisce about wedding photos,

Corresponding Author: J. Max Zubatsky, Ph.D., LMFT, Saint Louis University; Department of Family and Community Medicine; Medical Family Therapy Program; 3700 Lindell Blvd.; 1129 Morrissey Hall; St. Louis, MO 63108. E-mail: zubatskyjm@slu.edu.

memorable family reunions, and even embarrassing events. When friends invite us to parties nowadays, I often decline. Although I would enjoy the company of others, I can't put Don in a vulnerable position where he meets lifelong comrades for the first time again. I monitor his medications, doctor appointments, meals, and clothing for the day. Our house used to be clean and organized with family heirlooms and nice furniture. Now, certain rooms resemble the medical wing of a hospital.

I'm not sure how much more Don will remember from our years of marriage, let alone his life. The most difficult thing in the world is to hold the person you love the most, realizing that they will probably never remember that moment again. When I brush the palm of his hand across my cheek, I want him to remember how I feel. I want to believe there will be something in his memory that reminds him what I mean to him. This disease has made me re-prioritize my values in life. In a sense, I have to re-marry the one I love multiple times over. Yet, I wouldn't trade that love in the world for anything. When you're committed to someone and develop a lifetime bond, nothing replaces that promise."

One may read this story and think of the unique sadness and vulnerability that this wife is going through. How can she continue to be intimate with someone who often forgets her name or fails to recognize her face? The reality is that millions of individuals across the world endure this same vulnerability in relationships over time. The roads of relationships have unpredictable roadblocks, turns, and express lanes. With longer life expectancies anticipated over this next century come a greater frequency of chronic illnesses and diseases. Couples at different stages of life experience many celebrations, tragedies, stressors, and realizations about both themselves and their partners over the years.

We titled this chapter, "Relationships Across the Life Span" because individuals may choose to enter a relationship, partnership or marriage at different time points in life. Where one person may marry at 25 and want to raise children, another person may be single until they choose to date a widow at 55. The timeframe and course of relationships ebbs and flows based on many circumstances. We generally refer to "long-lived" relationships rather than "long-term" relationships.

In the pages that follow, we outline four principal areas relevant to relationships across the life span: (1) ways to sustain relationships across the life span, (2) theoretical approaches to viewing how couples and families move through the life course (and the adjustments and adaptations they make along the way), (3) major relationship decisions, and (4) stressors that affect relationships across biological, psychological, and social levels. We offer three case scenarios in conclusion that raise important family and ethical decision-making issues in relationships across the life span.

LONG-LIVED RELATIONSHIPS

Let's face it; commitment is a tough concept in our society. With the emergence of 24-hour media, constant advances in technology, and the connections we have globally, the world can be a pretty distracting place. We often want the latest and best thing, and are consistently "bettering" ourselves with the newest products on the

> A successful marriage requires falling in love many times, always with the same person.
>
> – *Mignon McLaughlin*

market. Relationships are not immune to these phenomena. Even in later life stages, people are now living longer and stay together for longer periods of time. Those whose initial courtship turns into cohabitation, marriage, or any other kind of long-lived union must embrace a relationship that requires dedication, trust, direction, and commitment. Successful relationships not only find ways to survive and thrive over time, but also ways to adjust to the increased, expected, and unexpected demands in life.

We view healthy long-lived relationships as persistent and emotionally close connections that span over several life stages. These relationships can be marital (or committed without marriage), familial, or close friendships. They are unique insofar as they are among the few relationships in a person's life that span several decades.

FIGURE 1   Trends in Cohabitating Couples in the United States

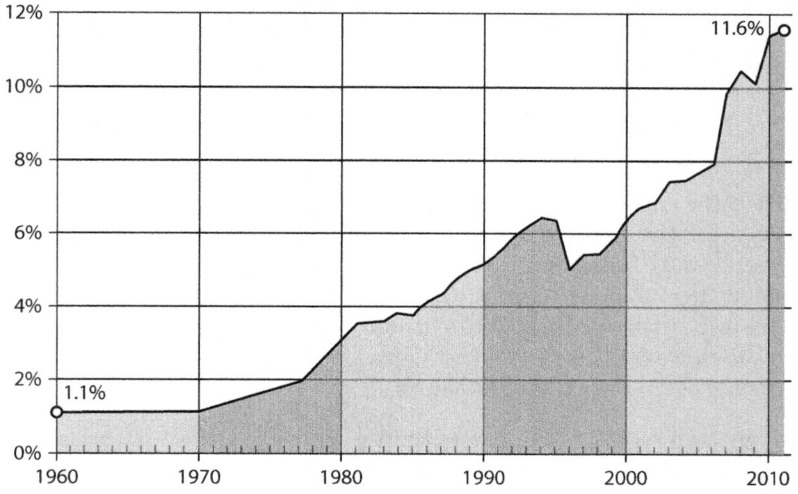

Source: U.S. Census Bureau, Current Population Survey, 2011

Statistics on Long-Lived Relationships

The landscape of long-lived relationships has changed significantly over the last 50 years. Since 2000, while the population in the United States has increased, the number of registered marriages has declined (CDC/NCHS National Vital Statistics System, 2012). Americans are putting off marriage at greater rates, and are identifying education, careers, and mobility as the major reasons. In the 1960s, it was common for individuals to first get married, and then form their life's goals (e.g., education, parenthood). Today, school, work, buying homes, and relocating often precede the formation of committed relationships, with marriage being the final milestone (Cherlin, 2009).

At the same time that marriage rates are declining, couples are increasingly starting to cohabitate. More men and women are living together for longer years, whether they decide to get married or not. Cohabitating couples have increased ten-fold in the past 50 years, from slightly more than 1% in 1960 to over 11% in 2010 (see Figure 1). Nearly half of women aged 15 to 44 years old cohabited outside of marriage between 2006 and 2010, compared with 43% in 2002 and only 34% in 1995. Along with this trend, fewer women reported getting married in the period from 2006 to 2010 than in either 2002 or 1995 (Copen, Daniels, & Moshler, 2013). Many couples who choose to cohabitate see this phase as the initial "courtship" in their relationship. Many others see it as an alternative to marriage.

SUSTAINING LONG-LIVED RELATIONSHIPS

Sustaining a long-lived relationship requires deliberate effort. In this section, we describe three key ways that couples can maintain and improve their relationships, including using the $1 + 1 = 2$ formula, goal setting, and establishing rituals. These perspectives and skills are particularly important as couples transition across major life events and stages.

The $1 + 1 = 2$ Formula

This simple mathematical equation can sometimes be very challenging for new couples. This formula gives insight into partners knowing not only their own role in the relationship, but what the relationship as a whole must build on. Couples who have a solid foundation in all three parts of the formula will be more likely to have longer relationship satisfaction than those who struggle in one or more parts. The following describes the three parts of this formula.

THE FIRST "1": HOW DO I SEE MYSELF IN THE RELATIONSHIP? It is important that individuals attend to how they see themselves in the context of the relationship. Many times, spouses will not recognize their own participation in problems or conflict. One must feel comfortable working on his or her own weaknesses and challenges in order to improve the quality of a marriage. Each partner in a struggling relationship has to look at how they need to communicate in a healthier and safer way. This may also entail finding ways that each person views their own self-worth and sets personal boundaries and limits in their life.

THE SECOND "1": HOW DO I SEE MY PARTNER IN THE RELATIONSHIP? In addition to how one sees one's self in a relationship, the individual must also be cognizant of his or her partner's needs. Awareness of these needs increases through effective communication and support for the partner's goals and making unconditional sacrifices. Both partners should give signs of affection and support for the other person, not just through difficult times, but during good times and accomplishments as well. Relationships work best when both individuals recognize that they must continually attend to and ask about their partner's needs and feelings.

THE "2": HOW DO BOTH PARTNERS WORK TOGETHER IN THE RELATIONSHIP? When relationships progress over time, both partners track where the context of the relationship stands. Both individuals are intentional about how the relationship needs to grow and continue to maintain intimacy and connection. Partners now see decision-making and goal setting as a team approach, not just two individual perspectives or separate roles. In a relationship where communication problems exist, both partners have to be—or learn to be—effective speakers and listeners. This may involve partners reflecting on what their partner has told them, instead of responding in a defensive or criticizing way.

Goal Setting

In the context of relationships, a goal is a mental representation of a desired outcome that a person is committed to (Norcross, 2012). When couples get stuck in the same routines and patterns over time, they often struggle in evolving their union. Couples benefit mentally and relationally when setting short-term (e.g., plan a vacation, chose a new apartment) and long-term (e.g., retirement planning, paying off financial aid debt) goals for their future. Goals help couples evolve as a partnership, achieve milestones, and celebrate achievements over the course of their lives. Furthermore, goals help couples learn more about one another and offer continual growth in the relationship.

Effective goals should be directly communicated, address key issues, and include both partners. For example, couples can discuss their weekly goals over coffee on a Sunday morning, meet with a financial advisor regarding how to outline their long-term savings or discuss possible relocation options if a new job arises or one wants to be closer to family. Regardless of the format in which couples form goals, there should be key issues addressed in the relationship that impact both individuals. The goals should be mutual and goal planning should give both partners the latitude to achieve the goal. Some examples of goals include: support goals (e.g., tending to medical issues in a partner's family), individual/growth goals (e.g., how each person can give intentional time to the relationship), family goals (e.g., what times families eat meals together), financial goals (e.g., when do partners purchase a new car or plan to retire together), intimacy goals (e.g., how often couples show signs of affection) and problem-solving goals (e.g., how couples manage time during a busy work week). Couples must be realistic at how much they can set forth to achieve, given the other demands and necessities in work, family, and social areas.

There are several benefits for couples to continue goal setting at different time points. Goal-setting:

- **Sparks and increases communication during challenging and difficult times:** It is one thing to communicate well when things in life are riding along. But when stressors (internal or external from the relationship) enter into the couple, this tests how well a couple connects. It is a very healthy sign when both partners can process difficult aspects in the relationship or in personal life and trust that the other person will listen. A husband is contemplating bringing his mother to stay with the couple because of her financial situation. The couple sits down multiple times at the dinner table to discuss the pros and cons of this decision in a clear and effective manner.

- **Strengthens the quality of the relationship over time:** Investing in a long-term relationship takes lots of effort. Couples who continue to set attainable goals keep the motivation level high for both partners. This agenda now becomes a team effort that the couple can strive for together. One partner wants the couple to start exercising more in order to improve their overall health. Over time, the couple wakes up earlier and spends more shared time around running before work.
- **Holds both partners accountable for working towards a desired interest or need:** Some couples fall into the "over-functioner/under-functioner" dance, wherein one partner will compensate the work in the relationship for the under-performing partner. With both people setting goals, accountability is in the open, with a greater understanding that both people must contribute to the end goal in mind. A couple who is struggling financially may benefit from using a plan that utilizes both partners' strengths. At the same time, both partners must execute their tasks separately in order for the couple to be financially sound in the long run.
- **Keeps the relationship a top priority in one's life:** Couples go through many stressors and distractions throughout their lives. When time passes so quickly, the intentional time to work on the relationship often times gets overlooked. Two partners can sit down and schedule time on the calendar to eat meals together around a busy work schedule. This way, the couple continues to put their priorities ahead of any life demands or tasks in the near future.

Establishing Rituals

Rituals (addressed more thoroughly in Chapter 14) are meaningful actions within the context of interpersonal relationships, and reflections of our common and varied history, culture, ethnicity, and social norms (Imber Black, Roberts, & Whiting, 2003). Rituals are grounded in our everyday routines. Routines are patterned behavioral interactions that are repeated over time. Rituals involve not only the practice of routines, but also the representation of one's beliefs concerning personal, family, or spiritual identity (Fiese et al., 2002). From brushing our teeth to checking email, we develop naturalistic habits that make us feel comfortable in our daily functioning. The same can be said for the interactional routines that couples and relationships go through. A ritual can be a specific routine that helps us feel connected or comfortable.

In relationships, the range of rituals can vary based on the level of connection individuals hope to achieve. A love ritual may involve a simple card or an act of physical affection, showing the other person how much they love them. A spiritual or religious ritual could be a couple attending a religious service or observing a holiday of sacred importance. A family ritual could involve annual Thanksgiving dinners, where the relationship is part of a larger group of familial and close relationships within the family system. These practices are necessary ways for couples to embrace the importance of their bond and re-shift life priorities back onto the relationship.

Rituals can help long-lived couples adjust to transitions, too. Whether it is work, children, hobbies, school commitments, or extended family, partners learn to adapt to these life themes over time. Healthy relationships grow not just with age, but through personal engagement as well. Couples learn to "re-discover" each other's life in new ways. But couples must make this time available in their relationship to provide fulfilling results. Couples can fall in love all over again through simple rituals such as going for walks, bike-riding, exchanging gifts, or making a romantic meal together. Couples also need intentional rituals, such as simply "checking-in" with each other ten minutes per day. With kids, busier work schedules, parental and extended family issues, and other life demands requiring greater time from couples, setting relationship routines become paramount in later stages of life.

With the consumer-based thinking of what marriage and relationships should look like, couples can get caught trying to "keep up with the Joneses" in the community. Our consumer culture has always been geared around individuals getting what they want, when they want it. And we never have enough of what we want in a culture where the newest and hottest thing on the market is always the most coveted. Why fix a broken mp3 player when you can get the newest ipod on the market? If a car has even minimal maintenance issues after three years, why not trade it in for an upgraded style? The same can be said of our relationships in the 21st century, where we are always

In the book, "Take Back Your Marriage" by William Doherty (2001), there are several tips for how couples can create rituals in their union. The following are some ideas:

- Establish a set time to talk everyday with no discussion of money, children, or chores
- Create a greeting ritual that marks the moment and has meaning for the couple
- Leave an affectionate note for your spouse that has no practical purpose
- Start dating again; go out on a spontaneous date
- Spend more quiet time together without the television on

looking around the corner to see what might be better. Rituals help couples view and remember what attracted them to one another in the first place, emphasizing the uniqueness of their relationship in a fast-paced ever-changing world.

The following is the narrative of a couple discussing rituals in a therapy session. This later life couple places importance on the ritual of remembering the loss of their son several years ago:

Therapist: "When did your child pass away?"

Wife: "Almost ten years ago. It's been very difficult to forget his death even after this many years. It helps that we created a ritual every year to remember him. On the anniversary of his death, we walk down to the park where we used to play and have picnics. My husband and I make the same meal that he used to enjoy so much and reminisce about the times we spent down there."

Husband: "Every time we go, we have a new story or memory that comes up. It's helped us in the grief process, but there are still the dates on the calendar that really hit me hard."

Therapist: "What are some of those times?"

Wife: "For me, it's the holidays, specifically Thanksgiving and Christmas. Cooking that day without him looking over my shoulder or making a funny comment is really tough to realize."

Husband: "I would agree. Especially when family comes over for holidays, the conversation at some point always comes up. Sometimes, it's like walking on eggshells when one person wants to give homage to Tommy, and others at the table seem uncomfortable."

Wife: "But you've said that it helps when others in the family think about him as well. It's not just us going through the coping of his death."

Husband: "That's true."

Therapist: "It looks like both of you have tried to navigate this road as best as possible. And the times you set aside to think about him are very important."

Wife: "You're right. Now, it's trying to move on with what we want to do as a couple nearing retirement. Yet, because this was our only child, you tend to think of scenarios regarding the grandchildren or future family that you'll never get now."

Rituals at many stages of life can help couples set routines and place importance on intentionality in their relationships. Many couples will carve out time to take a walk and discuss the events in their life outside of home or work

THEORIES ABOUT LONG-LIVED RELATIONSHIPS

Reflection Questions

1. What rituals do you feel comfortable sharing with a partner?
2. What types of rituals would you be open to learning about from your current or future partner?

There are several different conceptualizations about what factors influence the dynamics of relationships across time. Historical and cultural events can shape how families and couples adapt and adjust their paths. The quality and longevity of relationships can often be based on one's family of origin; experiences in one person's family of origin can carry important meanings through several generations. Individuals even relate to their partner and others in their environment based on their response to stress, crises, or lack of resources.

There is no right or wrong lens to frame how relationships form, sustain, or separate. The following represents three theoretical models that describe how couples and relationships evolve and grow.

Circumplex Model of Marital and Family Systems

Although several social science researchers explored the qualities that make healthy relationships (marital or family) work, prior to the 1980s few were able to specifically address communication and closeness patterns between two or more individuals (Emerson, 1976; Stryker, 1968). Furthermore, there was a gap in how to bridge the clinical and research sides of marital interaction. The Circumplex Model, first developed by Olson, Russell, and Sprenkle (1989), helped address this gap by looking at marital and family systems across different relational dimensions. This model has been addressed thoroughly in Chapter 7, but its elements will be described here as they relate to relationships across the life span.

ELEMENTS OF THE MODEL. Based on couples' research of over 50 concepts developed to describe marital and family dynamics, three specific dimensions became the cornerstone of the model: cohesion, flexibility, and communication. Each element is briefly described below.

COHESION (TOGETHERNESS). Cohesion refers to the amount of togetherness or bonding in a relationship (Olson, 2000; 2011, Olson & Lavee, 2013). Marriages and partnerships can range from being very connected (or enmeshed) to very disconnected (or disengaged). In the Circumplex Model, cohesion measures how marital and family systems balance separateness versus togetherness. The goal is for the couple and family to be able to strike a balance in bonding together, and to reach an equilibrium that fits their life stage and circumstances. The map has five levels, ranging from disengaged/disconnected type to enmeshed/overly connected type.

FLEXIBILITY. Flexibility in a family is the capacity for change in the relationships and rules in the relationships, as well as the quality of leadership and organization in the whole system. Couples and families must find productive ways to manage stability and change across time, despite the challenges or barriers that enter into a family system. Couples learn to adjust to stressors, new members in the family system or changes in the dynamics of either spouse. According to this model, the levels of flexibility range from rigid/inflexible (extremely low) to chaotic/overly flexible (extremely high) (Olson, 2000; 2011; Olson & Lavee, 2013).

COMMUNICATION. Communication in this model is considered to be a facilitating dimension to family and couple functioning over time (i.e., it is not visually depicted, but influences the flexibility and cohesion continua). It is defined as the communication skills utilized in the couple or family system (Olson, 2000; 2011; Olson & Lavee, 2013). By engaging in positive communication, couples can alter their levels of both flexibility and cohesion in response to changes in life circumstances. Specific skills such as listening, speaking, self-disclosure, clarity, tracking, and respect are all components of the communication dimension.

CRITIQUE OF THE MODEL. The Circumplex Model has been a valuable asset in the clinical work done with couples and families at various stages of their relationship(s). This model has been used in several premarital and family therapy studies, with strong clinical relevance and application. Clinicians and researchers are able to detect potential problematic areas in the functioning of a couple of family based on the scale of these dimensions and their point on the family life cycle. Additionally, the model has a strong conceptual framework in how family life evolves and adapts over time. The dimensions described in the model can be used for families with dysfunctional patterns or members with mental health or medical issues.

While the model aims to explain specific areas of functioning for couples and families, it lacks specific reasons why issues in these areas may exist. Some couples may have flexibility and communication problems as a result of financial issues, intimacy issues, parenting problems, or lack of adjusting to stressors of children. Caution should be used in assuming the "equilibrium" between dimensions results in successful coping for couples and families across time. Furthermore, the theory does not take into account some of the cultural themes in families related to functioning of its members. For example, traditional Latino families may have three or four generations in one home, wherein intense closeness between members is commonplace. In the Circumplex Model, this closeness could be classified negatively (i.e., as "enmeshment" because it is outside of "normal" ranges for ideal functioning).

Moreover, the model does not account for the unexpected stressors that could interfere with couples over time. When an individual suffers from a chronic illness or disability, the spouse or partner oftentimes sacrifices energy and resources to take care of their loved one. In these situations,

FIGURE 2 Circumplex Model of Marital and Family Systems (adapted from Olson & Gorall, 2003)

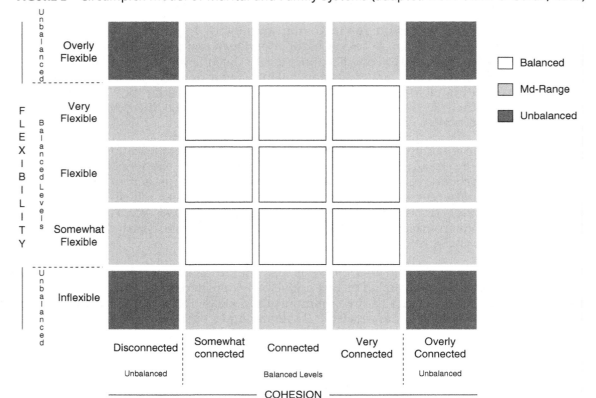

rigid flexibility and enmeshment may be warranted so that certain medical needs and caregiving tasks get addressed promptly and efficiently.

Family Life Cycle Theory

Even though all individuals are born into families, how one shapes the new course of his or her new family can vary significantly. Many factors come into play when we consider how the future of a marriage or family system will look. The Family Life Cycle Theory (McGoldrick & Carter, 1999; McGoldrick, Carter, & Garcia-Preto, 2010) is aimed to explore

Strategies for Managing Stressors (Olson et al., 2008)

- Look for something positive in each situation
- Don't push your partner away; pull together
- Share thoughts and feelings
- Be flexible in changing roles and tasks
- Take challenges head-on
- Go with the flow and take things day by day
- Allow yourself to cry, but also make sure you find humor
- Take one issue at a time
- Do not blame one another
- Find meaning and purpose
- Find strength in spiritual beliefs
- Show affection and love

not just individual identity, but the multigenerational process of how families evolve over time. According to the model, the main value of families is relationships. However, families also have specific roles and functions that guide the mechanisms of the unit. The theory takes both a multigenerational and family development perspective, where normative transitions through life are often determined by family of origin and child development factors (McGoldrick et al., 2010). This model includes six main stages, which are outlined below.

BETWEEN FAMILIES: YOUNG ADULTHOOD. In this first stage, young adults come to terms with their family of origin. A normative process for young adults is that they separate without cutting off from the family. The more adequate that young adults can make this separation, the fewer the stressors will follow them through other stages in the life cycle. Young people may need to re-evaluate the gender or cultural roles of their parents and grandparents, so as not to replicate themes in previous generations of inequality or dysfunction.

THE JOINING OF FAMILIES: THE YOUNG COUPLE. At the next stage, individuals are in the courtship phase of life, looking to find another partner to eventually form a new family. In current society, couples are less bound than previous generations by family traditions and themes of mate selection. Transitions to being a couple may be very challenging for some, given the trajectories of work, location, or family obligations. Couples will learn about how to negotiate patterns in their own relationship and to adapt to another family system: that of their partner.

FAMILIES WITH YOUNG CHILDREN. If the time comes when a couple decides to have a child, the family now becomes a unit of three, changing some of the roles in the family and creating a new family legacy. Through this stage, the couple now moves up a generation, caretaking for a younger generation in the family. Issues such as financial responsibility, childcare, parenting styles, extended family involvement, and living situation all have high levels of stress for new couples with children. Many of these issues also apply to couples that choose not to have children at this stage of life. When exploring family functioning at this phase, it is important to consider the boundaries and roles within the nuclear family and between generations.

FAMILIES WITH ADOLESCENTS. In the fourth stage, families must adjust to different priorities as children get older. Different boundaries must be established with older children. As adolescents bring in new friends and rituals from the outside, parents must learn to be consistent in structuring and parenting children. Fortunately, rituals and community are built in to help support the couple at this stage. It is during this phase that crucial, life-shaping decisions are made and communication and conflict resolution take place between children and parents.

FAMILIES AT MIDLIFE. In this phase, children are ready to launch. This phase can be the longest phase for both children and parents. The couple in midlife will experience the greatest number

FIGURE 3   Stages of the Family Life Cycle Theory Model (McGoldrick & Carter, 1999)

Between Families: Young Adulthood
(Accepting emotional and financial responsibility for self)

Joining of Families Through Marriage (The New Couple)
(Commitment to a new system)

Families with Young Children
(Accepting new members into the system)

Families with Adolescents
(Increasing flexibility with family boundaries)

Families at Midlife: Launching Children and Moving On
(Accepting a multitude of exits and entries from the family system)

Families in Later Life
(Accepting the shifting of generational roles)

of entries and exits within the family system. Additionally, it is a common time for couples to be sandwiched between taking care of their parents in later life years and facilitating healthy launching of their children as adults.

FAMILIES IN LATER LIFE. In the last phase of the model, couples learn to negotiate later years. Contrary to popular belief, most elderly individuals and couples have families of their own and interact with them frequently. Some of the tasks of later life couples include financial stability, clinical stability, and negotiations around caretaking and life priorities. When the first spouse dies, usually the remaining spouse will negotiate whether to remain single or find a mate as comfort in later years.

CRITIQUE OF THE MODEL. This model is evidenced-based from several years of research in the family field. It serves as an effective format for seeing how couples and families transition from one life stage to the next. Multiple generations of patterns and themes are addressed, where individuals and couples make decisions about what to hold on to and what to separate from. Additionally, many do not recognize the value of culture, religion, ethnicity, race, and religion in the context of couples in these life stages. These variables can be addressed in clinical contexts with couples and families at different time points of their lives.

This developmental model of family transitions is not without challenges, given the changing landscape of families in society. With more single parent and LGBT families raising children, the once standard two-parent structure in the home has now become only one of many definitions of a family system (Bronstein, Clauson, Stoll, & Abrams, 1993). Same-sex couples go through similar challenges—and some unique/different ones—as heterosexual couples in the decision to have children and how they grapple with the changing roles each partner must adopt over time (Goldberg, 2010).

Additionally, more macro level issues (e.g., economy, health issues, caregiving, education) have affected both younger adults and younger couples (Furstenberg, 2010). Many of these economic, social and cultural shifts in the twenty-first century have prolonged early adulthood and launching from the parental home (Furstenberg, Rumbaut, & Settersten Jr., 2005). Younger individuals, men and women alike, increasingly aspire to jobs that require postsecondary education and take more time to secure and support a family (Danziger & Rouse, 2007). Additionally, the growth of a consumer economy, stimulated by advertising and mass marketing, may contribute to the desire for adults and couples to increase earning potential before marriage (Mason & Jensen, 1995). With an increase in chronic illness and longer life expectancies in older adults come added responsibilities for younger adults to care for their family members in the home (Stajduhar, 2003). These evolving changes in society may impact how we view the "normative" process of individuals moving through phases of life.

Furthermore, in developed countries, there is a growing trend of postponing parenthood for newly married couples. There may be many reasons for this delay in childbirth, including couples' priorities relating to work, mobility, and family life (Schmidt, Sobotka, Bentzen, & Andersen, 2012). With infertility issues on the rise, women may not have the capability to bare children of their own (Sonfield, Hasstedt, & Kavanaugh, 2013). This model assumes that all couples intend to have children and want to follow a standard set of sequential stages throughout their lives. It is important to recognize is that there is no real definition of a "normal" family, and the goals of couples are an evolving process over time.

McMaster Model of Family Functioning

Many theories on family life highlight the dysfunctional and stressful parts of the system. Normalcy can be an ill-defined concept, given the complexities and changes that occur across time. While it is difficult to formulate a universal definition of normal family functioning, there are certain common elements that can help families avoid problems that occur down the road. The McMaster Model (MMFF) was an attempt to view dimensions of functioning that are seen to have the greatest emotional and physical impact on family members (Epstein, Bishop, & Levin, 1978). The model is derived largely from systems theory, where groups of individual units act as a whole. Assumptions of this model include: (a) one part of the system cannot be understood in isolation from the rest of the system, (b) family structure and organization are important factors in determining behavior, and (c) transactional patterns of the family system are among the most important variables that shape the behavior. There are six main dimensions of the model (Epstein et al., 1978; Epstein, Ryan, Bishop, Miller, & Keitner, 2003); they are outlined below.

PROBLEM SOLVING. Problem solving is marked by a family's ability to resolve problems to a level that maintains effective family functioning. Problems are subdivided into instrumental (e.g., negotiating schedules, paying bills) and affective (i.e., related to feelings) types. Families who have difficulties resolving both of these will function less effectively as a whole unit. There are seven stages in the problem-solving process for effective families, which include: (1) identifying the problem; (2) communicating about the problem; (3) developing action plans; (4) deciding what plan is best; (5) taking action; (6) monitoring the action; (7) evaluating the action's outcome(s).

COMMUNICATION. In this model, communication is the exchange of verbal information within a family (Epstein et al., 2003). Verbal communication can be easily measured in this context. It, too, is separated by instrumental and affective characteristics, and can be categorized as clear or masked, direct or indirect.

ROLES. Roles in this context are repetitive patterns of behavior by which family members fulfill family functions. There are five primary functions critical for role execution in a system: (1) provision of resources, (2) adult sexual gratification, (3) personal development, (4) nurturance and support, and (5) maintenance and management of the family system.

FIGURE 4 Dimensions of the McMaster Model of Family Functioning (Epstein et al., 2003)

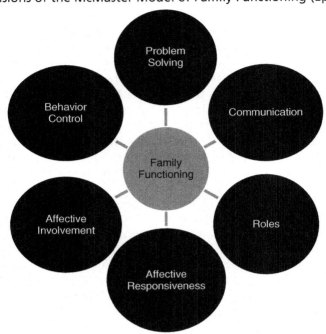

AFFECTIVE RESPONSIVENESS. This dimension can be seen as the ability to respond to a given stimulus with feelings that are appropriate in quantity and quality. The quality of affect depends on the capacity of family members to respond emotionally to a situation with genuine empathy. The quantity of affect is measured by the degree to which the affect exists along a continuum and how often the affective response is performed.

AFFECTIVE INVOLVEMENT. The involvement part of affect is the extent to which the family shows interest in the values, activities, and interests of other members. Families can be very involved in another's activities, or engage in activities very independently from one another. Level of involvement can range on a scale, from complete lack of involvement to total investment in others' lives.

WIFE: "What would you do if I died? Would you get married again?"
HUSBAND: "Definitely not!"
WIFE: "Why not? Don't you like being married?"
HUSBAND: "Of course I do."
WIFE: "Then why wouldn't you remarry?"
HUSBAND: "Okay, okay, I'd get married again."
WIFE: "Would you live in our house?"
HUSBAND: "Sure, it's a great house."
WIFE: "Would you give her my jewelry?"
HUSBAND: "No, I'm sure she'd want her own."
WIFE: "Would you take her golfing with you?"
HUSBAND: "Yes, those are always good times."
WIFE: "Would she use my clubs?"
HUSBAND: "No, she's left-handed."
WIFE: —silence—
HUSBAND: "Oh Boy."

BEHAVIOR CONTROL. Each family adjusts to behaviors in the system differently. In this context families handle behaviors in three areas: (1) dangerous situations, (2) meeting or expressing psychological needs, and (3) situations involving interpersonal socializing behavior. The model looks for the standards or rules that individuals place on others in this context, and how much latitude each person is given in the system.

CRITIQUE OF THE MODEL. This is an evidence-based model that has practical application in exploring family functioning. The model can be applied in teaching, research, and clinical work. Clinicians often utilize this framework when working with families with an individual with a mental health issue. For families with a member with mental illness, these dimensions can be critical assets in how the family responds and adjusts to a stressor. Family members can learn to identify these dimensions in family functioning and negotiate how the dimensions will be used to help deal with difficult issues moving forward. Several studies have integrated the model in their work to develop novel research in the family field, such as the Ontario Child Health Study (Boyle et al., 1988), the impact of parental training (Adams, 2001), and parent-adolescent acculturation (Crane, Ngai, Larson, & Hafen, 2005).

While this model has been viewed as a good basis for family functioning, there is some question as to what is considered "normal" in a family system. Because of the aforementioned changing landscapes of society, the normalcy in gender roles, mixed families, single parent homes, and parenting styles has been evolving rapidly (U.S. Census Bureau, 2013). Furthermore, much of the research on the MMFF has been on families with one member who has a mental illness. These dimensions could certainly exist for families with non-diagnosed family members or problems where a diagnosis is not necessarily applicable. Finally, some of the dimensional characteristics tend to overlap with one another. One of the aspects of problem solving, for example, involves communicating about the problem, while communication per se exists as a separate dimension in the model. The extensive criteria of functions make it difficult for any family at one time to perform at a "normative" level on all dimensions.

RELATIONSHIP DECISIONS

Every human faces the decision to be in a relationship. Whether one has been married for 40 years or decides to stay single, many factors come into play when deciding to enter a partnership. In this section, we focus on the various relationship choices that individuals can be involved in and what factors come into play when they take part in these choices.

> Staying married may have long-term benefits. You can elicit much more sympathy from friends over a bad marriage than you ever can from a good divorce.
>
> – *P.J. O'Rourke*

Marriage

Marriage is one of the most exciting, yet unpredictable, events and processes in a couple's life. Many individuals have dreams and aspirations of the ideal mate and the ideal ceremony. Navigating the decision-making process can be very challenging. It can be difficult even to picture what life might look like committed to just one person. Both individuals must be comfortable with their own expectations at this stage of their lives and with how far the relationship has progressed in order to consider marriage.

Consider these tips as you make decisions about marriage:

- Evaluate your partner not just with your heart, but with your head
- Identify what you need to feel comfortable in the decision to get married
- Pay attention to how you feel and act when you are with this person
- Know where you can compromise
- Do not be conflict avoidant; address concerns and conflicts with your partner

Several decisions are required prior to the legal contract of the marriage. Which of your family and friends will be invited? Which location or faith affiliation will the marriage be associated with? How do you and your partner want the process of the ceremony to go? It is important that couples discuss these issues in a collaborative manner during the wedding preparation. In a society where wedding planning, gift registries, and ceremonies have become more expensive and elaborate (Barash, 2012), what has sometimes been lost is the long-term intentions of the couple after the ceremony. *Couples should not worry about the 50 minutes of the wedding ceremony as much as the 50 years that a marriage may entail.*

FIGURE 5 Age of First Marriage in the United States

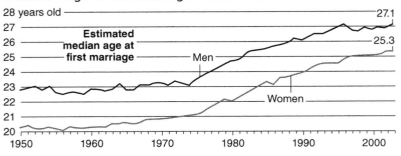

Percentage of men and women never married, by age

AGE	1970			2003		
20–24	54.7%		35.8	86.0		75.4
25–29	19.1		10.5	54.6		40.3
30–34	9.4		6.2	33.1		22.7
35–44	6.7		5.2	19.5		13.2

Researchers are starting to discover that not only are both men and women getting married at later ages, but the ages they have children have been delayed as well.

Over the past ten years, the rate of marriages in America has decreased, while age at which people get married has increased. Many factors contribute to these changes, including mobility of both partners, employment decisions, education, proximity to family, and financial concerns.

What's on your List?

What do you think are the most important factors in deciding whether to marry someone? Rank order your importance of these items from 1 (most important) to 10 (least important)

Wanting to have children	_____
Having the same faith	_____
Similar parenting styles	_____
Physical attraction	_____
Mutual respect	_____
Same moral values	_____
Financial stability	_____
Family background	_____
Career goals	_____
Proximity to family	_____

a distance is also becoming an everyday part of American and global life where couples can form a partnership without being in the same neighborhood, town, or state (Sahlstein & Stafford, 2010).

There is no longer as great a social pressure for couples to get married. The pressures of formalizing a wedding are not like they were in previous decades.

Because younger adults have witnessed divorce in their parents or other family, many are overly cautious of the decisions to get married.

For financial reasons, some couples choose to save costs at this point in life by not getting married.

Those who have been married already may have different priorities about re-marrying at later life stages.

Partnership

For some couples, choosing to not get legally married is an option. Individuals may have the same intentions to remain together and opt for a long-term partnership. Since the beginning of the 21st century, it has become more common for couples to cohabitate, either before getting married or as an alternative to marriage (Cherlin, 2005). For some, cohabitating in the same household for many years can satisfy the emotional, physical, social, and spiritual needs of partners. Relating from the same household for many years can satisfy the emotional, physical, social, and spiritual needs of partners. Relating from

The continuum of what constitutes long-term relationships will continue to evolve over future generations.

Gay, Lesbian, Bisexual, Transgender, and Queer (GLBTQ) couples have also increased attention to how we view relationship definitions differently in the 21st century. The Williams Institute analyses of newly released data from the 2009 American Community Survey show that the estimated number of same-sex couples who identified themselves as either spouses or unmarried partners increased at three times the rate of population growth from 2008 to 2009. An estimated 3.5% of adults in the United States identify as lesbian, gay or bisexual and an estimated 0.3% of adults identify as transgender (Williams Institute, 2011). This implies that there are roughly 9 million GLBTQ Americans today. Although the historical stigma of GLBTQ relationships and identity may have subsided in recent years, legislation for these couples to marry in some states is still being debated. Still, both same-sex and opposite sex couples choose never to get married at gradually increasing rates, highlighting the trend that long-term relationships outside of marriage have become more of a common path for Americans (Pew Research Center, 2011).

Singlehood Across Time

Compared to previous time periods in the United States, growing numbers of individuals are choosing not to partner with, or get married to, another person at all (Depaulo & Morris, 2005). And choosing singleness is not something to be looked down upon! The timing and trajectory of people's lives can profoundly influence whether a relationship is desirable (or even possible). For those who have divorced or lost a loved one, for example, being single could be a necessary break for their stage in life. Additionally, different family of origin issues could place pressure or strain on individuals getting married or being in a relationship. How many individuals in the family are currently married? Do members of the family have expectations for grandchildren? If someone has already gone through a divorce, is there pressure from the family to stay single henceforth? Do previous generations place greater emphasis on family or work? Does one's job or life circumstances make it difficult to be in a relationship?

The Experiences of Divorce

When a couple chooses to divorce, it may be among the most stressful experiences in one's life. The experience of divorce can be devastating for all parties involved, including family members and close friends. Partners envision a life together where they can share emotional, physical, social, and spiritual life needs. When this vision is no longer possible, partners must renegotiate their plans for the future. There are many ramifications that both people must realize if a marriage cannot be repaired. If the couple has children, there must be custody and legal issues to consider. If one person has been employed in the marriage, both individuals must now adjust financially in an independent manner.

Susan Pease Gadoua (2008), a licensed clinical social worker and author of "Contemplating Divorce", breaks down the main areas for couples to consider if a divorce can be avoided and what needs to be manageable for a marriage to survive:

1. **Safety Needs:** Mutual trust, honesty, sense of safety (mental, emotional, physical, financial), care and concern for each other, kindness.
2. **Love Needs:** Mutual love, shared interests, commitment to marriage, reciprocal relationship.
3. **Esteem Needs:** Self-esteem for both spouses, common goals, willingness of both to work on the marriage.

Sometimes, relationships face certain barriers that cannot be overcome. Whether couples are married for two years or 20 years, certain stressors can impact any relationship. Divorce has no single cause. Many factors contribute to divorce, including individual/personal, social, economic, and ethnic/cultural reasons (Clarke-Stewart & Brentano, 2006). Couples have disagreements that can escalate to long-term conflict problems. When anger and resentment surface, couples have a difficult time changing the course and perception of the marriage. This especially happens when one person may be "leaning in" to save the marriage while the other one is "leaning out" and is already considering (or made up their mind about) divorce. When it only takes one person to break a relationship apart, some of these mixed agenda couples may be too late to salvage.

Adjustments in Widowing

Losing a spouse who has passed away is a very challenging life process. One loses not just the physical presence of a husband, wife, best friend or life partner, but an emotional connection that they have developed over time. The surviving mate now must adapt to what life will look like being single. The experience for many is that they no longer have the same life as they did with their mate.

Newly bereaved spouses may have to adjust to the loss of an enduring emotional relationship, as well as manage daily decisions that were once accomplished by the deceased individual and/or within the teamwork of the couple (Carr, 2004a). Some of these daily decisions may include financial retirement and investments, bills, home maintenance, and business decisions.

How one copes with a loss will vary considerably based on individual circumstances. Some may take long periods of time to process the memories and life experiences that this relationship offered. Some may experience a period of loneliness or subjective sense of social isolation (Golden et al., 2009). Others may want to experience dating and connect with a new partner shortly after experiencing a loss. The guiding assumption is that people who remarry perceive the net benefits of marriage to be greater than the benefits of remaining widowed (Becker, 1981; Carr, 2004b). The openness to receiving social support from friends and family may depend on how the family system reacts to the loss, how close the couple was to both sides of the family, and proximity of family members to the survivor. For example, a widower may have more direct support from a partner's family if multiple members are currently living in their home. A couple who may be farther away from both sides of their families may be restricted to informal support either by phone or email.

There are still many stereotypes and myths about individuals who are widowed (Kamp, Nargi, & Drake, 2012). Much of the well-intentioned advice that friends or family offer are situated within these myths; examples include:

MYTH 1. When it comes to grieving, one size fits all. Different personalities, situations, and life experiences cause everyone to grieve and adapt to loss differently. Lots of different factors come into play, including age, the length of a marriage, the quality of the marriage, economic situations, number of children, and career status, to name a few.

MYTH 2. There is a time limit for grieving. When widows are given time limits to "get over their grief"—be it six months or two years—they may feel inadequate and abnormal if they have not "gotten over it" in the allotted time. At some point in the process, most widows/widowers realize that they need to learn new skills to adapt to the new realities of their lives. Some argue that "closure" is impossible, and perhaps even undesirable (Boss & Carnes, 2012). A widower may not want to close the door on the memories of his loved one. Instead, he may hope to find meaning and learn to live with the loss.

MYTH 3. You will "move on" or "get over it." Widowhood is not a disease, sickness or mental illness. It is a fact of life, where people learn to cope and survive in much different ways.

MYTH 4. Widowhood is reserved for the elderly. Contrary to popular belief, the average age of a woman who loses a spouse is 55. One third of those women will lose their spouse before they reach 45, and will raise children alone in the home.

STRESSORS IN LONG-LIVED RELATIONSHIPS

Relationships are not formed or nurtured in isolation. Couples are impacted by biological, psychological, social, and spiritual stressors and resources. Each of these types of stressors can be interconnected with the others. Individuals are contained within systems that come into constant contact with other systems, and couples will face many challenging stressors that they could not have planned for. Viewing a relationship from a biopsychosocial/spiritual lens (Engel, 1977; Wright, Watson & Bell, 1996) is the most holistic way to understand the unique stressors that couples may come across. This framework suggests that all human beings are biological creatures with psychological and spiritual experiences that are situated in larger social contexts.

When stressors are present in a relationship, there are circular impacts on a person's biological, social, psychological, and spiritual responses (see Figure 6). For example, a couple in a long-term committed relationship may face challenges when a male partner is newly diagnosed with testicular cancer. Almost immediately, this couple may begin to feel the strain of a biological stressor (i.e., cancer). Further, this diagnosis is likely to impact social aspects of this couple (e.g., economic strain from medical bills). If the pile up of stressors continues to build, they may lead to psychological

FIGURE 6   Biopsychosocial/spiritual Perspective in Relationships (Wright, Watson, & Bell, 1996)

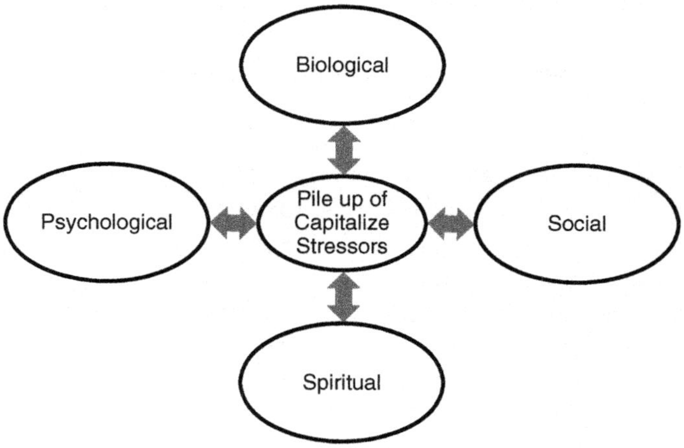

stressors (e.g., depression or addiction) and/or spiritual stressors (e.g., feeling disconnected from the higher power(s) the partners believe in). These processes work in bidirectional ways. A pile up of stressors may lead to increased stress in the four domains, and increased stress in one of the domains may lead to a pile up in others.

Coping and Resilience

Because struggles and adversities are unavoidable in couple relationships, fostering resilience may be the couple's best chance at not just getting through, but coming out stronger. Resilience is viewed as the "capacity to rebound from adversity strengthened and more resourceful" (Walsh, 2006, p. 4). When the couple is met with challenges, such as those listed above, there is the possibility for the couple to thrive during and after the crisis. Much of the time resilience is talked about as an individual trait—a strength that someone has within him or herself. However, resilience can also be seen as a dyadic or family trait. There is the possibility for growth between the couple, a chance to renew love, a chance to redefine what it means to be intimate, a chance to connect on a deeper level, a chance to gain perspective, and the opportunity to live life with intention.

Couples must not only cope with stress in their own lives, but also attend to crisis and loss within the couple or immediate family. Death and loss are both transactional processes that involve those who die and their survivors in a shared life cycle, acknowledging both the finality of death and the continuity of life (Walsh & McGoldrick, 2004). Death provides the opportunity for adaptive changes, requiring both short and long term reorganization and changes in the definition of the

EXAMPLES OF BIOLOGICAL STRESSORS ACROSS THE LIFE CYCLE
- Fertility issues, inability to get pregnant, or using assisted reproductive technology
- Diagnosis of a chronic illness such as diabetes, multiple sclerosis, or rheumatoid arthritis
- Diagnosis of a terminal illness such as a progressed stage of cancer

EXAMPLES OF PSYCHOLOGICAL STRESSORS ACROSS THE LIFE CYCLE
- Preexisting mental illness
- Diagnosis of mental illness such as depression or anxiety
- Addictions

EXAMPLES OF SOCIAL STRESSORS ACROSS THE LIFE CYCLE
- Employment loss
- Caregiving for aging family member(s)
- Economic strain

EXAMPLES OF SPIRITUAL STRESSORS ACROSS THE LIFE CYCLE
- Differing religious practices regarding how to raise children
- Selecting a mate different than the spirituality of one's family of origin
- Locus of control over a chronic or terminal illness ("It's in God's hands" vs. "I will be the only one in control of my body")

family system over time (Crenshaw, 1996; Shapiro, 2002). Within the couple, hidden losses such as stillbirths, miscarriages, and abortions can impact a couple's mindset, while these losses are sometimes unacknowledged by outsiders (Gilbert, 1989). When we foster relational resilience during loss, each individual and their relationships emerge strengthened and more resourceful in meeting future life challenges (Walsh, 2006).

Discussion Points for Couples to Discover Resilience

- Take a minute to think about what kind of caregiver you would be to your partner and write down your answer.
- Next, think about what type of care you would want to receive if you were to become ill or needed caring for. Share your answers.
- Discuss a time when you have had a challenge or a crisis occur.

- Discuss how you or your family coped.
- Discuss how you would have changed how you or your family coped.
- Discuss how you or your family coped well.
- Discuss your current resources (family, friends, work, school).

CONCLUSION

In this chapter, we discussed major relationship decisions and relationship states. We introduced three models that describe how relationships function and transition over the life span, and we described biological, psychological, and social stressors than can interfere with the connection between partners. However, families can be resilient in the face of these stressors. You have read in this chapter about several of the core skills that can help couples maintain a relationship across the life span.

This is an exhilarating time in family research. Across the life span, there are new trends in relationship states, decisions, and transitions. For example, we explored in this chapter how widows adjust to the loss of a loved one and make meaning of their lives moving forward. Yet, we still have little information regarding the decision-making process of young and older widows choosing to get remarried or have children in a new relationship. Additionally, many adults are delaying marriage and other life commitments in order to assume caregiving roles for their parents and family members. More research needs to explore how individuals in early and middle adulthood balance the roles between caring for a parent and entering a relationship.

Sustaining—and thriving in—a relationship over the long haul can be a lot of work. But it can be rewarding work. We will each face many relationship decisions and transitions, including some we could never have anticipated. Our relationships during and across these transitions can help us face and overcome stressors, understand ourselves, and build meaning in our lives. Our hope is that you can take the information we have presented in this chapter and make it your own. Grow as an individual, in the person you are. And grow as a couple, in all that you can be.

WHAT WOULD YOU DO?

The following scenarios are typical situations that happen for couples across different life stages. These situations will hopefully make you think critically about a tough ethical, medical, or family topic within a family. After reading each story, write down your answers to the questions we pose. Compare these answers with classmates to see on what topics you agree and disagree.

SCENARIO #1

Weighing all the Options

Gary and Sarah are a couple in their early 30s and have been married for five years. They have been trying to have a child and have been arguing about not being able to conceive. Sarah went into her doctor for a series of tests, and ultimately confirmed fertility problems. Sarah was devastated by the news and has been in numerous conversations with Gary. Sarah started some hormone treatments, but was still unable to conceive after a year. The couple has recently been talking about options and the possibility of adoption. Gary has wanted to adopt because he really wants to be a father and believes the couple can get their life started. Sarah still wants to continue trying to conceive and is insistent on having a biological child. The couple has been in conflict over this decision for the last two months. Sarah understands Gary's point, but says that the decision should ultimately come from the person experiencing the medical issues.

1. Which person are you more likely to side with in this case?
2. What issue(s) do you think the couple needs to explore going forward?

SCENARIO #2
Tough Love with Family

Maria (51) and Juan (53) have been married for 27 years and have three children. Their oldest child, Eva, is married and lives 15 miles from her parents. Recently, Eva and her husband, Jose, have been struggling financially and having trouble just affording their rent payments. Eva brought up the issue of moving into her parent's home temporarily. This is a difficult issue for her parents for two reasons. For one, Jose spent most of the trust fund that Eva inherited from her parents and grandparents on bad investments. Additionally, Juan and Maria have been caretaking for Juan's mother, who has just returned from the hospital. Juan and Maria have not been supportive of Jose and are at a crossroads of what to do. Jose tried to reach out to Juan for more help, but Juan has not responded to any of his calls or emails.

1. Do you think Maria and Juan should take Eva and Jose into their home?
2. What conversations need to take place to make this decision workable? And with whom?

SCENARIO #3
The Will to Live

Bill and Edna are in their 80s and have been married for 55 years. They have no children who are close by, but have a few childhood friends in the neighborhood. Just recently, Bill has been suffering from failing health. He suffered a severe stroke, and is currently recovering from being in a coma for a week. Bill is semi-conscious during the day, and very disoriented at times. He is still on a respirator and tells Edna, "I can't live like this anymore." Bill wants to die peacefully at home. Edna knows that these were his wishes in his will. But Edna, with a background in nursing, is aware that the hospital has over-medicated Bill after waking from the coma. Based on prior times that Bill has recovered from surgeries and procedures, she believes that Bill can come back from this. Her guilt lies in wanting to honor her husband's wishes, yet she can't live with the fact that he's giving up hope.

1. What decision would you make if you were Edna?
2. Who or what would you rely on to make this difficult choice?

REFERENCES

Adams, J. F. (2001). Impact of parent training on family functioning. *Child & Family Behavior Therapy, 23*(1), 29–42. doi:10.1300/J019v23n01_03

BBC News Magazine (2012). *Readers' stories of being single.* Retrieved from http://www.bbc.co.uk/news/magazine-20304302.

Barash, S. S. (2012). *The nine phases of marriage: How to make it, break it, keep it.* New York: Macmillan.

Baumrind, D. (1977). Some thoughts about childrearing. In S. Cohen & T. J. Comiskey (Eds.), *Child Development: Contemporary Perspectives* (pp. 248–258). Itaska, IL: Peacock.

Baumrind, D. (1978). Parental disciplinary patterns and social competence in children. *Youth and Society, 9,* 239–276. doi:10.1177/0044118X7800900302

Becker, G. S. (1981). *A treatise on the family.* Cambridge, MA: Harvard University Press. doi:10.2307/1973663

Boss, P., & Carnes, D. (2012). The myth of closure. *Family Process, 51*(4), 456–469. doi:10.1111/famp.12005

Boyle, M. H., Offord, D. R., Racine, Y. A., Fleming, J. E., Szatmari, P., & Links, P. S. (1993). Predicting substance use in early adolescence based on parent and teacher assessments of childhood psychiatric disorder: Results from the Ontario Child Health Study follow-up. *Journal of Child Psychology and Psychiatry, 34*(4), 535–544. doi:10.1111/j.1469-7610.1993.tb01034.x

Bronstein, P., Clauson, J., Stoll, M. F., & Abrams, C. L. (1993). Parenting behavior and children's social, psychological, and academic adjustment in diverse family structures. *Family Relations, 42,* 268–276. doi:10.2307/585556

Canary, D. J., & Dainton, M. (Eds.). (2002). *Maintaining relationships through communication: Relational, contextual, and cultural variations.* London, UK: Routledge.

Carr, D. (2004a). Gender, preloss marital dependence, and older adults' adjustment to widowhood. *Journal of Marriage and Family, 66*(1), 220–235. doi:10.1111/j.0022- 2445.2004.00016.x

Carr, D. (2004b). The desire to date and remarry among older widows and widowers. *Journal of Marriage and Family, 66*(4), 1051–1068. doi:10.1111/j.0022-2445.2004.00078.x

Cherlin, A. J. (2005). American marriage in the early twenty-first century. *The Future of Children, 15*(2), 33–55. doi:10.1353/foc.2005.0015

Cherlin, A. J. (2009). *The marriage go-round: The state of marriage and the family in America today.* New York: First Vintage Books.

Clarke-Stewart, A., & Brentano, C. (2006). *Divorce: Causes and consequences.* New Haven, CT: Yale University Press.

Cohn, D., Passel, J. S., Wang, W., & Livingston, G. (2011). *Barely half of U.S. adults are married- a record low.* Washington DC: Pew Research Social and Demographic Trends.

Copen, C.E., Daniels, K., & Mosher, W. D. (2013). First premarital cohabitation in the United States: 2006–2010 National Survey of Family Growth. *National Health Statistics Report, 64,* 1–16. Retrieved from http://www .cdc.gov/nchs/data/nhsr/nhsr064.pdf

Crane, D. R., Ngai, S. W., Larson, J. H., & Hafen, M. (2005). The influence of family functioning and parent-adolescent acculturation on north american chinese adolescent outcomes. *Family Relations, 54*(3), 400–410. doi:10.1111/j.1741-3729.2005.00326.x

Crenshaw, D. A. (1996). *Bereavement: Counseling the grieving throughout the life cycle.* (2nd ed.). New York: Crossroads.

Danziger, S., & Rouse, C. E. (Eds.). (2007). *The price of independence: The economics of early adulthood.* New York: Russell Sage Foundation.

DePaulo, B. M., & Morris, W. L. (2005). Singles in society and in science. *Psychological Inquiry, 16,* 57–83. doi:10.1080/1047840X.2005.9682918

Doherty, W. J. (2001). *Take back your marriage: Sticking together in a world that pulls us apart.* New York: Guilford Press.

Eden, K., & Reed, J. M. (2005). Why don't they just get married? Barriers to marriage among the disadvantaged. *The Future of Children, 15*(2), 117–137. doi:10.1353/foc.2005.0017

Emerson, R. M. (1976). Social exchange theory. *Annual Review of Sociology, 2,* 335–362. doi:10.1146/annurev .so.02.080176.002003

Engel, G. L. (1977). The need for a new medical model: A challenge for biomedicine. *Science, 196*(4286), 129–136. doi:10.1126/science.847460

Epstein N. S., Bishop, D. S., & Levin, S. (1978). The McMaster Model of family functioning. *Journal of Marital and Family Therapy, 4,* 19–31. doi:10.1111/j.1752-0606.1978.tb00537.x

Epstein, N. B., Ryan, C. E., Bishop, D. S., Miller, I. W., & Keitner, G. I. (2003). *The McMaster model: A view of healthy family functioning.* New York: Guilford Press.

Fiese, B. H., et al. (2002). A review of 50 years of research on naturally occurring family routines and rituals: Cause for celebration? *Journal of Family Psychology, 16*(4), 381–390. doi:10.1037/0893-3200.16.4.381

Furstenberg, F. F., Rumbaut, R. G., & Settersten Jr., R. A. (2005). *On the frontier of adulthood: Emerging themes and new directions.* Chicago, IL: University of Chicago Press. doi:10.7208/chicago/9780226748924.001.0001

Furstenberg, F. F. (2010). On a new schedule: Transitions to adulthood and family change. *The Future of Children, 20*(1), 67–87. doi:10.1353/foc.0.0038

Gadoua, S.P. (2008). *Contemplating divorce: A step by step guide to deciding whether to stay or go.* Oakland, CA: New Harbinger Publishing.

Gilbert, K. R. (1989). Interactive grief and coping in the marital dyad. *Death Studies, 13,* 605–626. doi:10.1080/07481188908252336

Goldberg, A. E. (2010). *Lesbian and gay parents and their children: Research on the family life cycle*. Washington, DC: American Psychological Association.

Golden, J., Conroy, R. M., Bruce, I., Denihan, A., Greene, E., Kirby, M., & Lawlor, B. A. (2009). Loneliness, social support networks, mood and wellbeing in community-dwelling elderly. *International Journal of Geriatric Psychiatry, 24*(7), 694–700. doi:10.1002/gps.2181

Imber-Black, E., Roberts, J., & Whiting, R. A. (Eds.). (2003). *Rituals in families and family therapy*. New York: W.W. Norton & Company.

Kastanis, A. & Gates, G. J. (2013). *Census & LGBT Demographic Studies*. Retrieved from *http://williamsinstitute. law.ucla.edu/category/research/census-lgbt-demographics-studies/*

Kamp, E., Nargi, D., & Drake, R. (2012). *W-Connection: Widows helping widows rebuild their lives*. Retrieved from http://www.wconnection.org/index.html

Lichter, D. T., Qian, Z., & Mellott, L. M. (2006). Marriage or dissolution? Union transitions among poor cohabiting women. *Demography, 43*(2), 223–240. doi:10.1353/dem.2006.0016

Mason, K. O., & Jensen, A. M. (Eds.). (1995). *Gender and family change in industrialized countries*. New York: Oxford University Press.

McGoldrick, M., & Carter, B. (1999). Self in context: The individual life cycle in systemic perspective. In B. Carter & M. McGoldrick (Eds.), *The exapnded family life cycle* (pp. 27–46). Boston: Allyn & Bacon.

McGoldrick, M., Carter, B. & Garcia-Preto, N. (2010). *The expanded family life cycle: Individual, family, and social perspectives* (4th Ed.). New York: Pearson Publication.

Miller, I. W., Ryan, C. E., Keiner, G. I., Bishop, D. S., & Epstein, N. B. (2000). The McMaster approach to families: Theory, assessment, treatment and research. *Journal of Family Therapy, 22*, 168–189. doi:10.1111/1467-6427.00145

Morris, W. L., Sinclair, S., & DePaulo, B. M. (2007). No shelter for singles: The perceived legitimacy of marital status discrimination. *Group Processes & Intergroup Relations, 10*, 457–470. doi:10.1177/1368430207081535

Norcross, J. (2011). *Psychotherapy relationships that work: Evidence based responsiveness* (2nd ed.). New York: Oxford University Press.

Olson, D. H., Russell, C. S., & Sprenkle, D. H. (1989). *Circumplex Model: Systemic assessment and treatment of families*. New York: Hawthorne Press.

Olson, D. H. (2000). Circumplex Model of Family Systems. *Journal of Family Therapy, 22*(2), 144–167. doi:10.1111/1467-6427.00144

Olson, D. H. (2011). FACES IV and the Circumplex model: Validation study. *Journal of Marital & Family Therapy, 3*(1), 64–80. doi:10.1111/j.1752-0606.2009.00175.x

Olson, D. H., & Lavee, Y. (2013). Family systems and family stress: A family life cycle. *Family Systems and Life-span Development,* 165–196. Retrieved from https://books.google.com/books?hl=en&lr=&id=Am2_fIS ZUKUC&oi=fnd&pg=PA165&dq=Family+systems+and+family+stress:+A+family+life+cycle&ots=p4Z9pQ LdRY&sig=FXJJjvcc-EHYkFqzCbr2Gdgy5Qg#v=onepage&q=Family%20systems%20and%20family%20 stress%3A%20A%20family%20life%20cycle&f=false

Papp, L. M., Cummings, E. M., & Goeke-Morey, M. C. (2009). For richer, for poorer: Money as a topic of marital conflict in the home. *Journal of Family Relations, 58*(1), 91–103. doi:10.1111/j.1741-3729.2008.00537.x

Pew Research Center (2011). *New facts about families: Recent findings on family meals, cohabitation and divorce*. Retrieved from http://www.pewresearch.org/2011/04/08/new-facts-about-families/

Sahlstein, E., & Stafford, L. (2010). Communication and distance: A special issue. *Journal of Applied Communication Research, 38*(1), 1–3. doi:10.1080/00909880903483607.

Schmidt, L., Sobotka, T., Bentzen, J. G., & Andersen, A. N. (2012). Demographic and medical consequences of the postponement of parenthood. *Human Reproduction Update, 18*(1), 29–43. doi:10.1093/humupd/dmr040

Shapiro, E. (2002). *Grief as a family process*. (Rev. ed). New York: Guilford Press.

Sonfield, A., Hasstedt, K., Kavanaugh, M. L., & Anderson, R. (2013). *The social and economic benefits of women's ability to determine whether and when to have children*. New York: Guttmacher Institute.

Stajduhar, K. I. (2003). Examining the perspectives of family members involved in the delivery of palliative care at home. *Journal of Palliative Care, 19*(1), 27–35. Retrieved from http://search.proquest.com/openview/ 3c09473c1f71c90f7fd27dc71f066ca0/1?pq-origsite=gscholar

Stryker, S. (1968). Identity salience and role performance: The relevance of symbolic interaction theory for family research. *Journal of Marriage and the Family, 30*, 558–564. doi:10.2307/349494

U.S. Census Bureau. (2000). *Current Population Reports*. Retrieved from http://www.census.gov/census2000/ states/us.html.

U.S. Census Bureau. (2011). *Current Population Survey*. Retrieved from http://www.census.gov/acs/www/ data_documentation/2011_release.

U.S. Census Bureau (2011). *Marital Events of Americans: 2009*. Retrieved from http://www.census.gov/ prod/2011pubs/acs-13.pdf

U.S. Census Bureau (2013). *Current Population Survey, Annual Social and Economic Supplements.* Retrieved from http://www.census.gov/hhes/www/poverty/publications/pubs-cps.html

U.S. Census Bureau (2013). *American Community Survey.* Retrieved from https://www.census.gov/acs/www/

Walsh, F. (2006). *Strengthening family resilience* (2nd ed.). New York: Guilford Press.

Walsh, F., & McGoldrick, M. (2004). *Living beyond loss.* New York: W.W. Norton and Company.

Weeks, G. R., & Treat, S. R. (2001). *Couples in treatment: Techniques and approaches for effective Practice* (2nd ed.). New York: Brunner-Routledge.

Williams Institute (2011). How many people are lesbian, gay, bisexual and transgender? Retrieved from http://williamsinstitute.law.ucla.edu/wp-content/uploads/Gates-How-Many-People-LGBT-Apr-2011.pdf

Wright, L.M., Watson, W.L. & Bell, J.M. (1996). *Belief: The heart of healing in families and illness.* New York: BasicBooks.

Zimbardo, P. G., Weber, A. L., & Johnson, R. L. (1999). *Psychology* (3rd ed.). Boston, MA: Addison Wesley Longman.

19

Are Intimate Relationships Good for Your Health?

Diego Garcia-Huidobro, M.D., M.S.
Department of Family Medicine
School of Medicine
Pontificia Universidad Catolica de Chile

Jerica M. Berge, Ph.D., MPH, LMFT, CFLE
Department of Family Medicine
and Community Health
University of Minnesota

LEARNING OBJECTIVES

- Understand how relationship health influences partners' physical health (and vice versa)
- Articulate how leading theories make sense of the reciprocal influences of relational and physical health
- Define strategies that couples can use to strengthen their relational and physical health

© Peter Bernik, 2014. Used under license from Shutterstock, Inc.

© auremar, 2014. Used under license from Shutterstock, Inc.

© wavebreakmedia, 2014. Used under license from Shutterstock, Inc.

Case Vignette

Sarah and Bob have been married 15 years. The 15 years have not been problem free. Bob was diagnosed with type 2 diabetes five years ago and initially struggled with the diagnosis both emotionally and physically. However, his hemoglobin A1c levels (a measure of metabolic control in diabetes management; low numbers are better) have been within a healthy range since his diagnosis. He also is medication free and has been able to control his disease via lifestyle management (e.g., healthy eating and regular physical activity).

Rebecca and Tim have been married 20 years. Tim was also diagnosed with type 2 diabetes five years ago. He has not fared as well as Bob. His A1c levels are consistently high when he goes to the doctor, his daily sugar levels (blood glucose; low numbers are better) are high, and he is on oral medications and daily insulin injections.

Why might Bob's prognosis be better than Tim's? There may be genetic reasons why Bob is able to manage his diabetes better; however, there is also evidence that Bob's intimate relationship influences his ability to manage his chronic condition well. Specifically, Sarah and Bob report high marital satisfaction. Bob reports that Sarah has been his partner in managing his diabetes. She changed her lifestyle to support Bob's lifestyle

Corresponding Author: Diego Garcia-Huidobro, M.D., M.S.; University of Minnesota; Department of Family Social Science; 1985 Buford Ave.; 290 McNeal Hall; Saint Paul, MN 55108. E-mail: garci506@umn.edu.

(e.g., eats diabetes-friendly meals the same as Bob, she exercises with him) and is supportive of his regular appointments with doctors. On the other hand, Tim and Rebecca report low marital satisfaction and high conflict. Tim has mostly managed his diabetes himself and claims that Rebecca is always nagging him to go to the doctor or check his sugars. Is it actually possible that an intimate relationship could make you healthier or less healthy?

THE INTERSECTION OF INTIMATE RELATIONSHIPS AND HEALTH

Intimate relationships are important for your health! A meta-analysis including 148 studies reported that strong intimate relations reduce mortality by almost 50% (Holt-Lunstad, Smith, & Layton, 2010). As a whole, individuals who are married live longer, are less likely to experience psychological distress and have fewer physical illnesses, including diabetes, cancer, heart disease, and others, compared to their divorced, widow, and single counterparts (Gardner & Oswald, 2004; Lorenz, Wickrama, Conger, & Elder, 2006; Manzoli, Villari, Pirone, & Boccia, 2007; Umberson, Williams, Powers, Liu, & Needham, 2006; Waite & Gallaher, 2000). However, it is not only about "being married," it is about being happily married. It is well known that people who are highly satisfied with their marital relationship enjoy better health outcomes compared to those who are less satisfied (Kiecolt-Glaser & Newton, 2001; Manzoli et al., 2007; Umberson et al., 2006). People in highly satisfied relationships take better care of themselves, have better mental health, don't engage in risky behaviors to cope with their marital distress (e.g., tobacco, alcohol, or substance use), and don't experience the detrimental physiological responses to chronic stress that their counterparts in low quality relationships do (Kiecolt-Glaser & Newton, 2001; Robles & Kiecolt-Glaser, 2003; Umberson et al., 2006; Waite & Gallaher, 2000).

In this chapter, we will review how intimate relationships affect health and illness, frameworks to explain the connections between health and intimate relationships, and how interpersonal communication is fundamental in maintaining good health. We conclude this chapter by highlighting an evidence-based program aiming to strengthen couple relationships to promote health and well-being. Make sure to complete the exercises at the end of the chapter so you can apply what you have learned.

INTIMATE RELATIONSHIPS AND HEALTH BEHAVIORS

Positive, supportive intimate relationships can promote healthy behaviors and discourage unhealthy practices. One interesting study examined the connection between a partner's day-to-day eating and physical activity patterns and their significant other's eating and physical activity patterns. This study included 1,212 young adults in the Midwest from diverse racial/ethnic and socioeconomic status backgrounds. The results showed that young adult women whose significant others had health promoting attitudes/behaviors were significantly less likely to be overweight/obese and were more likely to

©Monkey Business Images, 2014. Used under license from Shutterstock, Inc.

eat ≥5 fruits/vegetables per day, eat breakfast on a daily basis, and engage in ≥3.5 hours/week of physical activity compared to women whose significant others did not have health promoting behaviors/attitudes (Berge, Bauer, MacLehose, Eisenberg, & Neumark-Sztainer, In press; Berge, MacLehose, Eisenberg, Laska, & Neumark-Sztainer, 2012). Young adult men whose significant other had health promoting behaviors/attitudes were more likely to engage in ≥3.5 hours/week of physical activity compared to men whose significant others did not have health promoting behaviors/attitudes (Berge et al., 2012).

In addition, having a satisfactory intimate relationship is associated with lower use of tobacco, alcohol, and illicit drugs, and better dietary and sleeping patterns (Umberson et al., 2006; Kiecolt-Glaser & Newton, 2001; Wickrama, Lorenz, Conger, & Elder, 1997). Furthermore, individuals with high marital satisfaction have greater adherence to medications for both chronic condition management and short-term management of illness (Molloy, Perkins-Porras, Strike, & Steptoe, 2008), and utilize medical services less frequently than their unmarried or unhappily married counterparts (Prigerson, Maciejewski, & Rosenheck, 1999). However, marriage may not always promote healthy behaviors. Marriage may also promote unhealthy behaviors because partners tend to share their behaviors and they may be mutually reinforcing. For example, it is possible that both individuals could engage in unhealthy behaviors, such as smoking, drinking, gambling or sedentary behaviors, which could lead to unhealthy patterns overtime (Meyler, Stimpson, & Peek, 2007).

INTIMATE RELATIONSHIPS AND CHRONIC DISEASE

Chronic diseases, like hypertension, diabetes, heart disease or cancer, are health conditions that, at this point in time, have no cure. Therefore, the medical profession has highlighted the importance of managing health conditions/symptoms on a day-to-day basis, such as healthful eating and regular physical activity. This is also true of disease prevention. It is recommended by the American Medical Association (AMA, 2014) that adults should regularly engage in healthy eating patterns (e.g., more fruit and vegetable intake, less sugar-sweetened beverages and dense snacks consumption) and frequent physical activity

© spotmatik, 2014. Used under license from Shutterstock, Inc.

(e.g., at least five days a week). Spouses have been found to play an important role in their partners' daily chronic disease management and mental health treatment. Supportive activities include helping with medication or dietary adherence, attendance at medical visits, and providing advice when needed. Research looking at individuals' management of diabetes has shown that patients who included their spouse in their care had significantly better control of their diabetes compared to those who did not (Mendenhall et al., 2010; Umberson et al., 2006). As mentioned above, research also suggests that having a significant other who engages in healthful behaviors increases the likelihood that the partner will have a healthy weight status, eat fruits/vegetables, eat breakfast on a daily basis, and engage in frequent physical activity (Berge et al., 2012).

INTIMATE RELATIONSHIPS AND MENTAL HEALTH

It is well known that stress often leads to depression and anxiety (Timmermans, Xiong, Hoogenraad, & Krugers, 2013), and that these mental health diagnoses are strongly correlated with overall well-being. Experiencing marital distress increases the risk of experiencing depressive symptoms up to 10–25 times (Kiecolt-Glaser & Newton, 2001). However, research also shows that the relationship between depression and the quality of the marital relationship is reciprocal; being depressed also leads to poor quality relationships (Fincham & Beach, 1999). This reciprocal relationship is problematic either way because depression alters the cardiovascular, immune, and endocrine functions (Burke, Davis, Otte, & Mohr, 2005; Kiecolt-Glaser & Newton, 2001), which in turn has serious negative health consequences, such as higher rates of cancer, heart disease, stroke, and mortality (Reiche, Nunes, & Morimoto, 2004; Rugulies, 2002; Zheng et al., 1997). In addition, depressed people are more likely to engage in unhealthy behaviors including substance use, unhealthy dietary intake, reduced sleep, and physical activity, which can further increase their health risks

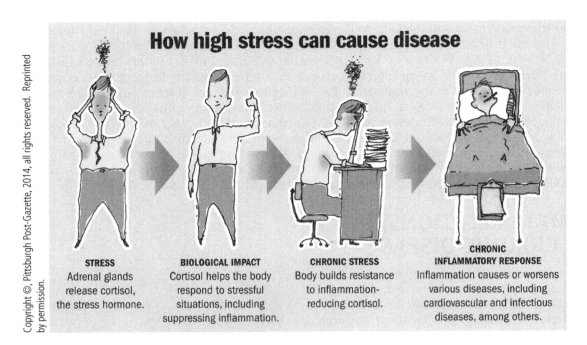

How high stress can cause disease

STRESS	**BIOLOGICAL IMPACT**	**CHRONIC STRESS**	**CHRONIC INFLAMMATORY RESPONSE**
Adrenal glands release cortisol, the stress hormone.	Cortisol helps the body respond to stressful situations, including suppressing inflammation.	Body builds resistance to inflammation-reducing cortisol.	Inflammation causes or worsens various diseases, including cardiovascular and infectious diseases, among others.

(Kiecolt-Glaser & Newton, 2001; Roberts, Shema, Kaplan, & Strawbridge, 2000). Research examining recovery from chemical dependency, treatment for depression, and treatment for compulsive gambling has suggested that involving a spouse or partner in the treatment increases the likelihood of treatment success (Ross & Mirowsky, 2002).

In summary, positive, satisfying relationships have been shown to be good for your health and negative, unsatisfying relationships have been found to be harmful for your health. Additionally, although the majority of the research has been conducted with married couples, some research suggests that couples in committed relationships also benefit from the health effects of having a significant other. In this section, we have briefly described what is known about the reciprocal relationship of intimate relationships and health. Now we will attempt to explain reasons for this connection.

THEORETICAL EXPLANATIONS REGARDING THE CONNECTION BETWEEN INTIMATE RELATIONSHIPS AND HEALTH

Many frameworks are useful in conceptualizing the impact of intimate relationships on health. In this section, we will review the biopsychosocial model, family systems theory, and family development theory to provide a holistic explanation regarding the connection between intimacy and health.

Biopsychosocial Model

This framework was proposed by George Engel in 1977 as a way to integrate the split between "mind" and "body" that was present during the time, and that persists to a certain degree today. Engel's model responded to the reductionist biomedical approach (mostly focused in the molecular and biological explanations of disease), by highlighting the social, psychological, and behavioral human dimensions of illness and integrating them into biological dimensions. He explained that the psychological and social facets of human life affect the underlying physiological and behavioral processes that lead to good or bad health outcomes. Therefore, by affecting biological processes, intimate relationships really can "get under our skin." Following these ideas, we will briefly describe how intimate relationships affect human physiology.

HOW INTIMATE RELATIONSHIPS AFFECT HUMAN PHYSIOLOGY. Research examining the connection between social relationships and physiological responses is a growing field of science. Researchers trying to understand the connection between neurobiology and intimate relationships have looked at stress. Human stress responses are primarily determined by the sympathetic-adrenomedulary (SAM) and the hypothalamic-pituitary-adrenocortical (HPA) systems, both of which are activated by the perception of stress in the central nervous system (Gunnar & Quevedo, 2007). When the brain perceives that something is stressful, the SAM system triggers a rapid release of adrenaline from the adrenal gland. This fast release of adrenaline is responsible for the increased arousal and vigilance characterized by the fight/flight response to a threat. Additionally, the brain also triggers the production of glucocorticosteroid hormones, mainly cortisol, which is responsible for a slower but longer sustained response to stress. This second response is commanded by the HPA system, and in the long run can become more detrimental to the person because the stress level is sustained for a longer period of time (i.e., chronic stress).

Low quality interpersonal relationships are an example of chronic stress that can continually activate the SAM and HPA systems (D'Onofrio & Lahey, 2010). The chronic, ongoing activation of the stress response mechanism increases cardiovascular reactivity (e.g., blood pressure and heart rate), produces endocrine dysregulation (e.g., abnormal levels of adrenaline, cortisol, oxci-tocine, prolactine, growth hormone, testosterone, and adenocorticotropin hormone (ACTH)—hormones responsible for different functions in the body), alters immune function (e.g., reduced natural killer cell clearance, increased antibody titers, increased interleukin-4, -5, and -6, and in-terferon-gamma production), and modifies brain activity and structure (e.g., prefrontal cortex and amygdala—brain structures involved in executive functioning, behavioral control, and emotional regulation) (D'Onofrio & Lahey, 2010; Kiecolt-Glaser & Newton, 2001; Miller & Chen, 2010; Robles & Kiecolt-Glaser, 2003; Tobin, Slatcher, & Robles, 2013; Whittle et al., 2008). These physiologically altered responses have been found to be significantly associated with worse health outcomes (e.g., inability to heal/recover, higher risk of mortality). Thus, because negative relationships can have potentially serious biological consequences, it is important to understand how to preserve and nurture positive intimate relationships, and to improve or end intimate relationships that are stressful or negative. Specifically, negative interpersonal relationships can deter physical and mental health, whereas positive relationships can promote better physical and mental health.

Another important issue to consider when trying to understand biological influences on in-terpersonal distress is intergenerational transmission of detrimental physiological states. Negative parent–child relationships also trigger similar biological responses as described above in intimate interpersonal relationships. These high-stressed, negative parent–child relationships expose and model for children development processes that could negatively affect their physiological responses in their current parent/child relationship and in future interpersonal relationships (Carr & Springer, 2010; D'Onofrio & Lahey, 2010; Tobin et al., 2013). Being aware of the physiological effects of positive and negative relationships is fundamental to fully understand the connection between healthy and unhealthy relationships on one's overall health and well-being.

Family Systems Theory

According to this theory, the interactions that occur within romantic relationships are reciprocal (Minuchin, 1974; Whitchurch & Constantine, 1993). That is, each partner is shaping and being shaped by the other part-ners' actions (e.g., via support, modeling). These mutual influencing patterns may give particular insight into the behaviors that ul-timately determine the relationship between health behaviors (e.g., dietary intake, physi-cal activity) and chronic disease manage-ment in adults and their relationship status (e.g., married or committed relationship). For example, healthful dietary intake modeled by a

© Monkey Business Images, 2014. Used under license from Shutterstock, Inc.

significant other may potentially influence a partner to engage in healthful eating as well. A spouse who decides to be more physically active may potentially influence the partner with type 2 diabetes to be more active, which will decrease the partner's overall hemoglobin A1c levels and improve his/her disease control. Keeping in mind this interdependence of family members is vital to understand the connection between health and family relations.

Family Development Theory

Family development theory emphasizes the impact of normal human development and family life cycle transitions in relation to environmental contexts where people live and carry out their lives (Bengston & Allen, 1993; Rodgers & White, 1993). As individuals experience normative transitions (e.g., adolescence) the family system changes accordingly (e.g., parents adjust their parenting practices to meet the innate desire of an adolescent to be more independent). Considering the intersection between normative individual development and family life cycle transitions is critical for better understanding how the family environment can affect individual health. *Critical developmental periods* are time points where an exposure has lifelong effects on individual development (e.g., *in utero* exposure to drugs has lifelong consequences for a child), while exposures during *sensitive periods* produce modifiable or reversible effects on individual development (Ben-Shlomo & Kuh, 2002). These individual and familial developmental considerations allow for a deeper understanding of how certain events in someone's life may differ depending on their developmental age and stage (e.g., the psychological consequences of the death of a parent are different for a child than for the spouse). In addition, these developmental periods (i.e., critical or sensitive periods) can guide professionals in identifying more salient time points in which to intervene with families (e.g., pregnant women are more likely to quit smoking than women who are not pregnant) (Hemsing, Greaves, O'Leary, Chan, & Okoli, 2012).

HOW DO FAMILY TRANSITIONS AFFECT HEALTH? All transitions affect health regardless of whether they are "positive" (e.g., marriage or having a newborn child) or "negative" (e.g., divorce or death of a family member). Why? All of these transitions increase stress levels. For example, having children increases the number of demands and decreases leisure time of the couple (Nomaguchi & Milkie, 2003). Additionally, parents have a hard time finding work/family balance, such as arranging daycare and carrying out household work. As a result, "couple time" is reduced, which can lead to diminished couple satisfaction (Demo & Cox, 2000). Even though parents enjoy their time with their children, the effects of parenthood persist throughout the child's upbringing, and parents report having lower levels of psychological well-being compared to nonparents (Nomaguchi, 2012; Nomaguchi & Milkie, 2003). However, psychological well-being increases as children grow (Nomaguchi, 2012).

Another well-known example of the influence of family life transitions on health and well-being is divorce. Evidence suggests that divorce not only affects the psychological well-being of the children, adolescents, and adults involved in the divorce, but also it increases the risk of other physical health problems, such as high blood pressure, headaches, and even mortality in the children, adolescents, and adults involved in the divorce (Amato, 2010; Lorenz, et al., 2006; Manzoli, et al., 2007; Umberson, et al., 2006). Many difficult issues occur simultaneously when children, adolescents, or adults experience divorce. For example, grief and loss occurs because one family member (or more) is no longer available for emotional or practical sources of support, and fear and stress occur because of the uncertainty of the unknown future. In addition, health behaviors are less frequently monitored and the family income is significantly reduced. All of these factors are detrimental for the health of the individual family members. Similar unfavorable health consequences are associated with the death of a parent or a spouse (Gardner & Oswald, 2004; Tyrka, Wier, Price, Ross, & Carpenter, 2008; Umberson et al., 2006).

Just as structural family transitions can affect well-being, health challenges can also impact family members' mental and physical health and well-being. As proposed by family systems theory (Whitchurch & Constantine, 1993), many studies have identified that family members experience distress when someone in the family is diagnosed with a medical condition (Miller-Day, 2011). In general, illnesses, especially chronic diseases, are considered "negative life events" that require adaptation. Depending on the disease type and severity, they might produce physical functioning limitations that require caregiver services, emotional concerns and distress, and increased monetary expenses or reduction in leisure time, all of which can have a negative impact on mental and physical health and well-being. To cope with these challenges, families may need to adjust their roles and responsibilities, which can be difficult and can result in reducing the overall quality and satisfaction of the relationship(s). As intimate relationships affect health, health also affects the quality of these relations. This reciprocal determinism should be attended to when considering the interplay between families and health.

Even though experiencing family transitions tend to increase the risk for negative health outcomes, it is important to note that the consequences can be modifiable. For example, first-time mothers who report having partners that are supportive experience lower levels of stress, compared to mothers who report their partners are not supportive (Nomaguchi, 2012; Nomaguchi & Milkie, 2003). Similarly, the mental and physical health consequences of divorce, death, or separation have been shown to be moderated by the quality of parent–child relationships, parenting practices, and by having additional sources of support (Amato, 2010; Carr & Springer, 2010; Walsh, 2006). Furthermore, research in the area of childhood trauma has shown that experiencing a serious childhood trauma (e.g., sexual and/or physical abuse) can lead to negative physiological and psychological problems as an adult, but that positive experiences, such as having a caring significant other, can increase emotional healing and even heal chronic physiological damage, altered patters of brain connections, and genetic expression that may have been a result of the childhood trauma (Bremner, Elzinga, Schmahl, & Vermetten, 2007; Cicchetti & Rogosch, 2012; D'Onofrio & Lahey, 2010).

Social Selection vs. Social Causation

In order to weave together the theoretical perspectives and research findings on the positive effects of committed relationships, there are two important concepts to introduce: social causation and social selection (Carr & Springer, 2010). *Social causation* implies that being married makes individual members of the couple healthier. For example, married people have more economic resources, monitor and engage in similar health behaviors, and provide psychosocial support when facing stressful events, which potentially contributes to better physical and emotional well-being overall. *Social selection* explains that healthy people are more likely to get and stay married, and therefore the health benefit of being married is not due primarily to their married condition, but to their health status previous to becoming married (Umberson et al., 2006; Waite & Gallaher, 2000). Both of these proposed mechanisms regarding the health transmission of intimate relationships/marriage are equally probable and should be used as backdrops when interpreting findings.

© kurhan, 2014. Used under license from Shutterstock, Inc.

FAMILY COMMUNICATION AND HEALTH

Through different communication practices, including verbal and nonverbal, we connect and interact with our significant others. Therefore, the way we communicate is vital for developing and maintaining healthy human relationships. An important body of research has assessed how interpersonal communication affects health. In this section, we will review how communication affects health and highlight recent research related to the communication around weight and health behaviors to exemplify how communication with one's significant other affects physical and mental health. We will end this section of the chapter by providing recommendations for positive communication when talking to significant others about health.

Couple Communication and Health

Partners communicate love and affection to one another in many ways, including expressing love, support and positive affect, physical emotional expressions (e.g., holding hands, hugging, kissing), self-disclosure, tolerating unpleasant aspects of the partner, and through material means (e.g., giving presents) (Segrin & Flora, 2011). All of these types of communication have been found to be significantly associated with greater relationship satisfaction for both partners (Segrin & Flora, 2011), which ultimately leads to better health.

© Blend Images, 2014. Used under license from Shutterstock, Inc.

John Gottman is a pioneer in the study of the relationship between physiological responses during couple interactions/communication (i.e., conflicts, fights) and overall couple relationship satisfaction. For more than 30 years, he analyzed the physiological effects of couple's arguments and discussions, finding that both men and women increase their heart rate and blood pressure when having marital conflict, with men having greater spikes in measures of cardiovascular reactivity (Gottman, 1990, 1991). Gottman explains that physiological arousal is what, in part, triggers stonewalling (presented in Chapter 9). When stonewalling occurs, a sequential dance is usually set off with the spouse avoiding conflict with the other partner (i.e., distancing), while the other partner, whose physiological arousal system has been activated, tries to continuously re-engage the spouse (i.e., "pursue") (Gottman, 1991). This cycle, termed the "Pursuer–Distancer" dance by Gottman, ends with one partner withdrawing from the interaction, which has been shown to be a strong predictor of divorce (Gottman, 1991).

It is essential for intimate partners to monitor and master healthy communication practices if they want to have a healthy, happy relationship. Key skills include: nurturing love, giving compliments/admiration, negotiating roles, problem-solving, respecting one another, accepting one another's influence, recognizing and repairing mistakes in the relationship, and sharing common activities. These communication characteristics have been found to distinguish happy and healthy marriages from relationships that are likely to end up in divorce (Gottman, 1999).

"You said what?": Communication regarding Health Behaviors

One aspect of communication that is bound to come up within an intimate relationship is conversations about weight and health behaviors (e.g., the way you eat, how physically active you are, your body shape and size). However, many sources seem to have differing opinions about whether you should or shouldn't bring these topics up in an intimate relationship. Luckily, there are research studies that have looked at these specific questions and can offer some insight into how to address these topics within intimate relationships.

TALKING TO YOUR SIGNIFICANT OTHER ABOUT THEIR WEIGHT, SHAPE, OR SIZE. Research with young or emerging adults (defined roughly as ages 18–25 years) has demonstrated that "weight talk" is common in this age group (Calogero, Herbozo, & Thompson, 2009; Herbozo & Thompson, 2006; Muscat & Long, 2008; Ousley, Cordero, & White, 2008; Thompson, Heinberg, Leslie, Altabe, & Tantleff-Dunn, 1999), in contrast to weight teasing, which is inherently negative and intentionally directed at the listener. Weight teasing is typically used to point out negative aspects of a persons' weight, shape or size (e.g., "You're muffin top is showing," "You're so fat!"). Alternatively, weight talk may be more general, may not refer to the listener, and may include both negative and positive comments regarding weight (e.g., "She looks terrible; she must have gained 20 pounds!" or "You look great—have you lost weight?"). Interestingly, weight talk has been found to have negative consequences, even when meant as a compliment. For example, Calogero and colleagues (2009) found that weight comments that were meant as positive compliments regarding one's weight, shape, or size were associated with higher body dissatisfaction in college women. Thus, it appears that talking about someone's weight, shape, or size, even when intending it to be a compliment, may come across as negative, because it may imply that there was something wrong with the person's weight, shape, or size previously.

Negative weight talk comments (e.g., "You're clothes are fitting tighter, it may be a good time to go to the gym," or "Look, she has no right wearing those jeans!") have been found to be even more strongly associated with negative consequences in one's significant other compared to weight talk that is meant to be a compliment. In two studies using longitudinal data sets with over 2000 young adults in the Midwest, researchers found that young adults whose significant others used negative weight talk were at an increased risk of having disordered eating behaviors, such as skipping meals, engaging in binging and purging (i.e., throwing up), and using diet pills or laxatives in both young adult women and men (Eisenberg, Berge, Fulkerson, & Neumark-Sztainer, 2011, 2012).

IS WEIGHT TALK EXPERIENCED THE SAME BY EVERYONE? Are women more affected by weight talk? Are people from higher socioeconomic status (SES) more worried about weight talk? Are there differences by race regarding who is affected more by weight talk? These are common questions asked when considering the far reaching effects of weight talk. Research has looked at these questions. One study found that Hispanic and Asian young adults reported a higher prevalence of receiving hurtful weight talk from significant others compared to white and African American young adults (Eisenberg et al., 2011). In addition, young adult males from lower SES families were significantly more likely to report receiving hurtful weight talk from significant others than young adult males from higher SES families; however, differences were not significant for females. Similarly, both male and female participants who were overweight or obese were more likely to report receiving hurtful weight-related comments from significant others than their male and female counterparts who were underweight or average weight.

INTIMATE RELATIONSHIPS AND BODY SATISFACTION. Existing research has found that general relationship quality, functioning, and satisfaction are associated with weight-related concerns. Specifically, women who are in more satisfying relationships tend to have greater body satisfaction and are less likely to use unhealthy weight control strategies (e.g., diet pills, vomiting) than those who are less satisfied (Friedman, Dixon, Brownell, Whisman, & Wilfley, 1999; Markey, Markey, & Birch, 2001; Morrison, Doss, & Perez, 2009). Several studies have also examined male partners' satisfaction with their female partner's body (Ambwani & Strauss, 2007; Morrison et al., 2009; Pole, Crowther, & Schell, 2004) and found that men's dissatisfaction with their partner's body was associated with women's own body dissatisfaction.

SAYING OR DOING: IS IT WORSE TO MODEL OR TALK ABOUT DIETING WITH YOUR SIGNIFICANT OTHER? It is also of interest to know whether modeling unhealthful behaviors (e.g., dieting) is as harmful for one's significant other's health behaviors as talking about their weight, shape, or size. One study conducted with over 2000 young adults in the Midwest found that perceived dieting behavior and encouragement to diet by significant others were common (Eisenberg, Berge, & Neumark-Sztainer, 2013). Specifically, three-quarters of males (n = 1500) reported that their significant others (predominantly female in this sample)

> **Take-home Messages about Talking with Your Significant Other about their Weight, Shape, or Size**
>
> - Weight talk that is negative, or even meant as a compliment, makes one's significant other feel unhappy about their body weight, shape, or size and can lead to disordered eating behaviors
> - Weight talk may be more harmful for some populations from certain race/ethnicities, socioeconomic status categories, or who are overweight/obese
> - Women and men are equally affected negatively by weight talk
> - When women aren't happy with how they look, their significant other is also not happy with how they look
> - Being in a satisfying relationship promotes body satisfaction
> - Modeling dieting and encouraging dieting in one's significant other are equally as harmful and promote disordered eating behaviors
> - When addressing a partner's weight, talk about the importance of health, rather than the importance of "losing weight"

dieted a little (23.7%), somewhat (33.7%) or very much (15.1%); 45.5% of females reported that their (predominantly male) significant others dieted. Approximately half of participants (51.2% of males and 44.1% of females) reported that their significant other encouraged them to diet. In addition, disordered eating behaviors were positively associated with significant other's dieting and encouragement to diet, particularly for females. For example, women's binge eating was almost doubled if their significant other encouraged dieting "very much" (25.5%) compared to "not at all" (13.6%).

IF NOT WEIGHT TALK, THEN WHAT? Researchers and therapists have suggested that in intimate relationships it is important to focus conversations related to weight or health behaviors on health, rather than the body weight, shape, or size of the significant other. For example, if a partner is worried about his or her significant other putting on weight, instead of saying, "I think you need to go on a diet," rather say, "I want us both to be healthy, let's help each other eat more healthfully and be more physically active." Using a positive undertone (i.e., both of us should work together for the sake of our health), rather than a negative undertone (i.e., you have a problem with your weight and need to fix it) in the message regarding one's significant other's health will increase the likelihood that the significant other will be motivated toward action, rather than be offended and either do nothing or do something harmful, such as engaging in disordered eating behaviors.

Recommendations for Positive Communication within Intimate Relationships

In general, open communication that avoids a negative undertone is better for intimate relationships and health. Here we provide some recommendations to improve your communication with your significant others (for details read Wahlroos, 1995):

- Actions are more important than words; nonverbal communication is more powerful than verbal communication
- Learn to listen, rather than talk, in order to really understand what your significant other is trying to say
- Recognize that each person has different viewpoints of the same situation
- Be aware that you might be wrong and your significant other is right
- Recognize that your significant other cares about you, and that they can give valuable information about you and your health behaviors
- Frame your communication in a positive tone (e.g., health vs. weight/fat)
- Emphasize what is important, and do not bring in irrelevant issues
- Be clear and specific
- Be realistic; base your statements on things that happened or that are likely to happen
- Be open about your thoughts and feelings and do not hide problems that are relevant for you
- Do not nag, shout, or harass!
- Learn how to disagree without destroying your relationship
- Do not bring up stuff that is unrelated to the conversation, especially if those things might hurt your significant other
- Try to understand the feelings behind the communication and show respect toward your significant other
- Do not lecture or preach, ask questions instead
- Use humor and avoid teasing
- Take responsibility for what you say or do
- Monitor the consequences of your communication. If the consequences are not what you intended revise your communication strategy

STRENGTHENING INTIMATE RELATIONSHIPS TO IMPROVE HEALTH

In order to ensure that the communication you are having with your significant other is beneficial to your and your partner's health, you must work on having good communication skills. In this section, we will briefly highlight one example of a couples program that has been well developed

Exercises after Reading this Chapter

1. Think of an intimate significant other relationship that you are currently in or one in the past. Make a list of examples where your mental or physical health were impacted either for the positive or negative by your significant other. Additionally, how did you positively or negatively impact your significant other's mental or physical health?
2. What's your opinion? Do you agree with the "social selection" or "social causation" depiction of why intimate relationships are good for your health?
3. Choose an individual or family life cycle transition that you went through (e.g., death of a loved one, divorce, birth of a child, transition into adolescence or young adulthood) and use Family Systems Theory, the Biospychosocial Framework, or the Family Development Theory to describe how your mental and physical health were impacted.
4. Write down an example of a time where you talked with an intimate significant other about their weight or health. How did it go? What would you do differently now, knowing the importance of communication and focusing on "health" versus "weight, shape or size" in your conversation?

to strengthen intimate relationships, which ultimately improves health outcomes. This program has been tested using a strong research design (e.g., well-executed randomized controlled trials), which increases the confidence in the findings. The program is called the "Prevention and Relationship Enhancement Program" (PREP).

Prevention and Relationship Enhancement Program (PREP)

The PREP is a cost-effective program focused on strengthening interpersonal couple relationships before or during marriage (Jakubowski, Milne, Brunner, & Miller, 2004). This program teaches participants how to communicate effectively, work as a team, manage conflicts without damaging the relationship, and promote affection and commitment. This program is carried out through weekly group sessions, followed by a weekend retreat. The content is constantly updated to reflect the current research in couple relationships and the program has been evaluated through multiple studies and across several countries. Research results examining the effectiveness of this program have shown improved couple's communication, conflict management, and connection, and lower divorce rates, all of which are related to health. More information about PREP is available at www .prepinc.com

Additional evidence-based couples programs can be found in repositories, such as the Substance Abuse and Mental Health Services Administration's National Registry of Effective Programs and Practices (http://nrepp.samhsa.gov).

SUMMARY

In this chapter, we have reviewed research showing a strong connection between intimate relationships and health, introduced theoretical frameworks that corroborate the research findings regarding intimate relationships and mental and physical health and well-being, emphasized that interpersonal communication is fundamental for positive couple relationships, and presented an evidence-based couples program that improves couples communication and strengthens intimate relationships. Overall, there is clear evidence that being in a married or committed relationship with a significant other is good for your health and well-being.

REFERENCES

Allen, M., Svetaz, M. V., Hardeman, R., & Resnick, M. D. (2008). *What research tells us about Latino parenting practices and their relationship to youth sexual behavior.* Washington, DC: National Campaign to Prevent Teen and Unplanned Pregnancy.

Amato, P. R. (2010). Research on divorce: Continuing trends and new developments. *Journal of Marriage and Family, 72*(3), 650–666. doi:10.1111/j.1741-3737.2010.00723.x

Amato, P. R., & Cheadle, J. (2005). The long reach of divorce: Divorce and child well-being across three generations. *Journal of Marriage and Family, 67*(1), 191–206. doi:10.1111/j.0022-2445.2005.00014.x

Ambwani, S., & Strauss, J. (2007). Love thyself before loving others? A qualitative and quantitative analysis of gender differences in body image and romantic love. *Sex Roles, 56,* 13–21. doi:10.1007/s11199-006-9143-7

American Medical Association (2014). Recommendations for managing chronic conditions and preventative living. http://www.ama-assn.org/ama. Accessed February 20, 2014.

Bhatia, S. K., & Bhatia, S. C. (2007). Childhood and adolescent depression. *American Family Physician, 75,* 1–8. Retrieved from https://vmw-lmsc.duhs.duke.edu/production/DUHS_Common/Peds_residency/adolescent/Child_Adol_Depression_Review09.pdf

Barker, D. J. (1997). Maternal nutrition, fetal nutrition, and disease in later life. *Nutrition, 13*(9), 807–813. doi:10.1016/s0899-9007(97)00193-7

Barnes, G. M., Hoffman, J. H., Welte, J. W., Farrell, M. P., & Dintcheff, B. A. (2006). Effects of parental monitoring and peer deviance on substance use and delinquency. *Journal of Marriage and Family, 68*(4), 1084–1104. doi:10.1111/j.1741-3737.2006.00315.x

Bengston, V. L., & Allen, K. R. (1993). The life course perspective applied to families over time. In P. Boss, W. J. Doherty, R. LaRossa, W. Schumm & S. Steinmetz (Eds.), *Boss, Doherty, LaRossa, Schumm, & Steinmetz book* (pp. 469–498). New York: Springer.

Ben-Shlomo, Y., & Kuh, D. (2002). A life course approach to chronic disease epidemiology: Conceptual models, empirical challenges and interdisciplinary perspectives. *International Journal of Epidemiology, 31*(2), 285–293. doi:10.1093/ije/31.2.285

Berge, J. M., Bauer, K. W., MacLehose, R., Eisenberg, M. E., & Neumark-Sztainer, D. (in press). Weight status and health behaviors among young adults who are single or in committed relationships. *Families, Systems, & Health.*

Berge, J. M., MacLehose, R., Eisenberg, M. E., Laska, M. N., & Neumark-Sztainer, D. (2012). How significant is the 'significant other'? Associations between significant others' health behaviors and attitudes and young adults' health outcomes. *International Journal of Behavioral Nutrition and Physical Activity, 9,* 35–43. doi:10.1186/1479-5868-9-35

Berge, J. M., & Saelens, B. E. (2012). Familial influences on adolescents' eating and physical activity behaviors. *Adolescent Medicine: State of the Art Reviews, 23*(3), 424–439. Retrieved from https://www.researchgate.net/publication/235727426_Familial_influences_on_adolescents'_eating_and_physical_activity_behaviors

Bremner, J. D., Elzinga, B., Schmahl, C., & Vermetten, E. (2007). Structural and functional plasticity of the human brain in posttraumatic stress disorder. *Progress in Brain Research, 167,* 171–186. doi:10.1016/s0079-6123(07)67012-5

Brown, W. J., Heesch, K. C., & Miller, Y. D. (2009). Life events and changing physical activity patterns in women at different life stages. *Annals of Behavioral Medicine, 37*(3), 294–305. doi:10.1007/s12160-009-9099-2

Burke, H. M., Davis, M. C., Otte, C., & Mohr, D. C. (2005). Depression and cortisol responses to psychological stress: A meta-analysis. *Psychoneuroendocrinology, 30*(9), 846–856. doi:10.1016/j.psyneuen.2005.02.010

Calogero, R. M., Herbozo, S., & Thompson, J. K. (2009). Complementary weightism: The potential costs of appearance-related commentary for women's self-objectification. *Psychology of Women Quarterly, 33,* 120–132. doi:10.1111/j.1471-6402.2008.01479.x

Carr, D., & Springer, K. W. (2010). Advances in families and health research in the 21st century. *Journal of Marriage and Family, 72*(3), 743–761. doi:10.1111/j.1741-3737.2010.00728.x

Chung, H. L., & Steinberg, L. (2006). Relations between neighborhood factors, parenting behaviors, peer deviance, and delinquency among serious juvenile offenders. *Developmental Psychology, 42*(2), 319–331. doi:10.1037/0012-1649.42.2.319

Cicchetti, D., & Rogosch, F. A. (2012). Gene × environment interaction and resilience: Effects of child maltreatment and serotonin, corticotropin releasing hormone, dopamine, and oxytocin genes. *Development and Psychopathology, 24*(2), 411–427. doi:10.1017/s0954579412000077

Cislak, A., Safron, M., Pratt, M., Gaspar, T., & Luszczynska, A. (2012). Family-related predictors of body weight and weight-related behaviours among children and adolescents: A systematic umbrella review. *Child: Care, Health and Development, 38*(3), 321–331. doi:10.1111/j.1365-2214.2011.01285.x

Clark, M. S., Jansen, K. L., & Cloy, J. A. (2012). Treatment of childhood and adolescent depression. *American Family Physician, 86*(5), 1–7. Retrieved from http://peds.stanford.edu.ezp3.lib.umn.edu/Rotations/adolescent_medicine/documents/depression/Treatment%20of%20Childhood%20and%20Adolescent%20Depression.pdf

Demo, D. H., & Cox, M. J. (2000). Families with young children: A review of research in the 1990s. *Journal of Marriage and Family, 62*(4), 876–895. doi:10.1111/j.1741-3737.2000.00876.x

D'Onofrio, B. M., & Lahey, B. B. (2010). Biosocial influences on the family: A decade review. *Journal of Marriage and Family, 72*(3), 762–782. doi:10.1111/j.1741-3737.2010.00729.x

Eisenberg, M. E., Berge, J. M., Fulkerson, J. A., & Neumark-Sztainer, D. (2011). Weight comments by family and significant others in young adulthood. *Body Image, 8*(1), 12–19. doi:10.1016/j.bodyim.2010.11.002

Eisenberg, M. E., Berge, J. M., Fulkerson, J. A., & Neumark-Sztainer, D. (2012). Associations between hurtful weight-related comments by family and significant other and the development of disordered eating behaviors in young adults. *Journal of Behavioral Medicine, 35*(5), 500–508. doi:10.1007/s10865-011-9378-9

Eisenberg, M. E., Berge, J. M., & Neumark-Sztainer, D. (2013). Dieting and encouragement to diet by significant others: Associations with disordered eating in young adults. *American Journal of Health Promotion. 27*(6), 370–377. doi:10.4278/ajhp.120120-QUAN-57

Engel, G. L. (1977). The need for a new medical model: A challenge for biomedicine. *Science, 196*(4286), 129–136. doi:10.1126/science.847460

Fincham, F. D., & Beach, S. R. (1999). Conflict in marriage: Implications for working with couples. *Annual Review of Psychology, 50*(1), 47–77. doi:10.1146/annurev.psych.50.1.47

Friedman, M. A., Dixon, A. E., Brownell, K. D., Whisman, M. A., & Wilfley, D. E. (1999). Marital status, marital satisfaction, and body image dissatisfaction. *International Journal of Eating Disorders, 26*(1), 81–85. doi:10.1002/(SICI)1098-108X(199907)26:1<81::AID-EAT10>3.0.CO;2-V [pii]

Gardner, J., & Oswald, A. (2004). How is mortality affected by money, marriage, and stress? *Journal of Health Economics, 23*(6), 1181–1207. doi:10.1016/j.jhealeco.2004.03.002

Gluckman, P. D., Hanson, M. A., Cooper, C., & Thornburg, K. L. (2008). Effect of in utero and early-life conditions on adult health and disease. *New England Journal of Medicine, 359*(1), 61–73. doi:10.1056/nejmra0708473

Gottman, J. M. (1990). Finding the laws of close personal relationships. In I. Sigel (Ed.), *Research programs from a personal perspective* (pp. 249–263). Hillsdale, NJ: Lawrence Erlbaum.

Gottman, J. M. (1991). Predicting the longitudinal course of marriages. *Journal of Marital Family Therapy, 17*, 3–7. doi:10.1111/j.1752-0606.1991.tb00856.x

Gottman, J. M. (1999). *The marriage clinic: A scientifically-based marital therapy.* New York: W.W. Norton & Company.

Gunnar, M., & Quevedo, K. (2007). The neurobiology of stress and development. *Annual Review of Psychology, 58*, 145–173. doi:10.1146/annurev.psych.58.110405.085605

Hemsing, N., Greaves, L., O'Leary, R., Chan, K., & Okoli, C. (2012). Partner support for smoking cessation during pregnancy: A systematic review. *Nicotine & Tobacco Research, 14*(7), 767–776. doi:10.1093/ntr/ntr278

Herbozo, S., & Thompson, J. K. (2006). Development and validation of the verbal commentary on physical appearance scale: Considering both positive and negative commentary. *Body Image, 3*(4), 335–344. doi:S1740-1445(06)00089-1 [pii] 10.1016/j.bodyim.2006.10.001

Hill, K. G., Hawkins, J. D., Catalano, R. F., Abbott, R. D., & Guo, J. (2005). Family influences on the risk of daily smoking initiation. *Journal of Adolescent Health, 37*(3), 202–210. doi:10.1016/j.jadohealth.2004.08.014

Holt-Lunstad, J., Smith, T. B., & Layton, J. B. (2010). Social relationships and mortality risk: A meta-analytic review. *PLoS Medicine, 7*(7), 1–20. doi:10.1371/journal.pmed.1000316

Jakubowski, S. F., Milne, E. P., Brunner, H., & Miller, R. B. (2004). A review of empirically supported marital enrichment programs. *Family Relations, 53*(5), 528–536. doi:10.1111/j.0197-6664.2004.00062.x

Kiecolt-Glaser, J. K., & Newton, T. L. (2001). Marriage and health: His and hers. *Psychological Bulletin, 127*(4), 472–503. doi:10.1037/0033-2909.127.4.472

Laursen, B., & Collins, W.A.(2004). Parent-child communication during adolescence. In A. Vangelisti (Ed.), *Handbook of family communication* (pp. 333–348). Mahwah, NJ: Lawrence Erlbaum Associates.

Lorenz, F. O., Wickrama, K. A. S., Conger, R. D., & Elder, G. H. (2006). The short-term and decade-long effects of divorce on women's midlife health. *Journal of Health and Social Behavior, 47*(2), 111–125. doi:10.1177/002214650604700202

Manzoli, L., Villari, P., M Pirone, G., & Boccia, A. (2007). Marital status and mortality in the elderly: A systematic review and meta-analysis. *Social Science & Medicine, 64*(1), 77–94. doi:10.1016/j.socscimed.2006.08.031

Markey, C. N., Markey, P. M., & Birch, L. L. (2001). Interpersonal predictors of dieting practices among married couples. *Journal of Family Psychology, 15*(3), 464–475. doi:10.1037/0893-3200.15.3.464

Mendenhall, T. J., Berge, J. M., Harper, P., GreenCrow, B., LittleWalker, N., WhiteEagle, S., & BrownOwl, S. (2010). The Family Education Diabetes Series (FEDS): Community-based participatory research with a midwestern American Indian community. *Nurse Inquiry, 17*(4), 359–372. doi:10.1111/j.1440-1800.2010.00508.x

Meyler, D., Stimpson, J. P., & Peek, M. K. (2007). Health concordance within couples: A systematic review. *Social Science & Medicine, 64*(11), 2297–2310. doi:10.1016/j.socscimed.2007.02.007

Miller, G. E., & Chen, E. (2010). Harsh family climate in early life presages the emergence of a proinflammatory phenotype in adolescence. *Psychological Science, 21*(6), 848–856. doi:10.1177/0956797610370161

Miller-Day, M. (Ed.). (2011). *Family comunication, connections, and health transitions.* New York: Peter Lang Publishing.

Minuchin, S. (1974). *Families and family therapy.* Cambridge, MA: Harvard University Press.

Molloy, G. J., Perkins-Porras, L., Strike, P. C., & Steptoe, A. (2008). Social networks and partner stress as predictors of adherence to medication, rehabilitation attendance, and quality of life following acute coronary syndrome. *Health Psychology, 27*(1), 52–58. doi:10.1037/0278-6133.27.1.52

Morrison, K. R., Doss, B. D., & Perez, M. (2009). Body image and disordered eating in romantic relationships. *Journal of Social and Clinical Psychology, 28*(3), 281–306. doi:10.1521/jscp.2009.28.3.281

Muscat, A. C., & Long, B. C. (2008). Critical comments about body shape and weight: Disordered eating of female athletes and sport participants. *Journal of Applied Sport Psychology, 20*, 1–24. doi:10.1080/10413200701784833

Nomaguchi, K. M. (2012). Parenthood and psychological well-being: Clarifying the role of child age and parent–child relationship quality. *Social Science Research, 41*(2), 489–498. doi:10.1016/j.ssresearch.2011.08.001

Nomaguchi, K. M., & Milkie, M. A. (2003). Costs and rewards of children: The effects of becoming a parent on adults' lives. *Journal of Marriage and Family, 65*(2), 356–374. doi:10.1111/j.1741-3737.2003.00356.x

O'Connell, M. E., Boat, T., & Warner, K. E. (Eds.). (2009). *Preventing mental, emotional, and behavioral disorders among young people: Progress and possibilities.* National Academies Press.

Olds, D. L. (2006). The nurse–family partnership: An evidence-based preventive intervention. *Infant Mental Health Journal, 27*(1), 5–25. doi:10.1002/imhj.20077

Olds, D., Henderson Jr, C. R., Cole, R., Eckenrode, J., Kitzman, H., Luckey, D., . . . & Powers, J. (1998). Long-term effects of nurse home visitation on children's criminal and antisocial behavior: 15-year follow-up of a randomized controlled trial. *Journal of American Medical Association, 280*(14), 1238–1244. doi:10.1001/jama.280.14.1238

Ousley, L., Cordero, E. D., & White, S. (2008). Fat talk among college students: How undergraduates communicate regarding food and body weight, shape & appearance. *Eating Disorders, 16*(1), 73–84. doi:789156439 [pii] 10.1080/10640260701773546

Pole, M., Crowther, J. H., & Schell, J. (2004). Body dissatisfaction in married women: The role of spousal influence and marital communication patterns. *Body Image, 1*(3), 267–278. doi:S1740-1445(04)00055-5 [pii] 10.1016/j.bodyim.2004.06.001

Prigerson, H. G., Maciejewski, P. K., & Rosenheck, R. A. (1999). The effects of marital dissolution and marital quality on health and health service use among women. *Medical Care, 37*(9), 858–873. doi:10.1097/00005650-199909000-00003

Reiche, E. M. V., Nunes, S. O. V., & Morimoto, H. K. (2004). Stress, depression, the immune system, and cancer. *The Lancet Oncology, 5*(10), 617–625. doi:10.1016/s1470-2045(04)01597-9

Resnick, M. D., Bearman, P. S., Blum, R. W., Bauman, K. E., Harris, K. M., Jones, J., . . . & Udry, J. R. (1997). Protecting adolescents from harm: Findings from the National Longitudinal Study on Adolescent Health. *Jama, 278*(10), 823–832. doi:10.1001/jama.278.10.823

Roberts, R. E., Shema, S. J., Kaplan, G. A., & Strawbridge, W. J. (2000). Sleep complaints and depression in an aging cohort: A prospective perspective. *American Journal of Psychiatry, 157*(1), 81–88. doi:10.1176/ajp.157.1.81

Robles, T., & Kiecolt-Glaser, J. (2003). The physiology of marriage: Pathways to health. *Physiological Behavior, 79*, 409–416. doi:10.1016/s0031-9384(03)00160-4

Rodgers, R. H., & White, J. M. (1993). Family development theory. In P. Boss, W. J. Doherty, R. LaRossa, W. Schumm, & S. Steinmetz (Eds.), *Boss, Doherty, LaRossa, Schumm, & Steinmetz book* pp. 225–254. New York: Springer.

Ross, C. E., & Mirowsky, J. (2002). Family relationships, social support and subjective life expectancy. *Journal of Health and Social Behavior, 43*(4), 469–489. doi:10.2307/3090238

Rueger, S. Y., Malecki, C. K., & Demaray, M. K. (2010). Relationship between multiple sources of perceived social support and psychological and academic adjustment in early adolescence: Comparisons across gender. *Journal of Youth and Adolescence, 39*(1), 47–61. doi:10.1007/s10964-008-9368-6

Rugulies, R. (2002). Depression as a predictor for coronary heart disease: A review and meta-analysis. *American Journal of Preventive Medicine, 23*(1), 51–61. doi:10.1016/s0749-3797(02)00439-7

Segrin, C., & Flora, J. (2011). *Family communication.* New York: Routledge.

Steinberg, L. (2001). We know some things: Parent–adolescent relationships in retrospect and prospect. *Journal of Research on Adolescence, 11*, 1–19. doi:10.1111/1532-7795.00001

Thompson, J. K., Heinberg, L., Leslie, J., Altabe, M., & Tantleff-Dunn, S. (1999). Appearance-related feedback. In J. K. Thompson, L. J. Heinberg, M. Altabe & S. Tantleff-Dunn (Eds.), *Exacting beauty: Theory, assessment, and treatment of body image disturbance* (pp. 151–174). Washington, DC: American Psychological Association.

Timmermans, W., Xiong, H., Hoogenraad, C. C., & Krugers, H. J. (2013). Stress and excitatory synapses: From health to disease. *Neuroscience, 248*, 626–636. doi:10.1016/j.neuroscience.2013.05.043

Tobin, E. T., Slatcher, R. B., & Robles, T. F. (2013). Family relationships and physical health: Biological processes and mechanisms. In M. L. Newman & N. A. Roberts (Eds.), *Health and social relationships: The good, the bad, and the complicated.* Washington, DC: American Psychological Association.

Tyrka, A. R., Wier, L., Price, L. H., Ross, N. S., & Carpenter, L. L. (2008). Childhood parental loss and adult psychopathology: Effects of loss characteristics and contextual factors. *International Journal of Psychiatry in Medicine, 38*(3), 329–344. doi:10.2190/pm.38.3.h

Umberson, D., Williams, K., Powers, D., Liu, H., & Needham, B. (2006). You make me sick: Marital quality and health over the life course. *Journal of Health and Social Behavior, 47*, 3–16. doi:10.1177/002214650604700101

Wahlroos, S. (1995). *Family communication: The essential rules for improving communication and making your relationships more loving, supportive, and enriching.* Chicago, IL: Contemporary Books.

Waite, L., & Gallaher, M. (2000). *The case for marriage: Why married people are happier, healthier, and better off financially* (1st edition ed.). New York: Doubleday.

Walsh, F. (2006). *Strengthening family resilience.* New York: Guilford Press.

Whitchurch, G. G., & Constantine, L. L. (1993). Systems theory. In P. G. Boss, W. J. Doherty, R. LaRossa, W. R. Schumm & S. K. Steinmetz (Eds.), *Sourcebook on family theories and methods: A contextual approach.* New York: Plenum Press.

Whittle, S., Yap, M. B., Yücel, M., Fornito, A., Simmons, J. G., Barrett, A., . . . & Allen, N. B. (2008). Prefrontal and amygdala volumes are related to adolescents' affective behaviors during parent–adolescent interactions. *Proceedings of the National Academy of Sciences, 105*(9), 3652–3657. doi:10.1073/pnas.0709815105

Wickrama, K. A. S., Lorenz, F. O., Conger, R. D., & Elder Jr., G. H. (1997). Marital quality and physical illness: A latent growth curve analysis. *Journal of Marriage and the Family*, 143–155. doi:10.2307/353668

Zheng, D., Macera, C. A., Croft, J. B., Giles, W. H., Davis, D., & Scott, W. K. (1997). Major depression and all-cause mortality among white adults in the United States. *Annals of Epidemiology, 7*(3), 213–218. doi:10.1016/s1047-2797(97)00014-8

20

Where have we been? Where are we going? Charting the Course in Our Intimate Journeys

Elizabeth J. Plowman, Ph.D.
Tai J. Mendenhall, Ph.D., LMFT
Lisa J. Trump, M.S.
Department of Family Social Science
University of Minnesota

Milkshakes on a rainy night. Holding her hand. Kissing him at every red light. Telling her your deepest secrets. Introducing him to your best friend. Wanting to be a better person. No makeup. Dressing up to keep the spark alive. Letting go. Letting her pick the restaurant—every time. The first "I love you." Being yourself. Laughing together. Nick names. Wanting to figure it out instead of wanting to win. Love. Keeping the lights on. Texting him when you get home at night. Leaving a rose on her windshield. Celebrating anniversaries—or treating every day like it's your anniversary. Helping him do his laundry. Editing her re'sume. A big bear hug. Being proud to call him your boyfriend or husband. Spending time with your friends—and not with your partner! Trust and honesty. Not being afraid to cry. Showing her your hometown. Showing him your favorite place. Carpet "picnics" in the living room. Hoping she gets promoted because you know it is her greatest wish. Cuddling under the covers. Stocking the fridge with his favorite snacks. Waiting patiently as she tries on an outfit . . . after outfit . . . after outfit. Dancing in the kitchen. Telling each other jokes. Leaving each other loving messages on hidden post-it notes or in cards "just because." Encouraging him to spend time with his friends. Driving her to the airport because she hates taking public transportation when she carries luggage. Breakfast for dinner. Taking care of him when he's sick. Forgiving her when she hurt you. Forgiving him when he hurt you. Playing board games every Sunday. Starting each morning with a kiss. Growing together and not apart. Feeling like you are a part of something special. Telling each other how you really feel.

Intimate relationships are a magical combination of all of these beautiful moments and experiences wrapped up into a complex, but meaningful, package. As we conclude this book, we revisit definitions of intimacy and explore the manners in which we develop and maintain it in our romantic relationships. It is here that we connect the dots for key takeaways that you can carry into your future as a person, partner, and potential helping professional.

WHAT IS INTIMACY?

In the early pages of this text, we discussed different approaches to revealing the "truth" in our quest to understand intimacy. Recognizing the importance of multiple perspectives, we embraced a post-modern approach whereby you are blessed with—and, indeed, tasked

---

in-ti-ma-cy
noun
\\'in-tə-mə-sē\\
1. the state of being intimate
2. something of a personal or private nature

Source: Merriam-Webster.com

Corresponding Author: Elizabeth J. Plowman, Ph.D., University of Minnesota; Department of Family Social Science; 1985 Buford Ave.; 290 McNeal Hall; Saint Paul, MN 55108. E-mail: eplowman@umn.edu

What does intimacy mean to you? Think about some of the concepts in this book that have rung most true for you. Then, define intimacy in your own words.

in·ti·ma·cy

noun

\ˈin-tə-mə-sē\

_____

_____

_____

with—creating your own reality. An individual's experience, and his or her personal truth, is different than the experience or truth of anyone else on Earth. As our introductory paragraph in this final chapter illustrates, our definitions of intimacy are comprised of what is most meaningful to us. For some, intimacy might mean sharing time and doing things together. For others, it might mean being able to be our true selves with another person, with all of the goods, the bads, and the imperfections that make us who we are. Mr. Webster—actually, Merriam-Webster.com (n.d.)—agrees; intimacy is "the state of being intimate," or "something of a personal or private nature."

It is important to note, too, that we are always growing—or least have the capacity to grow—in this amazing and difficult-to-define human and relational experience. In this sense, intimacy is a not only a state; it is a process—a journey—that can bring with it some of life's most extraordinary challenges, and its most amazing rewards.

Where does this journey begin? The answer is both simple and complex. It begins with us as individuals—with the person we are with 24 hours per day, and all that this means. All of our successes, failures, things that we are proud of, things that we are ashamed of, triumphs, and fears—these represent a culmination of where we have been, and a starting point for where we are going.

WHERE HAVE WE BEEN?

A common thread you may have noticed throughout this book is the (empirically supported) notion that our past experiences influence our current realities. Whether coming from early parent-child relationships, relationship sequences that challenged your primary attachment style, teachings from your faith community or cultural group, or any host of other influences, where you have been sets the stage for where you are going. And it can predestine it—for better or worse—unless you gain and act on insights about what you want to keep and what you want to change.

Think about it. If you were brought up by loving, responsive, and consistent parents, you likely developed secure attachments with them as you came to believe that the world around you was (is) a safe place—and that people, at least most of them, are good. The ways then, in which you engage in relationships with others today—from the vantage point that you are a good catch, and that they are too—will undoubtedly set the stage for a potentially healthy and solid union. But if your parents were inconsistent in their responsiveness to you, withheld love unless or until you acted "right," neglected or abused you—then you likely developed insecure attachments with them as you came to see the world around you as unpredictable, unstable, or unsafe. Engaging in adult relationships from a baseline sense that you are not loveable, or that others cannot be trusted to treat you well, can set the course of your union on a path that is doomed, or at least facing significant challenges, before it even begins.

Gaining awareness about where you have been—and why you do the things you do—is essential to setting a course whereby you live and "do" your relationships on purpose (not automatic pilot). For example, understanding how an insecure attachment likely fuels your constant need for reassurance, struggles with jealousy, and any host of mania love-style behaviors (e.g., constantly checking for texts, presuming personal fault or impending break-up whenever your partner is in a bad mood), can bring you to a crossroads at which now—today—you can *choose* how to act. Will you keep calling your partner when s/he doesn't call you at the exact time s/he said s/he would? Will you pine for words of affirmation or anything else that says "we're okay" because—once again—you are worried that maybe things are not okay? Or will you frame your worries and needy behaviors as things that you (not your partner) are responsible for changing? Will you challenge your own thinking that you are unworthy of love, or that others are a better catch than you are? Will you choose to put your phone down and trust that s/he will call you when s/he is able?

Will you then silently applaud your restraint—and take in your relief, telling yourself "I told you so; we're good!"—when s/he does?

If somebody has hurt you, abused you, betrayed your trust, or broken your heart—are you going to bring this experience into your next relationship, putting your new partner in a position of having to "fix" you or otherwise prove that s/he will not hurt you too? Are you going to live in fear of him or her cheating on you because your past partner cheated on you? Are you going make them profess and show their love and undying commitment to you—over and over again—only to doubt it because your past partner said that s/he loved you and would never leave you, but ultimately did? Or will you see these feelings and behaviors as yours—not your partner's—to face? Will you choose to not impose relational sanctions on one person for another person's wrongdoing(s)? Will you take the time to heal from a relationship that didn't work out before jumping—rebounding—into another one? Will you ultimately choose to try again, equipped with new insights and understandings?

WHERE ARE WE GOING?

Throughout this book, we highlighted ways for you to apply and act upon course material. We did this because we want to set you up for success in your current and future relationships by offering hands-on strategies—a toolbox of sorts—for building and sustaining intimacy. For example, in Chapter 2, we discussed why attachment during childhood is so relevant to (and informative of) adult functioning in relationships. We provided assessment tools to learn about one's own attachment style, and discussed ways to use this knowledge to maintain or change it. In Chapter 6, we discussed how intimacy "dances" can get us stuck in harmful patterns that can erode relationships in predictable ways. We described ways to identify these patterns and alter them into more healthy and satisfying sequences. In Chapter 9, we warned about intimacy "killers"

> How can we expect our partners to know us if we don't know ourselves?

across inter-relational processes (criticism, defensiveness, stonewalling, contempt) and common arenas in which these processes can play out (e.g., arguments about money, struggles with alcoholism or drug addiction). We offered strategies to disengage from these sequelae, alongside alternatives to begin resolving them. In Chapter 10, we built upon this as we discussed intimacy "healers" and ways that a couple can build a solid, loving, and enriching relational "house" together. In Chapter 17, we talked about the importance of compassion and forgiveness in human relationships. We described ways to develop and exercise empathy, and how partners' capacities for seeing the world through each other's eyes can be elemental to resolving conflict, negotiating change, and growing in togetherness. And across these chapters—and in each individual chapter in this text—we asked you, the reader, to go beyond simple reflections about how particular content fits or applies to you. We asked you to act upon your insights. We asked you do something—anything—different. We asked you to risk.

Sustaining Intimacy

Relationships in their early stages—with all of the excitement and mysteries of courtship, and before any of the day-to-day routines or schedules of being together over the long-haul have set in—can be very easy and fun to "do." This is what we see romanticized in popular media, with the only reference to a couple's future being some version of the clichéd "*And they lived happily-ever-after . . .*" narrative right before the final credits roll up.

Sustaining intimacy, however, requires consistent effort and stalwart commitment. And within our contemporary (Western) social contexts of instant-gratification and always-wanting-the-next-thing, hookups and serial monogamy, and knowing that half of all weddings we attend (or get married in) will end in divorce—many of us are quick to give up on a relationship that is in trouble before genuinely giving it a chance. The necessary work to resolve any of the challenges that a couple may face—finances, geographic distance, cultural differences, attachment issues, mismatches in sexual desire, health struggles, gender roles, troubles with communication, and so on—is more than many want to muster, and far less attractive than the lure of something (or someone) new.

What's in your healthy relationship toolbox?
Think about the concepts and skills we've highlighted throughout the book.

- Which skills do you currently possess? What are your relationship strengths?
  - Example: *"I believe I am my authentic self most of the time. I am in touch with my needs and wants in relationships. I feel comfortable being myself."*
- How do you plan to maintain this strength in your current or future relationship?
  - Example: *"I'm going to commit to spending one evening a week without my partner. 'Me time' helps me feel comfortable being on my own and lessens my insecurity about feeling alone."*
- Which tools do you need to work on? Based on what you've learned, what skills can you try to bring to future relationships?
  - Example: *"I could work on my receptive communication skills. I need to get better at actively listening to my partner."*
- How do you plan to develop these skills in your current or future relationship?
  - Example: *"The next time my partner and I argue and I feel like we are escalating, I'm going to request a 5-minute time-out. Taking a break will help me center and come back to the conversation with a solution-focused mindset. I'm going to ask my partner once a month if s/he feels like I listen to him/her. I need that type of reflective feedback to check in and make sure my improvements do not slip away."*

The "spark" that so many of us feel early-on in a relationship is fueled in large part by the attention and energy we put into it. Later on, it is easy to begin to take for granted the very thing that brought us so much novelty and joy in the beginning. Instead of saying "I love you" all the time, we begin reserving it for when we say goodbye in the morning on our way to work, at the end of a phone call, or in a birthday card. Instead of planning romantic dates across a variety of restaurants and activities, we begin going to the same diner and movie theater every weekend (or stop having regular dates altogether). Instead of having sex spontaneously and doing (and trying) lots of things together, love-making becomes routine—with the same sequence of events, at the same times and in the same place (and probably with less and less frequency). Instead of hugging and kissing each other at the door, or eating together and talking about anything and everything that is on our minds—we stop even getting up from the couch when our partner comes home, and we eat in silence—watching television. *Of course our "spark" burned out!* We stopped fueling its flame. And our relationship—whether we're still officially "together" or not—has died as a consequence of this neglect.

Couples who stay together in satisfying and enriching relationships do not neglect their union. Whether together for five, 10, or 50+ years—they consciously endeavor to make it work. And they do this every day. They communicate all the time (not just when there is trouble). They say "I love you" with their words and in their actions, their touches, and in the ways they smile and look at each other. They talk about their days and they share their worries, fears, hopes, dreams, certainties, and wonderings. They listen to each other. When they disagree, they work together as a team—instead of against each other—toward win/win solutions. They go out on dates, and they work to keep their romance alive in the same—and always evolving—ways that initially united them. And at the same time, they give each other space. They maintain their own (and some shared) hobbies, pursuits, and interests. They support each other when one is hurting. They are willing to risk being vulnerable so that they may be truly seen and understood. And they walk hand-in-hand—like they're still teenagers—into the sunsets of their own lives, and of the life they share together.

Final Thoughts

If you say "I love you" to someone, s/he might not say it back. If you allow yourself to be vulnerable with someone, s/he might hurt you. If you choose to trust someone, s/he might betray that trust. If you make a commitment to be with—and grow with—someone in a relationship, that union might ultimately fail.

But what is the alternative? If you choose not communicate what you are feeling, to not take a chance in allowing someone into your world and trying to grow in a relationship that could be extraordinary—you will, indeed, be safe. You won't get hurt. But you will never grow.

All growth involves risk. We want you to grow in your own personal self, and in the relationships you create, in ways that you cannot yet even imagine. Will you get hurt along the way? Probably. But if you fall down 10 times, get up 11 times. Learn. Reflect. Take action. Risk. And you will grow.

REFERENCES

Gottman, J.M. (2009). *The scientific basis for the orcas island couples' retreat: The Sound Relational House.* Gottman Institute. Retrieved from http://www.gottmancouplesretreats.com/about/sound-relationship-house-theory.aspx

Intimacy. (n.d.). Retrieved March 7, 2014, from http://www.merriam-webster.com/dictionary/intimacy

Author Bios

Tai J. Mendenhall, Ph.D., LMFT

Dr. Tai Mendenhall is a Medical Family Therapist and Associate Professor in the Couple and Family Therapy Program at the University of Minnesota (UMN) in the Department of Family Social Science. He is also the Associate Director of the UMN's Citizen Professional Center and Director of the UMN's Medical Reserve Corps' Mental Health Crisis-Response Teams. In scholarship, Tai works actively in the conduct of community-based participatory research (CBPR) targeting a variety of public health issues (e.g., diabetes and smoking cessation). He has authored more than 70 articles so far, half of which are peer-reviewed. He co-edited (and contributed to) a Special Issue regarding Medical Family Therapy for *Contemporary Family Therapy*, and has also authored or co-edited four books (two regarding Medical Family Therapy and two regarding contemporary understandings about intimate couple- and family-relationships). Outside of work, he enjoys motorcycling, running, and home-remodeling projects.

Elizabeth J. Plowman, Ph.D.

Dr. Elizabeth Plowman is an Adjunct Faculty Member in the School of Education at American Public University and American Military University. In addition to teaching, she works as an Account Supervisor at a small independent advertising agency in Chicago, IL and co-owns a small business dedicated to fund-raising for breast cancer research. Libby has co-authored several articles in peer-reviewed journals; her research interests center on innovative research designs in family science, the assessment of parent-child relationships, and parenting practices in at-risk families. She has presented her work across national and international conferences, and recently co-chaired the Developmental Methodology conference for the Society of Research in Child Development. Libby spends her time outside of the office practicing yoga, learning German, and connecting with family and friends.

Lisa J. Trump, M.S.

Lisa Trump is a Medical Family Therapist and doctoral candidate in the Couple and Family Therapy Program at the University of Minnesota (UMN) in the Department of Family Social Science. She is currently working at a UMN Family Medicine Residency Clinic in North Minneapolis, MN and has assisted in the implementation of an Integrated Care model. Lisa has published in our field's top journals and has presented her work across both local and national forums and conferences. Her research focuses on how couples and families manage chronic illness. In service to our field and community, Lisa is a student reviewer for the *Journal of Marital and Family Therapy*, Vice President for the Graduate Student Organization in Family Social Science, and an active member of the UMN's Crisis-Response Teams and Medical Reserve Corps. In her free time, she enjoys being outdoors and spending time with friends and family.

CPSIA information can be obtained
at www.ICGtesting.com
Printed in the USA
LVOW02s2301080716
495409LV00006B/21/P